$$a = \bar{y} - b\bar{x}$$

Sample y-intercept, simple linear regression

$$r^2 = \frac{b^2[\Sigma x_i^2 - (\Sigma x_i)^2/n]}{\Sigma y_i^2 - (\Sigma y_i)^2/n}$$

Sample coefficient of determination, simple linear regression

$$r = \frac{n\Sigma x_i y_i - (\Sigma x_i)(\Sigma y_i)}{\sqrt{n\Sigma x_i^2 - (\Sigma x_i)^2} \sqrt{n\Sigma y_i^2 - (\Sigma y_i)^2}}$$

Sample correlation coefficient

$$X^2 = \sum_{i=1}^{k} \left[\frac{(O_i - E_i)^2}{E_i} \right]$$

Statistic approximately distributed as χ^2, used as a test statistic in tests of goodness of fit, independence, and homogeneity

$$(r - 1)(c - 1)$$

Degrees of freedom for χ^2 in tests of independence and homogeneity (r = number of rows, c = number of columns)

KEY TO EXERCISE SYMBOLS

 Accounting

 Marketing

 Agribusiness

 Personnel/Human Resources

 Education/Training

 Production/Operations

 Government

 Real Estate

 Health/Safety

 Research and Development

 Management

 Transportation/Distribution

© Suitable for Computer Solution

ESSENTIALS OF BUSINESS STATISTICS

SECOND EDITION

ESSENTIALS OF BUSINESS STATISTICS

SECOND EDITION

WAYNE W. DANIEL
Georgia State University

HOUGHTON MIFFLIN COMPANY   **BOSTON**

Dallas   Geneva, Illinois   Lawrenceville, New Jersey   Palo Alto

To the memory of
Pickett H. Riggs, friend and colleague

Contents

7 Statistical Inference II: Hypothesis Testing 194

8 Hypothesis Tests for Three or More Populations: Analysis of Variance and Chi-Square 250

Preface

In a continuing effort to make available to undergraduate students of business the best possible textbook for their introductory statistics courses this second edition of Essentials of *Business Statistics* contains the following major changes and additions:

1. These new topics are discussed:
   graphical representation of qualitative data
   exploratory data analysis
   quality control
   systematic samples
   stratified random samples
   cluster samples
   judgment samples
   quota samples
   convenience samples
2. One-way analysis of variance and chi-square analysis are presented in the same chapter. The rationale for combining the two techniques in one chapter is the fact that they are both appropriate for hypothesis tests about three or more populations.
3. The following topics, covered in the first edition, have been deleted in the second edition:
   time-series analysis
   statistical decision theory
4. A large real data set has been added to the appendix. It consists of numerical data on six variables for each of more than 800 of the top-ranking business firms in the United States. Some of the exercises in the text require the student to analyze the data in samples selected from this population.
5. In the text there are an additional eight large data sets consisting of between 500 and 2,000 observations on from one to four variables. Accompanying exercises instruct students to select samples from these populations for analysis and to make inferences.
6. The text contains more than 180 new student exercises.
7. The *Instructor's Resource Manual* contains more than 350 new test items, bringing the total number of test items to more than 1200. The test questions

and answers are available to instructors on disks for microcomputer users or on tape for use with a main-frame computer.

8. STAT+, a computer software package containing computer programs that perform the calculations for most of the techniques presented in the text, is available to instructors for use with microcomputers. One disk is provided free to adopters of the text with permission to make additional copies for students.

This edition, like the first, is written for students of business—not for statisticians—on the assumption that these students have had only a minimum number of courses in mathematics. Consequently, the presentation has been made as simple as possible, with algebra as the highest level of mathematical sophistication needed. The emphasis is on an intuitive understanding of principles rather than an understanding based on a rigorous background in mathematics.

Essentials of Business Statistics, second edition, is designed for a one-term course. Some instructors, however, may find that they don't have enough time to cover all the material that has been included. Because of the way in which the text is written and organized, instructors may omit sections and/or chapters according to their individual preferences without destroying the overall continuity of the course.

Since the text is designed for business students, the many examples and exercises illustrate the application of statistical techniques in a wide variety of business settings (such as manufacturing, retail operations, transportation, real estate, and service industries) and functional areas (marketing, accounting, management, human resources, and research and development, for example).

Exercises appear at the ends of major sections. This placement has the effect of immediately reinforcing what has been learned in a given section. Review exercises and questions at the ends of chapters help the student master the content of one chapter before proceeding to the next.

To help the student quickly determine the area of application, there are descriptive symbols in the margins next to most of the exercises.

At the ends of most of the chapters there are suggested exercises to give students a chance to collect and analyze real data. The use of these exercises, called ''Practice with Real Data,'' helps make the course more realistic.

This book was written with the student in mind. The following are additional features that have been incorporated in this text to help students learn and to make it easier for the instructor to present the material in class.

1. *Chapter objectives.* These lists of objectives prepare the student for what is to be found in the chapter that follows. When students review the objectives after they have read the chapter, the objectives can help them to determine whether they learned what was expected of them.

2. *Small doses.* On the belief that statistics is best taught in small doses, broad topics—estimation, hypotheses testing, and regression analysis, for example—are broken down into several subtopics, each identified with an appropriate heading.

3. *Paragraph summaries.* To further help the student grasp important ideas, short summaries of some of the paragraphs are placed in the margins. These "one-liners" provide the students with a "handle" to hold onto as they read the complete paragraphs.

4. *Chapter summaries.* These help students as they review a chapter, before they begin a new one.

5. *Examples and solutions.* There is at least one example to illustrate each important topic. The solutions to these examples are clearly marked and serve further to break the textual material into more easily digestible chunks.

6. *Illustrations.* Drawings are used freely throughout the book to clarify concepts that benefit from such illustration.

7. *Color.* A second color is used to illuminate the text, and to emphasize certain salient points.

8. *Summation notation.* Appendix IV presents summation notation and explains the ways in which it is used in this book.

9. *Answers to exercises.* Answers to odd-numbered exercises appear at the end of the book. A separate *Solutions Manual,* available to instructors, provides worked-out solutions to all exercises, both odd- and even-numbered.

For students, a *Study Guide,* with a programmed-instruction format, is available as a companion piece to this text. The self-help features of the Study Guide enable students to check their ability to use computational techniques by comparing their step-by-step solutions on the right-hand side of a given page with step-by-step answers that appear on the left-hand side. To check their mastery of statistical concepts, students complete fill-in-the-blank questions. Again the answers are conveniently provided in the left-hand column.

The use of computers is emphasized throughout the text. The computer, like the old-fashioned slide rule and the modern hand-held calculator, is merely a tool that the student can use to advantage. A textbook such as this one should not be committed exclusively to one particular computer language or program package. Thus the remarks in the text regarding computers are expressed in general terms. This gives the individual instructor flexibility in integrating the text with available computer facilities. The exercises that are particularly appropriate for computer solution are marked with a ⓒ. For the convenience of text adopters whose students have access to microcomputers, the STAT+ statistical package is available free from the publisher.

In addition to the large data sets that are new in this edition, the large heads-of-households data set found in the first edition is retained in Appendix II of the present edition. Here the student finds data on 10 variables for each member of a population of 1000 fictitious heads of households. The data base is also available on computer tape for use with SPSS and other statistical packages. The student can draw samples from the population for the purpose of computing descriptive measures, constructing confidence intervals, testing hypotheses, and using all the statistical techniques described in the text. (In fact, some of the exercises direct the student to use Appendix II.)

I am grateful to many people for their help in the production of this book. The first edition manuscript was read by the following authorities in the field, whose helpful suggestions I greatly appreciate: Ralph Miller, California State Polytechnic University; Marlen Miller, Pacific Lutheran University; R. A. Johannsen, Miami Dade Community College; Walter C. Cornelison, Jr., Austin Community College; Benjamin N. Matta, New Mexico State University; and Michael E. Hanna, University of Texas at Arlington.

The second edition proposal received the critical scrutiny of another group of colleagues whose insightful suggestions were of tremendous help in the preparation of the book you are about to study. They were

Professor Mohammad S. Bajwa
Northampton County Area C.C.

Professor Bruce Bowerman
Miami University

Professor Dale M. Bryson
Umpqua Community College

Professor Kenneth O. Fladmark
Susquehanna University

Professor Michael S. Hanna
University of Houston Clear Lake

Professor Claire C. McAndrew
Fitchburg State College

Professor R. Allen Moran, Jr.
Lehigh University

Professor Jaqueline F. Redder
Virginia Polytechnic Institute and
State University

Professor Al Schainblatt
San Francisco State University

Professor Susan A. Simmons
Sam Houston State University

Professor Wayne A. Woodward
Southern Methodist University

I would like to thank my colleagues, Professors Geoffrey Churchill and Brian Schott, who wrote computer programs for generating several of the appendix tables.

Finally, I am grateful for the help of my wife Mary, without whose skills as a typist, proofreader, and critic this book could not have been published.

W.W.D.

ESSENTIALS OF BUSINESS STATISTICS

SECOND EDITION

1.

Introduction to Statistics

CHAPTER OBJECTIVES: This chapter introduces you to the field of statistics. It gives you some idea of the nature and usefulness of statistics, and why the study of statistics is important. After studying this chapter, you should be able to:

1. Define statistics
2. Distinguish between descriptive and inferential statistics
3. Discuss the different kinds of variables
4. Explain the difference between a population and a sample

At least one course in statistics is a standard requirement in most business curricula. There is a logical and pragmatic reason for such a requirement. Statistics is an essential research tool, and research is an important component of accounting, marketing, management, production, and other business disciplines.

We use statistics in research.

For example: The marketing researcher studies the life styles of certain consumer groups. The production supervisor investigates the effects that particular incentives have on output. The personnel director evaluates the relative effectiveness of several employee-training programs. All of these people use statistical procedures to analyze their findings.

We use statistics in management.

In addition to its role in research, statistics serves other purposes. A business firm, in its day-to-day operation, generates and collects a tremendous amount of data. Statistics provides the techniques for summarizing and describing these data in order to make them more easily understood by management and by those with whom the manager must communicate. Data that have been properly organized, summarized, and described provide a basis on which management can make sound decisions.

Marketing researchers may wish to describe their companies' customers with respect to such characteristics as median family income, age distribution, and education. Personnel directors find it helpful to have information on the number of employees who have responded favorably to each of several training programs. Production supervisors often want to know their employees' scores on personality, intelligence, and aptitude tests.

The role of statistics, then, is *to serve as a tool for those who collect, organize, summarize, analyze, and communicate quantitative information.*

Descriptive and Inferential Statistics   We can classify the results of the application of the tools of statistics into two categories: *descriptive statistics* and *inferential statistics*.

As the name implies, descriptive statistics is concerned with describing collections of persons, places, and things with respect to their characteristics.

We use statistics to describe.

One may describe a collection of *persons,* for example, by stating how many are males and how many are females, how many fall into various age categories, what the average level of education is, and what the average annual income is. As an example of *places,* cities may be described in terms of crime rate, unemployment rate, number of inhabitants, and average annual income of families living in the city. As an example of *things,* we may describe automobiles in terms of make, body style, weight, age, condition, and performance.

The techniques of inferential statistics make it possible to arrive at conclusions regarding a large collection of persons, places, or things on the basis of the information obtained from a small portion of the larger collection.

We use statistics to make inferences.

Many collections of persons, places, or things in which we are interested are so large that it is impractical to try to examine the entire collection. The ability to examine only a *part* of the larger collection and then draw conclusions about the large collection on the basis of the characteristics of the small portion is one of the researcher's most valuable tools. Suppose that a marketing researcher, for example, wants to know what proportion of the households in a large geographic area contain at least one teenager. Most researchers' budgets are not large enough to allow interviews to be conducted in each household. However, the researcher could conduct interviews in an appropriately selected portion of the households in the area and, on the basis of the results, arrive at a conclusion about what proportion of all households in the area contain at least one teenager.

In Chapter 2 we discuss various techniques of descriptive statistics. This chapter—along with Chapters 3, 4, and 5—provides the foundation for inferential statistics, which will be the topic of discussion in the remaining chapters of this book.

1.1 DATA SOURCES

Researchers and managers obtain the data they need for making decisions from three main sources: *sample surveys, designed experiments,* and the *routine operation* of their organizations.

Data come from sample surveys.

In a sample survey, data are collected from a subgroup of some larger group about which information is desired. Most people are familiar with the polls conducted by Gallup International, Inc., and other similar analyzers of public opinion. These are examples of organizations that use sample surveys to collect data.

Data come from designed experiments.

In a designed experiment, an experimenter manipulates and controls certain aspects of the environment. As a simple example of a designed experiment, consider a drug manufacturer whose objective is to learn the effect of a drug on the reaction time of the recipient. A laboratory technician might obtain the desired information through a designed experiment using two groups of laboratory animals. One group could be given the drug, while the other group was given an inert substance. Each group could then be observed and the individual reaction times measured.

Data come from routine records.

It is hard to think of a business organization that does not routinely generate data that are of interest to some researcher. The typical business firm collects data on employees, customers, and vendors. Such data provide the information on which to base decisions about hiring policies, purchasing decisions, and other functions that are critical to the firm's operation.

1.2 VARIABLES

Regardless of the source of the data used by the manager and researcher, the focus of inquiry is on characteristics (of persons, places, or things) called *variables*.

A *variable* is a characteristic that can assume different values when observed in different persons, places, or things.

Human intelligence is a variable, since it occurs in different amounts in different people. Marital status is another example of a variable: Some people are single, whereas others are married or divorced. Other variables that may be of interest to the business manager or researcher are age, sex, and occupation of employees and consumers; population density of defined geographic areas; and the quality of a manufactured product.

We use capital letters to represent variables.

To make it easier to discuss the statistical analysis of data, we use a kind of shorthand system of communication. We shall use various symbols and English and Greek letters to stand for words and phrases. We shall use capital letters near the end of the alphabet to designate variables. For example, when the variable of interest is the age of individuals, we may designate age by the capital letter X. Individual observed values of a variable are designated by lower-case letters with appropriate subscripts. The subscripts distinguish the value for one individual from the value for another. If, for example, the variable is age, designated by X, the ages of individuals in whom the variable is observed are designated by x_1, x_2, x_3, and so on. A typical age among those observed is designated by x_i. If the ages of certain adolescents within a group are of interest, we may, for example, observe the ages $x_1 = 13$, $x_2 = 16$, $x_3 = 15$, $x_4 = 17$, and so on.

We refer to an observed value of a variable as an *observation*.

Random Variables   When the values that a variable assumes cannot be predicted with certainty, the variable is called a *random variable*.

The occurrence of values of a random variable may be characterized as unsystematic, or lacking in apparent pattern. Examples of random variables are: the height attained by human adults; the length of life of humans; the number of children of a given sex occurring in families; and the IQs of assembly-line workers.

Quantitative Variables   Variables may be classified on the basis of whether they are *quantitative* or *qualitative*.

Quantitative variables yield measurements that are numerical in nature.

all numbers

The values that they can assume convey such concepts as quantity, amount, magnitude, or number. Examples of quantitative variables are: human intelligence; height; weight; number of daily admissions to a hospital; and the time it takes a person to react to some stimulus.

Qualitative Variables   *Qualitative variables*, in contrast to quantitative variables, assume values that convey the concept of *attribute*.

In fact, qualitative variables are sometimes referred to as *attribute variables*. Qualitative variables yield values that are not numerical or quantitative in nature. Examples of qualitative variables are: sex; occupation; and place of residence.

Discrete Variables   Variables may also be categorized on the basis of whether they are *discrete* or *continuous*.

A *discrete variable* is one that can assume only a finite number of values within some interval of values.

Consequently, a sequence of values that can be assumed by a discrete variable is characterized by the presence of gaps. These gaps represent the values that the variable cannot assume. An example of a discrete variable is the number of persons entering a grocery store on a given day. This variable can assume the values 0, 1, 2, . . . , and so on. The variable cannot assume the value 1/2 or the value 0.275, for example, since, from a practical point of view, it is impossible for a fractional part of a person to enter a grocery store. Other examples of discrete variables are: the number of trials required to correctly perform some task; scores in a basketball game; and number of correct answers on a true-false examination.

Whole numbers only [handwritten margin note]

Continuous Variables A *continuous variable* is one that can assume any value within a specified interval.

An example of a continuous variable is height. No matter how close in height two people may be, it is always theoretically possible to find a person whose height falls somewhere between them. Our ability to distinguish small differences in the heights of two people who seem to be the same height is hampered only by the precision of our measuring devices. The same problem arises in our attempts to obtain measurements of other continuous variables. Examples of other variables that are continuous are: the time required to complete a task; weight; and distance between two points.

1.3 POPULATIONS AND SAMPLES

Populations

Population is the main concern. [handwritten margin note]

Stacey! Dionne Lofton [handwritten margin note]

We have alluded to the fact that business managers are often interested in the characteristics of large collections of persons, places, or things. When a large collection of persons, places, or things in which one has an interest has been identified, it is referred to as a *population*. Thus a marketing researcher may want to know the educational level of a population of potential purchasers of some product. Or a personnel director may be concerned with the aptitude scores of a population of employees.

In a given situation, the extent of one's interest determines what constitutes the population to be studied. For example, a production supervisor's interest in some characteristic of employees may be limited to the employees on a single shift. These employees then constitute the relevant population. If the supervisor's interest is extended to all employees on all shifts, a new population is defined. We may, therefore, define a population as follows.

A population is the largest collection of persons, places, or things in which there is an interest in a given investigation.

It is convenient to refer to the individual persons, places, or things of which a population is composed as the *elements* of the population. Thus, in discussing a population of employees, we may refer to an individual employee as an element. Frequently, especially when the elements of a population are human beings, we refer to an individual member of the population as a *subject*.

We often use the term population to refer to a collection of measurements taken on the individual members of a population. We may, for example, refer to a collection of IQ scores of a population of subjects as ''a population of IQ scores.''

Populations may be either *infinite* or *finite*. Infinite populations are composed of a limitless number of elements. Consider some never-ending, element-yielding process. Such a process would produce an infinite population of elements. Imagine a manufacturing process that continues forever. If the products of the process are steel bolts, the process will yield an infinite population of steel bolts. The population of all humans who have ever lived, are now living, and ever will live in the future may be thought of as an infinite population.

When a population is finite, it is possible (though not always practical) to count the elements of which it is composed. Examples of finite populations are the students enrolled at a certain college, all employees of some firm, and the households located in a given census tract. We use the letter N to indicate the size of a finite population. If, for example, our population consists of 22,000 students enrolled at a state university, $N = 22,000$.

A population may be infinite or finite.

Samples

We reach conclusions about populations by studying samples.

As we noted earlier, populations are often so large that examining or measuring every element of which they are composed is either impossible or impractical. Consequently, with large populations we select a fraction of the elements for study. We then make inferences about the population on the basis of the information provided by the part of the population that we have examined.

The part of the population that is examined is called a *sample*.

We use the lower-case letter n to indicate the size of a sample.

Not all samples that one can select from a population are appropriate for use in making inferences about the population. In order for an investigator to make legitimate inferences about a population on the basis of sample data, the sample must meet certain scientific criteria. In particular, the manner in which the sample is selected is important. In Chapter 2, we discuss a proper method for selecting a sample so that valid inferences may be made about the population from which the sample was drawn.

Computers and Business Statistics

The enormous increase in the use of computers has had a tremendous impact on business management, on research in general, and on statistical analysis in particular. The computer has greatly reduced the need for laborious hand calculations. Computers can perform more calculations faster—and far more accurately—than humans. Through efficient use of computers, business researchers can devote more time to improving the quality of raw data and interpreting the results.

For those who use a mainframe computer, prewritten ("canned") computer programs are available that will do the calculations for most of the descriptive and inferential statistical procedures that the typical business researcher or decision maker is likely to need. Some widely used "packages" of statistical procedures are *BMDP: Biomedical Computer Programs, SPSS Statistical Package for the Social Sciences, The IMSL Library, Minitab,* and *SAS.*

Along with the current widespread use of personal computers has come the development of a large number of statistical software packages for use with these machines. One such package is STAT+, which is available for use with this book.

The computer is a useful tool for statistical analysis.

You can use canned programs and microcomputer software packages to perform the calculations for many of the exercises in this book. [*Note:* Such exercises are marked with a Ⓒ at the beginning of the exercise.] In particular, the computer is a useful tool for calculating descriptive measures and constructing frequency distributions from large sets of data.

Using Computers with this Text

Statistical programs differ with respect to their input requirements, their output formats, and the specific calculations they perform. If you wish to use a computer in solving the exercises in this book, you should become familiar with the programs that are available at your computer installation. You must determine, first of all, whether there is an existing program that will do the required calculations. Once you locate an appropriate program, study its input requirements carefully so that you can enter the data of the exercises into the computer correctly. Finally, study the program's output format to ensure that you will interpret the results properly. If you have studied a computer language, you may, in some instances, wish to write your own computer programs for use with the exercises.

Summary

This chapter introduced the subject of statistics. A discussion of the nature of statistics was followed by a discussion of variables, populations, and samples.

Review Questions

1. What is the role of statistics in business?
2. What is descriptive statistics?
3. What is inferential statistics?
4. What are the three main sources of data available to the business researcher or manager?
5. Define the following: (a) variable, (b) random variable, (c) quantitative variable, (d) qualitative variable, (e) discrete variable, (f) continuous variable.
6. Give three examples, not already mentioned in this book, of each of the following: (a) quantitative variable, (b) qualitative variable, (c) discrete variable, (d) continuous variable.
7. What is a population?
8. What is a sample?

2.
Organizing and Summarizing Data

CHAPTER OBJECTIVES: This chapter teaches you some of the basic techniques used in describing and summarizing important characteristics of a set of data. It will help you to understand and be able to use these techniques. These skills are essential for handling much of the material in the remainder of this text. After studying this chapter and working the exercises, you should be able to:

1. Obtain a simple random sample from a finite population
2. Organize and summarize data so that they can be better understood
3. Communicate, by means of graphs, the important information contained in a set of data
4. Compute numerical quantities that measure the central tendency and dispersion of a set of data

As we said in Chapter 1, we present the concepts and techniques of applied statistics under two broad headings: *descriptive statistics* and *inferential statistics*. This chapter introduces the more important methods and concepts of descriptive statistics. The next three chapters will present basic concepts necessary for understanding statistical inference, the subject of the rest of the book.

2.1 THE SIMPLE RANDOM SAMPLE

A simple random sample is the proper type of sample for many inference procedures.

As noted earlier, one of this book's primary concerns is to teach the concepts and techniques of statistical inference—of arriving at conclusions about a population on the basis of the information contained in a sample drawn from that population. In order for such inferences to be valid, the sample on which they are based must be of the proper type. For many situations involving the use of statistical inference procedures, a *simple random sample* is the proper type of sample to use.

A simple random sample is a sample that is selected from a population in such a way that each time an element is selected from the population, all elements available for selection have an equal chance of being selected.

A desirable characteristic of a sample is that it be representative of the population from which it was drawn. A simple random sample can be expected to be representative of the population from which it has been selected. This is not likely to be true of some other types of samples that one might draw. As we shall see, drawing a simple random sample is somewhat tedious, and those who are not convinced of the importance of making inferences on the basis of properly selected samples may be tempted to resort to easier methods of sample selection. In general, one cannot expect such "convenience samples" to be representative of the population from which they have been drawn. Suppose, for example, that a market researcher wished to draw a sample of homemakers living in a certain community in order to make an inference about the opinions of the population of homemakers regarding some new product to be placed on the market. The researcher might find it convenient to use the members of the community garden club as a sample. A close examination of the garden club membership, however, might show that the members do not represent the population of homemakers in the community with respect to such variables as age, education, and income.

Drawing a Simple Random Sample

The mechanics of drawing a sample that satisfies the definition of a simple random sample is called *simple random sampling*. When drawing a simple random sample, we can sample *with replacement* or *without replacement*.

When we sample *with* replacement, every element of the population is available each time an element to be in the sample is drawn.

Suppose, for example, that an accountant who wishes to analyze the purchases made during the year from a certain group of vendors decides to take a sample of vendor records that are filed sequentially in a filing cabinet. To sample with replacement, the accountant would proceed as follows: Select a record from the filing cabinet, record the desired information, and return the record to the filing cabinet. The record is back in the population and may be drawn again on some later draw. If a record that previously has been drawn is drawn again, the desired information is again taken for use in the analysis.

When we sample *without replacement,* we do not return an element to the population after it has been selected for inclusion in the sample.

For example, an accountant who samples *without* replacement does not return a selected record to the filing cabinet after recording the desired information. Thus, if the accountant samples without replacement, information on a given vendor can appear in the sample of data only once. In practice, sampling is almost always done without replacement.

In selecting a simple random sample from a population, in order to ensure true randomness, we must use some objective method. One such procedure involves the use of a *table of random numbers,* such as Table A of the Appendix. Using such a table ensures that every observation in the sampled population has an equal and independent chance of being selected. This is because each digit in the random-number table was generated in such a way that the values 0 through 9 had an equal and independent chance of occurring.

We may use a table of random numbers to select a sample.

EXAMPLE 2.1 Suppose that the population of interest consists of 200 workers at a certain firm. We want to draw a simple random sample of size 10 from this population in order to find out how many units these employees produced during the past week. For each employee there is a card on which the production data are recorded. These cards, which are filed alphabetically in a card file, are also numbered in sequence from 001 to 200. Table 2.1 represents our population of interest.

SOLUTION We can use Table A to draw a sample of size 10 without replacement from this population. Some samplers like to select a random starting point in the table of random numbers. However, since all the digits in the table are random, there is nothing wrong with starting with the very first number in the table. If we draw another sample from the same population later, and use the same table of random numbers, we begin drawing random numbers where we left off. This prevents us from drawing the same sample twice. Since we have 200 cards from which to choose, we can use only those three-digit numbers that are between 001 and 200, inclusive.

The first three-digit number in Table A is 859, a number we cannot use. As we proceed down the column, we find that we can use the second number, 074. Therefore, employee number 074 is the first employee we select for inclusion in the sample. This employee produced 49 units, as shown in Table 2.1. We record both the random number used and the number of units produced. (We record the random number so that we can keep track of the numbers used. Since we are

TABLE 2.1
Number of units produced by 200 employees

001.	30	041.	59	081.	65	121.	47	161.	62
002.	38	042.	56	082.	42	122.	64	162.	29
003.	33	043.	65	083.	73	123.	55	163.	37
004.	49	044.	50	084.	44	124.	50	164.	27
005.	33	045.	54	085.	54	125.	65	165.	36
006.	43	046.	61	086.	67	126.	53	166.	43
007.	60	047.	57	087.	49	127.	32	167.	30
008.	31	048.	55	088.	38	128.	44	168.	41
009.	34	049.	26	089.	59	129.	38	169.	59
010.	61	050.	41	090.	42	130.	37	170.	63
011.	49	051.	64	091.	46	131.	53	171.	55
012.	64	052.	25	092.	30	132.	44	172.	32
013.	62	053.	28	093.	64	133.	27	173.	32
014.	37	054.	49	094.	28	134.	40	174.	31
015.	25	055.	53	095.	64	135.	43	175.	35
016.	38	056.	25	096.	46	136.	45	176.	33
017.	65	057.	33	097.	59	137.	33	177.	58
018.	56	058.	28	098.	60	138.	60	178.	31
019.	55	059.	25	099.	46	139.	62	179.	38
020.	43	060.	60	100.	27	140.	30	180.	29
021.	58	061.	34	101.	59	141.	51	181.	43
022.	38	062.	25	102.	43	142.	49	182.	56
023.	71	063.	61	103.	50	143.	31	183.	53
024.	47	064.	42	104.	51	144.	29	184.	64
025.	65	065.	48	105.	39	145.	36	185.	38
026.	54	066.	57	106.	59	146.	50	186.	36
027.	74	067.	26	107.	33	147.	54	187.	59
028.	36	068.	55	108.	60	148.	38	188.	68
029.	62	069.	36	109.	26	149.	60	189.	26
030.	31	070.	33	110.	72	150.	65	190.	72
031.	48	071.	63	111.	25	151.	36	191.	29
032.	35	072.	48	112.	44	152.	25	192.	32
033.	26	073.	37	113.	58	153.	28	193.	73
034.	62	074.	49	114.	49	154.	56	194.	63
035.	51	075.	46	115.	31	155.	51	195.	69
036.	67	076.	31	116.	56	156.	53	196.	57
037.	30	077.	26	117.	37	157.	40	197.	38
038.	57	078.	28	118.	66	158.	33	198.	50
039.	50	079.	63	119.	55	159.	26	199.	60
040.	62	080.	37	120.	66	160.	42	200.	28

sampling without replacement, we do not want to use the same random number twice.) If we proceed down the column in this manner, we obtain the random numbers and corresponding numbers of units produced that are shown in Table 2.2. Note that when we get to the bottom of the column, we merely shift one digit to the right and move up the column. This is one of many alternatives. For example, we could start at the top of the next column.

This completes the drawing of our simple random sample. From now on, when we use the term *simple random sample,* we mean that the sample was drawn in this or an equivalent manner.

**TABLE 2.2
Sample of 10
employees,
showing number
of units produced
(from population
of Table 2.1)**

Random number	074	037	091	018	189	119	145	139	196	170
Sequence in sample	1	2	3	4	5	6	7	8	9	10
Units	49	30	46	56	26	55	36	62	57	63

Many computers now on the market are able to generate random numbers. Instead of using printed tables of random numbers, you may use a computer to generate random numbers. Actually, the ''random'' numbers generated by computers are *pseudorandom* numbers. They are the result of a deterministic formula. However, the numbers appear to be satisfactory for many practical purposes.

Exercise

2.1 Use the table of random numbers to select another sample of size 10 from the population in Table 2.1. You may begin selecting random numbers at the place where Example 2.1 left off.

2.2 OTHER KINDS OF SAMPLES

The basic techniques of sampling are illustrated by the procedures for selecting a simple random sample. A simple random sample, however, is not always the best kind of sample to use as a basis for making statistical inferences. When it is not, some other type of sample should be used. The other kinds of samples that are used instead of simple random samples can be classified into one of two categories: *probability samples* and *nonprobability samples*.

Probability Samples
Probability samples are selected in such a way that for each element in the population, one can determine in advance the chance, or probability, of its being selected for inclusion in the sample.

An advantage of probability samples is the fact that, when the data are analyzed, the results can be interpreted in certain important ways that are not possible with nonprobability samples. The simple random sample is a probability sample. Other frequently used probability samples are the *systematic sample,* the *stratified random sample,* and the *cluster sample.*

The Systematic Sample   If a sample must be drawn from a large population, selecting a simple random sample using a table of random numbers can prove to be a long and tedious procedure. One way to overcome this difficulty is to draw a systematic sample. To draw this type of sample, first select an element corresponding to a random starting point in the population, then draw successive elements in such a way that all elements in the sample are equidistant from each other. We may define a systematic sample more formally, then, as follows:

A systematic sample is obtained by selecting the first element from the first k elements in the population, then obtaining the remaining elements by selecting every kth element thereafter.

The result of following this procedure will be a 1 in k systematic sample. We may, for example, select an element at random from among the first 10 elements in a population, then select every tenth element thereafter. In that case $k = 10$, and we would, when finished, have a 1 in 10 systematic sample.

In addition to ease of selection, in many applications systematic sampling has the advantage of providing a sample that may be more representative of the population than a simple random sample because it is spread more evenly over the population.

The Stratified Random Sample Frequently the population about which we wish to make an inference is not homogeneous, so that it may not be represented adequately by a simple random sample or a systematic sample. Suppose, for example, that we are interested in making an inference about the amount of money spent for recreation by families in a certain community. The amount of money a family spends on recreation is certainly related to family income. In the typical community there are some families with very low incomes, some with very high incomes, and many with incomes in between. If we draw a simple random sample, there is a chance that none of the families—or a disproportionate number—with very low incomes or very high incomes will be included. Intuition suggests that a sample should be designed in such a way that all three groups are adequately represented. The procedure for accomplishing this objective is called *stratified random sampling,* and the resulting sample is called a *stratified random sample,* which we may define as follows:

A stratified random sample is a sample obtained by dividing the elements of a population into nonoverlapping and homogeneous subpopulations called strata, then selecting a simple random sample from each stratum.

Such a procedure ensures that each subpopulation or stratum is represented in the sample. To make inferences about the amount of money families spend for recreation, we could select a stratified random sample by first stratifying families into three strata—low, medium, and high—according to income, then selecting a simple random sample from each stratum. Note that stratification is carried out on the basis not of the variable of interest—amount of money spent on recreation, in the present example—but of another variable, in this case income. We believe that income is related to expenditures for recreation, the variable of interest. In general, the procedure involves stratifying the population on the basis of a variable that is closely related to the variable of interest, since we usually know little, if anything, about the variable of interest.

The Cluster Sample During the planning of sample surveys, we frequently encounter a problem when we try to obtain a list of the elements in our population of interest. Such a list is called a *sampling frame,* or *frame* for short. A ready-made frame that corresponds to the population may not be available, and the preparation of one may pose insurmountable problems. Imagine, for example, the difficulty of preparing a frame for the population of preschool children in a large community.

Another problem that may be encountered in sample surveys is widely scattered elements. This is a problem, for example, with sparsely settled rural areas in which the elements of interest are households. Widely scattered elements not only increase the cost of a survey, but also create administrative problems. These problems are not as grave when the populations involved are small, but for large populations they may be quite serious. A possible solution to problems such as these is to make use of *cluster sampling*.

A cluster sample is a sample that is drawn after the elements in the population have been subdivided into nonoverlapping and heterogeneous groups called clusters.

The drawing of the sample, then, proceeds in two stages: First, we select a sample of clusters, and second, we select a sample of elements from each of the clusters in the sample. Sometimes at the second stage we select all the elements in each cluster. Usually, however, we select only a sample of these elements. For example, suppose we want to make an inference about the number of children per family for the employees of a large company that has many branches located in many parts of the country. Rather than selecting a simple random sample or a systematic sample from a frame (which may be either not available or difficult and expensive to prepare), we may think of each branch's personnel roster as a cluster of employees. Suppose that the company has a total of 100 branches around the country. We might select a sample of 10 of these clusters in the first stage of sampling. In the second stage we would select a subsample of families from among the families in each of these 10 clusters.

In summary, cluster sampling should be considered when a frame is not available and when the elements of the population are located at great distances from each other. In such situations the proper use of cluster sampling usually provides maximum information at minimum cost.

Nonprobability Samples

Nonprobability samples include *judgment samples*, *quota samples*, and *convenience samples*.

Judgment Samples   When the subjective judgment of the sampler determines which elements are included in the sample, we call the result a *judgment sample*. Suppose that a market-research team wishes to use a judgment sample as the basis for making inferences about the buying habits of families living in a certain town. The researchers select what, in their judgment, is a sample of families representative of all families in the town. Another team of researchers would, no doubt, select a different judgment sample. It is unlikely that any two teams would ever agree on what constitutes a representative sample.

Quota Samples   A quota sample is selected on the basis of more specific guidelines concerning which elements should be drawn. The quota sampler must know, for the population of interest, the proportion of the elements that have certain characteristics. Suppose, for example, that a real estate appraiser wants to estimate the mean value of the houses in a population of single-family dwellings. If quota sampling is to be used, the appraiser may need to know, for the population, what proportion of houses are two-story, what proportion are split-level, what proportion have central air conditioning, and what proportion have swimming pools. A quota sample should contain dwellings with these characteristics in the same proportions as the population. Within each category, the appraiser, who must know which houses in the population have these characteristics, can use subjective judgment in deciding which ones to include in the sample.

Convenience Samples   As the name implies, convenience samples are used because of their convenience. A market researcher who wishes to draw a sample of families living in some subdivision might find it convenient to select those families living on the main street of the subdivision. Although convenience samples may serve some specialized purposes, we cannot, in general, depend on them for making inferences about populations.

Nonprobability samples do not have the objectivity of selection that is an essential characteristic of probability samples. When we make inferences based on probability samples, we can employ objective criteria to evaluate the usefulness of our inferences. It is not possible to do this when inferences are based on nonprobability samples. This is why probability samples rather than nonprobability samples are the primary focus of attention in this text.

2.3 SUMMARIZING DATA: THE ORDERED ARRAY

Data from a special study or from routine business records are usually available to a researcher or manager as an unorganized mass of observations, regardless of whether the data are a sample or a population. In order to better understand the nature of these ''raw'' data, one must organize and summarize them.

If the number of observations is not too great, a frequent first step in organizing the data is the preparation of an *ordered array*.

An ordered array is a list of the observations in order of increasing magnitude, from the smallest value to the largest.

By looking at an ordered array, the researcher can get a feel for the magnitude of the observations. If more calculations and further organization of the data have to be done with pencil, paper, and a calculator, these operations will be much easier if an ordered array has first been prepared. On the other hand, if all calculations are done by a computer, preparation of an ordered array may not be necessary.

EXAMPLE 2.2 A business firm wants to analyze the characteristics of its employees. A sample of 100 employees is selected, and the age at nearest birthday of each is determined. The ages are obtained from individual employee records filed

TABLE 2.3
Ages of 100
employees

Data

60	39	23	30	29	26	29	41	40	32
63	22	32	52	46	35	25	28	33	33
20	25	42	34	29	43	41	31	30	36
58	21	24	55	51	28	18	40	44	38
32	21	30	31	25	49	31	26	33	36
43	34	35	22	33	38	34	34	33	34
23	26	57	23	26	36	39	31	35	34
34	51	40	50	35	45	28	36	32	39
26	48	17	45	45	25	25	30	36	30
43	25	27	21	53	25	38	33	37	33

alphabetically in the personnel department. Table 2.3 shows the ages as recorded. Table 2.4 shows the ordered array that is prepared from the original list. According to this ordered array, the youngest employee in the sample is 17 and the oldest is 63. This information is hidden in Table 2.3. The ordered array also facilitates the tabular presentation of data, as we'll see in the next section.

2.4 SUMMARIZING DATA: THE FREQUENCY DISTRIBUTION

The ordered array helps to convey the information contained in a set of data, but it is hard to grasp a large number of observations, even when they are ordered according to magnitude. We can summarize further by grouping the data into *class intervals*. The result is called *grouped data*.

Class intervals are contiguous, nonoverlapping intervals selected in such a way that they are mutually exclusive and exhaustive. That is, each and every value in the set of data can be placed in one, and only one, of the intervals.

For example, you can summarize the individual incomes of a group of employees by showing the number falling into each of several class intervals, such as

< $5,000
5,000– 9,999
10,000–14,999
15,000–19,999
20,000–24,999
25,000–29,999
30,000 and over

After we have determined the class intervals, we examine the data and count the number of values falling into each interval. The result is a *frequency distribution*. It can be displayed as either a table or a graph. We can define it as follows:

A frequency distribution is any device, such as a graph or table, that displays the values that a variable can assume along with the frequency of occurrence of these values, either individually or as they are grouped into a set of mutually exclusive and exhaustive intervals.

INfORMatioN *RaNge is 46*

TABLE 2.4
Ordered array prepared from 100 ages in Table 2.3

17	23	26	29	32	33	35	38	43	50
18	24	26	30	32	34	35	39	43	51
20	25	26	30	32	34	36	39	43	51
21	25	26	30	32	34	36	39	44	52
21	25	27	30	33	34	36	40	45	53
21	25	28	30	33	34	36	40	45	55
22	25	28	31	33	34	36	40	45	57
22	25	28	31	33	34	37	41	46	58
23	25	29	31	33	35	38	41	48	60
23	26	29	31	33	35	38	42	49	63

*RaNge - is difference betweeN largest & smallest #'s iN aN oRdeRed aRRay

How many intervals should there be?

One of the first things to consider when data are to be grouped is k, the *number of intervals* to include. Using too few intervals results in an excessive loss of information. Using too many defeats the purpose of summarization. You usually should not use fewer than 6 intervals or more than 15. When deciding how many class intervals to have, you need to be familiar with the data and to understand the purposes of grouping.

Another decision to be made when grouping data concerns the *width of the intervals*. As a general rule, all the intervals should be the same width. We should also select a width that is convenient to work with.

How wide should the intervals be?

FiNal Sample Space CombiNatioN PeRMutatioN

We may approximate the width of the class interval by dividing the *range* by k. The range is the difference between the largest and the smallest values in a set of data. Let R be the range. The approximate width of the class interval is given by R/k. The class-interval width determined in this manner is often not an integer and must be rounded up or down. Also, R/k often yields a class-interval width that is undesirable because it is inconvenient to work with or because it is one that is not customarily used with the data under consideration. When the data permit, class-interval widths of 5 units, 10 units, or some multiple of 10 units are desirable, since people can grasp these intervals more readily.

EXAMPLE 2.3 To understand how to group data, consider the employee ages in Table 2.4.

SOLUTION Since we prefer intervals whose widths are 5 units or some multiple of 10 units, we have a choice here between using 5-year intervals and using 10-year intervals. If we were to use interval widths of 10 years, we would have only 5 class intervals, one fewer than the recommended minimum of 6. Hence 5-year intervals seem best here.

Specifying the intervals as suggested, and counting the number of observations that fall into each, gives the frequency distribution shown in Table 2.5. This table lets us ascertain, at a glance, various features of the data. For example, more employees are in the age group 30–34 than in any other group. The number in each group decreases in both directions from this interval. In Table 2.5 the numbers 15, 20, 25, 30, and so on, are the *lower class limits*. The numbers 19, 24, 29, 34, and so on, are the *upper class limits*. These numbers determine the magnitude of the observations that go into a given interval.

TABLE 2.5 Frequency distribution of the ages of 100 employees

Age (in years)	Frequency
15–19	2
20–24	10
25–29	19
30–34	27
35–39	16
40–44	10
45–49	6
50–54	5
55–59	3
60–64	2
Total	100

The choice of class limits reflects the extent to which the values being grouped are rounded off. The employee ages in the present example are rounded to the nearest year, since it was the age at the nearest birthday that was recorded. An employee between 24 and 24.5 would be counted in the second class interval, whereas one who is between 24.5 and 25 would be counted in the third. Thus 24.5 is really the boundary between the second and third class intervals. Similar boundaries between the other class intervals may be determined. These are sometimes referred to as the *class boundaries* or *true class limits*. For the employee ages, they are

| 14.5–19.5 | 19.5–24.5 | 24.5–29.5 | 29.5–34.5 | 34.5–39.5 |
| 39.5–44.5 | 44.5–49.5 | 49.5–54.5 | 54.5–59.5 | 59.5–64.5 |

The Cumulative Frequency Distribution

Sometimes one wants a *cumulative frequency distribution*. Table 2.6 shows this for the 100 employee ages.

We obtain a cumulative frequency distribution by adding the number of observations in each interval to the cumulated number of observations from the first interval through the preceding interval, inclusive.

The cumulative frequency distribution tells us quickly how many observations are below a certain value. For example, Table 2.6 shows that 74 employees are under 39.5 years old.

Relative Frequencies

We may at times wish to know what proportion of the observations under study fall within a certain class interval. We find this by dividing the number of values in that class interval by the total number of values. In Example 2.3, we find the proportion of observations in the class interval 15–19 by dividing 2 by 100. That is, $2 \div 100 = 0.02$. We refer to this as the *relative frequency* of occurrence of observations in that interval.

Just as we may construct cumulative frequency distributions, we may also construct *cumulative relative frequency* distributions. We can obtain cumulative

TABLE 2.6
Cumulative frequency distribution of the ages of 100 employees

Age (in years)	Frequency	Cumulative frequency
15–19	2	2
20–24	10	12
25–29	19	31
30–34	27	58
35–39	16	74
40–44	10	84
45–49	6	90
50–54	5	95
55–59	3	98
60–64	2	100
Total	100	

relative frequencies in one of two ways: We can cumulate individual relative frequencies, or we can divide cumulative frequencies by the total number of observations. Table 2.7 shows the relative frequency and cumulative relative frequency distributions for Example 2.3.

Effects of Too Few or Too Many Class Intervals

Let us now illustrate the effects of using too few or too many class intervals. Suppose that, in Example 2.3, we had used class-interval widths of 20. Table 2.8 shows the resulting frequency distribution. We can see that using only three class intervals results in too much loss of detail.

Now consider the same example, this time using three-year class intervals. Table 2.9 shows the results of using too many class intervals. The frequency distribution in Table 2.9 does not condense the original data enough to make clear the information they contain.

Unequal Class Intervals

As noted earlier, all class intervals for a frequency distribution should usually be of the same width. Sometimes, however, it may be impossible or undesirable to

TABLE 2.7
Relative frequency and cumulative relative frequency distributions of the ages of 100 employees

Age (in years)	Relative frequency	Cumulative relative frequency
15–19	0.02	0.02
20–24	0.10	0.12
25–29	0.19	0.31
30–34	0.27	0.58
35–39	0.16	0.74
40–44	0.10	0.84
45–49	0.06	0.90
50–54	0.05	0.95
55–59	0.03	0.98
60–64	0.02	1.00
Total	1.00	

TABLE 2.8
Frequency
distribution of ages
of 100 employees
using 20-year class
intervals

Usually, class-interval
widths should be equal.

Age (years)	15–34	35–54	55–74	
Frequency	58	37	5	Total: 100

have class intervals of equal width. Unequal class intervals are preferred, for example, when there are one or two extremely small or extremely large values in the set of data. In such cases, we may use an initial class interval labeled "less than . . ." or a terminal class interval labeled "greater than. . . ." This avoids having too many equal class intervals that contain zero frequencies. The disadvantage of such *open-end class intervals* is that there is no way of knowing their true widths unless we use some special notation to convey this information. In some instances we may need to use unequal class intervals at places other than the ends of a distribution to better communicate the true nature of the data.

2.5 SUMMARIZING DATA: THE HISTOGRAM AND FREQUENCY POLYGON

A frequency distribution may be portrayed graphically. This method of representing data has the usual advantages of graphical presentations. We can see the salient features of the data without having to interpret a column of numbers.

Histogram

A histogram is a special type of bar chart.

One way of graphically representing a frequency distribution or a relative frequency distribution is by means of a *histogram,* a special type of bar chart. In a histogram, we plot the variable under consideration on the horizontal axis, and the frequency (or relative frequency) on the vertical axis. We locate the class intervals on the horizontal axis, and above each we erect a vertical bar, or cell. The height of a bar corresponds to the frequency (or relative frequency) of observations in the class interval above which it is erected. We also make the adjacent cells of a histogram contiguous.

Figure 2.1 shows the histogram for the data in Table 2.5. Since there are two ages in the 15–19 interval, the height of the cell for that interval is two units. The next cell is 10 units high, since there are 10 ages in the interval 20–24. The

TABLE 2.9
Frequency
distribution of ages
of 100 employees
using three-year
class intervals

Age (years)	Frequency	Age (years)	Frequency
15–17	1	42–44	5
18–20	2	45–47	4
21–23	8	48–50	3
24–26	13	51–53	4
27–29	7	54–56	1
30–32	13	57–59	2
33–35	18	60–62	1
36–38	9	63–65	1
39–41	8		
		Total:	100

FIGURE 2.1
Histogram of ages
of 100 employees

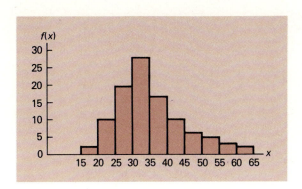

lower limits of the intervals show, on the horizontal axis, the points of separation between adjacent cells.

Frequency Polygon

A frequency polygon is a special type of line graph.

An alternative kind of graph for a frequency distribution is the *frequency polygon,* which is a special type of line graph. To construct this graph, we place a dot above the center of each class interval at a height that corresponds to the frequency for that interval. We then connect the dots with straight lines.

You can make a frequency polygon touch the horizontal axis at both ends by extending it to the center of an imaginary class interval at each end. Figure 2.2 shows a frequency polygon for the data in Table 2.5 superimposed over the corresponding histogram. This figure illustrates the relationship between these two graphic devices. Generally, the two graphs are not shown together in this manner. They are shown separately when both are desired, or alone when only one is wanted. Figure 2.3 shows, by itself, the frequency polygon for the frequency distribution of Table 2.5.

Ogive

An ogive is a graph of a cumulative frequency distribution.

Graphs of cumulative frequency distributions often help to describe the nature of data under analysis. This type of graph, which resembles a frequency polygon, is called an *ogive.* To construct an ogive, we place a dot above each lower class limit on the horizontal axis at a height corresponding to the cumulative frequency

FIGURE 2.2
Frequency polygon
and histogram of
ages of 100
employees

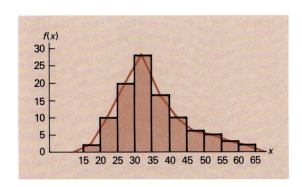

FIGURE 2.3
Frequency polygon
of ages of 100
employees

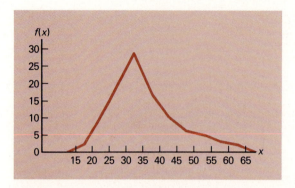

FIGURE 2.4
Ogive for
cumulative
frequency
distribution of
Table 2.6

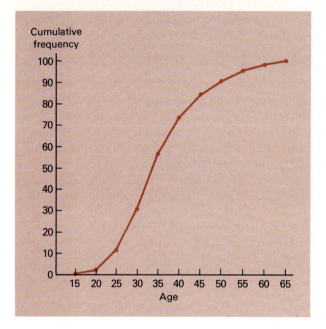

through the previous interval. We then connect these dots by straight lines. Any point on the ogive represents the number of observations that are less than the value directly below that point on the horizontal axis. Figure 2.4 shows the ogive for the cumulative frequency distribution of Table 2.6.

COMPUTER ANALYSIS

Many computer software packages that perform statistical analyses also contain routines for the construction of histograms. Figure 2.5 shows a computer-constructed histogram for the data in Table 2.4. The microcomputer software package STAT+ was used to construct this histogram.

**FIGURE 2.5
Computer-
constructed
histogram for the
data in Table 2.4
(software package
STAT+)**

RAW FREQUENCIES

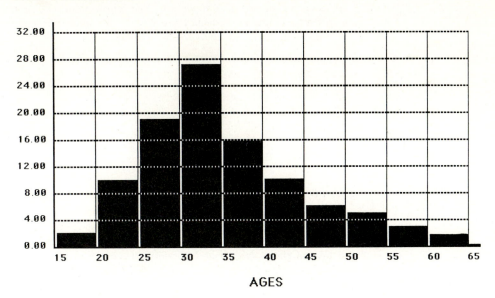

AGES

Exercises **2.2** Ⓒ The following are the number of miles (rounded to the nearest 1000) driven during a certain year by each of 110 salespeople. Prepare an ordered array, a frequency distribution, a cumulative frequency distribution, a histogram, and a frequency polygon for these data.

40	26	41	40	39	34	61	42	47	23	18
43	29	93	46	32	44	71	45	62	36	22
49	31	35	36	84	81	51	51	52	66	34
55	44	18	33	38	28	42	11	48	55	42
65	54	97	67	88	44	39	42	35	50	90
73	60	41	40	29	24	58	47	53	45	84
30	31	32	34	48	76	38	52	63	41	73
36	50	31	56	35	15	26	28	41	45	61
32	27	75	30	68	24	37	30	20	50	52
10	65	52	20	36	38	38	43	21	55	48

2.3 Ⓒ The following is an ordered array of the amounts of money (in millions of dollars) on deposit in each of 100 banks on a certain date. Prepare a frequency distribution, a cumulative frequency distribution, a histogram, and a frequency polygon for these data.

0.9	2.3	5.0	6.0	8.6	10.3	13.7	16.1	21.3	27.5
1.1	2.4	5.1	6.1	8.7	10.5	13.9	16.4	21.2	28.3
1.5	2.5	5.2	6.1	8.8	11.1	14.0	16.3	22.4	28.3
1.7	2.7	5.2	6.5	9.3	11.2	14.2	17.2	23.6	29.0
1.8	3.0	5.4	6.8	9.4	11.8	14.4	17.1	23.8	29.4
1.9	3.2	5.5	6.9	9.5	12.1	14.5	18.8	24.0	30.0
1.9	3.7	5.6	7.1	9.6	12.2	14.6	19.0	24.2	30.1
2.0	4.2	5.7	7.3	9.8	13.5	15.1	19.5	25.4	30.5
2.0	4.6	5.8	7.4	9.8	13.6	15.3	20.4	25.2	33.2
2.1	4.9	5.8	8.2	10.1	13.6	15.6	20.5	26.2	34.4

2.4 C As part of its screening process in hiring new assembly-line employees, a company gives each applicant an aptitude test. The following are the scores made by the last 100 applicants. Prepare a frequency distribution, a cumulative frequency distribution, a histogram, and a frequency polygon for these data.

49	86	40	45	48	93	97	58	58	98
58	82	52	56	50	85	80	60	62	80
62	72	65	60	64	70	78	67	69	88
60	72	66	66	65	75	78	62	64	74
68	72	67	61	62	72	79	71	74	73
76	69	73	78	73	78	78	74	73	69
76	65	74	75	78	60	62	72	74	72
70	66	77	78	77	64	65	77	82	61
88	51	87	84	84	54	50	82	88	65
81	46	87	83	94	41	49	90	98	52

2.5 C In a study of the history of small business firms in a certain area, researchers collect data on the length of time (in years) that 120 such firms existed before going out of business. The results are shown in the following table. **(a)** Construct a frequency distribution, a relative frequency distribution, a cumulative relative frequency distribution, and a histogram from these data. **(b)** Construct an ogive.

3	4	4	3	8	15	5	10	15	25	4	6
3	5	1	4	7	15	1	10	14	23	8	2
5	4	4	1	6	11	1	10	14	23	11	25
1	5	4	5	8	11	1	10	15	21	16	24
3	5	2	4	6	14	3	6	15	18	22	17
1	5	5	2	6	14	4	7	17	24	27	12
2	1	3	3	6	12	1	6	16	18	28	7
1	3	4	5	7	14	2	7	16	20	22	2
4	3	4	4	9	14	4	7	20	19	17	4
4	4	5	2	10	15	5	8	20	19	13	9

2.6 C The following are the lengths of service, in years, of 137 employees of a certain firm. Only employees with 10 or more years of service are included. From these data, construct the following: **(a)** a frequency distribution, **(b)** a cumulative frequency distribution, **(c)** a relative frequency distribution, **(d)** a cumulative relative frequency distribution, **(e)** a histogram, **(f)** an ogive.

10	10	19	17	21	22	20	24	25	33
12	13	19	15	24	21	22	26	29	32
11	12	17	16	23	21	24	26	27	31
12	12	17	17	20	24	24	29	25	33
12	10	17	15	22	22	20	25	27	31
10	14	19	19	22	22	22	25	27	34
11	13	17	15	20	20	24	29	28	37
11	13	17	18	20	20	23	29	26	35
14	11	16	18	20	20	22	26	28	35
14	19	19	17	24	24	20	26	27	44
13	15	15	23	21	21	20	26	29	42
14	19	15	23	20	20	21	27	31	
14	17	18	20	20	23	24	28	32	
11	15	18	22	24	24	20	27	33	

2.6 SUMMARIZING DATA: STEM-AND-LEAF DISPLAYS

Another graphical technique that is useful for representing quantitative data is the *stem-and-leaf* display. A stem-and-leaf display looks a lot like a histogram and serves the same purpose. That is, the display reveals the range of the data set, shows where the highest concentration of values occurs, provides information about the presence or absence of symmetry, and can indicate the degree to which the data are homogeneous.

In a stem-and-leaf display, each numerical value in a data set is partitioned into two parts. The first part is called the *stem,* and the second part is called the *leaf.* All the partitioned numbers are then shown together in a single display. The stem consists of one or more of the initial digits of the number, and the leaf is composed of one or more of the remaining digits.

Consider the number 12,375. In one situation we might make 12 the stem and 375 the leaf. The number, along with the other numbers in the data set, would be displayed as follows:

Stem	Leaf
12	375

In a different situation we might want to ignore the last two digits and form the following display:

Stem	Leaf
12	3

Numbers with the same stem are recorded in the same row of the completed display.

Suppose that the data set containing the number 12,375 also contains the number 12,376. Its stem is also 12, but its leaf is 376. In the first situation the two numbers would appear as

Stem	Leaf
12	375 376

and in the second situation they would appear as

Stem	Leaf
12	3 3

In the completed display the stems are arranged in order, from smallest to largest. If a data set contains the numbers 12,375; 12,376; and 13,250, these numbers might appear in a stem-and-leaf display as

Stem	Leaf
12	375 376
13	250

or as

Stem	Leaf
12	3 3
13	2

Although a stem-and-leaf display and a histogram communicate essentially the same information, there are some advantages to using a stem-and-leaf display. In the first place, when we use all the digits of a number in the display, the identities of the individual values are readily determined by inspection. In a histogram the individual identities of the numbers are obscured. A second advantage of using a stem-and-leaf display is the fact that its preparation automatically yields an ordered data set with respect to the digits used as stems. The choice of digits to serve as the stem is a matter of judgment; it depends, in part, on the sizes of the individual measurements and on the number of measurements in the data set. Stem-and-leaf displays are most effective with relatively small data sets.

As a rule, stem-and-leaf displays are not suitable for use in annual reports and other communications aimed at the general public. They are primarily of value for in-house use, as tools for helping managers and other decision makers to understand the nature of their data. Histograms are more appropriate for externally circulated publications.

EXAMPLE 2.4 Table 2.10 shows the number of employees under the supervision of 30 government department heads who responded to a survey. We wish to prepare a stem-and-leaf display from these data.

SOLUTION The stem-and-leaf display is shown in Figure 2.6.

TABLE 2.10 Number of employees under direct supervision of 30 government department heads

53	39	37	55	44	35
45	43	45	45	55	56
23	21	54	36	46	45
64	32	12	22	22	57
10	35	60	34	38	36

FIGURE 2.6 Stem-and-leaf display for the data in Table 2.10

Stem	Leaf
1	0 2
2	3 1 2 2
3	9 2 5 7 6 4 8 5 6
4	5 3 5 5 4 6 5
5	3 4 5 5 6 7
6	4 0

Exercises

2.7 The following are the number of microcomputers in use in a sample of 25 business firms in a large metropolitan area. Firms in suburban office parks are marked with asterisks.

7	21*	36*	26	35*
30	42*	40*	30	21
12	34	20*	46*	30
18*	35*	30	51*	30
25	27	17	27	16

Construct a stem-and-leaf display from these data and discuss the results. What does the display suggest regarding the firms located in suburban office parks as compared with the other firms?

2.8 The following are the paid circulations of a sample of 35 weekly newspapers. Those marked with an asterisk have been in existence 30 years or less.

5545*	5678	6414*	7549*	5908
1168	8165*	3949	6806*	4349
4268	4298	4004	7772*	7566
6001*	4853*	3112	2607	4780
3339	2892	3440	4145	9989*
8494*	3808	7701*	1998	3023
2891	5699*	4191	2485	6015

Construct a stem-and-leaf display from these data. What does the display suggest with respect to the "younger" newspapers as compared with the others?

 2.9 The following are the annual dollar sales per square foot of floor space as reported by a sample from each of two types of apparel store.

Adult Male:				
171.10	191.40	214.40	201.20	217.90
222.00	225.50	202.50	239.80	229.80
212.50	213.30	249.10	245.70	233.90
201.70	195.10	222.20	213.00	209.70
184.90	214.30	205.90	238.80	248.30

Adult Female:				
125.50	135.40	166.70	167.70	186.00
190.40	190.30	150.20	203.40	184.00
165.70	154.60	212.40	186.70	199.50
152.00	145.30	178.60	155.30	173.20
143.50	154.70	168.90	195.90	214.10

Construct a stem-and-leaf display for each set of data. What does a comparison of the two displays suggest regarding the two types of store?

2.7 GRAPHICAL REPRESENTATION OF QUALITATIVE DATA

When the variable in which we are interested is qualitative, the measurement procedure consists of determining the category of the variable to which a subject (or object) belongs. Suppose, for example, that the qualitative variable of interest is marital status. For each subject in the sample or population under study, we might determine whether he or she should be counted in the married, the never married, the widowed, or the divorced category. The numbers available for analysis, then, are the frequencies for the various categories. The resulting information can be presented either in the form of a frequency (or relative frequency) table or as a graph.

A frequency table for qualitative data consists of a list of the categories of the variable of interest along with the number (frequency) of subjects (or objects) that belong in each category.

EXAMPLE 2.5 In a survey of 40 business executives, respondents were asked to specify the primary business activity of their firm. The categories were manufacturing (M), transportation (T), communications (C), utilities (U), and other (O). The results are shown in Table 2.11. We wish to construct a frequency table from these data.

SOLUTION The frequency table for the data is shown as Table 2.12.

A relative frequency table for qualitative data contains a list of the categories of the qualitative variable of interest along with the *proportion* of subjects (or objects) that belong in each category.

The relative frequency table for the data of Example 2.5 is shown on page 29 as Table 2.13.

Bar Charts

The information contained in Tables 2.12 and 2.13 can be presented effectively in graphic form as a *bar chart*. When we prepare a bar chart for qualitative data,

TABLE 2.11 Primary business activity of 40 firms

Respondent	Activity	Respondent	Activity
1	C	21	T
2	T	22	M
3	M	23	C
4	C	24	M
5	T	25	M
6	M	26	O
7	C	27	C
8	M	28	T
9	U	29	O
10	T	30	M
11	T	31	C
12	M	32	O
13	M	33	T
14	C	34	M
15	M	35	M
16	O	36	C
17	M	37	T
18	C	38	U
19	M	39	M
20	U	40	C

TABLE 2.12
Frequency table
for the data of
Table 2.11

Primary business activity	Frequency
Manufacturing	15
Communications	10
Transportation	8
Utilities	3
Other	4
Total	40

we may represent the variable involved on either the horizontal or the vertical axis. The frequencies (or relative frequencies) are represented on the other axis. We list the various categories of the variable along the appropriate axis. When the horizontal axis is used to represent the variable, we place bars of equal width above the category labels; the bars are placed to the side of the category labels when the vertical axis is used to represent the variable. The height (or length) of a given bar is proportional to the frequency (or relative frequency) of the corresponding category. With qualitative data, the order in which the bars are placed is usually of no concern. Unlike in a histogram, the bars of a graph representing qualitative data should not touch each other.

EXAMPLE 2.6 Figure 2.7 shows a frequency bar chart and a relative frequency bar chart for the data of Table 2.11.

There are many effective ways of using bar charts to highlight important features of a set of data.

Grouped Bar Charts   Appropriate grouping of bars makes it possible to compare more than one characteristic for a given category at the same time. Figure 2.8 is an example of a grouped bar chart.

100% Bar Charts   Sometimes it is useful to portray in a single bar the percentages that various components are of a whole. This may be done in a single graph for the several levels of a qualitative variable. The result, called a *100% bar chart*, is illustrated in Figure 2.9.

Paired Bar Charts   Two different types of data may be represented effectively by a *paired bar chart*. Such a chart is shown in Figure 2.10.

TABLE 2.13
Relative frequency
table for the data
of Table 2.11

Primary business activity	Relative frequency
Manufacturing	0.3750
Communications	0.2500
Transportation	0.2000
Utilities	0.0750
Other	0.1000
Total	1.0000

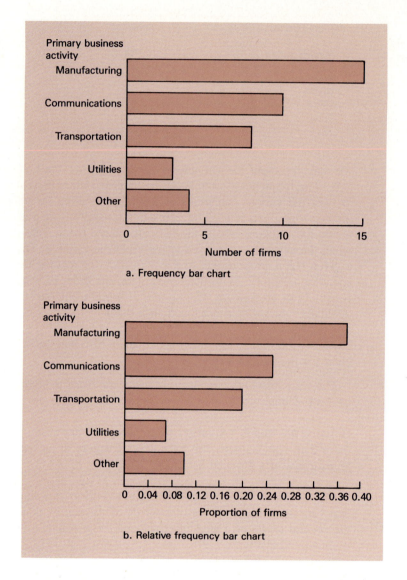

FIGURE 2.7
Bar charts for the data of Table 2.11

a. Frequency bar chart

b. Relative frequency bar chart

Deviation Bar Charts   When we wish to portray both positive and negative values in the same graph, we can use a *deviation bar chart*. Such a chart is suitable for showing the percentage change in some quantity from one year to the next. When possible, the bars in a deviation bar chart should be arranged in descending order of magnitude, as illustrated in Figure 2.11.

Pie Charts

An alternative to the 100% bar chart is the *pie chart*, which conveys the same information, but in a different form. In a pie chart the whole is represented by a

FIGURE 2.8
Ethnic groups of assembly-line employees at the five plants of a certain manufacturing firm

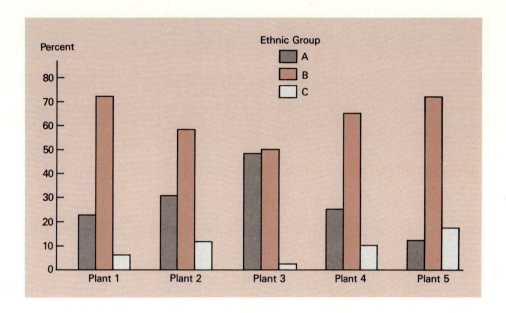

circle, or "pie," and the component parts are represented by "slices" of the pie. The size of a slice is proportional to the relative frequency of the component it represents. Since a complete circle contains 360 degrees, a component representing 25% of the total number of measurements, for example, will contain $(0.25)(360) = 90$ degrees. When possible, the largest slice of the pie should begin

FIGURE 2.9
Educational background of a sample of business executives by type of firm

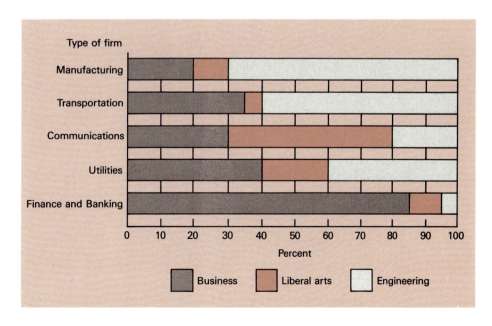

FIGURE 2.10
Number of items
produced and
number of items
replaced under
warranty for the
five plants of a
manufacturing
company

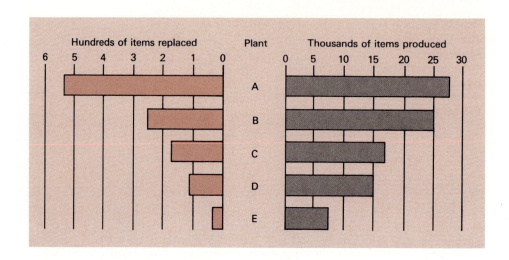

FIGURE 2.10
Number of items
produced and
number of items
replaced under
warranty for the
five plants of a
manufacturing
company

FIGURE 2.11
Percent change in
number of sickness
and accident
insurance claims
filed by employees
of ten large
business firms,
1987–1988

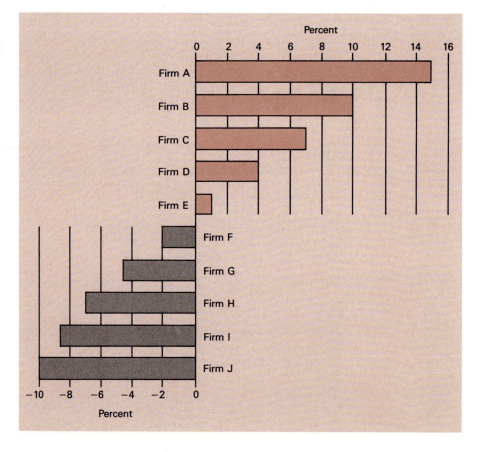

FIGURE 2.12
Estimated market
penetration
(percent of sales)
of five brands of
bath soap in two
geographic regions

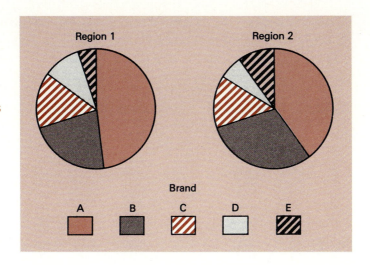

at the 12 o'clock position, and the other slices should follow, in a clockwise direction, according to size, with the smallest slice last. This rule may have to be violated when two or more pies are used, for comparison purposes, in the same graph. As a rule, the number of slices should not exceed five, and no slice should contain less than 5% (18 degrees) of the total pie. Figure 2.12 provides an example of the use of pie charts.

There are many other kinds of graphs that can be used to portray qualitative and quantitative data. When used properly, they are effective tools for bringing out the important characteristics of data sets. If they are not constructed and presented properly, however, they can create, in the minds of those who view them, false impressions about the data they represent.

Exercises

2.10 The following are a firm's quarterly sales in thousands of dollars in each of three major markets.

		Market	
Quarter	A	B	C
1	225	110	350
2	175	180	290
3	120	100	425
4	210	220	510

Using these data, construct the kind of bar chart that you think best communicates the information.

2.11 In a survey, the employees of a large firm were asked to state their opinion of the firm's health insurance plan. Of the 2500 female employees, 650 said they were satisfied, 975 said they were dissatisfied, and the remainder had no opinion. Of the 4300 male employees, 2279 said they were satisfied, 1720 said they were dissatisfied, and the remainder had no opinion. **(a)** Use what you consider to be the best type of bar chart to represent these data.   **(b)** Use a pie chart to portray the data.   **(c)** Which type of graph do you think is better for representing the data? Why?

2.12 The following housing data were reported by officials of 15 rural counties.

	Number of housing units		
County	Owner-occupied	Renter-occupied	Vacant
A	3828	1304	360
B	3838	1847	42
C	3708	2249	195
D	1358	800	413
E	5003	2471	100
F	3195	818	159
G	2896	1422	369
H	4127	1251	340
I	3054	898	191
J	4875	1760	404
K	4147	1104	254
L	4992	1307	125
M	2794	792	393
N	2688	974	488
O	2876	1412	318

Construct a single graph that you think best portrays this information.

2.13 The following data were reported by 10 business firms.

Number of persons employed on July 1

Firm	1987	1988
A	859	1031
B	962	977
C	491	481
D	973	924
E	904	904
F	285	295
G	252	265
H	287	270
I	847	847
J	410	381

Construct a single graph that you think best portrays this information.

2.14 The following table shows the number of housing units located in each of 12 geographic regions and the size of each region.

Region	Area (sq. mi.)	Number of housing units	Region	Area (sq. mi.)	Number of housing units
A	520	5,813	G	372	3,346
B	268	12,240	H	414	4,682
C	260	3,206	I	355	6,947
D	566	12,958	J	259	3,409
E	285	7,388	K	441	3,566
F	400	4,152	L	252	4,096

Construct a single graph that you think best portrays these data.

2.8 SUMMARIZING DATA: DESCRIPTIVE MEASURES

In addition to tabular and graphical methods of summarizing data, one also finds it useful to summarize data by methods that lead to numerical results, called *descriptive measures*. We shall discuss two types of descriptive measures: *measures of central tendency* and *measures of dispersion*. They may be computed from the data contained in a sample or from the data included in a finite population. In order to distinguish between the two types on the basis of whether they refer to a sample or a population, we use the following definitions:

A descriptive measure computed from or used to describe a sample of data is called a statistic.

A descriptive measure computed from or used to describe a population of data is called a parameter.

Throughout this text we will use different symbols to distinguish between descriptive measures that relate to a population and those that relate to a sample.

Measures of Central Tendency

Even when you draw a collection of data from a common source, individual observations are not likely to have the same value. It is impractical to keep in mind all the values that may be present in a set of data. What we need is some single value that we may consider typical of the set of data as a whole. The need for such a single value is usually met by one of the three measures of central tendency: the *sample mean*, the *median*, and the *mode*.

The Sample Mean The most familiar measure of central tendency is the arithmetic mean. Popularly known as the average, it is sometimes called the *arithmetic average*, or simply the *mean*. We find it by adding all the values in a set of data and dividing the total by the number of values that were summed.

EXAMPLE 2.7 A bus company uses extra drivers to handle demands for service beyond its routine schedule. A sample of five extra drivers drove the following numbers of hours during a certain week. What is the value of the sample mean?

Driver	A	B	C	D	E
Hours driven	17	28	35	42	45

SOLUTION To find the mean number of hours driven by this sample of drivers, add the five numbers showing the hours driven and divide by 5. Thus we have

$$Sample\ mean = \frac{\text{sum of all values in the sample}}{\text{number of values in the sample}} \qquad (2.1)$$

For the present example, we have

$$\text{Mean hours driven} = \frac{17 + 28 + 35 + 42 + 45}{5} = \frac{167}{5} = 33.4$$

We can do this in a more compact form by using the capital letter X to designate the variable of interest, which here is the hours driven by extra drivers during a week. As we noted in Chapter 1, particular values of this variable may be represented by lower-case letters as follows: $x_1, x_2, \ldots, x_n$, where the subscripts refer to the location of the value in the sequence of data. For example, x_1 refers to the first value, x_2 to the second value, and so on, to x_n, which represents the last value in a set of sample data. For the present example, $x_1 = 17$, $x_2 = 28$, $x_3 = 35$, $x_4 = 42$, and $x_5 = 45$. Note that the subscript n also indicates the size of the sample. If $\bar{x}$ denotes the mean of the sample, we can write Equation 2.1 as

$$\bar{x} = \frac{\sum_{i=1}^{n} x_i}{n} \tag{2.2}$$

where the symbol

$$\sum_{i=1}^{n} \qquad (\text{``summation from } i = 1 \text{ to } i = n\text{''})$$

$\bar{x}$ is the sample mean.

tells us to add the values of X from the first to the last. The subscript i on the x following Σ indicates a typical value from the series of values under study. From now on, we will omit the $i = 1$ and the n when it is clear from the context what they should be. We can write the formula for the sample mean, then, as

$$\bar{x} = \frac{\sum x_i}{n} \tag{2.3}$$

A more complete discussion of summation notation is given in Appendix III.

On occasion, we may have some finite population of values for which we want to compute the mean. The procedure for calculating the population mean is exactly the same as that for calculating the sample mean.

The Population Mean   To distinguish a sample mean from a population mean, we designate the population mean by the Greek letter μ (pronounced "mu"), and use the letter N to indicate the size of a finite population. Thus the formula for calculating the mean of a finite population is given by

$$\mu = \frac{\sum_{i=1}^{N} x_i}{N} \tag{2.4}$$

μ is the population mean.

or simply

$$\mu = \frac{\sum x_i}{N} \tag{2.5}$$

Since $\bar{x}$ is computed from a sample, it is called a *statistic*, whereas μ, computed from a population of data, is called a *parameter*.

Properties of the Mean The properties of the arithmetic mean include the three listed below:

1. For a given set of data, there is one, and only one, arithmetic mean.
2. Its meaning is easily understood.
3. Since every value goes into its computation, it is affected by the magnitude of each value.

Because of this last property, the arithmetic mean may not be the best measure of central tendency when there are one or two extreme values present in a set of data—that is, if a value in the set is unusually large or small.

The Mean as a Balance Point You can think of the mean as the *balance point* of a set of data. Think of the number line as a balance bar and the different values in the data set as cubes of equal weight. If you place each of the "cubes" on the "balance bar" at a position corresponding to its numerical value and place a fulcrum at the point on the balance bar corresponding to the numerical value of the mean, the bar will be in perfect balance.

EXAMPLE 2.8 Suppose that we have the following sample of values: 1, 1, 2, 5, 2, 2, 8. Using Equation 2.3, we find that

$$\bar{x} = \frac{1 + 1 + 2 + 5 + 2 + 2 + 8}{7} = \frac{21}{7} = 3$$

Figure 2.13 illustrates the concept that the mean is the balance point for the data. We can see here that the sum of the distances of the observations to the left of the mean plus the sum of the distances of the observations to the right of the mean equals zero. That is,

$$[3(-1) + 2(-2)] + [1(+2) + 1(+5)] = -7 + (+7) = 0$$

This demonstrates another property of the arithmetic mean: *The sum of the deviations* $(x_i - \bar{x})$ *of a set of observations about their mean is equal to zero.* We may express this property symbolically as follows:

$$\Sigma(x_i - \bar{x}) = 0$$

FIGURE 2.13
The mean is the balance point of a data set

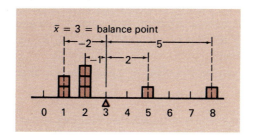

For our present example, as we have seen, we have

$$\Sigma(x_i - \bar{x}) = (1 - 3) + (1 - 3) + (2 - 3) + (5 - 3) + (2 - 3)$$
$$+ (2 - 3) + (8 - 3)$$
$$= (-2) + (-2) + (-1) + (+2) + (-1) + (-1) + (+5)$$
$$= 0$$

The Median Another useful measure of central tendency is the *median*.

The *median* is that value above which half the values lie and below which the other half lie.

If the number of items is odd, the median is the value of the middle item of an ordered array, when the items are arranged in ascending (or descending) order of magnitude. If the number of items is even, none of the items has an equal number of values above and below it. In this event, the median is equal to the mean, or average, of the two middle values.

EXAMPLE 2.9 Five households have annual total incomes of $10,000, $24,500, $15,000, $21,500, and $13,000. What is the value of the sample median?

SOLUTION To find the median total income for these five households, we first arrange the values in order of magnitude:

$10,000   13,000   15,000   21,500   24,500

The median is the middle value, $15,000. Suppose that there had been a sixth value of $9000. The ordered array would have been

$9000   10,000   13,000   15,000   21,500   24,500

and the median would have been ($13,000 + $15,000)/2 = $14,000.

Properties of the Median Properties of the median include the following:

1. The median can always be found for a set of numerical data. For a given set of data, there is only one median.
2. The median is not often affected by extreme values, as the mean is.
3. The median can be used to characterize certain qualitative data. For example, a product might be marketed in three quality categories—good, better, and best—where the quality of the product falling in the "better" category is considered "average."
4. The median is easy to calculate by hand unless a large number of values are involved.

The Mode The mode for ungrouped discrete data is the value that occurs most frequently. If all the values in a set of data are different, there is no mode. In the above family income example, there is no mode because all the values are dif-

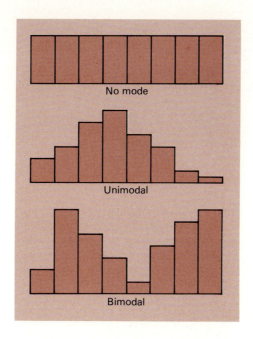

No mode

Unimodal

Bimodal

ferent. Some data sets may have more than one mode. Figure 2.14 shows the histograms of distributions with varying numbers of modes.

EXAMPLE 2.10 Here is a set of data that does have a mode. A clerical pool consists of 10 employees whose ages are 18, 19, 21, 22, 22, 22, 26, 32, 35, and 36. The most frequently occurring, or *modal,* age is 22. Some sets of data may have two modes, in which case the data are said to be *bimodal.* If the ages of the employees noted above had been 18, 19, 21, 22, 22, 22, 26, 32, 32, and 32, the two modes would be 22 and 32. Although a set of data can have more than two modes, the usefulness of indicating a large number of modes is questionable.

In symmetrical distributions, the mean and median are identical in value. In asymmetrical distributions, these values are not equal. Figure 2.15 shows the relative positions of the mean, median, and mode for a symmetrical distribution and for some asymmetrical distributions.

Of the three measures of central tendency we have discussed, the mean plays the most important role in the type of statistics presented in this text.

In a symmetrical distribution, the mean and median are equal.

Measures of Dispersion

Once we have computed the mean of a set of data, we want to know the extent to which the values differ from this mean.

We use the term *dispersion* to describe the degree to which values in a set vary about their mean.

Other terms that convey this same concept are *variation, scatter,* and *spread.* When the values in a sample or population are all close to the mean, they exhibit

FIGURE 2.15
Locations of mean, median, and mode for different distributions

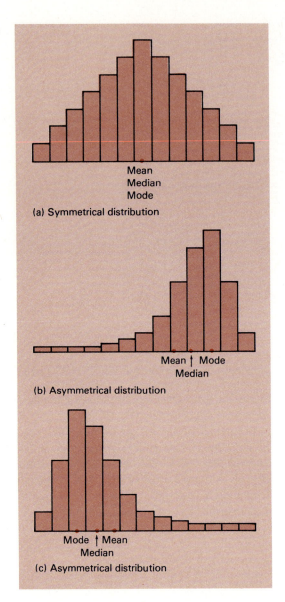

(a) Symmetrical distribution

(b) Asymmetrical distribution

(c) Asymmetrical distribution

less dispersion than when some of the values are much larger and/or much smaller than the mean. Figure 2.16 shows frequency polygons for two populations. They both have the same mean, but they have different amounts of dispersion. Population B has a greater amount of dispersion, or variation, than Population A. Four descriptive measures used to express the amount of dispersion present in a set of data are the *range,* the *average deviation,* the *variance,* and the *standard deviation.* We discuss each of these on the following pages.

FIGURE 2.16
Two frequency
polygons
representing
distributions with
equal means but
different amounts
of dispersion

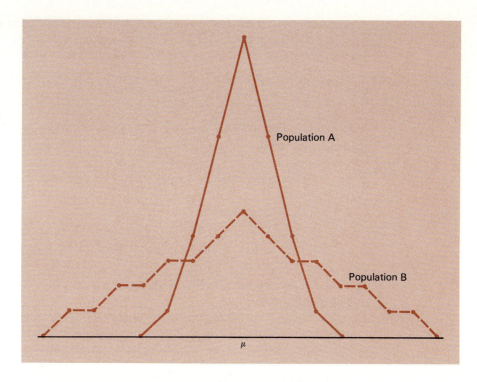

The Range   The *range,* as noted earlier, is defined as the difference between the largest and the smallest values in a set of data.

EXAMPLE 2.11 Ten typists applying for a job with a bank made the following scores on a typing speed test. What is the range for these data?

Applicant	1	2	3	4	5	6	7	8	9	10
Speed (words/min)	54	55	79	70	86	81	75	89	72	68

SOLUTION We compute the range by subtracting the smallest score from the largest score. That is, for these data, Range = 89 − 54 = 35.

The range is easy to compute. However, it's usually an unsatisfactory measure of dispersion, since only two values in a set of data are used in computing it. In other words, the range does not use all the information available in the data it is supposed to describe.

The Average Deviation   The *average deviation* expresses the average amount by which the values in a sample or population differ from their mean. When computed from a sample, the average deviation takes into account the deviation of each value from the mean, $x_i - \bar{x}$. However, as we have seen, the sum of these deviations, and hence their mean, is always equal to 0. We must modify this procedure if it is to lead to a valuable measure of dispersion. An appropriate modification is to take the mean of the deviations while ignoring the signs. That is, we add the absolute values of the deviations and divide by n to obtain the average deviation. The procedure is expressed in the following formula:

$$\text{Average deviation} = \frac{\Sigma|x_i - \bar{x}|}{n} \tag{2.6}$$

EXAMPLE 2.12 Let us use the data of Example 2.11 to show how to compute the average deviation.

SOLUTION Since the mean of these data is 72.9, we have

$$\text{Average deviation} = \frac{|54 - 72.9| + |55 - 72.9| + \cdots + |68 - 72.9|}{10}$$

$$= \frac{18.9 + 17.9 + \cdots + 4.9}{10} = 9.1$$

Thus we can say that, on the average, the values differ from their mean by 9.1 words per minute.

The average deviation is an intuitively satisfying measure of dispersion. But its usefulness is limited because it does not lend itself to further mathematical manipulation. Consequently, it is seldom used as a measure of dispersion.

The Variance The *variance,* like the average deviation, uses the deviations of all the values from their mean, that is, $x_i - \bar{x}$. In computing the variance, however, we avoid negative differences by squaring, rather than by taking absolute values. We may compute the variance of a sample of data, then, from the formula

$$\text{Sample variance} = \frac{\Sigma(x_i - \bar{x})^2}{n} \tag{2.7}$$

Thus the variance is also a kind of average. It is the average of the squares of the deviations of the individual values from their mean. The numerator of Equation 2.7 is called the *sum of squares about the mean.*

The sample variance s^2 has two functions in statistical analysis. First, it is used as a measure of the dispersion present in the sample. Second, it is used to *estimate* the variance of the population from which the sample was drawn. As a measure of the dispersion present in a sample, the variance computed by Equation 2.7 is perfectly adequate. However, when we use the sample variance as an estimate of the population variance, it is better to divide the sum of squares about the mean by $n - 1$ rather than n. (Chapter 6 will discuss this subject more fully.) Since the main object of computing a sample variance is usually to estimate the population variance, the following formula is almost always used in defining the sample variance:

s^2 is the sample variance.

$$s^2 = \frac{\Sigma(x_i - \bar{x})^2}{n - 1} \tag{2.8}$$

s is the sample standard deviation.

The Standard Deviation The variance is expressed in square units. Suppose that the data are measured in feet. The variance is expressed in feet *squared*. In statistical analysis you often want to have a measure of dispersion expressed in the same units as the original observations. We obtain such a measure, called the *standard deviation*, by taking the positive square root of the variance. That is, the standard deviation is equal to

$$s = \sqrt{\frac{\Sigma(x_i - \bar{x})^2}{n - 1}}$$

(2.9)

EXAMPLE 2.13 Let us compute the variance and standard deviation for the typing speed scores given in Example 2.11.

SOLUTION

$$s^2 = \frac{(54 - 72.9)^2 + (55 - 72.9)^2 + \cdots + (68 - 72.9)^2}{10 - 1}$$

$$= \frac{1248.9}{9} = 138.77$$

$$s = \sqrt{138.77} = 11.8$$

These formulas for the standard deviation and variance are known as *definitional* or *conceptual* formulas because they are literal representations of the definitions and concepts involved. Learning these formulas helps convey the concepts.

When there are a large number of values involved in the computations, using the definitional formulas without a computer may be tedious. There are alternative, less cumbersome formulas that we may use, called *computational formulas*, that yield exactly the same results as the definitional formulas. These are not approximations, but shortcut formulas algebraically derived from the definitional formulas. Their purpose is to lighten your burden, especially when you're using a desk calculator or working by hand.

The shortcut formula for the variance is

The computational formula for s^2.

$$s^2 = \frac{\Sigma x_i^2 - \dfrac{(\Sigma x_i)^2}{n}}{n - 1} = \frac{n\Sigma x_i^2 - (\Sigma x_i)^2}{n(n - 1)}$$

(2.10)

If we divide both the numerator and the denominator of Equation 2.10 by *n*, we obtain the following alternative form of the shortcut formula for the sample variance:

$$s^2 = \frac{\Sigma x_i^2 - n(\bar{x})^2}{n - 1}$$

(2.10a)

EXAMPLE 2.14 Let us again compute the variance for the data of Example 2.11, this time using Equation 2.10.

SOLUTION

$$s^2 = \frac{10(54^2 + 55^2 + \cdots + 68^2) - (54 + 55 + \cdots + 68)^2}{(10)(9)} = 138.77$$

and the standard deviation, as before, is

$$s = \sqrt{138.77} = 11.8$$

If we use Equation 2.10a, we obtain the same result:

$$s^2 = \frac{(54^2 + 55^2 + \cdots + 68^2) - 10(72.9)^2}{9}$$

$$= \frac{54{,}393 - 10(5314.41)}{9}$$

$$= 138.77$$

Population Variance and Standard Deviation   The variance and standard deviation of a *population* are designated, respectively, by the symbols σ^2 and σ (pronounced sigma). We compute the variance σ^2 of a finite population as follows:

σ^2 is the population variance.

$$\sigma^2 = \frac{\Sigma(x_i - \mu)^2}{N} = \frac{\Sigma x_i^2 - \frac{(\Sigma x_i)^2}{N}}{N} = \frac{N\Sigma x_i^2 - (\Sigma x_i)^2}{N \cdot N} \qquad (2.11)$$

We find the standard deviation of the population by taking the positive square root of σ^2. Suppose, for example, that we have a population of size $N = 4$ consisting of the values 10, 4, 3, and 7. By Equation 2.11, we find that

$$\sigma^2 = \frac{4(10^2 + 4^2 + 3^2 + 7^2) - (10 + 4 + 3 + 7)^2}{4(4)} = 7.5$$

σ is the population standard deviation.

The standard deviation, then, is $\sigma = \sqrt{7.5} = 2.74$.

Chebyshev's Theorem

We said earlier that when all the values in a set of data are located near their mean, they exhibit a small amount of variation or dispersion. And those sets of data in which some values are located far from their mean have a large amount of dispersion. Expressing these relationships in terms of the standard deviation, which measures dispersion, we can say that when the values of a set of data are concentrated near their mean, the standard deviation is small. And when the values of a set of data are scattered widely about the mean, the standard deviation is large. If the standard deviation computed from a set of data is small, the values are concentrated near the mean. And if the standard deviation is large, the values from which it is computed are dispersed widely about their mean.

A useful rule that illustrates the relationship between dispersion and standard deviation is given by *Chebyshev's theorem*, named after the Russian mathematician P. L. Chebyshev (1821–1894). This theorem enables us to calculate for any set of data (either a sample or a population) the minimum proportion of values that can be expected to lie within a specified number of standard deviations of the mean. The theorem tells us that at least 75% of the values in a set of data can be expected to fall within *two* standard deviations of the mean, at least 88.9% within *three* standard deviations of the mean, and at least 96% within *five* standard deviations of the mean. Chebyshev's theorem may be stated in general terms as follows:

Given a set of *n* observations $x_1, x_2, x_3, \ldots, x_n$, at least $(1 - 1/k^2)$ of the observations will fall within *k* (where $k > 1$) standard deviations of the mean of the set of observations.

Let us now see how we can apply Chebyshev's theorem in practice.

Suppose that a set of data has a mean of 150 and a standard deviation of 25. We can say that we can expect at least 75% of the values to be between 100 and 200, at least 88.9% to be between 75 and 225, and at least 96% to be between 25 and 275. Suppose that another set of data has the same mean, 150, but a standard deviation of 10. Applying Chebyshev's theorem, for this set of data we can expect at least 75% of the values to be between 130 and 170, at least 88.9% to be between 120 and 180, and at least 96% to be between 100 and 200. Thus the intervals computed for the latter set of data are all narrower than those for the former. Therefore we see that for a set of data with a small standard deviation, a larger proportion of values will be concentrated near the mean than for a set of data with a large standard deviation. We will discuss Chebyshev's theorem again later in the text.

Exercises

2.15 Ⓒ An office supply company has a fleet of 100 trucks that it uses for making local deliveries. During a recent month the number of miles each truck in a sample of 10 was driven was as follows. Compute the following descriptive measures: **(a)** the mean, **(b)** the median, **(c)** the mode, **(d)** the range, **(e)** the variance, **(f)** the standard deviation.

Truck number	1	2	3	4	5	6	7	8	9	10
Miles driven ($\times 100$)	23	34	20	18	30	30	30	38	25	27

2.16 Ⓒ The following are the amounts for food and lodging claimed on the expense accounts of a sample of 12 salespersons for the same day. For these data, compute: **(a)** the mean, **(b)** the median, **(c)** the mode, **(d)** the range, **(e)** the variance, **(f)** the standard deviation, **(g)** the average deviation.

Salesperson	1	2	3	4	5	6	7	8	9	10	11	12
Amount, $	55	84	63	57	52	70	56	68	74	66	68	64

2.17 Ⓒ The following are the prices (in thousands of dollars) of 15 condominiums in a sample selected from those in a new complex: 59, 52, 54, 56, 62, 62, 56, 56, 58, 55, 60, 54, 59, 55, 59. For these data, find: **(a)** the mean, **(b)** the median, **(c)** the mode, **(d)** the range, **(e)** the variance, **(f)** the standard deviation.

2.18 Ⓒ The following are the number of miles between home and office of a sample of 10 people who work for the same firm: 3, 16, 12, 11, 14, 5, 7, 14, 9, 8. For these data, find: (a) the mean, (b) the median, (c) the mode, (d) the range, (e) the variance, (f) the standard deviation.

 2.19 A grocer has determined that the mean daily sales of eggs is 100 dozen, with a standard deviation of 10. (a) What minimum percentage of the time can the grocer expect to sell between 80 and 120 dozen per day? (b) Between what two bounds can the grocer expect daily sales to lie at least 96% of the time?

2.9 DESCRIPTIVE MEASURES COMPUTED FROM GROUPED DATA

One sometimes needs to compute the various descriptive measures from data that have been grouped into class intervals and presented as a frequency distribution such as the one shown in Table 2.5. If the data consist of a large number of values, and if the computations have to be made by hand or on a calculator, we can save ourselves a great deal of labor by grouping the data before we compute the descriptive measures. If you have access to a computer, however, having a large number of values to analyze poses no particular problem. You can usually enter the raw data into the computer with little inconvenience.

Sometimes original data are inaccessible, but a frequency distribution based on the data is available in some published source, such as an annual report. In that case, if you need descriptive measures, use the techniques given in this section.

When data are grouped into class intervals, each observation loses its identity. We can determine the number of observations falling in each of the various class intervals from a frequency distribution, but we cannot determine the actual values associated with the observations. For this reason, when we compute descriptive measures from grouped data, we must make certain assumptions regarding the data. As a consequence of making these assumptions, we must regard the values of the descriptive measures computed in this manner as approximations to the true values. We will indicate the assumptions that have to be made as we consider each measure.

The Mean

When we compute the mean from grouped data, we make the assumption that each observation falling within a given class interval is equal to the value of the midpoint of that interval. The midpoint of a class interval is called the *class mark*. We obtain the class mark by adding the respective class limits and dividing by 2. Consider the data on employee ages in Table 2.5. To calculate the mean for this frequency distribution, we assume that the 2 observations in the first class interval are both equal to 17, the 10 observations in the second class interval are equal to 22, and so on. Of course, for a given frequency distribution, it is unlikely that all the observations in the class intervals have values that are actually equal to the class marks. We make this assumption with the hope that the errors that it intro-duces will average out. Experience has shown that the assumption is generally satisfactory, as are the assumptions made about the other descriptive measures computed from grouped data.

To compute the mean, assume that all values in an interval are equal to the class mark.

Since each observation takes on the value of the class mark of the interval in which it falls, we compute the mean by multiplying each class mark by its corresponding frequency. Then we add the resulting products, and divide the total by the number of observations. We may express the procedure for sample data by

$$\bar{x} = \frac{\sum_{i=1}^{k} x_i f_i}{n} \tag{2.12}$$

where k = the number of class intervals, x_i = the class mark of the ith class interval, and f_i = the frequency of the ith class interval.

Note that Equation 2.12 resembles Equation 2.2, the formula for computing the mean from ungrouped data. The numerator of Equation 2.12 illustrates an alternative way of finding the sum of a set of numbers when some of them are duplicated. For example, suppose we have the numbers 2, 2, 2, 3, 3, 6, 6, 6, 6. We can find the sum of these numbers by simple addition:

$$2 + 2 + 2 + 3 + 3 + 6 + 6 + 6 + 6 = 36$$

This is the procedure followed in obtaining the numerator of Equation 2.2. Alternatively, we can find the sum as follows:

$$3(2) + 2(3) + 4(6) = 6 + 6 + 24 = 36$$

This is the procedure followed in computing the numerator of Equation 2.12.

The mean computed by Equation 2.12 is an example of a *weighted mean*. It is a mean of the class marks in which each is weighted by the frequency with which it is represented in the frequency distribution.

The Variance and Standard Deviation

We make the same assumption regarding the values assumed by the observations when we compute the variance and standard deviation from grouped data. Consequently, the definitional or conceptual formula for the sample variance is

To compute the variance and standard deviation, assume that all values in a class interval are equal to the class mark.

$$s^2 = \frac{\sum_{i=1}^{k} (x_i - \bar{x})^2 f_i}{n - 1} \tag{2.13}$$

and the computational formula is

$$s^2 = \frac{n \sum_{i=1}^{k} x_i^2 f_i - (\sum_{i=1}^{k} x_i f_i)^2}{n(n - 1)} \tag{2.14}$$

or

$$s^2 = \frac{\sum_{i=1}^{k} x_i^2 f_i - n(\bar{x})^2}{n - 1} \tag{2.14a}$$

We find the standard deviation by taking the square root of s^2.

We may use the data of Table 2.5 to show how to compute the mean, variance, and standard deviation. Table 2.14 gives the necessary intermediate calculations.

TABLE 2.14
Intermediate calculations for computing descriptive measures for the frequency distribution of Table 2.5

Class interval	Class mark (x_i)	Frequency (f_i)	$x_i f_i$	$x_i^2 f_i$
15–19	17	2	34	578
20–24	22	10	220	4,840
25–29	27	19	513	13,851
30–34	32	27	864	27,648
35–39	37	16	592	21,904
40–44	42	10	420	17,640
45–49	47	6	282	13,254
50–54	52	5	260	13,520
55–59	57	3	171	9,747
60–64	62	2	124	7,688
Total		100	3,480	130,670

For the mean, we have

$$\bar{x} = \frac{3480}{100} = 34.8$$

For the variance, we have

$$s^2 = \frac{100(130,670) - (3480)^2}{(100)(99)} = 96.63$$

and for the standard deviation, $s = \sqrt{96.63} = 9.8$
    By Equation 2.14a we have

$$s^2 = \frac{130,670 - 100(34.8)^2}{99}$$

$$= 96.63$$

The Population Variance and Standard Deviation   The formulas in this section have implied that the values used in the calculations are those of a sample. To convert these formulas to formulas for computing the corresponding descriptive measures for a finite population, substitute μ for $\bar{x}$, σ^2 for s^2, and N for n and $n - 1$ wherever they appear in Equations 2.12 through 2.14. That is,

$$\mu = \frac{\sum_{i=1}^{k} x_i f_i}{N}$$

$$\sigma^2 = \frac{\sum_{i=1}^{k} (x_i - \mu)^2 f_i}{N}$$

$$= \frac{N \sum_{i=1}^{k} x_i^2 f_i - (\sum_{i=1}^{k} x_i f_i)^2}{N \cdot N}$$

The Median

We may also compute the median from grouped data. Earlier, we defined this measure of central tendency as the value, in a set of data, above and below which half the values lie. This definition holds when the data are in the form of a frequency distribution. But since the individual values in a frequency distribution are not identifiable, we cannot find the exact value of the median.

The median for a frequency distribution is that value, or point, on the horizontal axis of the histogram of the distribution at which a perpendicular line divides the area of the histogram into two equal parts.

For this definition to be valid, we must assume that the values in each class interval are evenly distributed over the entire interval. Figure 2.17 shows the location of the median of a set of data represented by a histogram.

To compute the median, assume that the values in a class interval are evenly distributed over the interval.

The first step in computing the median for a frequency distribution is to determine the class interval in which it is located. We do this by finding the interval that contains the $n/2$ value. For the employee-ages example, $n/2 = 50$. Table 2.6, the cumulative frequency distribution, shows that the fiftieth value is located in the fourth class interval. In Table 2.6, there are 31 values that are less than 29.5, the *true* upper limit of the third interval. Thus that point is only $50 - 31 = 19$ values away from the median. Assume that the values in the fourth class interval are evenly distributed throughout the interval. Then, since there are 27 values in the fourth interval, we can reason that the median is that value that is 19/27ths of the way into the fourth interval. To obtain the value of the median, we multiply 19/27 by 5, the width of the class interval, and add the product to 29.5, the true lower limit of the fourth class interval. We have, then, for the employee-ages data,

$$\text{Median} = 29.5 + \frac{19}{27}(5) = 33.0$$

In general, we find the median of a set of data, either a sample or a population, from

$$\text{Median} = L + \frac{j}{f}W \qquad\qquad (2.15)$$

FIGURE 2.17
Histogram showing median

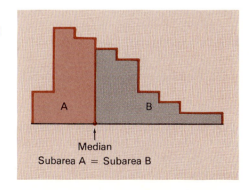

Median
Subarea A = Subarea B

where L = the true lower limit of the class interval in which the median is located

j = the number of values still needed to reach the median, after the lower limit of the interval containing the median has been reached

f = the frequency in the class interval containing the median

W = the width of the class interval

The Mode

When we want to find the mode of a frequency distribution, we usually just specify the *modal class,* which is defined as the *class interval containing the largest number of values.* The modal class for the employee-ages example is the fourth interval, whose limits are 30 and 34.

Percentiles and Quartiles

The mean and median are special cases of a family of parameters called *location parameters.* These parameters "locate" a distribution on the horizontal axis by designating certain positions in terms of the variable assigned to that axis when the distribution is graphed. For example, a distribution with a median of 50 is located to the right of a distribution with a median of 25 when the two distributions are graphed. Other location parameters include *percentiles* and *quartiles.* We define a percentile as follows:

Given a set of observations $x_1, x_2, \ldots, x_n,$ the pth percentile P is the value of X such that p percent of the observations are less than P and $(100 - p)$ percent are greater than $P.$

To distinguish one of the 99 possible percentiles from the others, we use appropriate subscripts on $P.$ For example, the tenth percentile is $P_{10},$ the sixty-fifth percentile is $P_{65},$ and so on. The median is the fiftieth percentile, $P_{50}.$

Suppose that we wish to find the sixtieth percentile of the distribution given in Table 2.5. Since 60% of 100 (the sample size) is 60, the sixtieth observation, when the observations are ordered, is $P_{60},$ the sixtieth percentile. When we consult the cumulative frequency distribution (Table 2.6), we note that the sixtieth observation is in the class interval 35–39. We assume that the values falling in, an interval are uniformly distributed over the interval. To find the sixtieth percentile, we use the procedure for computing the median:

$$P_{60} = 34.5 + \frac{60 - 58}{16}(5) = 35.125$$

We say that 60% of the observations are below and 40% are above 35.125.

The twenty-fifth percentile is often called the *first quartile* $Q_1.$ The fiftieth percentile (the median) is often called the second or *middle quartile* $Q_2,$ and the seventy-fifth is called the *third quartile* $Q_3.$

For ungrouped data, the quartiles may be conveniently found as follows:

$$Q_1 = \frac{n+1}{4} \text{ ordered observation}$$

$$Q_2 \text{ (the median)} = \frac{2(n+1)}{4} = \frac{n+1}{2} \text{ ordered observation}$$

$$Q_3 = \frac{3(n+1)}{4} \text{ ordered observation}$$

Box-and-Whisker Plots

The information about a data set that the quartiles provide can be portrayed graphically by what is known as a *box-and-whisker plot*. To construct a box-and-whisker plot, we proceed as follows.

1. The variable of interest is represented on the horizontal axis.
2. A box is drawn in the space above the horizontal axis in such a way that the left end of the box aligns with the first quartile Q_1 and the right end of the box is aligned with the third quartile Q_3.
3. The box is divided into two parts by a vertical line that aligns with the median.
4. A line, called a *whisker,* is extended from the left end of the box to a point that aligns with the smallest measurement in the data set.
5. Another line, or whisker, is extended from the right end of the box to a point that aligns with the largest measurement in the data set.

The following example illustrates the construction of a box plot.

EXAMPLE 2.15 Table 2.15 shows the downtime, in hours, recorded for 30 machines owned by a large manufacturing company. The period of time covered was the same for all machines.

We wish to construct a box-and-whisker plot for these data.

SOLUTION The smallest and largest measurements are 1 and 13, respectively. The first quartile is the $(30 + 1)/4 = 7.75$th ordered measurement and is equal to 4. The median is the $(30 + 1)/2 = 15.5$th measurement, or 5, and the third quartile is the $3(30 + 1)/4 = 23.25$th ordered measurement, which is 8.25. The resulting box-and-whisker plot is shown in Figure 2.18.

By looking at a box-and-whisker plot, one can quickly form impressions re-

TABLE 2.15 Downtime in hours of 30 machines						
4	4	1	4	1	4
6	10	5	5	8	2
1	6	10	3	13	5
8	4	3	9	4	9
6	4	4	11	8	9

**FIGURE 2.18
Box-and-whisker
plot of machine
downtime**

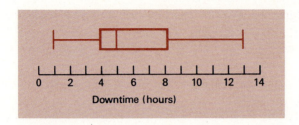

garding the amount of spread, location of concentration, and symmetry of the represented data set. A glance at Figure 2.18, for example, reveals that 50% of the measurements are between 4 and about 8. The median is 5, and the range is 12. Since the median line is closer to the left end of the box, we conclude that the data are skewed to the right. (In a perfectly symmetric data set, the median line will be exactly halfway between the two ends of the box, and in a data set that is skewed to the left, the median line will be closer to the right end of the box than it is to the left.)

COMPUTER ANALYSIS

Computers may be used to great advantage when descriptive measures are needed. The STAT+ microcomputer software package, for example, computes the mean, median, range, variance, and standard deviation for both grouped and ungrouped data.

Exercises

2.20 Ⓒ Refer to Exercise 2.2. Treat the data as a sample, and compute the mean, median, variance, and standard deviation by the methods of this section.

2.21 Ⓒ Repeat Exercise 2.20, using the data of Exercise 2.3.

2.22 Ⓒ Repeat Exercise 2.20, using the data of Exercise 2.4.

2.23 Ⓒ The following are the weights of 100 male first-year college students. **(a)** Prepare an ordered array, a frequency distribution, a histogram, and a frequency polygon. **(b)** Treat these data as a sample and compute the mean, median, variance, and standard deviation. (*Suggestion:* Use intervals of size 10 beginning with 110.)

119	183	147	148	143	153	163	169	149	153
126	191	143	156	145	151	163	166	135	152
139	200	133	151	143	161	157	169	137	143
130	202	136	161	143	173	152	162	142	143
142	190	123	191	124	176	142	155	140	137
140	180	117	184	134	184	143	143	150	144
158	171	122	175	130	187	137	146	156	139
159	164	139	160	140	172	132	143	154	145
162	157	139	151	148	164	145	144	154	148
170	152	149	150	155	151	147	148	154	153

2.24 Refer to Exercise 2.23. Compute **(a)** the first quartile and **(b)** the third quartile.

2.25 C The following is the distribution of commissions earned during a week by 160 salespersons. **(a)** Compute the sample mean, median, variance, and standard deviation for these data. **(b)** Determine the first and third quartiles and the ninety-fifth percentile.

Class interval, $	100–149	150–199	200–249	250–299	300–349	350–399	400–449	450–499
Frequency	19	25	30	25	20	17	14	10

2.26 The following are the odometer readings (in thousands of miles) for the last 40 cars an automobile dealer accepted as trade-ins:

36	64	76	68	64
76	34	31	53	67
93	40	46	69	32
19	25	67	65	54
81	39	41	54	37
41	79	69	55	55
36	48	46	54	36
57	70	35	51	31

Construct a box-and-whisker plot from these data. Describe the data set in light of the graph that you draw.

Summary

This chapter was concerned with techniques for organizing and summarizing data. People who wish to understand the true nature of their data and to communicate to others the information they contain must be able to use these techniques.

You learned in this chapter that making an ordered array may be a good first step in summarizing data. Frequency distributions, relative frequency distributions, and cumulative distributions make possible further organization and summarization of data. We can effectively communicate the information contained in large sets of data by using graphic procedures such as histograms, frequency polygons, and ogives.

You learned how to compute several descriptive measures that provide useful summary information about sets of data. The two broad categories of descriptive measures covered here are *measures of central tendency* (or measures of location) and *measures of dispersion*. You learned to compute and understand the meaning of the *mean,* the *median,* and the *mode* as measures of central tendency. The most important measures of dispersion you learned about in this chapter are the *variance* and the *standard deviation*. You learned to compute these descriptive measures using both grouped and ungrouped data.

Review Questions

1. Explain the difference between descriptive statistics and inferential statistics.
2. Define the following terms:
   - **(a)** ordered array
   - **(b)** frequency distribution
   - **(c)** histogram
   - **(d)** frequency polygon
   - **(e)** statistic
   - **(f)** parameter
   - **(g)** random sample
   - **(h)** ogive
   - **(i)** relative frequency distribution
   - **(j)** percentile
   - **(k)** quartile
   - **(l)** Chebyshev's theorem
   - **(m)** class-interval width
   - **(n)** class mark
   - **(o)** class limits

3. Compare and contrast the mean, median, and mode as measures of central tendency.

4. What is meant by the term *dispersion?*

5. Discuss the range, the average deviation, and the variance as measures of dispersion.

6. Explain how Chebyshev's theorem can be used to answer questions about a set of data.

7. Give two reasons why it is useful to be able to compute descriptive measures from grouped data.

8. State the assumptions made in computing each of the following descriptive measures from grouped data: **(a)** the mean, **(b)** the mode, **(c)** the variance, **(d)** the median.

9. What is a simple random sample?

10. What is a convenience sample?

11. Why is a simple random sample better than a convenience sample when you want to make inferences about the population from which the sample has been drawn?

12. Describe the relationships between the mean, the median, and the mode for the following types of distributions: **(a)** A symmetric mound-shaped distribution. **(b)** A distribution that is skewed to the left. **(c)** A distribution that is skewed to the right.

13. What do we call the numerator of the variance formula?

 14. Ⓒ Two regionally distributed general-interest magazines solicit advertising from the same clientele. The advertising rates and the total number of subscribers are the same for both magazines. The following table shows the age distributions of subscribers to the two magazines, in thousands of subscribers. **(a)** Construct a histogram for each set of data. **(b)** Prepare the relative frequency distribution for each set of data. **(c)** Prepare the cumulative relative frequency distribution for each set of data. **(d)** Suppose that you are a manufacturer of baby food. In which magazine would you advertise? Why? **(e)** Suppose that you are a real estate agent for a retirement community. In which magazine would you advertise? Why?

Age (years)	10–19	20–29	30–39	40–49	50–59	60–69	70–79
Magazine *A*	10	48	58	38	28	10	8
Magazine *B*	8	18	18	28	54	46	28

 15. Ⓒ A contest sponsored by a radio station drew 10,000 responses. The table below shows the age distribution of the contestants. **(a)** Construct a histogram from these data. **(b)** What is the approximate mean age of the contestants? **(c)** What proportion of the contestants are between 20 and 39 years of age, inclusive? **(d)** What proportion of the contestants are under 30 years of age? **(e)** What proportion are 40 or over?

Age (years)	10–14	15–19	20–24	25–29	30–34	35–39	40–44	45–49	50–54	55–59
Contestants (× 100)	4	8	15	19	21	12	8	6	4	3

 16. Ⓒ A market-research firm conducts a household survey in a certain community. One question asked is "Number of rooms per dwelling unit." The following table shows the results. Compute the mean, median, variance, and standard deviation.

3	2	4	4	1	6	3	6	6	6	7	6
5	7	5	2	7	5	4	6	8	4	5	7
4	3	6	6	4	3	6	5	5	6	7	6
5	5	2	5	8	6	6	3	7	7	7	5
6	1	5	6	5	4	3	4	3	6	5	4

17. [C] The weights, in micrograms, of 20 one-inch specimens of a certain synthetic fiber randomly selected from a day's production of a factory are as follows: 3.7, 3.1, 2.0, 2.8, 2.3, 4.5, 3.6, 3.0, 3.0, 2.3, 3.1, 2.6, 3.4, 4.8, 3.8, 4.2, 4.5, 3.5, 3.1, 4.6. Compute the measures that would be appropriate for describing these data.

18. [C] In a survey of small bakeries in the Southeast, 10 bakeries report the following numbers of employees: 15, 14, 12, 19, 13, 14, 15, 18, 13, 19. Find the mean, median, variance, and standard deviation.

19. [C] A sample of the records of an appliance dealer reveals the following ages (in years) of 15 refrigerators at the time of the first service call: 9.1, 2.5, 9.5, 1.1, 7.8, 7.0, 2.2, 4.4, 8.0, 6.4, 2.9, 7.4, 7.2, 4.3, 5.9. Compute the mean, median, variance, and standard deviation.

20. [C] A random sample of 10 college students reveals the following current balances in their bank accounts (in hundreds of dollars): 3.4, 1.8, 1.4, 3.6, 1.8, 3.7, 3.4, 2.9, 4.2, 2.8. Compute the mean, median, variance, and standard deviation.

21. [C] The following are the current prices per share (in dollars) of 20 stocks: 59, 97, 53, 83, 45, 47, 88, 51, 76, 64, 66, 92, 97, 55, 85, 108, 62, 55, 136, 51. Find the mean, median, variance, and standard deviation.

22. [C] For its quality-control program, a firm that makes spark plugs periodically draws samples of size 100 from the assembly line and inspects them. The numbers of defective spark plugs found in 25 such samples are as follows: 0, 1, 0, 0, 1, 5, 3, 0, 5, 5, 0, 0, 4, 4, 0, 3, 5, 0, 2, 3, 4, 2, 1, 5, 4. Find the mean, median, variance, and standard deviation.

23. [C] In a survey designed to learn more about the eating and drinking habits of urban employees, 15 secretaries reported the number of cups of coffee they drank each day to be as follows: 4, 2, 1, 3, 5, 6, 6, 3, 3, 2, 4, 3, 2, 0, 1. Compute the measures that would be appropriate for describing these data.

24. [C] The quality-control division of a light-bulb manufacturer conducted forced-life tests on a sample of 25 bulbs. The bulbs' lifetimes, in thousands of hours, were as follows: 1.1, 1.1, 1.2, 1.1, 1.4, 0.9, 1.2, 1.2, 1.3, 0.8, 1.2, 1.2, 1.2, 1.7, 1.5, 1.2, 0.8, 1.3, 0.9, 1.7, 1.3, 1.2, 1.2, 1.4, 1.0. Compute the mean, median, variance, and standard deviation.

25. [C] A sample of 20 car registrations selected by a certain county tax office reveals the following ages of cars (to the nearest year): 1, 3, 3, 3, 8, 7, 4, 6, 8, 5, 5, 5, 9, 9, 10, 10, 4, 2, 4, 2. Compute the mean, median, variance, and standard deviation.

26. [C] The following are the tensile strengths of 15 specimens of plastic: 37, 46, 45, 31, 32, 48, 44, 45, 35, 42, 42, 33, 35, 26, 47. The data have been coded for ease of calculation. Compute the mean, median, variance, and standard deviation.

27. [C] A sample of 20 cartons of household fuses reveals the following numbers of defectives per carton: 7, 6, 3, 4, 3, 9, 4, 4, 5, 5, 9, 4, 6, 9, 7, 0, 6, 1, 3, 0. Compute the mean, median, variance, and standard deviation.

28. [C] An estimator of timber yield selects a sample of 20 trees from a tract of land and estimates the following yields in board feet per tree: 385, 317, 326, 309, 595, 228, 241, 582, 411, 418, 305, 463, 482, 208, 503, 386, 329, 251, 193, 368. Compute the mean, median, variance, and standard deviation.

29. [C] A survey of 20 households reveals the following ages of refrigerators: 1, 1, 2, 2, 2, 2, 3, 3, 3, 3, 3, 4, 4, 4, 5, 5, 6, 7, 8, 10. **(a)** What is the mean age of the 20 refrigerators? **(b)** What is the median age? **(c)** Compute the variance and standard deviation of the ages.

30. Ⓒ The following are the times in seconds that a sample of 16 assembly-line employees take to perform a certain operation: 5.9, 7.2, 8.8, 7.0, 8.7, 6.3, 7.1, 5.1, 10.0, 8.5, 8.9, 9.3, 6.3, 6.9, 9.8, 6.7. Compute the mean, median, variance, and standard deviation.

 31. Ⓒ The following are the number of days elapsing between date of purchase and date of return of the first 110 items returned to a department store during the current fiscal year.

10	10	2	11	6	20	7	14	24	24	12
2	11	4	10	8	21	5	14	23	22	14
11	11	2	5	6	24	6	10	24	21	13
6	4	2	8	5	8	8	13	11	22	6
20	2	11	9	10	5	14	8	14	11	8
7	2	12	19	11	9	14	5	14	10	5
14	12	11	16	11	19	14	5	19	11	17
24	14	10	26	11	18	18	17	14	29	16
24	11	18	28	21	17	19	18	30	26	19
12	13	18	29	22	34	18	28	34	29	25

Summarize these data in the ways that you think would be appropriate for presentation to management.

32. Ⓒ The following are the annual salaries (in thousands of dollars) of the heads of household in two communities.

						Community A								
10	28	29	36	53	11	33	10	13	11	41	19	19	15	11
22	24	15	69	58	56	22	33	17	15	17	22	30	46	41
37	10	46	40	32	63	28	14	10	17	42	15	14	11	13
42	52	48	61	27	53	61	24	10	22	18	31	25	55	51
63	48	39	12	33	48	16	18	12	14	61	15	17	17	19
51	54	72	21	25	33	42	10	19	34	14	32	62	23	60
77	32	14	54	22	46	69	18	11	18	51	16	19	18	14

						Community B								
75	69	94	47	60	56	28	69	51	34	46	18	27	57	60
14	62	61	25	59	32	41	71	15	38	55	53	72	62	52
58	57	36	31	39	56	18	24	44	49	30	35	60	72	72
60	18	76	53	29	71	49	46	48	20	43	18	36	76	70
98	49	71	50	31	73	76	71	67	45	18	26	44	23	36
20	54	67	73	68	45	69	75	64	67	31	68	19	78	76
74	73	76	42	31	70	16	75	51	49	52	78	54	40	56
29	26	50	14											

(a) Organize and summarize these data as you would for presentation to the client of a market research firm. **(b)** The client, which specializes in expensive home furnishings, wants to open a new retail outlet in one of these communities. Which community would you recommend for the new store? Why? **(c)** Is the mean or the median a more appropriate measure of central tendency for the data of Community A? Community B? **(d)** Which set of data is more variable?

33. Ⓒ Refer to the population of employed heads of households given in Appendix II. Consider two groups: (1) widowed or divorced males and (2) widowed or divorced females. Compare the two groups with respect to mean annual income.

34. Ⓒ From the population of employed heads of households given in Appendix II, select a simple random sample of 150. For the variable "commuting distance to work," do the following: **(a)** Construct a frequency distribution, a relative frequency distribution, and a cumulative frequency distribution. **(b)** Construct a histogram and a frequency polygon. **(c)** Use grouped-data formulas to compute the mean, median, variance, and standard deviation. **(d)** Compare your results with those of your classmates.

35. C Refer to the population of employed heads of households given in Appendix II. Select a simple random sample of size 25. Compute the sample mean, median, variance, and standard deviation, using the variable "number of years with current employer."

36. C The following are the number of hours that 600 new photocopy machines operated before having to undergo unscheduled servicing. Construct a frequency distribution from these data.

1. 237	47. 236	93. 162	139. 169	185. 281
2. 280	48. 213	94. 231	140. 237	186. 228
3. 222	49. 231	95. 182	141. 253	187. 244
4. 250	50. 201	96. 209	142. 206	188. 212
5. 227	51. 220	97. 209	143. 225	189. 237
6. 304	52. 187	98. 233	144. 195	190. 208
7. 261	53. 211	99. 239	145. 253	191. 261
8. 201	54. 248	100. 197	146. 206	192. 249
9. 245	55. 219	101. 239	147. 156	193. 167
10. 250	56. 192	102. 194	148. 245	194. 215
11. 238	57. 158	103. 263	149. 240	195. 223
12. 212	58. 163	104. 223	150. 261	196. 184
13. 198	59. 221	105. 231	151. 184	197. 235
14. 193	60. 201	106. 212	152. 201	198. 187
15. 204	61. 171	107. 230	153. 254	199. 196
16. 193	62. 269	108. 236	154. 189	200. 209
17. 226	63. 267	109. 224	155. 259	201. 214
18. 217	64. 212	110. 224	156. 205	202. 205
19. 240	65. 223	111. 232	157. 214	203. 188
20. 285	66. 228	112. 238	158. 211	204. 223
21. 222	67. 129	113. 187	159. 264	205. 213
22. 224	68. 167	114. 222	160. 181	206. 190
23. 236	69. 227	115. 260	161. 202	207. 274
24. 224	70. 187	116. 221	162. 212	208. 237
25. 244	71. 207	117. 215	163. 232	209. 149
26. 162	72. 185	118. 252	164. 217	210. 193
27. 258	73. 194	119. 219	165. 239	211. 232
28. 270	74. 204	120. 207	166. 225	212. 246
29. 230	75. 169	121. 223	167. 194	213. 177
30. 179	76. 257	122. 233	168. 279	214. 271
31. 176	77. 221	123. 239	169. 253	215. 228
32. 196	78. 264	124. 238	170. 237	216. 219
33. 221	79. 195	125. 243	171. 242	217. 200
34. 178	80. 258	126. 276	172. 262	218. 226
35. 214	81. 236	127. 207	173. 215	219. 199
36. 232	82. 188	128. 200	174. 196	220. 219
37. 176	83. 225	129. 248	175. 194	221. 229
38. 174	84. 251	130. 229	176. 222	222. 166
39. 181	85. 197	131. 237	177. 227	223. 222
40. 234	86. 197	132. 204	178. 172	224. 189
41. 175	87. 309	133. 237	179. 212	225. 239
42. 258	88. 226	134. 229	180. 154	226. 203
43. 206	89. 232	135. 202	181. 176	227. 227
44. 220	90. 205	136. 232	182. 236	228. 223
45. 257	91. 312	137. 218	183. 266	229. 241
46. 230	92. 221	138. 222	184. 192	230. 247

231. 217	291. 206	351. 230	411. 158	471. 223
232. 228	292. 245	352. 224	412. 233	472. 206
233. 217	293. 266	353. 280	413. 237	473. 197
234. 189	294. 189	354. 200	414. 234	474. 179
235. 235	295. 195	355. 208	415. 200	475. 266
236. 197	296. 200	356. 250	416. 227	476. 236
237. 177	297. 184	357. 183	417. 195	477. 237
238. 246	298. 268	358. 243	418. 218	478. 219
239. 193	299. 248	359. 253	419. 267	479. 195
240. 250	300. 232	360. 263	420. 206	480. 218
241. 200	301. 201	361. 226	421. 264	481. 224
242. 232	302. 213	362. 243	422. 217	482. 208
243. 167	303. 219	363. 251	423. 225	483. 211
244. 215	304. 262	364. 234	424. 212	484. 248
245. 260	305. 205	265. 235	425. 242	485. 215
246. 196	306. 270	366. 286	426. 207	486. 209
247. 213	307. 222	367. 227	427. 153	487. 230
248. 202	308. 243	368. 229	428. 203	488. 227
249. 256	309. 249	369. 188	429. 208	489. 190
250. 193	310. 173	370. 250	430. 319	490. 259
251. 225	311. 251	371. 243	431. 225	491. 212
252. 264	312. 168	372. 231	432. 234	492. 238
253. 252	313. 236	373. 192	433. 247	493. 213
254. 224	314. 226	374. 216	434. 228	494. 200
255. 188	315. 233	375. 187	435. 236	495. 202
256. 214	316. 220	376. 237	436. 275	496. 212
257. 225	317. 229	377. 239	437. 216	497. 277
258. 210	318. 216	378. 261	438. 210	498. 208
259. 190	319. 211	379. 251	439. 204	499. 183
260. 224	320. 156	380. 224	440. 169	500. 211
261. 210	321. 202	381. 222	441. 211	501. 251
262. 253	322. 268	382. 238	442. 221	502. 250
263. 251	323. 217	383. 195	443. 153	503. 217
264. 216	324. 166	384. 249	444. 218	504. 169
265. 225	325. 239	385. 196	445. 276	505. 225
266. 209	326. 193	386. 240	446. 199	506. 259
267. 217	327. 195	387. 236	447. 202	507. 159
268. 236	328. 155	388. 261	448. 203	508. 267
269. 175	329. 244	389. 250	449. 232	509. 189
270. 172	330. 224	390. 163	450. 215	510. 183
271. 208	331. 187	391. 180	451. 209	511. 256
272. 225	332. 227	392. 187	452. 268	512. 197
273. 219	333. 206	393. 238	453. 197	513. 259
274. 184	334. 203	394. 235	454. 162	514. 231
275. 196	335. 193	395. 214	455. 204	515. 238
276. 191	336. 218	396. 245	456. 265	516. 234
277. 247	337. 230	397. 253	457. 222	517. 200
278. 214	338. 196	398. 222	458. 221	518. 202
279. 242	339. 250	399. 240	459. 201	519. 273
280. 188	340. 210	400. 196	460. 189	520. 187
281. 214	341. 223	401. 249	461. 253	521. 207
282. 244	342. 197	402. 208	462. 223	522. 254
283. 232	343. 241	403. 244	463. 192	523. 227
284. 281	344. 187	404. 203	464. 276	524. 293
285. 209	345. 237	405. 206	465. 250	525. 175
286. 226	346. 184	406. 214	466. 193	526. 249
287. 177	347. 224	407. 230	467. 229	527. 267
288. 132	348. 194	408. 252	468. 193	528. 233
289. 200	349. 236	409. 210	469. 201	529. 270
290. 232	350. 213	410. 206	470. 168	530. 224

531. 212	545. 205	559. 146	573. 249	587. 272
532. 238	546. 197	560. 227	574. 204	588. 230
533. 236	547. 216	561. 171	575. 166	589. 190
534. 211	548. 221	562. 242	576. 220	590. 220
535. 195	549. 244	563. 229	577. 213	591. 226
536. 207	550. 206	564. 229	578. 264	592. 210
537. 254	551. 213	565. 248	579. 244	593. 251
538. 189	552. 216	566. 229	580. 217	594. 187
539. 252	553. 255	567. 213	581. 189	595. 216
540. 248	554. 199	568. 256	582. 282	596. 222
541. 218	555. 216	569. 209	583. 201	597. 234
542. 256	556. 225	570. 209	584. 216	598. 245
543. 165	557. 188	571. 245	585. 229	599. 245
544. 215	558. 261	572. 211	586. 150	600. 247

37. Compute the mean for the grouped data in Exercise 36.

38. Compute the variance and standard deviation for the grouped data in Exercise 36. Treat the data both as a sample and as a population and compare the two results.

39. Construct a histogram and a frequency polygon from the results of Exercise 36.

40. Use the results of Exercise 36 to construct a relative frequency distribution.

41. Compute the median for the grouped data in Exercise 36.

42. Select a simple random sample of size 50 from the list of companies in Appendix III. For each company in your sample, record the information on assets, sales, market value, net profits, cash flow, and number employed. For the data on assets, do the following and compare your results with those of other students in your class: **(a)** construct a frequency distribution;   **(b)** construct a relative frequency distribution;   **(c)** construct a cumulative frequency distribution;   **(d)** construct a cumulative relative frequency distribution;   **(e)** draw a histogram;   **(f)** draw a frequency polygon.   **(g)** Use grouped data methods to compute the mean, median, variance, and standard deviation.

43. Repeat Exercise 42 using the data on sales.

44. Repeat Exercise 42 using the data on market value.

45. Repeat Exercise 42 using the data on net profit.

46. Repeat Exercise 42 using the data on cash flow.

47. Repeat Exercise 42 using the data on number employed.

48. Select a simple random sample of size 50 from the population of employed heads of households in Appendix II. Use the measurements for variables 6 (commuting distance) and 7 (number of years with current employer), and construct a box-and-whisker plot for each variable. Describe the sample in light of your graph. Compare your results with those of your classmates.

49. Select a simple random sample of size 30 from the list of companies in Appendix III. Use the assets measurements to construct a box-and-whisker plot. Describe the sample in light of your graph. Compare your results with those of your classmates.

PRACTICE WITH REAL DATA

Consult the homes-for-sale section of the Sunday edition of a large metropolitan newspaper. Select between 100 and 150 ads for homes for sale in a particular area, and record the advertised selling prices.

1. Use these data to construct a frequency distribution, as well as cumulative and relative frequency distributions.
2. Draw a histogram and frequency polygon for these data.
3. Compute the mean, median, variance, and standard deviation from your grouped data.

Do the same thing for a different geographic area and compare the results.

3.

Some Elementary Probability Concepts

CHAPTER OBJECTIVES: This chapter introduces you to the basic concepts and techniques of probability. These skills provide a mechanism that can help you understand much of the variability and complexity in the business world. This is the first of three chapters that tie together descriptive and inferential statistics. After studying this chapter and working the exercises, you should be able to do the following.

1. Determine the number of permutations that can be made from n objects taken r at a time

2. Determine the number of combinations that can be made from n objects taken r at a time

3. Construct a tree diagram to represent the possible choices available to a decision-maker, along with the associated possible outcomes

4. Understand the three recognized views of probability

5. Understand the elementary properties of probability

6. Compute the probability of an event

The next three chapters introduce the basic concepts of statistical inference. We can think of these chapters as bridging the gap between descriptive statistics (the topic of Chapter 2) and statistical inference.

The *theory of probability* is a branch of mathematics that is concerned with the concept and measurement of uncertainty. We cannot cover such a large subject in depth in a single chapter. However, since statistical inference is based on probability theory, it demands a rudimentary understanding of probability. The objective of this chapter, then, is to present the basic concepts of probability that are needed for an understanding of statistical inference. We shall introduce the subject by discussing probabilities that are based on observed data.

We obtain the observations we use in calculating probabilities in several different ways.

The process whereby we obtain these observations is called an *experiment.*

For many people the word experiment evokes visions of a scientific laboratory populated with technicians dressed in white coats scrutinizing test tubes and recording the behavior of white mice. We use the word here, however, in a much broader sense. For example, an experiment may consist of determining which brand of detergent a shopper in a certain area prefers. Recording the gasoline consumed by a car during a given week is another example.

The result of an experiment is called an *outcome.*

If an experiment consists of determining which brand of detergent a shopper prefers, the outcome might be ''Brand A'' or ''Brand B'' or any one of the brands that are available. If an experiment involves the assessment of an automobile's performance in terms of miles driven per gallon of gasoline, the outcome might be 20, or perhaps 25, or, in the case of superior performance, 40.

An *event* is a collection of one or more outcomes considered as a group.

An event is said to occur if an experiment yields at least one of its outcomes. Suppose, for example, that an experiment consists of determining the ages (at nearest birthday) of shoppers at a grocery store on a given day. Possible outcomes would include 16, 20, 30, 35, 50, 60, and so on. The event of interest to the experimenter might consist of the outcomes ''30 and under.'' If, during the day, only one person 30 years of age or under shopped at the store, the event would consist of one outcome. If 20 people in the designated age group shopped at the store while the experiment was in progress, the event would be composed of 20 outcomes.

The collection of all possible outcomes that may result when an experiment is conducted is called the *sample space* for that experiment.

In our example about grocery-store shoppers, the sample space consists of all possible ages, but in reality it might include only the ages 12 through 85, or 15 through 75, or some similar range.

We may now define probability as follows:

Probability is a number between 0 and 1 inclusive that measures the likelihood of the occurrence of some event.

The more likely the event, the closer the number is to 1. The more unlikely the event, the closer the number is to 0. An event that cannot occur has a probability of 0. An event that is certain to occur has a probability of 1.

Here are some examples of events for which we may be interested in computing probabilities: a defective item coming off an assembly line; the purchase of Product A; the arrival of a shipment of goods on time; Salesperson A selling more than 500 items during a given week.

3.1 COUNTING TECHNIQUES—PERMUTATIONS AND COMBINATIONS

Suppose that we are computing the probability of some event, or the probability of some combination of events, when the total number of possible events is large. We find it convenient to have some method of counting the number of such events. Let us now look at some techniques for facilitating the counting of events. These techniques are useful for computing probabilities.

Factorials

Given the positive integer n, the product of all the whole numbers from n down through 1 is called n factorial, written $n!$.

The following are examples of factorials:

$$10! = 10 \cdot 9 \cdot 8 \cdot 7 \cdot 6 \cdot 5 \cdot 4 \cdot 3 \cdot 2 \cdot 1$$
$$5! = 5 \cdot 4 \cdot 3 \cdot 2 \cdot 1$$
$$2! = 2 \cdot 1$$

In general, $n! = n(n - 1)(n - 2)(n - 3) \cdots 1$. By definition, $0! = 1$. Note that $10! = 10 \cdot 9!$, $5! = 5 \cdot 4!$, $n! = n(n - 1)!$.

By means of factorials, we can find the number of ways in which objects or persons can be arranged in a line.

EXAMPLE 3.1 In a certain company, four secretaries' desks are arranged in a line against a wall. Each secretary can sit at any desk. How many seating arrangements are possible?

SOLUTION The answer is $4! = 4 \cdot 3 \cdot 2 \cdot 1 = 24$ ways.

Using a graphic aid called a *tree diagram,* we can show the possibilities. Let us designate the positions as the first, second, third, and fourth positions, and the four secretaries as A, B, C, and D. Figure 3.1 is a tree diagram representing the possible arrangements.

Permutations

A permutation is an ordered arrangement of objects.

The 24 arrangements of secretaries shown in Figure 3.1 are the possible permutations of 4 objects taken 4 at a time. In certain situations there may be more objects available than positions to be filled. For example, we may wish to know

FIGURE 3.1
Tree diagram, showing possible arrangements of four objects taken four at a time

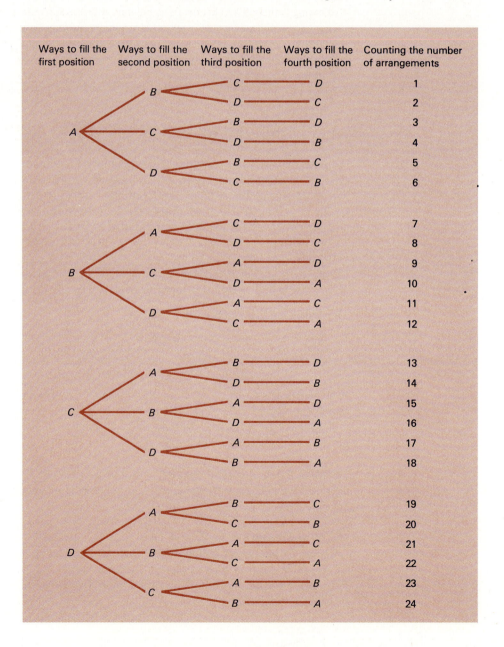

Ways to fill the first position	Ways to fill the second position	Ways to fill the third position	Ways to fill the fourth position	Counting the number of arrangements
	B	C	D	1
		D	C	2
A	C	B	D	3
		D	B	4
	D	B	C	5
		C	B	6
	A	C	D	7
		D	C	8
B	C	A	D	9
		D	A	10
	D	A	C	11
		C	A	12
	A	B	D	13
		D	B	14
C	B	A	D	15
		D	A	16
	D	A	B	17
		B	A	18
	A	B	C	19
		C	B	20
D	B	A	C	21
		C	A	22
	C	A	B	23
		B	A	24

how many permutations are possible if we have 5 objects and wish to take only 2 at a time. We may think of this problem as one in which we have 2 positions to fill and 5 objects from which to make selections to fill them. We can get the answer using the following line of reasoning: We can fill the first position in one of 5 ways, since initially there are 5 objects from which to select. Once we have selected an object to fill the first position, there are 4 remaining objects from which we can make a selection to fill the second position. Hence there is a total of 20 ways (5 $\times$ 4) to fill the two positions. Each of these ways of filling the two positions is a permutation, and consequently we may say that there are 20 permutations of 5 objects taken 2 at a time.

A key word in the definition of a permutation is the word "ordered." In determining the number of possible permutations in a given situation, we say that "order counts." By this we mean, for example, that a pair of adjacent positions filled with objects a and b and the same pair of adjacent positions filled with the same objects in the order b then a are two different permutations of the same two objects. Rearranging the order of two objects creates a new permutation.

In permutations, "order counts."

EXAMPLE 3.2 The telephone switchboard in the company referred to in Example 3.1 requires two operators whose chairs (positions) are side by side. When the telephone operators go to lunch, two of the four secretaries take their places. If we make a distinction between the two operators' positions, in how many ways can the four secretaries fill them?

SOLUTION We can answer this question by determining the number of possible permutations of 4 things taken 2 at a time. There are 4 secretaries, A, B, C, and D, to fill the first position. Once that position has been filled, there are only 3 secretaries to fill the second position. See Figure 3.2.

The tree diagram in Figure 3.2 illustrates that there are 4 · 3 = 12 possible permutations of 4 things taken 2 at a time. Suppose that n is the number of distinct objects from which an ordered arrangement is to be derived, and r is the number of objects in the arrangement. The number of possible ordered arrangements is the number of permutations of n things taken r at a time. This is written symbolically as $_nP_r$. In general,

$$_nP_r = n(n - 1)(n - 2) \cdots (n - r + 1) \tag{3.1}$$

We multiply the right-hand side of Equation 3.1 by $(n - r)!/(n - r)!$. This is equivalent to multiplying by 1. We obtain

$$_nP_r = n(n - 1)(n - 2) \cdots (n - r + 1)\frac{(n - r)!}{(n - r)!}$$

$$= \frac{n(n - 1)(n - 2) \cdots (n - r + 1)(n - r)!}{(n - r)!}$$

$$= \frac{n!}{(n - r)!} \tag{3.2}$$

FIGURE 3.2
Tree diagram, showing the number of permutations of four objects taken two at a time

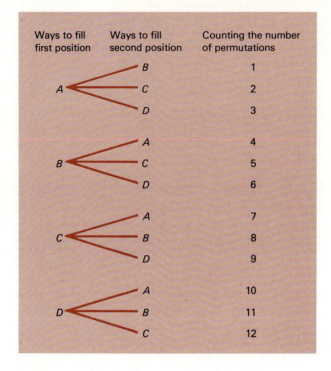

Ways to fill first position	Ways to fill second position	Counting the number of permutations
A	B	1
	C	2
	D	3
B	A	4
	C	5
	D	6
C	A	7
	B	8
	D	9
D	A	10
	B	11
	C	12

EXAMPLE 3.3 In a stock room, 5 adjacent bins are available for storing 5 different items. The stock of each item can be stored satisfactorily in any bin. In how many ways can we assign the 5 items to the 5 bins?

SOLUTION We get the answer by evaluating $_5P_5$, which is

$$_5P_5 = \frac{5!}{(5-5)!} = 5 \cdot 4 \cdot 3 \cdot 2 \cdot 1 = 120$$

Suppose that there are 6 different parts to be stocked, but only 4 bins are available. To find the number of possible arrangements, we need to determine the number of permutations of 6 things taken 4 at a time, which is

$$_6P_4 = \frac{6!}{(6-4)!} = \frac{6 \cdot 5 \cdot 4 \cdot 3 \cdot 2!}{2!} = 360$$

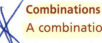

Combinations
A combination is an arrangement of objects without regard to order.

The number of combinations of n things taken r at a time may be written as $_nC_r$.

In Figure 3.2, the permutations of 4 things taken 2 at a time consist of the following 12 arrangements:

AB	AC	AD	BA	BC	BD
CA	CB	CD	DA	DB	DC

Six of the arrangements in this list are the same as the other six, except for the order in which the letters occur. They are:

AB	AC	AD	BC	BD	CD
BA	CA	DA	CB	DB	DC

In combinations, "order does not count."

Sometimes we may not need to distinguish between, for example, arrangement AB and arrangement BA. We may consider them as the same subset. That is, their order does not count. In that case, we refer to the arrangements as *combinations*. In the case of the 4 secretaries occupying 2 switchboard positions, there are 12 permutations, but only 6 combinations. That is, there are two permutations for each combination. In general, there are $r!$ permutations for each combination of n things taken r at a time. In other words, there are always $r!$ times as many permutations as combinations. We express this symbolically as

$$_nP_r = r! \, _nC_r \tag{3.3}$$

When we solve Equation 3.3 for $_nC_r$, the result is

$$_nC_r = \frac{_nP_r}{r!}$$

We rewrite the numerator of this last expression as the right-hand side of Equation 3.2 to get the formula for the number of combinations of n things taken r at a time:

$$_nC_r = \frac{n!}{r!(n-r)!} \tag{3.4}$$

Now let us use Equation 3.4 to obtain the number of combinations of 4 things taken 2 at a time. As expected, we get 6:

$$_4C_2 = \frac{4!}{2!2!} = \frac{4 \cdot 3 \cdot 2!}{2 \cdot 1 \cdot 2!} = 6$$

EXAMPLE 3.4 A perfume manufacturer who makes 10 fragrances wants to prepare a gift package containing 6 fragrances. How many combinations of fragrances are available?

SOLUTION The answer is

$$_{10}C_6 = \frac{10!}{6!4!} = \frac{10 \cdot 9 \cdot 8 \cdot 7 \cdot 6!}{6! \cdot 4 \cdot 3 \cdot 2 \cdot 1} = 210$$

Exercises

3.1 Evaluate the following: **(a)** $_8P_2$,   **(b)** $_5P_3$,   **(c)** $_9P_9$,   **(d)** $_{10}P_4$,   **(e)** $_6P_2$,   **(f)** $_{10}C_3$,   **(g)** $_{10}C_7$,   **(h)** $_7C_3$,   **(i)** $_5C_1$,   **(j)** $_8C_4$.

3.2 An office suite consists of 4 offices located side by side. These are to be occupied by 4 junior executives, A, B, C, and D. In how many ways can these executives be assigned to the four offices?

3.3 A supervisor has 7 workers available from which to form a 4-member production team. How many different teams are possible?

3.4 An advertising artist has 8 photographs from which to choose in designing a full-page magazine ad containing 3 photographs. Position on the page is immaterial. How many designs using different combinations of photographs are possible?

3.5 The president of a firm that produces 5 different kinds of soap has a sample of each displayed in a row on a credenza in her office.   **(a)** In how many different ways can she display the 5 products?   **(b)** Suppose that she wants to display only 3 of the products at a time (in a row). How many distinguishable arrangements are possible?

3.6 A salesperson has 7 products he wishes to display at a national convention. He can display only 4. The order in which he displays the products is immaterial. How many displays does he have to choose from?

3.7 An airline has 6 flights it wishes to advertise in one-page ads in a Sunday newspaper. It wants to feature a different flight each Sunday for 6 Sundays.   **(a)** How many different sequences of ads can the airline run?   **(b)** Suppose that the airline decides at the last minute to run only 4 ads. How many sequences of ads can it run?

3.8 A firm has 5 different positions to fill and 15 applicants from which to choose. All applicants are equally qualified for all 5 positions. In how many ways can the firm fill the positions?

3.2 DIFFERENT VIEWS OF PROBABILITY

We can discuss probability from two points of view: the *objective* and the *subjective*. Until recently, most statisticians have taken the objective point of view. We can also classify objective probability into two categories: (1) *a priori* or *classical* probability, and (2) *a posteriori* or the *relative frequency* concept. Classical probability has its origins in the seventeenth century and in the games of chance that were popular at that time. Examples from those games illustrate the principles: When a fair coin is tossed, the probability of observing a head is equal to one-half. This is equal to the probability of observing a tail. When a perfectly balanced die is rolled, the probability of observing a one equals one-sixth. The probability is the same for the other five faces. One can compute the probabilities of such events through abstract reasoning. One does not have to rely on the results of any experiment. A coin need never be tossed, nor a die rolled, to be able to calculate these probabilities. We can define probability from the classical point of view as follows:

If some event can occur in *N* mutually exclusive and equally likely ways, and if *m* of these ways have characteristic *E*, the probability of the occurrence of *E* is equal to *m/N*.

We can write this definition as a formula:

$$P(E) = \frac{m}{N}$$

(3.5)

Here $P(E)$ is read "the probability of E."

Mutually Exclusive and Equally Likely Events

Key phrases in this definition of probability are *mutually exclusive* and *equally likely*.

Two events are mutually exclusive if they cannot occur simultaneously. Two events are equally likely when there is no reason to expect one event rather than the other to occur.

The following example illustrates the classical concept of probability.

EXAMPLE 3.5 A magazine advertised that it would give a prize to 50 persons selected at random from those returning a completed entry form enclosed as part of an advertising brochure. As of the closing date for receipt of entries, the magazine had received 10,000 completed entry forms. What is the probability that a given individual who entered the contest will win a prize?

SOLUTION Using the classical concept of probability expressed by Equation 3.5:

$$P(\text{Winner}) = \frac{\text{number of prizes to be awarded}}{\text{total number of entries}} = \frac{50}{10,000} = 0.005$$

The Concept of Relative Frequency

There is another definition of probability, the *relative frequency* definition. It is similar to the classical definition. The relative frequency approach to probability depends on the repeatability of some process and the ability to count both the number of such repetitions and the number of times that some event of interest occurs. From the relative frequency point of view, we can define probability as follows:

Suppose that some process is repeated a large number of times n, and some resulting event with characteristic E occurs m times. The relative frequency of occurrence of E, m/n, will be approximately equal to the probability of E.

We can express this definition as a formula:

$$P(E) = \frac{m}{n}$$

(3.6)

EXAMPLE 3.6 A firm that makes soft drinks wants to estimate the probability that a customer of a certain grocery store will buy one of its products. A total of 1500 customers are observed over a period of time. Of these, 600 bought one or more of the firm's products. On the basis of this information, what is the best estimate of the desired probability?

SOLUTION By Equation 3.6,

$$P(E) = \frac{600}{1500} = 0.40$$

Bear in mind that m/n in Equation 3.6 is only an estimate of $P(E)$, the true probability of occurrence of event E.

Subjective Probability

The subjective approach to probability holds that probability measures the confidence that a given individual has in the truth of a certain proposition.

This view of probability does not depend on the repeatability of any process. In fact, we can apply the approach to events that can happen only once. An example would be the probability that the Los Angeles Rams will win the Super-bowl game this year. As another example, consider Salesperson A, who assesses the probability of winning the company sales contest this year to be 0.9. The sales manager assesses this salesperson's probability of winning to be only 0.5. The true probability is unknown. We say only that the salesperson is more optimistic than the sales manager.

3.3 ELEMENTARY PROPERTIES OF PROBABILITY

The following elementary properties of probability form the basis of the axiomatic approach to probability. From these three properties, one can construct a whole system of probability theory by using mathematical logic. The three properties are as follows:

1. *Given some process (or experiment) with n possible outcomes O_1, O_2, . . ., O_n, each outcome O_i is assigned a nonnegative number such that*

$$0 \leq P(O_i) \leq 1 \tag{3.7}$$

   Equation 3.7 is called the probability of outcome O_i. Simply stated, this property says that all outcomes must have a probability that is between 0 and 1, inclusive. This is a reasonable requirement, inasmuch as the concept of a negative probability has little intuitive appeal.

   The *probability of an event* is equal to the sum of the probabilities of the outcomes of which the event is composed. Given any event E_i, it is also true that $0 \leq P(E_i) \leq 1$.

2. *If all possible events E_1, E_2, . . . , E_n are mutually exclusive, the sum of their probabilities is equal to 1.*

$$P(E_1) + P(E_2) + \cdots + P(E_n) = 1 \tag{3.8}$$

This is the property of *exhaustiveness*. It refers to the fact that the observer of a probabilistic experiment must allow for all possible events. When all these events are taken together, their total probability is 1. The requirement that the events be mutually exclusive specifies that the events E_1, E_2, . . . , E_n be *disjoint,* that is, they do not overlap.

3. *Given any two mutually exclusive events E_i and E_j, the probability of the occurrence of either E_i or E_j is equal to the sum of their probabilities.*

$$P(E_i \text{ or } E_j) = P(E_i) + P(E_j) \tag{3.9}$$

To see the implication of this property more easily, think about what would be true if the two events were not mutually exclusive. What if E_i and E_j could happen at the same time? When we tried to find the probability of the occurrence of either E_i or E_j, we would have the problem of an overlap. Then it would not be so easy to calculate the probability. Given that E_i and E_j *cannot* occur at the same time—that they are mutually exclusive—we simply add the individual probabilities to find $P(E_i$ or $E_j)$.

EXAMPLE 3.7 A group of employees consists of Employees A, B, and C. Each has the same chance (probability) of being selected for promotion. One of them is definitely going to be promoted. What is the probability that Employee A will be promoted? Employee B? Employee C?

SOLUTION Each employee has one chance out of three of being promoted. Thus the probabilities are 1/3 for Employee A, 1/3 for Employee B, and 1/3 for Employee C. We can see that each of these probabilities is a number between 0 and 1.

Since only one person is to be promoted, the three possible events are mutually exclusive. Therefore their sum is equal to 1. That is, $1/3 + 1/3 + 1/3 = 1$.

The probability that either Employee A or Employee B will be promoted is equal to the sum of their individual probabilities, since the events are mutually exclusive. Thus the probability that either Employee A or Employee B will be promoted is equal to $1/3 + 1/3 = 2/3$.

3.4 CALCULATING THE PROBABILITY OF AN EVENT

Let us now use the concepts and techniques introduced in the previous sections to solve practical problems involving the calculation of specific probabilities.

We must first distinguish between two types of probability, *conditional probability* and *unconditional probability*. Suppose that all the possible outcomes of some experiment constitute the universal set U. We compute the probability of the occurrence of an event by forming the ratio of the number of favorable outcomes to the number of possible outcomes. This probability is called an *unconditional probability*. The discussion in this section assumes that each outcome is equally likely.

TABLE 3.1
Household appli-
ances classified by
color and style

	Color			
Style	C_1 (White)	C_2 (Copper)	C_3 (Green)	Total
S_1	1,400	450	900	2,750
S_2	1,300	350	800	2,450
S_3	900	700	750	2,350
S_4	1,000	250	1,200	2,450
Total	4,600	1,750	3,650	10,000

At times the set of all possible outcomes may constitute a subset of the universal set. The population of interest may be reduced by some set of conditions that are not applicable to the total population. When we calculate probabilities of occurrence using a subset of the universal set as the denominator in the ratio, the result is a *conditional probability*.

EXAMPLE 3.8 Table 3.1 shows 10,000 household appliances cross-classified by color and style. We let C_1 stand for the set composed of white appliances, S_1 stand for the set composed of style 1, and so on. We use the symbol $n(C_1)$ to indicate the number in set C_1, $n(S_1)$ to indicate the number in set S_1, and so on. Suppose that we want to calculate the probability that an appliance picked at random will be white.

SOLUTION This is an unconditional probability, since we have placed no restrictions on the set of all possible outcomes. We compute the probability as follows:

$$P(C_1) = \frac{n(C_1)}{n(U)} = \frac{4600}{10,000} = 0.46$$

Note that we calculate the probability by forming the ratio of two numbers. The denominator consists of the total number of appliances that could be selected $n(U)$. The numerator is the number of appliances with the characteristic of interest $n(C_1)$.

Conditional Probability

Now suppose that we reduce the set of all possible outcomes to S_1 appliances. What is the probability that an appliance picked at random will be white, given that it is type S_1? This is a conditional probability. In Table 3.1 there are 2750 members of set S_1. Of these, 1400 are white. These 1400 belong to the set $C_1 \cap S_1$.

The symbol $\cap$ is called the *intersection* symbol, and is read "intersection." The new set is referred to as the intersection of sets C_1 and S_1. It consists of those appliances that are *both* white (C_1) and of style S_1. The probability sought is given by $P(C_1|S_1)$, where the vertical line between C_1 and S_1 is read "given." The entire expression is read "the probability of C_1 given S_1." Thus we have

$$P(C_1|S_1) = \frac{n(C_1 \cap S_1)}{n(S_1)} = \frac{1400}{2750} = 0.51$$

Here is a further example of conditional probability.

EXAMPLE 3.9 Consider a class that consists of 30 students, of whom 10 are men and 20 are women. Five of the women and none of the men are out-of-state students. Thus the events "male" and "out-of-state" are mutually exclusive. (a) A student is selected at random from the class. What is the probability that the one selected will be an out-of-state student?

SOLUTION The answer is $5/30 = 0.17$.
(b) Now suppose that the student selected is a woman. What is the probability that she will be an out-of-state student?

SOLUTION Men are now no longer of interest, since one of the 20 women has been drawn. Since 5 of the women are out-of-state students, the probability that the one selected is from out of state is $5/20 = 0.25$. The occurrence of one event (a woman) increases the probability of the occurrence of the second event (an out-of-state student).
(c) Suppose that the student selected is a man. What is the probability that he is an out-of-state student?

SOLUTION Now women are eliminated from consideration in the calculation of the probability. Since no men are from out of state, the probability we seek is $0/10 = 0$. This time, the occurrence of the first event decreases the probability of the occurrence of the second event.

Now think about the three probabilities we have just computed. Why are they different? The probability computed in part (a) is an *unconditional probability*. No "conditions" were stipulated. The denominator of the probability consisted of all 30 students in the class.

The probabilities computed in parts (b) and (c) are *conditional probabilities*. We computed them under the stipulated "condition" that some preceding event had occurred. The denominators for these probabilities are subsets of the original 30 students. Figure 3.3 shows the situation described in this example.

The following is a general definition of conditional probability:

The conditional probability of *A* given *B* is equal to the probability *A* ∩ *B* divided by the probability of *B*, provided that the probability of *B* is not 0.

That is,

$$P(A|B) = \frac{P(A \cap B)}{P(B)}, \qquad P(B) \neq 0 \qquad \text{(3.10)}$$

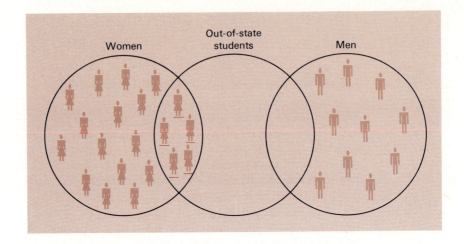

Joint Probability

A probability such as $P(A \cap B)$ is called a *joint probability*, since it gives the probability of the *joint*, or simultaneous, occurrence of two events or characteristics. Referring to Table 3.1, we see that $P(C_1 \cap S_1) = 1400/10{,}000$ is a joint probability, since it shows the probability of the joint occurrence of color C_1 and style S_1.

Marginal Probability

To illustrate the concept of marginal probability, let us again refer to Example 3.8. When we ask for the probability that an appliance in Table 3.1 is of style S_1, we are asking for a *marginal probability*. Interest centers on a probability associated with a marginal total. We disregard any other criterion of classification. When we compute

$$P(S_1) = \frac{2750}{10{,}000} = 0.275$$

this implies that we are not interested in the color. Similarly, if we are interested in the probability that an appliance picked at random is white, we use the marginal total, 4600, and ignore the style classification. These two examples suggest the following definition:

When we ignore one or more criteria of classification in computing a probability, the resulting probability is a marginal probability.

To gain further insight into the nature of marginal probabilities, let us refer again to Table 3.1. From the first row of the table, we may compute the following joint probabilities:

$$P(C_1 \cap S_1) = \frac{1400}{10,000} = 0.14$$

$$P(C_2 \cap S_1) = \frac{450}{10,000} = 0.045$$

$$P(C_3 \cap S_1) = \frac{900}{10,000} = 0.09$$

If we add these probabilities, we get $0.14 + 0.045 + 0.09 = 0.275$, which is the marginal probability we computed earlier. This result is not a coincidence, since, alternatively, we may define a marginal probability as follows:

A marginal probability is the sum of two or more joint probabilities taken over all values of one or more variables.

The Addition Rule

The probability of the occurrence of either one or the other of two mutually exclusive events is equal to the sum of their individual probabilities. When two events are *not* mutually exclusive, we use the *addition rule,* which may be stated as follows:

Given two events A and B, the probability that event A or event B or both occur is equal to the probability that event A occurs, plus the probability that event B occurs, minus the probability that both events occur.

We can write this as

$$P(A \cup B) = P(A) + P(B) - P(A \cap B) \tag{3.11}$$

The symbol $\cup$ is read "union" or "or," so that the notation $P(A \cup B)$ is read as either "the probability of the union of event A and event B" or "the probability of event A or event B."

Refer to Table 3.1 again. Let us compute the probability that an appliance picked at random will be either style S_1 or white or both. Using Equation 3.11, we obtain

$$P(C_1 \cup S_1) = P(C_1) + P(S_1) - P(C_1 \cap S_1)$$

$$= \frac{4600}{10,000} + \frac{2750}{10,000} - \frac{1400}{10,000} = \frac{4600 + 2750 - 1400}{10,000}$$

$$= \frac{5950}{10,000} = 0.595$$

The 1400 appliances that are *both* white *and* style S_1 are included both in the 2750 that are style S_1 and in the 4600 that are white. Since, in computing this probability, we have added these 1400 into the numerator twice, we must subtract them once to overcome the effect of duplication, or overlapping.

The Multiplication Rule

Another useful rule for computing the probability of an event is the *multiplication rule*. This rule is suggested by the definition of conditional probability. Recall that we compute the conditional probability of A given B from

$$P(A|B) = \frac{P(A \cap B)}{P(B)}, \qquad P(B) \neq 0$$

We may rewrite this equation to obtain

$$P(A \cap B) = P(B)P(A|B) \qquad (3.12)$$

This is the symbolic statement of the multiplication rule. In words it is:

The probability of the joint occurrence of event A and event B is equal to the conditional probability of A given B times the marginal probability of B.

As noted previously, this type of probability, which is the probability of the simultaneous occurrence of two events, is called a joint probability.

To illustrate the use of the multiplication rule, let us use Equation 3.12 to find the probability that an appliance picked at random from all appliances is both white and style S_1. The desired probability is

$$P(C_1 \cap S_1) = P(S_1)P(C_1|S_1) = \frac{2750}{10,000} \cdot \frac{1400}{2750} = \frac{1400}{10,000} = 0.14$$

We can also calculate this joint probability directly from the data of Table 3.1, as follows.

$$P(C_1 \cap S_1) = \frac{n(C_1 \cap S_1)}{n(U)} = \frac{1400}{10,000} = 0.14$$

Independent Events

Suppose that, in Equation 3.12, we are told that event B has occurred, but that this fact has no effect on the probability of A. That is, suppose that the probability of event A is the same regardless of whether or not B occurs. In this situation, $P(A|B) = P(A)$. We say that A and B are *independent events*. The multiplication rule for two independent events, then, may be written as

$$P(A \cap B) = P(B)P(A) \qquad (3.13)$$

Note that when two events are independent, each of the following statements is true:

$$P(A|B) = P(A), \qquad P(B|A) = P(B), \qquad P(A \cap B) = P(A)P(B)$$

In fact, two events are not independent unless all these statements are true.

As an illustration of independence, consider the following example.

EXAMPLE 3.10 A government agency employs 100 clerk-typists, classified by sex and marital status as shown in Table 3.2. If an employee is picked at random

TABLE 3.2
Data for
Example 3.10

Sex	Marital Status		Total
	Single	*Married*	*Total*
Male	16	24	40
Female	24	36	60
Total	40	60	100

from the 100 employees, the probability that he or she is single is $P(S) = (24 + 16)/100 = 40/100 = 0.4$. Now let us compute the probability that an employee picked at random is single, given that the employee is male.

Using the formula for computing a conditional probability (Equation 3.10),

$$P(S|M) = \frac{P(S \cap M)}{P(M)} = \frac{16/100}{40/100} = 0.4$$

Thus the additional information that a randomly selected employee is male does not alter the probability that he will be single, and $P(S) = P(S|M)$. Consequently, we can say that the two events—being single and being male—are, for this group, independent.

Joint Probability of Two Independent Events

We can show the calculation of the joint probability of two independent events by means of a tree diagram.

EXAMPLE 3.11 In a certain factory, an average of 1 out of every 20 items coming off an assembly line is defective. The quality-control supervisor wants to know the probabilities of the following joint events for two items randomly selected from the assembly line.

1. Both items are defective.
2. The first item is defective and the second is not.
3. The first item is not defective and the second is.
4. Neither item is defective.

The quality-control supervisor believes that whether or not a given item is defective is independent of whether or not any other item is defective.

SOLUTION We designate the probability of a defective item by $P(D)$ and the probability of a nondefective item by $P(N)$. We have $P(D) = 1/20$ and $P(N) = 19/20$. If the assumption of independence is correct, these probabilities hold for every item drawn from the assembly line. The four desired probabilities, then, are:

1. $P(D \cap D) = P(D)P(D) = (1/20(1/20) = 1/400$
2. $P(D \cap N) = P(D)P(N) = (1/20)(19/20) = 19/400$

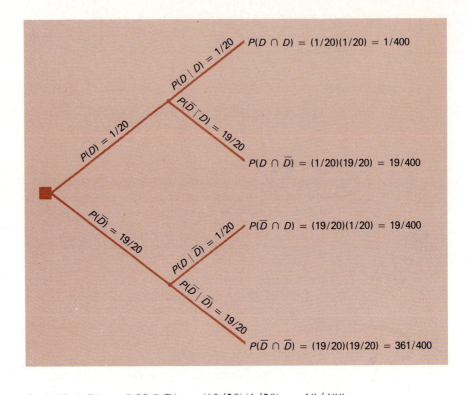

3. $P(N \cap D) = P(N)P(D) = (19/20)(1/20) = 19/400$
4. $P(N \cap N) = P(N)P(N) = (19/20)(19/20) = 361/400$

The total of the probabilities for these four mutually exclusive events is

$$\frac{1}{400} + \frac{19}{400} + \frac{19}{400} + \frac{361}{400} = \frac{400}{400} = 1$$

Figure 3.4 is a tree diagram representing these probabilities. If two events A and B are mutually exclusive, $P(A \cap B) = 0$.

Complementary Events

We must consider one more concept here. The probability of an event A is equal to 1 minus the probability of its complement $\bar{A}$, and therefore

$$P(\bar{A}) = 1 - P(A) \tag{3.14}$$

This result follows from the third property of probability, since the event A and its complement $\bar{A}$ are mutually exclusive.

Suppose, for example, that for some population the probability $P(A)$ that a person is a college graduate is 0.25. Then, for this population, the probability that a person is not a college graduate is

$$P(\bar{A}) = 1 - P(A) = 1 - 0.25 = 0.75$$

3.9 The following table classifies 1000 college graduates by area of concentration in college and type of employer for whom they went to work after graduation. **(a)** A graduate is picked at random from this group. Calculate the probability that he or she was: (1) an accounting major, (2) employed by a banking and finance firm, (3) an accounting major employed by a banking and finance firm, (4) an accounting major given that he or she was employed by a banking and finance firm, (5) an accounting major or an engineering major, (6) an accounting major or employed by a banking and finance firm. **(b)** Evaluate the following probabilities: (1) $P(B_3)$, (2) $P(A_4)$, (3) $P(B_3 \cap A_4)$, (4) $P(A_4)P(B_3|A_4)$, (5) $P(A_4 \cup B_3)$, (6) $P(A_4 \cup A_3)$, (7) $P(A_1|B_1)$. **(c)** Is type of employer independent of area of concentration? How do you support your answer mathematically?

Major		Type of employer					
		Public ac-counting A_1	Banking & finance A_2	Elec-tronics A_3	Merchan-dising A_4	All others A_5	Total
Accounting	B_1	60	15	10	5	10	100
General business	B_2	20	50	10	65	5	150
Humanities	B_3	1	2	2	10	60	75
Social science	B_4	2	20	8	20	70	120
Engineering	B_5	2	5	188	5	50	250
All others	B_6	30	50	55	60	110	305
Total		115	142	273	165	305	1,000

3.10 A company has two vacancies at the junior executive level. Ten people, seven men and three women, are eligible and equally qualified. The company has decided to draw two names at random from the list of eligibles. What is the probability that: **(a)** both positions will be filled by women? **(b)** at least one of the positions will be filled by a woman? **(c)** neither of the positions will be filled by a woman?

3.11 There are 300 homes in a neighborhood. On a certain evening, no one is at home at 100 of these. Of the remaining homes, the occupants of 50 will not participate in telephone surveys. On a particular evening, a person conducting a telephone survey calls one of these homes at random. What is the probability that: **(a)** the surveyor will call a home in which no one is present? **(b)** the surveyor will call a home in which someone is present, but the person will not participate in the survey? **(c)** the call will result in participation in the survey?

3.12 In a certain firm, the probability that an employee picked at random will be over 30 years of age is 0.58. What is the probability that an employee picked at random will be 30 years old or younger?

Summary

This chapter presented some of the basic concepts of probability.

To ease the task of counting certain events in order to compute their associated probabilities, we introduced some counting rules. You learned how to determine the number of *permutations* that can be made from *n* objects taken *r* at a time. You also learned about another type of arrangement called a *combination*. We showed how to find the number of combinations that can be made from *n* things taken *r* at a time.

You learned that we can discuss probability from three different points of view: the *a priori* or classical, the *a posteriori* or relative frequency, and the subjective.

You learned three elementary properties of probability for a given set of mutually exclusive events $E_1, E_2, \ldots, E_n$:

1. $0 \leq P(E_i) \leq 1$

2. $P(E_1) + P(E_2) + \cdots + P(E_n) = 1$

3. $P(E_i \text{ or } E_j) = P(E_i) + P(E_j)$

In calculating probabilities, one needs to understand the concepts of mutually exclusive events, independent events, unconditional probability, conditional probability, marginal probability, and joint probability.

You learned the addition rule and the multiplication rule, two rules that are helpful in calculating certain probabilities.

Review Questions

1. Define the following:
- **(a)** probability
- **(b)** objective probability
- **(c)** subjective probability
- **(d)** classical probability
- **(e)** relative frequency
- **(f)** mutually exclusive events
- **(g)** independence
- **(h)** marginal probability
- **(i)** joint probability
- **(j)** conditional probability

2. Name and explain the three properties of probability.

3. What is an experiment?

4. What is meant by the term "order counts" in an arrangement of objects?

5. What is an event?

6. What is a tree diagram?

7. Explain the meaning and use of the symbol $\cap$.

8. Explain the meaning and use of the symbol $\cup$.

9. Define and illustrate the following: **(a)** factorial,   **(b)** permutation,   **(c)** combination,   **(d)** addition rule,   **(e)** multiplication rule.

10. Make up a realistic problem from your area of interest to illustrate the use of as many probability concepts as possible.

11. A firm interviews 15 applicants for a position on its sales force. One question on the application form concerns leisure-time activities. Six applicants say they spend a major portion of their leisure time playing golf. Ten mention bowling. Three do not mention sports at all. How many applicants spend their leisure time both golfing and bowling? [*Hint:* $n(A \cup B) = n(A) + n(B) - n(A \cap B)$.]

12. A final examination consists of 20 questions. A student who takes the exam is told to select and answer 15. How many possible tests does a student have from which to choose?

13. Of 1000 items produced in a day in a certain factory, 400 are produced on the first shift, 350 on the second, and 250 on the third. An item is picked at random. What is the probability that it was produced on   **(a)** the first shift?   **(b)** the second shift?   **(c)** the third shift?   **(d)** either the first or the second shift?

14. In Question 13, suppose that the proportions of defective items produced on the first, second, and third shifts are 0.01, 0.02, and 0.04, respectively. An item is picked at random.   **(a)** What is the probability that it is defective?   **(b)** What is the probability that it is defective, given that it was produced on the third shift? **(c)** What is the probability that it is defective and also was produced on the first shift?

15. A hundred business people are asked to specify the type of magazine they prefer. The following table shows the 100 responses, cross-classified by educational level and type of magazine preferred. Find the probability that a person picked at random from the 100 will belong to each of the following sets: **(a)** S, **(b)** V ∪ C, **(c)** A, **(d)** $\overline{W}$, **(e)** U, **(f)** $\overline{B}$, **(g)** T ∩ B, **(h)** $(\overline{T ∩ C})$.

	Educational level			
Type of magazine	High school (A)	College (B)	Graduate school (C)	Total
Sports (S)	15	8	7	30
General news (T)	3	7	20	30
Travel (V)	5	5	15	25
Business news (W)	10	3	2	15
Total	33	23	44	100

16. An athletic team has 12 members. It plans to elect 4 officers—a captain, a co-captain, a manager, and a treasurer—by secret write-in ballot. All 12 members are eligible and willing to serve. How many possible sets of 4 members can serve? [Ignore the office held.]

17. In a certain computer center there are 7 keypunch operators who must sit at machines that are placed one behind the other. In how many ways can the 7 operators be assigned to the machines?

18. The probability that a salesperson making a call will make a sale is 0.8. What is the probability (assuming independence) that on two calls made in a day, the salesperson will make two sales?

19. The following table shows the outcome of 500 interviews attempted during a survey of opinions about big business held by residents of a certain city. The data are also classified by the area of the city in which the interview was attempted. A questionnaire is selected at random from the 500. **(a)** What is the probability that: (1) The questionnaire was completed? (2) The potential respondent was not at home? Refused to answer? (3) The potential respondent lived in area A? B? D? E? (4) The questionnaire was completed, given that the potential respondent lived in area B? (5) The potential respondent refused to answer the questionnaire or lived in area D? **(b)** Calculate the following probabilities: (1) $P(A ∩ R)$, (2) $P(B ∪ C)$, (3) $P(\overline{D})$, (4) $P(N|D)$, (5) $P(B|R)$, (6) $P(C)$.

	Outcome of interview			
Area of city	Completed (C)	Not at home (N)	Refused (R)	Total
A	100	20	5	125
B	115	5	5	125
D	50	60	15	125
E	35	50	40	125
Total	300	135	65	500

20. In a large city, 70% of the households receive a daily newspaper, and 90% have a television set. Suppose that these two events are independent. What is the probability that a randomly selected household will be one that both receives a daily newspaper and has a television set?

21. In a certain business firm, the probability that an employee picked at random is a college graduate is 0.55. What is the probability that an employee picked at random is not a college graduate?

22. In a government agency, 30% of the employees take public transportation to work. Also, 60% of the employees are female. It is assumed that these two characteristics are independent. Draw a tree diagram to illustrate and find the probability that an employee picked at random from this population will be: **(a)** female and take public transportation to work; **(b)** female and not take public transportation to work; **(c)** male and take public transportation to work; **(d)** male and not take public transportation to work.

23. In a certain firm, 6 persons (4 females and 2 males) are eligible for promotion to 2 higher-paying positions. **(a)** How many different combinations of these employees are possible? List them.

Assume that the persons who will be promoted are to be selected at random. Find the probability that: **(b)** at least one of the persons promoted will be a female, **(c)** exactly one female will be promoted, **(d)** no more than one female will be promoted, **(e)** no female will be promoted.

24. There are 50 applicants for a job, of whom 10 are members of ethnic group A, 15 of ethnic group B, and 25 of ethnic group C. The numbers of females (F) in the three groups are 2, 9, and 15, respectively. A person is selected at random to fill the job. Find the probability that this person will be **(a)** A and F, **(b)** A or F or both, **(c)** F given B, **(d)** A and B, **(e)** F and C.

25. Suppose that there are two events E_1 and E_2 such that $P(E_1) = 0.20$ and $P(E_2) = 0.30$. **(a)** Given that E_1 and E_2 are independent, what is $P(E_1 \cap E_2)$? **(b)** Given that E_1 and E_2 are mutually exclusive, what is $P(E_1 \cap E_2)$? **(c)** Given that E_1 and E_2 are mutually exclusive, what is $P(E_1 \cup E_2)$?

26. In a certain firm, 60% of the employees are male. Furthermore, 80% of the females and 60% of the males are high school graduates. Find the probability that an employee picked at random will be **(a)** a male high school graduate, **(b)** a female high school graduate.

27. An office supervisor claims to be a good judge of human intelligence. To test this claim, a psychologist asks the supervisor to pick the three most intelligent workers from a group of nine and rank them in order of intelligence. Suppose that the supervisor actually has no special ability to evaluate intelligence. **(a)** What is the probability that the supervisor will make a correct selection and ranking? **(b)** What is the probability that the supervisor will select at least one of the three most intelligent workers?

28. A personnel director has found that she can fill a certain type of position within one week 70% of the time. But she finds that 60% of the time, all applicants for the position are high school dropouts. The other 40% of the time, none of them are dropouts. When all applicants *are* high school dropouts, the position is filled within one week only 56% of the time. **(a)** What is the probability that the position is filled within one week, given that the applicants are not high school dropouts? **(b)** Is filling the position within a week independent of whether or not the applicants are high school dropouts?

29. The personnel director of a firm has determined the following probabilities for the length of time a certain type of employee remains with the firm after being hired.

Length of stay	Probability
Less than 1 year	0.05
1 year but less than 2	0.10
2 years but less than 3	0.10
3 years but less than 4	0.15
4 years but less than 5	0.20
5 years or longer	0.40
	1.00

Find the probability that a newly hired employee of this type will be with the firm **(a)** less than 5 years, **(b)** 3 years or more, **(c)** at least 2 but less than 4 years, **(d)** at least 4 years.

30. In a survey of business managers, 90% said they were covered by whole life insurance and 70% said they were covered by term insurance. In addition, 65% said they were covered by both types of insurance. Assume that these percentages apply to the sampled population. **(a)** What is the probability that a person selected at random from the sampled population will be covered by one or the other of the two types of insurance? **(b)** A person selected at random from the sampled population is covered by whole life insurance. What is the probability that he or she is also covered by term insurance? **(c)** What is the probability that a person randomly selected from the population will be covered by whole life insurance if he or she is covered by term insurance?

31. An instructor has a test bank that consists of 300 easy true-false questions, 200 difficult true-false questions, 500 easy multiple-choice questions, and 400 difficult multiple-choice questions. If a question is selected at random from the test bank, what is the probability that it will be: **(a)** an easy question? **(b)** an easy multiple-choice question? **(c)** an easy question, given that it is a multiple-choice question?

32. A market analyst claims to have an uncommon ability to predict the success of new products. He is asked to rank six new products in order of future success. If, in fact, he has no special ability to predict a product's success, what is the probability that he will correctly rank the products?

33. A personnel director must select from among 10 persons to fill 4 job openings. Four of the candidates belong to a minority group. If the 4 positions are filled at random from among the candidates, what is the probability that no minority group member will be selected?

34. Refer to Exercise 33. What is the probability that at least one minority group member will be selected?

35. The manager of a chain of fast-food restaurants found that 75% of the customers order a dessert with their meal, 60% order a certain brand of cola, and 40% order both. **(a)** What is the probability that a customer will order either a dessert or the particular brand of cola or both? **(b)** What is the probability that a customer who orders a dessert will also order the particular brand of cola? **(c)** What is the probability that a customer who orders the particular brand of cola will also order a dessert?

36. In a large business organization, 80% of the technical employees have met the training requirements for promotion, 70% have met the experience requirements, and 60% have met both requirements. If an employee is selected at random from the population, find the probability that the employee will: **(a)** meet at least one of the requirements; **(b)** not meet either of the requirements; **(c)** meet the training requirement, given that he or she meets the experience requirement.

37. In a survey of senior executives, it was found that 30% were recruited from outside their current firm; 20% of all the executives surveyed said that they would like to change firms, and 60% of those who said that they would like to change firms were recruited from outside their current firm. If we select an executive at random from this group, find the probability that he or she: **(a)** would like to change firms and was recruited from outside his or her current firm; **(b)** would like to change firms, or was recruited from outside his or her current firm, or both; **(c)** would like to change firms given that he or she was recruited from outside his or her current firm.

PRACTICE WITH REAL DATA

Conduct an experiment to estimate the probability that a customer having breakfast at the school cafeteria or some other nearby eating establishment will order coffee. Station yourself near the checkout counter. Of the first 25 customers, count the number who order coffee. Divide the number ordering coffee by 25 to estimate the probability that a breakfast customer will order coffee. Combine your results with those of your classmates. Obtain a new probability estimate by dividing the total number ordering coffee by the total number of customers observed.

4.

Some Important Probability Distributions

CHAPTER OBJECTIVES: This chapter deals with the basic concepts you need in order to understand random variables and probability distributions. These concepts and techniques provide the foundation for the statistical inference procedures that we discuss later. You will learn to use theoretical distributions that help you to get approximations of many probability distributions found in business situations. Distributions such as these are a necessary background for understanding a special type of probability distribution we shall encounter in Chapter 5. After studying this chapter and working the exercises, you should be able to do the following.

1. Distinguish between discrete and continuous random variables
2. Construct a probability distribution from raw data
3. Compute the mean and variance of a probability distribution
4. Use the binomial and normal distributions to calculate probabilities for appropriate random variables
5. Determine which model—the binomial or normal—is appropriate for describing a given situation

In Chapter 3 we presented the basic concepts of probability theory, as well as methods for computing the probability of an event. This chapter builds on those methods and concepts. It introduces techniques for calculating the probability of an event under more complicated circumstances.

We shall discuss the topic of this chapter, probability distributions, under two headings: probability distributions of *discrete random variables* and probability distributions of *continuous random variables*. Recall that Chapter 1 discussed discrete and continuous random variables.

4.1 PROBABILITY DISTRIBUTIONS OF DISCRETE RANDOM VARIABLES

Let us begin with the following definition:

The probability distribution of a discrete random variable is a table, graph, formula, or other device used to specify all possible values of the discrete random variable, along with their respective probabilities.

EXAMPLE 4.1 A certain firm employs 50 salespersons. Construct the probability distribution of the random variable X, the number of new customers each salesperson obtained during the past year.

SOLUTION We present the desired probability distribution by means of a table in which one column lists the possible values x_i that X can assume. Another column lists $P(X = x_i)$, the probability of X assuming each value. Table 4.1 shows the probability distribution of X for our firm. The entries in the last column are the relative frequencies of occurrence of values of X.

Alternatively, we may represent the probability distribution by a graph. In Figure 4.1, the length of each vertical line indicates the probability for the corresponding value of x in this example. The values of $P(X = x_i)$ are all positive, they are all less than 1, and their sum is equal to 1. These characteristics are not

TABLE 4.1
Probability distribution of number of new customers obtained by 50 salespersons

x_i	Frequency of occurrence of x_i	$P(X = x_i)$
0	1	1/50
1	2	2/50
2	4	4/50
3	3	3/50
4	6	6/50
5	8	8/50
6	10	10/50
7	7	7/50
8	5	5/50
9	3	3/50
10	1	1/50
Total	50	50/50

FIGURE 4.1
Probability distribution of number of new customers obtained by 50 salespersons

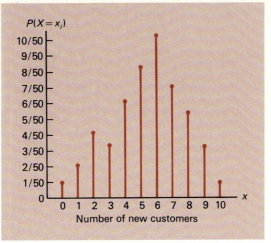

peculiar to this particular example. They are the essential properties of the probability distribution of a discrete random variable. This may be expressed more formally as follows:

Given a discrete random variable X that can assume only the k different values $x_1, x_2, \ldots, x_k$, the probability distribution of X must satisfy the following two conditions:

$$0 \le P(X = x_i) \le 1 \qquad i = 1, 2, \ldots, k \tag{4.1}$$

$$\sum_{i=1}^{k} P(X = x_i) = 1 \tag{4.2}$$

A probability distribution gives us $P(X = x)$.

We can make probability statements about the random variable X once we know its probability distribution. Suppose, for example, that a salesperson is picked at random from the 50. What is the probability of selecting a salesperson who got four new customers? The last column of Table 4.1 shows that the answer is $6/50 = 0.12$. That is, $P(X = 4) = 6/50 = 0.12$.

What is the probability that a salesperson selected at random is one who got either five or six new customers? To answer this question, we use the addition rule. The probability of selecting a salesperson who got five new customers is $8/50$. The probability of selecting a salesperson who got six new customers is $10/50$. Thus the probability of selecting a salesperson who got either five or six new customers is $8/50 + 10/50 = 0.16 + 0.20 = 0.36$. We express this more compactly as $P(X = 5 \text{ or } 6) = P(X = 5) + P(X = 6) = 0.36$.

Cumulative Distributions

At times it will be more convenient to compute probabilities using the *cumulative probability distribution* of a random variable. To obtain the cumulative probability distribution for the discrete variable whose probability distribution is given in

TABLE 4.2
Cumulative probability distribution of number of new customers obtained by 50 salespersons

x_i	Frequency of occurrence of x_i	$P(X = x_i)$	$P(X \le x_i)$
0	1	1/50	1/50
1	2	2/50	3/50
2	4	4/50	7/50
3	3	3/50	10/50
4	6	6/50	16/50
5	8	8/50	24/50
6	10	10/50	34/50
7	7	7/50	41/50
8	5	5/50	46/50
9	3	3/50	49/50
10	1	1/50	50/50
Total	50	50/50	

Table 4.1, we successively add the probabilities $P(X = x_i)$ in the last column. Table 4.2 shows the resulting cumulative probability distribution.

The graph in Figure 4.2 shows the cumulative probability distribution of X for this example. We call the cumulative probability distribution $F(x)$. That is, $F(x) = P(X \le x)$, the probability that X is less than or equal to any value of x. The graph of $F(x)$ consists of the horizontal lines only. The vertical lines only give the graph a connected appearance. The length of each vertical line is equal to that of the corresponding line in Figure 4.1. For example, the vertical line at $X = 6$ in Figure 4.2 is equal in length to the line erected at $X = 6$ in Figure 4.1, or 10/50 units on the vertical scale.

A cumulative probability distribution gives us $P(X \le x)$.

The cumulative probability distribution lets us answer such questions as:

1. What is the probability that the salesperson picked at random got fewer than four new customers during the past year? To answer this question, we need to

FIGURE 4.2
Cumulative probability distribution of number of new customers obtained by 50 salespersons

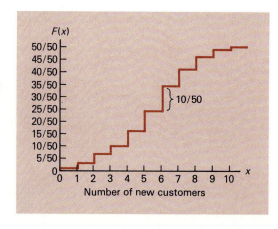

find $P(X < 4)$, or $P(X \le 3)$. We can find this in Table 4.2 by noting the value of $P(X \le x)$ for $x = 3$. We find this to be $10/50 = 0.20$.

2. What is the probability that a randomly selected salesperson got four or more new customers during the past year? The answer is the complement of the answer to the previous question. Since we have already found $P(X < 4) = 0.20$, we have $P(X \ge 4) = 1 - P(X < 4) = 1 - 0.20 = 0.80$.

3. What is the probability that a salesperson selected at random got between five and eight new customers, inclusive? To answer this, we need $P(5 \le X \le 8)$, which is equal to $P(X \le 8) - P(X < 5)$. From Table 4.2, we find $P(X \le 8) = 46/50$ and $P(X < 5) = 16/50$, so that $P(5 \le X \le 8) = 46/50 - 16/50 = 30/50 = 0.60$.

The probability distribution in Table 4.1 was developed from actual experience. Finding another variable that followed this distribution would be a coincidence. However, the probability distribution of a discrete random variable of interest often follows, or approximates, some probability distribution that has been named and extensively studied. The next section introduces a well-known distribution— the binomial distribution.

The Mean and Variance of Discrete Probability Distributions

We introduced the concepts of mean and variance in Chapter 2, and we discussed the calculation of their measures for samples and finite populations. This section treats these concepts in terms of discrete probability distributions.

The mean of a probability distribution is the *expected value* of the random variable that has the specified distribution. The expected value of a discrete random variable X is merely the arithmetic mean. Therefore it may be labeled μ. To obtain it, we multiply each value of the random variable by its probability of occurrence and sum the products. We express this procedure symbolically as follows:

$$E(X) = \Sigma x P(X = x) = \mu \tag{4.3}$$

Similarly, we define the variance of the probability distribution of the random variable X as the expected value of the squared deviations of the values of X from their mean. In symbols, we write this as

$$E(x - \mu)^2 = \Sigma(x - \mu)^2 P(X = x) = \sigma^2 \tag{4.4}$$

Alternatively, we may write the variance of X as

$$\sigma^2 = E(X^2) - [E(X)]^2 \tag{4.5}$$

where $E(X^2) = \Sigma x^2 P(X = x)$.

EXAMPLE 4.2 Suppose that the random variable X has the probability distribution shown in the first two columns of Table 4.3, shown at the top of page 90. What are the mean and variance of X?

TABLE 4.3
Calculations for obtaining the mean and variance of the random variable X

x	$P(X = x)$	$x - \mu$	$(x - \mu)^2$	$xP(X = x)$	$(x - \mu)^2 P(X = x)$	x^2
1	1/6	−2	4	1/6	4/6	1
2	1/6	−1	1	2/6	1/6	4
3	2/6	0	0	6/6	0	9
4	1/6	1	1	4/6	1/6	16
5	1/6	2	4	5/6	4/6	25
Total	1			$\sum xP(X = x) = 3$	$\sum (x - \mu)^2 P(X = x)$ $= 10/6 = 1.67$	

SOLUTION The mean and variance of X are computed as follows:

$$\mu = E(X) = \Sigma x P(X = x)$$
$$= 1(1/6) + 2(1/6) + 3(2/6) + 4(1/6) + 5(1/6) = 3$$
$$\sigma^2 = E(x - \mu)^2 = \Sigma (x - \mu)^2 P(X = x)$$
$$= (1 - 3)^2(1/6) + (2 - 3)^2(1/6) + (3 - 3)^2(2/6)$$
$$+ (4 - 3)^2(1/6) + (5 - 3)^2(1/6)$$
$$= 10/6 = 1.67$$

From the data in the last column of Table 4.3, we compute

$$E(X^2) = 1\left(\frac{1}{6}\right) + 4\left(\frac{1}{6}\right) + 9\left(\frac{2}{6}\right) + 16\left(\frac{1}{6}\right) + 25\left(\frac{1}{6}\right) = \frac{64}{6} = 10.67$$

By Equation 4.5, then, we may compute

$$\sigma^2 = 10.67 - (3)^2 = 1.67$$

This result agrees with that obtained using Equation 4.4.

EXAMPLE 4.3 Table 4.4 shows the results of a survey in which respondents were asked the number of times they had changed jobs during the past five years. We wish to find the mean and variance.

Using the information in Table 4.4, we compute the mean and variance as follows:

$$\mu = E(X) = \Sigma x P(X = x) = 0(0.30) + 1(0.40)$$
$$+ 2(0.20) + 3(0.05) + 4(0.03) + 5(0.02) = 1.17$$
$$\sigma^2 = E(X - \mu)^2 = \Sigma (x - \mu)^2 P(X = x)$$
$$= (0 - 1.17)^2(0.3) + (1 - 1.17)^2(0.4)$$
$$+ (2 - 1.17)^2(0.2) + (3 - 1.17)^2(0.05) + (4 - 1.17)^2(0.03)$$
$$+ (5 - 1.17)^2(0.02)$$
$$= 1.2611$$

TABLE 4.4 Probability distribution for Example 4.3	Number of job changes	0	1	2	3	4	5
	Proportion of respondents	0.30	0.40	0.20	0.05	0.03	0.02

Equations 4.3 and 4.4 are examples of weighted arithmetic descriptive measures in which the weights are probabilities. The calculations are similar to those for computing the mean and variance of grouped data, discussed in Chapter 2.

Exercises

4.1 The following table shows the distribution of the number of days of sick leave taken by 100 employees during a year. **(a)** Construct and graph the probability distribution of X = days of sick leave taken. **(b)** Construct and graph the cumulative probability distribution of X = days of sick leave taken.

x_i (Days of sick leave taken)	0	1	2	3	4	5	6	7	8	9	10
Number of employees	5	8	10	12	18	14	10	9	8	4	2

4.2 Find, for Exercise 4.1, the probability that a randomly selected employee will be one who took: **(a)** 3 days sick leave, **(b)** more than 5 days sick leave, **(c)** 6 to 8 days (inclusive) sick leave, **(d)** either 9 or 10 days sick leave.

4.3 For Exercise 4.1, find: **(a)** $P(X = 0)$, **(b)** $P(X = 10)$, **(c)** $P(X \geq 6)$, **(d)** $P(X < 6)$, **(e)** $P(3 \leq X \leq 7)$.

4.4 The following table shows the distribution of on-the-job accidents that befell 500 factory employees during a given year. **(a)** Construct and graph the probability distribution of X = number of accidents. **(b)** Construct and graph the cumulative probability distribution. **(c)** Find the probability that a randomly selected employee will be one who had (1) no accidents, (2) more than three accidents, (3) between two and four accidents, inclusive, (4) fewer than four accidents, and (5) four or more accidents. **(d)** Find the mean and variance.

Number of accidents	0	1	2	3	4	5	6
Number of employees	300	100	60	20	10	5	5

4.5 A sample of 80 customers at a department store were interviewed regarding their buying habits. One question asked was, "How many times did you shop at this store during the preceding month?" The responses were as follows:

x_i (Number of times shopped)	0	1	2	3	4	5	6	7
Number of customers	15	27	14	12	6	4	1	1

(a) Construct and graph the probability distribution of X = number of times shopped. **(b)** Construct and graph the cumulative probability distribution. **(c)** Find the probability that a randomly selected customer shopped: (1) more than once, (2) zero times, (3) more than four times, (4) fewer than three times. **(d)** Find the mean and variance.

4.6 A credit union has 400 members. A review of the membership account records reveals the following information regarding the number of transactions that occurred during the past quarter:

x_i (Transactions)	0	1	2	3	4	5	6	7	8	9	10
Number of members	146	97	73	34	23	10	6	3	4	2	2

(a) Construct and graph the probability distribution of X = number of transactions.   **(b)** Construct and graph the cumulative probability distribution.   **(c)** Find the probability that a randomly selected account record will have had: (1) no transactions, (2) at least one transaction, (3) more than five transactions, (4) fewer than six transactions. **(d)** Find the mean and variance.

4.2 THE BINOMIAL DISTRIBUTION

The *binomial distribution* is one of the most widely encountered probability distributions in applied statistics. It is derived from a process known as a *Bernoulli trial*. This is named for the Swiss mathematician James Bernoulli (1654–1705), who made many contributions to probability theory. A Bernoulli trial is a trial of some process or experiment that can only result in one of two mutually exclusive outcomes, such as defective or not defective, correct or incorrect, present or absent, acceptable or not acceptable.

Bernoulli Process

A sequence of Bernoulli trials forms a *Bernoulli process* when the following conditions are met:

1. Each trial results in one of two possible, mutually exclusive outcomes. One of the possible outcomes is denoted (arbitrarily) as a success, the other as a failure.
2. The probability of a success, p, remains constant from trial to trial. (The probability of a failure, $1 - p$, is denoted by q.)
3. The trials are independent; that is, the probabilities associated with any particular trial are not affected by the outcome of any other trial.

In n repetitions of a Bernoulli trial, the number of successes possible is 0, 1, 2, . . . , n. We want to be able to determine the probability of each possible number of successes in n repetitions, or trials. The distribution from which we determine these probabilities is called the *binomial distribution*.

EXAMPLE 4.4 A horticulturist knows from experience that 90% of a certain kind of seedling will survive being transplanted. A random sample of 5 seedlings is selected from current stock. What is the probability that exactly 3 will survive?

SOLUTION The probability of survival is 0.90 for each seedling. Let us call survival a *success* and nonsurvival a *failure*. Also, let us assign a value of 1 to a success (survival) and a value of 0 to a failure (nonsurvival). The actual random selection of a seedling is a Bernoulli trial.

Suppose that the first seedling survives (S), the second seedling fails to survive (F), the third and fourth survive, and the fifth fails to survive. We record the following sequence of outcomes: SFSSF. Using zeroes and ones, we may write the sequence of outcomes as 10110. We find the probability of this sequence of outcomes using the multiplication rule. It is given by

$$P(1, 0, 1, 1, 0) = pqppq = q^2 p^3$$

We are looking for the probability of a success, a failure, a success, a success, and a failure, in that order. In other words, we want the joint probability of the 5 outcomes. (For simplicity, we have used commas, rather than intersection notation, to separate the outcomes of the events in the probability statement.)

The resulting probability is the probability of obtaining the specific sequence of outcomes in the order shown. But we are not interested in the order in which the successes and failures occur. Rather, we are interested in the probability of the occurrence of *exactly* 3 successes (survivals) out of 5 randomly selected seedlings. In addition to the given sequence (call it sequence 1), 3 successes and 2 failures could also occur in any one of the sequences in Table 4.5. Each of these sequences has the same probability of occurring, $q^2 p^3$.

A single sample of size 5, drawn from the population specified, yields only one sequence of successes and failures. The question we must answer is: What is the probability of getting sequence 1, *or* sequence 2, . . . , *or* sequence 10? To find the answer, we use the addition rule to calculate the sum of the individual probabilities. In this example, we need to find the sum of the 10 $q^2 p^3$'s or, equivalently, multiply $q^2 q^3$ by 10.

We can now answer the original question: What is the probability that in a random sample of size 5, drawn from the specified population, there are 3 successes (survivals) and 2 failures (nonsurvivals)? Since $p = 0.90$, $q = (1 - p) = (1 - 0.90) = 0.10$, and so the answer is

$$10(0.10)^2(0.90)^3 = 10(0.01)(0.729) = 0.0729$$

Figure 4.3 illustrates the solution to this problem with a tree diagram. The probability of each individual event (S or F) is given in parentheses on the branch representing the event.

	Sequence number	Sequence	Sequence number	Sequence
TABLE 4.5	2	11100	6	10101
Additional	3	10011	7	01110
sequences for	4	11010	8	00111
3 successes and	5	11001	9	01011
2 failures			10	01101

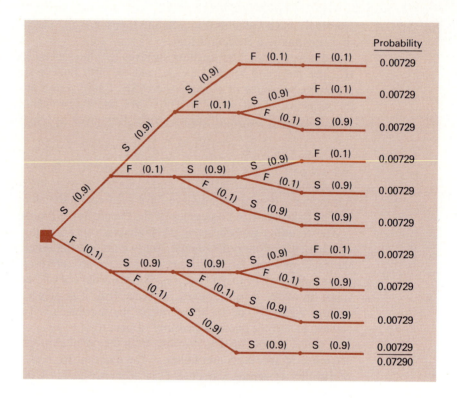

As the size of the sample increases, constructing a tree diagram or listing the sequences becomes more and more difficult. We need an easy method of counting the number of sequences. Since a sequence of outcomes consists of n things, some of which are of one type and the rest of which are of another type, we can use Equation 3.4 to count the number of sequences. Using this equation, we find the number of sequences to be

$$_5C_3 = \frac{5!}{3!2!} = \frac{120}{12} = 10$$

In general, if n equals the total number of objects, x the number of objects of one type, and $n - x$ the number of objects of the other type, the number of sequences is equal to

$$_nC_x = \frac{n!}{x!(n - x)!}$$

which is equal to the number of combinations of n things taken x at a time.

We can write the probability of obtaining exactly x successes in n trials, then, as

$$f(x) = _nC_x q^{n-x}p^x = _nC_x p^x q^{n-x} \qquad \text{for } x = 0, 1, 2, \ldots, n$$
$$= 0 \qquad\qquad\qquad\qquad \text{elsewhere} \qquad\qquad (4.6)$$

TABLE 4.6
The binomial distribution

Number of successes, x	Probability, $f(x)$
0	$_nC_0\, q^{n-0}p^0$
1	$_nC_1\, q^{n-1}p^1$
2	$_nC_2\, q^{n-2}p^2$
$\vdots$	$\vdots$
x	$_nC_x\, q^{n-x}p^x$
$\vdots$	$\vdots$
n	$_nC_n\, q^{n-n}p^n$
Total	1

This expression is the *binomial distribution*. In Equation 4.6, $f(x) = P(X = x)$, where X is the random variable, number of successes in n trials. We use $f(x)$ in this equation rather than $P(X = x)$ not only because it is shorter, but also because it is commonly used.

Table 4.6 shows the binomial distribution in tabular form.

Equation 4.6 has the two essential properties of a probability distribution. Consider the following:

1. $f(x) \geq 0$ for all real values of x.
2. $\Sigma f(x) = 1$.

EXAMPLE 4.5 In a certain community, on a given evening, someone is at home in 85% of the households. Suppose that a researcher conducting a telephone survey randomly selects 12 households to call that evening. What is the probability that someone will be at home in exactly 7 households?

SOLUTION The answer, by Equation 4.6, is

$$f(7) = {}_{12}C_7(0.15)^{12-7}(0.85)^7 = \frac{12!}{5!7!}(0.00007594)(0.320577) = 0.0193$$

The Binomial Table

When the sample size is large, using Equation 4.6 to calculate probabilities is tedious. Fortunately, probabilities for different values of n, p, and x have been tabulated. Thus, instead of calculating the probabilities, we may consult a table to find the desired result. Table B of the Appendix is one such table. This table gives the probability that X is *less than or equal to* some specified value.

Some additional examples illustrate the use of Table B.

EXAMPLE 4.6 An insurance company has found that 8% of its claims are for damages resulting from burglaries. What is the probability that a random sample of 20 claims will contain 5 or fewer that are for burglary damages?

SOLUTION We seek the probability that $X \leq 5$ when $n = 20$, $p = 0.08$, and $q = 0.92$. The table gives the probability that $X \leq x$, so we only need to locate the entry corresponding to $n = 20$, $p = 0.08$, and $X = 5$. We find this to be 0.9962. We can write the problem and its solution in a more compact notation as

$$P(X \leq 5 | n = 20, p = 0.08) = 0.9962$$

EXAMPLE 4.7 In the previous example, what is the probability that a sample of 20 claims will contain more than 5 claims for damages resulting from burglaries?

SOLUTION The answer to this question is the complement of the probability found in Example 4.6. Thus

$$P(X > 5 | n = 20, p = 0.08) = 1 - P(X \leq 5 | n = 20, p = 0.08)$$
$$= 1 - 0.9962 = 0.0038$$

EXAMPLE 4.8 For Example 4.6, let us determine

$$P(2 \leq X \leq 5 | n = 20, p = 0.08)$$

SOLUTION In this example we want the probability associated with an interval. To obtain the answer, we must find the probability that $X \leq 5$ and subtract from it the probability that $X < 2$ (or $X \leq 1$). Therefore, when $n = 20$ and $p = 0.08$,

$$P(2 \leq X \leq 5) = P(X \leq 5) - P(X \leq 1) = 0.9962 - 0.5169 = 0.4793$$

EXAMPLE 4.9 In Example 4.5, suppose that the researcher calls a random sample of 12 households in the community on the night that 85% of the households have someone at home. Use Table B to find the probability that the person conducting the telephone survey finds someone at home in exactly 7 households.

SOLUTION Table B does not give probabilities for values of p greater than 0.5. We can find the probability, however, by restating the problem as follows: What is the probability that the person conducting the telephone survey gets no answer from exactly 5 calls out of 12, if no one is at home in 15% of the households? We find the answer as follows:

$$P(X = 5 | n = 12, p = 0.15) = P(X \leq 5) - P(X \leq 4)$$
$$= 0.9954 - 0.9761 = 0.0193$$

There is a different binomial distribution for each different value of n or p.

This is the same answer we obtained previously. Thus the probability of finding someone at home in exactly 7 households is equal to the probability of finding no one at home in exactly 5 households, given the conditions specified in the example.

The binomial distribution is really a family of distributions. Each different value of either n or p specifies a different distribution. In this distribution n and p are called parameters. Figure 4.4 shows how the binomial distribution varies for different values of p and n. Regardless of the value of n, the distribution is

FIGURE 4.4
Binomial distributions for selected values of *p* and *n*

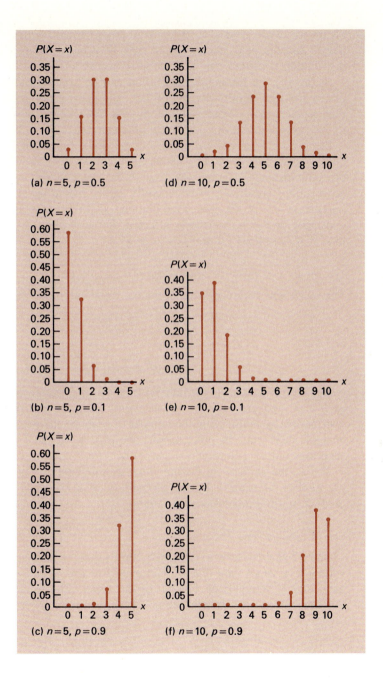

symmetric when $p = 0.5$. When p is greater than 0.5, the distribution is asymmetric and the peak occurs to the right of center. When p is less than 0.5, the distribution is asymmetric and the peak occurs to the left of center.

In theory, the binomial distribution can be applied only when the sample is drawn from an infinite population, or from a finite population when sampling is with replacement. (When sampling is with replacement, a selected unit is returned to the population before the next unit is selected.)

In practice, samples are usually drawn from finite populations. Therefore the question naturally arises of whether the binomial distribution is appropriate, given this circumstance. The answer depends on how constant p remains as succeeding observations are drawn. It is generally agreed that when n is small relative to the population size N, the use of the binomial distribution is appropriate. That is, the constancy of p is not seriously affected. Some writers say that n is small relative to N if N is at least 10 times as large as n.

The Mean and Variance of the Binomial Distribution

The mean and variance of the binomial distribution are

$$\mu = np \tag{4.7}$$

and

$$\sigma^2 = np(1 - p) \tag{4.8}$$

respectively, where n is the number of trials, p is the probability of a success for each trial, and the trials are independent. Thus we find the mean of a binomial distribution by multiplying the number of trials by the probability of a success on an individual trial. In other words, we *expect*, in the long run, to observe np successes out of n Bernoulli trials.

To find the variance of the binomial, as indicated by Equation 4.8, we multiply the number of trials n by the probability of a success. We then multiply this product by the probability of a failure.

Use of Chebyshev's Theorem

Chapter 2 showed how to use Chebyshev's theorem to calculate the proportion of values in a set of data that we can expect to fall within a specified distance (as measured in standard deviations) of the mean. The following is a statement of this theorem in probabilistic terms.

Given the probability distribution of the random variable X with mean μ and standard deviation σ, the probability of observing a value of X within k standard deviations of μ is at least $1 - 1/k^2$.

Alternatively, we may state Chebyshev's theorem as follows:

Given the probability distribution of the random variable X with mean μ and standard deviation σ, the probability of observing a value of X that differs from μ by k or more standard deviations cannot exceed $1/k^2$.

EXAMPLE 4.10 In a certain population, 60% are said to prefer a particular brand of toothpaste. We interview a random sample of 500 persons from this population. Within what interval would we expect the number of successes (persons who prefer the particular brand of toothpaste) in these 500 trials to lie with a probability of 0.96?

SOLUTION Since $1 - 1/k^2 = 0.96$ when $k = 5$, the probability is at least 0.96 that the number of successes we would observe is within five standard deviations of the mean. The probability that a given person prefers the brand of toothpaste is 0.6. And the number of successes out of 500 trials (interviews) is a random variable having a binomial distribution with $n = 500$ and $p = 0.6$. From Equations 4.7 and 4.8, we find the mean and standard deviation to be

$$\mu = np = (500)(0.6) = 300$$

and

$$\sigma = \sqrt{np(1 - p)} = \sqrt{(500)(0.6)(0.4)} = 10.95$$

Since $5(10.95) = 54.75$, the interval we want is 300 ± 54.75, or approximately 245 to 355.

Suppose that we find that only 240 of the 500 prefer the brand of toothpaste. What conclusion might we draw from this? We might question the truth of the statement that 60% of the population prefer the brand, since 240 is more than 5 standard deviations from the mean. Chebyshev's theorem tells us that the probability of this occurring is equal to $1/k^2 = 1/5^2 = 0.04$ or less.

Chebyshev's theorem applies to all random variables. However, it may provide weak information for the specific variable of interest. For many random variables, the probability of observing a value within two standard deviations of the mean is far greater than $1 - 1/2^2 = 0.75$. We have devoted so much time to the theorem in order to shed some light on the nature and importance of the standard deviation as a measure of dispersion.

Exercises

(In each of the following exercises, assume that N is sufficiently large relative to n, and use the binomial distribution to find the desired probabilities.)

 4.7 Over a long period of time, a salesperson has found that the probability of making a sale when calling on a customer is 0.5. If this salesperson calls on 5 customers on a given day, find the probability of making   **(a)** exactly 3 sales,   **(b)** 3 or more sales,   **(c)** fewer than 3 sales,   **(d)** no sales,   **(e)** 5 sales.

4.8 Of a certain group of people, it is estimated that 40% use a particular type of credit card primarily for installment buying. Suppose that this estimate is correct, and that 25 persons picked at random from this group are questioned on the matter. What is the probability that the number using the credit card in this manner is   **(a)** 5 or fewer?   **(b)** between 10 and 15, inclusive?   **(c)** 15 or more?

4.9 Given $n = 6$, $p = 0.2$, find   **(a)** $P(X > 3)$,   **(b)** $P(X \le 4)$,   **(c)** $P(2 \le X \le 4)$.

4.10 Given $n = 15$, $p = 0.3$, determine   **(a)** $P(X \ge 10)$,   **(b)** $P(X < 5)$,   **(c)** $P(X > 12)$,   **(d)** $P(7 \le X \le 10)$.

4.11 Refer to Exercise 4.8. Suppose that we review the records of 1000 holders of the credit card and find that 500 of them use the card primarily for installment buying. Is this sufficient evidence to indicate that the estimate of the true number using this credit card primarily for installment buying should be revised? [*Hint:* Use Chebyshev's theorem.]

4.12 In a certain town, 35% of the residents are opposed to the widening of Main Street. In a simple random sample of 20 residents, what is the probability that the number opposed to the widening is   **(a)** more than 10?   **(b)** between 15 and 18, inclusive?   **(c)** fewer than 8?   **(d)** at least 12?   **(e)** no more than 13?

4.13 Suppose that 72% of a certain population of drivers regularly use seat belts. You take a simple random sample of 15 of these drivers. What is the probability that the number regularly using seat belts is   **(a)** more than 10?   **(b)** fewer than 8?   **(c)** at least 11?   **(d)** 7 or more?

4.14 Suppose that 60% of the members of a credit union have loans with the credit union. If you select a random sample of 10 members, what is the probability that   **(a)** all will have loans?   **(b)** more than 5 will have loans?   **(c)** none will have loans?   **(d)** fewer than 6 will have loans?   **(e)** at least 1 has a loan?

4.15 The manager of a restaurant claims that only 3% of the customers are dissatisfied with the service. If this claim is true, what is the probability that the number of dissatisfied customers in a random sample of 25 customers will be   **(a)** zero?   **(b)** at least 1?   **(c)** between 1 and 5, inclusive?   **(d)** greater than 5?   **(e)** 25?

4.16 A manufacturer claims that 6% of her product is defective. If the claim is true, what is the probability that the number of defective products in a random sample of 20 will be   **(a)** exactly 2?   **(b)** 2 or more?   **(c)** zero?   **(d)** fewer than 5?   **(e)** between 2 and 5, inclusive?

4.17 In a survey of M.B.A. students, 75% said that they expect to be promoted within a month after receiving their degree. If this proportion holds for the population, find, for a sample of size 15, the probability that the number expecting a promotion within a month after graduation is   **(a)** 6,   **(b)** at least 7,   **(c)** no more than 5,   **(d)** between 6 and 9, inclusive.

4.3 PROBABILITY DISTRIBUTIONS OF CONTINUOUS RANDOM VARIABLES

In this section we consider the general idea of the distribution of a continuous random variable. In the following section we discuss in detail the most important special distribution of a continuous random variable—the *normal distribution*. The

**TABLE 4.7
Distribution of lengths of 200 aluminum-coated steel sheets**

Length (inches)	Frequency	Relative frequency
30.000–30.124	8	0.04
30.125–30.249	20	0.10
30.250–30.374	32	0.16
30.375–30.499	40	0.20
30.500–30.624	36	0.18
30.625–30.749	34	0.17
30.750–30.874	20	0.10
30.875–30.999	10	0.05
Total	200	1.00

FIGURE 4.5
Histogram of
lengths of 200
aluminum-coated
steel sheets

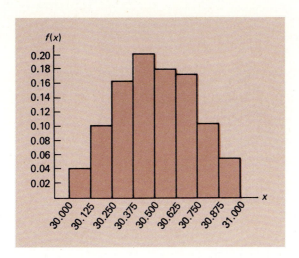

random variable X is continuous if it can assume all possible values between any two particular values x_a and x_b. To help understand the nature of the distribution of a continuous random variable, consider the following example.

EXAMPLE 4.11 Table 4.7 shows the frequency and relative frequency distributions of the lengths of a sample of 200 aluminum-coated steel sheets taken from a production lot of a certain factory. Since the probability associated with each interval of lengths shown in the first column is given by the relative frequency column, this column constitutes the probability distribution of the random variable, length of aluminum-coated steel sheet.

We can present the probability distribution as a histogram, as in Figure 4.5, or as a frequency polygon, as in Figure 4.6. The area within each cell of the histogram represents a certain proportion of the total area bounded by the histogram and the horizontal axis. The proportion of the total area contained within a par-

FIGURE 4.6
Relative frequency
polygon of lengths
of 200 aluminum-
coated steel sheets

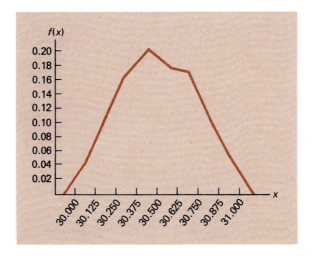

FIGURE 4.7
Histogram of
lengths of 2000
aluminum-coated
steel sheets (much
smaller class
intervals than in
Figure 4.5)

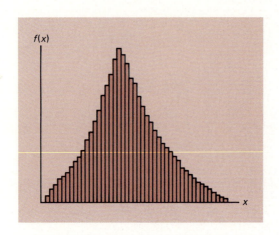

ticular cell is equal to the probability of observing a value between the boundaries of that cell. For example, Table 4.7 shows that the relative frequency, or probability, of occurrence of values between 30.000 and 30.125 inches is 0.04. The corresponding cell in Figure 4.5 has 4% of the total area of the histogram.

Given any histogram of a probability distribution, we can find the probability of occurrence of values between any two points on the horizontal axis. We do this by determining what proportion of the total area we enclose when we erect vertical lines at these points. For example, to find the probability of occurrence of values between 30.500 and 30.625 in Figure 4.5, we determine what proportion of the histogram's area is enclosed by vertical lines erected at these points. The values 30.500 and 30.625 define a class interval. Since the vertical lines erected at these points define a cell of the histogram, we consult Table 4.7, and we find the proportion of the area enclosed to be 0.18. The probability of occurrence of values between 30.500 and 30.625, then, is 0.18.

To find the area enclosed by two or more cells, we must find the sum of the individual areas. This total is equal to the probability associated with the corresponding class intervals. For example, to find the area between 30.500 and 30.750 in Figure 4.5, we add the areas of the two cells involved. From Table 4.7 we find this area to be $0.18 + 0.17 = 0.35$. Thus the probability of occurrence of values between 30.500 and 30.750 is 0.35.

FIGURE 4.8
Smooth curve
approximating a
histogram for data
with large *n* and a
large number of
class intervals

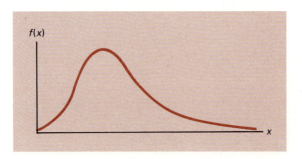

**FIGURE 4.9
Probability
distribution of the
continuous random
variable *X* showing
P(*a* ≤ *x* ≤ *b*)**

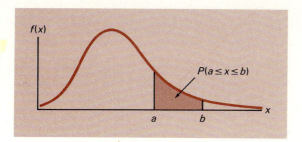

Now consider a situation in which the number of values of the random variable is very large and the width of the class intervals is very small. For example, suppose that we have 2000 aluminum-coated steel sheets instead of 200. And suppose that we prepare a histogram for these data using much smaller class intervals, perhaps 0.010 inch in width. The resulting histogram might look like the one in Figure 4.7.

Suppose that we were to construct a frequency polygon from the histogram of Figure 4.7. The figure would be much smoother than the one in Figure 4.6. In fact, as the number of values *n* approaches infinity, and the width of the class intervals approaches 0, the frequency polygon approaches a smooth curve, such as the one shown in Figure 4.8. We can use smooth curves as a graphical means of representing probability distributions of continuous random variables.

As with the histogram, the total area under a smooth curve used to represent a probability distribution is equal to 1. The probability of occurrence of values between any two points on the horizontal axis is equal to the area bounded by perpendicular lines erected at these points, the curve itself, and the horizontal axis. Figure 4.9 shows the graph of the probability distribution of a continuous random variable with the area between two points *a* and *b* shaded. This area is equal to the probability of occurrence of values between *a* and *b*.

We cannot find areas under a smooth curve the same way we find areas under a histogram. A smooth curve does not have delineated subareas corresponding to the cells of a histogram. We use integral calculus to find subareas under smooth curves. Methods of integral calculus are beyond the scope of this text. However, this is not a serious problem, since tables of values obtained by integration are available for those continuous distributions that are of interest to us.

4.4 THE NORMAL DISTRIBUTION

We now come to the most important distribution in statistics—the *normal distribution*. The equation for the normal distribution is

$$f(x) = \frac{1}{\sqrt{2\pi}\sigma} e^{-(x-\mu)^2/2\sigma^2}, \qquad -\infty < x < \infty \qquad (4.9)$$

FIGURE 4.10
A normal
distribution

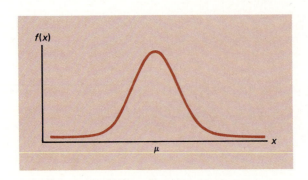

where π and e are the familiar constants 3.14159 and 2.71828, respectively. The distribution has two parameters: μ, the mean, and σ, the standard deviation. The graph of the normal distribution is the familiar bell-shaped curve shown above in Figure 4.10.

Characteristics of the Normal Distribution

The following are some important characteristics of the normal distribution:

1. It is symmetrical about its mean μ. As Figure 4.10 shows, the curve on either side of μ is a mirror image of the other side.
2. The mean, the median, and the mode are all equal.
3. The total area under the curve above the x axis is equal to 1. Because of the symmetry of the normal curve, 50% of the area is to the right of a perpendicular line erected at the mean, and 50% is to the left.
4. Suppose that we erect vertical lines one standard deviation from the mean in each direction. The area enclosed by these lines, the x axis, and the curve will be equal to approximately 68% of the total area. If we erect these lateral boundaries two standard deviations from the mean in each direction, they will enclose approximately 95% of the area. Perpendiculars erected three standard deviations on either side of the mean will enclose approximately 99.7% of the total area. Figure 4.11 illustrates these approximate areas.

   A *normally distributed* random variable is an example of a case in which Chebyshev's theorem provides weak information regarding the probability of observing a value within specified distances of the mean. Instead of the probabilities of 0.95 and 0.997, Chebyshev's theorem leads to probabilities of at least $1 - 1/2^2 = 0.75$ and at least $1 - 1/3^2 = 0.899$, respectively, of observing a value within two and three standard deviations of the mean. Chebyshev's theorem gives no information at all about the probability of observing a value within one standard deviation of the mean, since $1 - 1/k^2 = 0$ when $k = 1$. Thus, if we know that a random variable is normally distributed, we can make more powerful probability statements than we could using Chebyshev's theorem.
5. The normal distribution is completely determined by its parameters μ and σ. That is, each different value of μ or σ specifies a different normal distribution.

Interval	Approximate area
$\mu \pm \sigma$	0.68
$\mu \pm 2\sigma$	0.95
$\mu \pm 3\sigma$	0.997

FIGURE 4.11
Normal distributions, showing areas bounded by perpendiculars erected a distance of one, two, and three standard deviations on either side of the mean (areas are approximate)

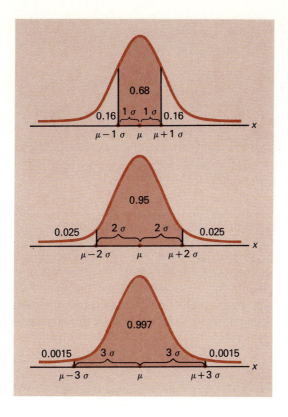

Figure 4.12 shows how different values of μ cause the graph of the distribution to be shifted along the x axis. Figure 4.13 shows how different values of the standard deviation σ, which is a measure of dispersion, determine the flatness or peakedness of the graph of the distribution.

The Standard Normal Distribution

The normal distribution is really a family of distributions in which one member is distinguished from another on the basis of the values of μ and σ. In other

FIGURE 4.12
Three normal distributions with different means

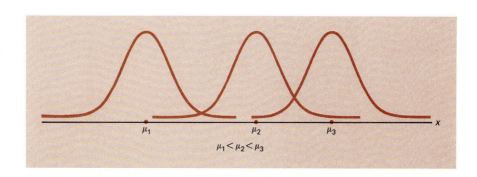

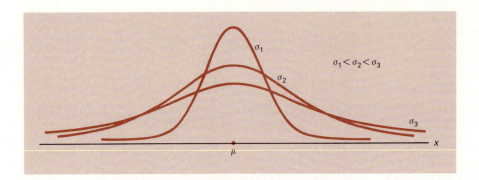

words, as already indicated, there is a different normal distribution for each different value of either μ or σ.

The most important member of this family of distributions is the one that has a mean of 0 and a standard deviation of 1. This distribution is called the *standard normal distribution*. We can obtain it from Equation 4.9 by letting $\mu = 0$ and $\sigma = 1$. We usually use the letter z for the random variable that results. Consequently the equation for the standard normal distribution is written

$$f(z) = \frac{1}{\sqrt{2\pi}} e^{-z^2/2}, \qquad -\infty < z < \infty \tag{4.10}$$

Figure 4.14 shows the graph of the standard normal distribution.

The probability that z lies between any two points on the z axis, say z_0 and z_1, is determined by the area bounded by perpendiculars erected at each of these points, the curve, and the horizontal axis. Table C of the Appendix gives the areas under the standard normal curve between $-\infty$ and the values of z shown in the marginal column of the table. The shaded area in Figure 4.15 represents the area listed in the body of Table C as being between $-\infty$ and $z = z_0$. The following examples illustrate the use of Table C.

EXAMPLE 4.12 Given the standard normal distribution, find the area under the curve above the z axis between $z = -\infty$ and $z = 2.5$.

FIGURE 4.14
The standard
normal distribution

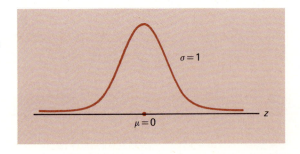

FIGURE 4.15
Standard normal
distribution
showing area
between $-\infty$
and z_0

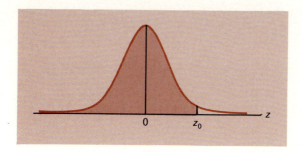

SOLUTION The area is shaded in Figure 4.16. Locating $z = 2.5$ in Table C and reading the corresponding entry in the body of the table, we find the desired area to be 0.9938. We can interpret this in several ways. It is the probability that a z picked at random from the population of z's will have a value between $-\infty$ and 2.5. It is also the relative frequency of occurrence (or proportion) of values of z between $-\infty$ and 2.5. Or we can say that 99.38 percent of the z's have a value between $-\infty$ and 2.5.

EXAMPLE 4.13 What is the probability that a z picked at random from the population of z's will have a value between -2.65 and $+2.65$?

SOLUTION Figure 4.17 shows the area desired. We find the area between $-\infty$ and 2.65 by locating 2.6 in the far left column of Table C, then moving across to the entry in the column headed by 0.05. The area at the intersection of 2.6 and 0.05 is 0.9960. Similarly we find the area from $-\infty$ to -2.65 to be 0.0040. We find the area we want by subtracting 0.0040 from 0.9960. That is,

$$P(-2.65 \leq z \leq 2.65) = 0.9960 - 0.0040 = 0.9920$$

EXAMPLE 4.14 What proportion of z values are between -2.78 and 1.47?

SOLUTION Figure 4.18 shows the area desired. The area between $-\infty$ and 1.47 is 0.9292. The area between $-\infty$ and -2.78 is 0.0027. To find the desired area,

FIGURE 4.16
Standard normal
distribution
showing area
between $-\infty$
and $z = 2.5$

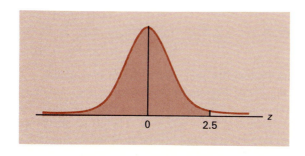

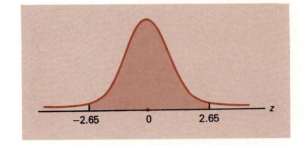

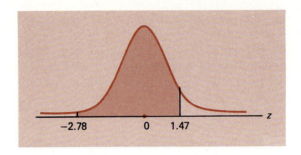

we subtract 0.0027 from 0.9292 to obtain 0.9265. That is,

$$P(-2.78 \le z \le 1.47) = 0.9292 - 0.0027 = 0.9265$$

EXAMPLE 4.15 Given the standard normal distribution, find $P(z \ge 1.73)$.

SOLUTION Figure 4.19 shows the area desired. We can obtain the area to the right of $z = 1.73$ by subtracting the area between $-\infty$ and 1.73 from 1. Thus

$$P(z \ge 1.73) = 1 - P(-\infty < z < 1.73) = 1 - 0.9582 = 0.0418$$

EXAMPLE 4.16 Given the standard normal distribution, find $P(0.79 \le z \le 2.37)$.

SOLUTION Figure 4.20 shows the area of interest. We first obtain the area between $-\infty$ and 2.37. From that area we subtract the area between $-\infty$ and 0.79. In other words,

$$P(0.79 \le z \le 2.37) = P(-\infty \le z \le 2.37) - P(-\infty \le z \le 0.79)$$
$$= 0.9911 - 0.7852 = 0.2059$$

Again, the probability that z is between two values z_a and z_b is equal to the area under the curve between perpendicular lines erected at z_a and z_b. The area above a point (with no width), say z_a, is equal to zero. Thus the probability that $z = z_a = 0$. That is, $P(z = z_a) = 0$. Therefore, the probability that z is greater than or equal to z_a is the same as the probability that z is greater than z_a. Using

FIGURE 4.19
Standard normal
distribution
showing area to
right of $z = 1.73$

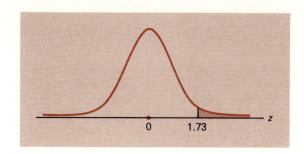

FIGURE 4.20
Standard normal
distribution
showing
$P(0.79 \leq z \leq 2.37)$

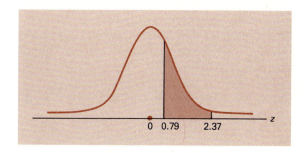

symbols, we can write $P(z \geq z_a) = P(z > z_a)$. For example, Table C tells us that $P(z \geq 1.5) = 0.0668$. Since $P(z = 1.5) = 0$, $P(z > 1.5) = 0.0668$, also. Similarly, $P(z_a \leq z \leq z_b) = P(z_a < z < z_b)$ and $P(z_a \leq z) = P(z_a < z)$.

Exercises

Given the standard normal distribution, find:

4.18 The area under the curve between $z = 0$ and $z = 1.54$.
4.19 The probability that a z picked at random has a value between $z = -2.07$ and $z = 2.33$.
4.20 $P(z \geq 0.65)$
4.21 $P(z \geq -0.65)$
4.22 $P(z < -2.33)$
4.23 $P(z < 2.33)$
4.24 $P(-1.96 \leq z \leq 1.96)$
4.25 $P(-2.58 \leq z \leq 2.58)$
4.26 $P(-3.10 \leq z \leq 1.25)$
4.27 $P(1.47 \leq z \leq 3.44)$

Given the following probabilities, find z_1:

4.28 $P(z \leq z_1) = 0.0055$
4.29 $P(-2.67 \leq z \leq z_1) = 0.9718$
4.30 $P(z > z_1) = 0.0384$
4.31 $P(z_1 \leq z \leq 2.98) = 0.1117$
4.32 $P(-z_1 \leq z \leq z_1) = 0.8132$

Applications of the Normal Distribution

The normal distribution is very important in statistical inference. We should realize, however, that it is not a natural law that we encounter each time we analyze a continuous random variable. The normal distribution is a theoretical, or ideal, distribution. No set of measurements conforms exactly to its specifications. Many sets of measurements, however, are *approximately* normally distributed. In such cases the normal distribution is quite useful when we try to answer practical questions regarding the data.

In particular, whenever a set of measurements is approximately normally distributed, we can find the probability of occurrence of values within any specific interval, just as we can with the standard normal distribution. We can do this because we can easily transform any normal distribution with a known mean μ and standard deviation σ to the standard normal distribution. Once we have made this transformation, we can use a table of standard normal areas, such as Table C, to find relevant probabilities.

Transforming x to z We can transform a normal distribution to the standard normal distribution using the formula

$$z = \frac{x - \mu}{\sigma} \tag{4.11}$$

This transforms any value of x in the original distribution to the corresponding value of z in the standard normal distribution.

Suppose, for example, that we have a population of measurements that are approximately normally distributed with a mean of 10 and a standard deviation of 2.5. Suppose, also, that we want to find the probability that a measurement selected at random from this population will have a value equal to or greater than 15. We first transform $x = 15$ to its corresponding z value. That is,

$$z = \frac{x - \mu}{\sigma} = \frac{15 - 10}{2.5} = \frac{5}{2.5} = 2$$

Figure 4.21 shows the relationship between the original distribution and the standard normal distribution, with the area of interest shaded. The figure shows that the distance from the mean, 10, to the value of interest, 15, is $15 - 10 = 5$. This is a distance of 2 standard deviations. When x values are transformed to z values, the distance of a z value from its mean, 0, is equal to the distance of the corresponding x value from its mean in standard deviation units. In the present example, x is 2 standard deviations from its mean. In the z distribution, a standard deviation is equal to 1. Therefore the point on the z scale located 2 standard deviations from 0 is $z = 2$. That is the same result that we obtained using the formula. From Table C, the area to the right of $z = 2$ is 0.0228. We can summarize this discussion as follows:

$$P(X \geq 15) = P\left(z \geq \frac{15 - 10}{2.5}\right) = P(z \geq 2) = 0.0228$$

FIGURE 4.21
Original distribution of X (approximately normal) and corresponding standard normal distribution. Note that the standard normal distribution is "skinnier" than the original distribution because σ = 1 is smaller than σ = 2.5

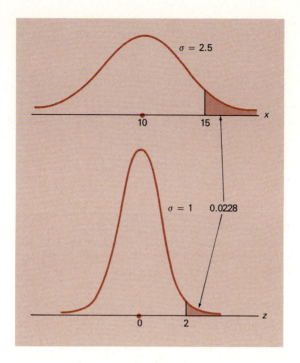

In Figure 4.21, the distribution of z is "skinnier" than the distribution of x. This is because the distribution of z has a smaller standard deviation (1) than does the distribution of x, which has a standard deviation of 2.5. Subsequent pictures of the standard normal distribution will not be drawn to scale.

EXAMPLE 4.17 Refer to Example 4.11. Suppose that the population of lengths of aluminum-coated steel sheets is approximately normally distributed with a mean of $\mu = 30.5$ inches and a standard deviation of $\sigma = 0.2$ inch. What is the probability that a sheet selected at random from the population is between 30.250 and 30.750 inches long?

SOLUTION First we transform each value of x to the corresponding value of z. Thus,

$$z_1 = \frac{30.250 - 30.500}{0.2} = \frac{-0.250}{0.2} = -1.25$$

and

$$z_2 = \frac{30.750 - 30.500}{0.2} = \frac{0.250}{0.2} = 1.25$$

Figure 4.22 shows the relationship between the original distribution and the standard normal distribution. The areas of interest are shaded. The probability we

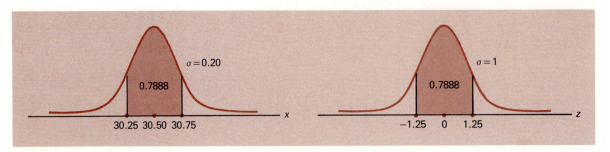

FIGURE 4.22
Normal distribution and corresponding standard
normal distribution, Example 4.17

seek can be calculated as follows:

$$P(30.250 \leq X \leq 30.750) = P(-1.25 \leq z \leq 1.25)$$
$$= P(z \leq 1.25) - P(z \leq -1.25)$$

Table C shows this to be $0.8944 - 0.1056 = 0.7888$.

The Normal Approximation to the Binomial

The normal distribution gives a good approximation to the binomial distribution when n is large and p is not too close to 0 or 1. This enables us to calculate probabilties for large samples from dichotomous populations for which binomial tables are not available. A good rule of thumb is that the normal approximation to the binomial is appropriate when np and $n(1 - p)$ are both greater than 5. To use the normal approximation, we use $\mu = np$ and $\sigma = \sqrt{np(1 - p)}$. We convert values of the original variable to values of z to find the probabilities of interest.

The Continuity Correction   The normal distribution is continuous and the binomial is discrete. Therefore we can get better results if we make an adjustment to account for this when we use the approximation. The need for such an adjustment, called the *continuity correction,* is evident when we compare a histogram constructed from binomial data with a superimposed smooth curve. Figure 4.23 illustrates this situation for $n = 20$ and $p = 0.3$.

In Figure 4.23, the probability that $X = x$ is equal to the area of the rectangle centered at x. For example, the probability that $X = 8$ is equal to the area of the rectangle centered at 8. We can see that this rectangle extends from 7.5 to 8.5. From Table B, we find that this area is equal to 0.1144. The corresponding area is shaded in Figure 4.23a.

When we use the normal approximation to the binomial distribution, we take into account the fact that for the binomial distribution, $P(X = x)$ is the area of a rectangle centered at x. When we convert values of x to values of z, the continuity correction consists of adding 0.5 to, and/or subtracting 0.5 from, x as appropriate.

FIGURE 4.23
Normal approximation to the binomial with $n = 20$, $p = 0.3$, and $\mu = np = 6$, showing $P(X = 8)$

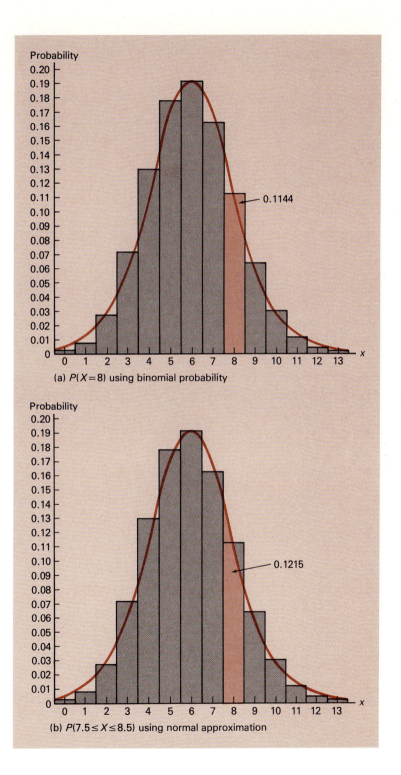

(a) $P(X=8)$ using binomial probability

(b) $P(7.5 \leq X \leq 8.5)$ using normal approximation

FIGURE 4.24
Normal approximation to the binomial with $n = 20$, $p = 0.3$, **and** $\mu = np = 6$, **showing** $P(5 \le X \le 10)$

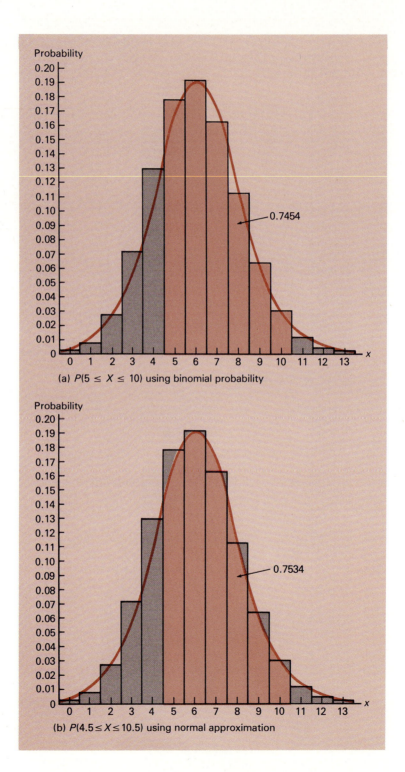

(a) $P(5 \le X \le 10)$ using binomial probability

(b) $P(4.5 \le X \le 10.5)$ using normal approximation

To illustrate, let us use the continuity correction and normal approximation to find the probability that X assumes a value between $x_a = 7.5$ and $x_b = 8.5$. Converting to z values, we have

$$z_a = \frac{7.5 - 6}{\sqrt{(20)(0.3)(0.7)}} = \frac{1.5}{2.05} = 0.73$$

$$z_b = \frac{8.5 - 6}{\sqrt{(20)(0.3)(0.7)}} = \frac{2.5}{2.05} = 1.22$$

From Table C, the probability we seek is 0.1215, which is reasonably close to the exact probability of 0.1144. The area under the normal curve corresponding to $P(7.5 \leq X \leq 8.5)$ is shaded in Figure 4.23b.

Let us use this same example to find $P(5 \leq X \leq 10)$. Using binomial probabilities from Table B, we find the answer to be 0.7454. The corresponding area is shaded in Figure 4.24a.

To use the normal approximation, we find

$$P(4.5 \leq X \leq 10.5) = P\left(\frac{4.5 - 6}{2.05} \leq z \leq \frac{10.5 - 6}{2.05}\right)$$

$$= P(-0.73 \leq z \leq 2.20)$$

$$= 0.9861 - 0.2327 = 0.7534$$

The corresponding area is shaded in Figure 4.24b.

Again we see that the normal approximation gives a result that is quite close to the exact probability. If we had not used the continuity correction, the normal approximation would have given

$$P(5 \leq X \leq 10) = P\left(\frac{5 - 6}{2.05} \leq z \leq \frac{10 - 6}{2.05}\right)$$

$$= P(-0.49 \leq z \leq 1.95)$$

$$= 0.9744 - 0.3121 = 0.6623$$

This approximation is not nearly as close to the true probability of 0.7454 as is the approximation obtained with the continuity correction. When n is large and p is not too close to 0 or 1, we usually omit the continuity correction when finding probabilities associated with such intervals as $P(x_a \leq X \leq x_b)$, $P(X \leq x)$, or $P(X \geq x)$.

Exercises

(In the following exercises, draw pictures to show areas and points of interest.)

4.33 Given a normally distributed population of values with a mean of 76 and a standard deviation of 10: **(a)** What proportion of values are between 71 and 82? **(b)** What proportion are greater than 75? **(c)** What is the probability that a value picked at random from this population is less than 78?

 4.34 Suppose that the diameters of lids for tin cans produced by a certain manufacturer are normally distributed with a mean of 4 inches and a standard deviation of 0.012 inch. What proportion of the lids produced are between 3.97 inches and 4.03 inches?

4.35 Given a normal distribution of values with a mean of 120 and a variance of 16, what proportion of the values are greater than 121?

4.36 The weights of a certain melon are normally distributed with a mean of 14 ounces and a standard deviation of 1.22 ounces. What is the probability that a melon drawn at random from this population will weigh less than 12 ounces?

4.37 A bank official finds that the lengths of time customers have to wait to be serviced by a teller are approximately normally distributed with a mean of 3 minutes and a standard deviation of 1 minute.   **(a)** What proportion of customers have to wait longer than 2 minutes but less than $3\frac{1}{2}$ minutes?   **(b)** What proportion of customers have to wait 1 minute or less?   **(c)** You are about to enter the bank. What is the probability that you will have to wait longer than 5 minutes?

4.38 A production supervisor found that employees, on the average, complete a certain task in 10 minutes. The times required to complete the task are approximately normally distributed, with a standard deviation of 3 minutes. Find the following: **(a)** the proportion of employees completing the task in less than 4 minutes;   **(b)** the proportion of employees requiring more than 5 minutes to complete the task;   **(c)** the probability that an employee who has just been assigned the task will complete it within 3 minutes.

4.39 In a certain large firm, 30% of the employees are females. A random sample of 50 is selected from this population. What is the probability that the number of females will be between 20 and 24, inclusive?

4.40 Suppose that only 40% of the residents of a city favor a certain zoning petition. What is the probability that a random sample of 100 citizens will contain between 30 and 50, inclusive, who favor the petititon?

Summary

This chapter introduced you to some important probability distributions. If you understand the basic concepts presented here, you will understand the ideas presented in the later chapters more easily. Chapter 3, this chapter, and the next chapter serve as a bridge connecting the methods and concepts of descriptive statistics with those of inferential statistics.

In this chapter you learned about discrete probability distributions and continuous probability distributions. You learned that *the probability distribution of a discrete random variable is a table, graph, formula, or other device used to specify all possible values of a discrete random variable along with their respective probabilities.*

You learned that if a random variable X is continuous, we cannot speak meaningfully of the probability that $X = x$. Thus the probability distribution of a continuous random variable must be defined differently. *A nonnegative function f(x) is called a probability distribution of the continuous random variable X if the total area bounded by its curve and the x axis is equal to 1, and if the subarea under the curve bounded by the curve, the x axis, and perpendiculars erected at any two points a and b gives the probability that X is between the points a and b.*

The discrete probability distribution covered in this chapter is the binomial distribution. This provides an appropriate means for analysis when the available data consist of n repetitions of a Bernoulli trial. A Bernoulli trial is one that can result only in one of two mutually exclusive outcomes.

The continuous probability distribution covered in this chapter is the normal distribution. This is the most important distribution we encounter in the study and practice of statistics. We shall use it often in later chapters.

Review Questions

1. What is a discrete random variable? Give three examples from the field of business.

2. What is a continuous random variable? Give three examples from the field of business.

3. Define the probability distribution of a discrete random variable.

4. Define the probability distribution of a continuous random variable.

5. What is a cumulative probability distribution?

6. What is a Bernoulli trial?

7. Describe the binomial distribution. What are its mean and variance?

8. Give an example of a random variable that you think follows a binomial distribution.

9. Explain the expression $E(X^2) - [E(X)]^2$.

10. Explain the expression $E(X) = \Sigma x P(X = x)$.

11. Describe the normal distribution.

12. Describe the standard normal distribution and tell how it is used in statistics.

13. Given an example of a random variable that you think is at least approximately normally distributed.

14. Using the example you gave in Question 13, demonstrate the use of the standard normal distribution in answering probability questions relating to this variable.

15. State Chebyshev's theorem and explain how it may be used.

16. Discuss the concept of expected value.

 17. The following is the frequency distribution of the number of times each of 100 machines in a factory broke down during the past year. **(a)** Construct the probability distribution of the random variable $X =$ number of machine breakdowns. **(b)** Draw a graph of the distribution. **(c)** Construct and graph the cumulative probability distribution of X.

x_i (Number of breakdowns)	0	1	2	3	4	5	6	7	8	9	10
Frequency of occurrence of x_i	10	15	20	25	15	5	3	2	2	2	1

18. In Exercise 17, find: **(a)** the probability that a machine picked at random is one that broke down 3 times; **(b)** the probability that a randomly selected machine is one that broke down 4 or fewer times; **(c)** the probability that a machine picked at random is one that broke down between 4 and 7 times, inclusive; **(d)** the probability that a randomly selected machine is one that broke down either 1 or 2 times; **(e)** $P(X > 5)$; **(f)** $P(X < 1)$; **(g)** $P(X \geq 5)$; **(h)** $P(0 < X \leq 3)$.

19. Customers entering a store have 5 brands (equal in price and weight) of a certain product from which to choose. Suppose that 30% of the customers prefer Brand A. What is the probability that of 20 customers making a selection from the available brands, Brand A is selected by **(a)** at least half? **(b)** more than half? **(c)** between 5 and 10, inclusive? **(d)** 14 or more?

20. You know that 5% of all items produced at a certain factory are defective. You select 25 items at random from a day's production. What is the probability that the number of defectives in the sample is: **(a)** at least 1? **(b)** no more than 5? **(c)** between 3 and 7, inclusive? **(d)** 10 or more? **(e)** 0?

21. Given the standard normal distribution, find $P(-1.65 \leq z \leq 1.65)$.

22. Given the standard normal distribution, find $P(z = 0.75)$.

23. A population of values is normally distributed with a mean of 25.5. It is known that 75.49% of the values are less than 27.8. What is the standard deviation of the population?

24. The inside diameters of metal washers produced by a certain factory are normally distributed with a mean of 0.5 inch and a standard deviation of 0.01 inch. Of all washers produced, 0.8% are rejected because they are too small for a bolt used to test them. What is the diameter of the bolt used for the test?

25. The breaking strengths of plastic bottles are normally distributed with a variance of 25. Approximately 1.97% of specimens produced are rejected because they fail a quality-control test that subjects them to 255 psi of pressure. What is the mean breaking strength of the bottles?

26. Agricultural experts have found that when a certain type of fertilizer is used, yields per acre of a certain grain are approximately normally distributed with a mean and standard deviation of 40 and 10 bushels per acre, respectively. **(a)** When this fertilizer is used, what proportion of the acreage planted in this grain yields more than 50 bushels per acre? **(b)** What is the probability that a randomly selected acre will yield less than 15 bushels?

27. Scores made by employees on a manual dexterity test are normally distributed with a mean of 600 and a variance of 10,000. **(a)** What proportion of employees taking the test score below 300? **(b)** An employee is about to take the test. What is the probability that the employee's score will be 850 or more? **(c)** What proportion of employees score between 450 and 700? **(d)** Management has decided that those employees whose scores are among the top 10% will be considered for promotion to a better job. What score must an employee make in order to be eligible for promotion? **(e)** Suppose that management decides to consider for promotion only those employees who make a score of 800 or more. What percentage of the employees will be eligible to be considered for promotion?

28. In a household survey, a market research firm found that family gasoline consumption per month was approximately normally distributed with a mean and standard deviation of 70 and 9 gallons, respectively. **(a)** What proportion of families use between 55 and 73 gallons per month? **(b)** A family is picked at random from this population. What is the probability that it uses more than 72 gallons per month? **(c)** What proportion of families in this population use less than 68 gallons?

29. In a suburban community, on a given weekday evening, the head of the household is at home in 65% of the households. A researcher conducting a telephone survey randomly selects 15 households to call that evening. What is the probability that the researcher will find the head of the household at home in exactly 8 households?

30. You know that 80% of the people applying for a certain job have had no previous experience in the job. You select a random sample of 5 current applicants. What is the probability that exactly 3 have had no previous experience in the job?

31. It is estimated that 30% of a certain group of truck drivers eat at a certain truck stop. Suppose that the estimate is correct. You question 25 drivers picked at random from this group. What is the probability that the number eating at the truck stop will be: **(a)** 5 or fewer? **(b)** between 19 and 15, inclusive? **(c)** 15 or more?

32. In a certain population of adolescents, the proportion who have their own cars is 0.40. A random sample of 20 is selected from the population. What is the probability that the number who have their own cars will be: **(a)** greater than 10? **(b)** fewer than 5? **(c)** between 5 and 15, inclusive?

33. In a population of executives, 40% are under 45. What is the probability that in a random sample of 15 of these executives, 8 or more are under 45?

34. You know that 20% of the salaried employees in a certain city have less than a high school education. You take a random sample of 20 of these employees. What is the probability that between 10 and 15, inclusive, have less than a high school education?

35. The standard deviation of employees' scores on an aptitude test is 10. What is the probability that the score of a randomly selected employee differs by more than 2 points from the mean score for all employees? Assume that scores are approximately normally distributed.

36. The mean breaking strength of a certain brand of plastic trash bag is 10 pounds per square inch. Breaking strengths are approximately normally distributed with a standard deviation of 0.1. In a shipment of 10,000 bags, how many would we expect to find with breaking strengths below 9.8 pounds per square inch? The manufacturer says that if 1% or more of the bags have breaking strengths below 9.75 pounds per square inch, the firm will look for a stronger raw material. Should the firm do so at this time?

37. On the average, a certain supermarket sells 250 quarts of milk per day. The standard deviation is 25. **(a)** On a given day, the supermarket stocks 300 quarts. What is the probability that all will be sold? Assume that the number of quarts sold per day is approximately normally distributed. **(b)** How many quarts should the supermarket stock if the proprietor wants the probability of not being able to meet the demand for quarts of milk to be 0.01?

38. Given the normally distributed random variable X, find the numerical value of k such that $P(\mu - k\sigma \leq X \leq \mu + k\sigma) = 0.754$.

39. Given the normally distributed random variable X with mean 100 and standard deviation 15, find the numerical value of k such that: **(a)** $P(X \leq k) = 0.0094$, **(b)** $P(X \geq k) = 0.1093$, **(c)** $P(100 \leq X \leq k) = 0.4778$, **(d)** $P(k' \leq X \leq k) = 0.9660$, where k' and k are equidistant from μ.

40. Given the normally distributed random variable X with $\sigma = 10$ and $P(X \leq 40) = 0.0080$, find μ.

41. Given the normally distributed random variable X with $\sigma = 15$ and $P(X \leq 50) = 0.9904$, find μ.

42. Given the normally distributed random variable X with $\sigma = 5$ and $P(X \geq 25) = 0.0526$, find μ.

43. Given the normally distributed random variable X with $\mu = 25$ and $P(X \leq 10) = 0.0778$, find σ.

44. Given the normally distributed random variable X with $\mu = 30$ and $P(X \leq 50) = 0.9772$, find σ.

45. Let $n = 20$. Find μ and σ^2 of the binomial distribution when **(a)** $p = 0.1$, **(b)** $p = 0.2$, **(c)** $p = 0.3$, **(d)** $p = 0.4$, **(e)** $p = 0.5$, **(f)** $p = 0.6$, **(g)** $p = 0.7$, **(h)** $p = 0.8$, **(i)** $p = 0.9$. For which value of p is σ^2 smallest? Largest?

46. In a population of heads of household, 38% own their homes. You select a simple random sample of size 15 from this population. What is the probability that the number in the sample who own their homes will be **(a)** exactly 8? **(b)** between 5 and 7, inclusive? **(c)** at least 12? **(d)** 9 or more?

47. In a population of executives, 10% have changed employers within the past 2 years. You select a simple random sample of 70 from this population. What is the probability that 12 or more in the sample will have changed employers within the past 2 years?

48. In a certain county, in 70% of the households, there is at least one person who is over 40. You draw a random sample of 200 from this population. What is the probability that the number of households with a person over 40 is between 150 and 155, inclusive?

5.
Some Important Sampling Distributions

CHAPTER OBJECTIVES: This chapter is the most important one in the book. It holds the key to statistical inference. Study this chapter very carefully. Pay special attention to the general discussion of sampling distributions. Before you can understand statistical inference, you must understand sampling distributions. After studying this chapter and working the exercises, you should be able to do the following.

1. Construct the sampling distribution of sample means computed from samples drawn from a small population
2. Determine the mean, standard error, and functional form of the sampling distribution of the mean, the difference between two means, a proportion, and the difference between two proportions
3. Explain the central limit theorem and discuss its importance in statistical inference
4. Use your knowledge of sampling distributions to compute the probability associated with specified sample results when the statistic of interest is the mean, the difference between two means, a proportion, or the difference between two proportions

Let us pause here and review briefly the material that we have covered so far. Chapter 1 emphasized the importance of statistics to the manager and the researcher. The object of that chapter was to justify statistics as a worthwhile subject for the student of business to study. Chapter 2 discussed the organization and summarization of data generated by the routine operation of a business firm or by a special study. It presented computations of the basic measures, such as the mean and standard deviation, used for describing a set of data. We learned that, when they are computed from the data of a sample, these descriptive measures are called statistics. When they are computed from a population of data, they are called parameters. Chapter 3, the first of three chapters designed to lay the foundation for statistical inference, was devoted to the basic concepts of probability. Chapter 4 expanded on these concepts and introduced the idea of a probability distribution. One distribution of discrete variables, the binomial, was discussed in detail, as was the normal distribution, a continuous distribution that we will refer to frequently in later chapters.

We come now to the last of the three chapters that link the descriptive material of Chapter 2 and the concepts of inference that begin in Chapter 6. You must understand the principles introduced here if you are to understand the inferential procedures that make up the major portion of this book.

The ideas presented in this chapter are based on the concept of *sampling*. Although we have already defined the word *sample*, here we shall discuss the concepts of a *sample* and *sampling* in greater detail and in more technical terms.

5.1 SIMPLE RANDOM SAMPLING

As noted in Chapter 2, it is important to distinguish between two types of sample, the *probability sample* and the *nonprobability sample*.

A probability sample is a sample of elements drawn from a population of elements in such a way that every element in the population has a known and nonzero probability of being selected.

All other methods of selecting a sample are known as *nonprobability* methods. The only type of sample we consider in this text is the probability sample. This is because only for probability samples are there statistically sound procedures that allow us both to infer from a sample to the population from which it is drawn and to obtain estimates of the sampling error involved.

We usually do not sample small populations. Instead, when we need to know their characteristics, we examine them in their entirety. As a rule, we use sampling only when the population of interest is so large that examining it completely is impractical.

A simple random sample is a probability sample.

From any finite population of size N, we can draw a finite number of different samples of size n. These samples are of interest when they are *simple random samples*, which are a special kind of probability sample. In Chapter 2, you learned how to draw a simple random sample, which we now define as follows:

If a sample of size *n* is drawn from a population of size *N* in such a way that every possible sample of size *n* has the same probability of being selected, the sample is called a simple random sample.

5.2 SAMPLING DISTRIBUTIONS

We can define a *sampling distribution* as follows:

The distribution of all possible values that can be assumed by some statistic, computed from samples of the same size randomly drawn from the same population, is called the sampling distribution of that statistic.

We can construct sampling distributions empirically from discrete, finite populations. The construction of a sampling distribution consists of the following steps.

Steps in constructing a sampling distribution.

1. From a discrete, finite population of size *N*, randomly draw all possible samples of size *n*.
2. Compute the value of the statistic of interest for each sample.
3. List in one column the different observed values of the statistic. In another column list the corresponding frequency of occurrence of each observed value of the statistic.

Three characteristics of a given sampling distribution are of interest to us: its mean, its variance, and its functional form (how it looks when graphed).

Given a sampling distribution, we want to know its mean, variance, and functional form.

We cannot construct exact sampling distributions empirically when the population we are sampling is infinite. In such a situation, we can only approximate the sampling distribution of the statistic of interest by taking a large number of samples. This is not a problem of any practical importance, since sampling distributions *per se* are of only theoretical interest.

5.3 DISTRIBUTION OF THE SAMPLE MEAN

As we have seen, the arithmetic mean is an important descriptive measure for characterizing the central tendency of a set of data. In many situations, we want to know the mean of a population. This information may not be available unless we draw a sample from the population and make an inference regarding the parameter μ based on analysis of the sample data. We shall consider this procedure in detail in Chapter 6. However, since the validity of this inferential procedure depends on knowing the sampling distribution of the statistic involved, that is, the sample mean, let's give some thought to this matter before we proceed.

The description that follows illustrates the construction of a sampling distribution of the sample mean computed from samples drawn from a very small population. It is important that you realize that this is for instructional purposes only. In practice, we do not actually construct a sampling distribution as a preliminary to statistical inference.

EXAMPLE 5.1 Suppose that a population consists of the 10 salespersons employed by a certain firm. The random variable of interest, X, is the number of years a salesperson has been with the firm. The values of the variable are as follows: $X_1 = 3$, $X_2 = 6$, $X_3 = 2$, $X_4 = 4$, $X_5 = 8$, $X_6 = 7$, $X_7 = 9$, $X_8 = 5$, $X_9 = 1$, $X_{10} = 10$. For this population, we may compute the following parameters:

$$\mu = \frac{\Sigma x_i}{N} = \frac{55}{10} = 5.5, \qquad \sigma^2 = \frac{\Sigma(x_i - \mu)^2}{N} = 8.25$$

Constructing the Sampling Distribution

To construct the sampling distribution of $\bar{x}$ computed from samples drawn from this population, we follow the steps outlined in Section 5.2.

1. We draw all possible samples of some size n. Suppose that we let $n = 2$. Table 5.1 shows the possible samples. Note that there are 100 samples. In general, when we sample with replacement, as we have done here, there will be N^n possible samples of size n.

2. We compute the mean $\bar{x}$ for each of these samples. The sample means are shown in parentheses in Table 5.1.

3. We list the different values of $\bar{x}$ that we observed, along with their frequencies of occurrence. The resulting table, Table 5.2, constitutes the sampling distribution of $\bar{x}$ for samples of size 2 from the specified population.

The individual probabilities (relative frequencies) shown in Table 5.2 are all greater than 0, and their sum is equal to 1. Thus the requirements for a probability distribution are met.

As stated earlier, we usually are interested in the *functional form,* the *mean,* and the *variance* of a sampling distribution.

Look at Figure 5.1 and compare the two distributions.

We can compare the functional form of the distribution for $\bar{x}$ that we just constructed with the distribution of the original population. Figure 5.1 shows both distributions. Observe that the two figures are very different. The population distribution is a uniform distribution (that is, each value occurs with the same frequency). The distribution of $\bar{x}$ is a symmetric distribution that is by no means uniform.

An impressive feature of the sampling distribution of $\bar{x}$, as Figure 5.1 shows, is the fact that the most frequently occurring value of $\bar{x}$ is 5.5. We also note the symmetric shape of the sampling distribution. We shall see shortly that these characteristics are not unique to these particular data. This is a general pattern of behavior that is inherent in sampling distributions of sample means.

TABLE 5.1
All possible samples of size n = 2 from a population of size N = 10

First draw	Second draw									
	1	2	3	4	5	6	7	8	9	10
1	1,1 (1)	1,2 (1.5)	1,3 (2)	1,4 (2.5)	1,5 (3)	1,6 (3.5)	1,7 (4)	1,8 (4.5)	1,9 (5)	1,10 (5.5)
2	2,1 (1.5)	2,2 (2)	2,3 (2.5)	2,4 (3)	2,5 (3.5)	2,6 (4)	2,7 (4.5)	2,8 (5)	2,9 (5.5)	2,10 (6)
3	3,1 (2)	3,2 (2.5)	3,3 (3)	3,4 (3.5)	3,5 (4)	3,6 (4.5)	3,7 (5)	3,8 (5.5)	3,9 (6)	3,10 (6.5)
4	4,1 (2.5)	4,2 (3)	4,3 (3.5)	4,4 (4)	4,5 (4.5)	4,6 (5)	4,7 (5.5)	4,8 (6)	4,9 (6.5)	4,10 (7)
5	5,1 (3)	5,2 (3.5)	5,3 (4)	5,4 (4.5)	5,5 (5)	5,6 (5.5)	5,7 (6)	5,8 (6.5)	5,9 (7)	5,10 (7.5)
6	6,1 (3.5)	6,2 (4)	6,3 (4.5)	6,4 (5)	6,5 (5.5)	6,6 (6)	6,7 (6.5)	6,8 (7)	6,9 (7.5)	6,10 (8)
7	7,1 (4)	7,2 (4.5)	7,3 (5)	7,4 (5.5)	7,5 (6)	7,6 (6.5)	7,7 (7)	7,8 (7.5)	7,9 (8)	7,10 (8.5)
8	8,1 (4.5)	8,2 (5)	8,3 (5.5)	8,4 (6)	8,5 (6.5)	8,6 (7)	8,7 (7.5)	8,8 (8)	8,9 (8.5)	8,10 (9)
9	9,1 (5)	9,2 (5.5)	9,3 (6)	9,4 (6.5)	9,5 (7)	9,6 (7.5)	9,7 (8)	9,8 (8.5)	9,9 (9)	9,10 (9.5)
10	10,1 (5.5)	10,2 (6)	10,3 (6.5)	10,4 (7)	10,5 (7.5)	10,6 (8)	10,7 (8.5)	10,8 (9)	10,9 (9.5)	10,10 (10)

TABLE 5.2
Sampling distribution of $\bar{x}$ computed from samples in Table 5.1

$\bar{x}$	Frequency	Relative frequency	$\bar{x}$	Frequency	Relative frequency
1	1	1/100	6	9	9/100
1.5	2	2/100	6.5	8	8/100
2	3	3/100	7	7	7/100
2.5	4	4/100	7.5	6	6/100
3	5	5/100	8	5	5/100
3.5	6	6/100	8.5	4	4/100
4	7	7/100	9	3	3/100
4.5	8	8/100	9.5	2	2/100
5	9	9/100	10	1	1/100
5.5	10	10/100	Total	100	100/100

**FIGURE 5.1
Distribution of
population and
sampling
distribution of $\bar{x}$
for $n = 2$**

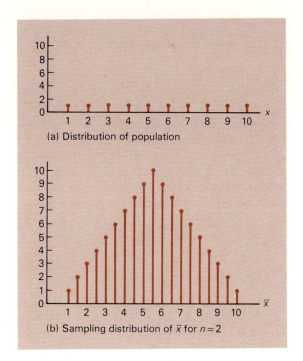

(a) Distribution of population

(b) Sampling distribution of $\bar{x}$ for $n=2$

Now we compute the mean $\mu_{\bar{x}}$ of the sampling distribution by adding the 100 sample means given in Table 5.1 and dividing by 100. That is,

$$\mu_{\bar{x}} = \frac{\Sigma \bar{x}_i}{N^n} = \frac{550}{100} = 5.5$$

This formula is a special case of Formula 2.4, which shows how to compute μ, the mean of a population of original observations. In the present case we are computing $\mu_{\bar{x}}$, the mean of a population of sample means. Therefore $\bar{x}_i$ in this formula has the same role as x_i in Formula 2.4, and N^n here has the same role as N in Formula 2.4.

$\mu_{\bar{x}} = \mu$

Note that the mean of the sampling distribution of $\bar{x}$ is equal to the mean of the original population.

Finally, we compute the variance of $\bar{x}$, $\sigma_{\bar{x}}^2$, as follows:

$$\sigma_{\bar{x}}^2 = \frac{\Sigma(\bar{x}_i - \mu_{\bar{x}})^2}{N^n}$$

$$= \frac{(1 - 5.5)^2 + (1.5 - 5.5)^2 + \cdots + (10 - 5.5)^2}{100} = \frac{412.5}{100} = 4.125$$

$\sigma_{\bar{x}}^2 = \dfrac{\sigma^2}{n}$

The variance of the sampling distribution is not equal to the variance of the population. However, the variance of the sampling distribution is equal to the *variance of the population divided by the size of the sample* used to obtain the sampling distribution. That is,

$$\sigma_{\bar{x}}^2 = \frac{\sigma^2}{n} = \frac{8.25}{2} = 4.125$$

The standard deviation of a sampling distribution is called the *standard error*.

The square root of the variance of the sampling distribution—that is, the standard deviation of the sampling distribution, $\sqrt{\sigma_{\bar{x}}^2} = \sigma/\sqrt{n}$—is called the *standard error of the mean*, or, simply, the *standard error*. It is written $\sigma_{\bar{x}}$. Variation in a sampling distribution represents estimation errors for the various possible samples. Thus we call the standard deviation of these errors the *standard error*.

Here is a summary of the symbols used to designate the mean, the variance, and the standard deviation of a sampled population, a single sample from the population, and the resulting sampling distribution of the sample mean.

Descriptive measure	Sampled population	Single sample	Sampling distribution of $\bar{x}$
Mean	μ	$\bar{x}$	$\mu_{\bar{x}}$
Variance	σ^2	s^2	$\sigma_{\bar{x}}^2$
Standard deviation	σ	s	$\sigma_{\bar{x}}$

Normally Distributed Populations

The fact that $\mu_{\bar{x}} = \mu$ and $\sigma_{\bar{x}}^2 = \sigma^2/n$ is not peculiar to this example. These results are characteristic of sampling distributions in general when sampling is with replacement from a finite population, or when the sampled population is infinite. We can also describe a sampled population according to whether it is normally or nonnormally distributed. The sampling distribution of $\bar{x}$ is different in the two cases. Actually, as noted in Chapter 4, no variables are exactly normally distributed, since the normal distribution is a mathematical ideal that is not realized in practice. In this text, when we speak of a normally distributed population, we mean one that approximates a normal distribution well enough for us to use the properties of a normal distribution in describing it.

Let us first describe the sampling distribution of the sample mean when sampling is from a normally distributed population.

The sampling distribution of $\bar{x}$ when the population is normal.

When sampling is from a normally distributed population, the sampling distribution of the sample mean will have the following properties:

1. The distribution of $\bar{x}$ will be normal, regardless of the size of the sample.
2. The mean $\mu_{\bar{x}}$ of the distribution of $\bar{x}$ will be equal to the mean of the population from which the samples were drawn.
3. The variance $\sigma_{\bar{x}}^2$ of the distribution of $\bar{x}$ will be equal to the variance of the population divided by the sample size.

In later chapters, when we make inferences about normally distributed populations, we shall use these properties of the sampling distribution of $\bar{x}$.

In many situations the normal distribution poorly approximates the population of interest. Consequently, when the sampled population is not normally distributed, we must know the nature of the sampling distribution of the sample mean.

The Central Limit Theorem

Knowledge of the sampling distribution of $\bar{x}$ when sampling is from a *non*normally distributed population comes from the proof of an important mathematical theorem, the *central limit theorem*. We can summarize this theorem as follows.

The sampling distribution of $\bar{x}$ when the population is not normal and *n* is large.

Given a population of any nonnormal functional form with a mean μ and finite variance σ², the sampling distribution of $\bar{x}$, computed from simple random samples of size *n* from this population, will be approximately normally distributed with mean μ and variance σ²/*n* when the sample size is large.

The central limit theorem guarantees that if we sample from a nonnormally distributed population, we will get approximately the same results as we would if the population were normally distributed, provided that we take a large sample. This is an important result. It is useful in applying the techniques of statistical inference.

To study the effect of the central limit theorem, we could draw *k* large sets of samples of varying sizes, $n_1 < n_2 < \cdots < n_k$, from a nonnormally distributed population and compare the resulting sampling distributions. We would find that the larger the value of *n*, the more closely the sampling distribution resembles a normal distribution. Figure 5.2 illustrates the general results of such a procedure.

**FIGURE 5.2
Illustration of effect of central limit theorem on the sampling distribution of $\bar{x}$**

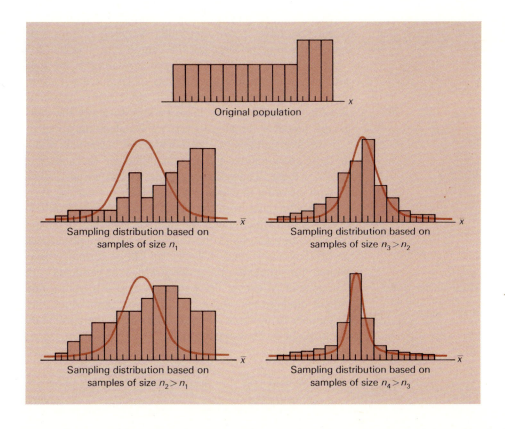

Original population

Sampling distribution based on samples of size n_1

Sampling distribution based on samples of size $n_3 > n_2$

Sampling distribution based on samples of size $n_2 > n_1$

Sampling distribution based on samples of size $n_4 > n_3$

The Meaning of "A Large Sample"

A "large" sample contains 30 or more observations.

The phrase "when the sample size is large" that appeared in our statement about the central limit theorem requires explanation. The size of the sample needed to achieve an approximately normal sampling distribution of $\bar{x}$ depends on how non-normal the original population is. The greater the departure of the population distribution from normal, the larger the sample must be. One rule of thumb states that the sample size should be 30 or more. We shall adopt this rule for the sake of convenience in later chapters when we apply inferential procedures.

Sampling Without Replacement

The previous results assume that the sample is drawn either from an infinite population or from a finite population with replacement. As we have pointed out, we do not sample with replacement in most practical situations. Because of this, we need to know how the sampling distribution of $\bar{x}$ behaves when we sample without replacement from a finite population. When we do so, we can describe the distribution of the sample mean as follows:

When sampling is without replacement from a finite population, the sampling distribution of the sample mean will have a mean $\mu_{\bar{x}}$ equal to the population mean μ and a variance $\sigma_{\bar{x}}^2$ equal to $[\sigma^2/n][(N - n)/(N - 1)]$.

When the sampled population is finite, the central limit theorem may not apply. Researchers have shown that when sampling is from a finite population, both n and $N - n$ must be large for the central limit theorem to apply.

Let us now try to verify the results relating to the mean and variance with a sampling experiment using the data of Example 5.1. We cannot verify that $\bar{x}$ is approximately normally distributed, since from a population of size 10 it is impossible to draw samples large enough to apply the central limit theorem. We should, however, be able to verify the statements about $\mu_{\bar{x}}$ and $\sigma_{\bar{x}}^2$.

If we take samples of size 2 without replacement, the resulting sample means are those shown above the principal diagonal in Table 5.1. We can see that there are 45 of these. The possible sample means are also shown below the diagonal, but with the order in which values are drawn reversed. We can compute the means below the diagonal from the samples that result when the order of selection is the reverse of that which yields the sample means above the diagonal. You may verify that you can also obtain the following means and variances if you use all 90 of the off-diagonal means in Table 5.1. In performing these calculations, we have ignored, for simplicity, the order in which the elements of the samples were drawn.

When sampling is without replacement, $_NC_n$ simple random samples of size n can be drawn from a population of size N.

In general, when we draw samples of size n from a finite population of size N without replacement, if we ignore the order in which the elements are selected, the number of possible samples is given by the combination of N things taken n at a time. In our present example,

$$_NC_n = \frac{N!}{n!(N - n)!} = \frac{10!}{2!8!} = \frac{10 \cdot 9 \cdot 8!}{2 \cdot 1 \cdot 8!} = 45$$

The mean of these 45 sample means is

$$\mu_{\bar{x}} = \frac{\Sigma \bar{x}_i}{_NC_n} = \frac{1.5 + 2 + \cdots + 9.5}{45} = \frac{247.5}{45} = 5.5$$

Thus we again see that $\mu_{\bar{x}} = \mu = 5.5$. The variance of this sampling distribution is found to be

$$\sigma_{\bar{x}}^2 = \frac{\Sigma(\bar{x}_i - \mu_{\bar{x}})^2}{_NC_n}$$

$$= \frac{(1.5 - 5.5)^2 + (2 - 5.5)^2 + \cdots + (9.5 - 5.5)^2}{45} = \frac{165}{45} = 3.67$$

This time, the variance of the sampling distribution is not equal to the population variance divided by the sample size, since $\sigma_{\bar{x}}^2 = 3.67 \neq 8.25/2 = 4.125$. But

$$\frac{\sigma^2}{n} \cdot \frac{N - n}{N - 1} = \frac{8.25}{2} \cdot \frac{8}{9} = \frac{66}{18} = 3.67$$

and we have verified the fact that in this example

$$\sigma_{\bar{x}}^2 = \frac{\sigma^2}{n} \cdot \frac{N - n}{N - 1}$$

Ignore the fpc when $n/N < 0.05$.

We may ignore the factor $(N - n)/(N - 1)$, which is called the *finite population correction* (fpc), when the sample size is small in comparison to the population size. When the population is a great deal larger than the sample, the difference between σ^2/n and $[\sigma^2/n][(N - n)/(N - 1)]$ is negligible. Suppose that a sample of size 25 is drawn from a population containing 10,000 observations. The finite population correction would be equal to $(10,000 - 25)/(9999) = 0.9976$. The product of 0.9976 and σ^2/n is almost equal to the product of σ^2/n and 1. Most statisticians do not use the finite population correction when the sample contains less than 5% of the observations in the population. Note that $\sigma_{\bar{x}}^2$ is always smaller when sampling is without replacement than when sampling is with replacement.

Applications

We have talked about the sampling distribution of $\bar{x}$ in detail here so that you will be able to apply the concept confidently later, in making inferences. We need not wait for Chapter 6, however, to apply this material. We can now answer questions such as this: "Given a population with mean μ and variance σ^2, what is the probability that a simple random sample of size n will yield a sample mean $\bar{x}$ as large as or larger than some specified value $\bar{x}_0$?"

EXAMPLE 5.2 The pressure, in pounds per square inch, required to rupture a certain type of fuel tank is an approximately normally distributed random variable with a mean of 2800 psi and a variance of 9216 psi squared. Suppose that we select a simple random sample of size 10 from this population and test each tank until it ruptures. What is the probability that the mean pressure required to rupture the tanks in the sample will be 2750 psi or less?

SOLUTION The single sample under consideration is one of the possible samples of size 10 that we can draw from the population. The mean of this sample is one of the $\bar{x}$'s that make up the sampling distribution of $\bar{x}$ that, theoretically, we could derive from this population.

If the population is approximately normally distributed, this assures us that the sampling distribution of $\bar{x}$ is, for all practical purposes, normally distributed. The mean and standard deviation of the sampling distribution are equal to 2800 and $\sqrt{9216/10} = 30.36$, respectively. We assume that the population is large relative to the sample, so that we can ignore the finite population correction.

From Chapter 4 we know that we can transform any normally distributed random variable to the standard normal distribution by means of a simple formula. In the present example, the random variable is $\bar{x}$, and the mean and standard deviation of its distribution are $\mu_{\bar{x}} = \mu$ and $\sigma_{\bar{x}} = \sigma/\sqrt{n}$, respectively.

Appropriate modification of the formula for z gives us the following formula for transforming the normal distribution of $\bar{x}$ to the standard normal distribution:

$$z = \frac{\bar{x}_0 - \mu_{\bar{x}}}{\sigma_{\bar{x}}} = \frac{\bar{x}_0 - \mu}{\sigma/\sqrt{n}} \qquad (5.1)$$

In this example, the probability is represented by the area to the left of $\bar{x} = 2750$ under the curve of the sampling distribution. This area is equal to the area to the left of

$$z = \frac{2750 - 2800}{\sqrt{9216}/\sqrt{10}} = \frac{-50}{96/3.16} = -1.65$$

Table C indicates that the area to the left of -1.65 is 0.0495. Thus we can say that the probability of drawing, from the specified population, a sample with a mean of 2750 or less is 0.0495. Figure 5.3 shows the relationship between the original population, the sampling distribution of $\bar{x}$, and the standard normal distribution.

EXAMPLE 5.3 The mean life of a certain saw blade is 41.5 hours, with a standard deviation of 2.5 hours. What is the probability that a simple random sample of size 50 drawn from this population has a mean of between 40.5 and 42 hours?

SOLUTION We are not told that the population is normally distributed. However, this does not prevent us from using the standard normal distribution as in Example 5.2. Because the sample size is large, the central limit theorem tells us that the sampling distribution of $\bar{x}$ is at least approximately normally distributed regardless of how the population is distributed. The mean and standard deviation of the sampling distribution of $\bar{x}$ are $\mu_{\bar{x}} = 41.5$ and $\sigma_{\bar{x}} = 2.5/\sqrt{50} = 0.35$, respec-

FIGURE 5.3
Distribution of a population, the sampling distribution of $\bar{x}$, and the standard normal distribution

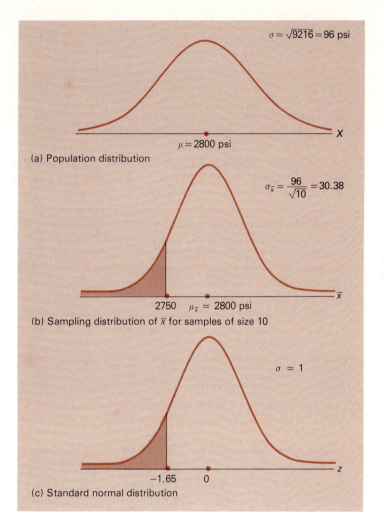

(a) Population distribution

$\sigma = \sqrt{9216} = 96$ psi

$\mu = 2800$ psi

(b) Sampling distribution of $\bar{x}$ for samples of size 10

$\sigma_{\bar{x}} = \dfrac{96}{\sqrt{10}} = 30.38$

2750 $\mu_{\bar{x}} = 2800$ psi

(c) Standard normal distribution

$\sigma = 1$

−1.65   0

tively. The probability we seek is

$$P(40.5 \leq \bar{x} \leq 42) = P\left(\frac{40.5 - 41.5}{0.35} \leq z \leq \frac{42 - 41.5}{0.35}\right)$$

$$= P(z \leq 1.43) - P(z \leq -2.86)$$

$$= 0.9236 - 0.0021 = 0.9215$$

To illustrate the use of the fpc, let us suppose that the population referred to in Example 5.3 consists of 800 tools. The standard error in that case would be

$$\sigma_{\bar{x}} = \sqrt{\frac{(2.5)^2(800 - 50)}{50(800 - 1)}} = \sqrt{(0.125)(0.938673)} = 0.34$$

The desired probability, then, would be

$$P(40.5 \leq \bar{x} \leq 42) = P\left(\frac{40.5 - 41.5}{0.34} \leq z \leq \frac{42 - 41.5}{0.34}\right)$$

$$= 0.9292 - 0.0016 = 0.9276$$

The result we find using the fpc is not very different from the result we find without it, even though the sample contains 6.25% of the population.

Exercises

5.1 The tensile strength of a certain type of wire is normally distributed with a mean of 99.8 and a standard deviation of 5.48.   **(a)** What are the mean and standard deviation of the sampling distribution of the sample mean based on simple random samples of size 100?   **(b)** You draw a single simple random sample of 16 values from this population. What is the probability that the mean of this sample will be between 98.8 and 100.9?

5.2 An employment agency has found that the mean time required for an applicant to take an aptitude test is 24.5 minutes, with a standard deviation of 4.5 minutes.   **(a)** What are the mean and standard deviation of the sampling distribution of the sample mean based on simple random samples of size 81 from this population?   **(b)** You draw a simple random sample of 81 applicant files. What is the probability that the mean time applicants in this sample need for taking the test is greater than 25 minutes?

5.3 A firm employs 1500 people. During a given year, the mean amount contributed to a charity drive per employee was $25.75. The standard deviation was $5.25. What is the probability that a simple random sample of 100 employees yields a mean between $25.00 and $27.00?

5.4 In a population of 1200 executives, the mean amount spent on lunch per day is $6.50. The standard deviation is $6.00. What is the probability that a simple random sample of 36 executives from this population yields a mean between $5.00 and $10.00?

5.5 Suppose that a population consists of the values 2, 4, 6, 8, and 10. Construct the sampling distribution of $\bar{x}$ based on samples of size 2 selected without replacement. Find the mean and variance of the original population and of the sampling distribution.

5.6 In a population of assembly-line workers, the mean length of employment with their present firm is 2.5 years. The standard deviation is 3 years. A simple random sample of 40 is drawn from this population. What is the probability that the mean will be more than 3.5 years?

5.4 DISTRIBUTION OF THE DIFFERENCE BETWEEN TWO SAMPLE MEANS

In practical situations we are often interested in the difference between two population means. In order to make inferences about this difference from sample data, we need to know the properties of the sampling distribution of the difference between two sample means, $\bar{x}_1 - \bar{x}_2$.

In practice, we would not try to actually construct the sampling distribution of the difference between two means. We can, however, easily conceptualize its

TABLE 5.3
Working table for constructing the distribution of the difference between two sample means

Samples from population 1	Samples from population 2	Sample means, population 1	Sample means, population 2	All possible differences between means
n_{11}	n_{12}	$\bar{x}_{11}$	$\bar{x}_{12}$	$\bar{x}_{11} - \bar{x}_{12}$
n_{21}	n_{22}	$\bar{x}_{21}$	$\bar{x}_{22}$	$\bar{x}_{11} - \bar{x}_{22}$
				.
				.
				.
n_{31}	n_{32}	$\bar{x}_{31}$	$\bar{x}_{32}$	$\bar{x}_{21} - \bar{x}_{12}$
.	.	.	.	.
.	.	.	.	.
.	.	.	.	.
$n_{N_1'1}$	$n_{N_2'2}$	$\bar{x}_{N_1'1}$	$\bar{x}_{N_2'2}$	$\bar{x}_{N_1'1} - \bar{x}_{N_2'2}$

construction when the two populations of interest are finite. First we select, without replacement, from population 1 all possible simple random samples of size n_1 and compute the mean for each sample. There are $_{N_1}C_{n_1}$ such samples, where N_1 is the population size and n_1 is the size of the sample drawn from population 1. Next we select, without replacement, all possible independent simple random samples of size n_2 from population 2 and compute the mean for each of these. Then we form all possible pairs of sample means, taking one mean from sample 1 and one mean from sample 2. We then compute the difference between each of these possible pairs of means. Table 5.3 shows the results. (Note that in Table 5.3, $N_1' = {_{N_1}C_{n_1}}$ indicates the number of samples drawn from population 1, and $N_2' = {_{N_2}C_{n_2}}$ indicates the number of samples drawn from population 2.)

The samples must be independent.

Sampling from Two Normally Distributed Populations

The distribution we seek is the distribution of the differences between these pairs of sample means. Assume that the two populations are approximately normally distributed. If we plotted the sample differences against their frequency of occurrence, the result, for all practical purposes, would be a normal distribution with a mean equal to $\mu_1 - \mu_2$, the difference between the true population means, and a variance equal to $(\sigma_1^2/n_1) + (\sigma_2^2/n_2)$.

This procedure is valid when the sample sizes n_1 and n_2 are either equal or different, and when the population variances σ_1^2 and σ_2^2 are either equal or different. Although we can construct the exact sampling distribution only with finite populations, the results of the outlined procedure also apply to infinite populations. We may summarize:

Given two normally distributed populations with means μ_1 and μ_2 and variances σ_1^2 and σ_2^2, respectively, the sampling distribution of the difference $\bar{x}_1 - \bar{x}_2$ between the means of independent samples of size n_1 and n_2 drawn from these populations is normally distributed with mean $\mu_{\bar{x}_1 - \bar{x}_2} = \mu_1 - \mu_2$ and variance $\sigma_{\bar{x}_1 - \bar{x}_2}^2 = (\sigma_1^2/n_1) + (\sigma_2^2/n_2)$.

FIGURE 5.4
**Two normal
distributions and
the sampling
distribution of the
difference between
sample means**

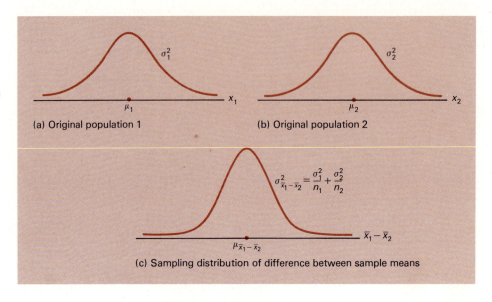

(a) Original population 1   (b) Original population 2

$$\sigma^2_{\bar{x}_1 - \bar{x}_2} = \frac{\sigma^2_1}{n_1} + \frac{\sigma^2_2}{n_2}$$

(c) Sampling distribution of difference between sample means

Figure 5.4 illustrates the sampling distribution of the difference between two sample means. This description specifies that the samples be *independent*.

Two samples are independent if the selection of elements to be included in one sample is in no way influenced by the selection of elements to be included in the other sample.

EXAMPLE 5.4 Two companies manufacture high-temperature lubricants aimed at the same market. Company A claims that the mean temperature at which its product ceases to be effective is 505°F. It quotes a standard deviation of 10°. Company B states that corresponding data for its product are a mean of 475°F and a standard deviation of 7°. Experience has shown that temperatures at failure for both products are approximately normally distributed. Suppose that a simple random sample of 20 specimens of Company A's product and an independent simple random sample of 25 specimens of Company B's product are tested. What is the probability that the difference between the mean temperature at failure for the two samples will be between 25 and 35 degrees?

SOLUTION From the data given here, we know that the sampling distribution of $\bar{x}_A - \bar{x}_B$ is normally distributed with mean $\mu_A - \mu_B$ and variance $(\sigma^2_A/n_A) + (\sigma^2_B/n_B)$. To find the desired probability, we transform this normal distribution to the standard normal distribution, using an adaptation of an earlier formula. The new formula is

$$z = \frac{(\bar{x}_1 - \bar{x}_2) - (\mu_1 - \mu_2)}{\sqrt{\dfrac{\sigma^2_1}{n_1} + \dfrac{\sigma^2_2}{n_2}}} \qquad (5.2)$$

For the present example, we compute two values of z as follows:

$$z_1 = \frac{25 - (505 - 475)}{\sqrt{\frac{(10)^2}{20} + \frac{(7)^2}{25}}} = -1.89, \qquad z_2 = \frac{35 - (505 - 475)}{\sqrt{\frac{(10)^2}{20} + \frac{(7)^2}{25}}} = 1.89$$

The probability we seek, then, is

$$P(-1.89 \leq z \leq 1.89) = P(z \leq 1.89) - P(z \leq -1.89)$$

$$= 0.9706 - 0.0294 = 0.9412$$

[handwritten annotation: op to chart keyt]

Sampling from Two Nonnormal Populations

In practice, the following problems often arise: (1) the need to sample from a nonnormally distributed population, and (2) the need to sample from a population of unknown functional form. We solve these problems by taking large samples. When the populations are not normally distributed and the sample sizes are large, the central limit theorem applies. The distribution of the difference between two sample means is then approximately normally distributed with a mean equal to $\mu_1 - \mu_2$ and a variance of $(\sigma_1^2/n_1) + (\sigma_2^2/n_2)$. In order to find the probabilities associated with specific values of the statistic, then, we proceed just as we do when sampling from populations that *are* normally distributed.

EXAMPLE 5.5 Two methods of performing a certain task in a manufacturing plant, Method A and Method B, are under study. The variable of interest is length of time needed to perform the task. It is known that σ_A^2 is 9 min^2 and σ_B^2 is 12 min^2. A simple random sample of 35 employees performed the task using Method A. An independent simple random sample of 35 employees, similar in all important aspects to the first group, performed the task using Method B. The average time the first group needed to complete the task was 25 min. The average time for the second group was 23 min. What is the probability of a difference $\bar{x}_A - \bar{x}_B$ this large or larger if there is no difference in the true average lengths of time needed for the task?

SOLUTION Since the functional form of the population is not specified, and since the sample sizes are large (greater than 30), we can use the central limit theorem. We compute

$$z = \frac{(25 - 23) - 0}{\sqrt{\frac{9}{35} + \frac{12}{35}}} = 2.58$$

Table C shows that the area to the right of $z = 2.58$ is 0.0049. Thus a difference between sample means as large as the one observed in this case is rather rare when the population means are equal.

Exercises

5.7 A market analyst studying the length of time shoppers spend in two types of grocery store observes a sample of 75 shoppers in each store. The mean time the sample of shoppers spends in Store A is 55 minutes. The mean time the sample of shoppers spends in Store B is 49 minutes. What is the probability of observing a sample difference $\bar{x}_A - \bar{x}_B$ at least as large as this if there is no difference in the true mean time shoppers spend in the two stores and if the standard deviation is 15 minutes for both populations? What assumptions are made regarding the samples?

5.8 An accountant for a department store is studying the characteristics of customers who have charge accounts. A customer may choose between two types of account, A and B. A simple random sample of 50 customers with Type A charge accounts has a mean age of 38 years. The mean age of an independent simple random sample of 50 customers with Type B accounts is 33 years. If both populations have the same mean age and a standard deviation of 10 years, what is the probability of drawing two samples with a difference $\bar{x}_A - \bar{x}_B$ in means at least as large as the one this accountant observed?

5.9 Scores on a motor-performance test for employees who hold nonsedentary jobs (group 1) are normally distributed with a mean and variance of 60 and 100, respectively. Scores for employees who hold sedentary jobs (group 2) are normally distributed with a mean of 50 and a variance of 121. A random sample of 10 employees is selected from group 1. An independent random sample of size 11 is selected from group 2. What is the probability that the difference between sample means $(\bar{x}_1 - \bar{x}_2)$ is between 8 and 14?

5.10 Researchers have determined that hostility scores among blue-collar workers are approximately normally distributed, with a variance of 400 for both high school dropouts and those who have finished high school. Random samples of 15 dropouts and 20 high school graduates yield sample means of $\bar{x}_d = 77.50$ and $\bar{x}_g = 62.75$, respectively. Assume that there is no difference between the population means. What is the probability of obtaining sample results $\bar{x}_d$ $\bar{x}_g$ as large as, or larger than, what was observed in these samples?

5.5 DISTRIBUTION OF THE SAMPLE PROPORTION

Sections 5.3 and 5.4 discussed the sampling distributions of measured variables. However, we often want to know the sampling distribution of statistics that arise when we count the number of subjects in a group who have a certain characteristic. We refer to such data as *count data*. An example of such a statistic is the *sample proportion,* which is a special case of the sample mean. Suppose that we know that in some population the proportion of elements with a particular characteristic is p. We are often interested in finding the probability of observing in a sample size n from this population a proportion of elements with the characteristic of interest as extreme as or more extreme than some specified value p_0. To do this, we need to know the properties of the sampling distribution of the sample proportion $\hat{p}$. The notation $\hat{p}$ is read "*p* hat."

   This problem is related to the problems in Chapter 4 that we solved by means of the binomial distribution. Those problems involved determining the probability of observing a certain number of elements with some characteristic in a sample

The sample proportion is equal to the number of sample elements with the characteristic of interest divided by the total number of elements in the sample.

of size n from a population in which a proportion p of the elements had that characteristic. Here we are interested in the proportion, rather than the number, that have the characteristic of interest. The two problems are related, since the sample proportion is equal to the number in the sample that have the characteristic divided by the sample size.

When the entities in a population can assume only one of two values, we usually call these values successes and failures. Suppose that we give the value 1 to an element in the sample that has the characteristic of interest (success), and the value 0 to an element in the sample that does not have the characteristic (failure). We compute the sample proportion $\hat{p}$ by

$$\hat{p} = \frac{\sum x_i}{n} \tag{5.3}$$

The numerator of Equation 5.3 is merely a count of the elements with the characteristic of interest (successes, or 1s). For example, suppose that in a simple random sample of 10 secretaries, 4 are married. The proportion married is given by

$$\hat{p} = \frac{\sum x_i}{n} = \frac{4}{10}$$

Observe the similarity between Equation 5.3 and the formula for the sample mean. In fact, since the sample proportion is a special case of the sample mean, it is not surprising that there are similarities between the sampling distributions of $\hat{p}$ and $\bar{x}$.

We can construct the sampling distribution of a sample proportion experimentally. We use the same method we used to construct the sampling distributions of the arithmetic mean and the difference between two means. From the population, which is assumed to be finite, we take all possible random samples of a given size. For each sample, we compute the sample proportion $\hat{p}$. We then prepare a frequency distribution of $\hat{p}$. Table 5.4 shows the results if the samples are drawn without replacement. We can summarize the characteristics of the sampling distribution presented in Table 5.4 as follows.

TABLE 5.4
Sampling distribution of a sample proportion

Sample	Sample size $n_1 = n_2 = \cdots = n_{N'}$	Sample proportion
1	n_1	$\hat{p}_1$
2	n_2	$\hat{p}_2$
3	n_3	$\hat{p}_3$
.	.	.
.	.	.
.	.	.
$_NC_n = N'$	$n_{N'}$	$\hat{p}_{N'}$

When the sample size is large, the distribution of sample proportions is approximately normally distributed by virtue of the central limit theorem. The mean of the distribution $\mu_{\hat{p}}$—that is, the average of all the possible sample proportions—is equal to the true population proportion p. The variance of the distribution $\sigma_{\hat{p}}^2$ is equal to $[p(1 - p)]/n$.

The sampling distribution of $\hat{p}$ is only *approximated* by a normal distribution. For this approximation to be achieved, n must be large. A common rule of thumb states that we should use the approximation only when the smaller of np and $n(1 - p)$ is greater than 5.

These results are known as the *normal approximation to the binomial,* which we discussed in Chapter 4.

EXAMPLE 5.6 A manufacturer of nails has found that 3% of the nails produced are defective. Suppose that a random sample of 300 nails is examined. What is the probability that the proportion defective is between 0.02 and 0.035?

SOLUTION Since $(0.03)(300) = 9$ is greater than 5, we may use the normal approximation. We conclude that $\hat{p}$ is approximately normally distributed with a mean of $\mu_{\hat{p}} = 0.03$ and a variance of $\sigma_{\hat{p}}^2 = p(1 - p)/n$. We can transform any value of $\hat{p}$ to a value of the standard normal distribution using the following modification of a now-familiar formula:

$$z = \frac{\hat{p} - p}{\sqrt{\dfrac{p(1 - p)}{n}}} \tag{5.4}$$

Applying this formula, we obtain the following two values of z:

$$z_1 = \frac{0.02 - 0.03}{\sqrt{\dfrac{(0.03)(0.97)}{300}}} = -1.02, \qquad z_2 = \frac{0.035 - 0.03}{\sqrt{\dfrac{(0.03)(0.97)}{300}}} = 0.51$$

The probability we seek, then, is

$$P(-1.02 \le z \le 0.51) = P(z \le 0.51) - P(z \le -1.02)$$

$$= 0.6950 - 0.1539 = 0.5411$$

which is found by referring to Table C.

Just as with the sampling distributions of $\bar{x}$, you should use the finite population correction factor in computing $\sigma_{\hat{p}}^2$ when n is more than 5% of N. When the finite population correction factor has to be used,

$$\sigma_{\hat{p}}^2 = \frac{p(1 - p)}{n} \cdot \frac{N - n}{N - 1}$$

*sampling
w/out replacement*

Exercises

5.11 An accounting firm has found that 60% of its clients' customers respond to initial requests for confirmation of their account balances. A simple random sample of 24 customers is sent requests for confirmation. What is the probability that 50% or more respond?

5.12 Suppose that we know that 5% of the forms processed by a clerical pool contain at least one error. If we examine a simple random sample of 475 forms, what is the probability that the proportion containing at least one error is between 0.03 and 0.075?

5.13 It is known that 25% of the people who saw a certain television program thought it contained too much violence. A random sample of 200 is selected from this population. What is the probability that the proportion in the sample with this opinion is between 0.24 and 0.28?

  5.14 An advertising agency claims that 20% of the members of a certain adult population have never heard a certain slogan created by the agency. In a random sample of 100 adults drawn from this population, 24 say that they have never heard the slogan. If the agency's claim is true, what is the probability of obtaining results as large as or larger than those found in this sample?

5.15 An opinion poll firm selects a simple random sample of size 250 from a population of 4000 households. Of the households in the sample, 143 report the presence of more than one television set. If the true population proportion is 0.55, what is the probability of obtaining a proportion as large as or larger than that obtained in this survey?

5.6 DISTRIBUTION OF THE DIFFERENCE BETWEEN TWO SAMPLE PROPORTIONS

Often there are two population proportions of interest and we wish to determine the probability associated with an observed difference between two sample proportions, where we draw an independent sample from each of the two populations. The relevant sampling distribution is the *sampling distribution of the difference between two proportions*. We can describe it as follows.

Suppose that independent random samples of size n_1 and n_2 are drawn from two populations, where the proportions of observations with the characteristic of interest in the two populations are p_1 and p_2, respectively. When n_1 and n_2 are large, the distribution of the difference between sample proportions $\hat{p}_1 - \hat{p}_2$ is approximately normal, with mean

$$\mu_{\hat{p}_1 - \hat{p}_2} = p_1 - p_2 \quad \text{and variance} \quad \sigma^2_{\hat{p}_1 - \hat{p}_2} = \frac{p_1(1 - p_1)}{n_1} + \frac{p_2(1 - p_2)}{n_2}$$

To answer probability questions about the difference between two sample proportions, we transform values of $\hat{p}_1 - \hat{p}_2$ to values of the standard normal distribution using the following formula:

$$z = \frac{(\hat{p}_1 - \hat{p}_2) - (p_1 - p_2)}{\sqrt{\dfrac{p_1(1 - p_1)}{n_1} + \dfrac{p_2(1 - p_2)}{n_2}}}$$

(5.5)

To construct the sampling distribution of the difference between two proportions for finite populations, we follow the same procedure used for the construction of the sampling distribution of the difference between two sample means.

EXAMPLE 5.7 It is claimed that 30% of the households in Community A and 20% of the households in Community B have at least one teenager. A simple random sample of 100 households from each community yields the following results: $\hat{p}_A = 0.34$, $\hat{p}_B = 0.13$. What is the probability of observing a difference $\hat{p}_A - \hat{p}_B$ this large or larger if the claims are true?

SOLUTION We assume that if the claims are true, the sampling distribution of $\hat{p}_A - \hat{p}_B$ is approximately normally distributed, with a mean of

$$\mu_{\hat{p}_A - \hat{p}_B} = 0.3 - 0.2 = 0.1$$

and a variance of

$$\sigma^2_{\hat{p}_A - \hat{p}_B} = \frac{(0.3)(0.7)}{100} + \frac{(0.2)(0.8)}{100} = 0.0037$$

The observed difference in sample proportions is

$$\hat{p}_A - \hat{p}_B = 0.34 - 0.13 = 0.21$$

The probability we want is represented by the area to the right of 0.21 in the sampling distribution of $\hat{p}_A - \hat{p}_B$. To find this area, we compute

$$z = \frac{0.21 - 0.10}{\sqrt{0.0037}} = \frac{0.11}{0.06} = 1.83$$

and consult Table C. We find that the area to the right of $z = 1.83$ is 0.0336. Thus, if the claim is true, the probability of observing a difference as large as or larger than that actually observed is 0.0336.

Exercises

5.16 A research group states that 16% of the firms of Type A increased their market research budgets in the past five years. For Type B firms, the figure was 9%. **(a)** What are the mean and standard deviation of the sampling distribution of the difference between sample proportions, based on independent simple random samples of 100 firms of each type? **(b)** What proportion of the sample differences $\hat{p}_A - \hat{p}_B$ would be between 0.05 and 0.10? **(c)** Suppose that you took a simple random sample of size 100 from each industry. What is the probability that the difference you would observe would be equal to or less than 0.02?

5.17 In a certain community, it is felt that 40% of the householders prefer a grocery store of a particular chain. In another community, it is felt that only 14% of the householders prefer a store of this chain. If these figures are correct, what is the probability that simple random samples of 100 from each community would yield a difference $\hat{p}_1 - \hat{p}_2$ in the proportion of householders preferring this type of store of 0.42 or more?

5.18 In a population of executives (Population A), 35% say that when they fly they prefer a certain airline. In another population of executives (Population B), 50% prefer this airline.

What is the probability that a simple random sample of size 100 from each population would yield a difference $\hat{p}_B - \hat{p}_A$ of 0.30 or more?

 5.19 A realtor claims that 40% of the homes in a certain neighborhood are appraised at $100,000 or more. A random sample of 75 homes from this area and 90 homes from another area yields a difference in proportion of homes appraised at $100,000 or more, $\hat{p}_1 - \hat{p}_2$, of 0.09. Suppose that there is actually no difference between the two population proportions. What is the probability of observing a difference $\hat{p}_1 - \hat{p}_2$ this large or larger?

5.20 In a simple random sample of 200 recent purchasers of a new Make A automobile, 120 said that they were satisfied with postpurchase service. In an independent simple random sample of 250 recent purchasers of a new Make B automobile, 180 said that they were satisfied with postpurchase service. If the proportion of satisfied purchasers is actually 0.70 in both populations, what is the probability of observing a difference $\hat{p}_B - \hat{p}_A$ as large as or larger than that obtained in these surveys?

Summary

This chapter is the most important one in the book. Unless you understand the concepts presented here, you can never truly understand statistical inference. For this reason, you should review this chapter carefully before you proceed further. Clear up *now* any points that you don't understand. Remember that knowing how to get correct answers to exercises does not mean that you understand the concepts they illustrate. The *why* of the exercises is just as important as the *how*.

This chapter introduced you to the concept of a probability sample. The statistical inference procedures discussed in the rest of this book depend for their validity on the assumption that the samples being analyzed are probability samples. You should now be familiar with the simple random sample, one of several kinds of probability samples. In Chapters 6 and 7, we assume that the samples on which our inferences are based are simple random samples.

The main concern of this chapter is sampling distributions. You should know what a sampling distribution is, and how to construct one from a small finite population. And, for the sampling distributions discussed, you should know the mean, the standard error, and the functional form. If you do not yet know these things, study this chapter some more before you begin Chapter 6.

Another important concept that you should now understand is the central limit theorem.

Finally, in this chapter you learned the characteristics of the sampling distributions of four statistics: the mean, the difference between two means, a proportion, and the difference between two proportions. You will encounter these sampling distributions again in Chapters 6 and 7.

Review Questions

1. Distinguish between probability and nonprobability sampling.

2. Why is nonprobability sampling not covered in this text?

3. What is a sampling distribution? What are the three important characteristics of a sampling distribution?

4. Explain how to construct a sampling distribution from a finite population.

5. Describe the sampling distribution of the sample mean when sampling is with replacement from a normally distributed population.

6. Explain the central limit theorem.

7. How does the sampling distribution of the sample mean when sampling is *without* replacement differ from the sampling distribution that we obtain when sampling is *with* replacement?

8. Describe the sampling distribution of the difference between two sample means.

9. Describe the sampling distribution of the sample proportion when large samples are drawn.

10. Describe the sampling distribution of the difference between two sample means when large samples are drawn.

11. Explain the procedure you would follow in constructing the sampling distribution of the difference between sample proportions based on large samples from finite populations.

12. A population consists of the values 5, 4, 7, 8, 6. Construct the sampling distribution of $\bar{x}$ for $n = 3$.

13. A population has a mean and standard deviation of 32 and 12, respectively. Consider the sampling distribution of the sample mean based on simple random samples of size 64. **(a)** What are the mean and standard deviation of the sampling distribution? **(b)** What proportion of sample means is between 30 and 35? **(c)** What is the probability that the mean of a single sample is greater than 35? **(d)** Less than 30? **(e)** Draw a picture of the sampling distribution and label the areas and points of interest as specified in (a) through (d). **(f)** What assumption is made about the sample specified in (c)?

14. Suppose that two normally distributed populations have the following parameters: Population I, $\mu = 60$, $\sigma = 8$; Population II, $\mu = 50$, $\sigma = 10$. A simple random sample of size 16 from population I and an independent simple random sample of size 20 from population II yield means of 61 and 45, respectively. What is the probability of observing a difference $\bar{x}_I - \bar{x}_{II}$ this large or larger between the sample means?

15. Suppose that 10% of all employees of a certain type who are fired during a certain period are fired because they violated company policy. In a simple random sample of 100 of these discharged employees, what is the probability that the proportion fired for violation of company policy is 0.15 or more?

16. Given the following population proportions: $p_1 = 0.6$, $p_2 = 0.5$. **(a)** Describe the sampling distribution of the difference $\hat{p}_1 - \hat{p}_2$ between sample proportions when $n_1 = 100$ and $n_2 = 50$. (Assume that the sample sizes are small relative to the population sizes.) **(b)** What proportion of sample differences would be between 0.03 and 0.24? **(c)** What is the probability that samples of these sizes would yield a difference in sample proportions greater than 0.31?

17. The mean time city bus drivers require to complete a round trip via Route 1 is 80 minutes with a standard deviation of 3 minutes. For Route 2, the mean and standard deviation are 75 minutes and 2 minutes, respectively. What is the probability that a random sample of 40 trips from Route 1 and an independent sample of 50 trips from Route 2 yield a difference $\bar{x}_1 - \bar{x}_2$ between sample means of 6 minutes or more?

18. A random sample of 50 reports by householders in City 1 yields a mean monthly utilities payment of $180. An independent random sample of 45 reports by householders in City 2 yields a mean monthly payment of $175. Suppose that there is no difference in the true mean monthly utilities payment for the two cities. What is the probability of observing a difference between sample means $\bar{x}_1 - \bar{x}_2$ as large as or larger than $5? Assume that $\sigma^2 = 225$ for both cities.

19. The mean yield per acre of a certain grain in one locality is 100 lb. The yield in another locality is 75 lb. Suppose that yields per acre in the two localities are normally distributed with a standard deviation of 20 lb. What is the probability that random and independent samples of 20 acres from each locality will yield a difference $\bar{x}_1 - \bar{x}_2$ between sample means of 10 or less?

20. Physical fitness scores of a certain population of executives are normally distributed with a mean and standard deviation of 75 and 10, respectively. What is the probability that a random sample of 25 such executives has a mean score between 70 and 78?

21. The mean number of years of experience of a certain population of salespersons is 10 years. The standard deviation is 3 years. What is the probability that a random sample of 81 of these salespersons yields a mean greater than 10 years and 8 months?

22. In a certain town, 18% of the teenage boys regularly ride a motorcycle. A random sample of 100 teenage boys is selected from this town. What is the probability that between 15 and 25% are regular motorcycle riders?

23. A study of a certain suburb reveals that 70% of the families moved into the town during the past 5 years. A random sample of 200 families is drawn from this town. What is the probability that the proportion who have moved into the town within the past 5 years is between 0.65 and 0.75? What is the probability that the proportion is greater than 0.75?

24. Of the 1150 middle managers in a certain area, 60% hold M.B.A. degrees. You select a random sample of 150 of them. What is the probability that the proportion in the sample with M.B.A. degrees is between 0.50 and 0.65?

25. It is believed that 0.16 of the households in Metropolitan Area I have at least one preschool child. The proportion in Metropolitan Area II is believed to be 0.11. If these figures are accurate, what is the probability that a simple random sample of 200 households from Area I and an independent simple random sample of 225 households from Area II will yield a difference in sample proportions $\hat{p}_I - \hat{p}_{II}$ as large as or larger than 0.10?

26. In a random sample of 150 children from Area A, 45 report that they regularly eat a certain breakfast cereal. In an independent random sample of 200 children from Area B, 20 say that they regularly eat the cereal. Suppose that the proportion who regularly eat the cereal is actually 0.15 in each population. What is the probability of observing a difference in sample proportions $\hat{p}_A - \hat{p}_B$ this large or larger?

27. Two drugs, A and B, are believed to be equally effective in preventing insomnia. The proportion of persons for whom the drugs are effective is believed to be 0.70. Of a random sample of 100 persons who are given Drug A, 75 experience relief. Drug B is effective with 105 of an independent random sample of 150 subjects. Suppose that the two drugs are, in fact, equally effective, as believed. What is the probability of observing a value of $\hat{p}_A - \hat{p}_B$ as large as or larger than that reported here?

28. It is believed that 15% of the members of Population A have tried a certain brand of shampoo, but only 8% of the people in Population B have tried it. Suppose that these figures are accurate. What is the probability that a random sample of 120 people from Population A and an independent random sample of 130 people from Population B will yield a value of $\hat{p}_A - \hat{p}_B$ equal to or greater than 0.16?

29. The weights of a certain kind of steel product are approximately normally distributed with a mean of 2800 lb and a variance of 9000 lb^2. Suppose that a random sample of size 10 is to be selected from this population. What is the probability that the mean weight of the sample is 2750 lb or less?

30. The mean weight gain of a certain breed of dog fed a given puppy chow for a year is 24.5 lb with a standard deviation of 4.5 lb.   **(a)** What are the mean and standard deviation of the sampling distribution of the sample mean, based on random samples of size 81 from this population? **(b)** A random sample of 81 puppies is fed the chow for a year. What is the probability that the mean weight gain in this sample is greater than 25 lb?

31. From Table A, select a simple random sample of 30 one-digit numbers. Compute the mean and variance for your sample. Using your results and those of the other students in your class, construct a frequency distribution of the sample means. Plot the distribution as a histogram. Compute the mean and variance of the sample means obtained by the class. Compare your results with the mean and variance of the true sampling distribution based on samples of size 30. They are $\mu_{\bar{x}} = 4.5$ and $\sigma_{\bar{x}}^2 = 8.25/30 = 0.275$.

32. For a population consisting of 1000 employees, the variable of interest is number of days of accrued annual leave. Suppose that the mean and variance are 12 and 144, respectively. What is the probability that a sample of size 100 will yield a mean greater than 9?

33. What is the probability that a sample of size 225 will yield a mean of 30 or less, given that the sampled population has a mean of 35 and a standard deviation of 30? The population size is 1500.

 34. ⓒ The following are the sizes, in square feet of living space rounded to the nearest hundred square feet, of the 724 dwelling units that compose a city housing development. Select a simple random sample of size 35 from this population.

1. 14	35. 15	69. 14	103. 13	137. 17	171. 15
2. 13	36. 14	70. 15	104. 12	138. 10	172. 14
3. 12	37. 13	71. 13	105. 15	139. 14	173. 14
4. 13	38. 14	72. 15	106. 13	140. 14	174. 16
5. 13	39. 17	73. 13	107. 12	141. 12	175. 12
6. 14	40. 15	74. 15	108. 17	142. 13	176. 15
7. 12	41. 14	75. 14	109. 14	143. 15	177. 17
8. 12	42. 14	76. 15	110. 13	144. 14	178. 16
9. 14	43. 14	77. 15	111. 13	145. 13	179. 13
10. 14	44. 13	78. 14	112. 14	146. 14	180. 12
11. 14	45. 17	79. 14	113. 15	147. 13	181. 12
12. 13	46. 14	80. 13	114. 15	148. 14	182. 14
13. 12	47. 12	81. 17	115. 14	149. 15	183. 15
14. 13	48. 15	82. 12	116. 15	150. 14	184. 15
15. 12	49. 16	83. 15	117. 15	151. 14	185. 13
16. 13	50. 12	84. 12	118. 13	152. 16	186. 15
17. 13	51. 14	85. 13	119. 14	153. 14	187. 13
18. 12	52. 14	86. 13	120. 14	154. 12	188. 15
19. 11	53. 12	87. 12	121. 13	155. 15	189. 12
20. 12	54. 15	88. 16	122. 13	156. 15	190. 14
21. 12	55. 16	89. 13	123. 13	157. 16	191. 15
22. 14	56. 14	90. 15	124. 13	158. 13	192. 13
23. 13	57. 13	91. 12	125. 14	159. 13	193. 14
24. 15	58. 14	92. 14	126. 13	160. 16	194. 13
25. 16	59. 12	93. 14	127. 12	161. 15	195. 12
26. 12	60. 15	94. 13	128. 13	162. 15	196. 14
27. 14	61. 14	95. 13	129. 15	163. 16	197. 15
28. 14	62. 15	96. 15	130. 16	164. 14	198. 15
29. 14	63. 14	97. 13	131. 17	165. 17	199. 12
30. 14	64. 12	98. 14	132. 14	166. 14	200. 13
31. 14	65. 15	99. 14	133. 14	167. 13	201. 14
32. 16	66. 14	100. 13	134. 14	168. 14	202. 12
33. 14	67. 14	101. 14	135. 18	169. 15	203. 14
34. 13	68. 14	102. 14	136. 16	170. 13	204. 14

205. 17	264. 12	323. 16	382. 15	441. 13	500. 14
206. 14	265. 15	324. 12	383. 16	442. 12	501. 13
207. 16	266. 13	325. 13	384. 16	443. 13	502. 14
208. 16	267. 14	326. 14	385. 16	444. 13	503. 16
209. 15	268. 13	327. 15	386. 13	445. 15	504. 15
210. 12	269. 13	328. 14	387. 13	446. 14	505. 15
211. 15	270. 14	329. 14	388. 15	447. 15	506. 13
212. 15	271. 16	330. 15	389. 12	448. 14	507. 13
213. 12	272. 14	331. 16	390. 14	449. 16	508. 13
214. 12	273. 16	332. 13	391. 15	450. 14	509. 14
215. 12	274. 13	333. 11	392. 15	451. 13	510. 14
216. 15	275. 15	334. 14	393. 11	452. 15	511. 16
217. 14	276. 17	335. 12	394. 12	453. 17	512. 13
218. 13	277. 13	336. 13	395. 14	454. 15	513. 13
219. 13	278. 11	337. 15	396. 14	455. 13	514. 14
220. 14	279. 12	338. 15	397. 15	456. 12	515. 12
221. 13	280. 15	339. 17	398. 14	457. 12	516. 15
222. 13	281. 16	340. 14	399. 14	458. 12	517. 15
223. 15	282. 15	341. 13	400. 12	459. 14	518. 13
224. 16	283. 11	342. 13	401. 13	460. 14	519. 17
225. 12	284. 14	343. 15	402. 16	461. 15	520. 15
226. 13	285. 13	344. 16	403. 14	462. 15	521. 16
227. 13	286. 13	345. 14	404. 16	463. 14	522. 14
228. 16	287. 11	346. 14	405. 14	464. 15	523. 13
229. 16	288. 12	347. 12	406. 13	465. 13	524. 15
230. 14	289. 14	348. 13	407. 16	466. 12	525. 14
231. 14	290. 14	349. 14	408. 15	467. 15	526. 12
232. 13	291. 14	350. 15	409. 12	468. 12	527. 16
233. 14	292. 16	351. 18	410. 17	469. 13	528. 15
234. 12	293. 15	352. 16	411. 12	470. 16	529. 13
235. 15	294. 15	353. 12	412. 14	471. 14	530. 12
236. 13	295. 16	354. 14	413. 15	472. 14	531. 13
237. 14	296. 17	355. 14	414. 12	473. 16	532. 12
238. 14	297. 14	356. 14	415. 15	474. 14	533. 15
239. 13	298. 12	357. 13	416. 15	475. 13	534. 13
240. 13	299. 13	358. 14	417. 15	476. 13	535. 15
241. 12	200. 17	359. 12	418. 16	477. 13	536. 12
242. 15	301. 11	360. 17	419. 14	478. 17	537. 15
243. 14	302. 14	361. 14	420. 13	479. 11	538. 14
244. 11	303. 14	362. 15	421. 16	480. 14	539. 13
245. 14	304. 14	363. 16	422. 14	481. 13	540. 13
246. 12	305. 13	364. 15	423. 13	482. 15	541. 13
247. 14	306. 14	365. 13	424. 16	483. 13	542. 11
248. 14	307. 16	366. 16	425. 13	484. 14	543. 15
249. 12	308. 13	367. 13	426. 14	485. 15	544. 15
250. 14	309. 13	368. 12	427. 14	486. 16	545. 15
251. 14	310. 11	369. 14	428. 15	487. 15	546. 16
252. 13	311. 12	370. 15	429. 15	488. 15	547. 12
253. 12	312. 11	371. 12	430. 15	489. 14	548. 13
254. 13	313. 15	372. 14	431. 12	490. 13	549. 16
255. 14	314. 13	373. 13	432. 13	491. 14	550. 11
256. 13	315. 13	374. 11	433. 16	492. 15	551. 13
257. 13	316. 13	375. 14	434. 13	493. 16	552. 11
258. 13	317. 14	376. 14	435. 14	494. 14	553. 14
259. 15	318. 14	377. 13	436. 12	495. 14	554. 15
260. 13	319. 13	378. 14	437. 15	496. 12	555. 14
261. 13	320. 14	379. 15	438. 16	497. 13	556. 12
262. 11	321. 15	380. 13	439. 12	498. 14	557. 14
263. 14	322. 15	381. 14	440. 15	499. 15	558. 14

559. 17	587. 15	615. 13	643. 14	671. 15	699. 12
560. 16	588. 18	616. 15	644. 15	672. 15	700. 17
561. 13	589. 14	617. 14	645. 15	673. 16	701. 12
562. 14	590. 13	618. 16	646. 12	674. 14	702. 15
563. 15	591. 14	619. 13	647. 13	675. 14	703. 13
564. 13	592. 11	620. 16	648. 15	676. 14	704. 14
565. 15	593. 13	621. 15	649. 17	677. 13	705. 16
566. 13	594. 13	622. 12	650. 12	678. 13	706. 14
567. 14	595. 14	623. 17	651. 12	679. 14	707. 16
568. 16	596. 14	624. 13	652. 12	680. 16	708. 13
569. 16	597. 12	625. 14	653. 14	681. 15	709. 15
570. 14	598. 12	626. 13	654. 16	682. 12	710. 14
571. 15	599. 12	627. 14	655. 14	683. 14	711. 14
572. 12	600. 12	628. 11	656. 12	684. 14	712. 14
573. 14	601. 15	629. 14	657. 14	685. 13	713. 15
574. 13	602. 14	630. 12	658. 14	686. 15	714. 14
575. 16	603. 15	631. 13	659. 16	687. 14	715. 14
576. 14	604. 14	632. 14	660. 15	688. 14	716. 16
577. 13	605. 13	633. 11	661. 15	689. 14	717. 16
578. 14	606. 13	634. 17	662. 14	690. 15	718. 14
579. 11	607. 14	635. 13	663. 14	691. 13	719. 16
580. 15	608. 16	636. 14	664. 14	692. 14	720. 13
581. 14	609. 13	637. 14	665. 14	693. 15	721. 14
582. 12	610. 16	638. 13	666. 10	694. 13	722. 11
583. 14	611. 12	639. 15	667. 15	695. 13	723. 14
584. 11	612. 17	640. 14	668. 15	696. 14	724. 14
585. 14	613. 16	641. 16	669. 15	697. 13	
586. 16	614. 14	642. 14	670. 15	698. 15	

35. Ⓒ Compute the mean and standard deviation for the sample you drew in Exercise 34. Compare your results with those of your classmates.

36. Ⓒ Select a simple random sample of size 10 from the population in Exercise 34. Compute the mean and variance for this sample and compare the results with those of Exercise 35.

6.

Statistical Inference I: Estimation

CHAPTER OBJECTIVES: This chapter discusses estimation, one of the two kinds of statistical inference procedures. (We shall discuss the other type—hypothesis testing—in Chapter 7.) There are two kinds of estimation: point estimation and interval estimation. Interval estimation is the more useful of the two. This chapter also gives you a chance to use what you learned earlier about probability, probability distributions, and sampling distributions. After studying this chapter and working the exercises, you should be able to do the following.

1. Define statistical inference
2. Discuss the properties of a good estimator
3. Construct confidence intervals for the following parameters: (a) a population mean, (b) a population proportion, (c) the difference between two population means, (d) the difference between two population proportions, and (e) a mean of a population of paired differences
4. Determine how large a sample to draw from a population when the objective is to estimate either a population mean or a population proportion
5. Describe the t distribution and discuss when its use is appropriate
6. Choose the correct reliability factor (z or t) for constructing a confidence interval
7. Explain the difference between probabilistic and practical interpretations of a confidence interval

We discussed the foundations of statistical inference in Chapters 3, 4, and 5, which were concerned with the concepts of probability, probability distributions, and sampling distributions.

In Chapter 2 we said that the motivation for analyzing data was the desire for insight into the nature of the data at hand. We computed a mean and a variance in order to describe a given set of data. Any conclusions we reached related only to those data. The calculation of a mean and a variance (and a standard deviation) takes on a new dimension in the area of *statistical inference*. Our interest now centers on what these measures can tell us about some larger body of data. Statistical inference, then, is defined as follows.

Statistical inference is the procedure whereby conclusions are reached about a population on the basis of the results obtained from a sample drawn from that population.

Why Sample?

There are several reasons why you may want to draw and analyze a sample in order to reach a decision about a population. A population may be so large that examining it in its entirety would require prohibitive amounts of money, time, or resources. Or the process of taking a measurement may be destructive. Consider, for example, a manufacturer of light bulbs who wants information on the average lifetime of the product. The impracticality of testing every element (light bulb) of the population is obvious. The manufacturer can get the desired information only by means of sampling and inference.

There are two types of statistical inference: (1) *estimation* and (2) *hypothesis testing*. We shall discuss the first of these in this chapter. We shall present hypothesis testing in Chapter 7.

Before we begin our discussion of estimation, consider the following examples of situations in which we might use sampling for the purpose of making inferences.

1. A firm is considering the establishment of a mobile home park in a certain area. The firm needs to know the average monthly rental fees for mobile homes in order to reach a decision on whether or not to develop the park.
2. The manager of a retail grocery chain is interested in knowing what proportion of the customers in a given week are regular shoppers at the chain's stores.
3. The personnel manager of a large organization wishes to know the average age of the employees.
4. An advertising executive wants to know what proportion of subscribers to a certain magazine remember a particular ad.
5. An employment agency wishes to know the average salary being paid to people employed in a certain job classification.

Sampled Populations and Target Populations

In applying statistical inference, you must know the difference between the *sampled* population and the *target* population. The sampled population is the population from which we actually draw the sample. The target population is the population about which we want information. The two may or may not be the same. Statistical inference, properly used, lets us make inferences about a properly sampled population. Statistical procedures do not help us to reach decisions about a target population if that target population is different from the sampled one.

Suppose that you wish to know what percentage of the households in a certain city have central air conditioning. Someone might propose that you select a simple random sample of households from the telephone book and base an inference about the population of households in the city on the information provided by this sample. You should ask yourself whether, in this case, the target population (households in the city) and the proposed sampled population (households listed in the phone book) are the same. A little reflection will probably convince you that they are not. What about households without phones? What about households with unlisted phone numbers?

In many situations the target population and the sampled population are the same. Then inferences about the target population are straightforward. You should, however, be aware that they may be different so that you do not fall into the trap of making unwarranted inferences about a population that is different from the one that you sampled.

The sampled population and the target population are not necessarily the same.

6.1 PROPERTIES OF GOOD ESTIMATORS

We can distinguish two types of estimates: *point estimates* and *interval estimates*.

A point estimate is computed from the data of a sample. It consists of a single value (of a statistic) used as the best conjecture as to what the corresponding population value (parameter) may be.

We shall define an interval estimate in Section 6.2.

Note that an estimate is a specific numerical value. We make a distinction between an estimate and an *estimator*. An *estimator* is the procedure or rule, usually expressed as a mathematical formula, that tells how an estimate is computed. An example of an estimator is

$$\bar{x} = \frac{\Sigma x_i}{n}$$

which is the estimator used to obtain an estimate of a population mean.

One aspect of point estimators has to do with whether a particular estimator is good or poor. Estimators are usually judged on the basis of the following criteria: (1) *unbiasedness*, (2) *consistency*, (3) *efficiency*, and (4) *sufficiency*. A rigorous treatment of these criteria is beyond the mathematical level of this text. However, a brief discussion will be of value.

Unbiasedness

An estimator is said to be an *unbiased* estimator of a population parameter if the mean value of the statistic computed from all possible simple random samples of a given size drawn from that population is equal to the corresponding parameter. That is, the estimator is unbiased if the *expected value* of the statistic is equal to the parameter. If θ is the parameter being estimated and $\hat{\theta}$ is an unbiased estimator of θ, we express this fact symbolically as

$$E(\hat{\theta}) = \theta$$

The left-hand term reads, ''the expected value of $\hat{\theta}$.'' The sample arithmetic mean $\bar{x}$ is an unbiased estimator of the population mean μ, since $E(\bar{x}) = \mu$. The example in Chapter 5 that showed the construction of the sampling distribution of the sample mean illustrated this fact.

The sample variance, computed by

$$\frac{\sum_{i=1}^{n}(x_i - \bar{x})^2}{n}$$

is not an unbiased estimator of σ^2. The sample variance calculated by this formula serves only as a measure of dispersion for the sample data. When we want to use sample data to compute an unbiased estimate of the population variance, we alter the estimator slightly. We divide the sum of the squared deviations of the values from their mean by $n - 1$ rather than n. An unbiased estimate of σ^2 is given by

$$s^2 = \frac{\sum(x_i - \bar{x})^2}{n - 1}$$

The denominator $(n - 1)$ is called the *degrees of freedom*. We can explain the concept of degrees of freedom as it applies to the calculation of the sample variance on an intuitive basis as follows: Since the sum of the deviations $x_i - \bar{x}$ must be 0, only $n - 1$ of these deviations are independent. The last deviation is automatically specified when $n - 1$ of them are known. Thus we say that only $n - 1$ degrees of freedom are available for estimating the population variance. You will encounter the concept of degrees of freedom *many* times in this text.

Consistency

A statistic is said to be a *consistent* estimator if, as the sample size increases, the estimator approaches the population parameter being estimated.

We have seen that the variance of $\bar{x}$, $\sigma_{\bar{x}}^2$, is equal to σ^2/n. This indicates that as n increases, we can expect the sample means to be closer to μ. Consequently $\bar{x}$ is a consistent estimator of μ.

Efficiency

The *efficiency* of an estimator depends on its variance: One estimator is more efficient than another if the variance of the former is less than the variance of the latter in repeated sampling. We can compute a measure of relative efficiency by forming the ratio of the variances of two estimators. In general, the relative efficiency of an unbiased estimator $\hat{\theta}_1$ with respect to another unbiased estimator $\hat{\theta}_2$ is given by

$$\frac{\text{Variance}\,(\hat{\theta}_2)}{\text{Variance}\,(\hat{\theta}_1)}$$

Sufficiency

An estimator is said to be *sufficient* if it utilizes all the information about the parameter being estimated that is contained in the sample. Admittedly, this is a rather vague statement. To be more specific, however, would require a more complex mathematical explanation than is desirable in this text. It is important to remember that if a sufficient estimator exists, it is useless to consider any other nonsufficient estimator. The sufficient estimator has exhausted all the information in the sample that is relevant to the estimation of the parameter of interest. The sample mean $\bar{x}$ and the sample proportion $\hat{p}$ are sufficient estimators, respectively, of μ and p.

6.2 ESTIMATING THE POPULATION MEAN— KNOWN POPULATION VARIANCE

In contrast to a point estimate, an *interval estimate* consists of an interval that we are willing to say, with varying degrees of conviction, contains the parameter being estimated. We may obtain both "one-sided" and "two-sided" interval estimates. However, since two-sided intervals are more often used, we shall consider only these. The bounds of a two-sided interval consist of two possible values of the parameter being estimated. It is a characteristic of point estimates that no statement of confidence can be attached to them. As we will show later, this is not true of interval estimates. We can obtain an interval that will satisfy any degree of confidence that the interval does contain the parameter of interest.

To consider the most extreme case, we may say with 100% confidence that the unknown mean of some population is contained in the interval $-\infty$ to $+\infty$. The uselessness of such an interval is obvious. Fortunately, we can obtain much narrower and, therefore, more useful intervals. The price we pay for a more useful interval is a reduction in confidence that it contains the parameter being estimated.

Since we can attach a statement of confidence to each interval estimate we obtain, we can refer to interval estimates as *confidence intervals* and to the bounds of the interval as *confidence limits*.

Obtaining Useful Confidence Intervals

To obtain a useful interval estimate, we draw on our knowledge of sampling distributions. For example, if we want to obtain an interval estimate of a population mean, we recall what we know about the sampling distribution of $\bar{x}$, the estimator of the population mean. Chapter 5 showed that when sampling is from

FIGURE 6.1
Sampling
distribution of $\bar{x}$,
showing $\mu_{\bar{x}} - 2\sigma_{\bar{x}}$
and $\mu_{\bar{x}} + 2\sigma_{\bar{x}}$

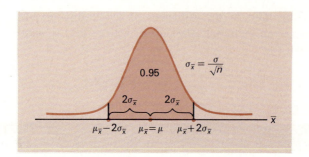

a normally distributed population, the sampling distribution of $\bar{x}$ is normally distributed with mean $\mu_{\bar{x}} = \mu$ and standard deviation $\sigma_{\bar{x}} = \sigma/\sqrt{n}$. Knowing that $\bar{x}$ is normally distributed lets us make further statements about the distribution of $\bar{x}$. For example, approximately 95% of all the values of $\bar{x}$ are within two standard errors of the mean μ, regardless of its numerical value. In other words, the interval bounded by $\mu - 2\sigma_{\bar{x}}$ and $\mu + 2\sigma_{\bar{x}}$ has μ as its center and contains approximately 95% of all values of $\bar{x}$.

Suppose that we draw a sketch of the sampling distribution of $\bar{x}$, showing the points that are two standard deviations from the mean. In any practical situation this would not be feasible, since μ, and hence $\mu_{\bar{x}}$, would be unknown. With $\mu_{\bar{x}}$ unknown, we would not know where on the $\bar{x}$ axis to center the distribution. In the general case, however, we can sketch the distribution as in Figure 6.1.

In a practical situation, the expression $\mu \pm 2\sigma_{\bar{x}}$ is not by itself informative, since μ is unknown. But if μ is replaced by its estimator $\bar{x}$, the picture changes completely. In $\bar{x} \pm 2\sigma_{\bar{x}}$ we have an interval estimate of μ. Furthermore, the nature of this interval is such that we can attach to it a statement of our degree of confidence that it actually contains the unknown parameter μ. We can change our degree of confidence simply by changing the value of the numerical coefficient accompanying $\sigma_{\bar{x}}$.

As you try to understand this confidence interval, consider the situation in which a confidence interval of the form $\bar{x} \pm 2\sigma_{\bar{x}}$ is computed for every possible value of $\bar{x}$. (If the population is infinite, imagine computing a large number of these confidence intervals.) The result would be a large number of intervals, all with widths equal to the width of the interval about the unknown μ. The centers of 95% of these intervals would fall within the interval about μ. Each of these intervals, therefore, would contain μ. Figure 6.2 shows the concept. It shows that $\bar{x}_1$, $\bar{x}_3$, and $\bar{x}_4$ all fall within the $2\sigma_{\bar{x}}$ interval about μ. Thus the $2\sigma_{\bar{x}}$ intervals about these sample means "cover," or include, μ. The sample means $\bar{x}_2$ and $\bar{x}_5$ do not fall within the $2\sigma_{\bar{x}}$ interval about μ. Therefore the $2\sigma_{\bar{x}}$ intervals about these sample means do not include μ.

Components of a Confidence Interval

Let us examine the composition of the interval estimate $\bar{x} \pm 2\sigma_{\bar{x}}$. The center of this interval is $\bar{x}$, the point estimator of μ. The 2 is a value from the standard

FIGURE 6.2
Sampling
distribution of $\bar{x}$,
showing several
confidence
intervals for μ

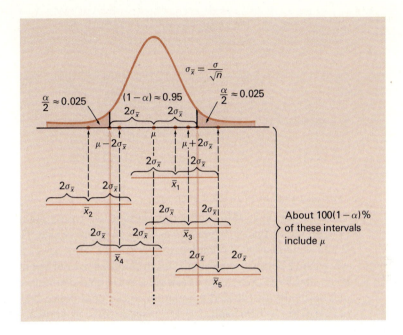

normal distribution that indicates within how many standard errors of the mean lie approximately 95% of the possible values of $\bar{x}$. This value of z is referred to as the *reliability coefficient*. The value of the reliability coefficient depends on the value of the *confidence coefficient*, which specifies the degree of confidence that we can attach to the interval estimate. If the reliability coefficient is 2, the level of confidence is approximately 95% and the confidence coefficient is approximately 0.95. In general, the confidence coefficient is equal to $1 - \alpha$, where α is the area under the curve of the sampling distribution of $\bar{x}$ that lies outside the interval about the unknown μ. This means that $1 - \alpha$ is equal to the area under the curve that is included in the interval about μ. See Figure 6.2.

The last component of the interval estimate, $\sigma_{\bar{x}}$, is the standard error, or standard deviation, of the estimator $\bar{x}$. In general, we may express a two-sided interval estimate as follows:

$$\text{Estimate} \pm (\text{reliability coefficient}) \times (\text{standard error}) \tag{6.1}$$

In particular, when sampling is from a normal distribution with a known variance, an interval estimate for μ is given by

$$\bar{x} \pm z_{1-\alpha/2}\sigma_{\bar{x}} \tag{6.2}$$

where $z_{1-\alpha/2}$ is the value of z to the right of which lies $\alpha/2$ of the area under the standard normal curve. Figure 6.3 shows $z_{1-\alpha/2}$ for the situation in which $\alpha = 0.05$. Table C shows that when $\alpha = 0.05$, $z_{1-\alpha/2} = z_{0.975} = 1.96$. That is, 0.975 of the area under the curve is to the left of 1.96.

FIGURE 6.3
Standard normal
distribution,
showing $z_{1-\alpha/2}$ for
$\alpha = 0.05$

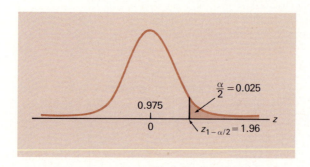

Selecting the Confidence Coefficient

Thus, for an exact 95% confidence interval, we would use a confidence coefficient of 1.96 rather than 2, which gives only an approximate 95% confidence interval. When we construct a confidence interval, we may select any level of confidence we wish. The most commonly used confidence coefficients, however, are 90%, 95%, and 99%. When we construct a two-sided confidence interval for the mean of a normally distributed population, these confidence coefficients yield z values of ± 1.645, ± 1.96, and ± 2.58, respectively, as shown in Figure 6.4. We also see in Figure 6.4 that, when all other things are equal, the more confidence we desire, the wider our confidence interval.

Confidence coefficient	z
0.90	± 1.645
0.95	± 1.96
0.99	± 2.58

Interpreting the Confidence Interval

We can interpret the confidence interval in one of two ways. The first, called the *probabilistic interpretation*, is based on the probability of occurrence of intervals about $\bar{x}$ that include μ. It may be stated as follows.

In repeated sampling from a normally distributed population, $100(1 - \alpha)\%$ of all intervals of the form $\bar{x} \pm z_{1-\alpha/2}\sigma_{\bar{x}}$ that may be constructed from simple random samples of size n will, in the long run, include the population mean μ.

The other interpretation, called the *practical interpretation*, may be stated as follows.

We are $100(1 - \alpha)\%$ confident that the single interval $\bar{x} \pm z_{1-\alpha/2}\sigma_{\bar{x}}$, computed from a simple random sample of size n from a normally distributed population, contains the population mean μ.

If we have constructed a 95% confidence interval, for example, we are 95% confident that this single interval contains the population mean. We can make this statement because we know that 95% of all possible intervals constructed in this manner will contain μ.

The following example illustrates the construction of a confidence interval. (In this chapter we will assume, unless otherwise indicated, that the population is large enough relative to the sample that the finite population correction can be ignored.)

FIGURE 6.4
Selection of *z* for 90, 95, and 99% confidence intervals for the mean of a normally distributed population

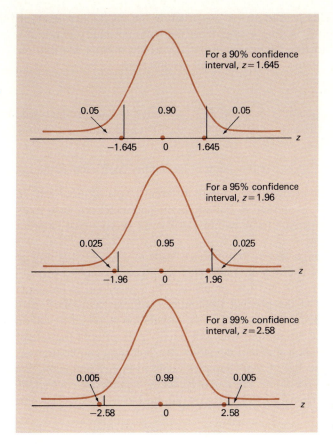

EXAMPLE 6.1 You are the quality-control supervisor for a wire manufacturing company. Periodically you select a sample of wire specimens to test for breaking strength. Experience has shown that the breaking strengths of a certain type of wire are normally distributed with a standard deviation of 200 lb. A random sample of 16 specimens yields a mean of 6200 lb. You want a 95% confidence interval for the mean breaking strength of the population.

SOLUTION The point estimate of μ is $\bar{x} = 6200$ lb, the *z* value corresponding to a confidence coefficient of 0.95 is 1.96, and the standard error of the estimate is $\sigma/\sqrt{n} = 200/\sqrt{16} = 50$. The population from which the sample was drawn is normally distributed. Thus you can use Equation 6.2 to obtain

$$6200 \pm 1.96(50), \qquad 6102, 6298$$

You are 95% confident that the population mean is contained in the interval 6102 to 6298. You can make this statement because you know that, in repeated sampling, 95% of the intervals that you can construct in this manner will, in the long run, contain the population mean.

This procedure for constructing the confidence interval for a population mean applies as long as the departure from normality is not too severe. If the sampled population deviates substantially from a normal distribution, we must take a further precaution, which we shall discuss later.

Precision

In Equations 6.1 and 6.2, we refer to the product we obtain by multiplying the reliability coefficient by the standard error as the *precision* of the estimator. That is,

$$\text{Precision} = (\text{reliability coefficient})(\text{standard error}) \qquad (6.3)$$

Different situations require different levels of precision. In one case in which the mean, expressed in dollars, is the parameter we wish to estimate, we might want the precision to be within 1 dollar. In another case, a precision of 5 dollars might suffice.

A high level of confidence leads to a large reliability coefficient. A large reliability coefficient, multiplied by a given standard error, yields a large product, which indicates low precision. High precision is indicated by a small numerical value of the product (reliability coefficient)(standard error). Remember that the standard error is equal to the population standard deviation divided by the square root of the sample size. For fixed values of both the reliability coefficient and the population standard deviation, the precision can be high or low, depending on the sample size. Larger samples result in higher precision. Smaller samples result in lower precision. For example, let the confidence coefficient be 0.95 (the reliability coefficient is 1.96), let $\sigma = 30$, and let $n = 25$. The precision is

$$\text{Precision} = 1.96\left(\frac{30}{\sqrt{25}}\right) = 1.96(6) = 11.76$$

Now suppose that we keep the same confidence coefficient and population σ, but increase the sample size to $n = 100$. We then have

$$\text{Precision} = 1.96\left(\frac{30}{\sqrt{100}}\right) = 1.96(3) = 5.88$$

Confidence Intervals for Means of Nonnormally Distributed Populations

In many, and perhaps most, practical cases, it is neither possible nor wise for you to assume that the population of interest is normally distributed, or even approximately normally distributed. This is not a problem as far as the use of Formula 6.2 is concerned, as long as it is possible to take a large sample. We are interested in the sampling distribution. We know that the sampling distribution of $\bar{x}$ is at least approximately normally distributed regardless of the functional form of the sampled population, provided that the sample size is large. This result is based on the central limit theorem (recall Chapter 5).

EXAMPLE 6.2 A counselor for an employment agency draws a simple random sample of previous applicants in order to estimate the mean score all previous applicants made on an aptitude test. The sample, which consists of 150 applicants, yields a mean score of $\bar{x} = 68$. The counselor knows from experience that the population variance is 100. The counselor also has evidence from experience that the population is not normally distributed. A 99% confidence interval for μ is desired.

SOLUTION Here we need to ask about the size of the population, to see whether we should use the finite population correction factor mentioned in Chapter 5. Suppose that the population consists of 1000 previous applicants. The sample then contains more than 5% of the population, and we must use the correction factor. The sample size is large, the central limit theorem applies, and we may use Formula 6.2, with $\sigma_{\bar{x}}$ adjusted by the finite population correction factor, to obtain the following interval:

$$68 \pm 2.58 \sqrt{\frac{100}{150}} \sqrt{\frac{1000 - 150}{1000 - 1}}, \qquad 68 \pm 2.58(0.82)(0.92), \qquad 66.05, 69.95$$

We say that we are 99% confident that the population mean is contained in the interval 66.05 to 69.95. But now suppose that the population had been much larger, say $N = 10,000$. We would not have needed the finite population correction factor, and the interval would have been

$$68 \pm 2.58(0.82), \qquad 65.88, 70.12$$

COMPUTER ANALYSIS

We may use STAT+ to construct confidence intervals. If, for example, we enter the information for Example 6.2 (ignoring the finite population correction factor) into the computer, STAT+ gives us the following printout:

```
 99% CONFIDENCE INTERVAL CONCERNING ONE MEAN
SAMPLE:
Xbar = 68                       Sigma = 10                    n = 150
Std error of the estimator = 0.8165

INFERENCE:
You are 99% confident that the interval
      65.8969 ,    70.1032
encloses the true population mean, using
z(1-.0100/2) = 2.576
```

Exercises

6.1 A frozen food company wishes to know the mean length of ears of corn received in a large shipment. A random sample of 200 is collected, and the ears are measured. The arithmetic mean of the lengths is found to be 8.8 in. The population has a standard deviation of 1.5 in. What are the 95% confidence limits for μ?

6.2 A telephone answering service, at the end of each call, completes a report in which the length of the call is recorded. A simple random sample of 9 reports yields a mean length of call of 1.2 minutes. Construct the 99% confidence interval for the population mean. It is known that the population is normally distributed with a standard deviation of 0.6 minute.

 6.3 The quality-control supervisor of a large manufacturing firm wishes to estimate the mean weight of 5500 packages of raw material. A simple random sample of 250 packages yields a mean of 65 lb. The population standard deviation is 15 lb. Construct a confidence interval for the unknown population mean μ. Assume that a 95% confidence interval is satisfactory.

 6.4 Ⓒ For males between the ages of 17 and 21, a physical fitness research team wishes to estimate the mean consumption of oxygen after a standard set of exercises. Previous research has indicated that the population variance is 0.0512. A random sample of 25 subjects yields the following results, in liters per minute: 2.87, 2.05, 2.90, 2.41, 2.93, 2.94, 2.26, 2.21, 2.20, 2.88, 2.51, 2.51, 2.56, 2.59, 2.52, 2.51, 2.50, 2.58, 2.52, 2.58, 2.44, 2.48, 2.43, 2.46, 2.46. Assume that the variable of interest is normally distributed. Obtain a 95% confidence interval for the population mean.

 6.5 You are an industrial psychologist who wants to estimate the mean age of a certain population of female employees. You draw a random sample of 60 females from the population. The sample yields a mean age of 23.67 years. You know that the population of ages is not normally distributed and that the population standard deviation is 15 years. Construct a 99% confidence interval.

6.3 ESTIMATING THE POPULATION MEAN— UNKNOWN POPULATION VARIANCE

The procedures in Section 6.2 for constructing a confidence interval for a population mean depend on knowing the numerical value of the population variance. But often you don't know the value of a population variance, nor do you know the value of the mean. In the typical situation, both will be unknown.

When we do not know the population variance, we cannot use Formula 6.2 to construct a confidence interval for μ, because we need σ to compute $\sigma_{\bar{x}} = \sigma/\sqrt{n}$. In that case, we compute the sample standard deviation s and use it to estimate σ, a procedure that leads to the following estimate of $\sigma_{\bar{x}}$:

$$s_{\bar{x}} = s/\sqrt{n} \tag{6.4}$$

We may now substitute $s_{\bar{x}}$ for $\sigma_{\bar{x}}$ in the formula for the confidence interval for μ. This procedure, however, does not completely solve the problem. The reliability coefficient z in the formula is no longer correct, since it is obtained from the relation

$$z = \frac{\bar{x} - \mu_{\bar{x}}}{\sigma_{\bar{x}}} = \frac{\bar{x} - \mu_{\bar{x}}}{\sigma/\sqrt{n}} \tag{6.5}$$

and z is normally distributed. In other words, we can no longer determine the appropriate z value accurately, since σ is unknown.

Student's *t* Distribution

When we use the estimate of $\sigma_{\bar{x}}$, $s_{\bar{x}}$, in Equation 6.5, the resulting variable is

$$t = \frac{\bar{x} - \mu_{\bar{x}}}{s_{\bar{x}}} = \frac{\bar{x} - \mu_{\bar{x}}}{s/\sqrt{n}} \tag{6.6}$$

which we use in place of z in the confidence interval for μ.

The next problem is to obtain a numerical value for t in a specific situation. We must consider the nature of the distribution of t. In other words, suppose that we take a very large number of samples of size n from a normally distributed population and use the mean and standard deviation of each to compute a value of t. The problem relates to the manner in which these values of t would be distributed.

The nature of the distribution of

$$t = \frac{\bar{x} - \mu_{\bar{x}}}{s/\sqrt{n}}$$

was first investigated and reported by William Sealy Gosset (1876–1937). Gosset published under the pseudonym ''Student.'' Consequently the distribution of t is frequently referred to as *Student's distribution*.

 Properties of the t Distribution   The properties of this distribution are as follows.

1. It has a mean of 0.
2. It is symmetrical about its mean.
3. In general, it has a variance greater than 1, but the variance approaches 1 as the sample size increases.
4. The variable t takes on values between $-\infty$ and ∞.
5. The t distribution is really a family of distributions, since there is a different distribution for each degrees-of-freedom value. In the one-sample case, this is $n - 1$, the divisor used in computing s^2.
6. In general, the t distribution is less peaked at the center and higher in the tails than the normal distribution.
7. The t distribution approaches the normal distribution as n increases.

Figure 6.5 compares the t distribution and the normal distribution.

The t distribution, like the standard normal distribution, has been extensively tabulated. Table D is one such table. To use it, we need to know the value of the confidence coefficient and the degrees of freedom.

FIGURE 6.5
The standard normal distribution and the t distribution

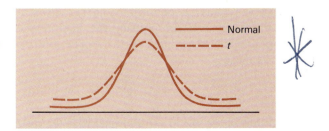

The general procedure for constructing confidence intervals for μ is not affected by the fact that we must obtain the reliability coefficient from the t table rather than from the z table. We still use the fact that we can express a confidence interval by the general relationship

$$\text{Estimate} \pm (\text{reliability coefficient}) \times (\text{standard error})$$

To be more specific, when we are sampling from a normally distributed population with unknown σ, the $100(1 - \alpha)\%$ confidence interval for the population mean is given by the following expression (in which $t_{1-\alpha/2}$ is the reliability coefficient):

$$\bar{x} \pm t_{1-\alpha/2} s/\sqrt{n} \tag{6.7}$$

In theory, we should use this formula only when sampling is from a normally distributed population. Experience has shown, however, that moderate departures from this assumption do not appreciably affect the results. Therefore, the t distribution is widely used even when it is known that the sampled population is not normally distributed. Most investigators require that the distribution of the population be at least mound-shaped. The following example shows the use of the t distribution.

EXAMPLE 6.3 In an effort to establish a standard time needed to perform a certain task, a production engineer randomly selects 16 experienced employees to perform the task. The mean time required by the 16 employees is 13 minutes. The standard deviation is 3 minutes. The production engineer wishes to construct a 95% confidence interval for the true mean length of time required to perform the task.

SOLUTION If we can assume that these 16 measurements constitute a simple random sample from a normally distributed population of times required to perform the task, we can use Formula 6.7. Assume that these assumptions are reasonable. The point estimate is 13 minutes. The standard error of the estimate is $s/\sqrt{n} = 3/\sqrt{16} = 0.75$. To find the reliability coefficient, we enter Table D with $n - 1 = 15$ degrees of freedom. The column containing the appropriate value of t is the one labeled $t_{0.975}$, since this is the one that contains t values with 0.025 of the area under the curve to their right. (The negatives of these values have 0.025 of the area under the curve to their left.) The appropriate t value is 2.1315. The desired interval is

$$13 \pm 2.1315(0.75), \qquad 11.4, 14.6$$

From the evidence this sample provides, we say that we are 95% confident that the true mean time required to perform the task is between 11.4 and 14.6 minutes. We can say this because of the probabilistic interpretation, which says that, in repeated sampling, 95% of the intervals that can be constructed in the same manner include the true mean.

Confidence Intervals for Means of Nonnormally Distributed Populations—Unknown Population Variance

We have said that, if we are to use Formula 6.7, the distribution of the sampled population must not deviate too much from a normal distribution. When sampling is from a nonnormally distributed population, the central limit theorem guarantees an approximately normally distributed sampling distribution of $\bar{x}$ when the sample size is large. We said earlier that when you are sampling from a nonnormally distributed population, you should draw a large sample and use Formula 6.2. But Formula 6.2 requires knowledge of σ, which is unknown under conditions of the type we are now discussing. Again we may use the sample standard deviation to estimate σ and use the resulting modification of Formula 6.2, which is as follows:

$$\bar{x} \pm z_{1-\alpha/2}s/\sqrt{n} \tag{6.8}$$

We can do this because we assume that, since the sample size is large, it provides an adequate estimate of σ. In fact, many people use Formula 6.8 when σ is unknown and n is large, whether or not they assume that the population is normally distributed. In other words, the size of the sample, rather than whether σ is known or unknown, is often used as the criterion for determining whether to use z or t as the reliability coefficient when constructing confidence intervals. This is reasonable, because the t distribution approaches the standard normal distribution as the size of the sample increases.

EXAMPLE 6.4 A real estate firm wants to develop a new shopping center. It wishes to know the average size of grocery stores in existing shopping centers. The firm's researchers are unwilling to assume that the population of store sizes is normally distributed. To obtain an interval estimate of μ, therefore, they decide to take a large sample. Then the central limit theorem will apply, and they can use the standard normal distribution to obtain their reliability coefficient. The population standard deviation is unknown, but they feel that a large sample will yield a satisfactory estimate of σ. The researchers draw a random sample of 50 grocery stores. They find the sample mean and standard deviation to be 10,000 and 4800 square feet, respectively. What is the 95% confidence interval for the population mean?

SOLUTION Under the circumstances, the appropriate formula for constructing a confidence interval for μ is Formula 6.8. Using this formula gives the following 95% confidence interval:

$$10,000 \pm 1.96\left(\frac{4800}{\sqrt{50}}\right), \qquad 8669; 11,331$$

Paired Observations

A special case of statistical inference about a single population mean occurs when the data for analysis consist of *paired observations*. We can generate paired observations in a variety of ways. We can take measurements on subjects before and after some intervening treatment, environmental alteration, and so forth. For example, we might gather individual production data on assembly-line employees before and after the initiation of measures designed to improve their working conditions. In the laboratory, we may divide individual specimens of material into two parts and subject each half to a different experimental procedure. For example, we can record tensile strengths for batches of plastic prepared according to the same formula, except that the two halves of each batch receive different amounts of a key ingredient. Another way to obtain paired observations is to match pairs of subjects according to as many relevant characteristics as possible. Then you apply one treatment to one member of each pair and a different treatment to the other member. For example, we pair salespersons by matching them according to age, years of experience, education, level of initiative, and so forth. Then we assign one member of each pair to a training course taught by one method and the other member to a training course taught by another method.

There are many ways to obtain paired observations.

In such situations, we are interested in the difference between the results produced under each of the two different conditions. We may, for example, want to determine the extent to which a change in working conditions causes a change in production volume. For individual employees, we can compare the number of units produced in a week before the change with the number produced during a week after the change. From the difference between these two observations, we can tell whether an individual employee's weekly production has increased, decreased, or remained the same. To assess the overall effect of the change, we examine the difference in production for the group as a whole. A measure that seems particularly relevant is the mean of the individual differences between before and after production figures. Indeed, this is a measure of considerable interest in analyzing paired observations.

Confidence Interval for a Mean Difference

Let d denote the difference between two paired observations x_1 and x_2. We may define the sample mean of the differences (*mean difference*) as

$$\bar{d} = \frac{\Sigma d_i}{n} \tag{6.9}$$

where n is the number of pairs of observations. The sample variance, denoted by s_d^2, may be computed as follows:

$$s_d^2 = \frac{\Sigma(d_i - \bar{d})^2}{n - 1} = \frac{n\Sigma d_i^2 - (\Sigma d_i)^2}{n(n - 1)} \tag{6.10}$$

We can use the sample mean difference $\bar{d}$ as a point estimator of the population mean difference μ_d. When the population of differences is normally distributed with unknown variance, a $100(1 - \alpha)\%$ confidence interval for μ_d is given by

$$\bar{d} \pm t_{1-\alpha/2}\frac{s_d}{\sqrt{n}} \tag{6.11}$$

where $s_d/\sqrt{n}$ is the estimated standard error of the mean difference. The degrees of freedom for t are $n - 1$. If the central limit theorem is applicable, we can use z in place of t in Equation 6.11.

TABLE 6.1
Amount of money spent on employee training by 10 firms (× $1000)

Firm	A	B	C	D	E	F	G	H	I	J
Current year (X_1)	12	14	8	12	8	10	8	9	10	10
Decade ago (X_2)	10	11	8	7	9	6	10	9	7	9
d_i	2	3	0	5	−1	4	−2	0	3	1

EXAMPLE 6.5 A simple random sample of 10 electronics firms is asked in a questionnaire to state the amount of money spent on employee training programs during the year just ended and during a year a decade ago. Table 6.1 gives the results (adjusted for inflation). We wish to construct a 95% confidence interval for the mean difference in expenditures for employee training programs by the 10 firms.

SOLUTION From the last row of Table 6.1, we compute

$$\bar{d} = \frac{2 + 3 + \cdots + 1}{10} = \frac{15}{10} = 1.5$$

$$s_d = \sqrt{\frac{10(2^2 + 3^2 + \cdots + 1^2) - (15)^2}{(10)(9)}} = \sqrt{5.17} = 2.3$$

$$s_{\bar{d}} = \frac{2.3}{\sqrt{10}} = 0.73$$

The 95% confidence interval for μ_d is

$$1.5 \pm 2.2622(0.73), \qquad -0.2, 3.2$$

When constructing confidence intervals for population means, we must decide whether to use z or t as the reliability factor. We can use Figure 6.6 as a guide in making the correct choice.

Exercises

 6.6 In a study to determine the feasibility of using a flexible plastic hose on a certain piece of machinery, engineers want to estimate the mean pressure to which the hose will be subjected. They take 9 pressure readings randomly throughout a 24-hour period of operation. The sample mean and standard deviation are 362 and 45, respectively. Assume that pressure readings are approximately normally distributed. Construct the 99% confidence interval for the true mean pressure.

 6.7 A simple random sample of 16 radio stations is selected in order to estimate the average charge for the same fixed-length spot announcement. The sample mean and standard deviation are $15.50 and $8.00, respectively. Assume that the amounts charged by all radio stations of the type sampled are approximately normally distributed. Construct the 95% confidence interval for the population mean.

 6.8 A record club wishes to know the average age of its members. A random sample of 100 members yields a mean age of 26 years with a standard deviation of 5 years. Assume that the population of ages is not normally distributed. Find the 95% confidence interval for μ.

 6.9 Ⓒ A soft-drink manufacturer wants to know the extent of customer preference for

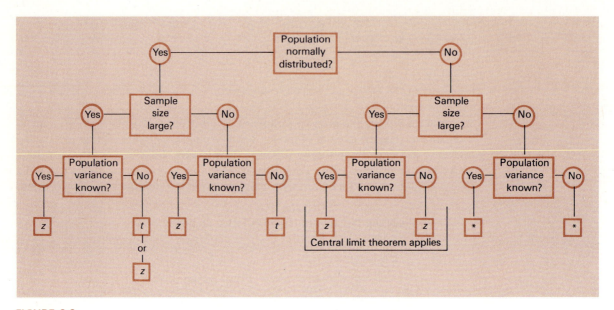

FIGURE 6.6
Flowchart for deciding between z and t when making inferences about population means [* = use a nonparametric procedure (Chapter 10)]

twist-off resealable tops for 32-ounce bottles. To investigate this, the manufacturer sets up a study in which the regular 32-ounce bottles are replaced by bottles with twist-off resealable tops in 16 randomly selected supermarkets in a certain area for a period of one month. The sales volume for each store for that month is compared with the same store's sales volume for the preceding month. The results (in hundreds of bottles) are as shown in the table. Construct a 95% confidence interval for μ_d based on $d_i = x_{1i} - x_{2i}$.

Store #	1	2	3	4	5	6	7	8	9	10	11	12	13	14	15	16
Test month (X_1)	44	61	46	55	49	50	45	64	40	62	53	54	57	55	61	52
Preceding month (X_2)	47	62	56	39	45	51	56	47	48	40	44	52	51	60	61	57

6.4 ESTIMATING THE DIFFERENCE BETWEEN TWO POPULATION MEANS—KNOWN POPULATION VARIANCES

We often want to know the difference between two population means, $\mu_1 - \mu_2$. In the absence of direct knowledge of this difference, we estimate it from sample data. Chapter 5 showed that $\bar{x}_1 - \bar{x}_2$ is an unbiased estimator of $\mu_1 - \mu_2$. It also showed that when two populations are normally distributed, the sampling distribution of $\bar{x}_1 - \bar{x}_2$, computed from *independent random samples,* is normally distributed, with a standard error given by

$$\sigma_{\bar{x}_1 - \bar{x}_2} = \sqrt{\frac{\sigma_1^2}{n_1} + \frac{\sigma_2^2}{n_2}}$$

We can construct a $100(1 - \alpha)\%$ confidence interval for $\mu_1 - \mu_2$, then, by

$$(\bar{x}_1 - \bar{x}_2) \pm z_{1-\alpha/2} \sqrt{\frac{\sigma_1^2}{n_1} + \frac{\sigma_2^2}{n_2}} \qquad (6.12)$$

This applies when the sampled populations are normally distributed, the population variances are known, and the samples are randomly and independently drawn from the two populations. Here is an example of the construction of such an interval.

EXAMPLE 6.6 A manufacturer produces a synthetic fiber at two factories located in different parts of the country. To help decide whether there is uniformity of production between the two factories with respect to the mean breaking strength of the fiber, he decides to construct a 95% confidence interval for the difference between population means.

SOLUTION To determine whether or not the two factories are maintaining uniformity of production, the manufacturer selects a sample of 25 specimens from Factory 1 and a sample of 16 specimens from Factory 2. The mean breaking strength of the sample from Factory 1 is 22 lb. The mean of the sample from Factory 2 is 20 lb. The variance in both factories is known to be 10. The populations are normally distributed. The following 95% confidence interval is constructed using Formula 6.12:

$$(22 - 20) \pm 1.96 \sqrt{\frac{10}{25} + \frac{10}{16}}, \qquad 0.0, 4.0$$

The usual probabilistic and practical interpretations may be given to this interval.

Exercises

6.10 A gasoline company wishes to compare credit-card holders in one area with those of another area. One question is how long the customers have held credit cards. A random sample of 100 card holders is selected from each area. The sample means are 156 months (Area 1) and 96 months (Area 2). The population variances for the two areas are 900 and 700, respectively. Construct a 95% confidence interval for the difference between population means.

6.11 A bank official who wants to know the difference between the average amount of money customers have on deposit in two branch banks selects a random sample of 25 customers from each branch. The sample means are: Branch A: \$450; Branch B: \$325. The two populations are normally distributed with variances $\sigma_A^2 = 750$ and $\sigma_B^2 = 850$. **(a)** Construct a 95% confidence interval for $\mu_A = \mu_B$; **(b)** construct a 99% confidence interval.

6.12 A firm hires a team of psychologists to study the differences between the characteristics of employees who attended a special training course and the characteristics of those who did not. The researchers examine a simple random sample of 50 employees who attended the course and an independent simple random sample of 60 who did not. At the end of six months, they give the employees a job-satisfaction test. Those who attended the course had a mean score of 4.50. Those who did not had a mean score of 3.75. Construct a 95% confidence interval for the difference between population means. On the basis of experience, the researchers assume that the two populations are approximately normally distributed. The variances are 1.8 for the population that attended the course and 2.1 for the population that did not.

 6.13 Ⓒ A researcher wants to construct a 95% confidence interval for the difference between the mean IQs of two groups of employees. The two populations of IQ scores are approximately normally distributed, with variances of $\sigma_1^2 = 100$ and $\sigma_2^2 = 144$. Independent simple random samples of sizes $n_1 = 25$ and $n_2 = 16$ yield the following results.

Sample 1	108	107	101	108	103	109	103	116	116	115	111	116	109
	111	120	102	119	124	101	114	128	111	115	129	126	
Sample 2	116	98	94	89	124	99	114	114	99	89	110	117	99
	94	92	117										

 6.14 A physical fitness counselor wishes to compare the muscular power of young executives who exercise regularly and that of executives of the same age and sex who do not exercise regularly. The subjects consist of 40 randomly selected exercisers and 50 randomly selected nonexercisers. The mean muscular endurance scores are 17.35 (for exercisers) and 15.19 (for nonexercisers). The counselor feels that the populations of scores are normally distributed. Experience shows that the variance for each group is about 2.25. The counselor would like to construct a 95% confidence interval for the difference between population means.

6.5 ESTIMATING THE DIFFERENCE BETWEEN TWO POPULATION MEANS—UNKNOWN POPULATION VARIANCES

Section 6.4 explained how to construct a confidence interval for the difference between two population means when the sampled populations are both normally distributed and the two population variances are known. But in real life, conditions are usually quite different. Sampled populations may be nonnormally distributed and/or population variances may be unknown. Here we consider two possible situations.

1. The populations are normally distributed, and the population variances are unknown but equal.
2. The populations are not normally distributed, and the population variances are unknown.

Normally Distributed Populations, Unknown but Equal Variances

When we want to estimate the difference between two population means, we cannot use Formula 6.12 if the population variances are unknown. Suppose that the populations are normally distributed, the *population variances are unknown, but known (or assumed) to be equal*, and we draw independent random samples from each of the two populations of interest. We may then construct a confidence interval for $\mu_1 - \mu_2$ by using the t distribution to obtain a reliability coefficient and estimating the population variances from sample data.

Pooling Sample Variances Say that the assumption of equal population variances is justified. Each of the sample variances computed from the two samples will be an estimate of the common variance σ^2. We capitalize on this fact by pooling the two sample estimates to obtain a single estimate of σ^2. To do this, we compute the weighted average of the two sample variances, where the weights are the degrees of freedom. If the sample sizes are equal, the weighted average is merely the arithmetic mean of the two sample variances. If, however, the two sample sizes are unequal, the weighted average takes advantage of the additional information provided by the larger sample. The pooled estimate of the common σ^2 is given by

s_p^2 is a weighted average of sample variances in which the weights are degrees of freedom.

$$s_p^2 = \frac{(n_1 - 1)s_1^2 + (n_2 - 1)s_2^2}{n_1 + n_2 - 2} \tag{6.13}$$

The estimated standard error of the estimator $\bar{x}_1 - \bar{x}_2$, then, is

$$\sqrt{\frac{s_p^2}{n_1} + \frac{s_p^2}{n_2}} = s_p \sqrt{\frac{1}{n_1} + \frac{1}{n_2}}$$

It can be shown that

$$t = \frac{(\bar{x}_1 - \bar{x}_2) - (\mu_1 - \mu_2)}{s_p \sqrt{\frac{1}{n_1} + \frac{1}{n_2}}}$$

follows the t distribution with $n_1 + n_2 - 2$ degrees of freedom. This justifies the use of t as a reliability coefficient in the confidence interval for $\mu_1 - \mu_2$ under the conditions mentioned.

In summary, we may state the following:

When random and independent samples of size n_1 and n_2, respectively, are drawn from two normally distributed populations with unknown but equal variances, the $100(1 - \alpha)\%$ confidence interval for $\mu_1 - \mu_2$ is given by

$$(\bar{x}_1 - \bar{x}_2) \pm t_{1-\alpha/2} s_p \sqrt{\frac{1}{n_1} + \frac{1}{n_2}} \tag{6.14}$$

EXAMPLE 6.7 Experimenters test two types of fertilizer for possible use in the cultivation of cabbages. They grow the cabbages in two different fields. One of the two fertilizers is applied in each field. To compare the two fertilizers, the researchers decide to construct a 95% confidence interval for the difference in the mean weight of cabbages grown with fertilizer I and the mean weight of those grown with fertilizer II.

SOLUTION At harvest time the experimenters select a random sample of 25 cabbages from the crop grown with fertilizer I. They also randomly select 12 cabbages from the crop grown with fertilizer II. The sample mean and variance of the weights of cabbages grown with fertilizer I are 44.1 oz and 36 oz^2. The mean weight computed from the second sample is 31.7 oz, and the variance is 44 oz^2. The experimenters assume that the two populations of weights are normally distributed. They also assume that the two population variances are equal. Therefore they compute the following pooled estimate of σ^2:

$$s_p^2 = \frac{24(36) + 11(44)}{25 + 12 - 2} = \frac{864 + 484}{35} = \frac{1348}{35} = 38.51$$

Formula 6.14 is used to compute the 95% confidence interval for $\mu_I - \mu_{II}$.

$$(44.1 - 31.7) \pm 2.0301\sqrt{38.51}\sqrt{\frac{1}{25} + \frac{1}{12}}, \qquad 8.0, 16.8$$

Nonnormally Distributed Populations and Unknown Variances

When we seek a confidence interval for the difference between two means, we may find that not only are the two population variances unknown, but the populations are not normally distributed. However, if n_1 and n_2 are both large, the central limit theorem applies, and we may use s_1 and s_2 to estimate σ_1 and σ_2. Under these circumstances, an approximate $100(1 - \alpha)\%$ confidence interval for $\mu_1 - \mu_2$ is given by

$$(\bar{x}_1 - \bar{x}_2) \pm z_{1-\alpha/2}\sqrt{\frac{s_1^2}{n_1} + \frac{s_2^2}{n_2}} \qquad (6.15)$$

When constructing confidence intervals for the difference between two population means, we must decide whether to use z or t as the reliability factor. We may use Figure 6.7 as a guide in making the correct choice.

Exercises

6.15 The difference in the ages of patients admitted to two different hospitals is of interest to an insurance company studying patterns of use of health facilities in a certain area. A simple random sample of discharge records is drawn from the files of each of the two hospitals, with the following results: For Hospital A, $n = 22$, $\bar{x} = 54.5$, $s^2 = 256$; for Hospital B, $n = 20$, $\bar{x} = 39.4$, $s^2 = 200$. It is felt that the two populations are approximately normally distributed. Assume that the two population variances are equal. Construct a 95% confidence interval for $\mu_A - \mu_B$.

6.16 A telephone answering service completes a report on each call received, noting the length of the call. The answering service serves only two types of clients. A simple random sample of 225 records for the type A client and an independent simple random sample of 100 records for the type B client give the following means and variances for length of call: $\bar{x}_A = 121.4$ seconds, $\bar{x}_B = 93.5$ seconds, $s_A^2 = 900$, $s_B^2 = 1200$. Assume that the populations are not normally distributed and do not have equal variances. Compute the 90% confidence interval for $\mu_A - \mu_B$.

6.17 In a certain factory, two machines are used to produce metal rods. A random sample of 11 rods from Machine A and a random sample of 21 rods from Machine B give these

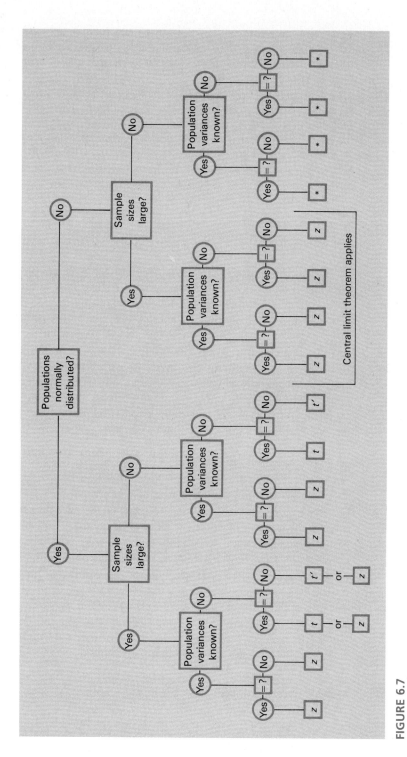

FIGURE 6.7

Flowchart for deciding between z and t when making inferences about the difference between two population means [* = use a nonparametric procedure (Chapter 10) For explanation of t′, see Daniel, Wayne W. and Terrell, James C., *Business Statistics*, 4e, Houghton Mifflin Company, Boston 1986, p. 193.]

results with respect to the lengths of metal rods produced: $\bar{x}_A = 5.95$ in., $\bar{x}_B = 6.01$ in., $s_A^2 = 0.018$, $s_B^2 = 0.020$. Assume that the populations are approximately normally distributed. Assume that the population variances are equal. Construct the 95% confidence interval for $\mu_A - \mu_B$.

 6.18 A research team wishes to know by how much, on the average, employees who have problems with alcohol and those who do not differ with respect to self-control. The researchers give a test designed to measure self-control to $n_1 = 21$ employees who do not have problems with alcohol and $n_2 = 16$ problem drinkers. The results are as follows: $\bar{x}_1 = 29.75$, $s_1^2 = 68.06$, $\bar{x}_2 = 24.50$, $s_2^2 = 47.61$. The researchers believe that the test yields scores that are approximately normally distributed. The sample variances are not equal, but the researchers believe that the population variances are equal. Construct a 95% confidence interval for the difference between population means.

6.6 ESTIMATING A POPULATION PROPORTION

In many business situations, we want to know what proportion of items in a population have a certain characteristic. A firm may want to find out what proportion of its customers would respond favorably to a change in the way service is provided. A company may want to know what proportion of its employees have not completed high school. A manufacturer may want to know what proportion of rejected items are rejected because of defective material.

To estimate a population proportion, we do the same things we did when we estimated a population mean. We randomly draw a sample of size n from the population of interest and compute the sample proportion $\hat{p}$. We use this sample proportion as a point estimate of the population proportion. We obtain a confidence interval for the population proportion by the general formula:

$$\text{Estimate} \pm (\text{reliability coefficient}) \times (\text{standard error})$$

Chapter 5 showed that when both np and $n(1 - p)$ are greater than 5, the sampling distribution of $\hat{p}$ is approximately normal with mean p and standard error $\sigma_{\hat{p}} = \sqrt{p(1 - p)/n}$. Since we are looking for an estimate of p, it must be unknown. Therefore, in practical situations we use $\hat{p}$ rather than p in the formula for the standard error. We obtain its estimate $s_{\hat{p}} = \sqrt{\hat{p}(1 - \hat{p})/n}$. When we can consider the sampling distribution of $\hat{p}$ approximately normal, we can obtain the reliability coefficient in the formula for the confidence interval from the table of the standard normal distribution. As indicated in Chapter 5, if the sample constitutes more than 5% of the population, we should use the finite population correction factor. The examples and exercises that follow assume that n is sufficiently small relative to N that the correction factor is not needed.

For estimating p, the reliability coefficient is z.

In summary, then, we may state the following:

When np and $n(1 - p)$ are both greater than 5, and when n is small relative to the size of the population, the approximate $100(1 - \alpha)\%$ confidence interval for p is given by

$$\hat{p} \pm z_{1-\alpha/2} \sqrt{\frac{\hat{p}(1 - \hat{p})}{n}} \qquad (6.16)$$

This interval is given the usual probabilistic and practical interpretations.

EXAMPLE 6.8 The personnel director of a large company, trying to find out what proportion of all persons who have ever been interviewed for any position have been hired, is willing to settle for a 95% confidence interval. A random sample of 500 interview records reveals that 76 (or 0.152) of the persons in the sample have been hired.

SOLUTION The 95% confidence interval for the population proportion, by Equation 6.16, is

$$0.152 \pm 1.96 \sqrt{\frac{(0.152)(0.848)}{500}}, \qquad 0.152 \pm 0.031, \qquad 0.121, 0.183$$

The interpretation of this interval is the same as the interpretation of the confidence interval for the arithmetic mean. In the long run, 95% of the intervals constructed in this manner include the population proportion. We are therefore 95% confident that the interval actually constructed contains the population proportion.

Exercises

 6.19 A consultant for an association of personnel directors wants to find what proportion of clerical personnel who change jobs do so because they are bored with their work. The consultant queries a random sample of 400 clerical workers who recently changed jobs. Two hundred state that they changed jobs because they were bored. The consultant prepares a 95% confidence interval for the true proportion changing jobs because of boredom. What are the lower and upper limits of this interval?

 6.20 A company wishes to estimate the proportion of its employees who have read with retention a safety leaflet that was distributed last week to all employees. A random sample of 300 employees is given a test to measure retention of the contents of the leaflet. Of those tested, 75 make a passing score. Construct a 95% confidence interval for the true proportion retaining sufficient knowledge of the contents of the leaflet to make a passing score.

 6.21 In a study of the reasons for employee turnover, an investigator draws a sample of 200 from a population of former employees of a firm. Of the 200, 140 say that they left because they couldn't get along with their supervisors. Construct a 95% confidence interval estimate of the true proportion who left the firm for this reason.

6.22 When you interview a random sample of 175 adults, 79 tell you that they feel that their community's most pressing social problem is drug and alcohol abuse. Construct a 95% confidence interval for the proportion in the population who hold that opinion.

6.7 ESTIMATING THE DIFFERENCE BETWEEN TWO POPULATION PROPORTIONS

It is often worthwhile to have some idea of the magnitude of the difference between two population proportions. For example, we may wish to compare—with respect to some characteristic of interest—men and women, two age groups, two types of firms, two socioeconomic groups, or two factories.

To estimate $p_1 - p_2$, the difference between the population proportions, we draw a simple random sample from each of the populations and use $\hat{p}_1 - \hat{p}_2$, the difference between the sample proportions. We may construct an interval estimate in the usual manner.

Chapter 5 showed that when n_1 and n_2 are both large, and the population proportions are not too close to 0 or 1, the sampling distribution of $\hat{p}_1 - \hat{p}_2$ for independent samples is approximately normally distributed with mean $p_1 - p_2$ and standard error

$$\sigma_{\hat{p}_1 - \hat{p}_2} = \sqrt{\frac{p_1(1 - p_1)}{n_1} + \frac{p_2(1 - p_2)}{n_2}}$$

Since p_1 and p_2 are unknown, the standard error has to be estimated by

$$s_{\hat{p}_1 - \hat{p}_2} = \sqrt{\frac{\hat{p}_1(1 - \hat{p}_1)}{n_1} + \frac{\hat{p}_2(1 - \hat{p}_2)}{n_2}}$$

For estimating $p_1 - p_2$, the reliability coefficient is z.

Under the given conditions, then, an approximate $100(1 - \alpha)\%$ confidence interval for $p_1 - p_2$ is given by

$$(\hat{p}_1 - \hat{p}_2) \pm z_{1-\alpha/2} \sqrt{\frac{\hat{p}_1(1 - \hat{p}_1)}{n_1} + \frac{\hat{p}_2(1 - \hat{p}_2)}{n_2}} \qquad (6.17)$$

EXAMPLE 6.9 An ad agency conducts a survey to study the characteristics of subscribers to two newspapers. A random sample of 500 subscribers to Newspaper A reveals that 300 have annual incomes in excess of $50,000. In the case of Newspaper B, 200 out of a random sample of 500 subscribers have annual incomes in excess of $50,000. Construct a 95% confidence interval for the difference between the two proportions of subscribers with annual incomes in excess of $50,000.

SOLUTION From the information given, we compute $\hat{p}_A = 300/500 = 0.6$ and $\hat{p}_B = 200/500 = 0.4$. Substituting in Equation 6.17 gives the desired interval:

$$(0.6 - 0.4) \pm 1.96 \sqrt{\frac{(0.6)(1 - 0.6)}{500} + \frac{(0.4)(1 - 0.4)}{500}}$$

$$0.2 \pm 1.96(0.03), \qquad 0.14, 0.26$$

We are 95% confident that the true difference is between 0.14 and 0.26, because in the long run approximately 95% of the intervals constructed in this manner would include the true difference.

Exercises

6.23 Doctors who have developed a new drug for the treatment of a certain disease treat a group of 400 patients suffering from the disease with the new drug. They treat another group of 400 patients with an alternative drug. At the end of two weeks, 320 of the patients receiving the new drug recover, whereas 240 of those taking the alternative drug recover. Construct the 95% confidence interval for the difference between the true proportions of patients who might be expected to respond to the two drugs.

6.24 A random sample of 350 salespersons and an independent random sample of 325 executives are questioned about their reading habits. Of the 350 salespersons, 105 say that they subscribe to car magazines. Of the executives, 130 say that they subscribe to car magazines. Construct the 90% confidence interval for the difference between the true proportions subscribing to car magazines.

 6.25 In a study of the types of errors made by employees in two factories owned by the same firm, researchers note the following facts. Construct a 95% confidence interval for $p_A - p_B$.

Factory	A	B
n	200	225
Proportion of errors due to employee carelessness	0.32	0.25

 6.26 A random sample of 200 female clerical workers and an independent random sample of 200 male clerical workers participate in a study conducted by a psychologist. In this study, 32 of the males and 11 of the females exhibit an intense dislike for their jobs. Construct a 99% confidence interval for the difference between the two population proportions. *99%*

6.8 DETERMINING SAMPLE SIZE FOR ESTIMATING MEANS

Up to this point, the problems and exercises have specified the sample size being used. But they have not mentioned how a particular sample size was decided on. One needs a method for determining how large a sample to take. Suppose that we want to estimate, with a confidence interval, the mean of a population. One of the first questions to arise is: How large should the sample be? We must consider this question seriously. Taking a larger sample than we need to achieve the desired results is a waste of resources. However, if the sample is too small, the results may be of no practical value. The key questions that bear on this problem are:

1. What precision is desired? That is, how close do we want our estimate to be to the true value? In other words, how wide would we like to make the confidence interval that we want to construct?
2. How much confidence do we want to place in our interval? That is, what confidence coefficient do we wish to employ?

To determine *n* for estimating μ, we need to know:
1. Desired precision
2. Desired confidence
3. σ^2

These questions bring to mind the nature of the confidence interval that we will eventually construct. This interval will be of the form

$$\bar{x} \pm z \frac{\sigma}{\sqrt{n}}$$

if we can ignore the finite population correction factor. The quantity

$$z \frac{\sigma}{\sqrt{n}}$$

is equal to one-half the confidence interval. If we can answer the first question, we can set up the following equation:

$$d = z \frac{\sigma}{\sqrt{n}} \qquad (6.18)$$

where d indicates how close to the true mean we want our estimate to be. That is, d is the precision of the estimator and is equal to one-half the desired interval width. If we solve Equation 6.18 for n,

$$n = \frac{z^2 \sigma^2}{d^2} \qquad (6.19)$$

Thus, if we can specify d, z, and σ^2 in advance, it is a simple matter to find n. We merely substitute the specified values into Equation 6.19.

   The value we specify for d varies from case to case. If we want a narrow interval, d will be small. The value of z depends on the level of confidence we want. And σ^2 depends on the variability present in the population of interest. As a general rule, σ^2 is unknown and has to be estimated.

Estimating σ^2

The most frequently used methods of estimating σ^2 are the following:

Sources of estimates
of σ:
1. Pilot sample
2. Similar studies
3. *R*/6

1. We may use the variance computed from a *pilot* or preliminary sample drawn from the population of interest, as an estimate of σ^2. We may count observations used in the pilot sample as part of the final sample. Therefore the number of observations we need after drawing the pilot sample is equal to $n - n_1$, where n is equal to the computed sample size and n_1 is the number of observations in the pilot sample.
2. We may have estimates of σ^2 from previous or similar studies.
3. If we feel that the population from which the sample is to be drawn is approximately normally distributed, we may use the fact that the range is approximately equal to 6 standard deviations to compute $\sigma \approx R/6$. This method requires some knowledge of the smallest and largest values of the variable in the population.

   When sampling is without replacement from a finite population, the finite population correction is appropriate. Equation 6.18 becomes

$$d = z \frac{\sigma}{\sqrt{n}} \sqrt{\frac{N - n}{N - 1}} \qquad (6.20)$$

which, when solved for n, gives

$$n = \frac{N z^2 \sigma^2}{d^2 (N - 1) + z^2 \sigma^2} \qquad (6.21)$$

Notice that if we ignore the finite population correction, Equation 6.21 can be reduced to Equation 6.19.

EXAMPLE 6.10 An advertising firm wants to estimate the average amount of money a certain type of store spent on advertising during the past year. Experience has shown the population variance to be about 1,800,000. How large a sample should the advertising firm take in order for the estimate to be within $500 of the true mean with 95% confidence?

SOLUTION Substituting the given data into Equation 6.19, we have

$$n = \frac{(1.96)^2(1,800,000)}{(500)^2} = 27.65 \approx 28$$

The advertising firm should take a sample of 28 establishments. (Note that n is always rounded up.)

Exercises

6.27 A plastics firm wishes to estimate the mean impact strength of a spool. How many spools should the company test if it wishes to be within 20 psi of the true value with 99% confidence? Previous experience indicates that an acceptable estimate of σ^2 is 4900.

6.28 A consultant for a chain of motels wants to estimate the average number of miles driven per day by families on vacation. The consultant obtains the names and addresses of vacationing families who stayed at motels in the chain during the past year. How large a sample should the consultant select in order to estimate the average daily mileage to within 25 miles with 95% confidence? It is felt that a reasonable estimate of σ^2 is 18,000.

6.29 A researcher with a company that employs 2500 workers wishes to estimate the mean travel time between the company and the employees' homes. The investigator wants a 99% confidence interval and an estimate that will be within 1 minute of the true mean. A small pilot sample yields a variance of 25 min^2. What size sample should the researcher draw?

6.30 A psychologist wants to construct an interval estimate of the mean IQ of a certain population of employees. The estimate is to be within 5 points of the true mean with 95% confidence. Previous experience indicates that the IQ's for the population of interest are approximately normally distributed with a variance of 100. The psychologist wants to know how large a sample to draw from the population.

6.9 DETERMINING SAMPLE SIZE FOR ESTIMATING PROPORTIONS

When we estimate a population proportion, we determine the sample size in about the same way as described above for estimating a population mean. We set half the desired interval d equal to the product of the reliability coefficient and the standard error. The assumption of random sampling and conditions warranting approximate normality of the distribution of $\hat{p}$ lead to the following formula for n, when sampling is with replacement or is from an infinite population:

$$n = \frac{z^2 pq}{d^2}$$

(6.22)

where $q = 1 - p$. If sampling is *without* replacement, the proper formula for n is

$$n = \frac{Nz^2pq}{d^2(N-1) + z^2pq}$$

(6.23)

When N is large in comparison to n (that is , $n/N \leq 0.05$), we may ignore the finite population correction, and Equation 6.23 reduces to Equation 6.22.

Both formulas require a knowledge of p, the proportion of elements in the population with the characteristic of interest. This is the parameter to be estimated. Obviously, it is unknown. Again, we may take a pilot sample and compute an estimate to use in place of p in the formula for n. Alternatively, we may have some good notion of the likely value of p that we can use in the formula. For example, a personnel director who wants to estimate the proportion of employees who have not completed high school may feel that p is about 0.10. In the formula for n, 0.10 would be used for p.

If we can't obtain a better estimate, we may set p equal to 0.5 in the formula for n. This gives a sample of sufficient size for the desired reliability and interval width, since it yields the maximum sample size. It may be larger than we need, however, in which case the sample will be more expensive than it would have been had we had a better estimate of p available. Use this procedure only if you cannot obtain a better estimate of p.

To determine n for estimating p, we need to know:
1. Desired precision
2. Desired confidence
3. An estimate of p

EXAMPLE 6.11 A market research firm wants to estimate the proportion of households in a certain area that have color television sets. The firm would like to estimate p to within 0.05 with 95% confidence. No estimate of p is available.

SOLUTION Since no better estimate of p is available, we must use 0.5. When appropriate substitutions are made in Equation 6.22, we have

$$n = \frac{(1.96)^2(0.5)(0.5)}{(0.05)^2} = 385$$

Exercises

6.31 An urban university will offer Saturday classes if student demand is sufficiently high. What size sample of students would you poll in order to estimate with 95% confidence, and to within 0.05, the proportion of students who would register for Saturday classes, if they were offered? Assume that no estimate of p is available.

6.32 A researcher in industrial medicine wants to determine what proportion of all shoe factories require that an employee provide a doctor's certificate after three or more days' absence for illness. What size sample should the researcher take in order to be within 0.05 of the true value with 95% confidence? The researcher feels that the true proportion cannot be more than 0.30.

6.33 A market-research analyst wishes to know how large a sample of the homes in a certain community to draw in order to find the proportion of the homes in which at least one member has seen a certain newspaper ad. There are 500 homes in the community. The analyst wants to be within 0.04 of the true proportion with 90% confidence. In a pilot

5.25

sample of 15 homes, 35% of the respondents indicate that someone in the home had seen the ad. How large a sample should be drawn?

Summary

This chapter introduced statistical inference procedures. The previous chapters provided the basic foundation for this and for the material in later chapters. In this chapter, the primary inference procedure discussed is estimation.

We first talked about point estimation and the properties of good estimators. You learned that a *point estimate* consists of a single numerical value computed from a sample. Since you cannot attach a statement of confidence to a point estimate alone, it is of limited value. *Interval estimates* or confidence intervals are of much greater use, since you can explicitly state the confidence you have that the interval contains the parameter you are estimating. The degree of confidence is equal to the percentage (or proportion) of all similarly constructed intervals that contain the parameter.

You learned that in many instances the general formula for a two-sided confidence interval is

$$\text{Estimate} \pm (\text{reliability coefficient}) \times (\text{standard error})$$

In this formula the degree of confidence we need determines the reliability coefficient. We compute the estimate and usually the standard error from sample data.

This chapter also introduced you to two possible *reliability coefficients, z* and *t.* Which reliability factor you should use depends on the specific situation. You learned the criteria for choosing between the two.

We can interpret a confidence interval in two ways. The *probabilistic interpretation* is stated in terms of what proportion of all similarly constructed intervals contain the estimated parameter. The *practical interpretation* is stated in terms of the degree of confidence we attach to the single interval that is computed.

In this chapter you learned to construct confidence intervals for population means, population proportions, the difference between two population means, the difference between two population proportions, and a mean of a population of paired differences.

You also learned how to compute the sample size you need to obtain a confidence interval for a population mean, a population proportion, the difference between two means, and the difference between two proportions.

Review Questions

1. What is statistical inference?

2. Why is estimation an important type of inference?

3. What is a point estimate?

4. Explain the meaning, as applied to estimators, of: **(a)** unbiasedness, **(b)** efficiency, **(c)** sufficiency, **(d)** consistency.

5. Define the following: **(a)** reliability coefficient, **(b)** confidence coefficient, **(c)** standard error, **(d)** estimator.

6. Give the general formula for a confidence interval.

7. State the probabilistic and practical interpretations of a confidence interval.

8. Of what use is the central limit theorem in estimation?

9. Describe the *t* distribution.

10. What are the assumptions underlying the use of the t distribution in estimating a single population mean?

11. What is the finite population correction? When can it be ignored?

12. What assumptions underlie the use of the t distribution to estimate the difference between two population means?

13. Explain the difference between a sampled population and a target population.

14. What is the rationale underlying the pooling of sample variances when one is testing the difference between means?

15. The widths of metal bars produced by a certain firm are normally distributed with a standard deviation of 0.02 in. A random sample of 25 bars is measured, and a mean of 2.49 in. is computed. Construct the 95% confidence interval for μ.

16. A quality-control engineer with a paper manufacturer wishes to estimate the mean diameter of a large shipment of logs. From a random sample of 49 logs, the engineer computes a mean of 32 in. and a standard deviation of 3.5 in.   **(a)** Construct the 95% confidence interval for μ.   **(b)** Construct the 99% confidence interval.   **(c)** Construct the 90% confidence interval.

17. Describe a situation from your particular area of interest in which a confidence interval for a mean difference would be meaningful. Use real or realistic data to obtain a sample of paired observations. Construct a 95% confidence interval for the mean difference.

18. A manufacturer designs a study to assess the effectiveness of an additive in prolonging the shelf life of bath salts. Two independent simple random samples consisting of 100 specimens with and 100 specimens without the additive are stored under identical conditions. The average life of the specimens with the additive is 32 months ($s^2 = 90$). For the specimens without the additive, the mean and variance are 24 and 160, respectively. The researcher is unwilling to assume that the populations are normally distributed.   **(a)** Construct the 95% confidence interval for the difference between the population means.   **(b)** Construct the 90% confidence interval.   **(c)** Construct the 99% confidence interval.

19. A random sample of 200 items produced in a certain factory is inspected for defectives. Ten defective items are discovered. Construct the 95% confidence interval for the true proportion defective.

20. A random sample of 100 people in a small town is asked to evaluate two brands of coffee. Of the sample, 70 say that they prefer Brand A.   **(a)** Construct the 95% confidence interval for the true proportion preferring Brand A.   **(b)** Construct the 90% confidence interval.   **(c)** Construct the 99% confidence interval.

21. Two apple orchards are sprayed with two different insecticides to prevent infestation of the mature fruit by fruit flies. At harvest time, a random sample of 500 apples from each orchard is examined, with the following results: Of the 500 apples from trees sprayed with Insecticide A, 50 are infested. Of those from trees sprayed with Insecticide B, 25 are infested. Construct the 95% confidence interval for the difference between the true proportions infested.

22. A firm specializing in direct-mail questionnaires has developed a new format and technique that it believes will get a higher response rate than the standard procedure. How large a sample of a particular type of respondent should the firm use in order to estimate within 0.03 the true proportion who would respond to the new procedure? The desired confidence level is 95%. Of those included in a pilot sample, 80% responded.

23. Each member of a random sample of 36 sixth-grade children keeps a record for one week of the amount of time spent watching television. The mean and standard deviation computed from the results are 15 hours and 6 hours, respectively. Construct a 99% confidence interval for the population mean.

24. A random sample of 100 records kept by a utility company on wood utility poles placed in service since 1900 reveals a sample mean life and standard deviation of 10.5 years and 5 years, respectively. Construct a 95% confidence interval for the population mean.

25. A researcher selects a random sample of 150 wood utility poles currently in service. The survey reveals that 15% of the poles need to be replaced. Construct a 99% confidence interval for the population proportion in need of replacement.

26. A random sample of 169 households in a certain area is selected as part of a study of the recreation habits of community residents. The respondents indicate a mean amount of $350 spent annually for recreation per family. The sample standard deviation is $65. Construct a 95% confidence interval for the population mean.

27. Of the households referred to in question 26, 60% had two or more children. Construct the 95% confidence interval for the proportion of households in the area with two or more children.

28. In a survey of adult residents of a rural area, 80 out of 150 respondents say that they prefer a certain type of music. Construct a 99% confidence interval for the population proportion.

29. Ⓒ A manufacturer of fire alarm systems makes an alarm that is sensitive to smoke. The quality-control department tests a random sample of 15 alarms to determine the level of smoke concentration required for activation. The results, coded for ease of calculation, are as follows: 3, 8, 8, 9, 9, 6, 9, 6, 2, 5, 6, 4, 8, 7, 5. Construct a 95% confidence interval for the population mean.

30. A radio station conducts a survey to determine what local citizens perceive to be the most pressing national problems. Of 350 adults contacted, 80 say that they feel that declining moral standards are the most serious problem. Construct the 90% confidence interval for the population proportion that holds this opinion.

31. The editor of a newspaper wishes to know what proportion of the subscribers regularly read the business news section. In a random sample of 500 subscribers, 200 state that they are regular readers of business news. Construct a 90% confidence interval for the true proportion of all subscribers who regularly read the business news.

32. The mean weight of a sample of 100 trucks weighed at a certain highway weigh station is found to be 50,000 lb with a standard deviation of 3600 lb. Construct a 95% confidence interval for the population mean.

33. During a winter shortage of natural gas, citizens are asked to lower the thermostats in their homes to 65° or lower. A random sample of 150 households in a certain town reveals that 130 have thermostats set at 65° or lower. Construct the 95% confidence interval for the proportion of all households in the community that have lowered thermostats.

34. A survey of 800 regular listeners to a certain radio station reveals that 600 are teenagers. Construct the 90% confidence interval for the true proportion of teenagers in the audience.

35. In a random sample of 100 households in a suburb, selected as part of a study of energy consumption, the mean amount spent for electricity during December is $42, with a standard deviation of $50. Construct a 90% confidence interval for the population mean.

36. A research chemist wishes to estimate the mean amount of oxygen (in liters) required to bring about a particular chemical reaction when the oxygen is mixed with a fixed amount of sulfur. He wants to be within 0.10 liter of the true mean with 95% confidence. Previous studies indicate that the variance of the oxygen requirements for this type of chemical reaction is about 0.09. What size sample does this investigator need?

37. A student working for a doctorate in education wishes to draw a sample of high school freshmen in order to estimate the average amount of time per day they spend studying. A standard deviation of 20 minutes is reported by a researcher who conducts a similar study. The student wants a 95% confidence interval for the population mean. How large should the sample be if the estimate should be within 3 minutes of the true value?

38. The following data give the means and standard deviations of nonverbal IQ scores obtained from independent simple random samples drawn from two populations of factory employees: For Sample I, $n = 19$, $\bar{x} = 110$, and $s = 10$; for Sample II, $n = 23$, $\bar{x} = 95$, and $s = 15$. Assume that each of the two populations of nonverbal IQ scores is approximately normally distributed and that the population variances are equal. Construct the 95% confidence interval for the difference between the two population means.

39. New employees hired to perform highly technical tasks are randomly assigned to one of two classes for training. Class A uses a computer-assisted instruction technique to teach employees the fundamentals of the job. Instruction in Class B follows traditional patterns. Performance tests are administered to each employee in the study after 6 months on the job. The results are as follows: For Class A, $n = 35$, $\bar{x} = 85$, and $s = 10$; for Class B, $n = 32$, $\bar{x} = 71$, and $s = 15$. Construct a 95% confidence interval for $\mu_A - \mu_B$.

40. Ⓒ A manufacturer who wishes to increase production per employee selects a department with 12 employees for an experiment. The manufacturer tries to improve working conditions in this department through renovation and employee incentives. The following table shows the mean number of items produced per day by each employee one month before and one month after the changes are made. Construct the 95% confidence interval for the mean difference.

Mean number of items produced per day

Employee	1	2	3	4	5	6	7	8	9	10	11	12
Before	75	61	62	68	58	70	59	79	68	80	64	75
After	82	70	74	80	65	80	70	88	77	90	75	87

41. An economist is studying the attitudes of local citizens toward the national energy program. As part of the proposed interview, respondents will be asked to indicate whether they agree or disagree with the statement, "The federal government should establish a strong energy department." She wants to know how large a sample to take in order to estimate the true proportion of citizens who agree with the statement. She wishes to be within 0.025 of the true value with 95% confidence. Researchers who conducted a similar study in another locality found that 60% of the people interviewed agreed with the statement. How large should the sample be?

42. The personnel director of a large firm wants to estimate the proportion of the 2000 employees of the firm who plan to go out of the state during vacation. How large a sample should the personnel director take if the estimate is to be within 0.05 of the true value with 99% confidence? Last year 70% of the employees polled went out of state during their vacations.

43. Researchers with an agrichemical company deliberately infect 200 plants with a certain disease. They then treat half the plants with Chemical A and half with Chemical B. Of the plants treated with Chemical A, 75 survive. Of those treated with Chemical B, 64 survive. Construct a 90% confidence interval for $p_A - p_B$.

44. A random sample of 300 blue-collar workers in a certain city reveals that 75% are planning to vote for a particular candidate for mayor. Of a random sample of 200 white-collar workers, 66% state that they are planning to vote for the candidate. Construct a 95% confidence interval for the difference between the two population proportions.

45. ⓒ A simple random sample of 15 employees who work downtown reports the following distances (in miles) traveled to work each day: 13, 21, 35, 10, 24, 35, 19, 11, 25, 17, 25, 11, 11, 6, 6. Construct a 95% confidence interval for the mean distance traveled by the population of employees from which the sample was drawn.

46. ⓒ Each of a random sample of 9 automobiles of a certain make is test-driven. The number of miles traveled per gallon of gasoline is recorded for each. The results are as follows: 23, 25, 21, 22, 23, 22, 21, 24, 22. Construct a 99% confidence interval for the population mean.

47. ⓒ During a local health fair, a simple random sample of 10 business executives suffering from hypertension yields the following systolic blood pressure readings: 171, 190, 157, 181, 178, 176, 167, 165, 198, 165. Construct a 90% confidence interval for the population mean.

48. ⓒ Researchers have found that it is not profitable for your firm to try to sell a new product to persons who live in houses that have fewer than 7 rooms. In fact, the researchers have recommended that at least 30% of houses in prospective market areas have 7 rooms or more. You want to know whether you should enter a new market area. You ask a market research firm to conduct a survey of households in the area to find out the number of rooms per dwelling unit. The results, for a random sample of 60 dwelling units, are as follows. Construct a 95% confidence interval for the proportion of dwelling units in the population with 7 or more rooms. Should you market your product in the area?

3	2	4	4	5	7	5	2	4	3	6	6	5	5	2	5	6	1	5	6
1	6	3	6	7	5	4	6	4	3	6	5	8	6	6	3	5	4	3	4
6	6	7	6	8	4	5	7	5	6	7	6	7	7	7	5	3	6	5	4

49. ⓒ A sample of 25 apples from a truckload shipment yields the following weights in ounces: 16, 11, 14, 20, 16, 13, 14, 17, 10, 18, 11, 20, 14, 15, 19, 16, 10, 15, 16, 14, 15, 20, 18, 18, 20. **(a)** Compute the mean weight of the apples in the sample. **(b)** Compute the median weight. **(c)** Compute the sample variance and standard deviation. **(d)** Use these data to construct a 95% confidence interval for the population mean. **(e)** Before vouching for the legitimacy of the inference procedure in part (d), is there any further information you would like to have? **(f)** The owner of the orchard in which the apples were grown claims that the mean weight of the apples in the truck is 16 ounces. Do you think that these data support the owner's claim? Explain.

50. ⓒ Quality-control experts with a garment manufacturer have found that, on the average, an employee performs 30 defective operations in a week when morale is high. When morale is low, the number of defective operations is higher. During a recent week a random sample of 12 employees performed the following number of defective operations: 40, 37, 32, 34, 31, 36, 34, 32, 33, 31, 35, 33. Construct a 99% confidence interval for the mean number of defective operations performed by the employees in the sampled population. On the basis of these data, does it appear that morale may be low?

51. ⓒ A sales manager has found that salespeople who spend more time per customer call are more successful. The most successful salespeople spend, on the average, 50 minutes per customer call. A random sample of 20 sales calls from the records of a new salesperson reveals the following amount of time in minutes spent on sales calls: 35, 41,

24, 26, 25, 53, 41, 40, 34, 39, 57, 23, 28, 53, 30, 79, 81, 90, 79, 88. Construct a 95% confidence interval for the population mean. Does it appear from these data that the new salesperson may become one of the firm's more successful salespeople?

 52. A researcher wants to estimate, for a large population of employees, the proportion who have ever sought professional help for an emotional or mental problem. Another researcher found the proportion in a similar population to be 0.15. The present researcher, who wants to be within 0.03 of the true proportion with 99% confidence, wants to know how large a sample to draw.

53. Ⓒ Select a simple random sample of size 50 from the population of employed heads of households given in Appendix II. Construct a 95% confidence interval for the proportion of women in the population. Compare your results with those of your classmates and determine how many of the intervals constructed by the class include the true proportion, which is 0.20.

54. Ⓒ Select a simple random sample of size 50 from the population of employed heads of households given in Appendix II. Then do the following: **(a)** Construct a 95% confidence interval for the population mean commuting distance to work, using the finite population correction factor. **(b)** From the same data, construct a 95% confidence interval for the same population mean, but ignore the finite population correction factor. Compare this interval with the one you found in step (a). **(c)** Construct a 95% confidence interval for the mean annual salary of the persons in the population.

55. Ⓒ From the population of employed heads of households given in Appendix II, select two simple random samples, one from the population of males and one from the population of females. **(a)** Construct a 95% confidence interval for the difference in population means (males versus females) for the variable "annual income." **(b)** Using the same two samples, construct a 95% confidence interval for the difference between the proportion of males who hold managerial positions and the proportion of females who hold managerial positions.

 56. Ⓒ In a survey of office workers in a large city, each subject in a random sample of 35 is asked to report the number of times during the previous month he or she has eaten an evening meal at a restaurant other than a fast-food establishment. The results were as follows. Construct a 95% confidence interval for the mean of the sampled population. Who do you think might be interested in the results of this survey? Define the sampled population.

5	0	9	1	9	8	5	5	2	6	4	9	0	3
7	1	9	7	2	3	5	2	8	5	9	4	7	3
1	3	4	3	8	1	7							

57. In a survey of college students who own automobiles, a random sample of 100 students is asked to report information on the following variables:

1. Gender—male, female

2. Resident—on campus, off campus

3. Type of car owned—foreign (F), American-made (A)

4. Number of miles driven during previous week

The responses are shown in the table that follows on pages 183 and 184.

Subject	1 Gender	2 Live on campus?	3 Type of car	4 Number of miles driven
1	F	Yes	A	43
2	M	Yes	A	77
3	M	No	F	91
4	F	No	A	48
5	F	Yes	F	39
6	M	No	A	72
7	M	No	A	99
8	F	Yes	A	56
9	M	No	A	100
10	M	Yes	A	86
11	M	No	A	99
12	M	No	F	78
13	F	Yes	A	45
14	F	No	F	64
15	F	Yes	F	67
16	M	No	F	99
17	M	Yes	A	88
18	M	No	F	81
19	M	No	A	98
20	F	Yes	F	67
21	M	No	A	88
22	M	Yes	A	98
23	M	No	A	85
24	F	Yes	F	58
25	M	No	A	99
26	F	No	A	58
27	M	Yes	F	84
28	M	Yes	A	73
29	M	No	A	76
30	M	No	F	87
31	F	Yes	F	55
32	M	Yes	F	72
33	M	No	F	81
34	F	Yes	A	68
35	M	Yes	A	61
36	F	Yes	A	67
37	M	No	F	85
38	M	Yes	A	68
39	M	No	F	99
40	F	Yes	A	40
41	M	Yes	A	70
42	M	No	F	90
43	F	Yes	A	44
44	F	No	F	51
45	F	No	A	64
46	F	Yes	A	47
47	M	Yes	A	75
48	M	No	A	91
49	F	Yes	A	39
50	M	No	A	102
51	M	Yes	F	87
52	M	No	A	97
53	F	Yes	A	54
54	M	No	F	89
55	M	No	A	87

Subject	1 Gender	2 Live on campus?	3 Type of car	4 Number of miles driven
56	F	No	F	82
57	M	Yes	A	64
58	M	No	A	40
59	F	Yes	A	62
60	M	No	F	78
61	M	No	A	82
62	M	No	A	78
63	F	Yes	F	52
64	M	Yes	A	56
65	M	Yes	F	57
66	M	Yes	A	56
67	M	No	A	75
68	F	Yes	F	47
69	F	Yes	A	45
70	M	Yes	A	59
71	F	No	F	60
72	M	Yes	A	47
73	M	No	A	75
74	F	Yes	A	42
75	F	Yes	A	38
76	F	No	A	90
77	F	Yes	A	54
78	M	Yes	F	50
79	M	No	A	68
80	F	No	F	75
81	F	Yes	A	66
82	M	Yes	A	30
83	F	No	A	58
84	M	No	A	54
85	M	No	A	64
86	F	Yes	F	56
87	F	Yes	A	60
88	M	Yes	F	26
89	M	No	A	73
90	M	Yes	A	27
91	M	No	A	80
92	F	Yes	F	51
93	M	No	A	62
94	M	Yes	F	20
95	F	Yes	F	60
96	M	Yes	A	28
97	M	No	A	59
98	F	Yes	A	38
99	F	No	F	38
100	F	No	A	62

Define the sampled population. Who do you think would be interested in the information collected in this survey? Explain how you think a survey of this type could best be conducted.

58. Ⓒ Refer to the data in Exercise 57. Construct a 95% confidence interval for the proportion of females in the sampled population.

59. Ⓒ Refer to the data in Exercise 57. Construct a 95% confidence interval for the proportion of males in the sampled population.

60. ⓒ Refer to the data in Exercise 57. Construct a 90% confidence interval for the proportion of students in the population who drive foreign cars.

61. ⓒ Refer to the data in Exercise 57. Construct a 90% confidence interval for the proportion of students in the population who drive American-made cars.

62. ⓒ Refer to the data in Exercise 57. Assume that the males constitute a simple random sample from one population and the females an independent simple random sample from another population. Define these two populations. From the information given, what is the best point estimate of the population proportion of males who drive foreign cars? What is the best point estimate of the population proportion of females who drive foreign cars?

63. ⓒ Construct a 90% confidence interval for the difference between the two population proportions for which point estimates were computed in Exercise 62.

64. ⓒ Refer to Exercise 57. Construct a 95% confidence interval for the mean number of miles driven during the previous week by the sampled population.

65. ⓒ Refer to Exercise 57. Assume that the females are a simple random sample from one population and the males are an independent simple random sample from another population. Define these two populations. What is the best point estimate of the mean number of miles driven by the population of females? What is the best point estimate of the mean number of miles driven by the population of males?

66. ⓒ Construct a 99% confidence interval for the mean number of miles driven by the population of females defined in Exercise 65.

67. ⓒ Construct a 99% confidence interval for the mean number of miles driven by the population of males defined in Exercise 65.

68. ⓒ Construct a 99% confidence interval for the difference between the mean number of miles driven by the two populations defined in Exercise 65.

69. ⓒ Refer to Exercise 65. For the population of females, construct a 95% confidence interval for the proportion who live on campus.

70. ⓒ Refer to Exercise 65. For the population of males, construct a 95% confidence interval for the proportion who live on campus.

71. ⓒ Construct a 95% confidence interval for the difference between the proportions who live on campus for the two populations defined in Exercise 65.

72. ⓒ The director of a city tourist bureau conducts a survey of a random sample of out-of-state tourists who visited the city during the previous year. The sampled population consists of individuals and families who traveled by automobile and stayed in motels or hotels. Among the questions asked on the survey were the following:

1. How many miles did you travel while on vacation last year?

2. What type of accommodations did you patronize?
    1 Economy-priced motel or hotel
    0 Regular-price or luxury motel or hotel

The following are the results.

Respondent	Miles driven	Type of accommodations	Respondent	Miles driven	Type of accommodations
1	1110	1	6	842	0
2	1499	1	7	2144	1
3	1316	0	8	1596	1
4	1190	0	9	1713	1
5	1097	0	10	1791	0

Respondent	Miles driven	Type of accommodations	Respondent	Miles driven	Type of accommodations
11	2047	1	68	2420	1
12	1463	1	69	1078	0
13	1417	1	70	1750	0
14	1576	1	71	1018	0
15	991	0	72	1811	0
16	1931	1	73	1680	1
17	1794	1	74	1162	1
18	998	1	75	1775	0
19	989	0	76	1501	0
20	994	1	77	1685	1
21	1129	0	78	2130	0
22	1518	0	79	1349	1
23	1513	1	80	1789	1
24	1290	0	81	1813	0
25	1659	1	82	1696	1
26	1918	1	83	1742	0
27	1401	0	84	1447	1
28	1837	0	85	2041	0
29	1799	1	86	1396	1
30	1242	0	87	1632	1
31	1683	1	88	1666	0
32	1544	1	89	1306	0
33	922	1	90	1546	0
34	1266	0	91	1246	1
35	1364	1	92	1333	1
36	1321	0	93	1755	0
37	1591	1	94	1521	0
38	1812	0	95	1473	0
39	1216	0	96	2068	1
40	1436	0	97	1111	0
41	1757	1	98	1568	1
42	1789	1	99	2099	0
43	1796	0	100	1713	1
44	1612	1	101	1426	1
45	950	1	102	1929	1
46	868	1	103	1097	0
47	1324	0	104	1172	0
48	1435	0	105	1717	1
49	1592	0	106	1658	1
50	1253	0	107	1968	1
51	2175	1	108	1402	0
52	1815	1	109	1839	0
53	980	1	110	1157	1
54	604	1	111	2085	0
55	1433	0	112	1692	1
56	1423	0	113	959	0
57	2186	1	114	1007	0
58	1411	1	115	1076	1
59	1310	0	116	1227	0
60	1131	0	117	1206	0
61	1368	1	118	2075	0
62	1577	1	119	1226	1
63	1549	1	120	1488	1
64	1025	1	121	1136	1
65	1399	1	122	1294	1
66	2018	1	123	1113	1
67	1722	1	124	1678	1

Respondent	Miles driven	Type of accommodations	Respondent	Miles driven	Type of accommodations
125	1888	0	182	1587	1
126	2125	0	183	1056	1
127	1690	0	184	1620	0
128	2043	1	185	1372	1
129	1267	1	186	1350	0
130	1723	0	187	1182	0
131	1013	1	188	1466	1
132	1371	0	189	1375	1
133	1490	0	190	1097	1
134	1135	0	191	1620	0
135	2170	1	192	1763	0
136	1793	1	193	1422	0
137	950	1	194	1290	0
138	1464	0	195	1364	1
139	1897	1	196	948	1
140	1456	0	197	1187	0
141	1687	0	198	445	1
142	996	1	199	1138	1
143	1405	1	200	1739	1
144	1286	1	201	1088	1
145	1521	1	202	2065	1
146	1598	0	203	2188	0
147	1421	0	204	1242	0
148	1204	1	205	1683	0
149	1390	1	206	707	1
150	1442	0	207	1658	0
151	1085	0	208	1483	1
152	791	0	209	1251	1
153	2542	1	210	1707	1
154	1776	1	211	1222	0
155	952	0	212	834	0
156	1103	0	213	843	1
157	1830	0	214	1404	1
158	1364	0	215	1344	1
159	1355	0	216	1905	0
160	805	1	217	1258	1
161	1052	1	218	1654	0
162	1697	1	219	2191	0
163	1673	1	220	1788	0
164	1591	1	221	1045	0
165	1488	1	222	971	1
166	1234	1	223	1561	0
167	1348	0	224	1877	1
168	1092	0	225	1542	1
169	1730	0	226	758	0
170	1821	0	227	1059	1
171	1780	0	228	1529	1
172	1360	0	229	1605	0
173	1403	0	230	1619	0
174	682	1	231	1615	1
175	1728	1	232	1339	1
176	1748	1	233	1579	0
177	1877	1	234	1851	1
178	1637	0	235	1535	1
179	1850	1	236	1834	1
180	1633	0	237	2019	1
181	1445	1	238	1097	1

Respondent	Miles driven	Type of accommodations	Respondent	Miles driven	Type of accommodations
239	1528	1	297	2034	1
240	1931	1	298	1109	0
241	1274	1	299	1661	0
242	886	0	300	1514	1
243	1282	0	301	1470	0
244	1323	1	302	2069	1
245	1014	1	303	1376	1
246	2230	0	304	1342	0
247	1859	0	305	1878	1
248	1920	1	306	1773	1
249	2055	0	307	1023	1
250	1502	1	308	871	0
251	1037	0	309	1255	1
252	1477	0	310	1103	0
253	2115	1	311	1511	0
254	1556	0	312	1266	0
255	1820	1	313	1007	1
256	1442	1	314	1684	1
257	1627	1	315	1437	1
258	1340	1	316	756	1
259	1329	0	317	1823	1
260	1400	1	318	1451	0
261	1349	1	319	1450	1
262	1746	0	320	1513	1
263	793	0	321	1995	1
264	1383	0	322	1468	1
265	1451	0	323	1578	0
266	1280	0	324	905	1
267	1420	0	325	1865	1
268	1497	1	326	1372	0
269	2076	1	327	1707	1
270	1078	1	328	696	1
271	1526	1	329	1655	0
272	1558	0	330	1785	0
273	1802	1	331	962	0
274	904	1	332	2010	0
275	858	0	333	712	1
276	1350	1	334	2128	0
277	1225	0	335	1146	1
278	1740	1	336	829	1
279	1075	0	337	1668	1
280	740	1	338	1453	0
281	1256	1	339	880	1
282	1453	0	340	1551	1
283	1167	0	341	2186	0
284	1583	0	342	1603	0
285	1733	1	343	2291	1
286	1726	0	344	2123	0
287	2258	1	345	1126	0
288	1093	0	346	1483	0
289	1766	0	347	1836	0
290	706	1	348	793	0
291	1630	1	349	1434	1
292	1487	1	350	862	1
293	1479	1	351	1610	0
294	1522	1	352	2053	1
295	1214	1	353	1472	0
296	2098	0	354	1286	1

Respondent	Miles driven	Type of accommodations	Respondent	Miles driven	Type of accommodations
355	1769	1	413	1339	1
356	1423	1	414	978	0
357	1793	0	415	150	0
358	1724	1	416	1703	0
359	1570	0	417	1879	1
360	1200	0	418	988	1
361	1020	0	419	1122	1
362	1730	0	420	1270	1
363	1955	0	421	1492	0
364	1498	0	422	1667	0
365	1521	0	423	2034	0
366	1403	1	424	729	1
367	1256	1	425	1759	1
368	1466	1	426	2588	1
369	1803	0	427	1162	1
370	2271	1	428	1494	1
371	1075	0	429	1218	0
372	2031	0	430	1364	1
373	1684	0	431	1359	1
374	750	1	432	1594	0
375	817	1	433	864	0
376	1626	1	434	1333	1
377	1723	1	435	1046	1
378	1220	0	436	2057	0
379	1679	1	437	2131	1
380	1052	1	438	1528	1
381	1790	0	439	2043	1
382	1555	0	440	2085	1
383	1350	1	441	992	0
384	1365	0	442	1806	1
385	1429	1	443	976	0
386	1418	0	444	336	1
387	1484	0	445	1196	1
388	1331	1	446	1782	0
389	1437	0	447	1625	1
390	1358	1	448	1229	1
391	1500	1	449	1108	0
392	1506	0	450	1648	0
393	1261	1	451	1528	0
394	1773	1	452	1071	1
395	1131	0	453	1357	0
396	1812	0	454	1231	1
397	871	0	455	2033	0
398	1074	1	456	1277	0
399	1827	1	457	1663	1
400	2090	1	458	1318	0
401	1796	1	459	1660	0
402	1352	0	460	1103	0
403	1987	0	461	1387	0
404	1934	1	462	1776	1
405	1229	1	463	620	1
406	1627	1	464	1354	0
407	1709	0	465	2024	0
408	1317	0	466	1004	1
409	1029	1	467	1749	1
410	1540	1	468	1166	1
411	1794	0	469	1848	1
412	1718	0	470	1393	1

Respondent	Miles driven	Type of accommodations	Respondent	Miles driven	Type of accommodations
471	1158	0	529	1117	1
472	769	0	530	1636	0
473	1060	0	531	2730	0
474	1301	1	532	1100	0
475	1711	1	533	1440	0
476	831	0	534	1290	0
477	1934	1	535	804	1
478	1210	1	536	1680	1
479	1705	1	537	2277	1
480	988	1	538	1402	1
481	1606	0	539	1474	1
482	1654	1	540	1951	1
483	962	0	541	980	1
484	1916	1	542	1152	1
485	1975	1	543	638	1
486	1351	1	544	2357	0
487	1854	1	545	1814	1
488	1723	1	546	504	1
489	1221	1	547	1917	0
490	2169	1	548	1633	1
491	1691	1	549	1651	0
492	1561	0	550	1447	1
493	1490	0	551	1350	1
494	1445	0	552	1508	1
495	2380	0	553	1524	0
496	1865	1	554	971	1
497	1214	1	555	1855	0
498	1475	1	556	1333	1
499	1049	0	557	1962	1
500	1550	1	558	1442	1
501	1819	1	559	1199	1
502	1214	0	560	1843	1
503	1651	0	561	1157	1
504	1288	0	562	2135	1
505	579	0	563	1741	0
506	1994	0	564	2106	1
507	1348	1	565	1446	0
508	1595	0	566	1483	1
509	1521	1	567	1590	1
510	2126	1	568	1765	1
511	1668	1	569	967	0
512	1257	1	570	1858	0
513	1693	1	571	1446	1
514	1681	1	572	889	1
515	1408	0	573	1418	1
516	1993	0	574	1802	1
517	1392	1	575	1817	1
518	1694	1	576	1456	1
519	464	1	577	1395	1
520	1607	1	578	1577	0
521	1925	0	579	1476	1
522	1782	1	580	1565	1
523	1630	0	581	2185	1
524	1200	0	582	1673	1
525	1659	0	583	1789	1
526	1518	1	584	1421	0
527	932	1	585	2060	1
528	1709	1	586	1608	1

Respondent	Miles driven	Type of accommodations	Respondent	Miles driven	Type of accommodations
587	1139	0	644	924	1
588	1915	1	645	925	1
589	1512	0	646	1497	1
590	1818	1	647	1885	0
591	2351	1	648	1240	1
592	1522	0	649	1083	1
593	1501	1	650	1908	1
594	1529	1	651	1403	0
595	1891	1	652	1484	1
596	1506	1	653	1606	1
597	905	1	654	1490	0
598	1884	1	655	2147	0
599	1000	1	656	1045	0
600	1359	1	657	1545	0
601	1004	1	658	1818	0
602	1555	1	659	859	0
603	1548	1	660	714	1
604	1993	0	661	1239	1
605	1412	0	662	1943	0
606	1833	1	663	1314	1
607	1374	1	664	1246	1
608	1487	0	665	1381	0
609	1137	1	666	1988	1
610	1547	0	667	719	1
611	1894	1	668	726	0
612	1454	0	669	2219	1
613	1835	1	670	1119	0
614	1575	1	671	1290	0
615	1124	0	672	1915	0
616	1944	0	673	1259	1
617	666	1	674	1486	0
618	1269	0	675	1164	1
619	1578	0	676	579	1
620	1144	0	677	1438	0
621	1550	1	678	2426	1
622	1552	1	679	1757	1
623	1837	0	680	1489	1
624	2137	1	681	1560	0
625	1314	0	682	916	1
626	1386	1	683	1971	1
627	2045	1	684	1339	1
628	1485	0	685	751	0
629	1895	0	686	1220	0
630	1764	1	687	1720	1
631	1913	1	688	1463	0
632	1586	1	689	2236	0
633	1217	1	690	1861	1
634	1674	1	691	1591	1
635	1086	1	692	1567	1
636	2056	1	693	1467	0
637	1622	0	694	1896	1
638	1746	1	695	1202	0
639	2124	1	696	1484	0
640	1430	1	697	1523	1
641	2052	0	698	2081	0
642	1352	0	699	1202	0
643	1721	1	700	1605	0

Construct a 95% confidence interval for the mean number of miles driven by the respondents in the sampled population.

73. ⓒ Construct a 95% confidence interval for the population proportion who stayed at economy-priced hotels and motels.

74. ⓒ Pretend that the data in Exercise 72 are for a population rather than a sample. Select a simple random sample of 15 respondents from this population. Construct a 95% confidence interval for the mean number of miles driven by the population. Does your confidence interval contain the true population mean? Compare your results with those of your classmates. What proportion of the intervals constructed by class members contain the true population mean?

75. ⓒ Pretend that the data in Exercise 72 are for a population. Select a simple random sample of 35 respondents from this population. Construct a 95% confidence interval for the proportion of the population that stayed at economy-priced motels and hotels.

76. Pretend that the data in Exercise 72 are for two populations: (1) vacationers who stayed at economy-priced motels and hotels, and (2) vacationers who stayed at regular-price or luxury motels and hotels. Select a simple random sample of size 15 from the respondents who stayed at economy-priced motels and hotels. Select an independent simple random sample of size 10 from the respondents who stayed at regular-price or luxury motels and hotels. Construct a 95% confidence interval for the difference between the two population means. On the basis of your confidence interval, do you believe that the population means are different? Compare your results with those of your classmates.

77. ⓒ Select a simple random sample from the list of companies in Appendix III. (Ask your instructor how large your sample should be.) For each company in your sample, record the data on each of the six variables. Construct a 95% confidence interval for the population mean assets. *Reminder:* You may need to use the finite population correction factor.

78. ⓒ Refer to Exercise 77. Construct a 95% confidence interval for the population mean sales.

79. ⓒ Refer to Exercise 77. Construct a 95% confidence interval for the population mean market value.

80. ⓒ Refer to Exercise 77. Construct a 95% confidence interval for the population mean net profits.

81. ⓒ Refer to Exercise 77. Construct a 95% confidence interval for the population mean cash flow.

82. ⓒ Refer to Exercise 77. Construct a 95% confidence interval for the population mean number employed.

83. ⓒ Refer to Exercise 77. Construct a 95% confidence interval for the proportion of companies in the population with assets of $1 billion or more.

84. ⓒ Refer to Exercise 77. Construct a 95% confidence interval for the proportion of companies in the population with sales of $1 billion or more.

85. ⓒ Refer to Exercise 77. Construct a 95% confidence interval for the proportion of companies in the population with a market value of $1 billion or more.

86. ⓒ Refer to Exercise 77. Construct a 95% confidence interval for the proportion of companies in the population with net profits of $100 million or more.

87. ⓒ Refer to Exercise 77. Construct a 95% confidence interval for the proportion of companies in the population with a cash flow of $1 billion or more.

88. Ⓒ Refer to Exercise 77. Construct a 95% confidence interval for the proportion of companies in the population with 50,000 or more employees.

PRACTICE WITH REAL DATA

Devise a scheme by which you can select a simple random sample of 40 magazines and journals (omit newspapers) currently available in your library. Obtain the annual subscription price for each. Construct a 95% confidence interval for the mean annual subscription price for all the magazines and journals available in the library.

7.

Statistical Inference II: Hypothesis Testing

CHAPTER OBJECTIVES: In this chapter we discuss the second type of statistical inference, hypothesis testing. You will note some similarities as well as differences between hypothesis testing and the interval estimation that you learned about in Chapter 6. The same parameters are of interest. However, in this chapter you will analyze sample data to see whether they support or fail to support a speculation (hypothesis) about the magnitudes of the parameters. In Chapter 6, you were not concerned with preanalysis conjectures about parameters. Instead, you used sample data to help you form an opinion about the magnitudes of parameters.

After studying this chapter and working the exercises, you should be able to do the following.

1. List seven steps that you can follow in testing a hypothesis
2. Conduct tests of hypotheses about values of the following parameters: (a) a population mean, (b) a population proportion, (c) the difference between two population means, (d) the difference between two population proportions, (e) a mean of a population of paired differences
3. Compute a *p* value for each test

There are two types of statistical inference—estimation, which was covered in Chapter 6, and hypothesis testing, which is the subject of this chapter.

The purpose of hypothesis testing, like that of estimation, is to help one reach a decision about a population by examining the data contained in a sample from that population.

In the examples and exercises of this chapter, the samples we refer to are simple random samples. In Section 7.1, we cover some general concepts of hypothesis testing. In succeeding sections of the chapter, we shall cover specific tests of hypotheses in detail.

Again, *the sampled population may not always be the same as the target population*. When using hypothesis testing, you should exercise the same caution in distinguishing between these two kinds of population that we suggested in connection with interval estimation.

7.1 HYPOTHESIS TESTING—SOME GENERAL CONSIDERATIONS

A hypothesis is a statement about one or more populations.

We may define a *hypothesis* simply as *a statement about one or more populations.* The hypotheses of interest here are those concerned with one or more parameters of the population or populations about which we are making the statement. An advertising executive may hypothesize that a certain type of newspaper ad attracts a larger proportion of readers than some other type of ad. A production supervisor may hypothesize that employees trained in a certain way need less time to do a task than employees trained in some other way. A marketing analyst may hypothesize that the mean family income in a certain area is some specific value μ_0. Or a company president may hypothesize that 60% of the company's employees have completed at least one year of college.

Given enough time, money, and other resources, each of these investigators could determine the truth of the hypothesis beyond doubt by examining the entire population to which the statement refers. But such an undertaking would cost a great deal. So investigators welcome a more economical means of testing the reasonableness of their hypotheses. And they are willing to settle for some degree of uncertainty in their conclusions.

The cases just described are typical of situations in which the concepts and techniques of sampling work well. The motivation for sampling may be a need to obtain estimates of population parameters, as discussed in Chapter 6, or to test hypotheses, as we shall see in this chapter. The advantages of sampling mentioned in Chapter 6 also apply in hypothesis testing. Therefore we shall not repeat them here. Here is a seven-step procedure for hypothesis testing.

Steps in Hypothesis Testing

1. Statement of the hypotheses
2. Identification of the test statistic and its distribution

3. Specification of the significance level
4. Statement of the decision rule
5. Collection of the data and performance of the calculations
6. Making the statistical decision
7. Conclusion

There is nothing sacred about this format. It just breaks the hypothesis-testing process into its basic components of acts and decisions. We can then analyze and understand each separately.

1. *Statement of the hypotheses.* You will ordinarily be concerned with two statistical hypotheses, the *null hypothesis* (designated H_0) and the *alternative hypothesis* (designated H_1).

The null hypothesis is the hypothesis that is tested.

The null hypothesis usually specifies one of the parameters of the population of interest. For example, the statement, or hypothesis, that 60% of the employees in a firm have had at least one year of college specifies that the parameter, the proportion of employees with at least one year of college, is 0.60. The null hypothesis is the hypothesis that is assumed to be true throughout the statistical analysis. The analysis is based on this assumption. Only after the analysis is complete, and there is evidence to warrant our doing so, do we entertain the idea that the null hypothesis is not true.

The null hypothesis
contains a statement
of equality.

The term *null hypothesis* reflects the concept that this is a *hypothesis of no difference*. For this reason, the null hypothesis always contains a statement of equality. When it is presented symbolically, it contains an equals sign.

The alternative hypothesis is the alternative available when the null hypothesis has to be rejected.

In the case of the company president's hypothesis about the education of the employees, we may state the alternative hypothesis in one of three ways: (1) the true proportion is not 0.60, (2) the true proportion is greater than 0.60, or (3) the true proportion is less than 0.60. In the case of the alternative, the statement of the hypothesis implies either a condition of not equal or an inequality. In the first case, if we reject the null hypothesis, we conclude that the true condition of the population with regard to the parameter is something other than that specified in the null hypothesis. However, this alternative does not indicate whether the true proportion is greater or less than that specified in the null hypothesis. In the second and third cases, when we reject the null hypothesis, we conclude that the true proportion is as specified by the alternative hypothesis. Which of the three alternative hypotheses we use is dictated by the nature of the problem.

Formulating the Hypotheses

An investigator may initially formulate a hypothesis in the null form or as the alternative. Thus the proportion of employees who have completed at least one year of college can be stated as 0.6 (null form) or not 0.6 (alternative form). Regardless of how we state the original hypothesis, however, we must specify both appropriate null and alternative hypotheses before we collect any data. In general, if we hypothesize that a population parameter θ is equal to some value θ_0, we may display the null and alternative hypotheses formally as follows:

$$H_0: \theta = \theta_0, \qquad H_1: \theta \neq \theta_0$$

What you want to con-clude goes in the alter-native hypothesis.

When setting up the null and alternative hypotheses, you must determine what you are trying to conclude. You should state this in the alternative hypothesis, unless this would violate the rule that the null hypothesis includes a statement of equality. You should state what you are trying to conclude in the alternative hypothesis because we want to reject the null hypothesis if at all possible.

Consider a situation in which you need to test a hypothesis about a population. If you want to know whether your sample data provide sufficient evidence to indicate that the population mean is not equal to some value μ_0, your alternative hypothesis is

$$H_1: \mu \neq \mu_0$$

and the null hypothesis, being the complement of the alternative, is

$$H_0: \mu = \mu_0$$

The null hypothesis and the alternative hypothe-sis are complements of each other.

The alternative hypothesis $H_1: \mu \neq \mu_0$ is an example of what is known as a two-sided alternative. You form a one-sided alternative if the question you want answered is one of the following: (1) Do the sample data provide sufficient evidence to indicate that the population mean is greater than μ_0? In this case the alternative hypothesis is $H_1: \mu > \mu_0$ and the null hypothesis is $H_0: \mu \leq \mu_0$. (2) Do the sample data provide sufficient evidence to indicate that the population mean is less than μ_0? In this case the alternative hypothesis is $H_1: \mu < \mu_0$ and the null hypothesis is $H_0: \mu \geq \mu_0$. We shall have more to say about two-sided and one-sided alternative hypotheses later in this chapter.

If we reject the null hypothesis, we can conclude with a high degree of conviction that the alternative hypothesis is true. If we cannot reject the null hypothesis, however, we do not conclude that the null hypothesis is true. We merely conclude that it *may be true*. This is because, in general, evidence compatible with a hypothesis is never conclusive, whereas contradictory evidence is sufficient to cast doubt on a hypothesis.

Consider an example. A firm that makes a headache remedy claims that the product always cures headaches within 15 minutes. This is the firm's hypothesis. You develop a headache and take the remedy. Your headache is gone within 15 minutes. You cannot conclude that the firm's hypothesis is true. If you have similar results with your next 25 headaches, will you conclude that the hypothesis is true? Although the evidence in favor of the hypothesis is now substantial, it is not sufficient for concluding that the manufacturer's hypothesis is true. On your twenty-seventh headache, relief does not come for 30 minutes. You can now conclude that the hypothesis is not true. This conclusion is based on a rejected hypothesis. You needed only one piece of contradictory evidence to reach this decision. And 26 pieces of evidence in favor of the hypothesis failed to establish its truth.

Decisions about statistical hypotheses of the type we consider here are never as clear-cut as in the headache example. The concept, however, is the same. To summarize, a decision based on a rejected null hypothesis is more conclusive than a decision based on evidence that is compatible with a null hypothesis. You'll realize the truth of this statement as you gain additional insight into the general nature of hypothesis testing.

The test statistic serves as a decision-maker.

2. *Identification of the test statistic and its distribution.* A *test statistic* is one that is used in statistical hypothesis testing. Generally the test statistic may assume many possible values. The particular value observed depends on the particular sample drawn. The test statistic serves as a decision-maker, since the decision to reject or not reject the null hypothesis depends on its magnitude.

When one is testing a hypothesis about a population mean, a possible test statistic is

$$z = \frac{\bar{x} - \mu_0}{\sigma/\sqrt{n}}$$

where μ_0 is the hypothesized value of the population mean. The subscript zero is used to indicate a hypothesized value of a parameter. This quantity follows the standard normal distribution when certain assumptions are met and the population mean is μ_0 as hypothesized. Some other test statistics with which we shall be concerned are

$$t = \frac{\bar{x} - \mu_0}{s/\sqrt{n}}$$

which is a possible test statistic that we use when we are testing a hypothesis about a population mean, and

$$t = \frac{(\bar{x}_1 - \bar{x}_2) - (\mu_1 - \mu_2)_0}{\sqrt{\dfrac{s_p^2}{n_1} + \dfrac{s_p^2}{n_2}}}$$

which we use when the parameter of interest is the difference between population means. Under certain conditions both of these statistics follow a t distribution.

When we test a hypothesis about a population proportion, the test statistic is

$$z = \frac{\hat{p} - p_0}{\sqrt{\dfrac{p_0(1 - p_0)}{n}}}$$

which is approximately normally distributed when certain conditions are met.

Many of the test statistics that we encounter will be of this form:

$$\text{Test statistic} = \frac{\text{sample statistic} - \text{hypothesized value of the parameter}}{\text{standard error of the statistic}}$$

3. *Specification of the significance level.* When the results are in, there are two possible actions: (1) *reject* H_0 or (2) *fail to reject* H_0. A hypothesis that is not rejected may be either true or false. Likewise, a rejected hypothesis may be either true or false. Thus, there are *four* possible outcomes when we test a hypothesis: (1) rejecting a false null hypothesis, (2) rejecting a true null hypothesis, (3) failing to reject a false null hypothesis, and (4) failing to reject a true null hypothesis. Outcomes (2) and (3) are undesirable. Outcomes (1) and (4) are desirable. We may classify the possible outcomes by the action taken and by the condition of the population relative to the null hypothesis. In tabular form, this two-way classification is as follows:

		Possible condition of null hypothesis	
		True	False
Possible action	Fail to reject H_0	Correct	Incorrect
	Reject H_0	Incorrect	Correct

We may think of the two undesirable outcomes as erroneous actions, or errors, and distinguish them by referring to them by type. That is, we may call the act of rejecting H_0 when it is true a Type I error, and the act of failing to reject H_0 when it is false a Type II error.

Bear in mind that in a hypothesis-testing situation there is always the probability that you will commit one or the other of these errors. We call the probability of committing a Type I error α, and the probability of committing a Type II error β. The larger α is, the more likely it is that we will commit a Type I error. That is, the larger α is, the more likely it is that we will reject a true null hypothesis. The larger β is, the more likely it is that we will commit a Type II error and fail to reject a false null hypothesis. We would like the probability of committing both errors to be as small as possible. For a given sample size, decreasing α causes an increase in β. Conversely, decreasing β causes an increase in α. The only way to reduce the likelihood of both types of error is to increase the sample size.

Choosing α

α = significance level = probability of committing a Type I error.

As we have noted, α is the probability of committing a Type I error. The quantity α is also called the *level of significance*. Before we collect the data, we specify that the level of significance, or probability of committing a Type I error, be some small probability. Once we have computed the test statistic, we determine the probability of obtaining a value as extreme as or more extreme than ours when the null hypothesis is true. If this probability is less than or equal to α, we reject

H_0 in favor of H_1. We then say that the computed value of the test statistic is *significant*. If the probability associated with the computed test statistic is greater than α, we cannot reject the null hypothesis. The value of the test statistic is then *not significant*. Although we could use any value of α between 0 and 1, the most common values are 0.05 and 0.01. These choices of α, though somewhat arbitrary, are based on tradition.

Consequences of a Type I Error

We choose the value of α in reference to the consequences of a Type I error. Consider the possible consequences of committing the two errors in an actual situation. Suppose that a firm that makes calculators has a policy of refusing to accept any shipment of microcircuits if there is reason to believe that more than 7% of them are of inferior quality. The manager selects a sample of microcircuits from each shipment and uses an appropriate hypothesis-testing procedure. Sometimes the hypothesis test indicates that a shipment should be rejected. By rejecting a shipment, the manager may commit a Type I error. Assume that when a shipment is rejected, the only alternative is to buy microcircuits from another supplier at a higher price. If the manager rejects a shipment of cheaper microcircuits that in fact do meet the specifications, and buys more expensive ones, this increases the cost of the calculators. A cost increase, then, is the consequence of rejecting a true null hypothesis in this case. If, on the other hand, the firm accepts a shipment as satisfactory, it may be committing a Type II error. That is, it may be accepting a shipment of inferior microcircuits, thus increasing the chance of producing inferior calculators. This may result in an added cost later if the firm has to make good its warranties. If it places too many inferior calculators on the market, the company may also face consumer ill will.

The manager must decide which of the two errors is more costly, then try to either minimize the probability of the more expensive error or strike a balance between the two errors on the basis of the costs involved.

Select α early.

Note that we select α early in the investigation. If we were to select α after we had completed the test, the results might influence our choice, and this would detract from the objectivity of the investigation.

Acceptance and Rejection Regions

The distribution of a test statistic includes all values that the statistic can assume when H_0 is true. In other words, we can imagine the set of all values of the test statistic that are possible when the null hypothesis is true. We call the subset of values of the statistic that are unlikely if the null hypothesis is true the *rejection region*. We call the remaining values the *acceptance region*. (However, it's better to avoid such phrases as "accept the null hypothesis." The word "accept" implies a greater degree of conviction than we should accord decisions based on hypotheses that we cannot reject. When we cannot reject the null hypothesis, we should characterize our action by saying that we "fail to reject the null hypothesis.") We call the values of the test statistic that separate the acceptance region

Critical values separate rejection regions from acceptance regions.

from the rejection region *critical values*. The value of α determines the delineation of the rejection and acceptance regions, in conjunction with the value of the hypothesized parameter and the relevant sampling distribution. This will become clearer when we consider a specific example.

4. *Statement of the decision rule.* We may state the decision rule, which is made before the data are gathered, in probabilistic terms, as follows:

If, when the null hypothesis is true, the probability of obtaining a value of the test statistic as extreme as or more extreme than the one actually obtained is less than or equal to α, we reject the null hypothesis. Otherwise, we do not reject the null hypothesis.

We may express this rule in terms of the computed test statistic, as follows:

If the computed value of the test statistic falls in the rejection region, we reject the null hypothesis. If the computed value of the test statistic falls in the acceptance region, we do not reject the null hypothesis. If the computed value of the test statistic is equal to the critical value, we reject the null hypothesis.

Regardless of how we state the decision rule, it will, if followed, lead to the same decision.

5. *Collection of the data and performance of the calculations.* Obtain the data to be analyzed as part of the decision-making process according to sound scientific principles. We cannot stress this point too much. The quality of a final decision depends on the quality of the raw data on which it is based. In Chapter 8 we shall discuss in more detail ways to improve the quality of basic data by using proper planning techniques. Once again, we emphasize that if the inferential procedures discussed here and in previous chapters are to be valid, *the sample must be random*.

Collect the data with the analysis in mind. Plan the analysis in detail before collecting the data. The nature of the calculations depends on the question being answered or the problem being solved. The method of analysis depends on the complexity of the calculations and the amount of data to be processed. For simpler problems, a desk calculator may be adequate. But for more complicated surveys, involving a large amount of data, you may need a computer.

6. *Making the statistical decision.* Evaluate the computed test statistic in light of the decision rule. The statistical decision consists of rejecting or not rejecting the null hypothesis based on this evaluation.

7. *Conclusion.* If the null hypothesis is rejected, we conclude that *the alternative hypothesis is true*. If the null hypothesis is not rejected, we conclude that *the null hypothesis may be true*.

To summarize the steps of a hypothesis test, let us consider a situation in which we wish to test a hypothesis about a population mean μ.

1. *Hypotheses*

$$\left.\begin{array}{l} H_0: \mu = \mu_0 \\ H_1: \mu \neq \mu_0 \end{array}\right\} \quad \text{or} \quad \left.\begin{array}{l} H_0: \mu \leq \mu_0 \\ H_1: \mu > \mu_0 \end{array}\right\} \quad \text{or} \quad \left.\begin{array}{l} H_0: \mu \geq \mu_0 \\ H_1: \mu < \mu_0 \end{array}\right\}$$

   (Two-sided alternative)   (One-sided alternatives)

   μ_0 is the hypothesized value of μ.

2. *Test statistic.* We decide between z and t.
3. *Significance level.* We select a value of α.
4. *Decision rule*
5. *Calculations.* We compute a z or t value.
6. *Statistical decision.* We decide whether or not to reject H_0.
7. *Conclusion*

   Figure 7.1 is a flowchart of the steps in testing a hypothesis.

**FIGURE 7.1
Flowchart for
hypothesis-testing
procedure**

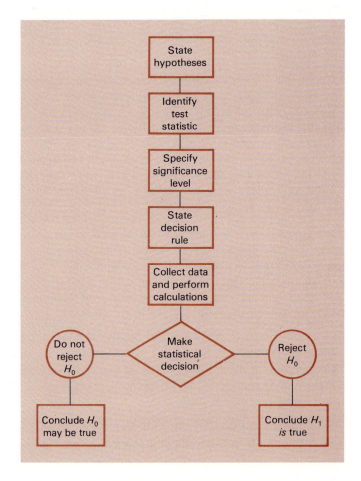

When testing hypotheses about population means and proportions, you must choose either z or t as the appropriate test statistic. The criteria for choosing between the two (as reliability factors) when constructing confidence intervals also apply in hypothesis-testing situations. Figures 6.6 and 6.7 summarize these criteria for cases in which the mean and the difference between two means are the parameters of interest.

The following sections are devoted to some specific hypothesis tests. The examples and exercises assume that the population is large enough relative to the sample that the finite population correction can be ignored.

7.2 TESTING HYPOTHESES ABOUT THE MEAN OF A NORMALLY DISTRIBUTED POPULATION—KNOWN POPULATION VARIANCE

This section considers examples of hypothesis testing that require the drawing of only one sample. We want to know whether or not the sample drawn is likely to have come from a population that has a specified mean.

EXAMPLE 7.1 A mail-order company that deals in small gifts charges a flat rate for postage, regardless of the weight of the package. This policy is based on the results of a study conducted several years ago. The study revealed that the mean weight of mailed packages was 17.5 ounces with a standard deviation of 3.6 ounces. The total flat postage rate is the current postage rate per ounce times 17.5. The company management assumed that in the long run the firm would break even on postage costs. The accounting department feels that the mean weight of packages being mailed today may not be 17.5 ounces and that the flat rate charged should perhaps be changed. It suggests that this hypothesis be tested. The volume of business has grown so large that doing a complete study, as was previously done, would be impractical. Therefore the management decides to take a random sample of the weights of 100 packages mailed and base the decision on the results from the sample. It is assumed that the weights of packages are approximately normally distributed.

SOLUTION We can reach a decision by following the seven steps of hypothesis testing discussed in Section 7.1.

1. *Hypotheses.*   We wish to test the hypothesis that the mean weight of packages being mailed today is the same as it was previously. The implied alternative hypothesis makes no suggestion as to the direction of any change. It merely suggests that the mean is now different from 17.5. We may state the null and alternative hypotheses symbolically as follows:

$$H_0: \mu = 17.5, \qquad H_1: \mu \neq 17.5$$

We state the two hypotheses in this manner because the firm presumably wants to reject the null hypothesis if the mean has either increased or decreased. That is, the firm wants to adjust its postage charges up or down, depending on the true state of affairs.

2. *Test statistic.* Since the parameter of interest is the population mean μ, the relevant statistic to be computed from the sample is $\bar{x}$. We know from Chapter 5 that when the sampled population is normally distributed, the sampling distribution of $\bar{x}$ is normal, with mean μ and variance σ^2/n. The test statistic that we can compute from the sample data, therefore, is

$$z = \frac{\bar{x} - \mu_0}{\sigma/\sqrt{n}}$$ (7.1)

which has the standard normal distribution.

3. *Significance level.* Assume that the consequences of committing a Type I error, rejecting H_0 when it is true, are such that we are willing to take a 1 in 20, or a 5 in 100, chance of committing this type of error. This decision sets the level of significance at $\alpha = 0.05$. Reference to the null and alternative hypotheses reveals that both extremely large and extremely small values of the test statistic will cause rejection of the null hypothesis. This is because the hypothesized sampling distribution of $\bar{x}$ is centered on 17.5, the hypothesized value of μ. Values of $\bar{x}$ that are sufficiently far from 17.5 in either direction, above or below, will cause z to fall in the rejection region. In other words, if the sample yields an extremely large value of $\bar{x}$, we shall compute an extremely large value of z. And if we obtain an extremely small value of $\bar{x}$ from the sample data, we shall compute an extremely small value of z. We know that in the standard normal distribution, extremely large values of z are located in the right tail and extremely small ones in the left tail. Half of α, therefore, is assigned to each tail of the distribution. A hypothesis test of this type is called a *two-sided test*.

This specification of α fixes the line of demarcation between the acceptance region and the rejection region. In other words, the values of z that have $\alpha/2 = 0.05/2 = 0.025$ of the area under the standard normal curve to their left and right, respectively, are -1.96 and $+1.96$. The rejection region consists of z values greater than or equal to $+1.96$ and smaller than or equal to -1.96. The acceptance region consists of the remaining values of z. Figure 7.2 shows the acceptance and rejection regions for $\alpha = 0.05$.

In a two-sided test about μ, $\alpha/2$ is assigned to each tail of the distribution of the test statistic.

**FIGURE 7.2
Standard normal distribution, showing acceptance and rejection regions for $\alpha = 0.05$ for a two-sided test**

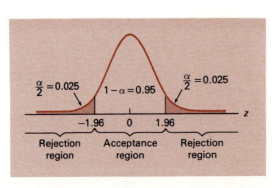

4. *Decision rule.* In the present example there is a two-sided test. Thus $\alpha = 0.05$ is divided equally between the two tails of the distribution of the test statistic. We must reflect this in the statement of the decision rule. In probabilistic terms, we may state the decision rule in two parts.
   (a) If the data yield a value of the test statistic so *large* that the probability of the occurrence of a value this large or larger when H_0 is true is less than or equal to $\alpha/2 = 0.025$, we reject the null hypothesis.
   (b) If the data yield a value of the test statistic so *small* that the probability of the occurrence of a value this small or smaller when H_0 is true is less than or equal to $\alpha/2 = 0.025$, we reject the null hypothesis.

   As we have already noted, the critical values of the test statistic are ± 1.96. We may state the decision rule in terms of these values as follows: If the computed value of the test statistic is either greater than or equal to $+1.96$ or less than or equal to -1.96, we reject the null hypothesis.

> The decision rule may be stated in terms of probability or in terms of values of the test statistic.

5. *Calculations.* The next step is to collect the data and perform the calculations. We have already decided to draw a sample of 100 packages to be weighed. The statistic of interest is the arithmetic mean $\bar{x}$. Suppose that the value of $\bar{x}$ computed from the sample is 18.4 ounces. From the sample, we may compute the following value of the test statistic:

$$z = \frac{18.4 - 17.5}{3.6/\sqrt{100}} = 2.5$$

6. *Statistical decision.* From the table of the standard normal distribution, the probability of obtaining a value of the test statistic this large or larger when the null hypothesis is true is less than 0.025. In fact, the probability of obtaining a value of 2.5 or larger is 0.0062. According to the decision rule, then, we reject the null hypothesis. Alternatively, we can say that we reject the null hypothesis because 2.5 is greater than 1.96.

7. *Conclusion.* The conclusion, based on the results of the study, is that the mean weight of mailed packages has changed. The firm should consider changing the amount charged for postage.

Relationship Between Hypothesis Testing and Interval Estimation

At this point let us consider the relationship between hypothesis testing and interval estimation. Specifically, we can use the interval estimation procedures discussed in Chapter 6 to test hypotheses. For example, suppose that we wish to test

$$H_0: \mu = \mu_0 \qquad \text{against the alternative} \qquad H_1: \mu \neq \mu_0$$

for some level of significance α. Instead of following the procedure just discussed, we can test this hypothesis by constructing the $100(1 - \alpha)\%$ confidence interval for μ. If μ_0 is contained in this interval, we fail to reject H_0. If, on the other hand, μ_0 is not contained in the interval, we reject H_0.

We can illustrate this by using the data of Example 7.1. The 95% confidence interval for μ in this example is

$$\bar{x} \pm 1.96 \frac{\sigma}{\sqrt{n}}, \qquad 18.4 \pm 1.96 \left(\frac{3.6}{\sqrt{100}}\right), \qquad 18.4 \pm 0.7, \qquad 17.7, 19.1$$

Since the interval does not contain $\mu_0 = 17.5$, we reject H_0. This is the same result we obtained by following the seven-step hypothesis-testing procedure.

A One-Sided Test

The test illustrated by Example 7.1 is a two-sided test. Now here is an example of a hypothesis test when a *one-sided* test is appropriate.

EXAMPLE 7.2 The quality-control department of a food-processing firm specifies that the mean net weight per package of cereal should not be less than 20 ounces. Experience has shown that the weights are approximately normally distributed with a standard deviation of 1.5 ounces. A random sample of 15 packages yields a mean weight of 19.5 ounces. Is this sufficient evidence to indicate that the true mean weight of the packages has decreased?

SOLUTION   We shall use a hypothesis test to help us answer this question.

1. *Hypotheses.* We can say that the sample data provide sufficient evidence that the mean has decreased if we can reject the null hypothesis that the mean has either remained the same or increased. This reasoning suggests the following hypotheses:

$$H_0: \mu \ge 20, \qquad H_1: \mu < 20$$

   Note one way in which these hypotheses differ from the hypotheses for the two-sided test: In the two-sided test, the null hypothesis specifies only *one* value of the parameter, whereas the null hypothesis of the one-sided test specifies a large number of values. Theoretically, then, in the case of a one-sided test, a large number of tests would be needed. Generally we perform only one test—a test at the point of equality. It can be shown, however, that if we reject H_0 at the point of equality, we will also reject H_0 for any other value implied by the null hypothesis.

2. *Test statistic.*   Since the population is approximately normally distributed and we know the population standard deviation, we can compute the following test statistic:

$$z = \frac{\bar{x} - \mu_0}{\sigma/\sqrt{n}}$$

3. *Significance level.*   Assume that a 0.05 level of significance is satisfactory.

4. *Decision rule.*   The fact that there is an inequality in the alternative hypothesis indicates that this is a one-sided test. All of $\alpha = 0.05$, therefore, will be in one tail of the distribution of the test statistic. Since computed values of the test statistic that are sufficiently small will cause rejection of the null hypothesis, the region of rejection will be in the left tail. The critical value of z, then, is that value of z to the left of which lies 0.05 of the area under the standard normal curve. Appendix Table C shows the critical value of the test statistic to be -1.645. We may state the decision rule as follows: If the value of z

In a one-sided test about μ, all of alpha is assigned to one tail of the distribution of the test statistic.

FIGURE 7.3
Standard normal distribution, showing acceptance and rejection regions for $\alpha = 0.05$ for a one-sided test

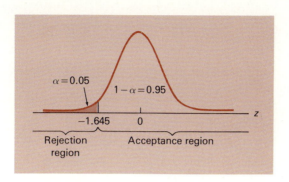

computed from the sample data is less than or equal to -1.645, we reject H_0. Otherwise we do not reject H_0. Figure 7.3 shows the acceptance and rejection regions for this example.

5. *Calculations.* A random sample of size 15 yielded a mean of 19.5. From these data we compute the following value of the test statistic:

$$z = \frac{19.5 - 20}{1.5/\sqrt{15}} = -1.29$$

6. *Statistical decision.* Since -1.29 is greater than -1.645, we cannot reject the null hypothesis.

7. *Conclusion.* Even though the sample mean is less than 20, the test result does not provide sufficient evidence to indicate that the true mean has decreased. We conclude that H_0 may be true.

p Values

In scientific journals, researchers usually report, as part of their research findings, a quantity known as the *p* value. A *p* value is a probability associated with a statistical hypothesis test.

A *p* value is the probability of obtaining a value of the test statistic as extreme as or more extreme (in the appropriate direction) than that actually obtained, given that the tested null hypothesis is true. It is also the smallest level of significance at which H_0 can be rejected.

When you read an article in *The Journal of Marketing Research*, for example, you are likely to see such compact statements as $p < 0.01$, $0.025 < p < 0.05$, and so on. The statement $p < 0.01$, for example, tells you that if the null hypothesis is true, the probability of obtaining a value of the test statistic (such as z) as extreme as or more extreme than that actually observed is less than 0.01. We interpret such a finding as evidence supporting the rejection of the null hypothesis and the acceptance of the alternative hypothesis.

A variety of symbols are used for the *p* value. We shall use the lowercase letter *p*, since this seems to be the most common. Do not confuse this *p* with the *p* used

FIGURE 7.4
p value for
Example 7.2

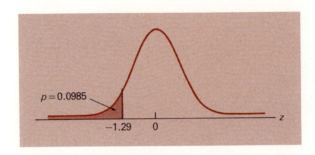

as the symbol for a population proportion. The context in which it appears will always make it clear whether *p* refers to the *p* value or to a population proportion.

Calculating a **p** *Value*   The *p* value associated with a given hypothesis test depends on three conditions: (1) the test statistic used, (2) the magnitude of the computed value of the test statistic, and (3) whether the alternative hypothesis is one-sided or two-sided. We find *p* values in a table of the applicable test statistic. As an example, let us refer to Example 7.2, in which we had a one-sided test and we computed the value of the test statistic as $z = -1.29$. From Table C, the probability of obtaining a value of z as small as or smaller than -1.29, if the null hypothesis is true, is equal to 0.0985. Since 0.0985 is greater than our chosen level of significance, 0.05, we would not reject H_0. Figure 7.4 shows the *p* value for Example 7.2.

The **p** *Value for a Two-sided Test*   When the alternative hypothesis is two-sided and the distribution of the test statistic is symmetric, as in the case of the z distribution, we double the *p* value that would apply if the alternative hypothesis were one-sided. A two-sided alternative hypothesis, you will recall, allows for a difference from the null hypothesis in either direction. That is, either a sufficiently large or a sufficiently small value of the test statistic causes rejection of the null hypothesis. Doubling the one-sided *p* value reflects this characteristic of a two-sided hypothesis test.

For a two-sided test, double the probability found in one tail of the z distribution.

Let us refer to Example 7.1, in which the test was two-sided and the computed value of the test statistic was 2.5. The sample data resulted in a test statistic that was located in the right tail of the distribution. However, we did not know that this would happen when we set up the test. To allow for the possibility of the test statistic's falling in either tail, we made the test two-sided. Just as α is divided between the two tails, the *p* value must also come from both tails. In this case the *p* value is equal to the area under the z curve to the right of $+2.5$ plus the area to the left of -2.5. When we consult Table C, we find that $p = 0.0062 + 0.0062 = 0.0124$. Since 0.0124 is less than 0.05, we reject H_0. Figure 7.5 shows the *p* value for Example 7.1.

FIGURE 7.5
p value for
Example 7.1

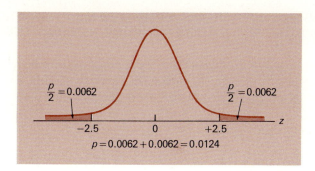

Advantage of Reporting p Values When researchers report a *p* value as part of their research findings, others can set their own level of significance. They can then use their own criterion, rather than that of the researcher, to reject or not reject the null hypothesis. The researcher who reports merely that the null hypothesis was rejected at, say, the 0.05 level is withholding information. This deprives the user of the findings of the ability to make an independent decision on whether or not to reject the null hypothesis.

Exercises

Carry out the seven-step hypothesis-testing procedure at the indicated level of significance and compute the *p* value for each test.

7.1 Suppose that a population is normally distributed with a standard deviation of 50. A random sample of size 25 is drawn from the population, and a sample mean of 70 is computed. Test at the 0.01 level of significance the null hypothesis that $\mu = 100$.

 7.2 A manufacturer of bolts claims that the mean length is 4.500 in. with a standard deviation of 0.020 in. A random sample of 16 bolts yields a mean of 4.512 in. Do these data provide sufficient evidence to indicate that the true mean length is greater than the manufacturer claims? Assume that the dimensions are normally distributed. Let $\alpha = 0.01$.

 7.3 A manufacturer of chemicals produces a certain compound by adding distilled water to fixed amounts of other ingredients. The amount of water needed depends on the purity of the other ingredients. As a result of using quality-control techniques, the manufacturer has determined that the mean amount of water needed to meet product standards is 6 liters with a standard deviation of 1 liter. A random sample of 9 batches required, on average, 7 liters of water. Do these data provide sufficient evidence to indicate that quality-control standards are not being met? Let $\alpha = 0.05$.

 7.4 Ⓒ A psychologist is conducting a research project in which the subjects are employees with a certain type of physical handicap. On the basis of past experience, the psychologist believes that the mean sociability score of the population of employees with this handicap is greater than 80. The population of scores is known to be approximately normally distributed with a standard deviation of 10. A random sample of 20 employees selected from the population yields the following results: 99, 69, 91, 97, 70, 99, 72, 74, 74, 76, 96, 97, 68, 71, 99, 78, 76, 78, 83, 66. The psychologist wants to know whether this sample result provides sufficient evidence to indicate that this belief about the population mean sociability score is correct. Let $\alpha = 0.05$.

7.3 TESTING HYPOTHESES ABOUT THE MEAN OF A NORMALLY DISTRIBUTED POPULATION—UNKNOWN POPULATION VARIANCE

We often need to test hypotheses about population means when we do not know the population variance. In such cases, even though the population may be approximately normally distributed, we cannot compute the test statistic

$$z = \frac{\bar{x} - \mu_0}{\sigma/\sqrt{n}}$$

because we do not know σ. When this is the case, we use the test statistic

$$t = \frac{\bar{x} - \mu_0}{s/\sqrt{n}} \tag{7.2}$$

When H_0 is true, this is distributed as Student's t with $n-1$ degrees of freedom.

In all respects other than choice of test statistic, the hypothesis-testing procedure appropriate under these conditions is the same as that outlined in Section 7.2.

EXAMPLE 7.3 A tire manufacturer claims that the average life of a certain grade of tire is greater than 25,000 miles under normal driving conditions on a car of a certain weight. A random sample of 15 tires is tested. A mean and standard deviation of 27,000 and 5000 miles, respectively, are computed. Assume that the lives of the tires in miles are approximately normally distributed. Can we conclude from these data that the manufacturer's product is as good as claimed?

SOLUTION We can decide by means of the following hypothesis test.

1. *Hypotheses.* We are asking whether we can conclude that μ, the true mean, is greater than 25,000. Thus a statement to this effect should go in the alternative hypothesis. The appropriate hypotheses, then, are

$$H_0: \mu \le 25,000, \qquad H_1: \mu > 25,000$$

2. *Test statistic.* The population is approximately normally distributed and the population standard deviation is unknown. Therefore the appropriate test statistic is

$$t = \frac{\bar{x} - \mu_0}{s/\sqrt{n}}$$

When H_0 is true, this is distributed as Student's t with $n-1$ degrees of freedom.

3. *Significance level.* Assume that a significance level of 0.05 is satisfactory.

4. *Decision rule.* The test is a one-sided test. Since only sufficiently large values of t will cause us to reject H_0, the region of rejection is in the upper tail of the distribution. The critical value of the test statistic, then, is the value of t with $n-1 = 14$ degrees of freedom that has to its right 0.05 of the area

under the curve of t. From Appendix Table D, we find this value to be 1.7613. The decision rule, then, may be stated as follows: If the computed value of t is greater than or equal to 1.7613, we reject H_0.

5. *Calculations.*   From the information given in the statement of the problem, we compute the following value of the test statistic:

$$t = \frac{27,000 - 25,000}{5000/\sqrt{15}} = 1.55$$

6. *Statistical decision.*   Since $1.55 < 1.7613$, we cannot reject H_0.
7. *Conclusion.*   Since we do not reject the null hypothesis, the data do not support the conclusion that the true mean life of the tires is as great as the manufacturer claims. Any action the tire firm takes that is incompatible with the hypothesis that $\mu \leq 25,000$ would not be warranted on the basis of these data.

Calculating the *p* Value

Readily available tables of the t distribution do not give us enough detail to determine the exact p value associated with the computed value of the test statistic. The table of Student's t distribution in Table D, for example, gives values of t only for selected percentiles: 0.90, 0.95, 0.975, 0.99, and 0.995. Unless the computed value of t happens to be exactly equal to a tabulated value, we cannot determine an exact p value from these tables. Thus, when the test statistic is a Student's t, the p value is usually reported as an interval, for example, $p < 0.05$ or $0.025 < p < 0.05$.

> When we use the t distribution, p is usually an interval.

Let us consider the value $t = 1.55$ that we computed in Example 7.3. When we enter Table D with 14 degrees of freedom, we find that 1.55 falls between 1.345 and 1.7613. If H_0 is true, the probability of obtaining a value of t as large as or larger than 1.345 is 0.10. The probability of obtaining a value as large as or larger than 1.7613 is 0.05. Then the probability, if H_0 is true, of obtaining a value of t as large as or larger than 1.55 is somewhere between 0.10 and 0.05. That is, for this test, $0.10 > p > 0.05$. Figure 7.6 shows the calculation of the p value for Example 7.3.

FIGURE 7.6
p value for
Example 7.3

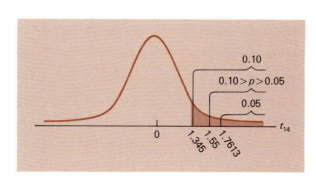

Paired Observations

Chapter 6 showed that in statistical inference, interest may focus on a population mean difference. It explained the construction of a confidence interval for the mean difference by using paired sample observations. We may also test hypotheses about the mean difference μ_d in a manner to be described in this section. We sometimes call such a test a *paired-comparisons test* or a *paired difference test*. Recall that the data for analysis consist of sample differences $d_i = x_{1i} - x_{2i}$, where x_{1i} and x_{2i} are observations taken on the ith pair of subjects under condition 1 and condition 2, respectively.

We may formulate any one of the following pairs of hypotheses:

1. $H_0: \mu_d = \mu_{d0},$ $H_1: \mu_d \neq \mu_{d0}$
2. $H_0: \mu_d \leq \mu_{d0},$ $H_1: \mu_d > \mu_{d0}$
3. $H_0: \mu_d \geq \mu_{d0},$ $H_1: \mu_d < \mu_{d0}$

When the population is normally distributed and the true variance of the difference is known, the test statistic is

$$z = \frac{\bar{d} - \mu_{d0}}{\sigma_{\bar{d}}} \tag{7.3}$$

When the variance is unknown, the test statistic is

$$t = \frac{\bar{d} - \mu_{d0}}{s_{\bar{d}}} \tag{7.4}$$

In practice, the most frequently hypothesized value of μ_{d0} is 0.

EXAMPLE 7.4 Nine pairs of salespeople are matched as to age, years of experience, level of initiative, and other variables. One member of each pair is randomly assigned to a training course taught by Method A. The other is assigned to the same type of training course taught by Method B. At the end of the course, each salesperson is given an examination to test retention of the material presented. Table 7.1 shows the results.

The investigator wishes to know whether Method A is better than Method B. If the methods are equally effective, we would expect, in the long run, to observe

TABLE 7.1
Scores made by nine pairs of salespersons, each member of which was trained by a different method

Pair	Method A	Method B	$d_i = x_{Ai} - x_{Bi}$
1	90	85	5
2	95	88	7
3	87	87	0
4	85	86	−1
5	90	82	8
6	94	82	12
7	85	70	15
8	88	72	16
9	92	80	12

an equal number of differences above and below 0. That is, we would expect the true mean difference μ_d to be 0. If, however, Method A is better than Method B, we would expect, in the long run, to find that Method A scores are higher than Method B scores. In this case μ_d, the mean of all $d_i = x_{Ai} - x_{Bi}$, will be greater than 0. The investigator in this example is asking whether this is so.

SOLUTION We carry out the hypothesis test by means of the following steps.

1. *Hypotheses.* Since, in Table 7.1, $d_i = x_{Ai} - x_{Bi}$, we have the following hypotheses:

$$H_0: \mu_d \leq 0, \qquad H_1: \mu_d > 0$$

2. *Test statistic.* Assume that the population of differences is approximately normally distributed. Then the test statistic is given by Equation 7.4.
3. *Significance level.* Let $\alpha = 0.05$.
4. *Decision rule.* H_1 implies a one-sided test with the rejection region in the upper tail of the distribution of t. Since there are 9 paired observations, we have $9 - 1 = 8$ degrees of freedom, and the critical value of t is 1.8595. If the computed value of t is greater than or equal to 1.8595, we reject H_0. Otherwise we do not reject H_0.
5. *Calculations.* From the data of Table 7.1, we compute

$$\bar{d} = \frac{\Sigma d_i}{n} = \frac{5 + 7 + \cdots + 12}{9} = \frac{74}{9} = 8.2$$

$$s_d = \sqrt{\frac{n\Sigma d_i^2 - (\Sigma d_i)^2}{n(n-1)}} = \sqrt{\frac{9(5^2 + 7^2 + \cdots 12^2) - (74)^2}{(9)(8)}} = 6.12$$

$$s_{\bar{d}} = \frac{s_d}{\sqrt{n}} = \frac{6.12}{\sqrt{9}} = 2.04$$

By Equation 7.4, we compute the following value of the test statistic:

$$t = \frac{8.2 - 0}{2.04} = 4.02$$

6. *Statistical decision.* Since the computed value of t exceeds the critical value of t, we reject H_0.
7. *Conclusion.* As we reject H_0, we conclude on the basis of these data, Method A instruction is superior to Method B. Since $4.02 > 3.3554$, $p < 0.005$.

A Reminder

Remember that this hypothesis-testing procedure rests on the assumption that the distribution of differences is at least approximately normal. All is not lost, however, if this assumption is not tenable. We may resort to one of two other alternatives. If the sample size is equal to or greater than 30, we can use the procedures of Section 7.4 regardless of the form of the population of differences. If the population of differences is not at least approximately normally distributed, and it is not possible to draw a large sample, we may use a test known as the *sign test*. This test, which does not depend on the functional form of the parent population, will be discussed in Chapter 10.

COMPUTER ANALYSIS

Computers may be used effectively to test hypotheses. Once we have written an appropriate program or located an existing one in a software package, we enter the raw data, give the computer the required commands, and obtain the resulting output. To illustrate the use of computers in testing hypotheses, consider the following example. We use the software package STAT+.

EXAMPLE 7.5 The following are the weights, in ounces, of 15 bags of raw nuts: 33.38, 32.15, 33.99, 34.10, 33.97, 34.34, 33.95, 33.85, 34.23, 32.73, 33.46, 34.13, 34.45, 34.19, 34.05. We wish to test at the 0.05 level H_0: $\mu = 34.5$ against H_1: $\mu \neq 34.5$. We presume that the assumptions for use of the t statistic are met.

After we key in the data, STAT+ computes the sample mean and standard deviation, performs the necessary calculations for the hypothesis test, and provides the following printout.

```
HYPOTHESIS TESTING CONCERNING ONE MEAN

      THE TEST
Ho : Mu = 34.5        H1 : Mu ≠ 34.5
Alpha = .05

Decision rule :
If the observed t <= -2.1448 or >= 2.1448 then reject Ho

      THE DECISION
Observed t = -4.314
Critical t = +/- 2.1448

Based on a random sample of 15 observations with sample s =
0.630224 and Xbar = 33.798, we reject the null hypothesis.

The P value (smallest Alpha to reject Ho) = .001
```

Exercises

Carry out the seven-step hypothesis-testing procedure at the indicated level of significance and compute the *p* value for each test.

 7.5 The mean operating temperature of a heat-sensing device, according to the manufacturer, is 190°F. A mean and standard deviation of 195° and 8°, respectively, are computed from the operating temperatures of a random sample of 16 devices. Do these data provide sufficient evidence to indicate that the mean operating temperature is higher than claimed? Let $\alpha = 0.05$, and assume that operating temperatures in the population are approximately normally distributed.

 7.6 Ⓒ A petroleum company has developed a gasoline additive that it feels will improve gasoline mileage. In order to get information to support the planned marketing program, the firm hires a testing organization to conduct a paired-comparisons test involving 16 pairs of cars. Each pair is identical with respect to make, model, engine size, and other relevant characteristics. One car of each pair is randomly selected and driven over a test course using gasoline with the additive. The other car of the pair is driven over the same course using a comparable gasoline without the additive. The mileage per gallon on the test course is shown here for all cars tested. Use the difference in gasoline mileage for a pair of cars as the variable of interest. Do the data provide sufficient evidence to indicate that the additive does increase gas mileage? Let $\alpha = 0.05$.

Pair #	With additive (X_1)	Without additive (X_2)	Pair #	With additive (X_1)	Without additive (X_2)
1	17.1	16.3	9	10.8	10.1
2	12.7	11.6	10	14.9	13.7
3	11.6	11.2	11	19.7	18.3
4	15.8	14.9	12	11.4	11.0
5	14.0	12.8	13	11.4	10.5
6	17.8	17.1	14	9.3	8.7
7	14.7	13.4	15	19.0	17.9
8	16.3	15.4	16	10.1	9.4

7.7 Ⓒ A study is conducted to investigate how effective street lighting placed at various locations is in reducing automobile accidents in a certain town. The following table shows the median number of nighttime accidents per week at 12 locations one year before and one year after the installation of lighting. Do these data provide sufficient evidence to indicate that lighting does reduce nighttime automobile accidents? Let $\alpha = 0.05$.

Location	A	B	C	D	E	F	G	H	I	J	K	L
No. before	8	12	5	4	6	3	4	3	2	6	6	9
No. after	5	3	2	1	4	2	2	4	3	5	4	3

7.8 A random sample of 25 hamburger patties sold by a fast-food restaurant yields a mean weight of 3.8 ounces with a standard deviation of 0.5 ounce. Can we conclude from these data that the population mean is less than 4 ounces? Let $\alpha = 0.05$. Weights of hamburger patties are approximately normally distributed.

7.9 Ⓒ The following are the weights of a random sample of 10 employees working in the shipping department of a wholesale grocery firm: 154, 154, 186, 243, 159, 174, 183, 163, 192, 181. On the basis of these data, can we conclude that the firm's shipping department employees have a mean weight greater than 160 pounds? Let $\alpha = 0.05$.

7.10 Ⓒ A hospital administrator states that emergency-room charges for a certain procedure must average at least $25 if the hospital is not to lose money on its emergency service. The hospital charged the following amounts for treating a sample of emergency-room patients with the procedure during a one-year period (rounded to the nearest dollar): 26, 20, 33, 25, 27, 30, 23, 27, 22, 38, 51, 60, 38, 56, 31. On the basis of these data, can we conclude at the 0.01 significance level that the mean charge for the sampled population of patients is greater than $25?

7.4 TESTING HYPOTHESES ABOUT THE MEAN OF A POPULATION THAT IS NOT NORMALLY DISTRIBUTED

Needless to say, not all populations are normally—or even approximately normally—distributed. Suppose that the sample on which a hypothesis test is based has been drawn from a population that is not normally distributed. If the sample is large (say, $n \geq 30$), we take advantage of the central limit theorem and use

$$z = \frac{\bar{x} - \mu_0}{\sigma/\sqrt{n}}$$

as the test statistic. If we do not know the standard deviation of the population, we use the sample standard deviation as an estimate. We reason that the large sample, which is necessary if the central limit theorem is to apply, will yield a satisfactory estimate of σ.

EXAMPLE 7.6 A market research firm is interested in the amount that households in a certain town spend on groceries each week. The firm believes that the average amount spent per household each week is less than $40. A random sample of 100 households yields a mean of $38 and a standard deviation of $10. Do these data support the firm's belief?

SOLUTION We can use the results of a hypothesis test to answer the question.

1. *Hypotheses*

$$H_0: \mu \geq \$40, \qquad H_1: \mu < \$40$$

2. *Test statistic.* The functional form of the population is not specified. However, since the sample size is large, we know that the sampling distribution of $\bar{x}$ is at least approximately normally distributed because of the central limit theorem. If σ were known, the test statistic would be

$$z = \frac{\bar{x} - \mu_0}{\sigma/\sqrt{n}}$$

However, since the sample size is large, it ought to yield a satisfactory estimate of σ. The test statistic we compute, then, is

$$z = \frac{\bar{x} - \mu_0}{s/\sqrt{n}}$$

We assume that when H_0 is true, this statistic will follow a normal distribution well enough for us to use a value from the standard normal distribution as the critical value of the test statistic.

3. *Significance level.* Let $\alpha = 0.05$.
4. *Decision rule.* If the computed value of z is less than or equal to -1.645, we reject H_0.
5. *Calculations.* From the information given, the computed value of the test statistic is

$$z = \frac{\$38 - \$40}{10/\sqrt{100}} = -2.0$$

6. *Statistical decision.* Since $-2.0 < -1.645$, we reject H_0.

7. *Conclusion.* Since we reject H_0, we conclude that the data support the firm's belief. For this test, $p = 0.0228$.

Exercises

Carry out the seven-step hypothesis-testing procedure at the indicated level of significance and compute the p value for each test.

7.11 An accountant for a certain firm has been told that in her section of the country the average weekly salary of typists is \$175. She wants to know whether she should doubt this information. She calls on you for help. You decide to use the procedures of hypothesis testing. Use the seven steps of hypothesis testing to arrive at a decision. Let $\alpha = 0.05$, use a sample of size 100, and use the sample standard deviation, $s = \$25$, to estimate the population standard deviation.

    If your sample yields an $\bar{x}$ of \$170, what advice would you give the accountant?

7.12 A real-estate agent claims that the average value of homes in a certain neighborhood is greater than \$45,000. A random sample of 36 homes has a mean value of \$48,000 and a standard deviation of \$12,000. Do these data support the agent's claim at the 0.05 level of significance?

7.13 The manager of a shopping mall hypothesizes that cars in the parking lot remain there, on the average, more than 90 minutes on weekends. A random sample of 100 cars arriving on weekends yields a mean parking time of 96 minutes with a standard deviation of 30 minutes. Do these data provide sufficient evidence to support the manager's contention? Let $\alpha = 0.05$.

7.14 Ⓒ An industrial psychologist who serves as consultant to many electronics firms has accused production supervisors of promoting unskilled assembly-line employees to a certain job for which they have no aptitude. A random sample of 40 of these employees yields the following aptitude scores. The population variance is known to be 280, and the population of scores is not normally distributed. The production supervisors contend that the mean aptitude score of all the employees they promoted is greater than 60. Do these data provide sufficient evidence to support their claim? Let $\alpha = 0.05$. Find the p value.

73	57	96	78	74	42	55	44	91	91
50	65	46	63	82	60	97	79	85	79
92	50	42	46	86	81	81	83	64	76
40	57	78	66	84	96	94	70	70	81

7.15 Ⓒ A firm that makes roofing tar wants the percentage of impurities not to exceed an average of 3%. A random sample of 30 one-gallon cans yields the following percentages of impurities. On the basis of these data, can one conclude that the population mean is less than 3 percent? Let $\alpha = 0.01$.

3	3	1	1	0.5	2	2	4	5	4	5	3	1	3	1
4	1	1	4	2	5	3	1	1	1	0.75	1.5	3	3	2

7.5 TESTING HYPOTHESES ABOUT THE DIFFERENCE BETWEEN THE MEANS OF TWO NORMALLY DISTRIBUTED POPULATIONS

The difference between two population means often interests researchers and managers. If we do not have direct knowledge of the true parameters, we make an inference on the basis of sample data. Two independent random samples, one from each of two populations, provide data on which we base the inference. In the most common situation involving the difference between two population means, we want to find whether or not it is reasonable to conclude that the two are not equal. In this situation the test may be either one-sided or two-sided. In the latter case, the hypotheses are of the form

$$H_0: \mu_1 - \mu_2 = 0, \qquad H_1: \mu_1 - \mu_2 \neq 0$$

and in the former case, the hypotheses are formulated as

$$H_0: \mu_1 - \mu_2 \leq 0, \qquad H_1: \mu_1 - \mu_2 > 0$$

or

$$H_0: \mu_1 - \mu_2 \geq 0, \qquad H_1: \mu_1 - \mu_2 < 0$$

However, in these hypotheses we can replace 0 with any value of interest. For example, we might want to test the null hypothesis that $\mu_1 - \mu_2 = 10$.

We shall discuss hypothesis tests involving the difference between two population means under three different circumstances: (1) when sampling is from normally distributed populations with known population variances; (2) when sampling is from normally distributed populations with unknown population variances; and (3) when sampling is from populations that are not normally distributed. The first two situations are discussed in this section. The third situation will be covered in Section 7.6.

Known Population Variances

For testing the difference between two population means when the populations are normally distributed and the population variances are known, the appropriate test statistic is based on

$$z = \frac{(\bar{x}_1 - \bar{x}_2) - (\mu_1 - \mu_2)}{\sqrt{\dfrac{\sigma_1^2}{n_1} + \dfrac{\sigma_2^2}{n_2}}} \tag{7.5}$$

This follows from our knowledge of the sampling distribution of $\bar{x}_1 - \bar{x}_2$, the difference between two sample means. Neither the sample sizes nor the variances need be equal.

EXAMPLE 7.7 Two procedures can be used to manufacture wire. Experience has shown that the tensile strengths that result from both procedures are approximately normally distributed. The standard deviation for Procedure 1 is 6 psi. For Procedure 2 the standard deviation is 8 psi. Management wishes to know whether the mean tensile strengths of wire produced by the two methods are different.

SOLUTION We can decide by means of the following hypothesis test.

1. *Hypotheses*

$$H_0: \mu_1 - \mu_2 = 0, \qquad H_1: \mu_1 - \mu_2 \neq 0$$

2. *Test statistic.* The test statistic is

$$z = \frac{(\bar{x}_1 - \bar{x}_2) - 0}{\sqrt{\dfrac{\sigma_1^2}{n_1} + \dfrac{\sigma_2^2}{n_2}}} \qquad \text{which is distributed as the standard normal}$$

3. *Significance level.* Let $\alpha = 0.05$.
4. *Decision rule.* Reject H_0 if the computed value of the test statistic is greater than or equal to $+1.96$ or less than or equal to -1.96.
5. *Calculations.* A random sample of 12 pieces of wire made by Procedure 1 gives a mean of 40 psi. A random sample of 16 pieces made by Procedure 2 yields a mean of 34 psi. From these data we can compute the following value of the test statistic:

$$z = \frac{(40 - 34) - 0}{\sqrt{\dfrac{36}{12} + \dfrac{64}{16}}} = 2.27$$

6. *Statistical decision.* Since $2.27 > 1.96$, we reject H_0.
7. *Conclusion.* On the basis of the sample data, we conclude that the two population means are different. That is, we conclude that the two procedures, on the average, do not yield wire with the same tensile strength. For this test, $p = 2(1 - 0.9884) = 2(0.0116) = 0.0232$.

Unknown but Equal Population Variances

In testing a hypothesis about the difference between the means of two normally distributed populations when the population variances are unknown, we distinguish between two cases: (1) the case in which the population variances are equal, and (2) the case in which they are not equal. We shall consider here only the case in which either the unknown population variances are known to be equal or the investigator is willing to assume that they are equal.

If the population variances, though unknown, are equal, then the correct test statistic for testing hypotheses about the difference between the means of two normally distributed populations is based on

$$t = \frac{(\bar{x}_1 - \bar{x}_2) - (\mu_1 - \mu_2)}{\sqrt{\dfrac{s_p^2}{n_1} + \dfrac{s_p^2}{n_2}}} \tag{7.6}$$

where

$$s_p^2 = \frac{(n_1 - 1)s_1^2 + (n_2 - 1)s_2^2}{n_1 + n_2 - 2}$$

is the pooled estimate of the common population variance.

EXAMPLE 7.8 Two machines are used in the making of steel rings. The quality-control department asks whether it should conclude that Machine 1 is producing rings with a larger inside diameter than Machine 2. Assume that the diameters are approximately normally distributed and $\sigma_1^2 = \sigma_2^2$.

SOLUTION We can decide by means of the following hypothesis test.

1. *Hypotheses*

$$H_0: \mu_1 - \mu_2 \leq 0, \qquad H_1: \mu_1 - \mu_2 > 0$$

2. *Test statistic.* Under the assumption that the two populations are normally distributed with equal variances, the appropriate test statistic is

$$t = \frac{(\bar{x}_1 - \bar{x}_2) - 0}{\sqrt{\dfrac{s_p^2}{n_1} + \dfrac{s_p^2}{n_2}}}$$

which, when H_0 is true, is distributed as Student's t with $n_1 + n_2 - 2$ degrees of freedom.

3. *Significance level.* Let $\alpha = 0.01$.

4. *Decision rule.* If the computed value of t is greater than or equal to the critical t for $n_1 + n_2 - 2$ degrees of freedom, and $\alpha = 0.01$, reject H_0.

5. *Calculations.* A random sample of 10 rings from Machine 1 and 15 rings from Machine 2 gives the following results: $\bar{x}_1 = 1.051$, $\bar{x}_2 = 1.036$, $s_1^2 = 0.000441$, and $s_2^2 = 0.000225$. The pooled estimate of the common population variance is

$$s_p^2 = \frac{9(0.000441) + 14(0.000225)}{23} = 0.000310$$

The value of the test statistic that we may compute from the sample data is

$$t = \frac{(1.051 - 1.036) - 0}{\sqrt{\dfrac{0.000310}{10} + \dfrac{0.000310}{15}}} = 2.09$$

6. *Statistical decision.* Since the computed t of 2.09 is less than the critical t of 2.5, we cannot reject the hypothesis.

7. *Conclusion.* Since we did not reject H_0, the quality-control department cannot conclude from the test results that Machine 1 is producing steel rings with a larger inside diameter than Machine 2. Since $2.0687 < t < 2.500$, for this test $0.025 > p > 0.01$.

Exercises

Carry out the seven-step hypothesis-testing procedure at the indicated level of significance and compute the p value for each test.

7.16 A textile manufacturer can buy a certain type of yarn from one of two vendors. The vendors' products appear to be comparable in all respects except price and, possibly, breaking strength. The manufacturer will buy from Vendor 1 (whose price is lower) unless there is reason to believe that Vendor 1's product has a lower mean breaking strength than Vendor 2's. Random samples are drawn from the two vendors' stocks, with the following results. Assume that breaking strengths are approximately normally distributed. Based on an appropriate hypothesis test with $\alpha = 0.05$, would you advise the manufacturer to buy the cheaper yarn? Assume that the population variances are equal.

Vendor 1	$n = 10$	$\bar{x} = 94$	$s^2 = 14$
Vendor 2	$n = 12$	$\bar{x} = 98$	$s^2 = 9$

 7.17 The following data are based on random samples taken from two shifts in a certain factory. The variable of interest is the length of time needed to do a certain task. Do these data provide sufficient evidence to indicate that the average time needed on Shift 2 is less than that on Shift 1? Let $\alpha = 0.05$. Specify all assumptions that you have to make in order to validate your procedure.

Shift 1	$n = 10$	$\bar{x} = 26.1$	$s^2 = 144$
Shift 2	$n = 8$	$\bar{x} = 17.6$	$s^2 = 110$

 7.18 A manufacturer of a sleeping medicine is comparing the effectiveness of a new formula, B, with Formula A, which is now on the market. For three nights 25 subjects try Formula B and 25 subjects in an independent sample try Formula A. The variable of interest is the average number of additional hours of sleep (compared with nights when no drug is taken) the subjects get for the three nights. The results are as follows. Do these data provide sufficient evidence to indicate that Formula B is better than Formula A? Let $\alpha = 0.01$.

$n = 25$
25

Medicine	A	B
$\bar{x}$	1.4	1.9
s^2	0.09	0.16

 7.19 Ⓒ An industrial psychologist feels that a big factor in job turnover among assembly-line workers is the individual employee's self-esteem. She thinks that workers who change jobs often (Population A) have, on the average, lower self-esteem, as measured by a standardized test, than workers who do not (Population B). To determine whether she can support her belief with statistical analysis, she draws a simple random sample of employees from each population, and gives a test measuring self-esteem. The results are as follows. The psychologist believes that the relevant populations of scores are normally distributed, with equal, although unknown, variances. At the 0.01 level of significance, what should she conclude? What use can she make of her findings?

Group A	60	45	42	62	68	54	52	55	44	41						
Group B	70	72	74	74	76	91	71	78	76	78	83	50	52	66	65	53	52

7.20 Ⓒ In a university finance class, an argument arises over the contention of some members of the class that men have a better knowledge of the stock market than women do. To settle the argument, the instructor gives a test to measure knowledge of the stock market to a random sample of 15 male students and an independent random sample of 15 female students. The results are as follows. Can one conclude on the basis of these data that male students, on the average, have a better knowledge of the stock market than female students do? Let $\alpha = 0.05$. What assumptions are necessary?

| Women: | 73 | 96 | 74 | 55 | 91 | 50 | 46 | 82 | 43 | 79 | 79 | 50 | 46 | 81 | 83 |
| Men: | 57 | 78 | 42 | 44 | 91 | 65 | 63 | 60 | 97 | 85 | 92 | 42 | 86 | 81 | 64 |

7.6 TESTING HYPOTHESES ABOUT THE DIFFERENCE BETWEEN THE MEANS OF TWO POPULATIONS NOT NORMALLY DISTRIBUTED

When samples are drawn from nonnormally distributed populations, we can use the results of the central limit theorem if the sample sizes are large. This lets us use normal theory, since the sampling distribution will be approximately normally distributed.

The appropriate test statistic for hypothesis-testing purposes is based on

$$z = \frac{(\bar{x}_1 - \bar{x}_2) - (\mu_1 - \mu_2)}{\sqrt{\dfrac{\sigma_1^2}{n_1} + \dfrac{\sigma_2^2}{n_2}}} \tag{7.7}$$

If the population variances are unknown, we use the sample variances as estimates. We do not pool the sample variances, however, since we don't need to assume equality of population variances when we use the z statistic.

EXAMPLE 7.9 A market-research firm wishes to know if it can conclude that the mean number of hours of television viewing per week by families in a certain type of community (Type A) is less than that in another type of community (Type B). Independent random samples give the following information:

	Type A	Type B
Number of families interviewed	100	75
Average number of hours of television viewing per week	18.50	27.25
Standard deviation	10	14

SOLUTION The results of the following hypothesis test will help answer the question.

1. *Hypotheses*

$$H_0: \mu_A \geq \mu_B, \qquad H_1: \mu_A < \mu_B$$

2. *Test statistic.* The functional forms of the populations are not given. However, since the sample sizes are large, we rely on the central limit theorem and assume that the statistic $\bar{x}_A - \bar{x}_B$ is approximately normally distributed. If σ_A^2 and σ_B^2 were known, the appropriate test statistic would be given by Equation 7.7. Since these parameters are unknown, we compute

$$z = \frac{(\bar{x}_A - \bar{x}_B) - 0}{\sqrt{\dfrac{s_A^2}{n_A} + \dfrac{s_B^2}{n_B}}}$$

which is approximately normally distributed when H_0 is true.

3. *Significance level.* Let $\alpha = 0.05$.
4. *Decision rule.* If the computed value of the test statistic is less than or equal to -1.645, reject H_0.
5. *Calculations.* From the data given in the problem statement, we may compute the following value of the test statistic:

$$z = \frac{(18.50 - 27.25) - 0}{\sqrt{\dfrac{100}{100} + \dfrac{196}{75}}} = -4.60$$

6. *Statistical decision.* Since $-4.60 < -1.645$, we reject H_0.
7. *Conclusion.* Since we reject H_0, we can conclude that μ_A is less than μ_B. For this test, $p < 0.001$.

Exercises

Carry out the seven-step hypothesis-testing procedure at the indicated level of significance and compute the p value for each test.

7.21 A paper manufacturer is thinking of buying one of two tracts of timberland. The size of the trees on each tract is important. Measurements of trunk diameter for a random sample of 50 trees from each tract give the following results. Do these data provide sufficient evidence at the 0.05 level of significance to indicate that trees on Tract B are, on the average, smaller than trees on Tract A?

Tract A	$\bar{x} = 28.25''$	$s^2 = 25$
Tract B	$\bar{x} = 22.50''$	$s^2 = 16$

7.22 An analyst is studying the advertising practices of two types of retail firms. One variable is the amount spent on advertising during the preceding year. An independent random sample is drawn from each type of firm, with the following results. Can we conclude from these data that Type A firms spent more for advertising, on the average, than Type B firms? Let $\alpha = 0.05$.

Type A	$n = 60$	$\bar{x} = \$14{,}800$	$s^2 = 180{,}000$
Type B	$n = 70$	$\bar{x} = \$14{,}500$	$s^2 = 133{,}000$

7.23 A random sample of 100 families from Community A and a random sample of 150 families from Community B yield the following data on length of residence in current home. Do these data provide sufficient evidence to indicate that, on the average, families in Community A have been living in their current homes for less time than families in Community B have? Let $\alpha = 0.05$.

Community A	$\bar{x} = 33$ months	$s^2 = 900$
Community B	$\bar{x} = 49$ months	$s^2 = 1{,}050$

7.24 An advertising analyst interviews a random sample of male executives and a random sample of married, unemployed, middle-class adult females regarding their exposure to advertising through radio, television, newspapers, and magazines. One variable is the number of ads to which each subject is exposed on a typical weekday. The results are shown in the following table. Do these data provide sufficient evidence to indicate that, on the average, the sampled female population is exposed to more ads than the sampled population of male executives? Let $\alpha = 0.01$.

Group	n	Mean number of ads to which exposed	Standard deviation
Male executives	100	200	50
Unemployed females	144	225	60

7.25 Ⓒ A manufacturer of electrical wire wants to compare two types of wire with respect to resistance per unit length. Thirty specimens of Wire 1 and 35 specimens of Wire 2 yield the following measurements in ohms $\times\ 10^2$. Can we conclude on the basis of these data that the populations differ with respect to mean resistance? Let $\alpha = 0.05$.

Wire 1	55.2	53.5	52.3	54.1	52.4	50.5	53.5	46.9	52.9	57.1	55.7	51.2	55.2
	57.4	53.9	58.1	50.6	59.4	51.8	50.8	56.9	56.3	59.1	52.7	56.1	58.2
	53.1	50.6	53.1	59.7									
Wire 2	46.9	50.6	47.3	48.0	49.2	48.4	48.5	48.6	48.2	50.2	47.2	50.3	49.1
	48.2	47.4	48.1	49.4	47.4	49.7	49.1	49.3	50.3	50.8	48.3	47.7	48.5
	51.1	50.9	49.5	49.7	51.4	48.1	49.7	50.9	48.6				

7.26 Ⓒ A manufacturer wants to compare the viscosity of two brands of motor oil. Thirty-two randomly selected specimens of each brand are analyzed, with the following results. (The data are coded for ease of computation.) Can one conclude on the basis of these data that the mean viscosity of the two brands differs? Let $\alpha = 0.05$.

Brand A	13	21	60	35	38	10	36	24	35	35	45	19	42	11	35	39	25
	17	51	25	52	25	11	11	55	44	25	41	16	47	50	18		
Brand B	46	52	66	65	71	67	47	48	58	42	66	69	60	80	45	47	69
	75	43	46	74	73	43	70	51	72	65	45	76	48	56	64		

7.7 TESTING HYPOTHESES ABOUT A POPULATION PROPORTION

We come now to hypothesis testing when the parameter of interest is the proportion of elements that have a given characteristic. We call the elements with the characteristic "successes," and designate the proportion of successes by p.

Chapter 4 showed that the binomial probability distribution is the correct model when we are considering the number of elements out of a total of n elements that have a certain characteristic.

When n is large, the work required to find the probability of some specified number of successes using the binomial formula is less than appealing. However, as we pointed out in Chapter 5, when np and $n(1 - p)$ are both greater than 5, the binomial distribution may be approximated by the normal distribution. When

When we test hypotheses about p, and n is large, the test statistic is z.

n/N is also ≤ 0.05, the appropriate test statistic for testing hypotheses about population proportions is

$$z = \frac{\hat{p} - p_0}{\sqrt{\dfrac{p_0 q_0}{n}}} \tag{7.8}$$

where p_0 is the hypothesized proportion, $q_0 = 1 - p_0$, and $\hat{p}$ is the sample proportion. This statistic is distributed approximately as the standard normal when H_0 is true. If n is large relative to N, we use a finite population correction in Equation 7.8. As we noted, in the examples and exercises of this chapter, we shall assume that n is small relative to N, so that we can ignore the correction factor. We use p_0 in the denominator of Equation 7.8 rather than $\hat{p}$ because we assume H_0 to be true while we are conducting the test.

EXAMPLE 7.10 The president of a certain firm, concerned about the safety record of the firm's employees, sets aside $15,000 a year for safety education. The firm's accountant believes that more than 75% of similar firms spend more than $15,000 a year on safety education. The president asks the accountant for evidence to support this belief.

SOLUTION The accountant responds with the following hypothesis test.

1. *Hypotheses*
$$H_0\!:p \leq 0.75, \qquad H_1\!:p > 0.75$$

2. *Test statistic.* The accountant decides to obtain information from a simple random sample of 60 firms. This sample is large enough to enable the accountant to use Equation 7.8.
3. *Significance level.* Let $\alpha = 0.05$.
4. *Decision rule.* If the computed value of the test statistic is greater than or equal to 1.645, reject H_0.
5. *Calculations.* Of the 60 firms, 50 state that they spend more than $15,000 per year on safety education. Therefore $\hat{p} = 50/60 = 0.83$, and the computed value of the test statistic is

$$z = \frac{0.83 - 0.75}{\sqrt{\dfrac{(0.75)(0.25)}{60}}} = 1.43$$

6. *Statistical decision.* Since $1.43 < 1.645$, we cannot reject the null hypothesis.
7. *Conclusion.* Even though the sample proportion is greater than 0.75, the test results do not support the accountant's hypothesis. We should conclude that the true proportion with the characteristic of interest may be less than or equal to 0.75. For this test, $p = 1 - 0.9236 = 0.0764$.

Exercises

Carry out the seven-step hypothesis-testing procedure at the desired level of significance and compute the *p* value for each test.

7.27 A self-help club is considering the promotion of a home study course leading to a high school diploma for members who have not finished high school. The president of the club thinks that fewer than 25% of the members have not completed high school, and would like to support this belief with an appropriate hypothesis test. Of a random sample of 200 members, 42 indicate that they have not completed high school. Do these data support the president's belief at the 0.05 significance level?

7.28 A college with an enrollment of approximately 10,000 students wants to build a new student parking garage. The administration feels that more than 60% of the students drive cars to school. If, in a random sample of 250 students, 165 indicate that they drive a car to school, is the administration's position supported? Let $\alpha = 0.05$.

7.29 The head accountant of a company is concerned about clerical errors on outgoing invoices, and believes that more than 20% of these invoices contain at least one error. In a random sample of 400 invoices, 100 are found to contain at least one error. Do these data support the accountant's belief? Let $\alpha = 0.05$.

7.30 In a study of job turnover, a researcher interviews a random sample of 200 top-level employees who have changed jobs during the past year. Thirty state that they changed jobs because they didn't see much prospect for advancement in their old jobs. Do these data provide sufficient evidence at the 0.05 level of significance to indicate that fewer than 20% of this type of employee changes jobs for this reason?

7.8 TESTING HYPOTHESES ABOUT THE DIFFERENCE BETWEEN TWO POPULATION PROPORTIONS

When n_1 and n_2 are large, and we test hypotheses about $p_1 - p_2$, the test statistic is z.

The manager or the researcher is often interested in the difference between two population proportions. We can test the null hypothesis that the difference between two population proportions is equal to any given value. The hypothesis we find most often in practice is that the difference is 0. The correct test statistic for testing hypotheses about the difference between two population proportions is based on

$$z = \frac{(\hat{p}_1 - \hat{p}_2) - (p_1 - p_2)}{\sqrt{\dfrac{p_1(1 - p_1)}{n_1} + \dfrac{p_2(1 - p_2)}{n_2}}} \tag{7.9}$$

where the samples are independent simple random samples.

Pooling Sample Results

Since p_1 and p_2, the true population proportions, are unknown, we must estimate them. The best available estimates usually are the sample proportions.

The null hypothesis that $p_1 - p_2 = 0$ is equivalent to the hypothesis that the two population proportions are equal. We may use this as justification for combining the results of the two samples. We thus obtain a pooled estimate of the hypothesized common proportion, which is given by

$$\bar{p} = \frac{x_1 + x_2}{n_1 + n_2} \tag{7.10}$$

where x_1 and x_2 are the numbers in the first and second samples, respectively, with the characteristic of interest. We use this pooled estimate of $p = p_1 = p_2$ to compute the following standard error:

$$s_{\hat{p}_1 - \hat{p}_2} = \sqrt{\frac{\bar{p}(1 - \bar{p})}{n_1} + \frac{\bar{p}(1 - \bar{p})}{n_2}} \tag{7.11}$$

The test statistic, then, is

$$z = \frac{(\hat{p}_1 - \hat{p}_2) - 0}{s_{\hat{p}_1 - \hat{p}_2}} \tag{7.12}$$

which is distributed approximately as the standard normal if the null hypothesis is true.

Suppose that n_1 and n_2 are fairly close in size, and neither p_1 nor p_2 is too close to 0 or 1. Then the results we obtain by pooling will, as a rule, not differ very much from the results we obtain when the data are not pooled. It is never wrong to pool the data under H_0: $p_1 = p_2$. Since in some cases it may make a difference, it is advisable always to pool the data when n_1 and n_2 are unequal.

Always pool the data when n_1 and n_2 are unequal.

EXAMPLE 7.11 A researcher studies the grocery-shopping habits of city residents. Interviews with the principal shopper in each of 400 households reveal the following: Of 225 shoppers with rural backgrounds and 175 shoppers with urban backgrounds, 54 and 52, respectively, state that they do most of their grocery shopping at chain stores. We want to decide, on the basis of this sample, whether or not the two groups differ with respect to where they do most of their grocery shopping.

SOLUTION We can decide on the basis of the following hypothesis test.

1. *Hypotheses*

$$H_0: p_1 = p_2, \qquad H_1: p_1 \neq p_2$$

2. *Test statistic.* The test statistic is given by Equation 7.12.
3. *Significance level.* Let $\alpha = 0.05$.
4. *Decision rule.* If the computed value of the test statistic is greater than or equal to $+1.96$ or less than or equal to -1.96, we reject H_0.
5. *Calculations.* From the information given in the problem statement, we compute the value of the test statistic as follows. By Equation 7.10, we have

$$\bar{p} = \frac{54 + 52}{225 + 175} = \frac{106}{400} = 0.265$$

The test statistic, by Equation 7.12, is

$$z = \frac{(0.240 - 0.297) - 0}{\sqrt{\dfrac{(0.265)(0.735)}{225} + \dfrac{(0.265)(0.735)}{175}}} = -1.28$$

6. *Statistical decision.* Since we find that $-1.28 > -1.96$, we do not reject the null hypothesis.

7. *Conclusion.* On the basis of the data given, we conclude that the two proportions may be equal. These data do not allow us to accept the alternative hypothesis. For this test, $p = 2(0.1003) = 0.2006$.

Sometimes the hypothesized difference between population proportions is other than 0. In these cases, it is not correct to pool the sample data. The following example shows this.

EXAMPLE 7.12 A market researcher believes that the proportion of households in Area A with two or more cars exceeds by more than 0.05 the proportion of households in Area B with two or more cars. To see whether the facts support this hypothesis, the researcher conducts a survey among Area A and Area B households, with the following results.

Area	Sample size	Number of households with two or more cars
A	$n_A = 150$	113
B	$n_B = 160$	104

SOLUTION The researcher conducts the following hypothesis test.

1. *Hypotheses*

$$H_0: p_A - p_B \leq 0.05, \qquad H_1: p_A - p_B > 0.05$$

2. *Test statistic.* The relevant statistic is $\hat{p}_A - \hat{p}_B$, which is considered to be approximately normally distributed (since n_1 and n_2 are large). If H_0 is true, the mean of the distribution is 0.05 or less (we test at 0.05). The test statistic is as follows:

$$z = \frac{(\hat{p}_A - \hat{p}_B) - 0.05}{\sqrt{\dfrac{\hat{p}_A(1 - \hat{p}_A)}{n_A} + \dfrac{\hat{p}_B(1 - \hat{p}_B)}{n_B}}}$$

When H_0 is true, the test statistic is distributed approximately as the standard normal.

3. *Significance level.* Let $\alpha = 0.05$.

4. *Decision rule.* If the computed value of the test statistic is greater than or equal to 1.645, reject H_0.

5. *Calculations.* From the sample data, we compute $\hat{p}_A = 113/150 = 0.75$ and $\hat{p}_B = 104/160 = 0.65$.

The standard error is

$$s_{\hat{p}_A - \hat{p}_B} = \sqrt{\frac{(0.75)(0.25)}{150} + \frac{(0.65)(0.35)}{160}} = 0.05$$

which allows us to compute

$$z = \frac{(0.75 - 0.65) - 0.05}{0.05} = 1.00$$

6. *Statistical decision.* Since the computed z of 1.00 is less than 1.645, we do not reject H_0.

7. *Conclusion.* We may not conclude, on the basis of the information contained in these data, that the market researcher's hypothesis is true. For this test, we have $p = 1 - 0.8413 = 0.1587$.

Exercises

Carry out the seven-step hypothesis-testing procedure at the desired level of significance and compute the p value for each test.

 7.31 A firm that makes carpeting is seeking a material that can withstand temperatures of up to 250°F. Two materials, one a natural material, the other a synthetic (and cheaper) material, are equally satisfactory in all respects except, possibly, heat tolerance. Simple random samples of 225 specimens of each of the two materials are tested for this characteristic. The samples are independently drawn. Thirty-six specimens of the natural material and 45 of the synthetic material fail at temperatures below 250°F. Can we conclude from these data that the two materials are different with respect to heat tolerance? Let $\alpha = 0.05$.

 7.32 A large corporation finds that 63% of the 150 salespeople who have never had a self-improvement course would like such a course. The firm did a similar study 10 years before. Then only 58% of 160 salespeople wanted a self-improvement course. At the 0.05 level of significance, test the null hypothesis that salespeople are no more eager for self-improvement courses this year than they were 10 years ago. The groups are assumed to constitute two independent simple random samples.

 7.33 A simple random sample of 200 Type A industrial firms shows that 12% of them spend more than 1% of their total sales for advertising. An independent simple random sample of the same size from Type B firms shows that 15% spend more than 1% of their sales for advertising. Let $\alpha = 0.05$, and test

$$H_0: p_B \leq p_A \qquad \text{against the alternative} \qquad H_1: p_B > p_A$$

7.34 You conduct a study of the leisure-time activities of business people in a certain city. A simple random sample of 400 salespersons and an independent simple random sample of 400 business people *not* engaged in selling yield the following results: 288 salespersons and 260 nonsales business people say that their leisure-time activities are mainly sports-oriented. Would you conclude on the basis of these data that a smaller proportion of nonsales business people than salespersons spend their leisure time in sports-oriented activities? Let $\alpha = 0.05$.

Summary

This chapter covered the basic concepts of hypothesis testing, the second type of statistical inference procedure. You learned that the hypothesis-testing procedure may be broken down into seven sequential steps.

1. Statement of the hypotheses
2. Identification of the test statistic and its distribution
3. Specification of the significance level
4. Statement of the decision rule
5. Collection of the data and performance of the calculations
6. Making the statistical decision
7. Conclusion

You learned how to carry out the seven-step hypothesis-testing procedure when the parameter of interest is one of the following:

1. The mean of a normally distributed population for which the population variance is known
2. The mean of a normally distributed population for which the population variance is unknown
3. The mean of a population that is not normally distributed (large-sample case)
4. The difference between the means of two normally distributed populations
5. The difference between the means of two populations that are not normally distributed (large-sample case)
6. A population proportion (large-sample case)
7. The difference between two population proportions (large-sample case)

You learned that in many hypothesis-testing procedures, we may compute the test statistic using the general formula

$$\text{Test statistic} = \frac{\text{sample statistic} - \text{hypothesized value of the parameter}}{\text{standard error of the statistic}}$$

You also learned how to determine a p value for each test conducted.

Now that you have completed this chapter, you should be able to distinguish between inference situations that require a z statistic and those that require a t statistic. The criteria for making the decision are summarized in Figures 6.6 and 6.7 on pages 164 and 169, respectively.

Review Questions

Where appropriate, carry out the seven-step hypothesis-testing procedure at the indicated level of significance and compute the p value for the test.

1. What is the purpose of hypothesis testing?
2. What is a hypothesis?
3. List and explain each step in the seven-step hypothesis-testing procedure.
4. What is a Type I error?
5. What is a Type II error?

6. Explain how to decide what statement goes into the null hypothesis and what statement goes into the alternative hypothesis.

7. What are the assumptions underlying the use of the *t* statistic in testing hypotheses about a single mean? the difference between two means?

8. When may the *z* statistic be used in testing hypotheses about: **(a)** a single population mean? **(b)** the difference between two population means? **(c)** a single population proportion? **(d)** the difference between two population proportions?

9. In testing a hypothesis about the difference between two population means, what is the rationale behind pooling the sample variances?

10. What is meant by the *p* value of a test?

11. Give an example from your field of interest in which it would be appropriate to test a hypothesis about the difference between two population means. Use real or realistic data and carry out the seven-step hypothesis-testing procedure.

12. Do Exercise 11 for a single population mean, a single population proportion, and the difference between two population proportions.

13. Explain the meaning of ''level of significance.''

14. Explain how confidence intervals can be used to test hypotheses.

15. What are critical values?

16. What is the general formula for a test statistic?

17. A manufacturer of strapping tape claims that the tape has a mean breaking strength of 500 psi. Experience has shown that breaking strengths are approximately normally distributed with a standard deviation of 48 psi. A random sample of 16 specimens is drawn from a large shipment of tape, and a mean of 480 psi is computed. Can we conclude from these data that the mean breaking strength for this shipment is less than that claimed by the manufacturer? Let $\alpha = 0.05$.

18. The mean length of time required to perform a certain task on an assembly line has been established as 15.5 minutes, with a standard deviation of 3 minutes. A random sample of 9 employees is taught a new method. After the training period, the average time these 9 employees take to perform the task is 13.5 minutes. Do these results provide sufficient evidence to indicate that the new method is faster than the old? Let $\alpha = 0.05$. Assume that the times required to perform the task are normally distributed.

19. A certain type of yarn is manufactured under specifications requiring the mean tensile strength to be 20 lb. A random sample of 16 specimens yields a mean tensile strength of 18 lb and a standard deviation of 3.2 lb. Can we conclude from these data that the true mean tensile strength is less than 20 lb? Assume that the tensile strengths are approximately normally distributed. Let $\alpha = 0.05$.

20. A manufacturer of electrical products will not accept a shipment of a certain part from a vendor if there is reason to believe that the mean resistance is not 70 ohms. A random sample of 25 selected from a large shipment yields a mean and standard deviation, respectively, of 66 and 10 ohms. Should the shipment be accepted? Let $\alpha = 0.05$. Assume that the resistances are approximately normally distributed.

21. The credit manager of a department store chain believes that the average age of charge-account customers is less than 30 years. A random sample of 100 charge-account customers reveals a mean age of 27 years and a standard deviation of 10 years. Do these data provide sufficient evidence to support the credit manager's belief? Let $\alpha = 0.05$.

22. A random sample of size 81 gives a mean and standard deviation, respectively, of 485 and 45. **(a)** Test the null hypothesis that $\mu = 500$. Let $\alpha = 0.01$. **(b)** Test the null hypothesis that $\mu \leq 500$ ($\alpha = 0.01$).

23. We test two brands of electric fuse by subjecting each to a fixed load and measuring the subsequent life of the fuse in seconds. We find the following test results. Can we conclude from these data that Brand B fuses have longer life, on the average, than Brand A fuses? Let $\alpha = 0.05$. What assumptions are necessary in order to carry out a valid hypothesis test?

Brand A	$n = 7$	$\bar{x} = 75$	$s^2 = 20$
Brand B	$n = 10$	$\bar{x} = 85$	$s^2 = 16$

24. The following results are based on independent simple random samples drawn from two normally distributed populations with variances $\sigma_1^2 = 135$ and $\sigma_2^2 = 91$. Can we conclude from these data that $\mu_2 < \mu_1$? Let $\alpha = 0.05$.

Sample 1	$n = 15$	$\bar{x} = 62$
Sample 2	$n = 13$	$\bar{x} = 50$

25. Explain the conditions under which a paired-comparisons test is appropriate.

26. The following data are obtained from independent simple random samples from two populations. Can we conclude from these data that the population means are different? Let $\alpha = 0.01$.

Population A	$n = 50$	$\bar{x} = 100$	$s^2 = 650$
Population B	$n = 50$	$\bar{x} = 107$	$s^2 = 600$

27. An official of a large paint factory believes that more than one-third of ordered raw materials are not delivered on time. She compares actual delivery date with promised delivery date on a random sample of 100 orders, and finds that 38 orders were not delivered on time. Do these data support her belief? Let $\alpha = 0.01$.

28. A simple random sample of size 210 yields a $\hat{p}$ of 0.7. Test the null hypothesis that $p = 0.75$. Let $\alpha = 0.01$.

29. It is hypothesized that the proportion of executives reared in cities of 100,000 or less population is greater for Industry A than for Industry B. Do the following sample results support this hypothesis at the 0.01 level?

	Industry A	Industry B
Sample size	150	100
Number of executives reared in cities of 100,000 population or less	78	48

30. An opinion poll firm has two mailing lists available for the distribution of a questionnaire. A simple random sample of 200 names and addresses is selected from each list, and a questionnaire covering general-interest topics is mailed to each person. Of the questionnaires sent to the sample from Mailing List A, 52% are returned, whereas only 40% of those sent to the B sample are returned. Do these data provide sufficient evidence to indicate that people on Mailing List A are more apt to respond to this type of questionnaire? Let $\alpha = 0.05$.

31. A random sample of 64 bank depositors reveals a mean checking account balance of $375 with a standard deviation of $80. Can we conclude from these data that the population mean is less than $400? Let $\alpha = 0.01$.

32. A sample of 9 high school seniors in a school system reports a mean of 5 hours worked at part-time jobs during a recent week. The sample standard deviation is 3 hours. Do these data provide sufficient evidence to indicate that the mean for the population is less than 8 hours? Assume a normally distributed population.

33. Draw a simple random sample of 30 one-digit numbers from Table A of Appendix I. Test the null hypothesis that $\mu = 4.5$ at the 0.05 level. Let $\sigma^2 = 8.25$. Compare your results with those of the other members of your class. Repeat the exercise, but this time use the sample variance in computing the standard error. Compare the results from the two procedures.

34. The owner of a shopping center claims that more than 50% of the households within a 3-mile radius of the shopping center have at least one member who shops at the center at least once a week. In a sample of 300 households in the area, an investigator finds that members of 171 households do so. Do these data provide sufficient evidence to support the shopping center owner's claim? Let $\alpha = 0.01$.

 35. Noting the declining popularity of public billiards parlors, a recreation specialist hypothesizes that more than 10% of the homes in a certain area have pool tables. In a random sample of 100 homes in the area, 18 are found to have pool tables. Do these data support the recreation specialist's contention? Let $\alpha = 0.05$.

36. Draw a simple random sample of 20 one-digit numbers from Table A. Compute $\hat{p} = $ number of odd digits/20. Test the null hypothesis that $p = 0.5$. Let $\alpha = 0.05$. Compare your results with those of the other members of your class.

 37. A researcher with a commercial nursery conducts an experiment to compare the characteristics of two kinds of tomato plants. The heights at a certain age are determined for a sample of each of the two kinds, grown under conditions that are as nearly identical as possible. The results are as follows: For Type A, $n = 15$, $\bar{x} = 11.5$, and $s = 3.2$; for Type B, $n = 22$, $\bar{x} = 13.2$, and $s = 3.8$. Do these data provide sufficient evidence to indicate that Type B plants are, on the average, taller than Type A plants at this age? Let $\alpha = 0.05$.

 38. A psychologist investigates the differences between high-performing and low-performing salespersons with respect to certain psychological factors. A random sample is selected from each of the two groups, and sampled subjects are given a battery of tests. The results of one such test, designed to measure subjects' need for security, are as follows: For the 16 high performers, $\bar{x} = 4.75$ and $s^2 = 2.25$; for the 21 low performers, $\bar{x} = 3.25$ and $s^2 = 2.00$. Can we conclude from these data that the two populations differ with respect to mean level of need for security? Let $\alpha = 0.05$.

39. Draw two simple random samples of one-digit numbers from Table A, letting $n_1 = n_2 = 30$ and $\sigma_1^2 = \sigma_2^2 = 8.25$. Test the null hypothesis that $\mu_1 - \mu_2 = 0$ at the 0.05 level of significance. Compare your results with those of other members of your class. Repeat the exercise, but this time use sample variances in computing the standard error. Compare the results from the two procedures.

 40. Ⓒ A factory manager wishes to know whether the efficiency of employees working in a high-noise area could be improved by reducing the noise level. The following table gives efficiency ratings taken before and after noise-reduction measures were introduced for 15 affected employees. Can we conclude from these data that reducing the noise level raises the efficiency level of employees? A higher number indicates a higher efficiency. Let $\alpha = 0.01$.

Employee	Efficiency rating		Employee	Efficiency rating	
	Before	*After*		*Before*	*After*
1	21	32	9	22	40
2	35	35	10	35	48
3	40	58	11	28	38
4	38	57	12	20	33
5	23	37	13	39	39
6	27	40	14	28	41
7	28	39	15	34	44
8	39	58			

41. Ⓒ A sample of 12 pairs of brothers, no more than two years apart in age, takes part in a study conducted by a high school guidance counselor. During his senior year in high school, each boy is given a business-knowledge test. The younger brothers, when they are seniors, all take a course in business practices that the older brothers did not take when *they* were seniors. The following table shows the scores. Should we conclude from these data that the course in business practices raises the level of a student's knowledge of business? Let $\alpha = 0.01$.

Pair	Older brother	Younger brother	Pair	Older brother	Younger brother
1	104	113	7	150	151
2	223	214	8	143	146
3	241	246	9	205	210
4	103	104	10	185	191
5	145	150	11	104	111
6	156	160	12	225	234

42. A random sample of 500 is selected from the subscribers to a sports magazine. The sample is then divided at random into two subsamples, A and B, of 250 each. Each subject is mailed a questionnaire seeking his or her opinions of certain sports teams. Each subject in Subsample A is sent a dollar bill with the questionnaire. Subjects in Subsample B are sent the questionnaire only. Then 212 persons in Subsample A and 150 in Subsample B return a completed questionnaire. Do these data provide sufficient evidence to indicate that paying people causes an increase in the rate of response to mailed questionnaires? Let $\alpha = 0.05$.

43. An ad agency testing its commercials inserts a Format A test commercial for a detergent into the normal Monday morning programming of a local radio station. The next day the agency telephones 100 listeners. Asked whether they recall the commercial, 25 out of the 100 say that they do recall it. The following Monday morning the ad agency inserts a Format B commercial for the same detergent into the radio station's normal programming. The next day the agency follows it up with telephone calls to 110 listeners. Of these, 40 are able to recall the Format B commercial. Do these data provide sufficient evidence to indicate that Format B is more easily recalled than Format A?

44. A random sample of households is selected from each of two communities, A and B. Each head of household is asked the question, "Is anyone in this household bothered by air pollution?'' In Community A, 80 out of 240 answer yes. In Community B, 90 out of 250 answer yes. Do these data provide sufficient evidence to indicate a difference in population proportions between the two communities?

45. An advertising executive believes that the proportion of adult females in Area A who regularly watch a certain soap opera on television exceeds by more than 0.10 the proportion in Area B who regularly watch it. Independent random samples of adult females from the two areas give the following information: In Area A, the sample size $n_A = 150$, and the number of respondents who regularly watch the program is 98. In Area B, the sample size $n_B = 200$, and the number who watch regularly is 80. Do these data provide sufficient evidence to support the advertising executive's belief? Let $\alpha = 0.05$.

46. An industrial psychologist with a large company believes that a certain employee orientation program will reduce the turnover rate among new employees by more than 15%. During a certain year, 100 new employees are chosen by random assignment to participate in the orientation program. Another 100 new employees are chosen by random assignment as a control group. Both groups are followed for a period of 5 years. At the end of this time, 22 persons in the experimental group and 45 in the control group have left the firm. Is the psychologist's belief about the orientation program justified? Let $\alpha = 0.05$.

47. Ⓒ A drug manufacturer wants to know whether two methods of producing headache tablets result in a difference in mean thickness of the tablets. A researcher draws a random sample from the items produced by the two methods, and records the following results (coded for computational convenience). Do these data provide sufficient evidence to indicate that the two population means are different? Let $\alpha = 0.05$.

Method A	39	46	35	38	36	45	42	54	52	55					
Method B	50	41	44	47	51	43	57	40	51	43	44	51	60	59	40

48. Ⓒ Simple random samples are selected from male factory workers in two industries. The variable of interest is a measure of lung health. The results are as follows. Can we conclude from these data that the two population means differ? Let $\alpha = 0.10$.

Industry A	3.44	3.81	2.05	3.01	2.42	2.12	2.83	3.26	3.69	2.46	2.72	3.39
	2.64	3.65	3.64	3.65								
Industry B	3.94	2.96	4.14	2.55	3.52	2.92	2.92	3.33	2.62	3.76	3.94	4.19
	2.62	4.31	2.55	3.51	4.31	4.15	3.51	3.14	3.89			

49. Ⓒ A firm makes soap using two different formulas. The firm wants to know the specific gravity of the soap produced by each of the two formulas. To compare the two formulas with respect to specific gravity of the product, a chemist draws simple random samples from production lots representing the two formulas. The results (coded for computational convenience) are as follows. Can we conclude from these data that the two population means are different? Let $\alpha = 0.05$.

Formula A	4	6	4	8	5	3	2	7	6	4				
Formula B	7	5	8	6	6	10	10	9	10	6	9	9	8	8	4

50. In a study comparing the attitudes of white-collar and blue-collar workers toward paid religious holidays, researchers with a large firm select a random sample of 150 white-collar workers and an independent random sample of 120 blue-collar workers. Of these, 29 of the white-collar and 34 of the blue-collar workers say that they think paid religious holidays are very important. Do these data provide sufficient evidence to indicate, at the 0.05 level, that the proportions of workers who think paid religious holidays are important are different in the two sampled populations?

51. © An industrial psychologist believes that a population of employees with a certain handicap has a mean test score for manual dexterity greater than 75. The population of scores, which has a standard deviation of 9, is assumed to be normally distributed. A random sample of 20 of these employees yields the following data: 77, 99, 96, 89, 85, 63, 51, 52, 54, 81, 91, 69, 91, 92, 98, 70, 53, 76, 90, 64. Do these data provide sufficient evidence to support the psychologist's belief? Let $\alpha = 0.01$.

52. © A drug manufacturer is concerned with the side effects of a depressant drug when it is used by normal adults. A researcher would like to find a dosage that will produce sedation, but that will not be strong enough to cause serious side effects. A random sample of 16 subjects taking part in an experiment with the drug achieves sedation with the following dosages, in milligrams per kilogram of body weight: 1.6, 1.8, 7.3, 5.7, 3.0, 1.6, 3.8, 3.1, 7.8, 7.4, 4.2, 1.6, 2.1, 2.1, 5.5, 4.4. Do these data provide sufficient evidence to indicate that the mean dosage required to produce sedation is greater than 2.5 milligrams per kilogram of body weight? Let $\alpha = 0.05$.

53. © Two researchers wish to know if they can conclude that high school seniors with a high aptitude for a career in law have higher IQs than seniors with a low aptitude for a law career. The subjects of their study consist of 12 pairs of seniors. The subjects within each pair are matched on as many relevant variables as possible, but differ with respect to their aptitude for a law career. The following table shows the IQs of the sample subjects. Do these data provide sufficient evidence to indicate that seniors with a high aptitude for law have, on the average, higher IQs than those who have a low aptitude for law? Let $\alpha = 0.05$.

Pair	1	2	3	4	5	6	7	8	9	10	11	12
High aptitude	129	103	123	118	99	95	126	115	110	122	127	135
Low aptitude	127	94	115	114	90	92	129	105	101	110	125	134

54. © The amount of a certain chemical in the raw material used to produce linoleum is a critical factor in the linoleum's durability. A researcher for a linoleum manufacturer believes that the mean concentration of the chemical is different in the raw material obtained from two suppliers. To find out whether or not this belief can be supported by objective data, the researcher takes random samples from the raw material provided by the two suppliers, and determines the concentration of the chemical in each specimen. The results are as follows. Do the data support the researcher's belief? Let $\alpha = 0.05$. State any assumptions that are necessary.

Supplier A	60.9	49.8	65.3	40.6	51.6	69.7	58.0	59.6	47.8	46.9	47.6	67.3
Supplier B	72.9	67.3	81.4	89.4	86.5	51.1	72.9	74.0	77.8	86.4	82.0	77.6
	74.8	50.7	61.0	57.4	61.0	57.8	74.7	89.4				

55. © Researchers give each of a random sample of 15 employees with high absenteeism records (Group A) a test to measure level of hostility. They give the same test to an independent random sample of 22 employees with low absenteeism records (Group B). The results are as follows. Do these data provide sufficient evidence to indicate that, on the average, employees who are often absent are more hostile than employees who are not? A high score indicates a high level of hostility. Let $\alpha = 0.01$. What use can the researchers make of their findings? What assumptions are necessary?

Group A	62	93	71	90	69	90	71	76	86	71	81	84	65	61	69	
Group B	55	56	57	60	48	60	53	65	64	46	41	67	66	64	42	59	70
	75	69	72	74	55											

56. A market research firm wants to find out whether the annual average household consumption of diet mayonnaise differs in two large market areas. The firm selects random samples of 100 households in each area, with the following results. What should the firm conclude from these results? Let $\alpha = 0.01$. What use can the researchers make of these results?

Area 1	$\bar{x}_1 = 10$ units	$s_1 = 6$
Area 2	$\bar{x}_2 = 14$ units	$s_2 = 8$

57. Ⓒ A sample of 100 orders received during a year by a mail-order house specializing in hobby and craft supplies shows the following receipts, rounded to the nearest dollar. Can we conclude on the basis of these data that the mean value of the company's receipts is greater than $20? Let $\alpha = 0.05$.

8	12	9	14	8	10	7	17	18	18	20	10	23	12	27	11	27	15	15	16
21	14	22	14	29	28	26	16	19	24	21	14	23	21	28	27	29	18	19	32
23	13	24	22	28	27	32	16	19	36	24	10	21	21	27	29	31	16	19	36
22	13	22	22	25	26	32	15	15	37	23	14	21	24	26	34	34	15	16	34
23	14	20	24	27	37	33	19	19	33	9	11	9	21	6	38	9	18	18	32

58. Ⓒ Consider the population of employed heads of household in Appendix II. Select a simple random sample of size 30 from the population, and perform an appropriate hypothesis test to see whether you can conclude that the mean age of the subjects in the population is greater than 30. Let $\alpha = 0.05$.

59. Ⓒ From the population in Appendix II, select a simple random sample of 100 subjects. Perform an appropriate hypothesis test to see whether you can conclude that the proportion of married persons in the population is not 0.50. Choose your own significance level.

60. Ⓒ From the population in Appendix II, select a simple random sample of 40 males and 40 females. Perform a hypothesis test to see whether you can conclude that the proportion of married persons is different for males and females. Use a 0.01 significance level, and find the p value. Compare your results with those of your classmates.

61. Ⓒ Using the samples from Exercise 60, test to see whether you can conclude that the populations of males and females differ with respect to mean number of years with current employer. Use a 0.05 significance level, and find the p value. Compare your results with those of your classmates.

62. Hypothesis testing is used extensively in industrial quality control. In order to maintain the quality of a given product, it is often necessary to test the same hypothesis again and again at successive points in time. To facilitate the procedure, quality-control technicians use a graphic device called a *control chart*. Control charts may be constructed for use with either sample means (the $\bar{x}$ chart) or sample proportions (the p chart). The $\bar{x}$ chart consists of three parallel horizontal lines. The middle line originates at the vertical axis at a point corresponding to μ_0, the hypothesized mean value of some measurement that can be made on a manufactured item. The measurement might be tensile strength, or weight, or length, or diameter, or any of a number of other critical measurements. The other two lines are located equally distant from the μ_0 line, one above and one below. The distance from the μ_0 line is usually three standard errors. That is, one line originates at the vertical axis at

FIGURE 7.7
Control chart for
the mean

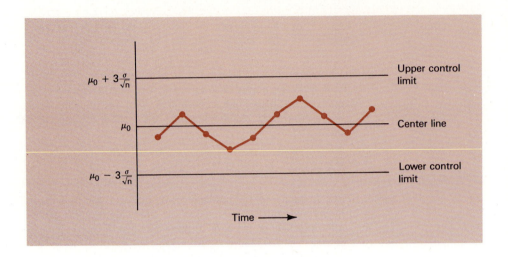

a point corresponding to $\mu_0 + 3(\sigma/\sqrt{n})$ and the other originates at a point corresponding to $\mu_0 - 3(\sigma/\sqrt{n})$. After the $\bar{x}$ control chart is constructed, samples are drawn periodically, and for each, $\bar{x}$ is computed and plotted on the chart. If a given $\bar{x}$ falls between the two outside lines, the manufacturing process for the product is considered to be under control with respect to the measurement, such as tensile strength, that is under consideration. In other words, when a sample mean falls within the two outside lines of the control chart, we are unable to reject the null hypothesis that $\mu = \mu_0$. If, on the other hand, a given $\bar{x}$ falls either above the $\mu_0 + 3(\sigma/\sqrt{n})$ line or below the $\mu_0 - 3(\sigma/\sqrt{n})$ line, the null hypothesis that $\mu = \mu_0$ is rejected. In that case there is cause to suspect that the manufacturing process is out of control, and the process is subjected to further examination to determine the cause of the likely lack of control. Figure 7.7 shows a typical $\bar{x}$ chart with several plotted sample means.

Suppose that a process for manufacturing metal bolts is considered to be under control if the mean length is $\mu = 4$ inches. Suppose also that the population standard deviation is known to be 0.015 inch. **(a)** Construct an $\bar{x}$ chart that a quality-control technician might use to monitor the process with regard to bolt length, using samples of size $n = 5$. **(b)** Suppose that the population of measurements is approximately normally distributed. What is the probability of committing a Type I error each time the control chart is used? **(c)** Suppose that selecting a sample of size 5 at each of 10 successive time periods yields the following means: 3.995, 4.015, 4.029, 4.012, 3.975, 4.010, 3.992, 4.019, 4.024, 4.005. Plot these means on the control chart you constructed in (*a*). Which sample means, if any, would cause you to conclude that the process is out of control?

63. Refer to Exercise 62. Suppose that the lengths of a sample of 5 bolts are as follows: 3.995, 4.012, 4.035, 3.804, 3.792. Do these data provide sufficient evidence for you to conclude that the process is out of control?

64. Sometimes quality-control technicians construct control charts to control the proportion of defective items produced. For this kind of control chart, the center line is p_0, the proportion of defectives produced when the manufacturing process is under control. The lower control limit is $p_0 - 3\sqrt{p_0(1 - p_0)/n}$, and the upper control limit is $p_0 + \sqrt{p_0(1 - p_0)/n}$. Samples are selected at successive time periods, and $\hat{p}$, the proportion

FIGURE 7.8
Control chart for proportion defective

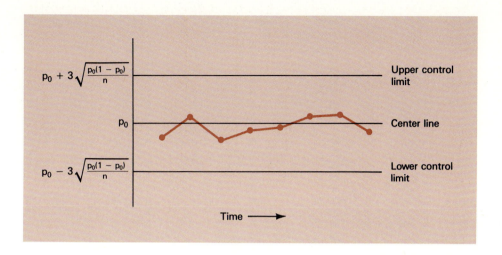

of defective items, is calculated for each. When $\hat{p}$ falls within the control limits, we conclude that the process is under control. When $\hat{p}$ falls outside the control limits, we conclude that the process is out of control. Figure 7.8 shows a control chart for the proportion of defective items with several plotted values of $\hat{p}$.

Suppose that a manufacturing process is considered to be under control when the proportion defective is 0.10. Construct a control chart for use with samples of size 100.

65. Suppose that in 10 samples of size 100, the following number of defective items are found: 5, 14, 2, 20, 12, 13, 22, 7, 11, 21.   **(a)** Plot the sample proportions on the control chart you constructed in Exercise 64.   **(b)** Was the process ever out of control? For which samples?

 66. Ⓒ A random sample of persons who regularly shop at Mall A and an independent random sample of persons who regularly shop at Mall B participate in a survey. Each person in the two samples answers the following questions:

1. About how many hours per day do you spend watching television?
2. How long have you lived at your present address?
3. How many cars are owned by members of your household?

The results are as follows.

Subject	Shopping mall	Hours TV per day	Length of residence	No. of cars
1	A	2	1	1
2	A	3	6	2
3	A	2	16	3
4	A	2	0.5	3
5	A	6	9	4
6	A	5	7	2
7	A	4	7	3
8	A	4	2	3
9	A	2	7	4
10	A	1	9	2
11	A	4	2	5
12	A	1	0.5	4

Subject	Shopping mall	Hours TV per day	Length of residence	No. of cars
13	A	0	9	5
14	A	2	2	2
15	A	5	8	2
16	A	5	19	3
17	A	5	8	4
18	A	6	5	4
19	A	1	7	2
20	A	4	7	2
21	A	4	5	2
22	A	2	8	3
23	A	5	8	3
24	A	4	3	4
25	A	0	9	4
26	A	5	8	3
27	A	6	18	1
28	A	0.5	1	2
29	A	0	7	2
30	A	3	3	3
31	A	0.5	14	2
32	A	5	2	3
33	A	1	13	2
34	A	9	12	3
35	A	2	3	3
36	A	6	7	2
37	A	0	16	2
38	A	0	5	3
39	A	0.5	12	3
40	A	1	2	2
41	A	6	11	2
42	A	7	16	3
43	A	0	5	3
44	A	2	2	3
45	A	4	7	3
46	A	0	3	3
47	A	2	5	3
48	A	4	15	3
49	A	7	15	2
50	A	1	10	2
1	B	6	0.5	1
2	B	5	15	2
3	B	7	7	2
4	B	7	1	3
5	B	7	16	2
6	B	3	13	2
7	B	7	4	3
8	B	6	3	1
9	B	4	15	2
10	B	7	3	2
11	B	7	16	3
12	B	2	11	4
13	B	3	11	2
14	B	5	12	3
15	B	4	15	1
16	B	4	10	3
17	B	6	2	2
18	B	11	7	2
19	B	7	10	2
20	B	2	17	4
21	B	8	13	1

Subject	Shopping mall	Hours TV per day	Length of residence	No. of cars
22	B	5	10	1
23	B	2	16	2
24	B	7	2	3
25	B	2.5	8	2
26	B	2.5	15	2
27	B	3	11	3
28	B	8	6	2
29	B	6	10	3
30	B	6	8	2
31	B	2	15	2
32	B	5	2	3
33	B	5	9	3
34	B	2	14	4
35	B	6	14	2
36	B	6	10	3
37	B	4	5	1
38	B	9	13	2
39	B	2	7	2
40	B	4	13	4
41	B	8	7	2
42	B	2	15	4
43	B	6	10	3
44	B	4	12	2
45	B	8	15	2
46	B	3	15	2
47	B	3	10	4
48	B	9	13	3
49	B	8	7	3
50	B	9	8	2

Calculate the variance and the mean for the number of hours per day spent watching television by the respondents in Sample A. Do the same for Sample B.

67. Ⓒ Refer to Exercise 66. For the respondents in Sample A, compute the variance and the mean for length of residence at present address. Do the same for Sample B.

68. Ⓒ Refer to Exercise 66. For the respondents in Sample A, calculate the proportion who have more than two cars. Do the same for Sample B.

69. Refer to Exercise 66. Can we conclude from these data that the population of shoppers at Mall A, on the average, spend less time per day watching television? Let $\alpha = 0.05$, and find the p value.

70. Refer to Exercise 66. On the basis of these sample data, can we conclude that the population of shoppers at Mall B, on the average, have lived at their present residences for a greater number of years than have shoppers at Mall A? Let $\alpha = 0.05$, and find the p value.

71. Refer to Exercise 66. Can we conclude on the basis of these sample data that for the population of shoppers at Mall B, the proportion who own more than two cars is less than for the population of Mall A shoppers? Let $\alpha = 0.05$, and find the p value.

 72. Ⓒ An executive with a hospitalization insurance company wishes to study the characteristics of policyholders aged 65 or over who filed claims during the previous year. A simple random sample of size 700 is selected from the relevant population. Two items of information collected from claims records are the number of days of hospitalization and whether or not the patient had surgery. The results are as follows: (1 = yes, surgery was performed; 0 = no, surgery was not performed).

Subject	No. of days	Surgery?	Subject	No. of days	Surgery?
1	11	1	58	2	0
2	6	1	59	14	1
3	15	1	60	10	0
4	10	0	61	12	1
5	13	0	62	8	0
6	13	1	63	10	1
7	12	1	64	9	1
8	14	1	65	8	1
9	12	1	66	12	1
10	10	0	67	10	1
11	15	1	68	11	1
12	12	1	69	11	1
13	13	1	70	9	0
14	9	1	71	12	1
15	16	1	72	9	0
16	14	1	73	12	1
17	5	1	74	12	1
18	12	1	75	12	0
19	11	0	76	6	0
20	8	0	77	10	0
21	14	1	78	7	1
22	8	1	79	9	1
23	8	1	80	8	0
24	6	1	81	14	0
25	13	0	82	6	1
26	11	0	83	16	0
27	10	1	84	17	1
28	16	1	85	13	1
29	7	1	86	12	1
30	12	0	87	17	1
31	11	1	88	15	1
32	9	0	89	14	1
33	15	1	90	8	1
34	14	1	91	4	1
35	10	1	92	5	1
36	10	1	93	13	1
37	12	0	94	7	0
38	10	1	95	11	1
39	8	0	96	8	1
40	9	0	97	7	1
41	13	0	98	10	1
42	11	1	99	12	1
43	7	1	100	4	1
44	8	1	101	5	1
45	9	1	102	9	1
46	8	1	103	12	0
47	12	0	104	6	1
48	11	1	105	13	0
49	14	1	106	14	1
50	12	1	107	8	1
51	13	0	108	8	1
52	13	1	109	7	1
53	8	1	110	12	1
54	6	1	111	13	1
55	6	1	112	12	1
56	16	0	113	9	1
57	12	1	114	10	1

Subject	No. of days	Surgery?	Subject	No. of days	Surgery?
115	7	0	172	9	1
116	7	0	173	11	1
117	8	0	174	5	0
118	12	1	175	6	1
119	9	1	176	12	0
120	8	0	177	10	1
121	9	1	178	10	1
122	11	1	179	15	1
123	6	1	180	7	1
124	18	1	181	12	1
125	6	1	182	10	0
126	7	1	183	15	0
127	4	1	184	9	1
128	12	1	185	8	0
129	8	1	186	11	1
130	10	0	187	12	1
131	6	1	188	15	1
132	14	1	189	9	1
133	7	0	190	8	0
134	13	1	191	5	1
135	16	0	192	5	0
136	7	1	193	13	1
137	9	1	194	6	1
138	12	0	195	4	1
139	10	1	196	13	1
140	9	1	197	8	1
141	11	1	198	7	1
142	6	0	199	16	1
143	8	1	200	11	0
144	10	1	201	4	1
145	4	0	202	10	1
146	10	0	203	10	1
147	4	1	204	6	1
148	8	0	205	9	0
149	10	0	206	9	0
150	5	1	207	15	0
151	10	1	208	17	1
152	9	0	209	15	1
153	11	0	210	8	0
154	7	1	211	7	1
155	7	0	212	11	1
156	11	1	213	9	1
157	6	0	214	15	1
158	7	1	215	11	0
159	10	1	216	8	1
160	14	1	217	6	1
161	13	0	218	12	0
162	7	1	219	6	1
163	7	1	220	8	1
164	3	1	221	11	1
165	13	1	222	6	1
166	13	1	223	17	1
167	7	0	224	9	0
168	6	1	225	7	1
169	10	1	226	10	1
170	7	0	227	13	1
171	9	1	228	9	0

Subject	No. of days	Surgery?	Subject	No. of days	Surgery?
229	10	1	287	15	0
230	1	0	288	12	1
231	9	1	289	8	0
232	5	1	290	15	1
233	9	1	291	8	1
234	14	1	292	10	1
235	11	0	293	14	1
236	11	1	294	6	1
237	8	0	295	9	1
238	6	0	296	14	1
239	12	0	297	10	1
240	14	1	298	9	1
241	12	1	299	8	1
242	9	0	300	12	1
243	11	1	301	11	0
244	7	1	302	15	1
245	8	0	303	12	1
246	8	1	304	11	1
247	9	1	305	12	1
248	9	1	306	6	0
249	11	1	307	11	0
250	13	1	308	5	1
251	14	0	309	17	1
252	13	0	310	13	1
253	10	1	311	11	0
254	10	1	312	13	1
255	12	1	313	6	0
256	8	1	314	11	1
257	11	1	315	12	1
258	7	0	316	5	1
259	9	1	317	10	1
260	8	1	318	12	1
261	4	1	319	11	1
262	12	1	320	9	1
263	8	0	321	12	1
264	3	1	322	11	1
265	7	1	323	10	1
266	9	1	324	14	1
267	10	0	325	8	1
268	10	1	326	7	0
269	12	1	327	9	1
270	11	0	328	15	1
271	14	1	329	5	1
272	13	1	330	9	0
273	11	1	331	16	1
274	7	1	332	9	1
275	11	1	333	8	1
276	5	1	334	5	0
277	8	1	335	9	1
278	11	0	336	11	1
279	8	1	337	5	1
280	8	1	338	11	0
281	8	1	339	10	1
282	7	0	340	14	0
283	9	1	341	11	1
284	10	1	342	10	1
285	12	1	343	11	1
286	11	1	344	6	0

Subject	No. of days	Surgery?	Subject	No. of days	Surgery?
345	6	0	403	8	0
346	14	1	404	11	1
347	7	0	405	9	1
348	7	1	406	7	1
349	9	1	407	8	0
350	10	0	408	13	1
351	11	0	409	11	1
352	13	1	410	9	0
353	8	1	411	7	1
354	14	1	412	7	0
355	8	0	413	11	1
356	11	0	414	13	0
357	12	1	415	9	0
358	12	1	416	10	0
359	8	0	417	12	0
360	9	1	418	11	0
361	11	1	419	3	1
362	12	1	420	11	1
363	14	1	421	14	0
364	9	1	422	12	1
365	10	0	423	8	1
366	5	1	424	8	1
367	8	0	425	6	1
368	10	1	426	13	1
369	6	1	427	10	0
370	11	0	428	4	1
371	9	0	429	8	1
372	11	1	430	16	1
373	10	1	431	7	1
374	6	1	432	8	0
375	6	0	433	8	1
376	7	1	434	6	0
377	13	1	435	8	1
378	7	0	436	8	1
379	13	0	437	8	1
380	21	1	438	11	1
381	15	0	439	9	0
382	17	1	440	9	0
383	10	0	441	9	1
384	8	1	442	6	0
385	10	0	443	10	0
386	6	1	444	11	1
387	5	0	445	10	1
388	9	0	446	11	1
389	8	1	447	14	1
390	9	0	448	9	1
391	7	1	449	5	1
392	11	1	450	12	1
393	10	1	451	11	1
394	8	1	452	10	0
395	8	0	453	13	1
396	12	1	454	13	0
397	10	1	455	10	1
398	12	1	456	8	0
399	9	0	457	13	1
400	8	0	458	10	0
401	12	1	459	18	1
402	17	1	460	9	0

Subject	No. of days	Surgery?	Subject	No. of days	Surgery?
461	13	0	519	8	1
462	13	1	520	7	0
463	5	1	521	10	1
464	10	1	522	14	1
465	10	1	523	12	1
466	8	1	524	8	1
467	9	0	525	12	1
468	8	1	526	9	0
469	9	1	527	14	0
470	8	0	528	5	1
471	12	0	529	9	1
472	15	0	530	14	0
473	10	1	531	10	1
474	8	1	532	12	1
475	7	1	533	15	1
476	11	0	534	5	1
477	7	1	535	7	1
478	16	1	536	18	1
479	6	1	537	10	1
480	8	1	538	7	1
481	8	0	539	10	0
482	13	1	540	9	0
483	7	1	541	12	0
484	14	0	542	11	0
485	10	1	543	16	1
486	12	1	544	10	1
487	13	1	545	10	1
488	7	1	546	5	1
489	10	1	547	12	0
490	4	0	548	9	1
491	11	1	549	13	0
492	8	1	550	13	1
493	11	1	551	7	0
494	9	0	552	12	1
495	9	1	553	10	1
496	11	1	554	2	1
497	17	1	555	12	1
498	9	1	556	11	0
499	13	0	557	17	1
500	16	1	558	9	1
501	9	1	559	9	1
502	7	0	560	11	1
503	9	1	561	14	0
504	11	0	562	15	1
505	5	1	563	10	0
506	14	1	564	11	1
507	7	1	565	11	1
508	11	1	566	7	1
509	11	1	567	5	1
510	7	1	568	14	0
511	11	1	569	6	1
512	14	0	570	7	1
513	7	1	571	14	1
514	10	1	572	11	1
515	11	0	573	11	1
516	7	0	574	6	0
517	7	0	575	3	0
518	12	1	576	10	0

Subject	No. of days	Surgery?	Subject	No. of days	Surgery?
577	15	1	635	6	0
578	11	0	636	12	1
579	13	1	637	14	1
580	8	1	638	9	1
581	19	1	639	10	0
582	11	0	640	8	1
583	12	1	641	12	1
584	7	0	642	12	0
585	11	1	643	11	1
586	9	1	644	16	1
587	8	1	645	5	0
588	4	0	646	13	0
589	11	1	647	11	1
590	8	1	648	9	1
591	12	1	649	11	1
592	4	0	650	12	1
593	10	1	651	7	0
594	6	1	652	11	1
595	10	0	653	12	1
596	13	0	654	17	1
597	11	1	655	5	1
598	7	0	656	11	0
599	12	0	657	8	0
600	12	1	658	9	0
601	9	1	659	9	1
602	11	1	660	11	1
603	7	1	661	13	0
604	9	0	662	9	1
605	11	0	663	11	1
606	7	1	664	10	1
607	7	1	665	8	0
608	6	1	666	16	1
609	9	1	667	12	1
610	6	0	668	10	0
611	13	1	669	11	1
612	10	1	670	10	1
613	17	0	671	10	1
614	10	1	672	5	1
615	12	1	673	6	0
616	11	1	674	12	0
617	16	1	675	16	0
618	11	1	676	5	1
619	9	1	677	11	1
620	9	1	678	10	1
621	12	0	679	7	1
622	10	1	680	7	0
623	14	0	681	6	1
624	15	1	682	11	1
625	11	1	683	15	0
626	3	0	684	11	1
627	11	1	685	12	0
628	10	0	686	6	1
629	11	0	687	7	1
630	14	1	688	13	1
631	11	1	689	13	1
632	6	1	690	15	1
633	10	1	691	2	0
634	4	1	692	9	1

Subject	No. of days	Surgery?	Subject	No. of days	Surgery?
693	9	1	697	4	1
694	7	0	698	10	1
695	10	1	699	14	0
696	16	0	700	12	1

Calculate the mean number of days spent in the hospital by the patients in the sample. Calculate the sample standard deviation.

73. [c] Refer to Exercise 72. What proportion of the patients in the sample had surgery?

74. [c] Refer to Exercise 72. Can we conclude from these data that the mean number of days of hospitalization for the sampled population is greater than 7? Let $\alpha = 0.05$, and determine the p value.

75. [c] Refer to Exercise 72. Can we conclude on the basis of these data that for the sampled population of patients, the proportion who had surgery is less than 0.75? Let $\alpha = 0.05$, and determine the p value.

76. [c] Refer to Exercise 72. Pretend that the data represent two populations: a population of patients who had surgery, and a population of patients who did not have surgery. Select a simple random sample of 10 patients from those who did not have surgery, and select an independent simple random sample of 15 patients from those who had surgery. On the basis of these data, can we conclude that the mean length of hospitalization for the two populations is different? Let $\alpha = 0.05$, and find the p value. Compare your results with those of your classmates.

For Exercises 77 through 88, do the following: Select a simple random sample from the population of companies listed in Appendix III. (Ask your instructor what size sample you should select.) For each company in your sample, record the data on each of the six variables.

77. [c] Formulate and test an appropriate null hypothesis about the population mean assets. Select your own significance level, and follow the seven-step hypothesis-testing procedure. Find the p value for your test.

78. [c] Repeat Exercise 77 using the sales variable.

79. [c] Repeat Exercise 77 using the market value variable.

80. [c] Repeat Exercise 77 using the net profits variable.

81. [c] Repeat Exercise 77 using the cash flow variable.

82. [c] Repeat Exercise 77 using the number employed variable.

83. [c] Formulate and test an appropriate null hypothesis about the proportion of companies in the population with assets of $1 billion or more. Select your own significance level, and follow the seven-step hypothesis-testing procedure. Find the p value for your test.

84. [c] Repeat Exercise 83 with a hypothesis about the proportion of companies in the population with sales of $1 billion or more.

85. [c] Repeat Exercise 83 with a hypothesis about the proportion of companies in the population with a market value of $1 billion or more.

86. [c] Repeat Exercise 83 with a hypothesis about the proportion of companies in the population with net profits of $100 million or more.

87. [c] Repeat Exercise 83 with a hypothesis about the proportion of companies in the population with a cash flow of $1 billion or more.

88. Ⓒ Repeat Exercise 83 with a hypothesis about the proportion of companies in the population with 50,000 or more employees.

PRACTICE WITH REAL DATA

Compare the readability levels of daily newspapers and news magazines with those of the core course textbooks required for freshman students at your college or university. Select a random sample from each, using the resources of your library and college bookstore. Use the Fog Index (Robert Gunning, *The Technique of Clear Writing,* revised edition, New York: McGraw-Hill, 1968) as the measure of readability. The Fog Index is computed as follows. For a selected passage:

1. Count the number of words and divide the total by the number of sentences. This gives the average sentence length for the passage.
2. For every 100 words, count the number of words of three syllables or more. Do not count proper names, words like *completed* or *exposes* that are formed from two-syllable words by adding *-ed* or *-es*, or words that are combinations of short, easy words (such as *underscore*).
3. Add the results from steps 1 and 2 and multiply the total by 0.4. This result is the Fog Index for the passage.

To compute the Fog Index for a given book, magazine, or newspaper, select a random sample of passages from each.

After you have collected your data, test the null hypothesis that the two populations of reading material have equal mean readability scores. Let $\alpha = 0.05$, and find the p value. Ask your instructor about the proper sample size.

8. Hypothesis Tests for Three or More Populations: Analysis of Variance and Chi-Square

CHAPTER OBJECTIVES: Now that you have learned the basic concepts and techniques of statistical inference, you can use these ideas and skills in more complex situations. In this chapter you learn to test hypotheses about three or more populations. The use of chi-square will also allow you to test other kinds of hypotheses.

After studying this chapter and working the exercises, you should be able to do the following.

1. Describe the completely randomized experimental design and use the appropriate analysis-of-variance technique to analyze the data generated by this design

2. Test the null hypothesis that

a. three or more population means are equal

b. three or more population proportions are equal

c. two variables are independent

d. a sample has been drawn from a population with specified characteristics

In Chapter 7 you learned to test five kinds of null hypotheses. They were: (a) a population mean is equal to some specified numerical value, (b) the mean of a population of differences between pairs of measurements is equal to zero, (c) two population means are equal, (d) a population proportion is equal to some specified numerical value, and (e) two population proportions are equal.

In this chapter we extend to more complex situations the concepts and techniques that we employed to test these five kinds of hypotheses. More specifically, in this chapter you will learn to test the null hypotheses that (a) three or more population means are equal, and (b) three or more population proportions are equal. The technique for testing the equality of three or more population means is called *analysis of variance*, and that for testing the equality of three or more population proportions is called the *chi-square test of homogeneity*. You will also learn to use the chi-square test to test two additional null hypotheses: (a) that two variables are independent (the *chi-square test of independence*), and (b) that a sample was drawn from a population with specified characteristics (the *chi-square goodness-of-fit test*).

We may view the preceding chapters, which covered the basic concepts and techniques of descriptive and inferential statistics, as providing the foundation for this and later chapters. The objective of this portion of the book is to help you understand some of the more widely used tools of statistical analysis.

8.1 ANALYSIS OF VARIANCE

This section is concerned with *analysis of variance*, which is defined as follows.

Analysis of variance is a technique whereby the total variation present in a set of data is partitioned into several components. Associated with each of these components is a specific source of variation, so that in the analysis, it is possible to ascertain the magnitude of the contribution of each of these sources to the total variation.

Analysis of variance is most often used to analyze data derived from designed experiments. Its use, however, is not restricted to this type of analysis. As some of the examples and exercises of this chapter show, we can also use analysis-of-variance techniques to analyze data from surveys.

When we design experiments with an analysis in mind—before we conduct the experiment—we identify those sources of variation that we consider important. We then choose a design that will let us measure the extent to which these sources contribute to the total variation.

We use analysis of variance to estimate and test hypotheses about both population variances and population means. Although this text deals with testing hypotheses about population means, the conclusions depend on the magnitudes of the observed variances.

The valid use of analysis of variance depends on a set of fundamental assumptions. We will state these briefly in the section that follows. Not all the assumptions will be met perfectly in a given situation. Thus, it is important that you be aware of the underlying assumptions so that you will be able to recognize serious departures from them.

We discuss analysis of variance as it is used to analyze data from a completely randomized design. We shall use the seven-step hypothesis-testing procedure introduced in Chapter 7 to illustrate the analysis-of-variance procedure.

In order to facilitate this discussion, we shall now define two terms. We shall define other terms as we introduce them.

A treatment is any factor that the experimenter controls.

The term *treatment* is broadly used in the design of experiments. It can refer to any factor that the experimenter controls. It may refer, for example, to a type of drug, one of several concentrations of a single drug, a new type of house paint, an advertising technique, or a particular training program. The term originated in the early days of analysis of variance, when different groups actually did have different treatments (in the usual sense of the word) applied to their respective experimental units.

Treatments are applied to experimental units.

We call an entity that receives a treatment an *experimental unit*. An experimental unit may be, for example, an individual, a single white mouse, a group of white mice, a plot of ground, a segment of the consuming public, a group of trainees, or an item of production. We may also think of it as that entity on which we take a measurement in order to obtain a value for the variable of interest.

Mean square = variance

In this chapter we will frequently use the expression "mean square," and the word "variance" synonymously. Thus, when we are speaking of a measure of variability for a data set, we may speak of the mean square of the set of data rather than the variance of the set of data.

8.2 THE COMPLETELY RANDOMIZED EXPERIMENTAL DESIGN

In Chapter 7, you learned how to use the t test to test the null hypothesis that two population means are equal. To refresh your memory on the use of the t test, consider the following example.

EXAMPLE 8.1 Researchers who work for a manufacturing firm wish to compare the effect of two different raw materials on the quality of their product. Length of life of the product is the criterion of interest. The researchers randomly select 10 specimens of the product made with raw material A and 8 specimens made with raw material B. The lifetimes of the specimens in hundreds of hours are as follows: raw material A: 5, 6, 5, 8, 6, 7, 6, 5, 6, 7; raw material B: 8, 9, 8, 7, 9, 9, 10, 8. The researchers wish to test the null hypothesis that the raw material used makes no difference in the quality of the product. That is, they wish to test the null hypothesis that the mean lifetime is the same regardless of which raw material is used.

SOLUTION We state the null and alternative hypotheses symbolically as follows:

$$H_0: \mu_A = \mu_B, \qquad H_1: \mu_A \neq \mu_B$$

Suppose we let $\alpha = 0.05$.

To test the null hypothesis, we first compute the following statistics from the sample data:

$$\bar{x}_A = 6.1, \qquad s_A^2 = \frac{\Sigma(x_{iA} - \bar{x}_A)^2}{n_A - 1} = \frac{8.9}{9} = 0.9889$$

$$\bar{x}_B = 8.5, \qquad s_B^2 = \frac{\Sigma(x_{iB} - \bar{x}_B)^2}{n_B - 1} = \frac{6.0}{7} = 0.8571$$

We now pool the sample variances to obtain

$$s_p^2 = \frac{9(0.9889) + 7(0.8571)}{16} = 0.9312$$

We now compute

$$t = \frac{6.1 - 8.5}{\sqrt{\dfrac{0.9312}{10} + \dfrac{0.9312}{8}}} = \frac{-2.4}{0.4577} = -5.2436$$

Since -5.2436 is smaller than the critical t of -2.1199, we reject H_0 and conclude that the two raw materials do have different effects on the mean lifetime of the product.

Solution Using ANOVA

We may also test the null hypothesis that $\mu_A = \mu_B$ by means of analysis of variance. For this problem we may identify two components of the total variation, each of which has its identifiable source. They are: (1) the *variation due to treatments,* or variation caused by the fact that two different raw materials are used, and (2) the *residual variation,* the variation resulting from all sources other than the treatments. Let us compute the variances associated with each of these sources. The variability due to treatments, which we may call the *mean square among treatments* (MSA), is given by

$$\text{MSA} = \frac{\Sigma n_i(\bar{x}_i - \bar{\bar{x}})^2}{k - 1} \tag{8.1}$$

where n_i and $\bar{x}_i$ are the size and mean, respectively, of the ith sample, $\bar{\bar{x}}$ is the weighted mean of the sample means, and k is the number of treatments.

For the present example, we have $n_A = 10$, $\bar{x}_A = 6.1$, $n_B = 8$, $\bar{x}_B = 8.5$, $k = 2$, and $\bar{\bar{x}} = [10(6.1) + 8(8.5)]/18 = 7.1667$. From these results we compute

$$\text{MSA} = \frac{10(6.1 - 7.1667)^2 + 8(8.5 - 7.1667)^2}{1} = 25.6$$

The variability resulting from all other sources, which we now call the *mean square within treatments* or *error mean square* (MSE), is the pooled sample variance s_p^2 that we have already computed. That is,

$$\text{MSE} = \frac{9(0.9889) + 7(0.8571)}{16} = 0.9312$$

The test statistic is

$$F = \frac{\text{MSA}}{\text{MSE}} \qquad (8.2)$$

For the present example, we have

$$F = \frac{25.6}{0.9312} = 27.4914$$

When the assumptions are met and when H_0 is true, the distribution of the statistic F of Equation 8.2 follows a distribution known as the F distribution. This distribution is given in Table E of the Appendix. The critical value of the test statistic, therefore, will come from Table E. Since the F statistic has a numerator (MSA) and a denominator (MSE), we must enter Table E with two degrees-of-freedom values (one for the numerator and one for the denominator) in order to obtain the critical value. The numerator degrees of freedom are equal to $k - 1$, the number of treatments minus one. The denominator degrees of freedom are equal to $n - k$, the total sample size minus the number of treatments. For the present example, the numerator degrees of freedom are $2 - 1 = 1$. The denominator degrees of freedom are $18 - 2 = 16$. When we enter Table E with 1 (numerator) and 16 (denominator) degrees of freedom and $\alpha = 0.05$, we find the critical value of F to be 4.49.

> We need two degrees-of-freedom values to find *F*, one for the numerator and one for the denominator.

Decision Rule   The decision rule for use in analysis of variance is as follows:

If the computed value of the test statistic is equal to or greater than the critical value, reject H_0.

Since, in our present example, the computed value of $F = 27.4914$ is greater than the critical value of $F = 4.49$, we reject H_0.

Note that the statistical decision that we reached using analysis of variance is the same as the statistical decision that we reached when we used the t test. This is not a coincidence, since the two tests are equivalent. Note that the critical F value of 4.49 is equal to the critical t value squared. That is, $4.49 = (-2.1199)^2$. Also, the computed F of 27.4914 is equal to the computed t squared. That is, $27.4914 = (-5.2436)^2$. These values may not be exactly equal in every instance because of rounding errors. In general, for the same α, F with 1 and $n - k$ degrees of freedom is equal to the square of t (two-sided test) with $n - k$ degrees of freedom. It is this relationship between the t distribution and the F distribution that makes the two tests equivalent.

Example with Three Treatments

Suppose, for the experiment described in this example, that there are three raw materials of interest: A, B, and C. That is, suppose that we wish to test the null hypothesis that three population means are equal against the alternative that they are not all equal. We may express these hypotheses as follows:

$$H_0: \mu_A = \mu_B = \mu_C, \qquad H_1: \text{Not all } \mu\text{'s are equal}$$

We cannot use the t test to test the null hypothesis that three or more means are equal. We can, however, use analysis of variance. Let us assume that the use of raw material C in the production of 12 specimens yields the following length of life values: 10, 10, 9, 8, 8, 9, 10, 9, 8, 9, 9, 8. We now compute

$$\bar{x}_C = 8.9, \ s_C^2 = 0.6291$$

$$\bar{\bar{x}} = \frac{10(6.1) + 8(8.5) + 12(8.9)}{30} = 7.86$$

$$\text{MSA} = \frac{10(6.1 - 7.86)^2 + 8(8.5 - 7.86)^2 + 12(8.9 - 7.86)^2}{2} = 23.616$$

$$\text{MSE} = \frac{9(0.9889) + 7(0.8571) + 11(0.6291)}{27} = 0.8081$$

$$F = \frac{23.616}{0.8081} = 29.22$$

Since our computation shows that 29.22 is greater than the critical F of 3.35 for $\alpha = 0.05$ and 2 and 27 degrees of freedom, we can reject the null hypothesis at the 0.05 level of significance and conclude that the three raw materials are not, on the average, of equal quality.

The use of analysis of variance in this example illustrates the application of the technique, which we call *one-way analysis* of variance, to the *completely randomized experimental design*.

Assumptions Underlying One-Way Analysis of Variance

The assumptions underlying one-way analysis of variance, which are extensions of the assumptions underlying the t test for two independent samples, are as follows: (a) The k sets of observed data constitute k independent random samples from the specified populations. (b) Each of the populations represented by a sample is normally distributed, with mean μ_j and variance σ_j^2. (c) Each of the populations has the same variance. That is, $\sigma_1^2 = \sigma_2^2 = \cdots = \sigma_k^2 = \sigma^2$, the common variance.

Figure 8.1 shows how the graph of the sampled populations would look in the case in which there are three samples to be analyzed, H_0 is true, and the assumptions are all met. Figure 8.2 pictures the populations represented by an experiment in which there are three samples to be analyzed and the assumptions of equal population variances and normally distributed populations are met, but H_0 is false because none of the three population means are equal.

When we use the *completely randomized design,* we assign the treatments at random to the experimental units. Suppose, for example, that we want to road-test four brands of tires, A, B, C, and D, to determine whether there are any

FIGURE 8.1
The populations represented by an experiment in which there are three samples to be analyzed, H_0 is true, and the analysis-of-variance assumptions are met

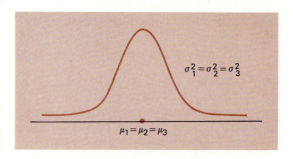

$$\sigma_1^2 = \sigma_2^2 = \sigma_3^2$$

$$\mu_1 = \mu_2 = \mu_3$$

FIGURE 8.2
Three samples: The assumptions of equal variances and normally distributed populations are met, but H_0 is false because none of the population means are equal

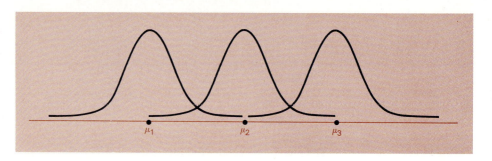

μ_1 μ_2 μ_3

differences among the brands with respect to expected tire mileage. We can assign 10 tires of each brand at random to the 40 rear wheels of 20 cars. We can then drive the cars until a predetermined amount of tread wear occurs. At that time we record the number of miles driven. We then use an analysis of variance to decide whether the brands differ with respect to expected tire mileage. As we have seen, the two sources of variation that we isolate are *variation due to treatment* (brand) *differences* and *residual variation,* which measures the variation resulting from all sources other than the tire brand.

We analyze data from an experiment that uses the completely randomized design by what is known as the *one-way analysis of variance.* This is so called because we classify the experimental units (and consequently the measurements obtained) according to only one criterion—the treatment group to which they belong.

We may also use one-way analysis of variance to analyze data from a sample survey in which we draw a random sample from each of several populations.

We use one-way analysis of variance to analyze data from a completely randomized experimental design.

Computational Formulas

The formulas calculating MSA and MSE that we used in Example 8.1 to illustrate the application of one-way analysis of variance are the definitional or conceptual formulas. They are too cumbersome for general use, especially when there are a large number of samples or when the sample sizes are large. We now present some computational formulas that greatly facilitate the calculations when they have to be performed by hand.

TABLE 8.1
Sample data for analysis by one-way analysis of variance

	Population sampled				
	1	2	3	$\cdots$	k
	x_{11}	x_{12}	x_{13}	$\cdots$	x_{1k}
	x_{21}	x_{22}	x_{23}	$\cdots$	x_{2k}
	x_{31}	x_{32}	x_{33}	$\cdots$	x_{3k}
	.	.	.	.	.
	.	.	.	.	.
	.	.	.	.	.
	$x_{n_1 1}$	$x_{n_2 2}$	$x_{n_3 3}$	$\cdots$	$x_{n_k k}$
Total	$T_{.1}$	$T_{.2}$	$T_{.3}$	$\cdots$	$T_{.k}$ $T_{..}$
Mean	$\bar{x}_{.1}$	$\bar{x}_{.2}$	$\bar{x}_{.3}$	$\cdots$	$\bar{x}_{.k}$ $\bar{x}_{..}$

We may display experimental or survey data that are to be analyzed by one-way analysis of variance as in Table 8.1. We define the symbols used in Table 8.1 as follows:

$$x_{ij} = \text{the } i\text{th observation that receives the } j\text{th treatment}$$

$$i = 1, 2, \ldots, n_j, j = 1, 2, \ldots, k$$

$$n_j = \text{the number of observations in the } j\text{th sample}$$

$$T_{.j} = \sum_{i=1}^{n_j} x_{ij} = \text{total of the } j\text{th column}$$

$$n = \sum_{j=1}^{k} n_j$$

The Total Sum of Squares We define analysis of variance as an arithmetic process by which we partition the *total variation* in a set of data into components that are attributable to different sources. In this context, variation refers to a *sum of squared deviations of values from their mean*, or *sum of squares*. The *total sum of squares* that we may compute from a set of data is the sum of the square of the deviation of each observation from the mean of all the observations taken together.

The computing formula for the total sum of squares is

$$\text{SST} = \sum_{j=1}^{k} \sum_{i=1}^{n_j} x_{ij}^2 - C \tag{8.3}$$

where

$$C = \frac{\left(\sum_{j=1}^{k} \sum_{i=1}^{n_j} x_{ij} \right)^2}{n}$$

and is called the correction term.

The Among-Treatments Sum of Squares   The computing formula for the among-treatments sum of squares, which reflects the variability among the sample or treatment means, is given by

$$\text{SSA} = \sum_{j=1}^{k} \left(\frac{T_{.j}^2}{n_j} \right) - C \tag{8.4}$$

The Error Sum of Squares   The error sum of squares SSE is sometimes called the *residual sum of squares* or *within-treatments sum of squares,* since it reflects the variability within the samples. Although it is possible to compute the error sum of squares directly, subtracting the among-treatments sum of squares from the total sum of squares is more convenient. That is,

$$\text{SSE} = \text{SST} - \text{SSA} \tag{8.5}$$

When the assumptions underlying one-way analysis of variance are met and the null hypothesis is true (that is, when $\mu_1 = \mu_2 = \cdots = \mu_k$), we can show that the among-treatments mean square

$$\text{MSA} = \frac{\text{SSA}}{k-1} \qquad \text{and the error mean square} \qquad \text{MSE} = \frac{\text{SSE}}{n-k}$$

both yield independent and unbiased estimates of σ^2, the population variance that is assumed to be common to all populations.

Suppose that the null hypothesis is true, that is, that there are no treatment effects. Then the two estimates of σ^2 ought to be fairly close in size, since they are independent estimates of the same parameter. Suppose, however, that the null hypothesis is false. Then the among-treatments mean square, which reflects variability among population means, ought to be larger than the error mean square, which is an unbiased estimate of the common population variance even when H_0 is not true.

We compare the two mean squares by forming their ratio, using Equation 8.2. If the numerator and denominator of Equation 8.2 are about equal, the variance ratio is close to 1. Then the hypothesis of equal population means is supported. If, however, the among-treatments mean square is much larger than the within-treatments mean square, the variance ratio is much greater than 1. In this case the hypothesis of equal population means becomes suspect.

Even when the null hypothesis is true, it is unlikely that the two estimates of σ^2 will be equal, because of the uncertainty (variation) of sampling. We must decide, then, how much greater than 1 the computed variance ratio has to be before we can conclude that something other than sampling fluctuation is operating. In other words, we wish to know how large F must be before we are willing to conclude that the observed difference between the two estimates of σ^2 is not due to chance alone.

The *F* Distribution

As we have already pointed out, the ratio of two sample variances, as defined by Equation 8.2, follows a distribution known as the *F* distribution when the sample

**TABLE 8.2
ANOVA table for
one-way analysis
of variance**

Source of variation	Sum of squares (SS)	Degrees of freedom (df)	Mean square (MS)	F
Among-treatments	SSA	$k - 1$	MSA = SSA/$(k - 1)$	$F = $ MSA/MSE
Error	SSE	$n - k$	MSE = SSE/$(n - k)$	
Total	SST	$n - 1$		

variances are computed from samples that have been randomly and independently drawn from normal populations. We need, then, to determine the appropriate F distribution by observing the degrees of freedom associated with the numerator and denominator of F. Once we have done this, the size of the observed F that will cause rejection of the hypothesis of equal population variances depends on the critical value selected. This, in turn, depends on the significance level. In other words, if the computed value of F is equal to or exceeds the critical value of F, we reject the null hypothesis of equal population variances. In the context of analysis of variance, rejecting this hypothesis is equivalent to rejecting the null hypothesis of equal population means.

We may summarize the results of a one-way analysis of variance in an analysis-of-variance (ANOVA) table, such as Table 8.2.

To further illustrate the use of one-way analysis of variance, we consider the following example.

EXAMPLE 8.2 Twenty-four freshman accounting students are randomly assigned to one of three computer-assisted instruction groups (treatments). In Group A, feedback from the computer is immediate. In Group B, there is a 10-second delay; and in Group C, a 20-second delay. At the end of 6 weeks, students are given a test to measure their knowledge of the material covered. The results (coded) are given in Table 8.3. We wish to know whether these data provide sufficient evidence to indicate a difference in treatment effects. We presume that the data comply with the assumptions underlying one-way analysis of variance.

SOLUTION

1. *Hypotheses*

$$H_0: \mu_A = \mu_B = \mu_C$$
$$H_1: \text{At least one population mean is not equal to}$$
$$\text{at least one other population mean}$$

2. *Test statistic.* The test statistic is F of Equation 8.2. When H_0 is true and the assumptions are met, the test statistic is distributed as F with 2 and 21 degrees of freedom. Since $n = 24$ and we have $k = 3$ treatments, the value of the

**TABLE 8.3
Data for
Example 8.2**

Group A	10	14	12	12	10	9	12	10	10
Group B	7	7	8	7	8	9	10	10	
Group C	7	6	9	7	8	9	5		

treatments degrees of freedom is 2, and the value of the error degrees of freedom is $24 - 3 = 21$.

3. *Significance level.*   Let $\alpha = 0.05$.
4. *Decision rule.*   Reject H_0 if the computed F is ≥ 3.47, the critical value of F found in Table E for 2 and 21 degrees of freedom and $\alpha = 0.05$.
5. *Calculations.*   We first compute the sample totals:

$$T_A = 10 + 14 + \cdots + 10 = 99$$

$$T_B = 7 + 7 + \cdots + 10 = 66$$

$$T_C = 7 + 6 + \cdots + 5 = 51$$

The correction term is

$$C = \frac{(99 + 66 + 51)^2}{24} = \frac{(216)^2}{24} = 1944$$

The total sum of squares, by Equation 8.3, is

$$\text{SST} = [(10)^2 + (14)^2 + \cdots + (5)^2] - 1944 = 2050 - 1944 = 106$$

Equation 8.4 yields the following among-treatments sum of squares:

$$\text{SSA} = \frac{(99)^2}{9} + \frac{(66)^2}{8} + \frac{(51)^2}{7} - 1944 = 61.0714$$

By subtraction, we find the error sum of squares to be

$$\text{SSE} = 106 - 61.0714 = 44.9286$$

Table 8.4 on page 261 shows the calculations, along with the mean squares and the computed F.

6. *Statistical decision.*   Since 14.273 is greater than 3.47, we reject H_0.
7. *Conclusion.*   We conclude that the three methods of instruction are not equally effective. Since 14.273 is greater than 6.89, the F for $\alpha = 0.005$, $p < 0.005$.

Computers and ANOVA

Computers make the calculations you need for analysis of variance much easier to do. You can work the exercises in this chapter using one of the computer statistical packages that are available. The input requirements and output formats for the various statistical packages vary somewhat, but anyone familiar with the general concepts of analysis of variance can easily understand them.

Figure 8.3 shows the output for Example 8.2 provided by a one-way analysis-of-variance program found in the STAT+ package. Compare the ANOVA table on the printout with the one given in Table 8.4. The printout gives the three population means and standard deviations. The STAT+ package can also provide additional analyses, including a graph of the data, through the use of appropriate commands.

TABLE 8.4
ANOVA table for
Example 8.2

Source	SS	df	MS	F
Among-treatments	61.0714	2	30.5357	14.273
Error	44.9286	21	2.1394	
Total	106.0000	23		

Exercises

Carry out the seven-step analysis-of-variance procedure at the indicated level of significance, and compute the p value for the test.

8.1 Ⓒ A company testing customer acceptance of a new product uses four different counter displays, A, B, C, and D. It selects 36 stores, matched on all relevant criteria. Each display is used in 9 of the stores. Total sales (coded) at the end of a week are as follows. At the 0.05 level of significance, test the null hypothesis of no difference among the four means.

$$\overset{3}{\underset{243}{}} \quad \overset{7}{\underset{1008}{}} \quad \overset{4}{\underset{484}{}} \quad \overset{4}{\underset{400}{}}$$

A	5	6	7	7	8	6	7	7	6
B	2	2	2	3	3	2	3	3	2
C	2	2	3	3	2	2	2	3	3
D	6	6	7	8	8	8	6	6	6

8.2 Ⓒ The following data give the production costs, in cents per pound, of broilers produced in three production areas, A, B, and C, as reported by 10 producers randomly selected from each area. Do these data provide sufficient evidence to indicate a difference in mean cost among the three regions? Let $\alpha = 0.05$.

A	11	10	12	10	11	9	8	13	12	12	10
B	12	10	9	11	10	12	12	14	8	9	
C	12	13	15	14	14	11	15	14	14	15	

8.3 Ⓒ The table at the top of the following page gives the production cost per dollar of net sales for 24 firms of different asset sizes. Do these data provide sufficient evidence to

FIGURE 8.3
Computer printout
for Example 8.2
using STAT+
microcomputer
package

```
              ONE WAY ANALYSIS OF VARIANCE

              SUM OF      DEGREES OF     MEAN      FISHER'S
   SOURCE     SQUARES      FREEDOM      SQUARE        F
AMONG GROUPS   61.07          2         30.54       14.27
ERROR          44.93         21          2.14
TOTAL         106.00         23

                            STANDARD
   GROUP        MEAN        DEVIATION
     A        11.0000        1.5811
     B         8.2500        1.2817
     C         7.2857        1.4960
```

indicate that firms of different sizes have different mean costs? Let $\alpha = 0.05$. (Assets are given in millions of dollars.)

$10–19.9	69	72	72	66	76	72	70	72
$20–49.9	75	70	80	74	68	80	72	76
$50 and over	83	77	80	74	86	75	85	80

8.4 © The following table shows the results, in miles per gallon, of an experiment conducted to compare three brands of gasoline. Each brand was used in seven different cars of the same weight and engine size, driven under similar conditions. Do these data provide sufficient evidence at the 0.01 level of significance to indicate a difference among brands of gasoline?

Brand A	14	19	19	16	15	17	20
Brand B	20	21	18	20	19	19	18
Brand C	20	26	23	24	23	25	23

8.5 © Researchers conducted a study to compare the characteristics of assembly-line employees of a watch factory. Employees were categorized into five achievement groups (populations): Very high, moderately high, average, low, and very low. Researchers selected a random sample from each population and interviewed and tested them in depth. The following table shows the self-concept scores of subjects in the five samples. Do these data provide sufficient evidence to indicate that the populations differ with respect to mean level of self-concept? Let $\alpha = 0.05$. What use can management make of the results of this experiment?

Very high	90	90	90	95	90	88		
Mod. high	79	83	85	75	93			
Average	77	66	85	87	67	73	75	82
Low	97	81	92	85				
Very low	66	63	83	65	74	64		

8.6 © Market researchers designed a study to compare the characteristics of people with high exposure to various media. Through intensive interviewing, they classified 40 randomly selected adults on the basis of the extent of their exposure to radio, TV, newspapers, and magazines. They included only subjects with "high" exposures to one of these media. For each subject, they obtained scores on a wide range of demographic and psychographic variables. The following table shows the subjects' scores on a test designed to measure knowledge of current events. Test for a difference among population means at the 0.05 level. Prepare a report on the results of this study for the president of the market research firm.

High exposure to											
Radio			*TV*			*Newspapers*			*Magazines*		
11	13	16	18	21	22	11	14	20	15	15	18
14	13	17	16	15	21	16	19	13	10	14	14
17	11	15	22	25	19	15	16	15	15	18	18
11			16			14			13		

8.3 CHI-SQUARE TESTS

For most of the statistical techniques you have studied so far, you need *measurements,* such as weight, length, diameter, distance, amount of money, or score on some type of test. But often the data available for analysis consist of *frequency counts* rather than measurements. The following examples illustrate the point.

Consider the case in which two or more factories produce some product under supposedly identical conditions. We examine a sample of items from each factory. For each sample, we count the number of items that fail to meet certain quality standards. Based on these results, should we conclude that the samples really come from different populations? That is, can we conclude that the factories are different with respect to the proportion of items that fail to meet the standards?

Or suppose that we wish to know, for a population of urban citizens, whether there is a relationship between area of residence and position on a proposal to install a mass rapid transit system. To reach a conclusion, we select a sample of subjects, then for each we ascertain his or her area of residence and position with respect to the mass rapid transit proposal. The sample subjects are then cross-classified according to the two variables, and the number falling into each residence/position category is determined. One such category might be Residence in Area A and Against the Mass Rapid Transit Proposal.

We compare observed frequencies with expected frequencies.

These examples have at least two things in common: (1) The raw data consist of *counts,* or *frequencies,* and (2) under the implied or stated hypotheses, there are *expected frequencies* with which we can compare the *observed frequencies.* Such a comparison can lead to some useful conclusions.

If conditions in the factories producing the same product are identical, and we take a sample of equal size from each of the factories, we would expect about the same number of items to fail to meet the standards. If there is no relationship between area of residence and position for or against the rapid transit proposal, we would expect this fact to be reflected by the number of subjects falling into the various categories.

The question to be answered in each of these cases is whether the discrepancies between the observed and expected frequencies are so large as to cast doubt on the assumptions that gave rise to the expected frequencies.

The statistical technique that we use to provide answers to such questions is based on the *chi-square distribution.* Specific values of the variable that is distributed as chi-square are designated by the Greek letter χ^2.

8.4 TESTS OF HOMOGENEITY

We often want to explore the proposition that several populations are homogeneous with respect to some characteristic. We may, for example, wish to know whether people in several age groups have the same television-viewing habits. Or we may want to know whether shoppers from different socioeconomic backgrounds have

TABLE 8.5
Two-way classification of sample subjects for chi-square test of homogeneity

Category of variable of interest	Population					Total
	1	*2*	*3*	$\cdots$	*c*	*Total*
1	O_{11}	O_{12}	O_{13}	$\cdots$	O_{1c}	$n_{1.}$
2	O_{21}	O_{22}	O_{23}	$\cdots$	O_{2c}	$n_{2.}$
3	O_{31}	O_{32}	O_{33}	$\cdots$	O_{3c}	$n_{3.}$
.	.	.	.	.	.	.
.	.	.	.	.	.	.
.	.	.	.	.	.	.
r	O_{r1}	O_{r2}	O_{r3}	$\cdots$	O_{rc}	$n_{r.}$
Total	$n_{.1}$	$n_{.2}$	$n_{.3}$	$\cdots$	$n_{.c}$	n

different reasons for buying a certain product. Finally, we may want to know whether some raw material that a manufacturer could purchase from several different vendors is homogeneous in quality.

Another way of stating the problem is to say that we are interested in testing the null hypothesis that several populations are homogeneous with respect to the proportion of subjects falling into each of two or more categories of some criterion of classification. We may test the hypothesis by means of a *chi-square test of homogeneity*. We draw a random sample from each of the populations of interest. Then we find the number in each sample that fall into each category. We can display the sample data in a *contingency table* like Table 8.5.

In Table 8.5, n is the total number of subjects in the sample, $n_{.1}$ is the number in the sample who are from population 1, $n_{1.}$ is the number in the sample who belong to the first category of the variable of interest, O_{11} is the observed number of subjects in the sample who are from population 1 and who belong to the first category of the variable of interest, and so on.

In such a contingency table, either the rows or the columns, depending on which we use to indicate the different populations, are *fixed*. This is because we determine the sample size before we obtain knowledge about the characteristic or variable of interest.

The rationale underlying the calculation of expected frequencies for the test of homogeneity is based on the assumption that if the sampled populations are homogeneous, we can get the best estimate of the probability that a member of a given population falls into a given category of the variable of interest by pooling the information from the available samples.

Suppose, for example, that the sampled populations are clerical workers, technicians, and salespersons employed by a large firm, and that the variable of interest is attitude toward management. Assume that there are two categories of the variable—satisfied with management and dissatisfied with management. Suppose that in a sample of 100 clerical workers, 30 are satisfied with management, whereas in a sample of 90 technicians and 70 salespersons, 50 and 60, respectively, are satisfied. The situation is summarized in Table 8.6.

If we hypothesize that clerical workers, technicians, and salespersons are homogeneous with respect to satisfaction, we can pool the three samples with respect to the variable of interest and consider them as a single sample from the same

**TABLE 8.6
Types of
employees
classified according
to attitude toward
management
(observed
frequencies)**

Attitude toward management	Type of employee			Total
	Clerical workers	Technicians	Salespersons	
Satisfied	30	50	60	140
Dissatisfied	70	40	10	120
Total	100	90	70	260

population. We will then get the best estimate of the true proportion of clerical workers, the best estimate of the true proportion of technicians, and the best estimate of the true proportion of salespersons who are satisfied by pooling the sample information. This gives $(30 + 50 + 60)/(100 + 90 + 70) = 0.5385$. Applying this proportion to the sample of 100 clerical workers gives an expected frequency of $(100)(0.5385) = 53.85$ satisfied clerical workers. Applying the proportion to the sample of 90 technicians yields an expected frequency of $(90)(0.5385) = 48.46$ satisfied technicians. Finally, applying the proportion to the sample of 70 salespersons yields an expected frequency of $(70)(0.5385) = 37.69$ satisfied salespersons. These results are shown in Table 8.7.

The chi-square test of homogeneity is an extension of the procedure for testing hypotheses about the difference between two population proportions (Chapter 7). When there are two populations involved and the characteristic of interest has two categories, the chi-square test of homogeneity is an alternative and equivalent way of testing the null hypothesis that two population proportions are equal.

The Chi-Square Test Statistic

Once we have computed the expected frequency for each cell, we compare each expected frequency with the corresponding *observed* cell frequency. If the agreement is sufficiently close between the observed frequencies and those that we expect, given that the null hypothesis of homogeneity is true, we do not reject the null hypothesis. On the other hand, if the agreement between the observed frequencies and those that we expect, given that H_0 is true, is sufficiently poor, we reject the null hypothesis that the populations are homogeneous. We then conclude that they are *not* homogeneous.

X^2 is a measure of how closely the expected frequencies agree with the observed frequencies.

**TABLE 8.7
Types of
employees
classified according
to attitude toward
management
(expected
frequencies)**

Attitude toward management	Type of employee			Total
	Clerical workers	Technicians	Salespersons	
Satisfied	53.85	48.46	37.69	140
Dissatisfied	46.15	41.54	32.31	120
Total	100	90	70	260

The overall closeness of agreement between the observed and expected frequencies is measured by the statistic

$$X^2 = \sum \left[\frac{(O_{ij} - E_{ij})^2}{E_{ij}} \right] \tag{8.6}$$

in which O indicates an observed frequency and E indicates an expected frequency. The subscript i indicates the row and the subscript j the column to which an observed or expected frequency belongs. The subscript i can be any number between 1 and r, and the subscript j can be any number between 1 and c, as shown in Table 8.5. O_{23}, for example, is the observed frequency for the cell formed by the intersection of row 2 and column 3.

Equation 8.6 tells us to perform the following arithmetic for each cell: First, subtract the expected frequency from the observed frequency. Second, square the difference and divide by the expected frequency. Finally, sum the results obtained from the various cells.

When there is close agreement between the observed and expected frequencies, X^2 is small. When there is poor agreement, X^2 is large. Consequently, only a sufficiently large value of X^2 causes rejection of H_0.

When the null hypothesis is true—that is, when the populations are homogeneous—the sampling distribution of X^2 follows approximately the distribution known as the chi-square distribution. Appendix Table F on page A-39 gives critical values of χ^2.

The following example illustrates the use of the chi-square test of homogeneity.

EXAMPLE 8.3 Let us consider further the example in which three samples of employees are classified according to their attitude toward management. We wish to know whether we can conclude, on the basis of the sample data, that the three sampled populations of employees are not homogeneous with respect to attitude toward management.

SOLUTION To reach a conclusion, we use the chi-square test of homogeneity.

1. *Hypotheses*

    H_0: Clerical workers, technicians, and salespersons are homogeneous with respect to their attitude toward management

    H_1: The three populations of employees are not homogeneous with respect to their attitude toward management

2. *Test statistic.*   The test statistic is given by Equation 8.6.
3. *Significance level.*   Suppose we let $\alpha = 0.05$.
4. *Decision rule.*   Our decision rule must contain the critical value of the test statistic.

    In order to determine the critical value of χ^2, we must decide how many degrees of freedom are at our disposal. In general, for a contingency table

When agreement between the observed and expected frequencies is poor, X^2 is "large"; when agreement is close, X^2 is "small."

consisting of r rows and c columns, the number of degrees of freedom equals $(r - 1)(c - 1)$. We can justify this method of calculating the degrees of freedom intuitively. Consider any $r \times c$ contingency table with fixed marginal totals. Within any column, we have complete freedom in assigning numbers to $r - 1$ of the cells of that column. Once we have filled these $r - 1$ cells, the frequency of the rth cell is automatically determined, since the sum of the cell frequencies must equal the fixed total. In other words, we have no freedom in assigning a number to the last cell. Similarly, for any row, we are free to assign numbers to only $c - 1$ of the cells in that row. Thus we can assign numbers to only $(r - 1) \times (c - 1)$ of the rc cells in the table. Hence the degrees of freedom associated with the table are $(r - 1)(c - 1)$.

$$df = (r - 1)(c - 1)$$

In the present example, $r = 2$ and $c = 3$. The degrees of freedom, then, are $(2 - 1)(3 - 1) = (1)(2) = 2$. From Table F we obtain the critical value $\chi^2_{(0.95,2)} = 5.991$. The decision rule, then, is as follows: Reject H_0 if the computed value of X^2 is equal to or greater than 5.991.

The chi-square tests discussed in this chapter are all one-sided tests in which the critical value and α are in the right tail of the distribution.

5. *Calculations.* We obtain the computed value of the test statistic using Equation 8.6. Table 8.6 contains the observed frequencies, and Table 8.7 contains the expected frequencies calculated earlier. In future calculations you may wish to use the following quick method of calculating the expected frequency for a cell: Multiply the corresponding row total by the corresponding column total and divide this product by the grand total. For Table 8.7, for example, the expected frequency for the cell formed by the intersection of row 2 with column 3 is obtained by multiplying the row total, 120, by the column total, 70, and dividing the product, 8400, by the grand total, 260. That is, $E_{23} = (120)(70)/260 = 32.31$.

Using the observed frequencies from Table 8.6 and the expected frequencies from Table 8.7, we compute

$$X^2 = \frac{(30 - 53.85)^2}{53.85} + \frac{(50 - 48.46)^2}{48.46} + \frac{(60 - 37.69)^2}{37.69} + \frac{(70 - 46.15)^2}{46.15}$$
$$+ \frac{(90 - 41.54)^2}{41.54} + \frac{(10 - 32.31)^2}{32.31}$$
$$= 10.56 + 0.05 + 13.21 + 12.32 + 56.53 + 15.40$$
$$= 108.07$$

6. *Statistical decision.* Since $108.07 > 5.991$, we reject H_0.
7. *Conclusion.* We conclude that the three populations of employees are not homogeneous with respect to their attitude toward management.

Since $108.07 > 10.597$, the p value for the test is less than 0.005.

The chi-square test of homogeneity can be used when the variable of interest has more than two categories. The following example illustrates this use of chi-square.

TABLE 8.8
Three samples of persons classified by type of television program preferred (expected frequencies in parentheses)

Population (ethnic group)	Type of program			Total
	A	*B*	*C*	
I	120(70)	30(67.50)	50(62.50)	200
II	10(35)	75(33.75)	15(31.25)	100
III	10(35)	30(33.75)	60(31.25)	100
Total	140	135	125	400

EXAMPLE 8.4 A market analyst wants to know whether different ethnic groups (populations) differ in the types of television programs they prefer. A random sample is selected from each of three ethnic populations. Each person is asked to specify which of three types of TV program he or she prefers. Table 8.8 shows the results.

SOLUTION

1. *Hypotheses*

   H_0: The three ethnic populations are homogeneous with respect to type of TV program preferred

   H_1: The three ethnic populations are not homogeneous

2. *Test statistic.* Equation 8.6 is the appropriate test statistic.
3. *Significance level.* Let $\alpha = 0.05$.
4. *Decision rule.* Reject H_0 if the computed value of X^2 is $\geq$ the critical value of χ^2.
5. *Calculations.* We find the expected frequencies by applying the rationale underlying the test of homogeneity. If the three sampled populations are homogeneous with respect to program preference, the best estimate of the true proportion of subjects in each ethnic group that prefer Type A is given by $140/400 = 0.35$. To find the expected frequency for Type A preference in each ethnic group, we multiply each sample total by 0.35. Thus $(200)(0.35) = 70$, $(100)(0.35) = 35$, and $(100)(0.35) = 35$. Similar reasoning yields the other two columns of expected frequencies shown in Table 8.8.

   From the data in Table 8.8, we compute

   $$X^2 = \frac{(120 - 70)^2}{70} + \frac{(10 - 35)^2}{35} + \cdots + \frac{(60 - 31.25)^2}{31.25} = 180.495$$

6. *Statistical decision.* From Table F, the critical value of χ^2 for $\alpha = 0.05$ and 4 degrees of freedom is 9.488. Since the computed value, 180.495, is larger than 9.488, we reject H_0.
7. *Conclusion.* We conclude that the populations are not homogeneous with respect to the type of TV program preferred ($p < 0.005$).

TABLE 8.9
A 2 × 2
contingency table

Second criterion of classification	First criterion of classification		
	1	*2*	*Total*
1	a	b	a + b
2	c	d	c + d
Total	a + c	b + d	n

Small Expected Frequencies

In contingency-table analysis, some cells may yield small expected frequencies. This poses a possible threat to the validity of a chi-square test. Writers disagree as to how to handle this problem. However, many follow the rule that says that for tables with more than 1 degree of freedom, a minimum expected frequency per cell of 1 is permissible if no more than 20% of the cells have expected frequencies of less than 5. If necessary, we may combine adjacent rows and/or columns to satisfy this rule, so long as this does not violate the logic of the classification scheme.

The 2 × 2 Contingency Table

When each criterion of classification has two levels, the resulting contingency table has two rows and two columns. Such a table is called a 2 × 2 or *fourfold contingency table*. Table 8.9 shows a typical 2 × 2 contingency table, where a, b, c and d are the observed frequencies in the four cells. We compute the X^2 value for a 2 × 2 contingency table by the following shortcut formula:

$$X^2 = \frac{n(ad - bc)^2}{(a + c)(b + d)(a + b)(c + d)}$$

(8.7)

This yields the same numerical result as Equation 8.6.

The 2 × 2 contingency table is not immune to the problem of small expected frequencies. We should not use the χ^2 test with 2 × 2 contingency tables if $n < 20$, or if $20 < n < 40$ and any expected frequency is less than 5. If n is greater than 40, no expected frequency in a 2 × 2 contingency table should be less than 1.

EXAMPLE 8.5 The chi-square test of homogeneity applied to a 2 × 2 contingency table is equivalent to a test of the equality of two population proportions. To show this, let us refer to Example 7.10.

SOLUTION We can display the data from that example in the 2 × 2 contingency table of Table 8.10. By Equation 8.7, we have

$$X^2 = \frac{400[(54)(123) - (171)(52)]^2}{(106)(294)(175)(225)} = 1.65$$

TABLE 8.10
Contingency-table display of data from Example 7.10

| | Type of store | | |
Background	Chain	Nonchain	Total
Rural	54	171	225
Urban	52	123	175
Total	106	294	400

Since $1.65 < 3.841$, we cannot reject the null hypothesis that the two populations are homogeneous. Recall that in Chapter 7 we computed a z value of -1.28, which did not allow us to reject $H_0: p_1 = p_2$. Note that $(-1.28)^2 = 1.64$, which, except for rounding error, is equal to our computed value of X^2. Also note that the critical value of $\chi^2 = 3.841$ is equal to the square of the critical value of $z = 1.96$.

Steps in the Test of Homogeneity

The following list is a summary of the steps involved in a chi-square test of homogeneity.

1. Identify the two or more populations to be sampled.
2. Draw a simple random sample from each of the populations.
3. For each sample, count the number falling into each category of the variable of interest. These are the observed frequencies.
4. Calculate the expected frequency corresponding to each observed frequency.
5. Compute X^2 by Equation 8.6 or, if the data conform to a 2×2 contingency table, by Equation 8.7.
6. Determine the critical value of χ^2 by referring to Table F.
7. If the computed value of X^2 is equal to or greater than the critical value of χ^2, reject the null hypothesis that the populations are homogeneous.

Exercises

Perform each test at the indicated level of significance. Determine the p value.

 8.7 Ⓒ In a study to evaluate instruction in technical writing, a group of firms submit 110 pieces of technical writing done by members of their staffs who have had training in technical writing. The firms also submit 120 pieces of technical writing by staff members without training in technical writing. A panel of judges rates each article as superior, acceptable, or inferior. The following table shows the number of articles from each group falling into each category. Do the data provide sufficient evidence to indicate that the samples came from different populations? Let $\alpha = 0.05$.

| Previous training | Rating | | | |
	Superior	Acceptable	Inferior	Total
Yes	48	39	23	110
No	12	36	72	120
Total	60	75	95	230

8.8 Ⓒ A national firm has a large plant in each of three sections of the country. Six months after a change in working conditions and employee benefits is introduced at the three factories, 250 employees from each plant are randomly selected and asked to rate their degree of satisfaction with the new system. The following table shows the results. Do these data provide sufficient evidence at the 0.05 level of significance to suggest that the employees at the different plants are not homogeneous with respect to satisfaction with the new system?

| | Degree of satisfaction | | | | |
Factory	Very satisfied	Satisfied	Dissatisfied	Very dissatisfied	Total
1	135	70	25	20	250
2	145	80	15	10	250
3	140	75	20	15	250
Total	420	225	60	45	750

 8.9 Ⓒ Managers may be characterized as traditional or democratic, depending on their management style. A professor of management at a university believes that employees working under democratic managers are more loyal to the organization for which they work than are employees working under traditional managers. To find out whether this theory would be supported, the professor conducts a study in which a sample of employees is selected from each of the two populations. Each employee is then classified as loyal or not loyal to the organization for which he or she works. The results are as follows. Can we conclude from these data that the professor's belief is correct? Let $\alpha = 0.05$.

| Loyal to organization? | Management style | | Total |
	Traditional	Democratic	
Yes	75	180	255
No	125	70	195
Total	200	250	450

 8.10 Ⓒ A management consultant wishes to know whether he can conclude that executives with a graduate degree in business administration are more innovative in the performance of their duties than executives who do not hold such a degree. A sample is selected from each of the two populations, and the performance of each executive in the two samples is analyzed by a management consulting firm. On the basis of these analyses, each executive is categorized as either innovative or not innovative. The results are as follows. Can we conclude from these data that the two populations differ with respect to the proportion of innovative executives? Let $\alpha = 0.05$.

| Innovative? | Graduate degree in business administration? | | Total |
	Yes	No	
Yes	120	90	210
No	50	120	170
Total	170	210	380

8.5 TESTS OF INDEPENDENCE

Two variables are independent if knowing the value of one doesn't help us make a better "guess" about the value of the other.

One of the most frequent uses of the chi-square distribution is for testing the null hypothesis that two criteria of classification, when applied to a population of subjects (or objects), are *independent*. Two criteria of classification are said to be independent if the distribution of one criterion in no way depends on the distribution of the other. If two criteria of classification are *not* independent, there is an *association* between the two criteria. Suppose, for example, that two criteria of classification are age and type of TV program preferred. Suppose that, for some population of people, knowing a person's age is of no help in predicting the type of program preferred, or vice versa. In such a case, age and type of program preferred are independent.

Typically, we make decisions about the independence of criteria in a population on the basis of sample data. We draw a random sample from the population of interest, and cross-classify the subjects according to the two criteria. We display the cross-classification in a contingency table. The *levels* of one criterion provide row headings, and the levels of the other criterion provide the column headings. Table 8.11 shows a contingency table in which a sample of n subjects has been cross-classified according to two criteria. There are r levels of the criterion forming the rows and c levels of the criterion forming the columns. We place the observed number O_{ij} of subjects that may be characterized by one level of each criterion in the cell formed by the intersection of the ith row and the jth column.

Expected Frequencies

In order to find the expected cell frequencies corresponding to those observed, we use the principles of probability. For the population represented by the sample in Table 8.11, suppose that we wish to know the probability that a subject picked at random is characterized by level 1 of the first (column) criterion. The best estimator of this probability is $n_{.1}/n$. Similarly, the estimator of the probability that a subject picked at random is characterized by level 1 of the second (row) criterion is given by $n_{1.}/n$. We can compute similar estimators for each level of

TABLE 8.11
Two-way classification of a sample of subjects for chi-square test of independence

Second criterion of classification	First criterion of classification					
	Level					
Level	1	2	3	$\cdots$	c	Total
1	O_{11}	O_{12}	O_{13}	$\cdots$	O_{1c}	$n_{1.}$
2	O_{21}	O_{22}	O_{23}	$\cdots$	O_{2c}	$n_{2.}$
3	O_{31}	O_{32}	O_{33}	$\cdots$	O_{3c}	$n_{3.}$
$\vdots$	$\vdots$	$\vdots$	$\vdots$	$\vdots$	$\vdots$	$\vdots$
r	O_{r1}	O_{r2}	O_{r3}	$\cdots$	O_{rc}	$n_{r.}$
Total	$n_{.1}$	$n_{.2}$	$n_{.3}$	$\cdots$	$n_{.c}$	n

each criterion. We call these probabilities *marginal probabilities* because they are computed from marginal totals. Now suppose that we wish to estimate the probability that a subject picked at random is characterized by level 1 of both criteria. In the absence of any hypothesis about the two criteria of classification, we estimate this probability by O_{11}/n. We call this a *joint probability*. Our objective, however, is to test the null hypothesis that the two criteria of classification are *independent*. Chapter 3 showed that if two events are independent, the probability of their joint occurrence is equal to the product of their individual probabilities. Applying this rule to a contingency table, we say the following:

If two criteria of classification are independent, a joint probability is equal to the product of the two corresponding marginal probabilities.

Under the hypothesis of independence, then, the estimator of the probability that a subject picked at random is characterized by level 1 of both criteria is given by $(n_1./n)(n_{.1}/n)$. We can find the probability for every other cell in the same way.

To convert any estimated or expected cell probability to an *expected cell frequency, we multiply the probability* by n. The expected frequency for the first cell, which is the expected number of subjects characterized by level 1 of both criteria, is

$$E_{11} = \left(\frac{n_1.}{n}\right)\left(\frac{n_{.1}}{n}\right)n \qquad (8.8)$$

if the criteria are independent. The n in the numerator will cancel one of the denominator n's, so that Equation 8.8 reduces to

$$E_{11} = \frac{(n_1.)(n_{.1})}{n} \qquad (8.9)$$

This leads to the shortcut procedure for computing expected cell frequencies. We simply divide the product of corresponding marginal totals by n.

EXAMPLE 8.6 A market research firm wishes to know whether they can conclude that, for adults in a certain city, the make of car driven is associated with the driver's area of residence. A random sample of 500 adult drivers is interviewed to determine what make of car they drive and in what area of the city they live. Table 8.12 shows the results.

TABLE 8.12
Five hundred drivers classified according to make of car driven and area of residence

| Area of residence | Make of automobile | | | |
	A	B	C	Total
1	52	64	24	140
2	60	59	52	171
3	50	65	74	189
Total	162	188	150	500

SOLUTION

1. *Hypotheses*

    H_0: Make of car driven and area of residence are independent

    H_1: The criteria of classification are not independent

2. *Test statistic.* Equation 8.6 is the appropriate test statistic.
3. *Significance level.* Let $\alpha = 0.05$.
4. *Decision rule.* In the present example, $r = 3$ and $c = 3$, so that the number of degrees of freedom available is $(3 - 1)(3 - 1) = 4$. The critical value of $\chi^2_{(0.95,4)}$ is 9.488. We will reject H_0, then, if the computed value of X^2 is equal to or greater than 9.488.
5. *Calculations.* Using the data from Table 8.12 and the shortcut rule, we compute the expected cell frequencies as follows:

$$E_{11} = \frac{(162)(140)}{500} = 45.36 \qquad E_{32} = \frac{(188)(189)}{500} = 71.06$$

$$E_{21} = \frac{(162)(171)}{500} = 55.40 \qquad E_{13} = \frac{(150)(140)}{500} = 42.00$$

$$E_{31} = \frac{(162)(189)}{500} = 61.24 \qquad E_{23} = \frac{(150)(171)}{500} = 51.30$$

$$E_{12} = \frac{(188)(140)}{500} = 52.64 \qquad E_{33} = \frac{(150)(189)}{500} = 56.70$$

$$E_{22} = \frac{(188)(171)}{500} = 64.30$$

We can display the observed and expected frequencies together in a table such as Table 8.13, where the expected frequencies are enclosed in parentheses. From the data in the table, we compute the following value of the test statistic:

$$X^2 = \sum \frac{(O_{ij} - E_{ij})^2}{E_{ij}} = \frac{(52 - 45.36)^2}{45.36} + \frac{(60 - 55.40)^2}{55.40}$$

$$+ \cdots + \frac{(74 - 56.70)^2}{56.70} = 19.825$$

TABLE 8.13
Observed and expected frequencies, Example 8.6

Area of residence	Make of automobile			Total
	A	*B*	*C*	
1	52(45.36)	64(52.64)	24(42.00)	140
2	60(55.40)	59(64.30)	52(51.30)	171
3	50(61.24)	65(71.06)	74(56.70)	189
Total	162	188	150	500

TABLE 8.14		Interviewer training	
Interviews by	Outcome of		
outcome and	interview	*Trained*	*Untrained*	*Total*
training of				
interviewer	*Successful*	176	188	364
	Unsuccessful	49	122	171
	Total	225	310	535

6. *Statistical decision.* Since the computed value of X^2 is greater than 9.488, we reject the null hypothesis.
7. *Conclusion.* We conclude, then, that in the city in which the study was conducted, the area of residence and the make of car a person drives are related ($p < 0.005$).

The rules for handling small expected frequencies, discussed in Section 8.4, apply when we use the chi-square test of independence.

When, in a chi-square test of independence, there are two categories of each variable, the sample data can be displayed in a 2×2 contingency table. The analysis is the same as that described for the test of homogeneity involving two populations and two categories of the variable of interest. The following is an example of a test of independence when the data can be displayed in a 2×2 contingency table.

EXAMPLE 8.7 A market research firm investigating the success of its interviewers finds that 176 out of 225 interviews attempted by trained interviewers are successfully completed. Of 310 interviews attempted by *un*trained interviewers, 188 are successfully completed. Table 8.14, at the top of the page, displays these data as a 2×2 contingency table.

The firm wishes to know whether these data provide sufficient evidence at the 0.05 level of significance to indicate a relationship between the training level of interviewers and the outcome of attempted interviews.

SOLUTION By Equation 8.7, we compute

$$X^2 = \frac{535[(176)(122) - (188)(49)]^2}{(225)(310)(364)(171)} = 18.522$$

The computed value of X^2 exceeds the critical value of χ^2 in Table F for 1 degree of freedom and $\alpha = 0.05$. We conclude, then, that the two criteria are related ($p < 0.005$).

Steps in Test of Independence

The following list is a summary of the steps involved in a chi-square test of independence.

1. From the population of interest, draw a simple random sample.

2. Display the data in a contingency table in which the rows represent one of the criteria of classification and the columns represent the other.
3. Compute the expected frequency for each cell using the probability law for independent events.
4. Compute X^2 by Equation 8.6 or 8.7 (for a 2×2 contingency table).
5. Determine the critical value of χ^2 from Table F.
6. If the computed X^2 is equal to or greater than the critical χ^2, reject H_0. Otherwise do not reject H_0.

Exercises

Perform each test at the indicated level of significance. Determine the p value.

8.11 Ⓒ During a market-research survey, a firm obtains information on the social class and major leisure-time activity of 375 heads of households. In the following table the respondents are cross-classified by the two criteria. Test at the 0.05 level the null hypothesis that social class and major leisure-time activity are independent.

Leisure-time activity	Social class					
	1	*2*	*3*	*4*	*5*	*Total*
A	10	7	3	4	1	25
B	14	10	7	4	2	37
C	9	25	13	18	3	68
D	7	9	38	44	6	104
E	3	8	14	18	62	105
F	2	3	8	10	13	36
Total	45	62	83	98	87	375

8.12 Ⓒ A government agency surveys unemployed persons who are seeking work. It prepares the following tabulation, by sex and skill level, of 532 interviewees. Do these data provide sufficient evidence to indicate that skill status is related to sex? Let $\alpha = 0.01$.

Skill level	Sex		
	Male	*Female*	*Total*
Skilled	106	6	112
Semiskilled	93	39	132
Unskilled	215	73	288
Total	414	118	532

8.13 Ⓒ A guidance counselor asks a group of 110 junior high school students how much time they spend reading books and how much time they spend watching television. The students are then classified as high or low with respect to each activity. The following table shows the number of students in each cell when cross-classified. Do these data provide sufficient evidence to suggest, at the 0.05 level of significance, that the amounts of book reading and television viewing are related?

Television viewing	Book reading		
	Low	*High*	*Total*
Low	11	41	52
High	18	40	58
Total	29	81	110

8.14 © A sample of 165 defective items produced in two factories operated by the same company are classified according to whether the defect is due to poor workmanship or inferior material. The data are shown in the following table. Test at the 0.05 level the null hypothesis that cause of defect and factory of production are independent.

Cause of defect	Factory		
	A	*B*	*Total*
Poor workmanship	21	72	93
Inferior material	46	26	72
Total	67	98	165

8.15 © In a transportation survey, 750 people employed in the downtown area of a large city are interviewed. They are cross-classified by their type of dwelling unit and their mode of travel to and from work. We want to see if there is a dependence between the two variables. The following table shows the number of interviewees falling into each cell after they are cross-classified. Test H_0: type of dwelling unit and mode of transportation to work are independent. Let $\alpha = 0.05$.

Mode of transportation	Type of dwelling unit				
	Single-family	*Two-family*	*Multiple-family*	*Other*	*Total*
Automobile	148	140	102	97	487
Public transportation	49	52	64	60	225
Other	7	8	9	14	38
Total	204	200	175	171	750

8.6 TESTS OF GOODNESS OF FIT

When we examine Equation 8.6, we see that we can think of X^2 as measuring the "goodness of fit" of the observed and expected frequencies in a contingency table. If the terms "tests of independence" and "test of homogeneity" were not more descriptive of the procedures to which they apply, we could use the term "goodness-of-fit test" in their stead. There are, however, many hypothesis-testing situations for which we use the term "goodness-of-fit test" to describe the testing procedure. In these situations some presumed underlying theory dictates what the expected sample frequencies should be in the several categories of the variable of interest. We draw a sample from the population of interest and determine the observed frequencies. We use Equation 8.6 to measure the goodness of fit of the observed and expected frequencies. We then compare the computed X^2 with the appropriate tabulated value of χ^2 to determine whether to reject the null hypothesis that the presumed underlying theory applies to the sampled population. The value of the relevant degrees of freedom is equal to the number of categories involved minus 1.

The following example illustrates the use of a chi-square goodness-of-fit test.

EXAMPLE 8.8 A research team concerned with occupational safety wishes to know whether they can conclude that the number of on-the-job accidents differs among the three shifts of a 24-hour day. A random sample of 240 accident reports selected from the files of participating industrial firms yields the following results: first shift, 50 accidents; second shift, 90 accidents; third shift, 100 accidents. If there were no tendency toward a greater proportion of accidents on at least one shift than on at least one other shift, the expected number of accidents per shift in a sample of 240 would be $240/3 = 80$. The objective, then, is to determine the goodness of fit of the observed frequencies to the expected frequencies.

SOLUTION

1. *Hypotheses*

> H_0: Industrial accidents occur with equal frequency on all three shifts
>
> H_1: Industrial accidents do not occur with equal frequency on the three shifts

2. *Test statistic.*   Equation 8.6 is the appropriate test statistic.
3. *Significance level.*   Let $\alpha = 0.05$.
4. *Decision rule.*   Since there are three categories, the degrees-of-freedom value is 2. From Appendix Table F, we find that the critical value of χ^2 is 5.991. We will reject H_0, then, if the computed value of X^2 is greater than or equal to 5.991.
5. *Calculations.*   By Equation 8.6, we have

$$X^2 = \frac{(50 - 80)^2}{80} + \frac{(90 - 80)^2}{80} + \frac{(100 - 80)^2}{80} = 11.25 + 1.25 + 5.00$$

$$= 17.50$$

6. *Statistical decision.*   Since our computed value of 17.50 is greater than 5.991, we reject H_0.
7. *Conclusion.*   We conclude that industrial accidents do not occur with equal frequency on the three shifts.

   Since 17.50 is greater than 10.597, $p < 0.005$.

COMPUTER ANALYSIS

Computers can be used to advantage in chi-square analysis. The STAT+ package, for example, allows the user to perform contingency table analyses and goodness-of-fit tests.

Exercises

For each of the following exercises, perform the chi-square test at the indicated level of significance and determine the p value.

 8.16 Each person in a random sample of 150 shoppers is allowed to choose one of three brands of facial tissue. The results are as follows: Shoppers chose Brand A 35 times, Brand B 55 times, and Brand C 60 times. Do these data provide sufficient evidence to indicate that the three brands are not equally preferred? Let $\alpha = 0.05$.

 8.17 A random sample of 125 absentee reports filed during a year by employees of a large firm yields the following information. Do these data provide sufficient evidence to indicate, at the 0.01 level of significance, that absenteeism tends to be higher on some days than on others?

Day of absence	Mon.	Tues.	Wed.	Thurs.	Fri.
Number of absences	35	20	15	15	40

 8.18 Interviewers ask each of a sample of 300 shoppers on which day he or she prefers to grocery-shop. The results are as follows. Do these data indicate that all days are not equally preferred by grocery shoppers? Let $\alpha = 0.05$.

Mon.	Tue.	Wed.	Thur.	Fri.	Sat.	Sun.	Total
10	20	40	40	80	60	50	300

 8.19 A market researcher believes that in a certain population the proportions of persons preferring brands A, B, C, and D of toothpaste are 0.30, 0.60, 0.08, and 0.02, respectively. A simple random sample of 600 people drawn from the population reveals the following preferences. Do these data provide sufficient evidence to cast doubt on the researcher's belief? Let $\alpha = 0.01$.

Brand	A	B	C	D
No. preferring this brand	192	342	44	22

8.20 Researchers ask each member of a random sample of 360 residents of a community to list which local television station he or she prefers to watch for national and international news. The results are as follows. Do these data provide sufficient evidence to indicate that the three stations are not equally preferred? Let $\alpha = 0.10$.

Station	A	B	C
No. preferring this station	190	30	140

Summary

This chapter covered the basic concepts and techniques of analysis of variance that we use to test for significant differences among several sample means. We discussed this topic in the framework of the completely randomized experimental design.

You learned that, when you wish to test the null hypothesis that two population means are equal, one-way analysis of variance and the t test will lead to identical conclusions. The t test for equal population means using data from two independent samples is a special case of one-way analysis of variance. As we have seen, one-way analysis of variance also allows us to test the null hypothesis that three or more population means are equal.

Also in this chapter you used the chi-square distribution to analyze frequency data. The chapter presented three types of test: tests of independence, tests of homogeneity, and tests of goodness of fit. It also presented methods of handling small expected frequencies.

The tests of independence and homogeneity are alike in that the arithmetic involved in calculating expected frequencies and the test statistic is the same. The two tests differ, however, with respect to the hypothesis they test, the rationale underlying the computation of relative frequencies, the way in which the data are typically collected, and the interpretation of the results.

The test of independence is concerned with the relationship between two variables in a single population, whereas the test of homogeneity is concerned with whether or not categories of a single variable are represented in the same proportions in two or more populations.

The rationale underlying the calculation of expected frequencies for the test of independence is based on a probability law that states that if two events are independent, the probability of their joint occurrence is equal to the product of the probabilities of the individual occurrences of the two events. The rationale underlying the calculation of expected frequencies for the test of homogeneity is as follows: If, as stated in the null hypothesis, the populations are homogeneous with respect to some variable, we can obtain the best estimates of the probabilities that sample entities fall into the various categories of the variable by pooling the sample data.

When we anticipate a test of independence, we select a random sample from a single population, then cross-classify the sample entities according to the two variables of interest. For the test of homogeneity, we identify two or more populations and draw a sample from each. We then classify sample entities in each sample on the basis of the single variable of interest.

We interpret the results of tests of independence and homogeneity, of course, in terms of independence and homogeneity, respectively.

You also learned that the test of goodness of fit is useful for testing the null hypothesis that data available for analysis were drawn from a population that follows some specified frequency distribution. Sufficiently poor agreement between observed frequencies and the frequencies we would expect if the null hypothesis is true is taken as an indication that the null hypothesis is false.

Review Questions   Where appropriate, do an analysis of variance or a chi-square test at the indicated level of significance and compute a p value for the test. If no level of significance is indicated, compute the p value and state whether or not you think the null hypothesis should be rejected.

1. Define analysis of variance.

2. Describe a situation in your particular field of interest in which the completely randomized experimental design would be appropriate. Use real or realistic data and do the appropriate analysis of variance.

3. What are the assumptions underlying one-way analysis of variance?

4. What is a treatment?

5. What is the correction factor? How is it computed? How is it used?

6. What are two other names for the error sum of squares?

7. What is an experimental unit?

8. What is the test statistic for analysis of variance?

9. Explain the relationship between the completely randomized design and the t test for two independent samples.

10. How do you compute degrees of freedom for the chi-square goodness-of-fit test?

11. What is a contingency table?

12. How are degrees of freedom computed for contingency tables?

13. Explain the rationale behind the method of computing the expected frequencies in a test of independence.

14. Explain the difference between a test of independence and a test of homogeneity.

 15. Ⓒ The following table shows the unit cost of producing a certain product by size of firm. Can we conclude at the 0.05 level of significance that there are differences among the three sizes of firm with respect to mean unit production cost?

Small	8	7	7	6	6	6	6	8	8	8
Medium	3	4	4	4	2	4	5	3	4	3
Large	4	5	5	5	3	4	5	4	5	6

 16. Ⓒ A psychologist is hired to compare the levels of job satisfaction of salespersons with three large companies. Ten salespersons from each firm are selected at random and given in-depth tests to ascertain their level of job satisfaction. The results are given in the following table. Do these data provide sufficient evidence to indicate a difference in mean job satisfaction among the three firms? Let $\alpha = 0.01$.

Firm A	67	65	59	59	58	61	66	53	51	64
Firm B	66	68	55	59	61	66	62	65	64	74
Firm C	87	80	67	89	80	84	78	65	72	85

 17. Ⓒ An advertising agency conducts an experiment to try to assess the effectiveness of various formats of TV commercials. Fifty regular television viewers are randomly assigned to view one of five formats of a TV commercial for a cold remedy. On the basis of an interview following the viewing, a score measuring the impact of the commercial on the participant is recorded. The results are as follows. Can we conclude on the basis of these data that the formats differ in their effectiveness? Let $\alpha = 0.05$.

TV commercial format														
A			*B*			*C*			*D*			*E*		
20	23	21	28	27	22	33	34	25	33	29	31	49	41	41
23	26	24	28	23	29	26	27	33	29	27	25	39	41	48
26	23	20	27	25	28	25	32	25	26	26	33	43	43	46
24			21			34			32			35		

 18. Ⓒ In a random sample of 30 junior executives, each is classified by potential for promotion: good, poor, or uncertain. Each subject is then given a test to measure his or her level of anxiety. The results (coded for ease of computation) are as follows. What are your conclusions about this study? Let $\alpha = 0.05$.

Potential												
Good	3	4	3	2	2	5	3	2	5	4	4	4
Poor	4	8	7	10	10	4	8	8				
Uncertain	4	5	3	4	3	3	4	4	6	5		

19. Ⓒ Researchers wish to study the effect of crowding on the productivity of office workers. Office workers of the same age, sex, and level of training and experience are randomly assigned to one of three treatment groups representing three levels of crowding: severe, moderate, or none. The following table shows the results. Can we conclude from these data that crowding affects productivity? Let $\alpha = 0.05$. What use can we make of the results of this experiment?

Severe	22	49	32	37	32	22
Moderate	31	30	43	30	46	
None	68	73	78	47	56	59

20. Ⓒ A publishing firm hires a reading specialist to assess the effects of three different typefaces—A, B, and C—on the reading comprehension scores of school children. The following table shows, for 20 subjects randomly assigned to a treatment, the difference in the reading scores of children given material set in a standard typeface and those given material set in experimental typefaces. The material was of equal difficulty. Can we conclude from these data that typeface has an effect on reading comprehension? Let $\alpha = 0.05$. What use can we make of the results of this experiment?

A	12	13	7	15	7		
B	15	11	15	15	14	17	18
C	16	18	24	18	24	23	24	22

21. Ⓒ Researchers conducted an experiment designed to evaluate the effectiveness of four different methods—A, B, C, and D—of teaching problem solving. The following table shows, by teaching method, the scores made by the participating subjects (who were randomly assigned to one of the treatments) following this training when they were forced to solve problems. Do these data provide sufficient evidence to indicate that the four teaching methods differ in effectiveness? Let $\alpha = 0.05$. Do the results of this experiment have any relevance to the world of business? Explain.

A	48	38	20	16	95		
B	91	37	53	91	80	38	
C	67	61	33	85	99	95	81
D	57	62	50	43	59	60	70

22. Ⓒ Four different samples of kittens were given food with four different flavors—A, B, C, and D. Kittens of the same age, sex, and breed were randomly assigned one of the four flavors. The following table shows the amount (coded) of food consumed by each kitten in each sample during a 24-hour period. Test to determine whether the kittens' acceptance of the four flavors differs significantly. Let $\alpha = 0.05$. How might management use the results of this experiment in deciding which flavor or flavors to market? Could the results of this experiment be used in advertising? Explain.

A	12	14	18	11	19	10
B	23	20	17	23	20	
C	29	27	30	35	33	
D	38	33	40	34	34	37

23. Ⓒ Researchers compared three brands of automobile tires of the same size. The criterion was length of life in thousands of miles. Six tires of each brand were tested. The following table shows the results. Can we conclude from these data that the three brands are not equal in quality? Let $\alpha = 0.05$. Prepare a report on the results of this experiment for the management of the firm that manufactures Brand B tires. Prepare advertising copy for Brand B tires using the results of this experiment.

Brand A	43	44	42	50	46	48
Brand B	51	49	52	45	48	50
Brand C	47	41	42	45	43	42

24. Complete the following ANOVA table.

Source	SS	df	MS	F	p
Treatments	154.9199	4			
Error	_____	__			
Total	200.4773	39			

25. Consider the following ANOVA table.

Source	SS	df	MS	F
Treatments	5.05835	2	2.52917	1.0438
Error	65.42090	27	2.4230	

(a) How many treatments were compared? **(b)** How many observations were analyzed? **(c)** At the 0.05 level of significance, can we conclude that there is a difference among treatments? Why?

26. Ⓒ The manager of a health club wishes to compare four physical fitness programs designed for young adult females. Thirty new members are given physical fitness tests at the time they join. Each is then randomly assigned to one of the four programs. At the end of six months each subject is again given the physical fitness test. The following table shows the gains in scores made by the 30 subjects. Construct an analysis-of-variance table from these data, and compute the four sample means.

	Program		
A	*B*	*C*	*D*
13	11	12	22
24	13	19	26
19	20	9	22
18	14	14	22
9	11	21	26
21	21	7	19
17	14	6	
22	8		
24			

27. Ⓒ Refer to Exercise 26. Can the manager conclude from the sample results that the four programs differ in effectiveness? Let $\alpha = 0.05$, and find the p value.

28. Ⓒ The following table contains data on the following four populations of subjects.

Population	Subjects
A	Male clerical workers
B	Female clerical workers
C	Male executives
D	Female executives

	Population			
Row No.	A	B	C	D
1	43	48	71	61
2	41	55	52	70
3	51	48	70	60
4	48	50	67	65
5	44	28	75	54
6	30	28	71	69
7	57	35	66	56
8	40	34	49	79
9	46	47	60	78
10	59	53	71	67
11	39	42	53	61
12	48	45	64	72
13	51	37	76	72
14	42	34	44	71
15	51	47	58	64
16	52	29	51	51
17	44	38	52	62
18	55	28	58	68
19	36	39	60	57
20	53	32	67	63
21	41	37	67	61
22	59	27	73	62
23	46	39	61	59
24	65	49	46	79
25	49	52	65	66
26	46	44	59	60
27	57	26	52	70
28	55	40	74	52
29	44	45	63	70
30	47	34	64	76
31	32	61	92	55
32	44	37	53	72
33	43	20	69	64
34	51	39	74	62
35	40	49	75	55
36	44	48	62	69
37	44	47	81	60
38	67	36	55	83
39	42	34	67	76
40	50	45	61	64
41	41	54	58	69
42	44	27	69	66
43	55	30	53	82
44	49	32	75	47
45	52	38	66	68

	Population			
Row No.	A	B	C	D
46	54	38	73	63
47	59	34	66	73
48	59	54	69	75
49	47	58	55	62
50	61	49	65	58
51	49	36	52	47
52	43	18	56	65
53	52	25	64	73
54	62	44	56	55
55	52	58	32	70
56	37	32	75	55
57	56	23	88	71
58	51	10	68	57
59	58	47	66	42
60	64	51	66	75
61	48	49	63	80
62	47	52	70	56
63	39	46	59	76
64	62	48	59	76
65	63	48	78	63
66	53	39	43	75
67	41	53	71	69
68	53	23	76	71
69	61	50	82	68
70	35	27	73	88
71	50	36	72	67
72	64	26	53	54
73	44	56	77	59
74	53	57	69	58
75	60	56	67	70
76	55	46	53	53
77	37	30	64	73
78	49	43	69	55
79	40	22	83	65
80	51	21	50	86
81	37	55	55	85
82	40	48	64	74
83	51	43	89	52
84	59	45	59	73
85	48	37	78	64
86	45	41	51	79
87	59	41	70	65
88	50	48	50	85
89	66	32	67	67
90	39	35	68	66
91	66	37	83	68
92	45	49	72	63
93	41	27	35	75
94	60	54	63	49
95	54	58	70	73
96	46	30	69	53
97	46	27	59	69
98	69	47	58	76
99	46	40	55	57
100	44	26	66	61
101	62	44	62	60

	Population			
Row No.	A	B	C	D
102	44	25	78	76
103	60	39	79	66
104	46	55	66	63
105	33	32	52	47
106	48	56	68	58
107	44	40	56	61
108	71	45	51	65
109	60	50	67	59
110	40	40	63	54
111	44	42	67	55
112	40	47	83	75
113	46	25	45	55
114	34	37	74	52
115	54	32	56	94
116	59	13	69	65
117	43	47	76	78
118	43	21	56	75
119	38	45	60	62
120	61	35	71	53
121	32	45	49	61
122	57	35	42	75
123	47	37	56	65
124	57	47	87	53
125	61	49	64	57
126	47	44	70	68
127	53	32	51	75
128	69	31	71	74
129	46	41	74	50
130	58	38	67	77
131	39	30	70	66
132	39	36	43	60
133	70	34	69	73
134	57	36	95	52
135	51	39	64	58
136	56	56	49	68
137	57	42	65	67
138	58	41	87	50
139	52	42	52	62
140	54	48	64	68
141	40	30	59	55
142	52	48	52	60
143	42	21	84	77
144	48	39	59	61
145	59	41	66	80
146	54	48	58	60
147	65	35	71	61
148	72	31	47	60
149	35	35	68	58
150	55	42	54	67
151	34	34	29	58
152	33	25	88	47
153	54	48	60	61
154	54	34	79	62
155	53	44	80	62
156	46	39	75	75

Row No.	Population			
	A	B	C	D
157	57	32	54	51
158	46	51	59	51
159	49	42	68	69
160	39	35	60	56
161	53	36	83	55
162	44	36	69	59
163	44	33	57	60
164	43	44	64	63
165	44	52	55	61
166	37	46	62	58
167	48	38	69	92
168	39	70	81	78
169	39	40	84	61
170	49	35	58	61
171	46	33	58	78
172	43	48	73	69
173	59	31	60	76
174	47	52	60	78
175	38	30	70	75
176	48	47	62	51
177	75	29	65	65
178	36	35	71	56
179	61	37	68	53
180	38	25	64	68
181	41	48	78	66
182	56	21	61	70
183	59	28	70	66
184	38	31	60	67
185	36	42	72	86
186	44	52	75	90
187	51	42	62	58
188	57	50	73	77
189	54	51	54	62
190	71	46	62	64
191	46	35	61	58
192	54	26	56	66
193	50	46	72	75
194	53	45	59	48
195	58	50	60	71
196	60	36	83	59
197	55	39	72	50
198	41	42	58	61
199	57	42	46	49
200	57	33	54	58
201	63	52	64	71
202	51	43	76	56
203	59	38	69	66
204	40	35	69	69
205	33	63	66	66
206	40	36	72	52
207	33	18	66	67
208	53	39	56	56
209	63	39	64	89
210	54	50	85	76
211	33	31	49	65

| | Population | | | |
Row No.	A	B	C	D
212	49	49	58	59
213	43	39	63	70
214	55	34	80	72
215	72	34	62	82
216	46	55	71	61
217	57	40	56	73
218	44	30	61	68
219	53	30	63	67
220	64	43	67	72
221	37	39	85	72
222	49	43	59	70
223	51	45	58	73
224	59	30	59	83
225	55	40	39	66
226	59	42	69	73
227	47	33	60	57
228	58	40	66	79
229	48	52	80	73
230	52	47	68	52
231	41	24	71	55
232	23	60	63	72
233	63	48	56	75
234	72	31	51	57
235	40	42	73	78
236	56	34	63	82
237	74	35	65	63
238	46	35	64	60
239	42	54	60	70
240	32	42	56	68
241	32	22	77	76
242	35	37	62	75
243	54	11	77	64
244	55	38	76	70
245	62	38	58	71
246	38	47	56	69
247	50	29	64	61
248	43	45	64	46
249	49	44	63	76
250	53	55	60	69
251	56	34	81	60
252	55	64	53	75
253	46	47	51	57
254	60	59	49	56
255	40	42	71	58
256	65	46	54	62
257	53	35	60	51
258	54	66	71	74
259	55	30	58	66
260	55	42	51	55
261	37	17	66	67
262	58	44	52	82
263	49	42	65	46
264	25	48	68	71
265	61	36	80	90
266	54	33	72	60

Row No.	Population			
	A	*B*	*C*	*D*
267	41	54	65	64
268	58	52	69	58
269	45	38	79	72
270	58	40	73	82
271	51	43	73	57
272	46	51	72	50
273	47	44	72	62
274	57	33	63	55
275	37	38	65	72
276	63	22	61	75
277	55	44	71	66
278	68	49	63	63
279	53	33	80	67
280	56	33	60	55
281	50	37	64	69
282	68	23	59	58
283	48	39	64	67
284	62	25	60	68
285	58	38	77	83
286	56	11	70	70
287	48	38	74	75
288	59	41	86	61
289	57	47	75	53
290	56	53	51	76
291	46	40	69	64
292	41	47	73	79
293	40	36	81	69
294	43	59	70	46
295	41	39	59	64
296	44	36	75	76
297	46	38	63	44
298	53	36	64	59
299	55	30	54	67
300	40	29	64	62
301	43	44	58	57
302	35	44	71	91
303	47	55	61	54
304	49	26	67	60
305	63	25	76	66
306	76	31	75	73
307	47	40	70	68
308	48	17	50	54
309	52	46	66	56
310	41	27	68	90
311	58	46	75	78
312	44	42	72	68
313	38	46	53	73
314	55	33	75	74
315	50	45	65	66
316	50	48	75	72
317	62	48	81	72
318	49	45	47	79
319	50	33	56	76
320	34	29	58	67
321	59	25	64	94

Row No.	Population			
	A	B	C	D
322	50	40	83	69
323	59	47	84	57
324	51	45	62	69
325	55	39	81	80
326	45	42	56	64
327	67	40	73	72
328	39	57	66	49
329	46	52	62	57
330	45	41	72	73
331	56	39	74	62
332	49	48	70	69
333	42	51	79	54
334	39	47	70	79
335	30	51	62	60
336	40	45	72	56
337	70	35	60	68
338	40	53	59	71
339	27	47	45	64
340	34	44	65	61
341	53	52	71	63
342	53	48	64	58
343	43	60	74	76
344	38	47	67	75
345	53	35	65	87
346	46	48	69	78
347	47	41	72	63
348	60	44	55	61
349	46	35	60	70
350	44	40	43	63
351	50	27	65	66
352	45	36	56	71
353	61	46	75	57
354	63	30	58	61
355	61	30	52	66
356	58	25	68	63
357	60	37	70	65
358	27	37	69	73
359	34	50	66	68
360	46	35	90	83
361	47	22	55	45
362	46	63	46	60
363	61	49	49	66
364	54	30	77	78
365	32	53	47	63
366	54	34	72	74
367	40	38	77	85
368	65	24	47	67
369	49	24	64	63
370	69	46	80	66
371	55	41	70	76
372	66	40	64	78
373	76	47	81	64
374	44	45	60	69
375	45	36	58	49
376	57	37	69	63

Row No.	Population			
	A	B	C	D
377	48	36	62	59
378	49	31	81	69
379	43	47	68	62
380	59	32	72	70
381	44	33	59	65
382	48	30	58	62
383	45	43	66	81
384	51	47	56	54
385	45	27	76	53
386	66	41	79	72
387	53	52	59	61
388	45	27	54	68
389	50	36	87	76
390	67	48	49	50
391	62	29	67	67
392	49	51	50	62
393	47	37	50	74
394	71	47	60	73
395	50	63	62	56
396	45	51	63	65
397	50	49	57	66
398	62	47	50	78
399	52	34	62	56
400	29	51	68	67
401	59	42	64	51
402	39	38	62	68
403	59	35	62	80
404	56	42	56	73
405	38	44	70	67
406	51	34	52	63
407	43	28	70	58
408	19	48	62	85
409	74	37	62	77
410	61	31	74	62
411	31	44	70	52
412	67	42	67	61
413	54	34	64	49
414	49	19	59	64
415	57	22	68	69
416	56	40	69	72
417	56	57	66	46
418	39	44	66	81
419	65	34	66	71
420	47	23	81	66
421	64	17	62	52
422	38	50	72	50
423	64	31	65	66
424	55	41	76	57
425	56	43	65	67
426	43	35	73	83
427	51	28	60	79
428	64	43	54	49
429	39	27	67	69
430	55	27	45	72
431	43	30	62	84

	Population			
Row No.	A	B	C	D
432	55	57	68	62
433	50	21	64	66
434	26	37	59	80
435	44	56	57	53
436	66	33	60	70
437	58	34	62	58
438	51	42	78	74
439	47	34	70	57
440	57	52	64	76
441	49	42	73	70
442	66	43	74	62
443	55	34	62	58
444	48	39	61	73
445	42	26	62	68
446	50	60	75	76
447	39	66	70	69
448	60	43	73	63
449	59	35	73	73
450	47	41	57	54
451	67	38	59	50
452	42	30	51	63
453	51	36	60	56
454	53	29	78	77
455	39	39	68	71
456	63	34	64	75
457	32	57	75	66
458	53	37	51	59
459	53	56	68	66
460	40	37	58	51
461	60	24	77	63
462	43	51	85	63
463	34	41	55	56
464	54	51	63	74
465	46	35	64	74
466	51	46	55	55
467	35	52	74	73
468	48	49	65	63
469	46	24	62	65
470	39	39	68	61
471	61	42	61	71
472	43	29	49	78
473	58	31	81	71
474	52	48	58	41
475	55	55	76	70
476	28	38	64	60
477	50	38	55	66
478	42	37	68	62
479	59	42	62	59
480	51	40	66	64
481	58	39	58	61
482	62	41	65	59
483	45	51	60	61
484	48	31	63	76
485	40	39	50	67
486	37	38	74	63

Row No.	Population			
	A	*B*	*C*	*D*
487	55	38	75	74
488	44	19	54	75
489	50	45	74	66
490	28	37	88	58
491	51	45	52	69
492	52	55	63	63
493	48	64	66	84
494	53	41	81	85
495	49	37	47	58
496	48	44	76	65
497	67	40	60	79
498	35	35	64	66
499	52	54	68	67
500	68	38	65	35

The measurements are scores made on a test designed to measure the level of stress experienced by the subjects. Select four independent simple random samples, one sample from each of the four populations, and perform an analysis to determine whether we may conclude that the four population means are not equal. Let $\alpha = 0.05$, and find the *p* value. Compare your results with those of your classmates.

29. Ⓒ In a certain firm the health records of 280 employees who were ill during a year show the following distribution by sex and severity of illness. Do these data provide sufficient evidence at the 0.05 level of significance to indicate that sex and severity of illness are related? Determine the *p* value.

Severity of illness	Sex		
	Male	*Female*	*Total*
Nondisabling	90	90	180
Disabling but mobile	36	25	61
Confined to bed	24	15	39
Total	150	130	280

30. Ⓒ In a study of the price–quality relationship of certain household products, a market research firm has a team of homemakers test a sample of 135 products and rate them as poor, mediocre, or superior. The following table shows the 135 products cross-classified by the homemakers' ratings and the price category. Test at the 0.05 level the null hypothesis that price and quality are unrelated. Determine the *p* value.

Rating	Price category			
	Low	*Medium*	*High*	*Total*
Poor	15	8	7	30
Mediocre	10	40	14	64
Superior	5	12	24	41
Total	30	60	45	135

31. Ⓒ A researcher selects a random sample from the regular customers of each of three shopping centers. The researcher then determines the area of residence of each customer.

The following table shows the distribution by area of residence for the 500 customers of the three shopping centers. Do these data provide sufficient evidence to suggest that these shopping centers are not homogeneous with respect to area of residence of their regular shoppers? Let $\alpha = 0.05$. Determine the p value.

Area of residence	Shopping center			
	A	*B*	*C*	*Total*
X	110	80	87	277
Y	40	55	57	152
Z	20	25	26	71
Total	170	160	170	500

32. © In a study of outdoor recreation, researchers select a random sample from among the adult males working in a metropolitan area. Subjects are classified on the basis of their occupation and the extent to which they pursue outdoor activities such as hunting, fishing, camping, and outdoor sports. The results are given in the following table. Do these data provide sufficient evidence to indicate a lack of independence between occupation and extent of participation in outdoor activities? Let $\alpha = 0.05$, and determine the p value.

Occupation	Extent of participation				
	Seldom or never	*Occasionally*	*Frequently*	*Very frequently*	*Total*
Professional	10	10	20	60	100
Executive	10	10	25	65	110
Other white collar	25	30	30	65	150
Skilled labor	25	20	35	40	120
Unskilled labor	45	40	25	20	130
Total	115	110	135	250	610

 33. © Market researchers select samples of adults from each of two communities. Respondents are asked to indicate the extent to which they are satisfied with the shopping facilities available to residents of their community. The results are given in the following table. Do these data provide sufficient evidence to indicate a lack of homogeneity between the two communities with regard to extent of residents' satisfaction with available shopping facilities? Let $\alpha = 0.05$, and determine the p value.

Degree of satisfaction	Community	
	A	*B*
Very satisfied	40	60
Satisfied	70	90
Dissatisfied	60	30
Very dissatisfied	30	20
Total	200	200

34. © An economist selects a sample of 200 executives from each of five industries. A questionnaire mailed to each executive asks, "Do you believe that the rate of inflation will be higher during the coming year than last year?" The following table shows the results. Can we conclude that there is a lack of homogeneity among industries with regard to the executives' opinions on inflation? Let $\alpha = 0.05$.

Response to question	Industry				
	A	*B*	*C*	*D*	*E*
Yes	150	100	75	170	90
No	50	100	125	30	110
	200	200	200	200	200

35. A firm has found that about 85% of its accounts receivable are paid on time, 8% are paid after becoming 1 through 30 days delinquent, 6% are paid within the 31- through 60-day delinquency period, and 1% are paid after becoming 60 days delinquent or are not paid at all. A random sample of 500 of this year's accounts reveals the following payment status: Paid on time, 405; 1–30 days delinquent, 50; 31–60 days delinquent, 40; over 60 days delinquent, 5. Does it appear that current accounts receivable conform to the prior payment experience? Let $\alpha = 0.05$, and determine the p value.

36. In a certain area the population consists of four ethnic groups in the following proportions:

Ethnic group	A	B	C	D
Proportion of population	0.13	0.05	0.08	0.74

A survey of 1000 persons in the area employed in managerial and professional positions gives the following results:

Ethnic group	A	B	C	D	
Number	145	45	75	735	Total: 1000

Do these data indicate that the ethnic-group composition of persons employed as managers and professionals in the area is different from the ethnic-group composition of the area's population? Let $\alpha = 0.05$, and determine the p value.

37. Ⓒ Market researchers select a random sample from each of two populations of recent purchasers of new cars. Subjects in Population A have recently bought a Make A car, and those in Population B have recently bought a Make B car. Subjects are asked to indicate the degree to which they are satisfied or dissatisfied with their new car. The results are given in the following table. Do these data provide sufficient evidence to indicate a lack of homogeneity between the two populations with respect to degree of satisfaction or dissatisfaction? Let $\alpha = 0.05$, and determine the p value.

Degree of satisfaction/dissatisfaction	Make of automobile purchased	
	A	*B*
Extremely satisfied	62	28
Mildly satisfied	24	18
Neutral	20	28
Mildly dissatisfied	8	10
Extremely dissatisfied	6	16
	120	100

38. Ⓒ A team of industrial psychologists selects a random sample from among the middle- and lower-echelon white-collar workers in a certain industry. Subjects are asked to indicate the strength of their expectation of achieving a top-level position in their firm. The results by age of respondent are shown in the following table. Do these data provide sufficient evidence to indicate a relationship between age and strength of expectation of achieving a top-level position? Let $\alpha = 0.05$, and determine the p value.

	Strength of Expectation			
Age	Low	High	Uncertain	Total
< 25	10	95	20	125
25–34	20	110	20	150
35–44	20	60	20	100
44 or more	50	40	35	125
Total	100	305	95	500

39. Ⓒ A sociologist selects a sample of 200 ads from the media available in a city. The ads are then categorized on the basis of sex orientation and content. The results are as follows. Do these data provide sufficient evidence to indicate a lack of independence between the two variables? Let $\alpha = 0.05$.

	Sex orientation			
Content	Masculine	Feminine	Neutral	Total
Adventure	60	10	5	75
Domestic	5	50	10	65
Nostalgic	15	10	35	60
Total	80	70	50	200

40. Ⓒ Each of a sample of 400 adults residing in the home city of a professional football team is asked, "Do you think that this city should continue to be the home of a professional football team?" The responses by age of respondent are shown in the following table. Do these data suggest a lack of independence between age and attitude toward the professional football team? Let $\alpha = 0.01$, and determine the p value.

Age of respondent	Response		
	Yes	No	Total
Under 30	50	75	125
30–49	130	45	175
50 and older	60	40	100
Total	240	160	400

41. Ⓒ Market researchers conduct a study of shoppers at the four leading department stores of a city. They select independent random samples of shoppers who shop primarily at each store. The following table shows the age distribution of shoppers. Do these data provide sufficient evidence to indicate a lack of homogeneity with respect to age among the sampled populations? Let $\alpha = 0.05$, and determine the p value.

Age group	Store A	B	C	D	Total
< 25	80	40	90	50	260
25–35	60	60	80	40	240
36–45	30	50	45	75	200
Over 45	30	50	35	85	200
Total	200	200	250	250	900

42. © An ecologist investigates the extent to which officials of industrial firms in a certain area are concerned with control of environmental pollution. One of the questions asked is, ''Does your firm have a policy regarding the implementation and/or maintenance of environmental pollution-control measures?'' The following table shows responses by major industry type. Do these data suggest a lack of independence between type of industry and the presence or absence of a policy on pollution-control measures? Let $\alpha = 0.01$, and find the p value.

Industry type	Response Yes	No	Total
A	5	35	40
B	15	15	30
C	10	15	25
D	15	45	60
E	35	15	50
Total	80	125	205

43. © Select a simple random sample of size 100 from the population of employed heads of households in Appendix II. Can you conclude from the information in your sample that sex and occupation are independent? Let $\alpha = 0.05$, and find the p value. Compare your results with those of your classmates.

44. © During a market-research survey, a firm obtains information on the social class and major leisure-time activity of 375 heads of household. In the following table, the respondents are cross-classified by the two criteria. Test at the 0.01 level the null hypothesis that social class and major leisure-time activity are independent. What use can be made of the results of this study?

Leisure-time activity	Social class 1	2	3	4	5	Total
A	10	7	3	4	1	25
B	14	10	7	4	2	37
C	9	25	13	18	3	68
D	7	9	38	44	6	104
E	3	8	14	18	62	105
F	2	3	8	10	13	36
Total	45	62	83	98	87	375

45. A random sample of 150 shoppers is allowed to choose one of three brands of facial tissue. The results are as follows: Brand A is chosen 35 times; Brand B, 55 times; and

Brand C, 60 times. Do these data provide sufficient evidence to indicate that the three brands are not equally preferred? Let $\alpha = 0.05$.

46. Ⓒ One of the biggest problems with which users of sample surveys have to contend is that of nonresponse to mailed surveys. Many solutions to the problem have been proposed. One market-research analyst believes that mailed questionnaires printed on colored paper are more likely to be returned than those printed on white paper. Each subscriber in a random sample of 500 subscribers to a general-interest magazine is sent the same questionnaire. Half are printed on white paper and half on colored paper. The results are as follows. Do these data provide sufficient evidence to indicate that people are more likely to respond to questionnaires printed on colored paper? Let $\alpha = 0.01$.

	Type of paper		
Response	White	Colored	Total
Returned	75	158	233
Not returned	175	92	267
Total	250	250	500

47. Ⓒ The president of a large national firm wishes to know whether the firm's white-collar and blue-collar employees differ with respect to their opinions on a proposed change in certain fringe benefits. A random sample drawn from each of the two populations yields the following results. Can we conclude from these data that the two populations differ with respect to their opinions regarding the proposal? Let $\alpha = 0.05$.

	Employee category		
Opinion	White-collar	Blue-collar	Total
For	70	55	125
Against	30	95	125
Total	100	150	250

48. Ⓒ A survey is conducted among employees of two different nonunionized firms. One of the questions on the survey is, "Are you in favor of unionization of your firm?" Of the 190 Firm A employees completing the questionnaire, 70 said no. Of 220 Firm B employees completing the questionnaire, 122 said no. On the basis of these results, can we conclude that the two populations differ with respect to their feelings about unionization? Let $\alpha = 0.05$.

49. Ⓒ The manufacturer of a certain household appliance includes with each of its products a customer information/warranty card for the purchaser to return to the manufacturer. Two items of information requested on the card are:

1. The appliance was purchased by a
Man ————
Woman ————

2. The appliance was purchased at a
Department store ————
Other type of store ————

In a random sample of 350 returned cards, 130 state that the appliance had been purchased by a man. Of these purchases by men 40 were made at department stores. Of the women respondents, 184 indicated that their purchase was made at a department store. Do these data provide sufficient evidence to indicate a lack of independence between place of purchase and gender of purchaser? Let $\alpha = 0.05$.

 50. Ⓒ The following table contains information on a population of 2000 adults. A toothpaste manufacturer collected the data to determine whether the subjects' reaction to a new kind of toothpaste is related to their sex. Variable 1 is sex and is coded as follows:

Male $= 1$
Female $= 2$

Variable 2 is the subjects' reaction to the new toothpaste and is coded as follows:

Likes new toothpaste $= 1$
Indifferent $= 2$
Does not like new toothpaste $= 3$

Select a simple random sample of size 50 from this population and perform an appropriate test to determine whether your sample data provide sufficient evidence to enable you to conclude that there is a relationship between sex and reaction to the toothpaste. Let $\alpha = 0.05$, and find the p value for the test.

Subject	Sex	Reaction	Subject	Sex	Reaction
1	1	3	32	2	1
2	1	2	33	1	1
3	1	1	34	2	1
4	2	1	35	1	1
5	1	1	36	1	1
6	2	3	37	1	1
7	2	1	38	2	1
8	2	1	39	1	2
9	1	1	40	2	1
10	2	1	41	2	1
11	2	2	42	1	1
12	2	1	43	1	1
13	1	1	44	2	3
14	2	1	45	2	1
15	2	2	46	1	1
16	2	3	47	2	3
17	2	1	48	1	1
18	1	1	49	2	1
19	2	3	50	1	1
20	1	1	51	1	2
21	2	1	52	1	3
22	2	1	53	1	1
23	2	3	54	1	1
24	1	1	55	2	1
25	1	1	56	1	2
26	1	1	57	2	1
27	2	2	58	2	1
28	2	3	59	2	3
29	2	1	60	2	2
30	1	1	61	1	1
31	2	1	62	2	2

Subject	Sex	Reaction	Subject	Sex	Reaction
63	2	1	121	2	1
64	1	1	122	1	1
65	1	3	123	2	3
66	2	1	124	2	3
67	1	1	125	2	2
68	2	1	126	1	2
69	2	1	127	2	2
70	1	2	128	1	3
71	1	2	129	2	3
72	2	1	130	2	2
73	1	1	131	2	3
74	2	2	132	1	1
75	1	2	133	2	3
76	2	1	134	2	1
77	2	1	135	1	1
78	1	3	136	2	1
79	2	1	137	2	1
80	2	1	138	1	1
81	1	1	139	1	3
82	2	1	140	1	2
83	2	1	141	2	1
84	1	2	142	1	2
85	2	2	143	2	2
86	1	2	144	2	3
87	1	2	145	2	1
88	2	2	146	2	1
89	2	3	147	1	2
90	1	3	148	1	3
91	1	1	149	2	1
92	2	1	150	1	1
93	2	3	151	2	1
94	2	1	152	2	1
95	2	3	153	2	1
96	1	1	154	1	1
97	2	2	155	2	1
98	2	2	156	2	1
99	1	3	157	1	2
100	2	2	158	1	2
101	1	2	159	1	1
102	1	3	160	1	2
103	1	1	161	1	3
104	2	1	162	2	3
105	1	1	163	2	1
106	1	1	164	2	3
107	2	1	165	2	1
108	1	1	166	2	2
109	1	1	167	2	3
110	1	3	168	1	1
111	1	2	169	1	3
112	1	2	170	1	1
113	1	3	171	1	1
114	2	3	172	1	3
115	1	1	173	1	2
116	2	2	174	1	1
117	2	1	175	2	1
118	1	1	176	2	2
119	2	3	177	2	1
120	1	1	178	2	2

Subject	Sex	Reaction	Subject	Sex	Reaction
179	1	1	237	2	1
180	1	1	238	1	3
181	1	1	239	2	3
182	2	3	240	2	1
183	1	3	241	1	1
184	2	1	242	1	1
185	2	1	243	2	1
186	1	1	244	2	2
187	2	3	245	2	2
188	1	3	246	2	2
189	1	1	247	1	3
190	2	1	248	2	1
191	1	2	249	2	1
192	1	1	250	2	2
193	2	1	251	2	2
194	1	2	252	1	3
195	2	1	253	1	1
196	2	1	254	1	1
197	1	2	255	2	1
198	1	1	256	2	3
199	1	1	257	2	1
200	2	2	258	2	2
201	1	1	259	1	1
202	1	1	260	1	1
203	2	1	261	2	1
204	1	3	262	1	2
205	2	3	263	2	1
206	2	1	264	1	1
207	2	1	265	1	1
208	2	1	266	2	1
209	2	1	267	2	3
210	2	1	268	1	1
211	1	1	269	1	1
212	1	1	270	2	1
213	1	1	271	2	1
214	1	3	272	2	2
215	2	1	273	2	3
216	2	1	274	1	2
217	2	2	275	2	1
218	2	1	276	2	1
219	2	2	277	1	3
220	2	3	278	2	2
221	2	1	279	2	2
222	1	2	280	1	1
223	2	1	281	1	1
224	2	1	282	1	1
225	1	2	283	1	1
226	1	3	284	2	1
227	2	1	285	2	2
228	1	1	286	2	1
229	2	1	287	2	1
230	2	3	288	1	3
231	1	1	289	1	1
232	2	3	290	1	1
233	1	2	291	1	1
234	2	1	292	1	2
235	1	3	293	1	2
236	2	1	294	2	1

Subject	Sex	Reaction	Subject	Sex	Reaction
295	1	1	353	1	1
296	1	1	354	2	1
297	2	2	355	1	1
298	1	3	356	1	1
299	1	2	357	1	1
300	1	1	358	1	1
301	1	1	359	2	3
302	1	1	360	1	1
303	2	1	361	1	1
304	1	1	362	2	2
305	1	3	363	1	1
306	2	3	364	1	1
307	1	1	365	2	1
308	2	1	366	2	1
309	2	1	367	2	1
310	1	3	368	1	1
311	1	1	369	1	3
312	1	2	370	1	1
313	2	1	371	1	1
314	2	1	372	2	2
315	1	1	373	2	1
316	1	1	374	2	1
317	1	2	375	1	2
318	1	1	376	2	1
319	1	3	377	1	1
320	2	1	378	2	2
321	2	2	379	2	2
322	2	1	380	1	1
323	1	1	381	2	2
324	2	1	382	1	1
325	1	1	383	1	3
326	1	1	384	1	1
327	2	1	385	2	1
328	2	3	386	2	3
329	2	1	387	1	2
330	2	3	388	2	3
331	2	1	389	1	1
332	1	1	390	2	1
333	2	2	391	2	1
334	1	2	392	2	1
335	1	2	393	1	1
336	2	3	394	1	2
337	2	3	395	1	1
338	2	1	396	2	1
339	2	1	397	1	3
340	2	2	398	2	2
341	1	3	399	2	3
342	1	2	400	2	1
343	1	1	401	2	2
344	2	1	402	1	1
345	2	1	403	2	2
346	1	1	404	1	1
347	1	3	405	2	1
348	1	1	406	1	1
349	1	1	407	2	2
350	2	1	408	1	2
351	1	1	409	1	1
352	1	3	410	2	1

Subject	Sex	Reaction	Subject	Sex	Reaction
411	1	2	469	2	1
412	1	2	470	2	1
413	2	1	471	2	2
414	1	1	472	2	2
415	1	3	473	1	3
416	1	1	474	2	1
417	2	1	475	2	1
418	2	1	476	1	2
419	2	1	477	1	3
420	2	1	478	2	1
421	1	2	479	1	2
422	1	1	480	2	1
423	2	2	481	1	2
424	1	2	482	2	1
425	1	1	483	2	1
426	1	1	484	1	1
427	1	1	485	2	2
428	1	1	486	2	1
429	1	3	487	1	3
430	1	2	488	2	1
431	1	3	489	1	1
432	2	1	490	1	1
433	2	1	491	1	2
434	1	3	492	2	1
435	1	1	493	2	3
436	1	3	494	2	2
437	2	3	495	1	1
438	1	1	496	1	1
439	1	2	497	2	1
440	1	1	498	1	1
441	1	1	499	2	3
442	1	2	500	2	2
443	2	2	501	1	1
444	2	1	502	1	1
445	2	2	503	2	1
446	1	2	504	1	3
447	1	1	505	2	1
448	1	1	506	1	1
449	1	1	507	1	1
450	2	1	508	2	1
451	2	1	509	2	1
452	2	1	510	1	2
453	1	1	511	1	1
454	2	2	512	2	1
455	2	1	513	1	3
456	2	1	514	1	2
457	2	1	515	2	1
458	1	1	516	2	1
459	1	1	517	2	3
460	2	1	518	1	2
461	2	1	519	2	1
462	1	1	520	2	1
463	1	2	521	2	2
464	1	3	522	2	1
465	2	1	523	1	1
466	1	1	524	1	2
467	2	1	525	1	1
468	2	1	526	1	2

Subject	Sex	Reaction	Subject	Sex	Reaction
527	1	1	585	1	2
528	1	2	586	2	2
529	1	1	587	1	1
530	2	1	588	2	3
531	1	2	589	2	3
532	1	1	590	1	1
533	2	2	591	1	1
534	2	1	592	1	1
535	1	1	593	2	3
536	1	2	594	1	1
537	1	3	595	2	3
538	2	2	596	2	1
539	2	3	597	1	3
540	1	1	598	2	1
541	2	1	599	1	1
542	2	1	600	2	2
543	1	1	601	2	1
544	1	3	602	1	1
545	1	1	603	1	1
546	1	3	604	2	3
547	2	1	605	1	1
548	1	1	606	1	1
549	2	3	607	2	2
550	1	1	608	2	1
551	2	1	609	1	3
552	2	1	610	2	1
553	1	2	611	2	1
554	1	1	612	2	3
555	2	3	613	1	1
556	1	1	614	2	1
557	2	2	615	2	1
558	1	2	616	2	1
559	2	1	617	1	1
560	2	3	618	2	2
561	1	1	619	1	1
562	1	2	620	2	3
563	2	1	621	1	1
564	1	1	622	1	1
565	2	1	623	1	1
566	2	1	624	1	1
567	1	1	625	1	1
568	1	1	626	2	2
569	2	3	627	2	1
570	1	2	628	1	1
571	1	1	629	1	1
572	1	1	630	1	3
573	1	2	631	2	1
574	2	1	632	1	1
575	2	2	633	2	3
576	1	1	634	2	2
577	2	1	635	1	3
578	1	3	636	2	1
579	2	1	637	1	1
580	2	1	638	1	1
581	2	1	639	1	3
582	2	3	640	2	2
583	2	3	641	1	1
584	1	2	642	1	1

Subject	Sex	Reaction	Subject	Sex	Reaction
643	2	1	701	2	1
644	2	3	702	1	1
645	2	1	703	2	1
646	2	1	704	2	1
647	1	1	705	2	3
648	1	2	706	2	1
649	1	3	707	1	1
650	1	1	708	2	1
651	2	2	709	1	1
652	2	1	710	2	2
653	1	1	711	2	1
654	1	1	712	1	3
655	1	1	713	2	3
656	2	1	714	1	1
657	2	3	715	2	1
658	1	1	716	2	1
659	2	2	717	1	1
660	1	2	718	2	1
661	1	3	719	2	3
662	1	1	720	2	1
663	1	1	721	1	3
664	1	1	722	1	1
665	2	2	723	1	3
666	1	1	724	2	1
667	1	1	725	2	1
668	2	1	726	2	1
669	1	2	727	1	3
670	2	1	728	2	2
671	1	1	729	2	3
672	1	3	730	2	1
673	2	1	731	2	1
674	1	1	732	1	3
675	1	2	733	2	3
676	1	2	734	1	3
677	1	3	735	1	3
678	1	2	736	2	1
679	2	2	737	1	1
680	1	3	738	2	3
681	2	1	739	2	1
682	2	1	740	2	1
683	1	1	741	1	3
684	2	3	742	1	3
685	2	1	743	1	3
686	1	1	744	2	1
687	2	2	745	2	3
688	1	2	746	2	1
689	2	1	747	1	2
690	1	1	748	1	1
691	2	1	749	2	1
692	2	1	750	2	2
693	1	1	751	2	1
694	2	1	752	2	2
695	1	1	753	2	1
696	1	2	754	1	1
697	1	1	755	2	1
698	2	1	756	1	2
699	1	2	757	1	2
700	1	1	758	2	2

Subject	Sex	Reaction	Subject	Sex	Reaction
759	2	1	817	1	2
760	1	1	818	2	1
761	1	3	819	1	3
762	2	1	820	2	1
763	2	1	821	1	1
764	1	3	822	2	1
765	2	1	823	1	1
766	1	1	824	1	3
767	2	3	825	2	1
768	1	3	826	2	1
769	2	3	827	1	1
770	2	1	828	1	2
771	2	1	829	1	2
772	1	3	830	1	1
773	1	1	831	2	1
774	1	3	832	1	1
775	2	3	833	2	3
776	1	1	834	2	2
777	2	1	835	2	1
778	2	1	836	1	1
779	2	2	837	1	2
780	1	1	838	2	2
781	1	1	839	1	1
782	2	3	840	2	3
783	2	1	841	1	3
784	1	3	842	2	1
785	2	1	843	2	1
786	1	3	844	1	1
787	2	1	845	1	1
788	1	1	846	1	1
789	1	1	847	2	1
790	2	1	848	2	1
791	1	1	849	1	1
792	1	3	850	1	1
793	1	1	851	1	1
794	2	1	852	1	1
795	1	2	853	2	1
796	2	1	854	1	1
797	1	1	855	2	1
798	2	3	856	1	1
799	2	1	857	1	1
800	1	1	858	1	1
801	1	1	859	1	1
802	2	3	860	1	3
803	1	3	861	1	1
804	2	1	862	2	2
805	1	1	863	2	1
806	1	1	864	1	2
807	2	3	865	1	1
808	2	3	866	1	3
809	2	1	867	2	1
810	1	1	868	1	1
811	2	1	869	1	1
812	1	2	870	2	1
813	1	1	871	2	2
814	1	1	872	2	1
815	1	2	873	2	1
816	2	2	874	2	1

Subject	Sex	Reaction	Subject	Sex	Reaction
875	2	1	933	1	1
876	2	3	934	1	3
877	1	3	935	2	2
878	1	3	936	1	1
879	2	1	937	1	1
880	1	2	938	2	1
881	1	1	939	2	3
882	1	2	940	2	1
883	2	1	941	2	1
884	2	2	942	2	3
885	2	1	943	2	1
886	2	3	944	2	2
887	2	1	945	2	2
888	1	2	946	1	2
889	1	2	947	2	1
890	2	1	948	2	1
891	2	1	949	1	1
892	1	3	950	1	1
893	2	3	951	1	2
894	2	2	952	1	1
895	1	1	953	2	1
896	2	1	954	1	1
897	1	1	955	2	1
898	2	3	956	2	3
899	2	1	957	1	3
900	2	2	958	2	1
901	1	2	959	2	3
902	1	3	960	2	1
903	2	3	961	2	1
904	1	2	962	2	3
905	1	1	963	1	1
906	1	1	964	1	2
907	2	3	965	1	1
908	1	1	966	1	3
909	2	1	967	1	2
910	2	1	968	1	2
911	1	3	969	2	1
912	1	1	970	1	1
913	2	3	971	1	2
914	1	2	972	1	1
915	2	1	973	1	3
916	1	3	974	2	1
917	1	1	975	1	1
918	1	2	976	1	1
919	1	1	977	1	1
920	1	3	978	2	3
921	2	2	979	2	2
922	2	3	980	2	1
923	2	1	981	2	2
924	1	1	982	1	1
925	2	2	983	1	1
926	1	2	984	1	1
927	2	2	985	2	1
928	1	1	986	1	1
929	1	1	987	2	3
930	2	1	988	1	1
931	2	1	989	1	1
932	1	1	990	2	1

Subject	Sex	Reaction	Subject	Sex	Reaction
991	2	3	1049	2	3
992	1	2	1050	2	1
993	2	1	1051	2	1
994	2	1	1052	1	1
995	2	1	1053	1	3
996	1	1	1054	1	3
997	1	1	1055	1	2
998	2	1	1056	2	1
999	2	3	1057	1	1
1000	1	1	1058	2	1
1001	2	3	1059	1	2
1002	1	1	1060	2	1
1003	2	1	1061	2	1
1004	2	1	1062	2	1
1005	1	1	1063	2	3
1006	2	3	1064	1	2
1007	1	2	1065	1	1
1008	1	1	1066	2	1
1009	1	3	1067	2	1
1010	2	1	1068	2	1
1011	1	3	1069	1	1
1012	1	1	1070	2	1
1013	2	1	1071	1	1
1014	1	1	1072	1	3
1015	1	1	1073	1	2
1016	1	2	1074	1	1
1017	2	3	1075	1	1
1018	1	1	1076	2	1
1019	2	3	1077	1	3
1020	2	1	1078	1	1
1021	2	1	1079	1	1
1022	2	1	1080	1	1
1023	1	1	1081	2	3
1024	1	1	1082	1	1
1025	1	3	1083	2	1
1026	2	2	1084	1	1
1027	1	1	1085	2	1
1028	1	1	1086	1	1
1029	2	1	1087	1	1
1030	2	3	1088	1	2
1031	1	2	1089	2	2
1032	1	3	1090	1	1
1033	2	3	1091	1	2
1034	2	1	1092	1	3
1035	2	1	1093	2	1
1036	1	1	1094	2	1
1037	2	1	1095	2	1
1038	1	1	1096	1	1
1039	1	2	1097	1	1
1040	1	2	1098	1	1
1041	1	1	1099	1	1
1042	1	1	1100	1	1
1043	2	3	1101	1	1
1044	2	3	1102	1	1
1045	1	3	1103	1	2
1046	2	1	1104	2	1
1047	2	1	1105	1	3
1048	1	1	1106	1	3

Subject	Sex	Reaction	Subject	Sex	Reaction
1107	2	1	1165	1	2
1108	1	1	1166	1	3
1109	1	1	1167	2	1
1110	2	2	1168	1	3
1111	2	1	1169	1	1
1112	2	1	1170	2	2
1113	2	1	1171	2	3
1114	1	3	1172	2	2
1115	2	1	1173	1	1
1116	2	1	1174	2	1
1117	2	1	1175	1	1
1118	1	2	1176	2	1
1119	1	1	1177	2	1
1120	2	3	1178	2	3
1121	2	1	1179	1	3
1122	1	2	1180	1	1
1123	1	3	1181	1	2
1124	1	1	1182	1	3
1125	1	1	1183	2	1
1126	2	1	1184	1	1
1127	1	1	1185	2	1
1128	1	3	1186	2	3
1129	2	2	1187	1	1
1130	2	1	1188	2	1
1131	2	1	1189	2	2
1132	1	1	1190	1	3
1133	1	1	1191	1	1
1134	1	1	1192	1	3
1135	1	1	1193	2	2
1136	1	2	1194	2	1
1137	1	1	1195	1	3
1138	2	3	1196	1	1
1139	1	1	1197	2	2
1140	1	1	1198	2	3
1141	1	1	1199	2	1
1142	1	1	1200	1	1
1143	2	2	1201	2	1
1144	2	3	1202	2	1
1145	2	3	1203	1	3
1146	1	1	1204	2	1
1147	1	3	1205	1	2
1148	1	1	1206	2	1
1149	1	1	1207	2	1
1150	2	1	1208	1	1
1151	2	3	1209	1	1
1152	1	1	1210	2	1
1153	2	2	1211	1	2
1154	2	1	1212	1	2
1155	1	3	1213	1	1
1156	2	3	1214	1	3
1157	2	1	1215	1	1
1158	2	2	1216	2	1
1159	1	1	1217	1	3
1160	2	1	1218	2	1
1161	1	3	1219	1	1
1162	1	1	1220	1	1
1163	2	1	1221	2	2
1164	2	2	1222	1	1

Subject	Sex	Reaction	Subject	Sex	Reaction
1223	2	1	1281	1	2
1224	1	2	1282	2	1
1225	2	1	1283	2	1
1226	1	1	1284	2	2
1227	1	2	1285	2	1
1228	1	3	1286	1	2
1229	1	2	1287	1	2
1230	1	3	1288	2	2
1231	1	2	1289	2	2
1232	1	1	1290	2	1
1233	2	2	1291	1	2
1234	1	1	1292	2	1
1235	2	1	1293	2	1
1236	2	3	1294	1	1
1237	1	3	1295	1	2
1238	2	1	1296	2	1
1239	2	2	1297	2	1
1240	2	1	1298	1	1
1241	2	2	1299	1	2
1242	2	1	1300	1	3
1243	1	2	1301	1	1
1244	1	1	1302	1	2
1245	2	1	1303	1	2
1246	2	1	1304	2	2
1247	1	1	1305	2	1
1248	2	1	1306	1	1
1249	2	2	1307	2	1
1250	2	1	1308	2	3
1251	1	1	1309	2	1
1252	2	2	1310	2	3
1253	1	1	1311	2	1
1254	2	3	1312	2	1
1255	1	2	1313	2	2
1256	2	1	1314	2	2
1257	2	2	1315	1	3
1258	1	3	1316	1	1
1259	2	1	1317	2	1
1260	1	3	1318	1	1
1261	1	1	1319	1	1
1262	1	1	1320	1	1
1263	1	3	1321	1	2
1264	2	3	1322	2	1
1265	1	3	1323	1	2
1266	1	1	1324	2	1
1267	2	1	1325	2	1
1268	2	3	1326	1	1
1269	2	1	1327	1	3
1270	2	1	1328	1	1
1271	2	1	1329	1	3
1272	2	1	1330	1	1
1273	2	1	1331	2	1
1274	2	1	1332	2	3
1275	1	1	1333	1	1
1276	2	1	1334	2	3
1277	2	3	1335	1	2
1278	1	2	1336	1	2
1279	1	1	1337	2	2
1280	1	1	1338	2	3

Subject	Sex	Reaction	Subject	Sex	Reaction
1339	2	1	1397	1	1
1340	2	1	1398	1	3
1341	2	1	1399	1	1
1342	2	3	1400	2	1
1343	2	2	1401	1	3
1344	1	1	1402	2	2
1345	2	3	1403	2	1
1346	1	1	1404	1	3
1347	2	1	1405	1	1
1348	2	2	1406	2	1
1349	1	2	1407	2	3
1350	2	1	1408	1	1
1351	1	2	1409	2	1
1352	1	1	1410	1	3
1353	2	1	1411	2	3
1354	2	1	1412	2	3
1355	2	1	1413	1	1
1356	2	3	1414	2	1
1357	1	1	1415	2	2
1358	2	1	1416	1	1
1359	2	1	1417	2	1
1360	2	1	1418	1	3
1361	1	3	1419	1	3
1362	2	1	1420	2	1
1363	2	1	1421	2	2
1364	2	3	1422	2	1
1365	1	1	1423	1	1
1366	1	1	1424	2	1
1367	1	1	1425	2	1
1368	1	3	1426	2	1
1369	2	1	1427	2	2
1370	1	1	1428	2	1
1371	1	1	1429	1	2
1372	2	1	1430	2	1
1373	2	1	1431	2	1
1374	2	1	1432	2	1
1375	2	1	1433	1	3
1376	2	2	1434	2	1
1377	2	2	1435	2	1
1378	1	2	1436	2	3
1379	1	2	1437	2	1
1380	1	1	1438	1	2
1381	2	2	1439	2	2
1382	1	1	1440	2	3
1383	2	1	1441	1	1
1384	1	3	1442	1	1
1385	1	1	1443	1	3
1386	1	2	1444	1	1
1387	2	1	1445	1	2
1388	2	1	1446	2	1
1389	1	1	1447	2	1
1390	1	1	1448	2	2
1391	2	2	1449	2	1
1392	1	1	1450	1	3
1393	1	1	1451	1	1
1394	2	3	1452	2	1
1395	1	3	1453	1	1
1396	2	1	1454	2	1

Subject	Sex	Reaction	Subject	Sex	Reaction
1455	1	1	1513	2	1
1456	2	3	1514	1	1
1457	1	1	1515	2	1
1458	1	2	1516	1	1
1459	1	3	1517	1	3
1460	2	1	1518	2	3
1461	1	1	1519	1	3
1462	2	3	1520	1	1
1463	2	2	1521	2	1
1464	2	3	1522	2	1
1465	1	3	1523	2	1
1466	1	1	1524	2	1
1467	1	3	1525	1	1
1468	2	1	1526	1	1
1469	2	1	1527	1	1
1470	2	1	1528	2	3
1471	1	1	1529	1	2
1472	1	1	1530	1	1
1473	1	1	1531	1	1
1474	1	1	1532	2	2
1475	1	2	1533	1	2
1476	2	1	1534	2	1
1477	1	3	1535	2	1
1478	1	3	1536	2	1
1479	2	1	1537	2	1
1480	1	1	1538	1	2
1481	1	3	1539	2	3
1482	1	3	1540	1	2
1483	1	1	1541	1	1
1484	1	1	1542	2	2
1485	1	1	1543	2	3
1486	2	1	1544	2	1
1487	2	3	1545	2	3
1488	1	1	1546	1	2
1489	2	1	1547	2	1
1490	2	1	1548	2	1
1491	2	3	1549	1	1
1492	1	3	1550	1	1
1493	1	1	1551	2	1
1494	2	3	1552	2	1
1495	1	1	1553	1	3
1496	2	1	1554	2	1
1497	2	1	1555	2	1
1498	2	2	1556	2	3
1499	2	2	1557	2	1
1500	1	3	1558	1	2
1501	2	1	1559	1	2
1502	2	1	1560	2	1
1503	1	1	1561	1	2
1504	1	3	1562	2	1
1505	1	1	1563	1	3
1506	1	2	1564	1	1
1507	2	1	1565	1	1
1508	1	3	1566	2	3
1509	2	1	1567	1	1
1510	1	2	1568	2	1
1511	2	1	1569	2	1
1512	2	1	1570	2	1

Subject	Sex	Reaction	Subject	Sex	Reaction
1571	1	3	1629	1	2
1572	2	1	1630	2	2
1573	1	2	1631	1	1
1574	1	1	1632	2	1
1575	1	1	1633	2	1
1576	2	1	1634	2	1
1577	1	3	1635	2	1
1578	2	1	1636	2	2
1579	2	3	1637	1	1
1580	1	1	1638	1	1
1581	1	2	1639	2	2
1582	2	2	1640	2	1
1583	2	1	1641	1	1
1584	1	1	1642	1	1
1585	2	2	1643	1	1
1586	1	1	1644	2	3
1587	2	2	1645	1	1
1588	2	1	1646	1	1
1589	1	1	1647	1	3
1590	2	1	1648	1	1
1591	2	1	1649	2	1
1592	1	1	1650	1	1
1593	1	1	1651	1	3
1594	2	1	1652	1	2
1595	2	1	1653	2	2
1596	1	1	1654	2	1
1597	1	1	1655	1	3
1598	1	1	1656	2	1
1599	2	1	1657	2	1
1600	1	2	1658	1	3
1601	1	1	1659	1	2
1602	1	1	1660	1	1
1603	1	1	1661	2	1
1604	2	1	1662	2	1
1605	2	3	1663	1	1
1606	2	3	1664	1	1
1607	2	1	1665	1	1
1608	2	1	1666	2	3
1609	2	3	1667	1	3
1610	1	1	1668	2	1
1611	1	3	1669	1	1
1612	1	1	1670	1	3
1613	2	1	1671	1	1
1614	1	2	1672	1	1
1615	2	2	1673	1	3
1616	1	1	1674	2	1
1617	1	1	1675	1	2
1618	1	1	1676	1	1
1619	2	2	1677	1	1
1620	1	3	1678	1	3
1621	1	3	1679	2	2
1622	2	1	1680	2	2
1623	2	1	1681	1	2
1624	1	2	1682	2	3
1625	1	1	1683	2	1
1626	1	1	1684	1	1
1627	1	1	1685	1	1
1628	2	1	1686	1	1

Subject	Sex	Reaction	Subject	Sex	Reaction
1687	1	1	1745	1	1
1688	1	1	1746	2	1
1689	1	1	1747	2	1
1690	1	2	1748	2	2
1691	1	1	1749	1	1
1692	2	2	1750	2	2
1693	2	1	1751	2	1
1694	1	1	1752	2	3
1695	2	1	1753	2	2
1696	2	3	1754	2	3
1697	2	2	1755	1	2
1698	2	1	1756	1	1
1699	1	1	1757	2	2
1700	1	1	1758	2	1
1701	1	2	1759	2	3
1702	2	1	1760	1	3
1703	2	3	1761	1	1
1704	2	1	1762	1	2
1705	1	1	1763	1	1
1706	2	1	1764	1	2
1707	2	2	1765	1	1
1708	2	1	1766	2	1
1709	1	1	1767	1	1
1710	1	1	1768	1	1
1711	2	3	1769	2	1
1712	1	1	1770	1	3
1713	2	3	1771	1	1
1714	1	2	1772	1	2
1715	1	3	1773	2	1
1716	1	1	1774	2	2
1717	1	1	1775	1	1
1718	2	3	1776	2	2
1719	2	1	1777	2	1
1720	2	1	1778	1	1
1721	1	1	1779	1	1
1722	2	1	1780	2	3
1723	2	1	1781	2	1
1724	1	3	1782	1	2
1725	1	1	1783	1	2
1726	1	1	1784	1	1
1727	1	1	1785	1	2
1728	1	2	1786	1	3
1729	1	3	1787	2	1
1730	2	3	1788	2	1
1731	1	1	1789	2	1
1732	2	3	1790	1	1
1733	2	2	1791	1	1
1734	2	1	1792	1	3
1735	1	3	1793	2	1
1736	1	1	1794	2	1
1737	1	1	1795	1	3
1738	1	1	1796	2	1
1739	2	1	1797	2	2
1740	2	2	1798	2	3
1741	2	2	1799	1	3
1742	1	1	1800	1	1
1743	2	2	1801	2	1
1744	1	1	1802	1	2

Subject	Sex	Reaction	Subject	Sex	Reaction
1803	2	3	1861	1	1
1804	1	2	1862	1	1
1805	2	3	1863	2	1
1806	1	1	1864	1	1
1807	2	1	1865	1	1
1808	2	2	1866	1	3
1809	1	1	1867	2	1
1810	2	1	1868	2	1
1811	2	3	1869	2	3
1812	1	1	1870	1	1
1813	1	3	1871	2	1
1814	2	1	1872	1	1
1815	1	1	1873	1	3
1816	2	1	1874	1	3
1817	1	1	1875	2	1
1818	1	1	1876	1	1
1819	2	2	1877	1	2
1820	1	1	1878	2	1
1821	2	2	1879	1	1
1822	2	1	1880	2	1
1823	2	2	1881	2	3
1824	1	1	1882	2	2
1825	2	1	1883	1	1
1826	1	1	1884	1	1
1827	1	2	1885	1	3
1828	2	2	1886	2	1
1829	1	3	1887	1	2
1830	2	2	1888	1	1
1831	2	1	1889	2	1
1832	1	1	1890	2	1
1833	2	3	1891	2	1
1834	1	1	1892	1	1
1835	2	1	1893	1	2
1836	2	2	1894	2	1
1837	1	1	1895	1	3
1838	2	2	1896	1	2
1839	1	1	1897	2	1
1840	1	1	1898	1	1
1841	1	1	1899	2	1
1842	2	2	1900	1	1
1843	1	3	1901	2	2
1844	1	1	1902	2	1
1845	1	1	1903	1	2
1846	1	1	1904	1	1
1847	2	1	1905	2	1
1848	2	1	1906	2	2
1849	2	2	1907	2	1
1850	2	1	1908	1	3
1851	1	2	1909	2	1
1852	2	1	1910	1	1
1853	1	3	1911	2	1
1854	2	1	1912	1	2
1855	1	1	1913	2	2
1856	1	1	1914	1	1
1857	2	2	1915	1	1
1858	1	2	1916	2	1
1859	1	1	1917	1	3
1860	1	1	1918	2	1

Subject	Sex	Reaction	Subject	Sex	Reaction
1919	1	1	1960	2	1
1920	2	1	1961	2	3
1921	2	1	1962	2	2
1922	1	1	1963	1	1
1923	2	1	1964	2	1
1924	2	1	1965	1	3
1925	1	1	1966	1	1
1926	2	3	1967	1	2
1927	2	1	1968	1	1
1928	2	2	1969	1	1
1929	1	1	1970	1	2
1930	2	1	1971	1	3
1931	2	1	1972	1	3
1932	1	3	1973	2	1
1933	1	1	1974	2	1
1934	1	1	1975	2	3
1935	1	2	1976	1	1
1936	1	1	1977	1	3
1937	2	1	1978	2	1
1938	1	3	1979	2	2
1939	2	1	1980	2	1
1940	2	3	1981	2	1
1941	1	1	1982	1	1
1942	1	1	1983	1	3
1943	2	2	1984	1	2
1944	1	2	1985	1	1
1945	1	2	1986	1	3
1946	2	3	1987	2	1
1947	2	3	1988	1	1
1948	1	1	1989	1	1
1949	2	1	1990	2	2
1950	2	1	1991	2	1
1951	1	1	1992	2	3
1952	1	1	1993	1	1
1953	2	2	1994	1	1
1954	2	1	1995	1	2
1955	2	2	1996	2	1
1956	2	3	1997	2	1
1957	1	1	1998	1	2
1958	2	3	1999	2	1
1959	1	1	2000	1	1

For Exercises 51 through 65, do the following: Select a simple random sample of size 200 from the population of companies in Appendix III. Formulate and test an appropriate hypothesis about the independence of pairs of variables as indicated in the exercises that follow. Form appropriate categories for the two variables, and prepare a contingency table containing observed frequencies. Select the level of significance of your choice, follow the seven-step hypothesis-testing procedure, and find the p value for the test.

51. ⓒ Can we conclude that assets and sales are related?

52. ⓒ Can we conclude that assets and market value are related?

53. ⓒ Can we conclude that assets and net profits are related?

54. ⓒ Can we conclude that assets and cash flow are related?

55. ⓒ Can we conclude that assets and number employed are related?

56. © Can we conclude that sales and market value are related?
57. © Can we conclude that sales and net profits are related?
58. © Can we conclude that sales and cash flow are related?
59. © Can we conclude that sales and number employed are related?
60. © Can we conclude that market value and net profits are related?
61. © Can we conclude that market value and cash flow are related?
62. © Can we conclude that market value and number employed are related?
63. © Can we conclude that net profits and cash flow are related?
64. © Can we conclude that net profits and number employed are related?
65. © Can we conclude that cash flow and number employed are related?

PRACTICE WITH REAL DATA

1. From your student directory, select a simple random sample of students from each of three or more categories, such as class (freshman, sophomore, junior, senior), major (accounting, marketing, management, etc.), school or college (business, arts and sciences, engineering, etc.), or home residence (in-state, out-of-state, foreign). Contact the students in the samples by telephone or in person and collect appropriate information so that you can use one-way analysis of variance to test the null hypothesis of equal population means for some variable, such as: amount of money spent for books during the current school term, amount of money spent for recreation so far during the current school term, number of miles traveled on vacations during the past year, age of father, number of siblings, or number of movies attended during the past month.

   Consult with your instructor regarding sample sizes and the design of your questionnaire.

2. From the help-wanted section of the Sunday edition of a metropolitan newspaper, select a simple random sample of 100 or more ads. Use the information in the ads to test the null hypothesis that two variables are independent. Possible variables for use in this assignment include type of position, type of firm, location of firm, experience required (yes or no), fringe benefits mentioned (yes or no), required skills mentioned (yes or no), and type of application required (call, write, or apply in person).

9.

Regression and Correlation Analysis

CHAPTER OBJECTIVES: This chapter introduces you to two of the most widely used of all statistical techniques—regression analysis and correlation analysis. After studying this chapter and working the exercises, you should be able to do the following.

1. Discuss applications of simple linear regression and correlation analysis

2. State the assumptions underlying the two methods of analysis

3. Obtain an equation that you can use for prediction and estimation

4. Perform hypothesis tests to determine whether you should conclude that two variables are linearly related

5. Compute a measure of the strength of the correlation between two variables

6. Perform hypothesis tests to determine whether you should conclude that two variables are correlated

7. Use a computer to analyze the data of a multiple-regression study and interpret the computer printout

In analyzing data generated by a business or industrial operation, we often want to know something about the relationship between two variables, X and Y. Is there a relationship between the sales of a certain product and the age of persons in the various market areas? Do employees who score high on a certain aptitude test perform well on the job? What is the nature of the relationship between the amount of a certain chemical in some material and the material's optical density? Between the price of a product and demand for that product? Between the hardness and the tensile strength of a certain metal? The list of pairs of variables with a relationship that is of potential interest is almost limitless.

One approach to studying such relationships is the analysis of variance, discussed in Chapter 8. This chapter will show that we can also examine the nature of the relationships between variables such as those listed using *regression analysis* and *correlation analysis*. Although regression and correlation are related, they serve different purposes.

We use regression to *predict* and to *estimate*.

Regression analysis helps one determine the probable *form* of the relationship between variables. The objective of this method of analysis is usually to *predict* or *estimate* the value of one variable that corresponds to a given value of another variable. The English scientist Sir Francis Galton (1822–1911) first proposed the ideas of regression in reports of his research in the area of heredity—first in sweet peas and later in human stature. Galton used first the word *reversion* and later the word *regression* to describe a tendency of adult offspring, even those with short or tall parents, to revert back toward the average height of the general population.

Correlation measures the strength of a relationship.

Correlation analysis is concerned with measuring the *strength* of the relationship between variables. When we compute measures of correlation from a set of bivariate ("two variables") data, our interest focuses on the degree of *correlation* between the variables. The concepts and terminology of correlation analysis also originated with Galton, who first used the word *correlation* in 1888. In business applications, one uses regression analysis more often than correlation analysis. This is so because there are so many business operations that depend on the ability to predict the future. For that reason, we shall devote more space in this text to regression analysis.

In our discussion of regression and correlation analysis, the order of presentation is as follows:

1. Simple linear regression analysis
2. The assumptions underlying simple linear regression
3. Obtaining the regression equation
4. Evaluating the regression equation
5. Using the regression equation
6. Correlation analysis
7. A measure of the strength of a relationship
8. Multiple-regression analysis
9. Some precautions

9.1 SIMPLE LINEAR REGRESSION ANALYSIS

The typical regression problem is like most problems in applied statistical inference. We have available for analysis a sample of observations from some real or hypothetical population. On the basis of our analysis of these data, we want to reach decisions about the population from which we presume the sample was drawn. In order to handle the analysis of the sample intelligently and interpret the results properly, we must understand the nature of the population from which the sample was drawn.

Measurements are made on the unit of association.

The type of relationship between two variables X and Y that we are concerned with here is a *linear* relationship. This implies that the relationship of interest has something to do with a straight line. The measurements that are available for analysis come in pairs, (x_1, y_1), (x_2, y_2), . . . , (x_n, y_n), where the measurements (x_i, y_i) are taken on the same entity.

The entity on which measurements are made is called the *unit of association.*

Suppose, for example, that we want to study the relationship between workers' aptitude for a certain job and their satisfaction in that job. After we observe that employees who have a greater aptitude for the job also seem to be better satisfied with the job, we might suspect that the relationship between the two variables is linear. If we can learn enough about this suspected relationship, we may be able to predict a prospective employee's level of job satisfaction on the basis of knowledge of his or her level of aptitude for the job.

In this case, the unit of association is the employee. We can designate the variable *aptitude* by X and the variable *job satisfaction* by Y. To obtain data on which to base our study of the relationship between the two variables, we select a random sample of employees and give each of them two tests—one to measure aptitude for the job and one to measure level of job satisfaction.

Two variables X and Y are linearly related if their relationship can be expressed by the following equation:

$$y_i = \alpha + \beta x_i + e_i \qquad (9.1)$$

where y_i is the value of the Y variable for a typical unit of association from the population, x_i is the value of the X variable for that same unit of association, α and β are parameters called the *regression constant* and the *regression coefficient,* respectively, and e_i is a random variable with a mean of 0 and a variance of σ^2.

In order to understand simple linear regression more thoroughly, we need to look at some of the assumptions that underlie it.

9.2 THE ASSUMPTIONS UNDERLYING SIMPLE LINEAR REGRESSION

As we have said, simple linear regression analysis is concerned with the relationship between two variables, X and Y. For reasons that will become apparent, the variable X is called the *independent variable,* and Y is called the *dependent vari-*

able. In discussing the linear relationship between X and Y, given in Equation 9.1, we speak of the *regression of Y on X.*

Regression Assumptions

The following assumptions underlie simple linear regression analysis.

1. Values of the independent variable X may be either ''fixed'' or random. That is, we may select the values of X in advance (''fixed''), so that as we collect the data, we control the values of X. Or we may obtain the values of X without imposing any restrictions, in which case X is a random variable.

2. The variable X is measured without error. From a practical point of view, this means that the magnitude of the measurement error in X is negligible.

3. For each value of X there is a subpopulation of Y values. For most of the inferential procedures of estimation and hypothesis testing to be valid, these subpopulations must be normally distributed. To demonstrate inferential procedures, we shall assume in the examples and exercises that follow that the Y values are normally distributed.

4. The variances of the subpopulations of Y are all equal.

5. The means of the subpopulations of Y all lie on the same straight line. This assumption is known as the *assumption of linearity*. It may be expressed symbolically as

$$\mu_{y|x} = \alpha + \beta x_i \tag{9.2}$$

where $\mu_{y|x}$ is the mean of the subpopulation of Y values that is assumed to exist for x_i, a particular value of X. When viewed geometrically, as in Figure 9.1, α and β represent the Y intercept and slope, respectively, of the line on which all the subpopulation means are assumed to lie.

6. The Y values are statistically independent. This means that in drawing the sample, the values of Y chosen at one value of X in no way depend on the values of Y chosen at another value of X.

We are now in a position to shed some more light on the term e_i in Equation 9.1. If we solve the equation for e_i, we have

$$e_i = y_i - (\alpha + \beta x_i) \tag{9.3}$$

Thus e_i shows the amount by which y_i deviates from the mean of the subpopulation of Y values from which it is drawn, since, by Equation 9.2, $\mu_{y|x} = \alpha + \beta x_i$. The subpopulations of Y values are assumed to be normally distributed with equal variances. Thus the e_i's for each subpopulation are also normally distributed, with a variance equal to σ^2, the common variance of the subpopulations of Y values. The e_i's are independent, and their distribution has a mean of 0.

Figure 9.2 shows e_i for y_i in the first subpopulation of Y values shown in Figure 9.1.

FIGURE 9.1
Representation of
the assumptions
underlying simple
linear regression
analysis

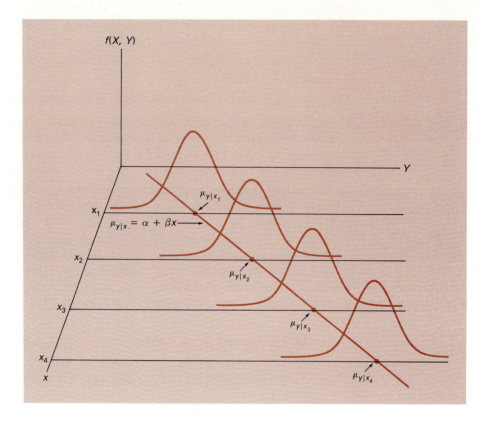

FIGURE 9.2
e_i **for first**
subpopulation of
Y **values shown in**
Figure 9.1

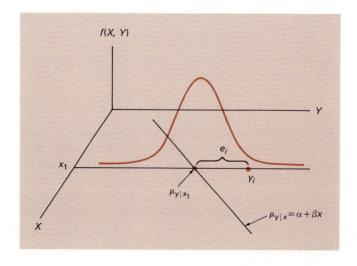

9.3 OBTAINING THE SAMPLE REGRESSION EQUATION

Equation 9.1 is not an equation for a straight line. It is a symbolic representation of a typical value of the dependent variable Y. Equation 9.2, however, *is* an equation for a straight line. It is the line that describes the true relationship between X and $\mu_{y|x}$. The true position of this line is unknown because α and β are unknown. The objective of regression analysis is to estimate α and β in order to make inferences about the true line of regression of Y on X.

We can explain the procedures involved in regression analysis more easily by means of a numerical illustration.

EXAMPLE 9.1 An operations analyst conducts a study to analyze the relationship between production and manufacturing expenses in the electronics industry. A sample of $n = 10$ firms, randomly selected from within the industry, yields the data in Table 9.1. ''Manufacturing expenses'' is considered to be the dependent variable. It changes as the volume of production varies. On the other hand, a change in manufacturing expenses would not necessarily cause a change in volume of production.

Note that X, as well as Y, is a random variable here, since we made no effort to collect sales figures only for firms with preselected values of the independent variable, production. In this example, we call the firm the *unit of association*. It is important that we preserve the pairwise identity of the measurements throughout the analysis.

SOLUTION A good first step in a study of the relationship between two variables is to make a *scatter diagram,* a graph of the observed pairs of observations. We assign values of the independent variable X to the horizontal axis. We place a dot on the graph at the intersection of each pair of values of X and Y. Figure 9.3 shows the scatter diagram for these data. The pattern made by the points on the scatter diagram usually suggests the basic nature of the relationship between two variables. The points in Figure 9.3, for example, appear to be scattered around an invisible straight line. The scatter diagram also shows that, in general, firms with high production tend to have high manufacturing costs. These impressions suggest that the relationship between production and manufacturing expenses may be described by a straight line crossing the Y axis above the origin and making less than a 45-degree angle with the X axis.

We could draw a freehand line through the data. The question is: Would this be the best possible line for describing the relationship that exists? It probably would not be. Any such freehand line would be subjective, and would reflect any defects in the vision or judgment of the person drawing it. We need some objective

A scatter diagram gives us clues regarding the likely form and strength of the relationship between two variables.

TABLE 9.1
Production (X) and manufacturing expenses (Y) for 10 selected firms

X (thousands of units)	40	42	48	55	65	79	88	100	120	140
Y (thousands of dollars)	150	140	160	170	150	162	185	165	190	185

FIGURE 9.3
Scatter diagram for
Example 9.1

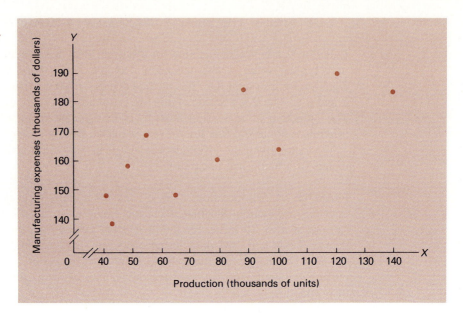

method of drawing a line that, by some criterion, we could call the *best line* to describe the relationship between the two variables.

The Least-Squares Line

The objective method that we use here to find a line to describe the relationship between the variables is called the *method of least squares*. The line obtained by this method is called the *least-squares line*.

We may write the equation for a straight line as

$$y = a + bx \tag{9.4}$$

Here a is the point at which the line crosses the Y axis and b is the amount by which the line changes per unit change in x. We refer to a as the *Y intercept* and to b as the *slope* of the line. To draw a straight line for the sample data, then, we need only numerical values for a and b. Once we have these values, we can substitute two different values of X into the equation and get corresponding values of Y. If we plot the resulting coordinates (x_1, y_1) and (x_2, y_2) on the graph and connect them, we have a straight line.

Figure 9.4 is a graph of a straight line. Here we see the geometric relationships between the slope, the Y intercept, and a unit change in x.

We can find numerical values for a and b for any set of data such as that in the present example by simultaneously solving the following two equations:

$$\sum y_i = na + b \sum x_i \tag{9.5}$$

$$\sum x_i y_i = a \sum x_i + b \sum x_i^2 \tag{9.6}$$

These equations, obtained by differential calculus, are called the *normal equa-*

a is the Y intercept and b is the slope of the sample regression line.

FIGURE 9.4
A linear regression
equation
illustrating the
geometrical
interpretations of
a and *b*

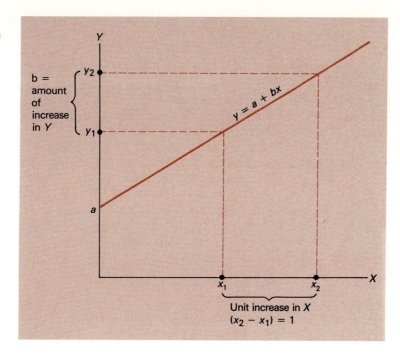

tions. Their solution yields the equation for the least-squares line describing the relationship between X and Y. The equation is of the form

$$\hat{y} = a + bx \qquad (9.7)$$

where $\hat{y}$ denotes the calculated value of Y for a given X, and a and b are estimates of α and β, respectively.

Table 9.2 gives the values of Σy_i, Σx_i, $\Sigma x_i y_i$, Σx_i^2, and n, which are needed to solve the equations. Substituting values from Table 9.2 into Equations 9.5 and 9.6 gives

$$1657 = 10a + 777b, \qquad 132{,}938 = 777a + 70{,}903b$$

TABLE 9.2
Intermediate
computations for
normal equations,
Example 9.1

	x_i	y_i	x_i^2	xy	y_i^2
	40	150	1,600	6,000	22,500
	42	140	1,764	5,880	19,600
	48	160	2,304	7,680	25,600
	55	170	3,025	9,350	28,900
	65	150	4,225	9,750	22,500
	79	162	6,241	12,798	26,244
	88	185	7,744	16,280	34,225
	100	165	10,000	16,500	27,225
	120	190	14,400	22,800	36,100
	140	185	19,600	25,900	34,225
Total	777	1,657	70,903	132,938	277,119

We may solve these equations by any familiar method to get

$$a = 134.79, \qquad b = 0.3978$$

The following formulas for a and b are usually computationally more convenient:

$$b = \frac{\Sigma x_i y_i - \dfrac{\Sigma x_i \Sigma y_i}{n}}{\Sigma x_i^2 - \dfrac{(\Sigma x_i)^2}{n}} = \frac{n\Sigma x_i y_i - \Sigma x_i \Sigma y_i}{n\Sigma x_i^2 - (\Sigma x_i)^2} \qquad (9.8)$$

$$a = \frac{\Sigma y_i}{n} - b\left(\frac{\Sigma x_i}{n}\right) = \bar{y} - b\bar{x} \qquad (9.9)$$

For the present example, we have

$$b = \frac{132{,}938 - \dfrac{(777)(1657)}{10}}{70{,}903 - \dfrac{(777)^2}{10}} = 0.3978$$

$$a = 165.7 - 0.3987(77.7) = 134.72$$

The two results for a do not agree exactly, due to rounding errors.

The equation for the least-squares line that describes the relationship between production and manufacturing expenses is

$$\hat{y} = 134.79 + 0.3978x$$

If we let $x = 0$, $\hat{y} = 134.79$. And if $x = 100$, $\hat{y} = 174.57$. These two points are sufficient for plotting the line, as we have done in Figure 9.5. This line is the sought-after "best" line for describing the relationship between the sample values of X and Y. Before we say by what criterion we judge it to be best, let us look at Figure 9.5. None of the points actually falls on the line that was drawn. That is, the points *deviate* from the line. It's obvious that we can't draw a straight line that will pass through all the points. Some deviation of points from any straight line is inevitable. The line drawn through the points is best in this sense:

The sum of the squared deviations of the observed data points y_i from the least-squares line is smaller than the sum of the squared deviations of the data points from any other line that can be drawn through the data points.

Suppose that we square the vertical distance from each observed point y_i to the least-squares line, and add these squared distances for all the points. The total we get will be smaller than the similarly computed total for any other line that we could draw through the original points. That is why we call the line the *least-squares line*.

If, in our sample regression equation, we set x equal to $\bar{x}$, the mean of X, we find that $\hat{y}$ is equal to $\bar{y}$, the mean of Y. Hence we see that the plotted line passes through the point $(\bar{x}, \bar{y})$.

**FIGURE 9.5
Scatter diagram
and least-
squares line
for Example 9.1**

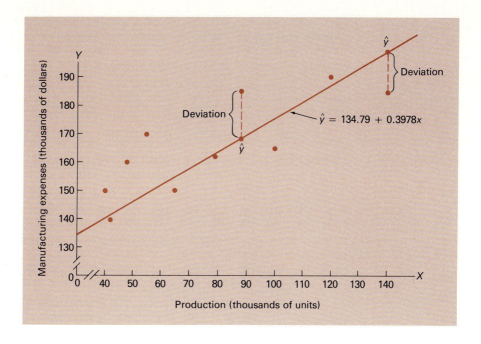

Exercises   In these exercises: **(a)** plot the data as a scatter diagram,   **(b)** obtain the least-squares regression equation, and   **(c)** draw the regression line on the scatter diagram.

9.1 Ⓒ A firm that sells office supplies wants to expand. The head of the firm wants to know what sales volume can be expected in various market areas. Regression analysis, with sales as the dependent variable, is suggested. It is decided that effective buying income would be the best independent variable. A sample of 15 trade areas in which the firm now does business gives the following results.

Amount of sales $(Y)(\times \$100{,}000)$	Effective buying income $(X)(\times \$1{,}000{,}000)$
0.5	11
2.3	69
9.4	168
1.1	22
2.9	38
2.5	30
3.0	51
3.4	61
5.8	83
6.1	91
6.8	101
6.9	124
7.2	159
11.4	176
14.3	201

$$\sum x_i = 1385 \quad \sum y_i = 83.6 \quad \sum x_i y_i = 10{,}917.6 \quad \sum x_i^2 = 179{,}661 \quad \sum y_i^2 = 681.32$$

9.2 Ⓒ A research analyst is studying the relationship between shopping-center traffic and a department store's daily sales. The analyst develops an index to measure the daily volume of traffic entering the shopping center, and an index of daily sales. The following table shows the index values for 10 randomly selected days.

Traffic index (X):	71	82	111	85	89	110	111	121	129	132
Sales index (Y):	250	280	301	325	328	390	410	420	450	475

$\sum x_i = 1041$ $\sum y_i = 3629$ $\sum x_i y_i = 390{,}918$ $\sum x_i^2 = 112{,}359$ $\sum y_i^2 = 1{,}369{,}435$

 9.3 Ⓒ The following data show the daily wages (X) and amount of monthly rent payments (Y) for a random sample of 15 unskilled workers who live alone.

(Y), $	120	130	135	138	142	149	155	158	160	169	170	175	182	190	195
(X), $	34	37	39	42	41	45	40	52	50	62	68	65	70	68	75

$\sum x_i = 788$ $\sum y_i = 2368$ $\sum x_i y_i = 128{,}592$ $\sum x_i^2 = 44{,}162$ $\sum y_i^2 = 380{,}858$

9.4 Ⓒ The following table shows the hardness (in Brinell hardness numbers) and the tensile strength (in thousands of pounds per square inch) of 10 specimens of an alloy.

Hardness (X)	20	30	40	50	60	70	80	90	100	25
Tensile strength (Y)	10	16	22	30	35	40	45	50	60	15

9.4 EVALUATING THE SAMPLE REGRESSION EQUATION

After we have determined the regression equation, we must evaluate it to find out whether it adequately describes the relationship between the two variables, and to see whether we can use it effectively for prediction and estimation.

Partitioning the Total Sum of Squares

One method of evaluating the regression equation is to compare the scatter of the points about the regression line with the scatter about $\bar{y}$, the mean of the sample values of Y. Figure 9.6 shows the regression line and the relative magnitudes of the scatter of the points from $\bar{y}$ for Example 9.1. It shows the line representing $\bar{y}$ as a horizontal line. This is because, regardless of the value of X, $\bar{y}$ remains constant. For these data, the dispersion of the points about the regression line is much less than the dispersion about the $\bar{y}$ line. So it seems that the regression line provides a good fit for the data.

$y_i - \bar{y}$ is the *total deviation.*

We get the amount by which any observed value of Y, y_i, deviates from $\bar{y}$ by measuring the vertical distance between y_i and $\bar{y}$ as shown in Figure 9.6. This difference $y_i - \bar{y}$ is called the *total deviation.* Consider, for example, the ninth value of Y. In Table 9.2 you will find that $y_9 = 190$. Since $\bar{y} = 165.7$, the total deviation of this Y value is $190 - 165.7 = 24.3$. Figure 9.7 shows the total deviation for each observation.

FIGURE 9.6
Scatter diagram for
Example 9.1,
showing deviations
about $\bar{y}$ and the
regression line

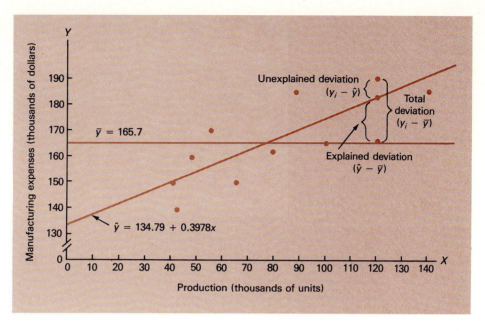

FIGURE 9.7
Total deviations
$y_i - \bar{y}$ for
Example 9.1

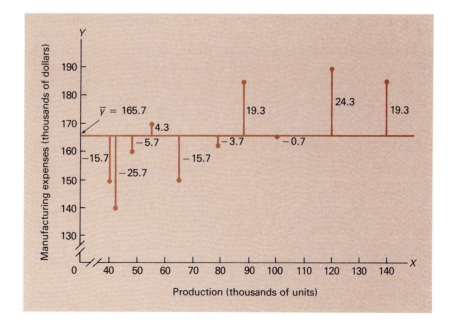

FIGURE 9.8
Explained
deviations $\hat{y} - \bar{y}$
for Example 9.1

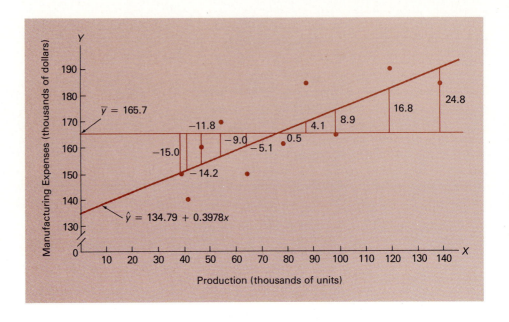

$\hat{y} - \bar{y}$ is the explained deviation.

$y_i - \hat{y}$ is the unexplained deviation.

The vertical distance from the regression line to the $\bar{y}$ line is given by $\hat{y} - \bar{y}$. This is called the *explained deviation*. It shows the amount by which we reduce the total deviation when we fit the regression line to the points. For example, for $y_9 = 190$, $\hat{y} = 182.5$. The explained deviation is $\hat{y} - \bar{y} = 182.5 - 165.7 = 16.8$. Figure 9.8 shows the explained deviation for each observation.

Finally, the vertical distance of the observed Y from the regression line $y_i - \hat{y}$ is called the *unexplained deviation*. It represents that portion of the total deviation that is not "explained" or accounted for by the fitting of the regression line. In the case of $y_9 = 190$, there is an unexplained deviation of $y_9 - \hat{y} = 190 - 182.5 = 7.5$. Figure 9.9 shows the unexplained deviation for each observation.

Figure 9.6 shows the three deviations for y_9.

Thus the total deviation for a particular y_i is equal to the sum of the explained and unexplained deviations. That is,

$$\underset{\substack{\text{Total} \\ \text{deviation}}}{(y_i - \bar{y})} = \underset{\substack{\text{Explained} \\ \text{deviation}}}{(\hat{y} - \bar{y})} + \underset{\substack{\text{Unexplained} \\ \text{deviation}}}{(y_i - \hat{y})} \tag{9.10}$$

In the case of $y_9 = 190$, we have $24.3 = 16.8 + 7.5$. We can perform similar calculations for each y_i.

If we square each of the deviations in Equation 9.10 and sum for all observations, we get three sums of squared deviations. Their relationship may be expressed as follows:

$$\underset{\substack{\text{Total sum} \\ \text{of squares}}}{\sum(y_i - \bar{y})^2} = \underset{\substack{\text{Explained sum} \\ \text{of squares}}}{\sum(\hat{y} - \bar{y})^2} + \underset{\substack{\text{Unexplained sum} \\ \text{of squares}}}{\sum(y_i - \hat{y})^2} \tag{9.11}$$

FIGURE 9.9
Unexplained deviations $y_i - \hat{y}$ **for Example 9.1**

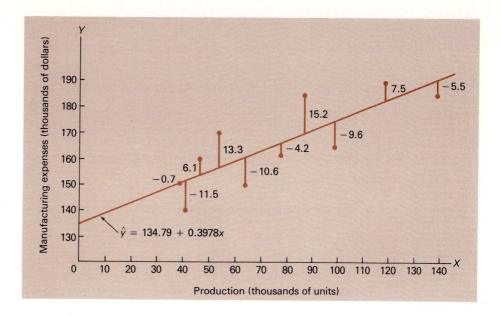

The Total Sum of Squares

Each of the terms in Equation 9.11 is a measure of dispersion. The *total sum of squares* measures the dispersion of the observed values of Y about their mean $\bar{y}$. That is, this term is a measure of the total variation in the observed values of Y. It is the numerator of the familiar formula for the sample variance.

The Explained Sum of Squares

The *explained sum of squares* is a measure of the portion of the total variability in the observed values of Y that is accounted for by the linear relationship between the observed values of X and Y. This quantity is sometimes referred to as the *sum of squares due to linear regression*.

The Unexplained Sum of Squares

The *unexplained sum of squares* measures the dispersion of the observed Y values about the regression line. It is sometimes referred to as the *sum of squares of deviations from linearity*. The unexplained sum of squares is the quantity that we minimize when we find the least-squares line. It is usually called the *error sum of squares*.

Computing the Sums of Squares

We may write Equation 9.11 in a more compact form, as follows:

$$\text{SST} = \text{SSR} + \text{SSE} \tag{9.12}$$

where SST = total sum of squares; SSR = sum of squares due to regression (explained sum of squares); SSE = error sum of squares (unexplained sum of squares).

We can compute the total sum of squares by the following formula:

$$\text{SST} = \sum (y_i - \bar{y})^2 = \sum y_i^2 - \frac{(\Sigma y_i)^2}{n} \qquad (9.13)$$

We can compute the explained sum of squares by

$$\text{SSR} = \sum (\hat{y} - \bar{y})^2 = b^2 \sum (x_i - \bar{x})^2 = b^2 \left[\sum x_i^2 - \frac{(\Sigma x_i)^2}{n} \right] \qquad (9.14)$$

We can get the *un*explained sum of squares by subtraction. That is,

$$\text{SSE} = \text{SST} - \text{SSR}$$

For the data on production and manufacturing expenses, we may compute

$$\text{SST} = 277{,}119 - \frac{(1657)^2}{10} = 2554.10$$

Alternatively, we may compute SST by squaring and summing the individual total deviations $y_i - y$, as shown in Figure 9.7. When we do this, we have

$$(-15.7)^2 + (-25.7)^2 + \cdots + (19.3)^2 = 246.49 + 660.49 + \cdots + 372.49$$
$$= 2554.10$$

By Equation 9.14, the explained sum of squares, or sum of squares due to regression, is

$$\text{SSR} = (0.3978)^2 \left[70{,}903 - \frac{(777)^2}{10} \right] = 1666.33$$

Or we can get the explained sum of squares by squaring and summing the explained deviations $\hat{y} - \bar{y}$, shown in Figure 9.8, to give

$$\text{SSR} = (-15)^2 + (-14.2)^2 + \cdots + (24.8)^2$$
$$= 225.0 + 201.64 + \cdots + 615.04 = 1666.44$$

The unexplained, or error, sum of squares, obtained by subtraction, is

$$\text{SSE} = 2554.10 - 1666.33 = 887.77$$

Alternatively, we can compute SSE by squaring and summing the individual unexplained deviations $y_i - \hat{y}$, shown in Figure 9.9. Thus

$$\text{SSE} = (-0.7)^2 + (-11.5)^2 + \cdots + (-5.5)^2$$
$$= 0.49 + 132.25 + \cdots + 30.25 = 886.54$$

Note that there is a slight discrepancy, due to rounding, in the results for SSR and SSE computed by the two methods.

Analysis of Variance

When the assumptions we gave in Section 9.2 hold, we may use analysis of variance to test for the presence of regression. In this process, the total sum of

TABLE 9.3
ANOVA table for simple linear regression

Source of variation	SS	df	MS	F
Linear regression	SSR	1	MSR = SSR/1	MSR/MSE
Deviation from linearity (error)	SSE	$n-2$	MSE = SSE/$(n-2)$	
Total	SST	$n-1$		

squares $\Sigma(y_i - \bar{y})^2$ is a measure of the total *variability* present in the data. The explained sum of squares $\Sigma(\hat{y} - \bar{y})^2$ is a measure of the *variability due to linear regression*. And the unexplained sum of squares $\Sigma(y_i - \hat{y})^2$ is a measure of the *variability left unexplained* after regression has been considered. This last sum of squares is also called the *deviations from regression* or *error sum of squares*. We can also subdivide the total degrees of freedom $n - 1$ into two components, 1 for regression and $(n - 1) - 1 = n - 2$ associated with the error sum of squares. Dividing the sums of squares by their associated degrees of freedom yields corresponding mean squares. If there is no linear regression (that is, if $\beta = 0$), and if the stated assumptions apply, the ratio of the regression mean square to the error mean square is distributed as F with 1 and $n - 2$ degrees of freedom.

We can, therefore, test the null hypothesis that $\beta = 0$ using analysis of variance. Table 9.3 shows the analysis-of-variance table that we can construct.

EXAMPLE 9.1 CONTINUED We illustrate the hypothesis-testing procedure with the data on production and manufacturing expenses.

SOLUTION

1. *Hypotheses*

    H_0: There is no linear regression between X and Y ($\beta = 0$)

    H_1: There is a linear regression of Y on X ($\beta \neq 0$)

2. *Test statistic.* The test statistic is $F = \text{MSR}/\text{MSE}$, which, if H_0 is true and the assumptions are met, follows the F distribution with 1 and 8 degrees of freedom.

3. *Significance level.* Let $\alpha = 0.01$.

4. *Decision rule.* Reject H_0 if the computed value of F is ≥ 11.26.

5. *Calculations.* Table 9.4 below shows the analysis-of-variance table that we can construct from the sample data. When we use a computer in regression

TABLE 9.4
Analysis of variance for Example 9.2

Source	SS	df	MS	F
Regression	1,666.33	1	1,666.33	15.02
Error	887.77	8	110.97	
Total	2,554.10	9		

analysis, the ANOVA table is usually part of the computer output. When we use a calculator, Formulas 9.12 through 9.14 yield the sums of squares given in the table.

6. *Statistical decision.* Since $15.02 > 11.26$, we reject H_0.
7. *Conclusion.* We conclude that the data of this sample provide sufficient evidence of the presence of regression. Since $15.02 > 14.69$, we have, for this test, $p < 0.005$.

When we can't reject H_0: $\beta = 0$, we can't be certain that X and Y are unrelated. Aside from the fact that we may have committed a Type II error, we must be aware that, although they may not be linearly related, X and Y may have a non-linear relationship. Even when we can reject H_0: $\beta = 0$, we can't be certain that the strongest form of relationship between X and Y is a linear one. The two variables may be more strongly related in a nonlinear way, although a linear model gives a satisfactory approximation to the true relationship. Of course, a rejected null hypothesis that $\beta = 0$ may very well indicate that there is a true linear relationship between X and Y.

Another Hypothesis Test about β

An alternative way to evaluate the sample regression equation is to use b, the slope of the sample line, as a basis for testing the null hypothesis of no regression.

When the assumptions in Section 9.2 are met, a and b are unbiased point estimators, respectively, of α and β. When, under these assumptions, the subpopulations of Y values are normally distributed, the sampling distributions of a and b are each normal, with means and variances as follows:

$$\mu_a = \alpha \tag{9.15}$$

$$\sigma_a^2 = \frac{\sigma_{y|x}^2 \Sigma x_i^2}{n\Sigma(x_i - \bar{x})^2} \tag{9.16}$$

$$\mu_b = \beta \tag{9.17}$$

$$\sigma_b^2 = \frac{\sigma_{y|x}^2}{\Sigma(x_i - \bar{x})^2} \tag{9.18}$$

In Equations 9.16 and 9.18, $\sigma_{y|x}^2$ is the variance about the population regression line. We also call $\sigma_{y|x}^2$ the *unexplained variance of the population*. It is the common variance σ^2 of the subpopulations of Y as specified in the initial assumptions. The definitional equation for this quantity, for a finite population of size N, is

$$\sigma_{y|x}^2 = \frac{\Sigma_{i=1}^{n}(y_i - \mu_{y|x})^2}{N} \tag{9.19}$$

When the assumptions are met, then, we can construct confidence intervals for, and test hypotheses about, α and β in the usual way. In most cases, inferences

FIGURE 9.10
Scatter diagrams
showing different
types of linear
relationships

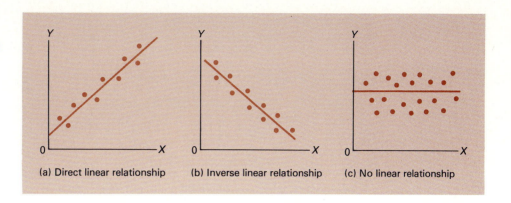

(a) Direct linear relationship   (b) Inverse linear relationship   (c) No linear relationship

Variables may be
related directly or
inversely.

about α are not of great interest. The parameter β, however, *is* of great interest. If $\beta = 0$, the regression line is horizontal, and an increase or decrease in X is not associated with a change in Y. In this situation, we conclude that X and Y are not linearly related. A positive β indicates that, generally, Y tends to increase as X increases. In this situation, there is a *direct linear relationship* between X and Y. A negative β indicates that values of Y tend to decrease as values of X increase, and so there is an *inverse linear relationship* between X and Y. Figure 9.10 illustrates these three situations.

We want to determine whether the sample data provide sufficient evidence to indicate that β is different from 0. Suppose that we can reject the null hypothesis that $\beta = 0$. Then we can conclude that β is not equal to 0, and therefore that there is a linear relationship between X and Y. Whether this suggested linear relationship is presumed to be direct or inverse depends on the sign of b, the estimate of β.

The test statistic, when $\sigma_{y|x}^2$ is known, is

$$z = \frac{b - \beta_0}{\sigma_b} \tag{9.20}$$

In the usual case, $\sigma_{y|x}^2$ is unknown and the test statistic is

$$t = \frac{b - \beta_0}{s_b} \tag{9.21}$$

where s_b is the estimator of σ_b. The associated degrees of freedom are $n - 2$, the error degrees of freedom from the ANOVA table.

To find s_b, we must first estimate $\sigma_{y|x}^2$. An unbiased estimator of this is given by

$$s_{y|x}^2 = \frac{\Sigma(y_i - \hat{y})^2}{n - 2} \tag{9.22}$$

An alternative formula for $s^2_{y|x}$ is

$$s^2_{y|x} = \frac{1}{n-2}\left\{\left[\sum y_i^2 - \frac{(\sum y_i)^2}{n}\right] - \frac{\left[\sum x_i y_i - \frac{(\sum x_i)(\sum y_i)}{n}\right]^2}{\sum x_i^2 - \frac{(\sum x_i)^2}{n}}\right\}$$

$$= \frac{1}{n-2}\left\{\left[\sum y_i^2 - \frac{(\sum y_i)^2}{n}\right] - \frac{b[n\sum x_i y_i - (\sum x_i)(\sum y_i)]}{n}\right\} \qquad (9.23)$$

The estimator, $s^2_{y|x}$, is the same as the error mean square appearing in the analysis-of-variance table. An unbiased estimator of σ^2_b, then, is

$$s^2_b = \frac{s^2_{y|x}}{\sum(x_i - \bar{x})^2} \qquad (9.24)$$

The following formula takes less work:

$$s^2_b = \frac{s^2_{y|x}}{\sum x_i^2 - (\sum x_i)^2/n} \qquad (9.25)$$

EXAMPLE 9.1 CONTINUED Let us now use the example of production and manufacturing expenses to show how to test the null hypothesis that $\beta = 0$.

SOLUTION

1. *Hypotheses*

$$H_0: \beta = 0, \qquad H_1: \beta \neq 0$$

2. *Test statistic.* The test statistic is t, as given by Equation 9.21. If H_0 is true and the assumptions are met, it follows the t distribution with 8 degrees of freedom.
3. *Significance level.* Let $\alpha = 0.01$ as before.
4. *Decision rule.* Reject H_0 if the computed t is ≤ -3.3554 or ≥ 3.3554.
5. *Calculations.* We obtain $s^2_{y|x}$, which, from Table 9.4, is

$$s^2_{y|x} = \text{MSE} = 110.97$$

We may now compute

$$s^2_b = \frac{110.97}{70{,}903 - (777)^2/10} = 0.0105 \qquad \text{and} \qquad s_b = \sqrt{0.0105} = 0.102$$

The figures in the denominator of s^2_b come from Table 9.2.
   The test statistic that we may compute is

$$t = \frac{0.3978 - 0}{0.102} = 3.9$$

6. *Statistical decision.* We reject H_0, since $3.9 > 3.3554$.
7. *Conclusion.* We conclude that β is not 0 and that there is a linear relationship between X and Y. Since b is positive, we conclude that the relationship is direct, not inverse. Since $3.9 > 3.3554$, $p < 2(0.005) = 0.01$.

Note that the decision resulting from testing H_0: $\beta = 0$ by means of the t test is the same as that reached using analysis of variance. In fact, the value of t computed from Equation 9.21 is equal to the square root of the F computed in the analysis of variance. (In practice, small differences may occur because of rounding.)

We can also use Equation 9.21 to test the null hypothesis that β is equal to some value other than 0. In that case the hypothesized value for β, β_0, replaces 0 in the equation. All other quantities, computations, degrees of freedom, and methods of determining significance are the same as in the example.

A Confidence Interval for β

Alternatively, we can test the null hypothesis that $\beta = 0$ by means of a confidence interval for β. We use the general formula for a confidence interval,

$$\text{Estimate} \pm (\text{reliability factor}) \times (\text{standard error})$$

When we construct a confidence interval for β, the estimator is b. The reliability factor is some value of z or t (depending on whether or not $\sigma^2_{y|x}$ is known). And the standard error of the estimator is

$$\sigma_b = \sqrt{\frac{\sigma^2_{y|x}}{\Sigma(x_i - \bar{x})^2}}$$

When $\sigma^2_{y|x}$ is unknown, we estimate σ_b by

$$s_b = \sqrt{\frac{s^2_{y|x}}{\Sigma(x_i - \bar{x})^2}}$$

Thus, in most practical cases, the $100(1 - \alpha)\%$ confidence interval for β is given by

$$b \pm t_{1-\alpha/2}s_b \tag{9.26}$$

If the confidence inter-
val contains 0, we can-
not reject H_0: $\beta = 0$.

If the confidence interval that we construct includes 0, we conclude that 0 is a candidate for β. Therefore we cannot rule out the possibility that β is 0. This conclusion corresponds to the statistical decision of failing to reject H_0: $\beta = 0$. If, on the other hand, the interval does not contain 0, we reject the null hypothesis that $\beta = 0$. We conclude that X and Y are linearly related. The strength of this conclusion is related to the confidence coefficient that we select when we construct the confidence interval.

EXAMPLE 9.1 CONTINUED Let us construct a 95% confidence interval for β, using the production and manufacturing expenses data.

SOLUTION We can construct the following 95% confidence interval using Expression 9.26:

$$0.3978 \pm 2.306(0.102)$$

$$0.3978 \pm 0.2352, \qquad 0.1626, 0.6330$$

We interpret this interval in the usual way. From the probabilistic point of view, we say that if we were to draw samples of size 10 repeatedly from the population and from each compute a confidence interval for β, 95% of these intervals would, in the long run, include the parameter β. From a practical standpoint, we say that we are 95% confident that the single interval that we have constructed includes β.

The interval 0.1626 to 0.6330 does not include 0. We therefore conclude that β is not 0 and that there is a linear relationship between X and Y. This is the same conclusion that we reached by means of the hypothesis tests described earlier. The three inferential procedures always lead to the same conclusion.

The Coefficient of Determination

Another measure of how well the least-squares line fits the observed data is the *coefficient of determination*. If you interpret this descriptive measure properly, it helps you decide whether the regression equation you have obtained is likely to be useful for prediction and estimation.

Let us define the sample coefficient of determination as

$$r^2 = \frac{\Sigma(\hat{y} - \bar{y})^2}{\Sigma(y_i - \bar{y})^2} \tag{9.27}$$

A useful computing formula for r^2 is given by

$$r^2 = \frac{b^2\Sigma(x_i - \bar{x})^2}{\Sigma(y_i - \bar{y})^2} = \frac{b^2[\Sigma x_i^2 - (\Sigma x_i)^2/n]}{\Sigma y_i^2 - (\Sigma y_i)^2/n} \tag{9.28}$$

In words, we say that the coefficient of determination is equal to the ratio of the explained sum of squares to the total sum of squares. As such, it indicates the proportion of the total variation in Y that is explained by the regression of Y on X. Thus, since we compute r^2 from sample data, it measures a characteristic of these sample data. And it is not the measure of that characteristic for the total population of data. The population counterpart of r^2 is usually designated by ρ^2. Thus we use r^2 to estimate ρ^2, the population coefficient of determination. We define ρ^2 the same way we define r^2 for a sample. That is,

$$\rho^2 = \frac{\Sigma(\hat{y} - \mu_y)^2}{\Sigma(y_i - \mu_y)^2}$$

Interpretations of r^2

We can interpret the sample coefficient of determination in the following ways.

1. We may interpret r^2 as a *measure of the closeness of fit of the regression*

FIGURE 9.11
Scatter diagrams illustrating different values of r^2

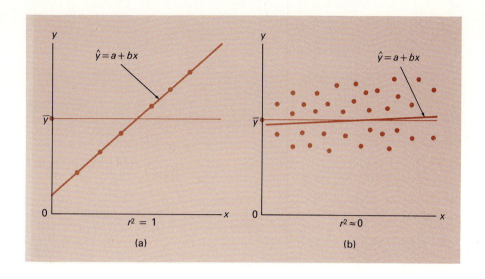

equation to the sample data. The better the fit of the *computed* regression line, the closer r^2 will be to 1. In other words, if the regression line provides a perfect fit, the total variation in Y is completely explained, and r^2 is exactly equal to 1. If, in Equation 9.11, the unexplained sum of squares is 0, the total sum of squares and the explained sum of squares are equal. Figure 9.11a shows this situation. On the other hand, if the regression line is very close to the $\bar{y}$ line, it will explain only a small proportion of the total variation in Y, and r^2 will approach 0. Figure 9.11b illustrates this concept.

r^2 measures closeness of fit.

2. We may also think of r^2 as a *measure of the relative reduction in the total sum of squares achieved by fitting a regression line.* As we have implied, the relative reduction may be 0, 1, or any amount in between.

r^2 measures relative reduction in SST.

3. Finally, we may interpret r^2 as a *measure of the linearity of the data points.* When the regression line fits the data well, the data points are such that their scatter diagram gives the impression of a straight line. On the other hand, when the fit is not good, the points are so widely scattered that the diagram does not suggest a straight line. Figure 9.12a and b illustrates this. This interpretation requires that the points have a distribution and that $b \neq 0$. When all values of Y are the same, $b = 0$, y is a constant, the variables X and Y are unrelated, and r^2 is zero. In other words, if $y_i = \bar{y}$ for all y_i, then $\Sigma(y_i - \bar{y})^2$, the denominator of the formula for r^2, is equal to 0, and r^2 has no meaning. Figure 9.12c illustrates this.

r^2 measures linearity.

EXAMPLE 9.1 CONTINUED Let us illustrate the calculation of r^2 using the data on production and manufacturing expenses. Look back at Table 9.2 on page 325 to get the needed preliminary calculations.

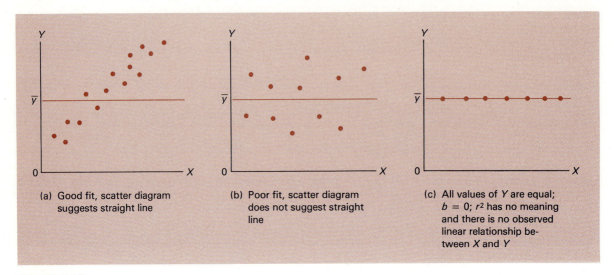

(a) Good fit, scatter diagram suggests straight line

(b) Poor fit, scatter diagram does not suggest straight line

(c) All values of Y are equal; $b = 0$; r^2 has no meaning and there is no observed linear relationship between X and Y

FIGURE 9.12
Scatter diagrams illustrating different degrees of closeness of fit of observed values of Y to a regression line

SOLUTION By Equation 9.28, we compute

$$r^2 = \frac{(0.3978)^2[70{,}903 - (777)^2/10]}{277{,}119 - (1657)^2/10} = 0.65$$

Thus the regression of Y on X explains 65% of the total variability in Y.

Using r^2 to Estimate ρ^2

The sample coefficient of determination r^2 provides a point estimate of ρ^2, the population coefficient of determination. When the number of degrees of freedom is small, however, r^2 is positively biased. An unbiased estimator is provided by

$$\bar{r}^2 = 1 - \frac{\Sigma(y_i - \hat{y})^2/(n-2)}{\Sigma(y_i - \bar{y})^2/(n-1)} \tag{9.29}$$

The numerator of this fraction is the unexplained mean square, and the denominator is the total mean square. Thus the difference between r^2 and $\bar{r}^2$ is due to the factor $(n-1)/(n-2)$. When n is large, this factor approaches 1 and the difference between r^2 and $\bar{r}^2$ approaches 0.

For the example, we may compute

$$\bar{r}^2 = 1 - \frac{(887.77)/8}{(2554.10)/9} = 0.61$$

In this example, the difference between r^2 and $\bar{r}^2$ is small.

Residual Plots

As noted in Section 9.2, for the use of inferential procedures in regression analysis to be valid, certain assumptions about the sampled population must be met. We

FIGURE 9.13
Some typical
residual plots

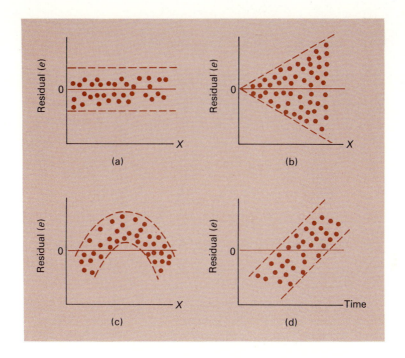

may state these assumptions in terms of e_i of Equation 9.1. We refer to the e_i component as the *error term*. The calculated residuals are estimates of these error terms in the population. The residuals in a given application are the unexplained components of the individual total deviations. That is, $\hat{e}_i = y_i - \hat{y}$. Figure 9.9 shows the residuals for Example 9.1.

If, then, we wish to determine whether or not the data satisfy the assumptions, we focus on the residuals.

We may use a simple technique to help us decide whether or not it appears likely that the assumptions have been violated. The technique consists of plotting the residuals. We may plot the residuals in many ways. One way is to plot them against the independent variable X. That is, we plot values of X on the horizontal axis and the residuals on the vertical axis.

Residual plots provide clues about the nature and strength of the relationship between variables.

If a scatter diagram of sample residuals has a pattern that suggests a horizontal band centered on 0, this is taken as a lack of evidence that the assumptions have been violated. Figure 9.13a shows a scatter diagram that is compatible with the assumptions. You must realize that we are not saying that such a scatter diagram indicates that the assumptions have been met. Rather, we are saying that this particular plot does not indicate that they have been violated.

A scatter diagram that conforms to the pattern in Figure 9.13b suggests that the variances in the subpopulations are not all equal. This scatter diagram suggests that $\sigma^2_{y|x}$ increases as X increases. When the scatter diagram resembles Figure 9.13c, this indicates that the relationship between X and Y is curvilinear rather than linear.

FIGURE 9.14
Residual plot for
Example 9.1

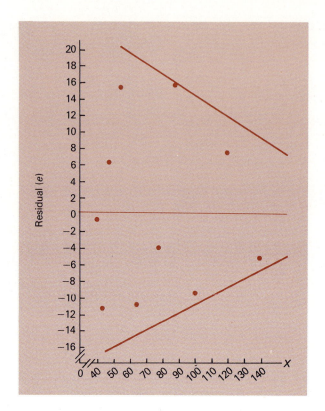

When error terms are correlated, the correlation is often due to a dependence between successive values. This type of correlation is called *autocorrelation* or *serial correlation*. If we suspect that the assumptions have been violated because of autocorrelation, a plot of the residuals against time may prove helpful. A scatter diagram resembling that of Figure 9.13d suggests the presence of autocorrelated error terms.

To illustrate a plot of sample residuals, let us refer to the residuals of Example 9.1, which are shown in Figure 9.9. When we plot these residuals, we have the scatter diagram shown in Figure 9.14. This scatter diagram suggests that the subpopulation variances may not be equal, but tend to decrease as X increases.

Exercises

9.5 Ⓒ Refer to Exercise 9.1.   **(a)** Compute the coefficient of determination.   **(b)** Prepare an ANOVA table and test the null hypothesis of no linear relationship between the two variables.   **(c)** Test the null hypothesis that $\beta = 0$ using a 0.05 level of significance.   **(d)** State your conclusions in terms of the problem.   **(e)** Construct the 95% confidence interval for β.   **(f)** Determine the p value for each test.   **(g)** Arrange the residuals in order of their corresponding X values and sketch the relationship.

9.6 Ⓒ Repeat steps **(a)** through **(f)** of Exercise 9.5, using the data of Exercise 9.2. Assume that the sample values were collected in the sequence 1, 2, 3, . . . , 10 (time = 1, 2, 3, . . . , 10) and sketch the residuals accordingly, with time as the independent variable.

9.7 ⒸRepeat steps **(a)** through **(f)** of Exercise 9.5, using the data of Exercise 9.3.

9.8 ⒸRepeat steps **(a)** through **(f)** of Exercise 9.5, using the data of Exercise 9.4.

9.5 USING THE SAMPLE REGRESSION EQUATION

Once we have decided that the data at hand provide sufficient evidence to indicate that there is a linear relationship between X and Y, we can use the sample regression equation. We can use it in two ways. First, we can use it to *predict* what value Y is likely to assume for a given value of X. When the assumptions of Section 9.2 are met, we can construct a *prediction interval* for Y. Second, we can use it to *estimate* the mean of the subpopulation of Y values for a particular value of X. Again, if the assumptions of Section 9.2 are met, we can construct a confidence interval for the mean.

We make predictions about individual subjects.

When we use a regression equation to make an inference about the Y value of a single subject (or other entity), given the subject's X value, we call the procedure *predicting*. For example, suppose that we have a regression equation that describes the relationship between the grade-point averages (X) of college students and their scores on the Scholastic Aptitude Test (Y). We may wish to use the equation to *predict* the grade-point average of a given student about to enter college.

We make estimates about populations.

When we use a regression equation to make an inference about the mean Y score of a population of subjects, all of whom have the same X value, we call the procedure *estimating*. We may, for example, want to use the regression equation describing the relationship between college students' grade-point averages and their SAT scores to estimate the mean grade-point average of a population of college-bound students, all of whom have the same SAT score.

For any given value of X, the predicted value of Y and the point estimate of the mean of the subpopulation of Y are numerically the same. However, the two intervals are not of the same width. This seems reasonable, since the estimate of the mean ought to be subject to less variation than the estimate of a single value.

Predicting *Y* for a Given *X*

We get a point prediction of the value Y is likely to assume for a given X by substituting a particular value of X, x_p, into the sample regression equation and solving for $\hat{y}$. If the assumptions of Section 9.2 are met, and if $\sigma^2_{y|x}$ is unknown, the $100(1 - \alpha)\%$ prediction interval for Y is given by

$$\hat{y} \pm t_{1-\alpha/2} s_{y|x} \sqrt{1 + \frac{1}{n} + \frac{(x_p - \bar{x})^2}{\Sigma(x_i - \bar{x})^2}} \qquad (9.30)$$

We can evaluate the denominator, $\Sigma(x_i - \bar{x})^2$, by means of the formula

$$\Sigma x_i^2 - \frac{(\Sigma x_i)^2}{n}$$

The degrees of freedom used in selecting t are $n - 2$.

EXAMPLE 9.1 CONTINUED Suppose, for our production and manufacturing expenses example, that we wish to predict the manufacturing expenses for a firm that produces 50,000 units.

SOLUTION Substituting 50 for x in the sample regression equation gives

$$\hat{y} = 134.79 + 0.3978(50) = 155$$

Using Expression 9.30 and the data from Tables 9.2 and 9.4, we construct the following 95% prediction interval:

$$\$155 \pm 2.306(\sqrt{110.97})\sqrt{1 + \frac{1}{10} + \frac{(50 - 77.7)^2}{70,903 - (777)^2/10}}$$

$$\$155 \pm \$26, \qquad \$129, \$181$$

Interpreting a prediction interval is like interpreting a confidence interval. If we repeatedly draw samples, do a regression analysis, and construct prediction intervals for firms that produce 50,000 units, 95% of the intervals will include the manufacturing expenses. This is the probabilistic interpretation. The practical interpretation is that we are 95% confident that the single prediction interval constructed includes the true manufacturing expenses.

Estimating the Mean of *Y* for a Given *X*

To estimate the mean $\mu_{y|x}$ of a subpopulation of Y values for a certain value of X, x_p, we substitute x_p into the sample regression equation and solve for $\hat{y}$.

The $100(1 - \alpha)\%$ confidence interval for $\mu_{y|x}$, when $\sigma^2_{y|x}$ is unknown and the assumptions of Section 9.2 are met, is given by

$$\hat{y} \pm t_{1-\alpha/2}s_{y|x}\sqrt{\frac{1}{n} + \frac{(x_p - \bar{x})^2}{\Sigma(x_i - \bar{x})^2}} \tag{9.31}$$

EXAMPLE 9.1 CONTINUED Suppose that, for the production and manufacturing expenses example, we wish to estimate the mean of the subpopulation of Y values for firms that produce 50,000 units.

SOLUTION We obtain the point estimate as follows:

$$\hat{y} = 134.79 + 0.3978(50) = 155$$

Using Expression 9.31, we obtain the 95% confidence interval for $\mu_{y|x}$:

$$\$155 \pm 2.306(\sqrt{110.97})\sqrt{\frac{1}{10} + \frac{(50 - 77.7)^2}{70,903 - (777)^2/10}}$$

$$\$155 \pm \$10, \qquad \$145, \$165$$

If we were to repeatedly draw samples of size 10 from the population, perform a regression analysis, and construct confidence intervals for $\mu_{y|x}$ for $X = 50$, 95%

TABLE 9.5
95% confidence limits for selected values of X, Example 9.1

x	40.0	50.0	60.0	77.7	100.0	120.0	140.0
Lower limit	139	145	150	158	166	170	173
Upper limit	163	165	168	174	184	196	207

TABLE 9.5
95% confidence limits for selected values of X, Example 9.1

of such intervals would include the true mean. Thus we are 95% confident that the single interval constructed contains the true mean.

Constructing a Confidence Band for $\mu_{y|x}$

Suppose that we construct confidence intervals for several subpopulation means and plot the upper and lower limits on a scatter diagram with the regression line. We may construct a *confidence band* by connecting all the upper limits with one curve and all the lower limits with another curve. Table 9.5 gives the upper and lower 95% confidence limits for $\mu_{y|x}$ for selected values of X in the example of production versus manufacturing expenses. Figure 9.15 shows the 95% confidence band that results when we plot these values.

Note that the confidence band of Figure 9.15 is wider at the ends than in the middle. In fact, the band is narrowest for $x_p = \bar{x}$, since the quantity under the radical of Expression 9.31 is smallest when we use the mean of the X values as the particular value of X. As x_p increases or decreases, the quantity under the radical becomes larger and the corresponding intervals become wider. We can construct *prediction bands,* using prediction intervals, in a similar manner.

FIGURE 9.15
Regression line and 95% confidence band for Example 9.1

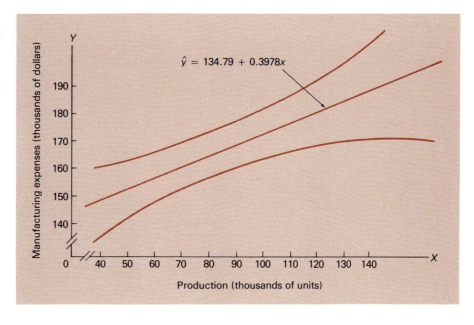

$\hat{y} = 134.79 + 0.3978x$

FIGURE 9.16
Computer printout
for analysis of data
of Example 9.1
using STAT+

```
VARIABLE I      B(I)         BETA(I)       XBAR(I)       S(I)

1             134.7893      N.D.          165.7000      15.98153
2               0.397821    0.807766       77.70001     32.45011


          INDEX OF DETERMINATION (R-SQ) = 0.65248


          CORRELATION COEFFICIENT (R) =   0.80777


       C O R R E L A T I O N   M A T R I X
1.0000   0.8078
0.8078   1.0000


          A N A L Y S I S   O F   V A R I A N C E

SOURCE           SS        DF       MS          F

REGRESSION    1666.508      1     1666.508    15.021    **
ERROR          887.586      8      110.948
TOTAL         2554.094      9


STANDARD DEVIATION OF ERROR TERM   10.5332


** SIGNIFICANT AT 1% LEVEL


                                                        95%
                                                     CONFIDENCE
VARIABLE  COEFFICIENT      STD ERROR    T STATISTIC   LIMITS (+,-)

   2         0.3978          0.1026        3.876         0.237


D.F.= 8


       A C T U A L   V S   C A L C U L A T E D

  ACTUAL       CALCULATED       RESIDUAL     PCT RESIDUAL

 150.0000      150.7021        -0.7021       -0.4000
 140.0000      151.4978       -11.4978       -7.5000
 160.0000      153.8847         6.1153                 3.9000
 170.0000      156.6695        13.3306                 8.5000
 150.0000      160.6477       -10.6477       -6.6000
 162.0000      166.2172        -4.2172       -2.5000
 185.0000      169.7976        15.2025                 8.9000
 165.0000      174.5714        -9.5714       -5.4000
 190.0000      182.5278         7.4722                 4.0000
 185.0000      190.4843        -5.4843       -2.8000
```

COMPUTER ANALYSIS

A computer is a valuable tool for regression analysis.

The computations needed for carrying out a complete regression analysis can take time, especially if there are many observations and if the numbers are large or involve many decimal places. But this is not a major problem now that most people have access to a computer. Even if you don't write your own computer programs, there are many software packages available that will perform all the calculations you need for a complete regression analysis. The printed output from these programs includes such calculated measures as numerical values for a, b, r^2, $\bar{x}$, $\bar{y}$, Σx, and Σy; explained, unexplained, and total sums of squares; confidence intervals for α and β; and predicted values of Y. When you have a computer to provide such output, you can concentrate on improving the quality of the raw data and interpreting the output, rather than spending hours on tedious calculations.

Figure 9.16 shows part of the printout available from STAT+ when the data of Example 9.1 are analyzed. When we compare the results given on the computer printout with the calculations given earlier, we note some differences due to rounding errors. On the printout, the dependent variable Y and the independent variable X are referred to as variables 1 and 2, respectively. The entries in the "Residual" column are the sample residuals. Beta is a standardized regression coefficient obtained by dividing the standard deviation of X by the standard deviation of Y and multiplying the result by the slope. For the present example we have

$$\text{Beta} = \frac{32.45011}{15.98153}(0.397821) = 0.807766$$

Note that the word BETA on the printout is not the same as the symbol β that is used to designate the slope coefficients in the population regression equation.

Exercises

In each of these exercises, construct **(a)** the 95% confidence interval and **(b)** the 95% prediction interval, using the indicated value of X to obtain $\hat{y}$.

9.9 Ⓒ Refer to Exercise 9.1 and let $X = 50$.

9.10 Ⓒ Refer to Exercise 9.2 and let $X = 100$.

9.11 Ⓒ Refer to Exercise 9.3 and let $X = 60$.

9.12 Ⓒ Refer to Exercise 9.4 and let $X = 75$.

9.13 Ⓒ Construct the 95% confidence band for Exercise 9.4.

9.6 LINEAR CORRELATION ANALYSIS

As we have seen, regression analysis requires only that Y be a random variable. The variable X may be either random or nonrandom. Correlation analysis, however, requires that both X and Y be random variables.

FIGURE 9.17
Scatter diagram of sample data from a bivariate distribution, showing regression lines of Y on X and X on Y

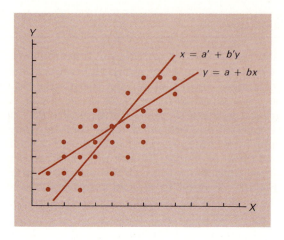

For correlation analysis, both X and Y must be random variables.

When we choose correlation analysis, we obtain sample observations by selecting a random sample of units of association and taking a measurement of both X and Y on each. In this procedure, values of X are not selected in advance but occur at random. Their values depend on the unit of association randomly selected in the sample.

In regression analysis, you will recall, one variable is referred to as the dependent variable and the other as the independent variable. Correlation analysis involving two variables implies that both variables have equal status. It does not distinguish between them on the basis of dependence and independence. In other words, we may do a regression of X on Y or of Y on X. The fitted lines in the two cases, in general, will be different. Thus a logical question arises as to which line to fit.

If our objective is only to measure the strength of the relationship between the two variables, it doesn't matter which line we fit, since the computed measure of correlation will be the same in either case. If, however, we wish to use the equation describing the relationship between the two variables for estimation and prediction, which line we fit does make a difference. We should treat the variable for which we wish to estimate means or make predictions as the dependent variable. That is, we should regress this variable on the other variable.

Figure 9.17 shows a scatter diagram of sample data from a population of X and Y values and the two regression lines that we can obtain from the data.

9.7 THE CORRELATION COEFFICIENT

The population *correlation coefficient,* designated by the Greek letter ρ, measures the strength of the relationship between X and Y.

The population correlation coefficient is the square root of ρ^2, the population coefficient of determination, which we discussed in Section 9.4. Since ρ^2 can assume values between 0 and 1, inclusive, ρ can take on values between -1 and

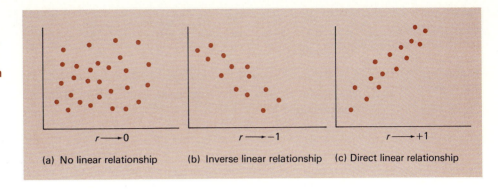

FIGURE 9.18
Scatter diagrams illustrating different values of the sample correlation coefficient

(a) No linear relationship   (b) Inverse linear relationship   (c) Direct linear relationship

+1, inclusive. When $\rho = +1$, there is perfect direct linear correlation between X and Y. When $\rho = -1$, there is perfect inverse linear correlation between them. A ρ of 0 indicates that X and Y are not linearly correlated.

The slope of the regression line and the correlation coefficient always have the same sign.

The sign of ρ is always the same as the sign of β, the slope of the regression line for X and Y. The sample correlation coefficient r, the square root of the sample coefficient of determination, measures the strength of the relationship between the sample observations on two variables in the same way that ρ describes the relationship in a population. The scatter diagrams in Figure 9.18 represent situations in which r is approaching 0, -1, and $+1$, respectively.

A Hypothesis Test for ρ

We usually want to know whether a set of sample data provides sufficient evidence to indicate that $\rho \neq 0$. If we can reject the null hypothesis that $\rho = 0$, we can conclude that there is a linear relationship between X and Y.

Correlation Assumptions   The following assumptions are necessary if inferences about the population correlation coefficient are to be valid.

1. For each value of X there is a normally distributed subpopulation of Y values.
2. For each value of Y there is a normally distributed subpopulation of X values.
3. The joint distribution of X and Y is a normal distribution called the bivariate normal distribution.

The hypothesis-testing procedure requires the following calculations:

1. Obtain b by solving Equations 9.5 and 9.6 or Equation 9.8.
2. Compute r^2 by Equation 9.27.
3. Compute the following test statistic:

$$t = r\sqrt{\frac{n-2}{1-r^2}} \tag{9.32}$$

This is distributed as Student's t distribution with $n-2$ degrees of freedom when $\rho = 0$ and the distribution of X and Y is bivariate normal. In using Equation 9.32,

TABLE 9.6
Sales volume and size of shopping center, selected shopping centers for a given year

X	40	600	60	72	400	90	200	70	80	84	Total: 1696
Y	3.5	25.0	4.8	3.5	30.0	5.0	12.0	4.5	5.0	6.0	Total: 99.3

$\Sigma x_i^2 = 596{,}840$ $\Sigma y_i^2 = 1822.79$ $\Sigma x_i y_i = 31{,}749$

be careful to give r the appropriate sign, which is the same as the sign of the sample slope b.

An alternative formula for r is

$$r = \frac{n\Sigma x_i y_i - (\Sigma x_i)(\Sigma y_i)}{\sqrt{n\Sigma x_i^2 - (\Sigma x_i)^2}\sqrt{n\Sigma y_i^2 - (\Sigma y_i)^2}} \qquad (9.33)$$

When we use this formula, we do not need to compute b first. It is usually better to use Equation 9.33 when we do not need the regression equation. When we use Equation 9.33, the value of r that results will have the correct sign.

When $\beta_0 = 0$, the t value computed by Equation 9.32 is identical to the t computed by Equation 9.21.

We can illustrate these procedures by an example.

EXAMPLE 9.2 A study is made of the relationship between the annual sales volume of shopping centers and their size. Table 9.6 shows data on a sample of 10 shopping centers. Here X denotes thousands of square feet of building space and Y denotes volume of sales in millions of dollars. Can we conclude on the basis of these data that X and Y are linearly correlated?

SOLUTION
1. *Hypotheses*

$$H_0{:}\,\rho = 0, \qquad H_1{:}\,\rho \neq 0$$

2. *Test statistic*.   We compute the test statistic by Equation 9.32:

$$t = r\sqrt{\frac{n-2}{1-r^2}}$$

If H_0 is true and the assumptions are met, the test statistic is distributed as Student's t with $n - 2$ degrees of freedom. For this example, $n - 2 = 8$.
3. *Significance level*.   Let $\alpha = 0.05$.
4. *Decision rule*.   Reject H_0 if the computed t is either ≤ -2.306 or ≥ 2.306.
5. *Calculations*.   The normal equations for these data are

$$99.3 = 10a + 1696b \qquad \text{and} \qquad 31{,}749 = 1696a + 596{,}840b$$

When these equations are solved, they yield

$$b = 0.048$$

Using Equation 9.27, we compute

$$r^2 = \frac{(0.048)^2[596{,}840 - (1696)^2/10]}{1822.79 - (99.3)^2/10} = 0.8514$$

and we wind up with

$$r = \sqrt{0.8514} = 0.9227$$

When we compute r by the alternative formula, using the data of this example, we have

$$r = \frac{10(31,749) - (1696)(99.3)}{\sqrt{10(596,840) - (1696)^2}\sqrt{10(1822.79) - (99.3)^2}} = 0.9268$$

Except for rounding error, this is the value we found using Equation 9.27. The test statistic is

$$t = 0.9227\sqrt{\frac{10 - 2}{1 - 0.8514}} = 6.7701$$

6. *Statistical decision.* Since $6.7701 > 2.306$, we reject H_0.

7. *Conclusion.* We conclude that X and Y are linearly related; $p < 0.010$.

Since F with 1 and $n - 2$ degrees of freedom is equal to t^2 with $n - 2$ degrees of freedom, we can carry out an alternative test of H_0: $\rho = 0$. We use as the test statistic

$$F = t^2 = \left(r\sqrt{\frac{n - 2}{1 - r^2}}\right)^2 = r^2\left(\frac{n - 2}{1 - r^2}\right) = \frac{r^2(n - 2)}{1 - r^2}$$

This is the F that appears in the analysis of variance in Table 9.3. For this example, we have

$$F = (6.7701)^2 = \frac{0.8514(8)}{1 - 0.8514} = 45.8358$$

Exercises

9.14 © The following table shows the amount spent for safety and insurance during a year (Y) and the volume of business (X) in tons hauled for a random sample of trucking firms of a certain type. All figures are in thousands.   **(a)** Plot the data as a scatter diagram. **(b)** Test H_0: $\rho = 0$ at the 0.05 significance level.   **(c)** Determine the p value for the test.

Y, $	13	18	14	18	23	21	14	25	23	14
X, tons	10	16	12	18	17	17	9	19	17	11

$\Sigma x_i = 146$ $\Sigma y_i = 183$ $\Sigma x_i y_i = 2804$ $\Sigma x_i^2 = 2254$ $\Sigma y_i^2 = 3529$

9.15 © The following table shows the scores on a clerical aptitude test (X) and grades in a clerical skills course (Y) for 10 business students.   **(a)** Plot the data as a scatter diagram. **(b)** Perform the correct hypothesis test to determine whether the data provide sufficient evidence to indicate that X and Y are linearly correlated. Let $\alpha = 0.05$.   **(c)** Determine the p value for the test.

X	60	70	65	72	75	75	82	84	90	95
Y	68	72	76	78	80	86	82	90	96	93

$\Sigma x_i = 768$ $\Sigma x_i y_i = 63,885$ $\Sigma y_i^2 = 68,153$ $\Sigma x_i^2 = 60,064$ $\Sigma y_i = 821$

9.16 ⓒ The following table shows the expenditures for equipment maintenance (X) and net income before taxes (Y) for a random sample of 10 firms of a certain type. All figures are coded for ease of calculation.   **(a)** Plot the data as a scatter diagram.   **(b)** Determine whether we can conclude from these data that the two variables are linearly related. Let $\alpha = 0.05$.   **(c)** Determine the p value for the test.

X, $	10	20	25	30	36	42	54	62	74	82
Y, $	12	24	14	18	18	28	26	40	38	54

$$\Sigma x_i = 435 \qquad \Sigma y_i = 272 \qquad \Sigma x_i y_i = 14{,}438 \qquad \Sigma x_i^2 = 24{,}045 \qquad \Sigma y_i^2 = 8984$$

9.8 MULTIPLE-REGRESSION ANALYSIS

One would think that if we can predict the value of a variable on the basis of knowing *one* associated variable, we might be able to make an even better prediction given knowledge of *several* associated variables. We also often want to obtain some measure of the strength of the relationship among several variables rather than between only two. A market analyst, for example, may correctly predict sales of a company's product in a given area from a knowledge of such things as the age composition of the population in the area, per capita income, population density, and the amount of money the firm spends on advertising. A personnel director may find that the productivity of employees is related to such factors as their experience, education, intelligence, emotional stability, and aptitude. A quality-control engineer may find that the quality of the product depends on such variables as the temperature, humidity, and pressure under which it is produced, as well as the quality of the raw material and the amount of some key ingredient. We can study relationships such as these by means of *multiple-regression* analysis. The techniques are logical extensions of those used in simple linear regression analysis.

Multiple-Regression Analysis and Underlying Assumptions

The population multiple-regression equation is given by

$$\mu_{y|x_{1j},x_{2j},\ldots,x_{kj}} = \beta_0 + \beta_1 x_{1j} + \beta_2 x_{2j} + \cdots + \beta_k x_{kj} \tag{9.34}$$

where $\mu_{y|x_{1j},x_{2j},\ldots,x_{kj}}$ is the mean of the subpopulations of Y values for a given combination of X values; β_0, β_1, . . ., β_k are the population *partial regression coefficients;* and x_{1j}, x_{2j}, . . ., x_{kj} are observed values of the independent variables X_1, X_2, . . ., X_k, respectively.

   The following are the necessary assumptions underlying multiple regression when inference is an objective of the analysis:

1. The X_i may be either random or nonrandom (fixed) variables. Because of their role in explaining the variability in the dependent variable Y, they are sometimes referred to as *explanatory variables*. The X_i also are sometimes referred to as *predictor variables,* because of their role in predicting Y.
2. For each combination of X_i values, there is a normally distributed subpopulation of Y values.

3. The variances of the subpopulations of Y values are all equal.

4. The Y values are independent. This means that the value of Y selected for one value of X does not depend on the value selected for another value of X.

You know that we can describe the linear relationship between two variables by a straight line. But how can we describe the linear relationship among *several* variables? We do so by means of a *regression surface:* a *plane* when three variables are involved, or a *hyperplane* when there are more than three variables.

Obtaining the Sample Multiple-Regression Equation

To find the sample multiple-regression equation, we must first get a set of normal equations by minimizing the sum of the squared deviations of the observed values of Y from the regression surface. Thus the *method of least squares* is used for multiple regression, just as it was for simple linear regression.

The normal equations for k variables are as follows:

$$\left. \begin{array}{l} nb_0 + b_1 \Sigma x_{1j} + b_2 \Sigma x_{2j} + \cdots + b_k \Sigma x_{kj} = \Sigma y_j \\ b_0 \Sigma x_{1j} + b_1 \Sigma x_{1j}^2 + b_2 \Sigma x_{1j}x_{2j} + \cdots + b_k \Sigma x_{1j}x_{kj} = \Sigma x_{1j}y_j \\ b_0 \Sigma x_{2j} + b_1 \Sigma x_{2j}x_{1j} + b_2 \Sigma x_{2j}^2 + \cdots + b_k \Sigma x_{2j}x_{kj} = \Sigma x_{2j}y_j \\ \cdots \quad \cdots \quad \cdots \quad \cdots \quad \cdots \quad \cdots \quad \cdots \\ b_0 \Sigma x_{kj} + b_1 \Sigma x_{1j}x_{kj} + b_2 \Sigma x_{2j}x_{kj} + \cdots + b_k \Sigma x_{kj}^2 = \Sigma x_{kj}y_j \end{array} \right\} \quad (9.35)$$

Note that the number of equations is the same as the number of parameters to be estimated. Solving these normal equations, which can best be done by a computer, leads to the following sample regression equation:

$$\hat{y}_j = b_0 + b_1 x_{1j} + b_2 x_{2j} + \cdots + b_k x_{kj} \quad (9.36)$$

The regression equation with two independent variables defines a plane.

When there are only two independent variables, the sample regression equation is given by

$$\hat{y}_j = b_0 + b_1 x_{1j} + b_2 x_{2j} \quad (9.37)$$

where b_0 is the Y intercept of the plane, and b_1 and b_2 are the slopes of the plane associated with X_1 and X_2, respectively. The amount by which $\hat{y}$ changes for a unit change in x_1, with x_2 held constant, is given by b_1. Similarly, b_2 is the amount by which $\hat{y}$ changes for each unit change in x_2 when x_1 is held constant. It is for this reason that the b_i and the parameters they estimate are referred to as *partial regression coefficients*.

Figure 9.19 shows a typical scatter diagram of sample values and the corresponding regression plane for the case of two independent variables.

To illustrate the use of multiple-regression techniques, we present the following example, which includes a partial printout from STAT+.

EXAMPLE 9.3 A market-research firm wants to predict weekend circulation of daily newspapers in various market areas. The firm selects two variables, total retail sales and population density, as the independent variables. A random sample of $n = 25$ trade areas gives the results shown in Table 9.7.

**FIGURE 9.19
Scatter diagram
and regression
plane for multiple
regression**

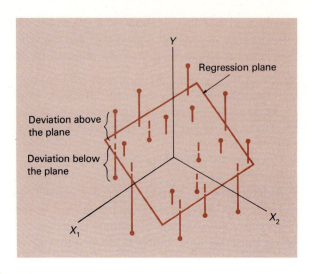

**TABLE 9.7
Sample data,
Example 9.3**

(1)	(2) Daily newspapers, weekend circulation (× 1,000) y_j	(3) Total retail sales ($1,000,000) x_{1j}	(4) Population per sq. mi. x_{2j}
Trade area			
1	3.0	21.7	47.8
2	3.3	24.1	51.3
3	4.7	37.4	76.8
4	3.9	29.4	66.2
5	3.2	22.6	51.9
6	4.1	32.0	65.3
7	3.6	26.4	57.4
8	4.3	31.6	66.8
9	4.7	35.5	76.4
10	3.5	25.1	53.0
11	4.0	30.8	66.9
12	3.5	25.8	55.9
13	4.0	30.3	66.5
14	3.0	22.2	45.3
15	4.5	35.7	73.6
16	4.1	30.9	65.1
17	4.8	35.5	75.2
18	3.4	24.2	54.6
19	4.3	33.4	68.7
20	4.0	30.0	64.8
21	4.6	35.1	74.7
22	3.9	29.4	62.7
23	4.3	32.5	67.6
24	3.1	24.0	51.3
25	4.4	33.9	70.8

SOLUTION Figure 9.20 shows a STAT+ computer printout containing numerical values of the coefficients for the equation.

We assume that multiple-regression assumptions apply here.

How to read the computer printout. On the computer printout, the dependent variable Y and the independent variables X_1 and X_2 are referred to as variables 1, 2, and 3, respectively. The correlation matrix on the printout shows the simple correlation coefficients for each pair of variables. The simple correlation between Y and X_1, for example, is 0.9875, and for Y and X_2, $r = 0.9849$. The correlation coefficients are repeated below the diagonal of 1's.

The "Actual versus calculated" values are the observed and calculated values of Y. For each observed (actual) value of Y (y_j), the computer substitutes the accompanying observed values of X_1 and X_2 into the regression equation to obtain $\hat{y}$, the calculated value of Y. The "Residual" column contains the residuals $y_j - \hat{y}_j$. Finally the computer constructs the analysis-of-variance table and does the calculations necessary to test the null hypothesis that each slope coefficient (β_i) is equal to 0.

**FIGURE 9.20
Partial STAT+
computer printout
of analysis of data
for Example 9.3
(Figure continues
on page 356)**

```
VARIABLE I        B(I)        BETA(I)       XBAR(I)       S(I)

   1           0.382152       N.D.         3.928000      0.548831
   2           0.067766      0.581634     29.58000       4.710577
   3           0.024441      0.412136     63.06400       9.254847


        INDEX OF DETERMINATION (R-SQ) = 0.98026


        CORRELATION COEFFICIENT (R) =   0.99008


        C O R R E L A T I O N  M A T R I X
  1.0000    0.9875    0.9849
  0.9875    1.0000    0.9847
  0.9849    0.9847    1.0000


        A N A L Y S I S  O F  V A R I A N C E

  SOURCE           SS          DF        MS              F

  REGRESSION      7.382         2       3.691        546.255  @
  ERROR           0.149        22       0.007
  TOTAL           7.530        24


  STANDARD DEVIATION OF ERROR TERM   0.0822
```

FIGURE 9.20
(continued)

```
@  CONSULT F TABLE TO DETERMINE SIGNIFICANCE


                                                          95%
                                                      CONFIDENCE
        VARIABLE  COEFFICIENT    STD ERROR   T STATISTIC  LIMITS (+,-)


           2         0.0678        0.0201       3.377       0.042
           3         0.0244        0.0102       2.393       0.021


        D.F.= 22



            A C T U A L  V S  C A L C U L A T E D

         ACTUAL       CALCULATED     RESIDUAL    PCT RESIDUAL


        3.000000      3.020940     -0.020940    -0.6000
        3.300000      3.269122      0.030879          0.9000
        4.700000      4.793648     -0.093648    -1.9000
        3.900000      3.992448     -0.092447    -2.3000
        3.200000      3.182136      0.017864          0.5000
        4.100000      4.146644     -0.046644    -1.1000
        3.600000      3.574072      0.025929          0.7000
        4.300000      4.156198      0.143802          3.4000
        4.700000      4.655116      0.044884          0.9000
        3.500000      3.378437      0.121563          3.5000
        4.000000      4.104429     -0.104429    -2.5000
        3.500000      3.496751      0.003249           .0
        4.000000      4.060770     -0.060770    -1.4000
        3.000000      2.993722      0.006278          0.2000
        4.500000      4.600236     -0.100236    -2.1000
        4.100000      4.067213      0.032787          0.8000
        4.800000      4.625788      0.174212          3.7000
        3.400000      3.356552      0.043448          1.2000
        4.300000      4.324615     -0.024615    -0.5000
        4.000000      3.998891      0.001109           .0
        4.600000      4.586461      0.013539          0.2000
        3.900000      3.906906     -0.006906    -0.1000
        4.300000      4.236740      0.063260          1.4000
        3.100000      3.262345     -0.162345    -4.9000
        4.400000      4.409823     -0.009823    -0.2000
```

From the printout, we obtain the following sample multiple-regression equation:

$$\hat{y}_j = 0.382152 + 0.067766x_{1j} + 0.024441x_{2j}$$

Evaluating the Regression Equation

Before we can feel confident about using a sample multiple-regression equation for prediction and estimation, we must be assured that it adequately represents the relationship among the variables. The *coefficient of multiple determination* provides an overall measure of the adequacy of the equation. Also, we can use analysis of variance and the F test as an overall significance test for regression. We can evaluate the importance of individual explanatory variables by examining the sample *partial regression coefficients* associated with each.

The Coefficient of Multiple Determination   The *coefficient of multiple determination* is defined as

$$R^2_{y.12\ldots k} = \frac{\Sigma(\hat{y}_j - \bar{y})^2}{\Sigma(y_j - \bar{y})^2}$$

(9.38)

The numerator is the explained sum of squares, or the *sum of squares due to regression,* as it is sometimes called. The denominator is the total sum of squares. The subscript on R^2 indicates that Y is the dependent variable and X_1, X_2, . . ., X_k are independent variables.

On the computer printout (Figure 9.20), we see that the coefficient of multiple determination is

$$R^2_{y.12} = 0.98026$$

Thus the regression of Y on X_1 and X_2 explains 98% of the total variation in Y. We also may interpret $R^2_{y.12}$ as a measure of the goodness of fit of the regression plane to the observed points.

The printout displays the results in an analysis-of-variance table. We can then carry out an F test to determine whether the overall regression of Y on the independent variables is significant. We can state the hypotheses formally as follows:

We use F to test for overall significance among all the variables.

H_0: there is no linear relationship between Y and the set of independent variables

H_1: there is a linear relationship between Y and the set of independent variables

Suppose we let $\alpha = 0.01$. We see that the computed F of 546.255 is considerably larger than 5.72, the tabulated F for $\alpha = 0.01$ and 2 and 22 degrees of freedom. Therefore we would reject the hypothesis of no regression at the 0.01 level. We would conclude that the data at hand provide evidence to support, at the 0.01 level of significance, the contention that there is a linear regression between Y and the two independent variables ($p < 0.005$). When the analysis of variance leads to a significant computed F, we say that a significant proportion of the variation in Y is explained by the regression of Y on the independent variables. Or we simply say that $R^2_{y.12\ldots k}$ is significant.

Inferences About Individual Partial Regression Coefficients We can make inferences about individual population partial regression coefficients when the previously stated assumptions apply. When these assumptions hold, the b_i are each normally distributed, with mean β_i and a standard error of s_{b_i}. To test the null hypothesis that β_i is equal to some particular value β_{i0}, we use the following test statistic:

$$t = \frac{b_i - \beta_{i0}}{s_{b_i}}$$

(9.39)

The test statistic is distributed as Student's *t* with $n - k - 1$ degrees of freedom.

To illustrate inferential procedures with respect to β's, let's take the newspaper-circulation example. Test the null hypothesis that $\beta_1 = 0$ against the alternative that $\beta_1 \neq 0$. The hypotheses, stated formally, are

$$H_0: \beta_1 = 0, \qquad H_1: \beta_1 \neq 0$$

Suppose that $\alpha = 0.05$. From the computer printout, we see that

$$t = \frac{b_1 - 0}{s_{b_i}} = 3.377$$

Since 3.377 is greater than the tabulated value of *t*, 2.0739, for $\alpha = 0.05$ and 22 degrees of freedom, we reject H_0. We conclude that X_1, total retail sales, is linearly related to newspaper circulation ($p < 0.01$). We conclude that this variable in the presence of X_2 is useful in predicting and estimating the dependent variable.

We can carry out a similar test for β_2. Suppose, for this example, that we test

$$H_0: \beta_2 = 0 \qquad \text{against} \qquad H_1: \beta_2 \neq 0$$

at the 0.05 level of significance. The computed value of the test statistic is

$$t = 2.393$$

Since the computed *t* of 2.393 is greater than 2.0739, we again reject the null hypothesis. We conclude that population density, when it is used as an explanatory variable in the presence of X_1, has a significant influence on weekend circulation of daily newspapers ($p < 0.01$).

Using the Sample Multiple-Regression Equation

We use the sample multiple-regression equation for the same purposes as the simple linear regression equation: (1) to *predict* the value Y is likely to assume for given values of the independent variables, and (2) to *estimate* the mean of the subpopulation of Y values for a given combination of values of the independent variables.

When the assumptions stated earlier are met, we may also construct *prediction intervals* and *confidence intervals* by methods that are straightforward extensions of those used in simple linear regression.

Predicting Y for Given Values of the Independent Variables To predict the value
Y is likely to assume for given values of the independent variables, we substitute
the values of interest into the regression equation.

To illustrate the use of the regression equation for predicting purposes, let us
go back to our newspaper-circulation example. The equation is

$$\hat{y}_j = 0.382152 + 0.067766x_{1j} + 0.024441x_{2j}$$

Suppose that, from the population of trade areas from which the sample was
drawn, we draw another trade area with total retail sales of $25,000,000 and
population density of 52 persons per square mile. We wish to predict the weekend
circulation of daily newspapers for this trade area.

Substituting $X_1 = 25$ and $X_2 = 52$ into the regression equation gives

$$\hat{y} = 0.382152 + (0.067766)(25) + (0.024441)(52) = 3.347$$

Our prediction of the weekend circulation of daily newspapers for this trade area
is 3347.

Estimating the Mean of a Subpopulation of Y Values To get a point estimate of
the mean of a subpopulation of Y values, we substitute the X values into the
sample regression equation. The numerical value of the estimate will be the same
as that of the prediction. Suppose, for our newspaper-circulation example, that
we wish to estimate the mean circulation for all trade areas with total retail sales
of $25,000,000 and a population density of 52 persons per square mile. As we
have seen, the point estimate is 3347.

Exercises

For each of the following exercises, use a computer to   (a) obtain the multiple-regression
equation,   (b) compute the coefficient of multiple determination,   (c) use analysis of
variance to test for a relationship among all the variables,   (d) test each b_i for significance,
and   (e) predict Y and estimate the mean of Y for selected values of the independent
variables.

9.17 © In a study of the yield of a certain grain, in bushels per acre (Y), researchers
obtain the following data from 10 farms. Here X_1 is fertilizer applied, in pounds per acre,
and X_2 is an index of soil quality.

Y	50	52	56	59	62	64	68	69	70	71	Total = 621
X_1	38	39	39	41	44	42	43	46	48	47	Total = 427
X_2	50	50	54	56	56	60	64	63	62	60	Total = 575

9.18 © The following table shows the scores (Y) made by 10 assembly-line employees
on a test designed to measure job satisfaction. It also shows the scores made on an aptitude
test (X_1) and the number of days absent (X_2) during the past year (excluding vacations).
All employees were on the payroll during the entire year.

Y	70	60	80	50	55	85	75	70	72	64	Total = 681
X_1	6	6	8	5	6	9	8	6	7	6	Total = 67
X_2	1	2	1	8	9	0	1	1	1	2	Total = 26

9.19 Ⓒ The following table shows, for a particular week, the sales (Y) of a certain product, advertising expenditures (X_1), and population density (X_2) for 10 market areas. Sales and advertising expenditures are in tens of thousands of dollars, and population density is in people per square mile.

Y	20	25	24	30	32	40	28	50	40	50	Total = 339
X_1	0.2	0.2	0.2	0.3	0.3	0.4	0.3	0.5	0.4	0.5	Total = 3.3
X_2	50	50	50	60	60	70	50	75	70	74	Total = 609

9.9 SOME PRECAUTIONS

When properly used, regression and correlation analysis are powerful statistical techniques. Their inappropriate use, however, can lead only to meaningless results. We offer the following suggestions:

1. Carefully review the assumptions underlying regression and correlation analysis before you collect the data. It is rare for assumptions to be met to perfection. However, you should have some idea of the magnitude of the gap between the data to be analyzed and the assumptions of the proposed analysis.

2. No matter how strong the indication of a relationship between two variables, do not interpret it as one of cause and effect. For example, suppose that you observe a significant sample correlation coefficient between two variables X and Y. This can mean one of several things: (a) X causes Y. (b) Y causes X. (c) Some third factor either directly or indirectly causes both X and Y. (d) An unlikely event has occurred, and a large-sample correlation coefficient has been generated by chance from a population in which X and Y are in fact not correlated. Or: (e) The correlation is purely nonsensical, a situation that may arise when measurements of X and Y are not taken on a common unit of association.

3. Do not use the sample regression equation to predict or estimate outside the range of values of the independent variable represented in the sample. This practice, called *extrapolation*, can have dangerous consequences. The true relationship between two variables may be linear over an interval of the independent variable, but may best be described by a curve outside this interval. If the sample happens to be drawn only from the interval in which the relationship is linear, it provides only a limited representation of the population. Projecting the sample results beyond the interval represented by the sample may lead to false conclusions. Figure 9.21 shows one of the possible pitfalls of extrapolation.

Summary

This chapter presented two important tools of statistical analysis, linear regression and correlation. It suggested the following outline for the application of regression techniques:

1. Review the assumptions.
2. Obtain the regression equation.

FIGURE 9.21
Example of the possible danger of using extrapolation in linear regression

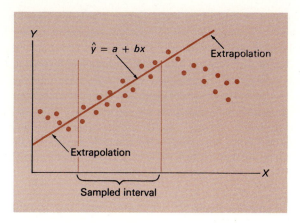

3. Evaluate the equation.

4. Use the equation.

You saw how you can use an analysis of residual plots to determine whether or not it is likely that the data violate the assumptions underlying regression analysis.

You saw that correlation analysis, though closely related to regression analysis, is used for a different purpose: to study the strength of the relationship between two variables. Correlation analysis is strictly valid only when both X and Y are continuous random variables. However, regression analysis is valid when X is either fixed or random. You learned that you can use regression analysis to predict the value that Y is likely to assume for a given X. You can also use it to estimate the mean of the subpopulation of Y values at a given value of X. We discussed methods of testing hypotheses and constructing confidence intervals in both regression and correlation situations.

Review Questions

1. In the equation $\hat{y} = a + bx$, explain: **(a)** two ways we may interpret $\hat{y}$, **(b)** the meaning of a, and **(c)** the meaning of b.

2. What is a scatter diagram?

3. Why is the regression line called the least-squares line?

4. What are the basic assumptions underlying regression analysis?

5. Give three interpretations of the coefficient of determination.

6. For the following expression, explain each of the terms, express each term symbolically, and draw a picture to illustrate the relationship:

Total sum of squares = explained sum of squares + unexplained sum of squares

7. What is the function of the analysis of variance in regression analysis?

8. Describe three ways of testing the null hypothesis that $\beta = 0$.

9. What are the assumptions underlying simple correlation analysis when inference is an objective?

10. What is meant by the unit of association in regression and correlation analysis?

11. What are the possible explanations for a significant sample correlation coefficient?

12. Explain why it is risky to use a sample regression equation to predict or estimate outside the range of values of the independent variable represented in the sample.

13. Describe a situation in your area of interest in which simple regression analysis would be useful. Use real or realistic data and do a complete regression analysis.

14. Describe a situation in your area of interest in which simple correlation analysis would be useful. Use real or realistic data and do a complete correlation analysis.

15. Ⓒ The following table shows the age and efficiency rating of each of a random sample of 20 assembly-line employees. **(a)** Obtain the equation describing the linear relationship between age and efficiency rating. **(b)** Compute r. **(c)** Do the data provide sufficient evidence to indicate that the two variables are correlated? **(d)** Determine the p value for the test.

Age	Efficiency rating	Age	Efficiency rating
44	61	51	60
44	41	50	78
45	89	61	78
43	76	47	74
40	79	62	82
52	67	34	70
43	73	51	60
47	94	48	67
54	96	51	72
43	77	57	80

16. Ⓒ A survey is conducted among customers holding charge cards from a certain department store. Researchers ask each of a random sample of 16 customers to estimate the amount he or she charged at the store during the past month. The estimates and actual charges obtained from store records are as follows (amounts are rounded to the nearest dollar). **(a)** Compute r and test for significance at the 0.05 level. **(b)** Find the p value for the test.

Customer	Actual	Estimate	Customer	Actual	Estimate
1	85	85	9	84	75
2	96	100	10	41	50
3	49	50	11	67	75
4	97	100	12	72	75
5	90	75	13	92	100
6	28	50	14	29	30
7	25	30	15	74	60
8	28	35	16	75	90

17. Ⓒ A garment manufacturer wants to know the relationship between the age and annual maintenance costs of sewing machines. A sample of 16 machines reveals the following ages and maintenance costs during the past year. **(a)** Find the sample regression equation. **(b)** Do the data provide sufficient evidence at the 0.05 level to indicate that the two variables are related? Use ANOVA. **(c)** Determine the p value for the test. **(d)** What is the expected annual maintenance cost for a 7-year-old machine?

Age (years)	Maintenance costs (dollars)	Age (years)	Maintenance cost (dollars)
8	109	1	25
3	75	3	70
1	21	6	126
9	135	2	58
5	67	1	30
7	125	2	47
5	71	6	120
2	52	8	105

 18. Ⓒ The following are scores made by 15 salespersons on a sales aptitude test, and their performance ratings as given by their supervisor. **(a)** Find the sample regression equation. **(b)** Use ANOVA to evaluate the equation. Let $\alpha = 0.05$. **(c)** Determine the p value for the test.

Aptitude test score (X)	Performance rating (Y)	Aptitude test score (X)	Performance rating (Y)
92	70	84	63
77	57	70	51
83	65	85	66
72	55	81	62
81	62	76	53
90	79	76	52
79	57	70	59
91	73		

 19. Ⓒ The following table shows the hardness, measured in units of Brinell hardness, and tensile strength, in thousands of pounds per square inch, of 15 specimens of a metal alloy. **(a)** Plot a scatter diagram of these data. **(b)** Find the sample regression equation. **(c)** Test the null hypothesis that $\beta = 0$. **(d)** Compute r^2. **(e)** Suppose that a new specimen has a hardness of 50. Estimate the tensile strength with a 95% confidence interval.

Hardness	Tensile strength	Hardness	Tensile strength
41	27	41	23
74	42	96	51
100	62	20	15
72	43	45	22
67	37	38	19
55	31	26	17
71	45	29	17
35	21		

20. Ⓒ A professor is doing a study of the relationship between students' grades and their part-time work. She analyzes data from a random sample of 15 college students. The numbers of hours worked per week and the grade-point averages of these students are as follows. **(a)** Plot a scatter diagram of these data. **(b)** Find the least-squares regression equation. **(c)** Do these data provide sufficient evidence to indicate a relationship between grade-point average and number of hours worked?   **(d)** Determine the p value for the test.

Hours/week worked (X)	G.P.A. (Y)	Hours/week worked (X)	G.P.A. (Y)
10	2.5	32	3.9
22	3.0	29	2.7
24	2.3	29	1.4
28	3.5	5	2.4
9	4.0	25	1.8
10	1.8	9	1.7
7	2.8	17	2.9
7	3.2		

21. Ⓒ From Table A in the Appendix, select a random sample of 15 pairs of one-digit numbers. Compute the sample correlation coefficient. Test H_0: $\rho = 0$ against the alternative H_1: $\rho \neq 0$ at the 0.05 level of significance. Compare your results with those of other members of the class.

22. For each of the following situations, indicate whether one should use regression analysis or correlation analysis.   **(a)** An industrial psychologist wants to know the relationship between intelligence and job satisfaction of assembly-line employees.   **(b)** In a factory, there are two methods for measuring the durability of a certain product. One (the direct method) is expensive and hard to perform, but gives a true measure of durability. A second (the indirect method) provides an indirect measure of durability. Officials will switch to the less expensive indirect method if it can be shown that this method is a good predictor of the results that the direct method would give.   **(c)** A drug company wants to know the average reduction in reaction time to a certain stimulus of people who take various strengths of their drug. The strengths are 1-, 2-, 3-, and 4-milligram doses.   **(d)** Medical researchers wish to know whether high levels of exercise are associated with low levels of serum cholesterol in adults.

23. The president of a firm wants to find the relationship between the effectiveness of salespersons, as measured in dollar volume of sales, and their aptitude for selling. Data on a sample of 15 salespersons are collected and analyzed by means of regression analysis. The independent variable is the salesperson's score on a sales aptitude test. The dependent variable is mean annual sales, in $10,000 units, over the past five years. The following computer printout (in a format similar to that of STAT+) shows the results of the analysis. (On the printout, E-01 instructs you to move the decimal to the left one place. For example, .897939E-01 = 0.0897939.)   **(a)** Write out the sample regression equation.   **(b)** Should H_0: $\beta = 0$ be rejected at the 0.05 level of significance? Why?

```
VARIABLE        REGR COEFF      MEAN VALUE      STD DEV

1 (CONSTANT =   4.78001)        11.4667         2.47301

2               .897939E-01     74.4666         18.2939

      INDEX OF DETERMINATION (R-SQ) = .441219

CORRELATION MATRIX
 1                    .664244
 .664244             1
DO YOU WISH TABLE OF VALUES PRINTED? YES
```

```
              A C T U A L    V S    C A L C U L A T E D
  ACTUAL          CALCULATED        RESIDUAL          PCT RESIDUAL

    11            12.2329          -1.23291           -10
    13            13.3104          -.310435           -2.3
     8             9.3595          -1.3595            -14.5
    14            13.6696           .330389                      2.4
    14            11.1554          2.84462                       25.4
    15            12.1431          2.85689                       23.5
    10            10.0779          -.778542E-01       -.7
    13            11.1554          1.84462                       16.5
    13             9.98806         3.01194                       30.1
    11            10.9758           .242071E-01                  .2
     6             9.4493          -3.4493            -36.5
     8             8.64115         -.641151           -7.4
    13            13.2206          -.220641           -1.6
    11            12.9513          -1.95126           -15
    12            13.6696          -1.66961           -12.2
```

```
         A N A L Y S I S   O F   V A R I A N C E

  SOURCE           SS              DF             MS             F

  REGRESSION      40.476           1             40.476        10.2649**
  ERROR           51.2608         13              3.94314
  TOTAL           91.7368         14

  **SIGNIFICANT AT 1% LEVEL

  VARIABLE        COEFFICIENT     STD ERROR      T STATISTIC

     2            .897939E-01     .280274E-01    3.20379
  D.F. = 13
```

24. Ⓒ Select a simple random sample of size 30 from the population of employed heads of household in Appendix II. **(a)** Find the simple linear regression equation with annual salary as the dependent variable and education as the independent variable. **(b)** Find the coefficient of determination. **(c)** Do an analysis of variance to test the null hypothesis that the slope of the regression line equals zero. **(d)** Plot a scatter diagram from the sample data. Draw the regression line through the points. **(e)** Construct a 95% confidence interval for the population slope. **(f)** Suppose that a person picked at random from the population has completed 12 years of school. Predict his or her annual salary.

25. Ⓒ The following data are based on a survey conducted in 10 market areas. The dependent variable is the proportion of adults who say they prefer a certain brand of toothpaste. The independent variables are per capita income (X_1) and a measure of the educational level (X_2) of residents of the market areas. **(a)** Do a complete regression analysis of these data. Let $\alpha = 0.05$, and determine the p value for each test. **(b)** Let $x_1 = 5$ and $x_2 = 6$ and predict Y. **(c)** Using the values of x_1 and x_2 specified in (b), estimate the mean of Y.

Market area	Proportion preferring the brand (Y)	Per capita income $(\times 5000)(X_1)$	Index of education (X_2)
1	61.6	6.0	6.3
2	53.2	4.4	5.5
3	65.5	9.1	3.6

(continued)

Market area	Proportion preferring the brand (Y)	Per capita income ($\times$ 5000)(X_1)	Index of education (X_2)
4	64.9	8.1	5.8
5	72.7	9.7	6.8
6	52.2	4.8	7.9
7	50.2	7.6	4.2
8	44.0	4.4	6.0
9	53.8	9.1	2.8
10	53.5	6.7	6.7

26. Ⓒ In a study of the sales of a certain product by market area, a market researcher collects the following data on a sample of market areas. All observations are coded for ease of calculation. **(a)** Find the sample coefficient of multiple determination and test the null hypothesis that the variables are not linearly related. **(b)** Find each of the partial regression coefficients and test each for significance. Let $\alpha = 0.05$ for all tests. **(c)** Determine the p value for each test. **(d)** State your conclusions.

Sales (Y)	Advertising expenditures (X_1)	Market share (X_2)	Sales (Y)	Advertising expenditures (X_1)	Market share (X_2)
149.0	21.00	42.50	169.0	24.92	48.95
152.0	21.79	43.70	172.0	25.50	49.90
155.7	22.40	44.75	174.5	25.80	50.30
159.0	23.00	46.00	176.1	26.01	50.90
163.3	23.70	47.00	176.5	26.15	50.85
166.0	24.30	47.90	179.0	26.30	51.10

27. Ⓒ An education researcher collects the following data on a sample of 11 college seniors majoring in accounting. **(a)** Compute the coefficient of multiple determination and test for significance, using F. **(b)** Compute each of the partial regression coefficients and test for significance. Let $\alpha = 0.05$ for all tests. **(c)** Determine the p value for each test. **(d)** What are your conclusions? In the table, Y denotes students' scores on a verbal reasoning test, X_1 their scores on a mathematics aptitude test, and X_2 their IQ scores.

Y	162.2	158.0	157.0	155.0	156.0	154.1	169.1	181.0	174.9	180.2	174.0
X_1	51.0	52.9	56.0	56.5	58.0	60.1	58.0	61.0	59.4	56.1	61.2
X_2	108	111	115	116	117	120	124	127	122	121	125

28. In a study of variables thought to be related to scholastic aptitude, a team of education researchers collects data on a sample of 15 students in their first year of college. The variables are as follows.

Y = scholastic aptitude scores of students entering college
X_1 = pupil–teacher ratio in high school from which student graduated
X_2 = median family income of student's community of residence
X_3 = size of high school graduating class
X_4 = student's high school grade-point average

On page 367 is a partial computer printout (in a format similar to STAT+) of the results of the multiple-regression analysis. Prepare a verbal interpretation.

```
VARIABLE      REGR COEFF    MEAN VALUE    STD DEV

1 (CONSTANT = 2.0886 )      10.0667       2.40743
2             -.244325E-02  30.2666       6.75783
3              .175112      12.4          6.60102
4              .259161       4.53333      2.9409
5             1.72162        2.73333       .771729

        INDEX OF DETERMINATION (R-SQ) = .91937

                   CORRELATION MATRIX
      1           -.771389        .875112      .402715E-01   .870786

  -.771389         1           -.68683       -.171496     -.689374

   .875112       -.686831        1           -.241071      .845416

   .420715E-01   -.171495      -.241071       1           -.289815

   .870786       -.689374       .845416      -.289815       1
```

DO YOU WISH TABLE OF VALUES PRINTED? YES

```
              A C T U A L   V S   C A L C U L A T E D
ACTUAL      CALCULATED    DIFFERENCE      PCT DIFFER

 14          14.9571      -.957058           -6.3
 13          11.4745      1.52546        13.2
  6           6.85242     -.852423          -12.4
 11          11.8923      -.892345           -7.5
 10           9.28295      .717051       7.7
  9           9.10082     -.100823           -1.1
  8           8.39517     -.395173           -4.7
 11          10.5895       .410474       3.8
 13          12.2341       .765889       6.2
 12          12.313       -.312957           -2.5
  7           7.44439     -.44439            -5.9
  7           6.99089      .911331E-02   .1
  8           7.43738      .562624       7.5
 12          11.705        .294983       2.5
 10          10.3304      -.330365           -3.1
```

```
            A N A L Y S I S   O F   V A R I A N C E
SOURCE        SS          DF            MS           F

REGRESSION    79.9264     4             19.9816      28.5059**
ERROR          7.00964    10             .700964
TOTAL         86.936      14
```

**SIGNIFICANT AT 1% LEVEL

```
VARIABLE    COEFFICIENT   STD ERROR    T STATISTIC

2           -.244325E-02  .550838E-01  -.443552E-01
3            .175112      .645715E-01  2.71191
4            .259161      .922597E-01  2.80904
5           1.72162       .584559      2.94516
D.F. = 10
```

 29. A management consultant conducts a performance study of salespersons in a large firm. Data are collected on a sample of 10 salespersons. These variables are studied:

Y = annual sales (in $10,000 units)

X_1 = sales experience (in years)

X_2 = score on a sales aptitude test

A partial computer printout (in a format similar to that of STAT+) of the results of the multiple-regression analysis follows. Prepare a verbal interpretation of these results.

VARIABLE	REGR COEFF	MEAN VALUE	STD DEV
1 (CONSTANT = .395081)		20.5	7.00368
2	.257827	7.79999	3.68241
3	2.96621	6.09999	1.81387

INDEX OF DETERMINATION (R-SQ) = .7526

CORRELATION MATRIX

1	.666929	.861978
.66693	1	.691797
.86198	.691697	1

DO YOU WISH TABLE OF VALUES PRINTED? YES

A C T U A L   V S   C A L C U L A T E D

ACTUAL	CALCULATED	DIFFERENCE	PCT DIFFER
22	16.7731	5.22693	31.1
15	13.0334	1.96661	15
18	13.8069	4.19312	30.3
10	15.9996	-5.9996	-37.4
16	19.4814	-3.48145	-17.8
29	26.1873	2.81265	10.7
35	33.6667	1.33327	3.9
15	18.32	-3.32004	-18.1
22	23.479	-1.47897	-6.2
23	24.2525	-1.25246	-5.1

A N A L Y S I S   O F   V A R I A N C E

SOURCE	SS	DF	MS	F
REGRESSION	369.162	2	184.581	10.6472*
ERROR	121.354	7	17.3362	
TOTAL	490.516	9		

*SIGNIFICANT AT 1% LEVEL

VARIABLE	COEFFICIENT	STD ERROR	T STATISTIC
2	.257827	.495103	.520753
3	2.96621	1.00514	2.95103
D.F. = 7			

 30. A health research team collects data on 10 communities. Measurements are obtained on the following variables:

$$Y = \text{health care facility utilization index}$$
$$X_1 = \text{median family income}$$
$$X_2 = \text{proportion of workers with health insurance}$$
$$X_3 = \text{doctor–population ratio}$$

A partial computer printout (in a format similar to that of STAT+) of the results of multiple-regression analysis follows. Prepare a verbal interpretation of these results.

```
VARIABLE       REGR COEFF     MEAN VALUE    STD DEV

1 (CONSTANT =  7.62552 )       20.1          6.90586

2                .621658       8.19999       4.42268
3               16.9724        .574999        .202794
4               -.313452       7.59999       4.07923

        INDEX OF DETERMINATION (R-SQ) = .814088

                   CORRELATION MATRIX
 1               .804793        .805102       -.49909
 .804794        1              .646684       -.455618
 .805102         .646684       1             -.265937
 -.499089       -.455618       -.265937       1

DO YOU WISH TABLE OF VALUES PRINTED? YES


              A C T U A L   V S   C A L C U L A T E D

ACTUAL         CALCULATED     DIFFERENCE    PCT DIFFER

  20           12.691         7.309          57.5
  15           15.5608        -.560793                -3.6
  17           19.6529        -2.65291                -13.4
  10           13.1827        -3.18268                -24.1
  16           19.026         -3.02602                -15.9
  28           26.7931        1.20692         4.5
  35           34.1717         .828293        2.4
  15           16.3832        -1.38318                -8.4
  22           22.5882        -.588226                -2.6
  23           20.9502        2.04979         9.7


              A N A L Y S I S   O F   V A R I A N C E

SOURCE         SS             DF            MS               F

REGRESSION     388.246        3             129.415          8.75775*
ERROR          88.6636        6             14.7773
TOTAL          476.91         9

*SIGNIFICANT AT 5% LEVEL

VARIABLE       COEFFICIENT    STD ERROR     T STATISTIC
2                .621658       .390581       1.59162
3               16.9724        7.86578       2.15774
4               -.313452       .33507        -.935481
D.F. = 6
```

31. Ⓒ A sample survey is conducted to study the relationship between the amount of life insurance held by business executives and several other variables. The following data are collected. **(a)** Find the least-squares multiple-regression equation. **(b)** Compute $R^2_{y.123}$ and test for significance at the 0.05 level. Determine the p value. **(c)** Test $H_0: \beta_1 = 0$, $H_0: \beta_2 = 0$, $H_0: \beta_3 = 0$. Let $\alpha = 0.05$, and determine the p value for each test. In the table, Y denotes the amount of life insurance held by the executives ($\times$ \$10,000), X_1 denotes their annual incomes ($\times$ \$1000), X_2 denotes the number of children they have, and X_3 denotes their ages.

Y	30	60	75	70	50	50	20	40	45	50	50	20	20	30	25
X_1	25	42	37	57	52	48	28	53	51	52	54	32	29	29	25
X_2	2	3	3	3	4	2	1	4	3	2	4	2	1	1	1
X_3	31	35	42	60	58	49	28	55	52	35	38	41	31	32	30

32. ⓒ Select a simple random sample of size 40 from the population of employed heads of households in Appendix II. Do a complete multiple-regression analysis of the data, using size of residence as the dependent variable and age, salary, education, length of time with current employer, and size of family as the independent variables.

 33. ⓒ The measurements in the following table were made on 40 geographic regions. The variable X is a measure of the extent of industrialization (the higher the value of X, the greater the industrialization). The variable Y is an overall measure of the extent of air and water pollution (the higher the value of Y, the greater the pollution). Plot a scatter diagram of these data.

X	Y	X	Y	X	Y
85	118	82	101	48	50
73	90	80	89	86	82
88	123	76	85	68	89
52	74	86	82	76	88
85	98	55	52	77	96
68	91	91	105	91	97
109	113	81	92	89	102
47	62	67	76	69	80
79	76	63	73	74	84
60	63	73	82	87	87
54	67	69	81	81	84
71	78	71	93	77	95
62	74	61	75		
67	60	57	73		

34. ⓒ Refer to Exercise 33. Obtain the least-squares regression equation for these data and plot the line on your scatter diagram.

35. ⓒ Refer to Exercise 33. Compute the coefficient of determination for these data.

36. ⓒ Refer to Exercise 33. Construct the ANOVA table. Can we conclude, at the 0.05 level of significance, that, in the population, X and Y are linearly related? What is the p value for the test?

37. ⓒ Refer to Exercise 33. Use the t test to determine whether you may conclude that $\beta \neq 0$. Let $\alpha = 0.05$, and find the p value.

38. ⓒ Refer to Exercise 33. Construct a 95% confidence interval for β.

39. ⓒ Refer to Exercise 33. What is the correlation coefficient for these data? Do you think that the correlation coefficient is an appropriate measure in this case?

40. ⓒ Refer to Exercise 33. Can we conclude that the correlation coefficient in the sampled population is not 0? Let $\alpha = 0.05$, and find the p value.

41. ⓒ Refer to Exercise 33. Suppose that an area has an industrialization score of 80. What do you predict the pollution score to be?

42. ⓒ Refer to Exercise 41. Construct the 95% prediction interval for the predicted Y.

 43. ⓒ The following is a population of measurements on two variables. The data were collected as part of a study a firm is conducting to analyze and subsequently estimate the costs associated with the repair of customer-returned products. The independent variable X is the amount of time involved in a major repair operation, in thousandths of an hour, and the dependent variable Y is the total cost of repair for each product. Select a simple random sample of size 25 from this population, and plot a scatter diagram of the resulting data points.

Item No.	X	Y	Item No.	X	Y
1	166	17.23	57	183	19.03
2	143	12.51	58	185	18.58
3	263	23.21	59	203	13.95
4	177	10.57	60	167	12.94
5	147	13.69	61	93	7.99
6	184	17.08	62	148	10.04
7	158	15.50	63	187	18.49
8	149	17.17	64	88	10.25
9	203	16.75	65	202	16.56
10	144	13.24	66	211	19.76
11	162	13.83	67	205	17.47
12	175	19.47	68	196	12.00
13	173	14.15	69	202	20.82
14	163	16.22	70	158	14.46
15	148	8.69	71	233	23.47
16	146	18.87	72	167	13.66
17	79	8.39	73	128	11.01
18	166	13.30	74	162	12.49
19	174	14.39	75	173	17.08
20	161	15.29	76	117	15.99
21	211	16.64	77	128	15.51
22	166	13.49	78	214	19.44
23	121	8.41	79	168	17.05
24	171	18.94	80	212	17.40
25	167	15.39	81	182	13.49
26	221	22.18	82	218	23.34
27	103	8.67	83	188	15.08
28	173	16.05	84	200	15.87
29	170	13.80	85	153	10.38
30	187	17.24	86	193	15.97
31	165	14.89	87	155	15.28
32	228	20.87	88	164	13.77
33	143	12.18	89	170	16.68
34	141	12.36	90	197	11.70
35	152	12.50	91	119	14.71
36	167	14.98	92	113	6.79
37	216	21.41	93	111	8.63
38	149	14.71	94	228	17.66
39	205	17.40	95	185	12.75
40	99	7.29	96	213	20.28
41	186	19.13	97	223	15.05
42	210	19.23	98	190	16.65
43	122	10.82	99	163	16.25
44	159	15.99	100	225	21.55
45	150	15.04	101	101	6.25
46	125	10.99	102	86	8.26
47	237	21.95	103	195	16.03
48	138	12.64	104	125	11.35
49	112	6.52	105	192	17.46
50	189	20.59	106	146	14.61
51	137	13.97	107	139	14.45
52	138	10.07	108	157	13.10
53	162	15.65	109	213	20.24
54	183	15.44	110	203	17.36
55	205	24.24	111	202	18.87
56	113	11.30	112	211	18.71

Item No.	X	Y	Item No.	X	Y
113	170	15.07	170	194	18.10
114	198	16.77	171	144	17.76
115	124	10.89	172	132	12.34
116	125	14.86	173	142	12.45
117	191	15.84	174	159	11.14
118	229	23.17	175	92	11.30
119	156	15.48	176	201	15.11
120	132	12.14	177	167	14.49
121	143	14.05	178	96	9.41
122	126	13.77	179	158	13.74
123	143	6.41	180	90	6.53
124	155	15.39	181	191	19.69
125	175	15.53	182	185	16.44
126	133	10.36	183	88	9.53
127	172	13.50	184	206	17.81
128	130	9.46	185	249	25.29
129	156	11.52	186	194	21.57
130	183	15.24	187	231	22.38
131	205	16.85	188	166	17.82
132	126	14.61	189	130	12.62
133	184	13.01	190	161	12.94
134	208	14.24	191	111	10.56
135	112	9.47	192	181	16.32
136	207	18.25	193	121	10.70
137	143	11.21	194	172	12.93
138	218	16.90	195	145	15.57
139	137	10.83	196	148	12.75
140	191	14.35	197	149	16.37
141	182	17.18	198	218	20.57
142	163	16.17	199	239	17.59
143	134	11.73	200	249	22.90
144	125	11.82	201	211	20.26
145	154	16.15	202	223	22.95
146	173	14.05	203	154	15.23
147	100	10.64	204	155	12.36
148	160	17.08	205	121	7.59
149	193	19.33	206	195	14.56
150	178	14.63	207	166	12.19
151	108	5.70	208	135	12.03
152	147	13.30	209	164	15.49
153	172	15.45	210	179	12.08
154	174	16.95	211	164	14.76
155	162	12.54	212	132	9.74
156	194	17.04	213	150	15.33
157	170	13.54	214	113	9.48
158	176	14.58	215	146	14.81
159	176	14.15	216	167	17.50
160	165	13.34	217	180	15.29
161	199	21.00	218	221	18.63
162	216	17.01	219	225	18.89
163	192	17.28	220	130	10.82
164	209	17.54	221	137	6.65
165	173	18.06	222	138	14.07
166	177	12.96	223	100	14.09
167	207	18.72	224	248	23.07
168	123	6.32	225	204	18.11
169	95	9.35	226	222	11.42

Item No.	X	Y	Item No.	X	Y
227	188	19.56	284	158	16.36
228	175	11.73	285	189	14.70
229	182	16.15	286	191	15.02
230	165	13.63	287	143	10.10
231	113	8.91	288	217	19.21
232	212	19.76	289	245	19.72
233	165	16.18	290	253	25.97
234	207	15.64	291	233	24.51
235	203	16.13	292	200	15.28
236	101	8.94	293	184	14.03
237	135	10.62	294	153	14.88
238	164	15.14	295	218	16.75
239	237	23.02	296	181	13.96
240	197	18.78	297	217	15.80
241	188	16.16	298	139	14.08
242	134	12.17	299	226	17.30
243	244	23.11	300	151	11.28
244	106	11.67	301	164	16.54
245	176	15.68	302	157	14.04
246	176	15.36	303	208	22.73
247	182	12.46	304	176	13.18
248	248	18.47	305	184	17.07
249	247	25.28	306	176	14.54
250	90	3.87	307	209	18.61
251	156	16.77	308	205	22.18
252	159	14.76	309	150	13.61
253	210	18.16	310	183	17.99
254	216	19.31	311	176	15.98
255	182	18.57	312	208	21.11
256	107	8.51	313	126	11.76
257	198	18.48	314	217	18.15
258	137	9.64	315	127	13.15
259	252	20.47	316	174	13.03
260	188	16.67	317	201	18.66
261	225	17.56	318	204	16.16
262	141	10.61	319	229	17.14
263	141	13.05	320	264	26.48
264	201	20.41	321	226	16.95
265	187	16.52	322	170	15.61
266	167	16.61	323	179	15.92
267	88	10.27	324	249	23.14
268	238	21.32	325	124	12.86
269	107	8.22	326	175	13.06
270	121	12.35	327	189	15.12
271	160	13.32	328	111	10.14
272	222	20.34	329	191	15.86
273	125	9.62	330	192	18.57
274	167	13.21	331	141	9.06
275	167	15.79	332	176	12.11
276	127	11.60	333	163	11.45
277	213	16.45	334	128	13.02
278	114	7.97	335	214	23.67
279	215	17.70	336	159	15.58
280	147	13.17	337	231	16.72
281	170	15.50	338	200	17.74
282	178	12.25	339	219	15.97
283	142	13.19	340	200	15.55

Item No.	X	Y	Item No.	X	Y
341	159	15.62	398	133	13.27
342	209	17.55	399	94	12.03
343	184	15.17	400	145	14.33
344	160	15.75	401	191	16.77
345	144	11.18	402	108	12.88
346	170	14.47	403	207	18.03
347	191	15.40	404	171	13.75
348	143	13.81	405	238	14.76
349	217	21.86	406	198	14.72
350	159	16.52	407	214	16.43
351	214	21.32	408	153	10.62
352	132	12.37	409	170	14.79
353	198	15.61	410	205	17.52
354	157	15.81	411	239	19.97
355	210	16.49	412	183	9.94
356	216	16.11	413	249	20.92
357	183	16.53	414	141	11.77
358	219	23.80	415	197	15.74
359	128	11.10	416	129	10.02
360	243	17.56	417	247	20.19
361	155	12.57	418	148	13.08
362	197	19.15	419	74	8.01
363	126	13.04	420	170	16.96
364	137	8.01	421	220	22.59
365	209	19.91	422	144	14.15
366	165	12.10	423	136	11.49
367	148	13.64	424	154	9.58
368	130	9.44	425	250	17.74
369	125	12.05	426	220	19.81
370	200	15.55	427	204	16.55
371	206	17.43	428	168	13.40
372	164	16.18	429	169	13.37
373	137	12.59	430	180	13.68
374	214	16.46	431	223	21.14
375	215	15.24	432	179	13.55
376	149	12.67	433	108	7.42
377	226	19.27	434	117	7.88
378	107	10.25	435	200	17.07
379	203	15.56	436	105	13.44
380	206	18.80	437	155	10.87
381	95	9.48	438	169	13.55
382	172	16.87	439	100	5.29
383	165	11.67	440	206	19.97
384	118	11.21	441	93	5.87
385	142	11.94	442	181	17.12
386	126	10.51	443	88	9.03
387	185	15.21	444	184	12.82
388	212	20.36	445	190	17.33
389	225	15.75	446	236	18.39
390	217	25.52	447	198	16.21
391	222	15.64	448	105	11.42
392	148	18.59	449	175	13.90
393	202	16.38	450	141	10.32
394	171	13.63	451	98	11.50
395	201	17.29	452	132	12.16
396	165	10.84	453	164	15.36
397	187	14.84	454	122	8.32

Item No.	X	Y	Item No.	X	Y
455	155	10.30	512	181	15.49
456	172	19.44	513	219	19.16
457	169	14.67	514	228	20.86
458	130	12.79	515	181	14.33
459	115	10.62	516	162	14.95
460	169	19.25	517	201	18.84
461	222	21.23	518	194	19.79
462	150	13.68	519	106	8.45
463	197	17.25	520	218	18.92
464	117	7.15	521	269	24.01
465	171	16.95	522	131	12.15
466	220	14.48	523	184	14.05
467	143	14.19	524	211	16.86
468	178	15.12	525	202	19.64
469	138	16.42	526	116	2.87
470	145	10.34	527	203	17.91
471	190	18.37	528	199	16.69
472	173	12.87	529	214	18.10
473	158	13.03	530	158	14.20
474	164	15.89	531	169	10.63
475	215	17.42	532	169	13.74
476	133	11.07	533	174	16.35
477	167	13.71	534	217	19.23
478	152	12.46	535	153	15.72
479	118	14.13	536	232	21.47
480	183	20.19	537	182	8.92
481	170	13.86	538	119	7.65
482	217	18.48	539	188	15.76
483	205	14.21	540	255	20.20
484	157	12.71	541	199	16.77
485	230	22.86	542	132	10.72
486	175	16.27	543	174	14.76
487	215	18.53	544	214	14.30
488	144	15.32	545	254	19.86
489	157	12.05	546	139	9.09
490	121	6.41	547	227	24.38
491	226	18.28	548	118	8.29
492	180	12.30	549	205	21.59
493	213	18.27	550	134	5.20
494	170	15.97	551	201	13.94
495	92	4.33	552	169	14.92
496	227	18.76	553	147	13.20
497	173	17.96	554	89	9.47
498	168	17.76	555	180	16.04
499	163	15.48	556	249	21.51
500	141	10.85	557	187	19.90
501	136	14.07	558	164	15.52
502	230	19.99	559	127	14.23
503	176	17.18	560	180	16.00
504	170	16.28	561	180	16.42
505	154	16.15	562	140	14.86
506	256	25.40	563	126	15.26
507	203	17.40	564	104	8.42
508	257	17.72	565	198	16.62
509	215	16.58	566	169	16.07
510	190	13.67	567	116	9.68
511	178	18.55	568	196	16.93

Item No.	X	Y	Item No.	X	Y
569	163	15.37	626	202	17.74
570	238	18.38	627	195	13.31
571	170	17.99	628	147	14.51
572	195	15.42	629	233	19.87
573	107	9.16	630	147	12.48
574	199	18.70	631	246	20.23
575	175	14.10	632	201	19.03
576	162	17.03	633	209	18.39
577	211	19.49	634	228	23.59
578	129	15.45	635	198	17.02
579	158	14.90	636	225	18.27
580	165	13.85	637	163	11.29
581	155	13.77	638	191	15.31
582	216	19.87	639	186	13.78
583	153	14.10	640	138	14.14
584	141	7.46	641	171	13.89
585	104	12.06	642	220	17.67
586	182	18.96	643	171	12.78
587	170	15.83	644	132	9.52
588	141	8.85	645	182	17.52
589	176	13.06	646	199	20.82
590	121	10.76	647	214	18.46
591	169	11.24	648	208	20.95
592	214	17.56	649	163	13.96
593	230	16.10	650	236	18.38
594	123	11.60	651	218	20.43
595	166	13.12	652	142	14.35
596	184	14.65	653	161	10.77
597	182	13.09	654	156	13.97
598	199	14.46	655	137	11.50
599	148	11.86	656	214	15.88
600	157	17.15	657	153	14.37
601	219	17.49	658	261	23.25
602	170	14.94	659	192	15.91
603	196	16.25	660	177	13.56
604	191	16.75	661	171	16.75
605	163	14.61	662	231	21.74
606	191	20.50	663	158	14.57
607	137	9.91	664	182	17.04
608	234	20.08	665	158	16.12
609	87	6.81	666	119	10.46
610	131	12.41	667	209	20.75
611	120	9.71	668	216	21.38
612	185	16.50	669	116	8.83
613	161	13.85	670	240	17.01
614	131	11.01	671	99	6.38
615	139	11.32	672	170	13.22
616	195	20.12	673	124	7.82
617	197	16.12	674	184	13.82
618	153	19.36	675	165	13.93
619	134	11.88	676	131	14.05
620	175	12.36	677	55	2.57
621	182	18.71	678	113	10.88
622	164	13.44	679	196	18.30
623	130	16.83	680	220	19.89
624	172	8.40	681	161	14.28
625	164	14.43	682	176	18.52

Item No.	X	Y	Item No.	X	Y
683	168	17.93	740	154	14.95
684	178	17.70	741	170	15.03
685	157	13.17	742	192	10.99
686	179	18.13	743	139	10.21
687	120	7.86	744	171	14.70
688	220	19.33	745	137	13.62
689	178	14.58	746	136	9.07
690	195	13.07	747	186	16.96
691	290	29.32	748	104	9.71
692	192	13.52	749	165	9.02
693	182	13.98	750	200	15.24
694	151	15.25	751	240	20.79
695	235	20.33	752	253	22.83
696	226	16.14	753	198	18.35
697	230	19.86	754	207	14.45
698	207	16.35	755	174	13.76
699	151	13.52	756	119	10.57
700	144	12.40	757	151	12.55
701	219	18.48	758	193	12.54
702	183	13.02	759	168	16.39
703	216	20.40	760	225	20.76
704	153	10.54	761	150	17.84
705	188	17.89	762	124	14.40
706	98	10.42	763	140	8.51
707	238	17.48	764	201	14.53
708	150	10.65	765	193	15.80
709	146	13.73	766	191	14.38
710	160	17.72	767	210	19.14
711	191	19.88	768	94	4.63
712	140	13.20	769	175	12.11
713	147	13.67	770	182	15.48
714	190	19.44	771	125	11.84
715	170	13.83	772	146	9.35
716	174	15.79	773	241	21.83
717	171	16.68	774	165	11.93
718	248	21.42	775	181	17.26
719	224	19.36	776	200	18.94
720	167	10.99	777	248	22.55
721	167	16.34	778	167	13.65
722	120	11.31	779	177	18.73
723	98	8.51	780	173	13.17
724	88	6.40	781	110	8.57
725	189	15.08	782	214	15.57
726	121	15.85	783	163	15.01
727	224	18.45	784	77	7.55
728	142	11.62	785	171	17.84
729	203	18.15	786	110	12.10
730	153	13.53	787	135	13.39
731	236	23.63	788	159	11.29
732	211	17.08	789	201	14.85
733	146	12.78	790	214	21.06
734	188	17.41	791	151	9.24
735	107	11.27	792	192	23.04
736	199	17.98	793	149	7.85
737	208	14.22	794	183	17.07
738	189	15.06	795	181	19.39
739	201	17.28	796	157	14.53

Item No.	X	Y	Item No.	X	Y
797	152	13.89	854	240	21.09
798	174	14.48	855	187	16.91
799	157	13.03	856	104	8.69
800	181	11.90	857	203	15.96
801	156	12.36	858	122	8.66
802	144	14.94	859	202	16.69
803	184	16.54	860	194	16.86
804	158	11.16	861	149	10.77
805	219	19.31	862	170	13.23
806	199	16.72	863	144	12.60
807	231	15.54	864	176	16.78
808	172	19.81	865	184	18.28
809	136	12.79	866	160	14.84
810	143	8.84	867	165	15.60
811	107	8.93	868	211	21.05
812	204	18.22	869	137	10.72
813	181	18.75	870	177	14.60
814	181	18.69	871	161	14.25
815	186	19.91	872	140	12.90
816	160	9.21	873	147	11.04
817	202	13.82	874	129	10.53
818	197	19.96	875	191	16.38
819	114	5.40	876	152	8.80
820	174	13.18	877	168	12.39
821	195	16.04	878	115	8.18
822	195	17.99	879	113	11.67
823	214	17.34	880	219	17.85
824	164	13.94	881	181	16.22
825	172	12.70	882	148	14.96
826	209	18.90	883	168	15.00
827	204	21.79	884	101	8.01
828	186	18.73	885	200	15.89
829	219	18.81	886	220	16.42
830	223	17.86	887	217	19.92
831	160	14.53	888	87	3.20
832	122	8.96	889	108	10.04
833	160	10.03	890	221	21.85
834	257	20.39	891	110	4.90
835	202	18.41	892	229	21.94
836	125	13.62	893	254	20.07
837	186	19.46	894	175	12.34
838	166	13.76	895	197	11.87
839	209	15.86	896	153	14.18
840	191	19.01	897	139	14.09
841	107	11.38	898	140	8.84
842	165	16.55	899	229	24.02
843	178	15.42	900	185	20.82
844	219	19.40	901	195	18.57
845	131	12.26	902	245	17.88
846	205	16.64	903	194	20.93
847	163	10.08	904	128	6.93
848	144	12.34	905	190	14.45
849	217	18.97	906	222	17.40
850	168	16.23	907	146	8.51
851	223	19.83	908	223	19.98
852	135	12.91	909	146	12.55
853	90	9.82	910	236	26.19

Item No.	X	Y	Item No.	X	Y
911	174	20.94	968	234	22.25
912	148	14.95	969	102	8.38
913	231	17.26	970	198	14.13
914	196	20.53	971	229	21.00
915	184	14.94	972	155	12.83
916	159	16.88	973	260	22.24
917	211	14.19	974	200	19.57
918	102	7.87	975	116	10.55
919	165	18.27	976	215	15.35
920	201	14.57	977	130	11.41
921	133	13.03	978	219	17.57
922	178	13.54	979	196	19.98
923	137	12.68	980	136	14.12
924	138	8.26	981	159	12.28
925	227	24.31	982	142	16.05
926	79	4.11	983	175	10.98
927	167	13.54	984	117	9.10
928	153	9.49	985	151	13.20
929	122	8.55	986	209	18.43
930	219	20.94	987	208	20.31
931	169	16.44	988	214	17.26
932	187	17.46	989	167	17.05
933	124	8.03	990	168	14.12
934	166	16.36	991	159	12.47
935	221	15.70	992	161	13.07
936	232	19.38	993	131	12.71
937	155	12.95	994	224	18.09
938	205	19.58	995	124	11.71
939	180	15.98	996	131	11.50
940	205	15.92	997	188	19.88
941	128	14.85	998	206	17.44
942	175	17.17	999	214	16.79
943	178	16.50	1000	162	11.89
944	170	15.53	1001	231	20.72
945	139	9.78	1002	150	15.23
946	150	12.44	1003	125	9.78
947	136	10.16	1004	146	15.40
948	168	13.43	1005	159	15.71
949	219	20.39	1006	123	8.96
950	180	15.23	1007	239	22.35
951	189	10.54	1008	163	12.50
952	172	12.77	1009	200	13.62
953	174	14.95	1010	140	11.70
954	148	15.70	1011	226	21.75
955	130	8.97	1012	196	18.53
956	222	20.17	1013	181	16.05
957	156	14.89	1014	225	19.09
958	131	9.94	1015	166	18.19
959	114	8.39	1016	241	18.70
960	121	12.25	1017	276	25.04
961	204	18.65	1018	178	18.67
962	108	6.87	1019	119	9.76
963	186	17.01	1020	199	18.61
964	175	14.82	1021	140	9.02
965	143	11.09	1022	127	11.11
966	114	9.78	1023	195	13.53
967	130	11.16	1024	221	16.18

Item No.	X	Y	Item No.	X	Y
1025	225	23.33	1038	211	15.80
1026	207	17.88	1039	175	20.58
1027	175	17.51	1040	242	17.18
1028	109	9.05	1041	104	8.73
1029	158	9.15	1042	190	14.89
1030	273	19.52	1043	204	18.14
1031	206	19.20	1044	209	19.58
1032	212	18.82	1045	147	15.01
1033	121	11.58	1046	177	14.70
1034	207	15.91	1047	185	14.98
1035	227	18.33	1048	119	12.71
1036	125	11.01	1049	179	18.70
1037	169	15.89	1050	169	13.20

44. ⓒ Refer to Exercise 43. Obtain the least-squares regression equation for your sample and plot the line on your scatter diagram.

45. ⓒ Refer to Exercise 43. Compute the coefficient of determination for your sample. Compare your results with those of your classmates.

46. ⓒ Refer to Exercise 43. Construct the ANOVA table for your sample. Can we conclude, at the 0.05 level of significance, that, in the population, X and Y are linearly related? What is the p value for the test? Compare your results with those of your classmates.

47. ⓒ Refer to Exercise 43. Use the t test to determine whether you can conclude that $\beta \neq 0$. Let $\alpha = 0.05$, and find the p value.

48. ⓒ Refer to Exercise 43. Construct a 95% confidence interval for β.

49. ⓒ Refer to Exercise 43. What is the correlation coefficient for your sample? Do you think that the correlation coefficient is an appropriate measure for these data?

50. ⓒ Refer to Exercise 43. Can we conclude that the correlation coefficient in the sampled population is not 0? Let $\alpha = 0.05$, and find the p value.

51. ⓒ Refer to Exercise 43. Predict Y for a selected value of X, and construct the 95% prediction interval.

52. ⓒ Refer to Exercise 43. Estimate the mean Y value for a subpopulation of time studies in which the value of X was the same. You choose the value of X. Construct the 95% confidence interval for the mean.

For Exercises 53 through 67, do the following: Select a simple random sample from the population of companies in Appendix III. (Ask your instructor how large your sample should be.) For each company in your sample, record the information on each of the six variables.

53. ⓒ With sales as the dependent variable and assets as the independent variable, do a regression analysis that includes at least the following calculations and procedures. **(a)** Find the simple linear regression equation. **(b)** Compute r^2 and r. **(c)** Use ANOVA to determine whether you can conclude that, in the population, the two variables are linearly related. **(d)** Use the t test to test the null hypothesis that the population slope is equal to 0. **(e)** Construct a 95% confidence interval for the population slope. **(f)** Use the regression equation to predict Y for selected values of X. **(g)** Use the regression equation to estimate $\mu_{y|x}$ for selected values of X.

54. ⓒ Repeat Exercise 53 with sales as the dependent variable and market value as the independent variable.

55. Ⓒ Repeat Exercise 53 with sales as the dependent variable and net profits as the independent variable.

56. Ⓒ Repeat Exercise 53 with sales as the dependent variable and cash flow as the independent variable.

57. Ⓒ Repeat Exercise 53 with sales as the dependent variable and number employed as the independent variable.

58. Ⓒ Repeat Exercise 53 with net profits as the dependent variable and assets as the independent variable.

59. Ⓒ Repeat Exercise 53 with net profits as the dependent variable and sales as the independent variable.

60. Ⓒ Repeat Exercise 53 with net profits as the dependent variable and market value as the independent variable.

61. Ⓒ Repeat Exercise 53 with net profits as the dependent variable and cash flow as the independent variable.

62. Ⓒ Repeat Exercise 53 with net profits as the dependent variable and number employed as the independent variable.

63. Ⓒ Repeat Exercise 53 with cash flow as the dependent variable and assets as the independent variable.

64. Ⓒ Repeat Exercise 53 with cash flow as the dependent variable and sales as the independent variable.

65. Ⓒ Repeat Exercise 53 with cash flow as the dependent variable and market value as the independent variable.

66. Ⓒ Repeat Exercise 53 with cash flow as the dependent variable and net profits as the independent variable.

67. Ⓒ Repeat Exercise 53 with cash flow as the dependent variable and number employed as the independent variable.

The exercises that follow should not be attempted without the aid of a computer. The use of STAT+ with a microcomputer is recommended.

68. Ⓒ A real estate broker is interested in knowing what variables are associated with the appraised selling price of single-family dwellings located in a certain area. The data shown in the following table were collected on each of the 1050 dwellings in the population. The variables are as follows:

$$Y = \text{Appraised selling price in thousands of dollars}$$
$$X_1 = \text{Size in hundreds of square feet}$$
$$X_2 = \text{Age in years}$$
$$X_3 = \text{Lot size in acres}$$

Select a simple random sample of size 25 from the population and find the sample least-squares regression equation.

Dwelling	Y	X_1	X_2	X_3
1	80	17	12	1.36
2	125	25	15	1.52
3	97	22	11	1.34
4	87	19	11	1.33

(continued)

Dwelling	Y	X_1	X_2	X_3
5	81	17	19	1.36
6	132	25	20	1.79
7	83	19	23	1.18
8	105	23	24	1.31
9	90	18	24	1.36
10	115	23	25	1.52
11	84	18	24	1.23
12	113	21	22	1.59
13	93	21	20	1.24
14	106	19	21	1.57
15	85	16	11	1.53
16	123	22	16	1.85
17	88	17	22	1.45
18	113	25	19	1.24
19	103	22	17	1.38
20	107	17	10	1.91
21	109	19	18	1.77
22	67	17	23	1.03
23	78	17	24	1.29
24	108	20	19	1.65
25	82	18	28	1.24
26	56	18	14	0.78
27	72	14	20	1.37
28	109	22	22	1.43
29	103	17	23	1.67
30	125	20	16	1.94
31	112	19	16	1.77
32	112	20	21	1.75
33	94	20	17	1.28
34	76	16	25	1.28
35	96	22	14	1.21
36	106	20	20	1.56
37	74	15	27	1.30
38	106	24	18	1.15
39	142	23	29	1.96
40	95	20	20	1.38
41	85	17	14	1.45
42	81	20	18	1.19
43	59	15	15	1.04
44	76	16	20	1.32
45	126	22	21	1.83
46	107	19	19	1.73
47	100	18	25	1.59
48	82	18	22	1.26
49	92	16	16	1.61
50	90	18	16	1.44
51	110	23	19	1.51
52	100	20	19	1.43
53	69	13	14	1.42
54	101	18	28	1.62
55	87	17	19	1.46
56	111	17	19	1.88
57	79	15	15	1.45
58	163	27	21	2.19
59	89	21	21	1.15
60	87	19	19	1.27
61	118	21	19	1.75

Dwelling	Y	X_1	X_2	X_3
62	121	23	20	1.66
63	95	18	17	1.61
64	102	18	18	1.70
65	119	20	19	1.86
66	100	19	22	1.52
67	106	21	24	1.50
68	74	15	19	1.37
69	59	13	19	1.20
70	74	14	21	1.43
71	107	21	21	1.48
72	114	21	21	1.61
73	68	16	19	1.19
74	91	17	21	1.56
75	119	24	20	1.49
76	86	20	14	1.29
77	87	19	21	1.27
78	123	22	21	1.72
79	93	20	15	1.29
80	78	18	12	1.22
81	81	18	23	1.17
82	94	18	19	1.58
83	98	22	14	1.24
84	52	13	15	1.06
85	88	19	19	1.35
86	122	22	19	1.67
87	101	18	21	1.62
88	119	23	26	1.60
89	74	17	16	1.18
90	105	20	14	1.63
91	101	21	18	1.45
92	111	20	16	1.69
93	126	23	26	1.67
94	71	17	21	1.10
95	103	23	19	1.27
96	127	25	23	1.64
97	148	25	23	1.97
98	108	20	23	1.64
99	64	16	18	1.08
100	94	22	23	1.18
101	128	25	25	1.54
102	133	26	17	1.67
103	103	19	27	1.57
104	121	24	13	1.55
105	71	17	20	1.16
106	79	18	18	1.16
107	97	21	25	1.28
108	106	20	18	1.63
109	82	17	21	1.35
110	119	24	27	1.38
111	85	18	23	1.25
112	117	21	19	1.70
113	91	18	21	1.43
114	81	16	19	1.37
115	105	20	21	1.54
116	100	21	19	1.36
117	88	21	23	1.13
118	104	22	18	1.46

Dwelling	Y	X_1	X_2	X_3
119	95	17	20	1.71
120	82	19	21	1.15
121	132	23	21	1.83
122	106	18	22	1.64
123	100	20	18	1.49
124	77	17	18	1.24
125	76	15	23	1.35
126	82	21	16	1.09
127	61	12	17	1.33
128	141	26	24	1.79
129	111	25	14	1.28
130	142	25	18	1.93
131	101	18	18	1.64
132	71	19	13	1.03
133	116	24	23	1.50
134	140	25	28	1.71
135	86	16	16	1.53
136	113	22	22	1.51
137	111	20	17	1.68
138	84	19	15	1.32
139	110	19	25	1.69
140	75	19	12	1.06
141	84	21	20	1.15
142	108	21	16	1.68
143	94	20	26	1.32
144	116	20	10	1.82
145	101	19	18	1.55
146	101	17	22	1.70
147	104	21	10	1.57
148	96	20	21	1.38
149	99	18	12	1.63
150	107	23	20	1.36
151	64	12	20	1.42
152	84	17	17	1.47
153	80	20	14	1.07
154	108	21	15	1.57
155	71	19	12	1.03
156	126	25	20	1.64
157	132	24	27	1.78
158	99	18	14	1.66
159	81	16	22	1.38
160	78	18	12	1.26
161	108	19	26	1.69
162	67	16	20	1.06
163	55	12	13	1.26
164	85	19	19	1.25
165	113	20	20	1.78
166	105	20	11	1.73
167	107	21	29	1.43
168	100	19	20	1.52
169	108	21	20	1.59
170	84	18	20	1.28
171	95	18	22	1.47
172	100	23	17	1.23
173	92	17	28	1.51
174	107	21	22	1.50
175	118	24	18	1.56

Dwelling	Y	X_1	X_2	X_3
176	91	20	17	1.29
177	108	24	18	1.41
178	131	24	17	1.74
179	117	18	26	1.93
180	118	21	19	1.74
181	83	14	21	1.56
182	77	16	19	1.32
183	107	20	15	1.63
184	88	18	19	1.38
185	125	21	12	1.97
186	113	19	21	1.82
187	114	21	23	1.69
188	63	14	14	1.23
189	86	17	21	1.37
190	121	20	20	1.97
191	80	14	23	1.54
192	115	20	18	1.78
193	59	16	19	0.97
194	100	18	27	1.59
195	101	19	24	1.52
196	84	17	23	1.27
197	88	19	17	1.33
198	85	19	20	1.25
199	94	25	21	0.96
200	73	12	18	1.53
201	99	20	21	1.48
202	107	20	25	1.54
203	98	21	18	1.35
204	80	20	24	1.01
205	45	14	23	0.81
206	92	18	13	1.42
207	83	15	14	1.54
208	130	23	19	1.80
209	106	19	24	1.62
210	105	20	20	1.65
211	109	21	15	1.59
212	92	21	13	1.25
213	125	24	22	1.58
214	103	20	21	1.58
215	126	18	18	2.21
216	111	19	20	1.77
217	112	24	24	1.33
218	98	23	19	1.23
219	108	19	19	1.69
220	118	25	17	1.41
221	76	16	17	1.37
222	120	22	19	1.62
223	91	15	19	1.67
224	108	20	12	1.65
225	88	20	19	1.24
226	114	20	20	1.78
227	116	20	21	1.72
228	119	22	20	1.70
229	128	23	22	1.77
230	150	27	20	1.88
231	75	17	20	1.19
232	93	20	24	1.27

Dwelling	Y	X_1	X_2	X_3
233	112	19	24	1.77
234	102	19	17	1.57
235	134	25	25	1.74
236	110	20	24	1.64
237	112	23	19	1.48
238	115	23	25	1.45
239	78	17	17	1.39
240	121	21	21	1.82
241	122	22	21	1.70
242	96	20	18	1.41
243	89	18	21	1.35
244	109	22	23	1.44
245	87	17	15	1.50
246	130	23	18	1.89
247	107	19	22	1.64
248	90	20	19	1.28
249	128	23	22	1.70
250	82	16	22	1.37
251	123	21	23	1.90
252	117	22	23	1.67
253	94	16	20	1.66
254	92	20	22	1.25
255	121	22	21	1.73
256	40	13	13	0.92
257	81	19	21	1.15
258	71	18	16	1.07
259	109	22	15	1.55
260	97	17	18	1.61
261	148	24	18	2.18
262	113	17	17	1.95
263	74	17	14	1.21
264	79	17	15	1.36
265	95	22	15	1.20
266	105	19	21	1.61
267	75	17	25	1.23
268	108	22	11	1.53
269	93	16	21	1.65
270	106	18	21	1.72
271	128	23	20	1.70
272	98	20	20	1.39
273	85	16	15	1.46
274	77	16	23	1.31
275	116	21	22	1.72
276	67	19	12	1.03
277	137	24	15	1.84
278	105	19	20	1.61
279	86	17	18	1.42
280	115	25	22	1.34
281	80	15	22	1.42
282	112	23	22	1.43
283	103	21	22	1.44
284	101	20	25	1.40
285	58	14	11	1.21
286	83	14	30	1.51
287	112	24	23	1.34
288	107	19	23	1.59
289	101	17	18	1.65

Dwelling	Y	X_1	X_2	X_3
290	80	14	20	1.54
291	75	17	16	1.25
292	91	20	18	1.40
293	66	15	26	1.10
294	90	19	22	1.40
295	109	17	20	1.87
296	73	15	15	1.26
297	91	21	21	1.16
298	106	19	17	1.71
299	107	17	22	1.81
300	90	19	22	1.36
301	93	17	26	1.56
302	95	17	13	1.65
303	95	19	20	1.44
304	125	24	16	1.72
305	96	21	18	1.31
306	93	17	15	1.57
307	95	18	22	1.52
308	133	24	21	1.81
309	128	25	20	1.64
310	60	14	18	1.12
311	81	14	25	1.50
312	108	21	16	1.52
313	105	19	19	1.68
314	98	18	18	1.59
315	77	20	17	1.00
316	87	18	28	1.35
317	93	17	18	1.60
318	102	20	17	1.53
319	85	20	15	1.23
320	125	24	20	1.63
321	80	18	17	1.24
322	109	22	16	1.61
323	94	23	26	1.21
324	95	17	23	1.57
325	116	23	22	1.56
326	76	14	20	1.42
327	86	22	14	1.13
328	107	20	17	1.63
329	74	18	21	1.02
330	83	17	24	1.41
331	110	17	22	1.91
332	88	15	18	1.69
333	106	20	24	1.51
334	90	20	25	1.22
335	109	22	16	1.47
336	91	17	17	1.56
337	101	23	19	1.25
338	76	12	20	1.51
339	83	17	19	1.37
340	117	20	17	1.82
341	75	16	24	1.35
342	95	21	14	1.32
343	118	21	13	1.75
344	93	17	23	1.55
345	96	20	13	1.45
346	140	24	24	1.93

Dwelling	Y	X_1	X_2	X_3
347	107	19	14	1.76
348	112	25	21	1.33
349	59	13	20	1.19
350	108	21	19	1.58
351	86	22	17	1.00
352	104	20	18	1.60
353	152	25	27	2.09
354	104	21	17	1.41
355	127	24	29	1.63
356	146	25	26	1.84
357	149	25	26	1.93
358	91	18	18	1.48
359	104	19	26	1.63
360	101	18	12	1.63
361	99	21	14	1.40
362	72	18	16	1.02
363	76	16	16	1.36
364	109	25	19	1.28
365	111	22	19	1.52
366	105	22	21	1.33
367	88	15	21	1.64
368	117	21	24	1.68
369	79	18	18	1.29
370	82	20	17	1.20
371	111	22	22	1.47
372	69	12	16	1.55
373	98	17	23	1.62
374	93	18	23	1.57
375	110	24	27	1.21
376	126	24	25	1.66
377	104	20	24	1.53
378	80	16	29	1.29
379	91	18	18	1.51
380	82	18	23	1.14
381	81	18	17	1.28
382	116	22	25	1.60
383	129	24	18	1.65
384	80	20	25	0.97
385	74	18	13	1.16
386	121	23	24	1.56
387	75	16	15	1.35
388	56	11	10	1.34
389	93	17	20	1.55
390	94	19	15	1.42
391	128	26	22	1.53
392	146	27	19	1.83
393	119	20	14	1.91
394	98	16	18	1.78
395	75	16	17	1.37
396	76	18	17	1.16
397	76	18	22	1.14
398	114	22	16	1.55
399	79	17	22	1.28
400	87	17	18	1.49
401	99	18	18	1.67
402	86	19	17	1.33
403	103	22	18	1.35

Dwelling	Y	X_1	X_2	X_3
404	79	19	24	1.11
405	74	14	23	1.49
406	128	22	16	1.87
407	90	20	16	1.31
408	68	15	18	1.27
409	96	21	18	1.25
410	92	20	19	1.18
411	102	19	12	1.66
412	97	18	17	1.53
413	106	19	19	1.60
414	115	20	23	1.71
415	90	16	17	1.57
416	155	25	18	2.08
417	97	17	10	1.79
418	103	21	23	1.41
419	112	19	24	1.74
420	93	20	21	1.25
421	97	20	25	1.30
422	31	13	19	0.62
423	95	18	16	1.51
424	94	19	22	1.39
425	80	19	17	1.15
426	91	18	21	1.53
427	103	21	23	1.40
428	78	18	14	1.28
429	84	15	21	1.53
430	75	17	17	1.25
431	107	21	18	1.56
432	54	15	14	1.02
433	84	19	16	1.26
434	106	20	25	1.57
435	101	18	22	1.68
436	100	20	20	1.47
437	84	19	21	1.19
438	142	25	26	1.81
439	85	16	23	1.47
440	98	19	21	1.56
441	111	21	23	1.56
442	99	19	22	1.48
443	75	14	20	1.42
444	66	17	19	0.99
445	93	17	25	1.56
446	128	21	25	1.87
447	102	21	24	1.43
448	122	23	17	1.63
449	94	18	22	1.44
450	73	15	17	1.33
451	124	23	17	1.68
452	85	15	16	1.59
453	124	20	27	1.95
454	141	25	17	1.95
455	105	20	18	1.59
456	106	20	19	1.59
457	132	23	17	1.88
458	60	14	20	1.08
459	95	20	29	1.37
460	90	16	22	1.49

Dwelling	Y	X_1	X_2	X_3
461	94	17	21	1.64
462	99	20	26	1.40
463	104	21	17	1.44
464	96	20	18	1.42
465	75	16	16	1.36
466	115	16	17	2.06
467	90	17	20	1.46
468	117	23	20	1.56
469	95	19	15	1.45
470	128	26	23	1.59
471	62	15	14	1.14
472	119	21	22	1.77
473	112	21	15	1.65
474	107	22	22	1.43
475	118	23	17	1.60
476	59	18	15	0.87
477	108	20	14	1.62
478	103	21	27	1.38
479	93	20	17	1.34
480	76	17	27	1.19
481	76	16	13	1.32
482	97	20	23	1.37
483	139	24	21	1.92
484	79	18	18	1.22
485	77	18	17	1.22
486	106	22	16	1.45
487	110	21	21	1.58
488	86	16	18	1.53
489	99	19	15	1.49
490	107	22	23	1.49
491	123	22	21	1.85
492	90	18	14	1.54
493	99	21	13	1.39
494	100	18	19	1.66
495	132	23	15	1.87
496	105	20	18	1.57
497	110	21	18	1.56
498	95	18	15	1.52
499	55	13	15	1.19
500	105	22	21	1.45
501	105	20	14	1.60
502	108	20	21	1.61
503	118	21	13	1.75
504	99	21	23	1.43
505	89	19	21	1.35
506	106	18	23	1.70
507	86	17	21	1.41
508	105	20	20	1.55
509	70	16	17	1.18
510	78	15	15	1.47
511	117	23	21	1.57
512	102	21	15	1.45
513	109	17	21	1.83
514	106	18	22	1.81
515	131	24	18	1.80
516	96	20	21	1.29
517	73	16	21	1.25

Dwelling	Y	X_1	X_2	X_3
518	104	21	13	1.53
519	74	17	10	1.32
520	70	15	15	1.28
521	99	20	12	1.45
522	101	24	22	1.06
523	106	19	24	1.59
524	111	20	16	1.64
525	94	23	19	1.19
526	60	14	23	1.13
527	57	13	13	1.21
528	117	20	23	1.85
529	100	19	22	1.41
530	95	20	17	1.31
531	91	19	18	1.34
532	80	14	21	1.48
533	91	20	21	1.37
534	118	21	23	1.69
535	62	14	20	1.08
536	101	17	15	1.75
537	110	19	21	1.81
538	66	16	14	1.22
539	81	16	16	1.43
540	115	21	17	1.70
541	88	17	14	1.54
542	123	22	19	1.78
543	84	18	22	1.31
544	110	24	20	1.35
545	91	20	20	1.37
546	89	17	15	1.58
547	67	19	17	0.91
548	93	20	19	1.29
549	116	19	16	1.92
550	101	20	23	1.46
551	63	13	20	1.31
552	47	14	10	0.92
553	121	23	15	1.74
554	124	22	33	1.70
555	97	19	12	1.54
556	97	20	22	1.36
557	111	21	19	1.61
558	120	22	12	1.72
559	118	24	17	1.57
560	96	21	23	1.26
561	92	19	17	1.42
562	123	25	27	1.49
563	107	20	23	1.62
564	113	24	21	1.42
565	94	21	12	1.29
566	102	17	21	1.74
567	102	21	17	1.34
568	100	22	17	1.42
569	124	21	17	1.91
570	115	22	20	1.62
571	92	18	17	1.46
572	121	17	21	2.13
573	122	19	18	1.98
574	109	21	17	1.50

Dwelling	Y	X_1	X_2	X_3
575	98	21	11	1.41
576	65	14	13	1.32
577	96	20	19	1.44
578	77	15	15	1.44
579	69	14	20	1.29
580	113	20	23	1.63
581	113	22	16	1.52
582	99	21	13	1.47
583	76	18	11	1.26
584	123	21	18	1.82
585	123	24	20	1.53
586	91	20	20	1.27
587	93	21	16	1.28
588	95	18	24	1.47
589	108	23	15	1.43
590	130	22	19	1.89
591	93	19	15	1.51
592	81	17	27	1.25
593	108	20	17	1.64
594	96	19	23	1.38
595	99	20	26	1.35
596	92	16	18	1.65
597	108	22	21	1.48
598	90	20	16	1.34
599	74	16	18	1.39
600	133	26	24	1.65
601	108	20	26	1.61
602	100	16	21	1.75
603	61	15	19	1.10
604	95	18	18	1.59
605	111	20	20	1.65
606	102	17	23	1.74
607	92	16	15	1.70
608	116	25	23	1.36
609	62	16	18	1.00
610	72	12	23	1.49
611	102	22	22	1.38
612	96	18	25	1.57
613	60	16	14	1.00
614	103	18	16	1.70
615	76	17	14	1.31
616	56	15	17	0.97
617	115	20	23	1.81
618	69	16	19	1.24
619	124	22	19	1.78
620	90	17	17	1.52
621	77	17	20	1.19
622	73	14	21	1.46
623	108	21	18	1.57
624	108	17	13	1.87
625	108	20	24	1.69
626	92	17	23	1.56
627	115	23	12	1.51
628	102	21	19	1.37
629	96	23	21	1.04
630	89	17	19	1.49
631	86	20	16	1.12

Dwelling	Y	X_1	X_2	X_3
632	71	18	16	1.12
633	103	17	18	1.77
634	115	19	32	1.69
635	99	19	26	1.45
636	110	21	29	1.50
637	89	17	23	1.45
638	115	22	21	1.50
639	83	15	18	1.57
640	102	24	16	1.19
641	90	16	16	1.62
642	71	17	18	1.11
643	107	21	21	1.56
644	80	15	18	1.40
645	124	24	22	1.64
646	87	18	21	1.39
647	79	19	11	1.04
648	124	18	31	2.02
649	76	15	18	1.38
650	131	25	24	1.68
651	139	25	23	1.84
652	89	19	28	1.21
653	82	18	22	1.28
654	112	21	19	1.66
655	89	19	22	1.27
656	104	21	24	1.39
657	113	24	24	1.40
658	127	24	19	1.80
659	103	21	15	1.41
660	99	20	17	1.50
661	27	10	13	0.97
662	144	24	27	1.99
663	127	24	16	1.75
664	64	17	14	1.04
665	75	17	27	1.19
666	98	19	25	1.43
667	85	20	18	1.14
668	96	24	14	1.06
669	86	18	25	1.35
670	112	22	15	1.63
671	91	19	25	1.32
672	82	19	20	1.18
673	124	19	26	1.99
674	105	23	23	1.33
675	88	17	21	1.42
676	103	21	15	1.52
677	93	20	22	1.27
678	102	21	24	1.36
679	127	23	22	1.67
680	90	19	14	1.26
681	116	20	22	1.76
682	137	29	14	1.53
683	116	24	27	1.42
684	85	16	13	1.57
685	106	21	13	1.51
686	134	23	24	1.83
687	97	16	15	1.81
688	130	23	27	1.74

Dwelling	Y	X_1	X_2	X_3
689	75	17	16	1.27
690	77	15	23	1.43
691	105	21	17	1.51
692	63	14	20	1.22
693	100	16	19	1.73
694	90	22	19	1.12
695	103	19	18	1.65
696	76	17	21	1.24
697	118	20	19	1.85
698	106	20	21	1.59
699	95	21	28	1.08
700	100	22	18	1.31
701	88	21	16	1.15
702	116	19	24	1.84
703	109	22	23	1.54
704	88	19	24	1.35
705	106	24	8	1.27
706	97	20	18	1.46
707	110	20	18	1.67
708	69	17	20	1.02
709	116	23	10	1.63
710	127	24	20	1.68
711	90	17	20	1.54
712	163	27	23	2.06
713	79	21	16	1.04
714	96	20	19	1.38
715	167	27	22	2.20
716	112	21	19	1.66
717	83	17	19	1.38
718	102	17	26	1.68
719	91	17	19	1.51
720	93	20	17	1.37
721	100	19	22	1.54
722	87	20	19	1.28
723	124	24	27	1.49
724	93	22	14	1.17
725	106	20	20	1.62
726	109	24	22	1.36
727	114	21	19	1.66
728	98	20	25	1.45
729	99	22	18	1.20
730	94	18	10	1.70
731	116	19	23	1.84
732	94	17	20	1.49
733	92	18	16	1.45
734	110	22	17	1.50
735	96	21	17	1.26
736	74	16	12	1.34
737	98	20	24	1.32
738	119	24	17	1.44
739	96	21	18	1.31
740	112	19	22	1.77
741	96	22	15	1.36
742	74	17	12	1.28
743	123	24	27	1.57
744	103	20	20	1.42
745	94	21	19	1.25
746	95	18	18	1.63

Dwelling	Y	X_1	X_2	X_3
747	78	19	23	1.07
748	96	17	20	1.61
749	77	17	11	1.33
750	101	21	16	1.45
751	89	20	14	1.31
752	75	15	19	1.36
753	86	19	14	1.39
754	104	21	19	1.53
755	94	22	30	1.09
756	107	21	16	1.53
757	95	23	26	1.12
758	113	21	22	1.49
759	110	23	16	1.48
760	92	20	17	1.38
761	76	17	20	1.22
762	116	19	23	1.81
763	84	18	23	1.31
764	113	18	18	1.91
765	120	21	25	1.71
766	106	18	20	1.81
767	117	18	28	1.87
768	74	14	18	1.40
769	101	22	19	1.31
770	75	19	14	1.09
771	98	21	21	1.36
772	116	24	18	1.45
773	97	20	18	1.37
774	95	19	14	1.46
775	122	24	19	1.65
776	87	21	17	1.14
777	113	26	20	1.24
778	128	24	25	1.64
779	77	18	21	1.20
780	98	20	17	1.43
781	88	21	22	1.16
782	104	21	17	1.53
783	83	17	19	1.27
784	62	15	16	1.11
785	105	19	18	1.66
786	85	12	20	1.75
787	84	18	20	1.26
788	101	20	24	1.52
789	93	21	18	1.24
790	76	16	15	1.29
791	124	25	13	1.57
792	80	17	12	1.36
793	103	21	19	1.39
794	71	16	15	1.23
795	120	19	22	1.92
796	94	16	26	1.62
797	41	12	15	1.07
798	94	18	20	1.52
799	86	20	18	1.16
800	78	18	17	1.12
801	122	24	23	1.55
802	89	18	24	1.43
803	80	13	16	1.69
804	112	20	22	1.69

Dwelling	Y	X_1	X_2	X_3
805	73	14	21	1.42
806	113	24	23	1.35
807	91	21	20	1.23
808	76	18	18	1.23
809	108	20	21	1.70
810	80	17	23	1.22
811	111	23	22	1.39
812	102	23	23	1.31
813	111	22	17	1.54
814	101	22	18	1.32
815	94	18	20	1.56
816	66	16	18	1.19
817	101	17	29	1.67
818	97	18	30	1.50
819	103	21	18	1.43
820	125	20	21	1.89
821	114	22	19	1.57
822	128	22	17	1.90
823	136	24	17	1.86
824	106	19	21	1.65
825	122	22	21	1.75
826	127	27	20	1.36
827	118	17	19	2.01
828	114	24	26	1.27
829	140	25	17	1.97
830	113	22	16	1.68
831	90	21	19	1.24
832	86	14	13	1.70
833	90	14	15	1.76
834	109	22	17	1.50
835	94	20	19	1.29
836	102	17	20	1.61
837	96	19	22	1.46
838	93	19	16	1.48
839	95	19	16	1.45
840	99	24	17	1.21
841	115	22	22	1.56
842	72	16	27	1.10
843	73	18	24	1.05
844	62	16	21	1.04
845	162	25	29	2.28
846	94	20	24	1.32
847	98	20	19	1.46
848	85	19	18	1.24
849	117	21	19	1.70
850	142	25	19	1.92
851	113	20	30	1.59
852	92	20	24	1.25
853	62	12	18	1.40
854	84	18	18	1.33
855	111	25	13	1.40
856	56	16	17	0.90
857	89	18	11	1.41
858	80	14	20	1.51
859	84	16	15	1.52
860	89	21	17	1.20
861	117	21	13	1.81
862	90	18	15	1.48

Dwelling	Y	X_1	X_2	X_3
863	83	18	18	1.39
864	77	14	14	1.58
865	56	13	16	1.14
866	133	24	14	1.79
867	86	20	21	1.13
868	84	20	19	1.16
869	91	17	24	1.46
870	110	19	21	1.80
871	76	16	18	1.24
872	77	18	23	1.17
873	82	17	26	1.37
874	85	19	12	1.35
875	114	24	18	1.49
876	104	22	22	1.40
877	137	26	24	1.71
878	71	17	14	1.08
879	100	21	9	1.53
880	116	21	27	1.73
881	77	14	10	1.56
882	92	14	25	1.77
883	94	18	14	1.48
884	81	17	21	1.28
885	59	15	20	1.04
886	114	19	22	1.72
887	73	17	21	1.16
888	114	21	23	1.61
889	128	24	22	1.74
890	145	26	17	1.91
891	81	16	11	1.49
892	85	20	19	1.20
893	94	20	17	1.36
894	62	14	20	1.19
895	102	17	17	1.77
896	105	17	18	1.80
897	95	18	30	1.40
898	65	15	12	1.23
899	96	19	20	1.47
900	104	23	25	1.29
901	119	20	17	1.81
902	87	14	17	1.81
903	117	23	14	1.56
904	76	15	18	1.41
905	92	16	15	1.65
906	115	23	20	1.49
907	81	16	27	1.29
908	86	19	19	1.30
909	103	20	15	1.57
910	95	16	16	1.68
911	75	16	19	1.32
912	108	22	20	1.45
913	82	16	19	1.41
914	86	16	31	1.41
915	138	24	17	1.88
916	92	18	16	1.53
917	107	19	15	1.73
918	88	20	19	1.25
919	89	20	22	1.18
920	49	12	12	1.22

Dwelling	Y	X_1	X_2	X_3
921	111	24	14	1.34
922	95	19	23	1.46
923	123	22	23	1.74
924	87	20	17	1.14
925	107	23	11	1.45
926	111	18	17	1.82
927	109	21	14	1.59
928	81	17	27	1.38
929	94	15	15	1.72
930	85	18	19	1.40
931	75	19	18	1.01
932	103	21	23	1.37
933	92	18	16	1.61
934	63	17	11	1.04
935	95	19	19	1.47
936	96	20	18	1.45
937	89	18	13	1.40
938	92	20	12	1.36
939	78	18	20	1.18
940	102	18	17	1.65
941	78	20	18	1.03
942	119	19	17	1.95
943	97	19	22	1.47
944	141	25	27	1.79
945	69	14	19	1.30
946	78	19	17	1.13
947	95	17	15	1.64
948	81	14	23	1.55
949	87	17	15	1.44
950	103	21	21	1.49
951	115	23	23	1.55
952	133	23	25	1.86
953	70	17	13	1.21
954	140	20	21	2.16
955	101	22	14	1.35
956	108	20	23	1.54
957	94	20	14	1.39
958	102	19	20	1.58
959	73	16	11	1.23
960	129	24	26	1.64
961	97	20	18	1.39
962	89	19	17	1.39
963	106	20	17	1.69
964	67	16	20	1.15
965	124	24	12	1.67
966	75	16	18	1.32
967	113	20	20	1.71
968	116	20	27	1.66
969	105	21	20	1.47
970	105	21	29	1.42
971	94	21	24	1.27
972	101	16	16	1.80
973	101	19	22	1.60
974	111	21	11	1.72
975	84	16	21	1.48
976	119	20	18	1.86
977	93	20	20	1.31
978	83	16	19	1.46

Dwelling	Y	X_1	X_2	X_3
979	81	17	18	1.31
980	78	14	17	1.51
981	90	12	18	1.91
982	104	22	17	1.39
983	123	21	18	1.87
984	121	21	12	1.88
985	130	24	18	1.75
986	70	17	16	1.10
987	94	19	23	1.32
988	93	19	16	1.44
989	96	20	25	1.34
990	87	18	18	1.42
991	133	25	20	1.77
992	73	19	17	1.01
993	82	17	14	1.44
994	70	19	23	0.90
995	123	23	20	1.71
996	106	17	23	1.75
997	81	16	12	1.41
998	122	23	22	1.67
999	128	26	23	1.59
1000	129	22	18	1.92
1001	87	18	19	1.26
1002	90	19	19	1.29
1003	114	21	13	1.71
1004	93	20	20	1.28
1005	90	20	12	1.24
1006	88	19	18	1.29
1007	130	25	16	1.65
1008	113	23	24	1.42
1009	98	18	15	1.57
1010	98	18	22	1.61
1011	123	23	19	1.62
1012	93	19	18	1.46
1013	67	19	21	0.85
1014	100	20	19	1.42
1015	139	26	19	1.78
1016	62	19	19	0.76
1017	80	18	9	1.28
1018	103	20	23	1.49
1019	114	22	17	1.60
1020	84	20	18	1.10
1021	124	23	17	1.69
1022	93	20	22	1.38
1023	85	20	18	1.13
1024	81	16	23	1.44
1025	80	19	14	1.23
1026	64	12	22	1.36
1027	111	19	21	1.71
1028	134	23	28	1.77
1029	112	21	21	1.59
1030	89	17	13	1.59
1031	70	16	23	1.20
1032	95	16	25	1.66
1033	102	20	22	1.46
1034	92	22	20	1.18
1035	97	19	21	1.38
1036	98	18	21	1.55

Dwelling	Y	X_1	X_2	X_3
1037	105	22	21	1.43
1038	94	20	17	1.38
1039	81	18	22	1.23
1040	91	19	22	1.38
1041	139	21	19	2.28
1042	123	24	19	1.66
1043	78	16	16	1.33
1044	85	14	22	1.68
1045	71	17	16	1.16
1046	91	19	15	1.39
1047	86	19	27	1.24
1048	69	15	20	1.29
1049	88	18	14	1.37
1050	118	21	20	1.76

69. Ⓒ Refer to Exercise 68. Find the coefficient of multiple determination. What does this measure tell you about your sample? Compare your results with those of your classmates.

70. Ⓒ Refer to Exercise 68. Use your sample data to construct an ANOVA table. Can we conclude that, in the population, the four variables are related? Let $\alpha = 0.05$, and find the p value.

71. Ⓒ Refer to Exercise 68. Test each of your sample slope coefficients for significance. Let $\alpha = 0.05$ for each test, and find the p value.

72. Ⓒ Refer to Exercise 68. Use your sample regression equation to estimate the mean Y value for selected values of the independent variables. Construct a confidence interval for the mean of Y.

73. Ⓒ Refer to Exercise 68. Use your sample regression equation to predict Y for selected values of the independent variables.

74. Ⓒ Select a simple random sample from the population of companies listed in Appendix III. (Ask your instructor how large your sample should be.) Do a multiple-regression analysis of the data with sales as the dependent variable. Cover at least the following calculations and procedures. **(a)** Find the multiple-regression equation. **(b)** Compute R^2 and R. **(c)** Use ANOVA to determine whether the six variables are linearly related in the population. **(d)** Use a t test to test H_0: $\beta = 0$ for each slope coefficient. **(e)** Use the sample regression equation to predict values of Y for selected values of the X's. **(f)** Use the sample regression equation to estimate the means of the subpopulations of Y for selected values of the X's.

75. Ⓒ Repeat Exercise 74 with cash flow as the dependent variable.

76. Ⓒ Repeat Exercise 74 with net profits as the dependent variable.

PRACTICE WITH REAL DATA

Select a random sample of college textbooks. For each book in the sample, determine the price of the book and the number of pages. Do a complete regression and correlation analysis of your data. Ask your bookstore manager or reference librarian about the best source of the information you need and available lists from which you may select your sample.

10. Nonparametric Statistics

CHAPTER OBJECTIVES This chapter introduces you to some statistical techniques that are often characterized as "quick and dirty" because you can usually do the calculations quickly, and because the assumptions underlying their use are not as stringent as those underlying most of the other procedures discussed in this text. After studying this chapter and working the exercises, you should be able to do the following.

1. Name and describe the four measurement scales
2. List the advantages and disadvantages of nonparametric statistical procedures
3. Determine when nonparametric statistical procedures are appropriate
4. Perform the analysis for each of the following statistical procedures: (a) the one-sample runs test, (b) the sign test, (c) the Spearman rank correlation analysis, (d) the Wilcoxon signed-rank test, and (e) the Mann–Whitney test

Most of the inferential procedures we have discussed have had two characteristics in common. First, they were concerned with population *parameters*. Second, their validity depended on a set of rigid *assumptions*. The objectives of estimation and hypothesis testing were to estimate and test hypotheses about such parameters as a population mean, a population proportion, and a population variance. As an example of a set of assumptions underlying an inferential procedure, consider the *t* test for testing the null hypothesis that two population means are equal. The use of this test rests on the assumption that the populations of interest are normally distributed with equal variances.

The one inferential procedure covered earlier that was not concerned with population parameters and that did not rest on a rigid set of assumptions was the use of the chi-square distribution in tests of goodness of fit and independence.

We refer to inferential procedures such as the *t* test and analysis-of-variance methods as *parametric procedures,* because they are concerned with population parameters. The body of statistical theory and methodology of which they are a part is called *parametric statistics*. Inferential procedures such as the chi-square tests of goodness of fit and independence, which are not concerned with population parameters or do not depend on rigid assumptions about the distribution of the relevant population, are called *nonparametric procedures*. The statistical theory and methodology relating to these procedures is called *nonparametric statistics*.

10.1 WHEN TO USE NONPARAMETRIC STATISTICS

Nonparametric statistics are most often used in four situations, as follows.

1. *The data do not meet the assumptions for a parametric test.* For example, the nature of the hypothesis to be tested may suggest the use of the *t* test. But this test may not be appropriate because the sample on which the test is to be based was drawn from a population that is known to be substantially nonnormally distributed. In such a case, we may use an alternative nonparametric test that does not depend on the assumption of a normally distributed parent population.

2. *The data consist merely of ranks.* For example, consumers may be asked to indicate how much they like several brands of coffee. They may not be able to assign each brand a numerical score representing how much they like it, but they may be able to rank the brands in order of preference. The analysis, then, is based on ranks. Data consisting of ranks are said to be measured on a weak measurement scale. Most parametric tests require a stronger measurement scale, but generally the nonparametric tests do not. Section 10.2 gives a more complete discussion of measurement scales.

3. *The question to be answered does not involve a parameter.* For example, if we wish to reach a decision about whether a sample is a random sample, we use the appropriate nonparametric test.

4. *We need results quickly.* As a rule, the calculations required by the nonparametric procedures can be carried out more quickly and easily than those required by parametric ones. The calculations for some of the nonparametric procedures are so easy that they can be done right at the data-collection site—in a manufacturing plant, for example—by someone relatively unskilled in statistics or mathematics.

10.2 MEASUREMENT AND MEASUREMENT SCALES

We define *measurement* as "the assignment of numerals to objects or events according to rules." Here *numeral* is used to mean any symbol, not necessarily a number, that we may assign to an object or event. The use of different rules for the assignment of numerals leads to different types of measurement, which, in turn, lead to different *measurement scales*. There are four measurement scales: *nominal, ordinal, interval,* and *ratio*. We discuss each one briefly here.

The Nominal Scale

The weakest of the four measurement scales is the *nominal* scale. We use this when one object or event is distinguished from another by names. For example, the names *desk, chair,* and *file cabinet* are assigned to objects in an office to distinguish one from the other. Another example of nominal measurement occurs when numerals are assigned to football players for identification purposes. When objects or events are measured on a nominal scale, we can say that one is *different* from another.

The Ordinal Scale

When one object not only differs from another with respect to some characteristic, but also has more or less of the characteristic than another, we have at least an *ordinal* scale. There are many instances in business in which we use an ordinal measurement scale. We may categorize accounts receivable as large, medium, and small. We may label typists as fast, average, and slow. We may rate different sources of raw material for the manufacture of some product as good, better, and best. We may rank salespersons according to the strength of their personalities. When we rank items, it is possible to tell which ones have more or less of the characteristic on which the ranking is based (except in the case of ties). But it is not possible to tell how much more or less of the characteristic one object has than another.

The Interval Scale

When we can say not only that one object is greater or less than another, but also that one is greater or less by a specified amount, we have achieved measurement on at least an *interval scale*. A characteristic of the interval scale is the presence of a *unit of measurement*. Temperature as measured on a Fahrenheit thermometer is an example of measurement on an interval scale. We can say that it is warmer today than yesterday. We can also say that it is five degrees warmer.

The Ratio Scale

The *ratio scale* is characterized by the use of both a unit of measurement and a true zero point. The fact that a thermometer shows the temperature to be zero degrees does not mean that there is a complete absence of temperature. On the other hand, we measure weight on a ratio scale. When a weighing device shows 0, this indicates an absence of weight. Measurement on a ratio scale allows us to say that one object is so many times as great as (or less than) another, and that it is so many units more than (or less than) another. For example, suppose that a man weighs 180 pounds and his child weighs 60 pounds. We can say that (1) the father weighs *three times as much* as the child, and (2) the father weighs 120 pounds *more than* the child. The ratio scale is the ''strongest'' of the four measurement scales.

10.3 ADVANTAGES AND DISADVANTAGES OF NONPARAMETRIC STATISTICS

The advantages and disadvantages of nonparametric statistical procedures are as follows.

Advantages

1. The probability statements accompanying the statistical tests are usually exact.
2. The calculations are usually easily and rapidly performed.
3. The assumptions are usually few and easily met.
4. As a consequence of (3), nonparametric procedures are widely applicable.
5. We can analyze data measured on a weak measurement scale by nonparametric techniques.

Disadvantages

1. Nonparametric procedures, because of their simplicity and ease of computation with small samples, may be applied in cases in which parametric procedures would be more appropriate. Such a practice is inefficient and should be avoided.
2. For large samples, the calculations may become burdensome unless one uses approximations.

10.4 THE ONE-SAMPLE RUNS TEST

We have shown the importance of random samples in statistical inference. It is valuable to have a procedure for testing the null hypothesis that a sample is indeed a random sample. This section presents a test based on the number of *runs* present in the sample. A run is defined as a sequence of like symbols preceded and followed by either a different symbol or no symbol at all. Two types of symbols are used. One or the other is assigned to each observation in the sample, depending on whether the observation is greater than or less than the sample median or mean. If we display the symbols in the order in which the numerical values they represent were selected, we can easily recognize the number of runs in the data. Suppose, for example, that we observe the following sequence of symbols in a sample of size 10, where *B* stands for a value below the median and *A* represents a value above the median:

BBBBB AAAAA

In this sequence there are only two runs. This seems to be too few to support a hypothesis of randomness. By contrast, consider the following sequence:

B A B A B A B A B A

This sequence contains 10 runs. Again we suspect a lack of randomness. Intuitively it seems that some systematic, rather than random, procedure is operative. In a particular sequence, then, we suspect a lack of randomness if there appear to be either too few or too many runs.

Finally, suppose that we observe the following sequence, which contains six runs:

B A BB A BB AAA

This sequence seems to be rather well mixed. There does not appear to be any reason to suspect a lack of randomness.

To determine whether an observed number of runs is small enough or large enough to cause rejection of the null hypothesis that the sample is a random one, we can consult Appendix Table G. To use Table G, we designate the number of symbols of one kind as n_1 and the number of symbols of the other kind as n_2. (The total sample size is $n_1 + n_2 = n$.) Table G gives critical values of r, the number of runs, for values of n_1 and n_2 through 20. If the observed number of runs is less than or equal to the appropriate critical value of r in Table Ga or greater than or equal to the appropriate critical value of r in Table Gb, we can reject the null hypothesis of randomness at the 0.05 level of significance.

In the first sequence given above, we have n_1 = number of *B*'s = 5, n_2 = number of *A*'s = 5, and r = 2. Table Ga indicates that we can reject the hypothesis of randomness in that sequence at the 0.05 level of significance, since the critical value is 2. For the second sequence, where n_1 = 5, n_2 = 5, and r = 10, Table Gb shows that we can reject the hypothesis of randomness at the 0.05 significance level, since here the critical value is 10. The last sequence, where n_1 = 5, n_2 = 5, and r = 6, may be in random order, since, from Tables Ga and Gb, r = 6 is not significant.

The use of the runs test is not limited to testing the null hypothesis that a sample is random. We can use it to test any sequence for randomness, no matter how the sequence is generated. Sequences that we may test for randomness include, for example, the arrangement of males and females in a cafeteria line, the presence and absence of rain over a period of several days, the wins and losses of an athletic team, or the sequence of correct answers in a true-false quiz.

EXAMPLE 10.1 The quality-control department of a bubble-bath company requires the mean weight of packages of its product to be 17 ounces. A sample of 20 consecutive packages filled by the same machine is taken from the assembly line and weighed, with the following results (in ounces): 17.9, 17.5, 17.2, 17.3, 16.5, 16.8, 16.7, 17.2, 17.4, 17.6, 17.5, 17.8, 16.8, 16.5, 16.6, 17.7, 17.6, 17.7, 17.8, 17.2. Do these data provide sufficient evidence to indicate a lack of randomness in the pattern of over and under fills?

SOLUTION

1. *Hypotheses*

H_0: Over fills and under fills occur at random

H_1: Over fills and under fills do not occur at random

2. *Test statistic.*   The test statistic is r, the number of runs present in the sample data.
3. *Significance level.*   Let $\alpha = 0.05$.
4. *Decision rule.*   Suppose that we let n_1 be the number of weights less than the mean ($n_1 = 6$) and n_2 be the number of weights greater than the mean ($n_2 = 14$). Reference to Table G shows that the critical values of r are 5 and 13. The decision rule, then, is: Reject H_0 if the observed value of r is either ≤ 5 or ≥ 13.
5. *Calculations.*   Examination of our sample data shows that they contain 5 runs.
6. *Statistical decision.*   We can reject the null hypothesis of randomness at the 0.05 level of significance.
7. *Conclusion.*   We conclude that over fills and under fills do not occur at random.

The Large-Sample Case

When either n_1 or n_2 is larger than 20, we cannot use Table G to test for significance. For samples that are too large to use Table G, we can compute the following test statistic:

$$z = \frac{r - \left(\dfrac{2n_1 n_2}{n_1 + n_2} + 1 \right)}{\sqrt{\dfrac{2n_1 n_2 (2n_1 n_2 - n_1 - n_2)}{(n_1 + n_2)^2 (n_1 + n_2 - 1)}}} \tag{10.1}$$

The z of Equation 10.1 is compared for significance with tabulated values of the standard normal distribution of Appendix Table C.

EXAMPLE 10.2 At a certain gasoline station, two grades of gasoline are available, A and B. On a certain day the first 50 gasoline purchases are of grades A and B in the following order: AA B AA B A BB AAA BB A BB A BB A BB A BB AA BBBB AA B A B A B AAA B AAAAA BB. Does this sequence of purchases appear to indicate a random selection of grades of gasoline? Let $\alpha = 0.05$.

SOLUTION We have n_1 = number of A's = 26, n_2 = number of B's = 24, and $r = 28$. Since n_1 and n_2 are both greater than 20, we cannot use Table G. Thus we use Equation 10.1 to compute

$$z = \frac{28 - \left(\dfrac{2(26)(24)}{26 + 24} + 1\right)}{\sqrt{\dfrac{2(26)(24)[2(26)(24) - 26 - 24]}{(26 + 24)^2(26 + 24 - 1)}}} = 0.58$$

Table C shows that a z of 0.58 is not significant at the $\alpha = 0.05$ level of significance. We are therefore unable to reject the null hypothesis that the sequence of gasoline purchases is in random order.

Exercises

10.1 In a large company, the last 15 promotions to top-level jobs were males and females in the following order: M FF MMMMM FFF MMM F. Test for randomness. Let $\alpha = 0.05$.

10.2 A sample of 60 consecutively produced bolts is selected from an assembly line and measured. The following are the deviations, in thousandths of an inch, of the lengths of the bolts from 3.000 inches: -5, 4, 2, -2, 3, 8, 4, 3, 3, 1, 4, 1, 1, 5, 3, -2, 6, 1, 3, -11, -10, 12, 5, 3, 7, 8, -9, 3, 3, -2, 10, -1, 4, -5, 6, -3, 1, 5, 3, 5, 3, -1, -5, 3, -7, -4, 4, -2, -1, -2, -1, 10, -5, -5, 5, -2, 1, -7, 4, 4. Divide the measurements on the basis of whether they are above or below 3.000 inches. Test for randomness. Let $\alpha = 0.05$.

10.3 Figure 9.9 shows the residuals resulting from the regression analysis of Example 9.1. They are -0.7, -11.5, $+6.1$, $+13.3$, -10.6, -4.2, $+15.2$, -9.6, $+7.5$, -5.5. Can we conclude from these data that the residuals are independent? Use the runs test to test for randomness in the sequence of plus and minus signs. Randomness is compatible with independence. Let $\alpha = 0.05$.

10.5 THE SIGN TEST

We often want to analyze two sets of data that are composed of measurements from two related samples. The data may be "before and after" scores for the same subject or scores for matched subjects that have been treated in different ways. When the necessary assumptions are met, we can analyze the data of two related samples by the parametric paired-comparisons test that is used to test null hypotheses about the mean difference in the two sets of observations. (See Chapter 7.)

When the assumptions underlying the parametric paired-comparisons test are not met, however, or when the observations are based on a weak measurement scale, we must use an alternative test. A simple nonparametric test that we can use is the *sign test*, which focuses on the median, rather than the mean, as a measure of central tendency. As we have seen, the median and mean coincide in symmetric distributions. Specifically, we use the sign test to test hypotheses about median differences, where we obtain differences by comparing various pairs of observations. Examples would be "before and after" scores made by the same subject or the two scores made by paired subjects. Let us call the values of one set of scores X_i and the values of the other set Y_i. We observe the differences $X_i - Y_i$. If $X_i > Y_i$, we record the difference as $+$. If $X_i < Y_i$, we record the difference as $-$. The test uses the resulting sample of pluses and minuses.

The Hypotheses

Perhaps the most common use of the sign test is to test the null hypothesis that the median difference is 0. This may be stated more compactly as follows:

$$H_0: P(X_i > Y_i) = P(X_i < Y_i) = 0.5$$

The null hypothesis states that a positive difference is as likely to occur as a negative one. In a random sample of pluses and minuses obtained by computing $X_i - Y_i$ for each pair of observations, then, we would expect about as many pluses as minuses when the null hypothesis is true. Alternatively, we can state the null hypothesis as

$$H_0: P(+) = P(-) = 0.5$$

We can think of obtaining a series of pluses and minuses in this manner as a binomial experiment with parameters n and p, where n is the number of pairs of observations and $p = 0.5$.

The Test Statistic

The test statistic for the sign test is either the observed number of plus signs or the observed number of minus signs. The nature of the alternative hypothesis determines which of these test statistics is appropriate.

In a given test, any one of the following alternative hypotheses is possible:

$$H_1: P(+) > P(-) \qquad \text{one-sided alternative}$$

$$H_1: P(+) < P(-) \qquad \text{one-sided alternative}$$

$$H_1: P(+) \neq P(-) \qquad \text{two-sided alternative}$$

If the alternative hypothesis is

$$H_1: P(+) > P(-)$$

a sufficiently large number of plus signs causes rejection of H_0. The test statistic is the number of plus signs. Suppose that the chosen level of significance is α. We reject H_0 if the probability (when H_0 is true) of obtaining as many plus signs as we actually obtain, or more, is equal to or less than α. Thus if $\alpha = 0.05$ and we observe 7 plus signs, we reject H_0 if the probability (when H_0 is true) of obtaining 7 or more plus signs is equal to or less than 0.05.

Similarly, if the alternative hypothesis is

$$H_1: P(+) < P(-)$$

a sufficiently large number of minus signs causes rejection of H_0. The test statistic is the number of minus signs.

If the alternative hypothesis is

$$H_1: P(+) \neq P(-)$$

either a sufficiently large number of plus signs or a sufficiently large number of minus signs causes rejection of the null hypothesis. We may take as the test statistic the more frequently occurring sign. For a two-sided test with a significance level α, we reject H_0 if the probability, when H_0 is true, of obtaining as many of the more frequently occurring sign as we actually obtained, or more, is equal to or less than $\alpha/2$.

If a difference $X_i - Y_i$ is equal to 0, we eliminate the pair from the sample and reduce the value of n accordingly.

EXAMPLE 10.3 The following experiment is designed to compare the effectiveness of two detergents in cleaning cotton fabric. Twelve pieces of fabric are uniformly soiled and then cut in half. One half of each piece is randomly assigned to be washed in Detergent A. The other half is washed in Detergent B. After the fabric specimens have been washed and dried, each piece is tested to determine the effectiveness of the detergent. We wish to know whether we can conclude, at the 0.05 level of significance, that the median difference is negative. The results are shown in Table 10.1.

SOLUTION

1. *Hypotheses*

H_0: The median of the differences is 0 $\qquad [P(+) = P(-)]$

H_1: The median of the differences is negative $\qquad [P(+) < P(-)]$

2. *Test statistic.* Since the alternative hypothesis is $P(+) < P(-)$, we have a one-sided test, and the test statistic is the number of minus signs.
3. *Significance level.* Let $\alpha = 0.05$.
4. *Decision rule.* Reject H_0 if the probability, when H_0 is true, of obtaining as many minus signs as we observe, or more, is ≤ 0.05.
5. *Calculations.* Table 10.1 shows one 0, which we eliminate from the analysis, and 9 minus signs.

TABLE 10.1
Results of experiment described in Example 10.3

Specimen	1	2	3	4	5	6	7	8	9	10	11	12
Detergent A (X)	9	8	7	9	7	7	7	8	7	9	7	8
Detergent B (Y)	8	10	8	8	9	9	8	10	9	9	8	9
Sign of (X_i − Y_i)	+	−	−	+	−	−	−	−	−	0	−	−

6. *Statistical decision.* We wish to know the probability of obtaining 9 or more minus signs when the probability of a minus sign is 0.5. That is, we wish to determine $P(k \geq 9|11, 0.5)$, where k is the test statistic, the number of minus signs. Appendix Table B shows this probability to be 0.0327. Since 0.0327 is less than 0.05, we reject H_0.

7. *Conclusion.* We conclude that the median of the differences is negative. The p value is 0.0327.

Large Samples

For samples of size 11 or larger, we can use the normal approximation to the binomial (recall Chapters 5, 6, and 7). The transformed test statistic is

$$z = \frac{(k \pm 0.5) - 0.5n}{0.5\sqrt{n}} \tag{10.2}$$

where k = the original test statistic, the number of plus or minus signs, whichever is appropriate. In Equation 10.2, $k + 0.5$ is used when $k < n/2$, and $k - 0.5$ is used when $k > n/2$. We compare the computed z with the appropriate z value from the standard normal distribution for significance.

The following example illustrates the use of Equation 10.2 with a large sample.

EXAMPLE 10.4 To investigate the effectiveness of different kinds of advertising, the market research department of a chain of discount stores conducts the following experiment in a random sample of 15 stores. During a certain week, automotive department specials are advertised by periodic announcements over the stores' loudspeaker systems. During the following week, automotive department specials are advertised by window displays and other storewide visual advertising. The variable of interest is total dollar sales volume for the automotive department during the week. Table 10.2 shows the results.

**TABLE 10.2
Dollar volume
of sales for
automotive
departments of 15
discount stores
under two
experimental
advertising
conditions**

Store number	Announcements (X)	Visual displays (Y)	Sign of $(X_i - Y_i)$
1	$4,127	$4,147	−
2	4,288	4,048	+
3	4,024	4,853	−
4	3,627	4,865	−
5	4,813	4,376	+
6	3,925	4,838	−
7	4,840	3,526	+
8	3,731	4,300	−
9	3,779	4,672	−
10	4,229	4,721	−
11	3,977	4,770	−
12	3,778	4,484	−
13	3,602	4,389	−
14	3,959	4,560	−
15	4,918	3,848	+

SOLUTION The hypotheses are as follows. Let $\alpha = 0.05$.

H_0: The median of the differences is 0 $[P(+) = P(-)]$

H_1: The median of the differences is not 0 $[P(+) \neq P(-)]$

By Equation 10.2, we compute

$$z = \frac{(11 - 0.5) - 0.5(15)}{0.5\sqrt{15}} = 1.55$$

Since the computed value of $z = 1.55 < 1.96$, we do not reject the null hypothesis. We conclude that the two methods of advertising may have equal effects $[p = 2(0.0606) = 0.1212]$.

Exercises

 10.4 A firm wants to study the effect of piped-in music on the productivity of employees. One department of a certain factory is selected at random to receive piped-in music for 30 working days. There are 10 employees in the department. The following table shows the average daily output for 30 days before the introduction of music and the average daily output for the 30 days during which music is piped into the department. Can we conclude from these data that music increases productivity? Let $\alpha = 0.05$. Determine the p value.

Employee	A	B	C	D	E	F	G	H	I	J
Before music	90	80	92	85	81	85	72	85	70	88
During music	99	85	98	83	88	99	80	91	80	94

 10.5 In a study designed to test the effect of packaging on consumer acceptance of a certain candy bar, 27 candy bars are wrapped in a colorful wrapper (Method A) and 27 identical candy bars are wrapped in a plain wrapper (Method B). Then 27 subjects are asked to eat one of each type of bar and indicate their preference. The following table shows the results. Let the event "A preferred over B" be designated by a plus, and the event "B preferred over A" by a minus. Test to see whether the data provide sufficient evidence to indicate that the candy bar packaged by Method A is preferred over the bar in the plain wrapper. Let $\alpha = 0.05$. Determine the p value. (n.p. = no preference)

Subject	Bar preferred	Subject	Bar preferred	Subject	Bar preferred	Subject	Bar preferred
1	A	8	A	15	n.p.	22	A
2	A	9	A	16	A	23	A
3	A	10	A	17	A	24	A
4	B	11	A	18	A	25	A
5	B	12	B	19	A	26	A
6	n.p.	13	A	20	A	27	B
7	A	14	A	21	B		

10.6 A consumer-affairs investigator conducts an experiment to probe the possibility of differential pricing by retail stores in a metropolitan area. At different times two subjects visit 12 retail stores in which prices are not posted. One subject projects the image of a member of the upper socioeconomic stratum of the area. The second subject projects the image of a member of the low socioeconomic stratum of the area. In 10 instances the upper socioeconomic subject is quoted a lower price. Do these data provide sufficient evidence to indicate that more than 50% of the sampled firms practice differential pricing? Let $\alpha = 0.05$, and determine the p value.

10.6 THE SPEARMAN RANK CORRELATION COEFFICIENT

When the assumptions underlying the parametric correlation coefficient introduced in Chapter 9 are not met, there are several measures of correlation that we can use. One of the simplest and most widely used is the *Spearman rank correlation coefficient,* designated by r_s. As the name implies, r_s is computed from data consisting of ranks. If the observations in their original form are not ranks, we can use the Spearman rank correlation coefficient as a measure of correlation if we can rank the observations according to magnitude from smallest to largest.

The data consist of a bivariate random sample of size n. One variable is designated X, and the ranks consist of 1 (the rank of the observation on X that is smallest in magnitude), 2, . . . , i, . . . , n (the rank of the observation on X that is largest). The other variable is designated Y and ranked 1, 2, . . . , i, . . . , n, according to the relative magnitude of the observations. Alternatively, we may assign the rank of 1 to the largest value of X (and Y), and so on to the rank of n, which we assign to the smallest value of X (and Y). The direction of the ranking is immaterial so long as we rank both X and Y in the same direction.

If the two rankings are perfectly and directly correlated, the rank of X_i will equal the rank of Y_i for all pairs of X_i, Y_i. If the rankings are perfectly and inversely correlated, the ranks of X will run from 1 to n and the matching ranks of Y will run from n to 1. That is, the order of the ranks of the Y_i will be the reverse of that of the X_i.

The Test Statistic

The Spearman rank correlation coefficient focuses on the differences between the ranks of each $(X_i \ Y_i)$ pair as a measure of the extent to which the paired rankings depart from perfect direct or inverse correlation. We call the difference between a pair of ranks d_i. We use the values of the d_i^2 in the computation of r_s, which is given by

$$r_s = 1 - \frac{6 \Sigma \, d_i^2}{n(n^2 - 1)}$$

(10.3)

The larger the differences between the ranks of X and Y, the larger will be Σd_i^2. If all the differences are 0, Σd_i^2 will equal 0, r_s will equal 1, and we consider the rankings perfectly and directly correlated. If we observe the maximum possible differences between the ranks of X and Y—that is, if the ranking of X is the reverse of the ranking of Y in each case—Σd_i^2 will be a maximum and r_s will equal -1. When the rankings are less than perfectly correlated, r_s will be somewhere between $+1$ and -1. Remember that r_s measures the strength of the association between ranks, not the values of the variates that have been ranked.

The Hypotheses

We can use the Spearman rank correlation coefficient to test any one of the following hypotheses:

TABLE 10.3
Scores of 15 employees evaluated by peers (X) and supervisors (Y)

Employee	1	2	3	4	5	6	7	8	9	10	11	12	13	14	15
Peers (X)	90	83	60	95	84	68	93	55	79	78	71	80	87	76	89
Supervisors (Y)	90	89	63	87	85	57	81	68	60	65	67	76	70	55	69

1. H_0: The X_i and Y_i are mutually independent
   H_1: Either large values of X_i tend to be paired with large values of Y_i or large values of X_i tend to be paired with small values of Y_i
2. H_0: The X_i and Y_i are mutually independent
   H_1: Large values of X_i tend to be paired with large values of Y_i
3. H_0: The X_i and Y_i are mutually independent
   H_1: Large values of X_i tend to be paired with small values of Y_i

The first pair of hypotheses specifies a two-sided test. The last two pairs specify one-sided tests. If we wish to know whether we can conclude that large values of X_i tend to be paired with small values of Y_i, we test the H_0 specified in 3. If we wish to know whether we can conclude that large values of X_i tend to be paired with large values of Y_i, we test the H_0 specified in 2. If we wish to detect a departure from independence in either direction, we test the H_0 specified in 1.

The procedure for testing r_s for significance depends on the sample size. If n is less than or equal to 30, we can consult Appendix Table H. Table H contains critical values of r_s for various values of α. For values of n greater than 30, we can compute the statistic

$$z = r_s \sqrt{n - 1} \qquad (10.4)$$

and compare it for significance with values of the standard normal distribution.

Ties may occur in the rankings of X, Y, or both. In such cases, the mean of the ranks that would have been assigned had no ties occurred is assigned to the tied ranks.

EXAMPLE 10.5 A random sample of 15 assembly-line employees of a large manufacturing firm are evaluated by their peers and their supervisors as to their congeniality and cooperativeness on the job. Table 10.3 shows the scores. The firm's personnel director wishes to know whether he can conclude that the two measures are directly correlated. Table 10.4 shows the resulting ranks.

TABLE 10.4
Fifteen employees ranked as to congeniality and cooperativeness by peers and supervisors

Employee	1	2	3	4	5	6	7	8	9	10	11	12	13	14	15
X rank	13	9	2	15	10	3	14	1	7	6	4	8	11	5	12
Y rank	15	14	4	13	12	2	11	7	3	5	6	10	9	1	8
d_i	-2	-5	-2	2	-2	1	3	-6	4	1	-2	-2	2	4	4
d_i^2	4	25	4	4	4	1	9	36	16	1	4	4	4	16	16

SOLUTION

1. *Hypotheses*

H_0: The X_i and Y_i are mutually independent

H_1: Large values of X_i tend to be paired with large values of Y_i

2. *Test statistic.* The test statistic is given by Equation 10.3.

3. *Significance level.* Let $\alpha = 0.05$.

4. *Decision rule.* Reject H_0 if the computed value of r_S is ≥ 0.4429.

5. *Calculations.* By Equation 10.3, we compute

$$r_S = 1 - \frac{6(148)}{15(15^2 - 1)} = 0.7357$$

6. *Statistical decision.* Table H indicates that the probability of obtaining a value of r_S as large as or larger than 0.7357 when the null hypothesis is true is less than 0.005. Therefore we reject the null hypothesis at the 0.05 level of significance.

7. *Conclusion.* We conclude that the two rankings are directly correlated ($0.005 > p > 0.001$).

Exercises

10.7 ©️ The personnel department of a large firm gives a test to 20 employees to measure their degree of job satisfaction. The following table gives the results, along with the employees' average daily production (in units) during the past year. Convert the original observations to ranks and test to see whether we can conclude that the two rankings are directly correlated. Let $\alpha = 0.05$. Find the *p* value.

Employee	1	2	3	4	5	6	7	8	9	10
Job satis. score	97	83	73	88	69	70	76	60	73	99
Ave. daily production	166	174	111	189	106	129	159	136	153	160
Employee	11	12	13	14	15	16	17	18	19	20
Job satis. score	97	62	87	89	98	93	85	79	64	85
Ave. daily production	165	121	166	169	189	161	195	145	138	174

10.8 ©️ A panel of 5 men and another panel of 5 women are asked to rank 10 ideas for a new television program on the basis of their relative appeal to a general audience. The results are shown in the following table. Test the null hypothesis that the rankings are mutually independent against the alternative that they are inversely correlated. Let $\alpha = 0.05$. Determine the *p* value.

Program idea	1	2	3	4	5	6	7	8	9	10
Men	6	4	8	7	2	1	3	5	9	10
Women	6	10	8	2	7	1	5	9	4	3

10.9 ©️ A panel of small-business experts ranks 15 small businesses on the basis of their employees' job-satisfaction scores and on the basis of growth potential of the businesses. The results are given in the following table. Can we conclude from these data that there is a direct relationship between employee satisfaction within a firm and that firm's growth potential? Let $\alpha = 0.01$. Find the *p* value.

Employee satisfaction	1	2	3	4	5	6	7	8	9	10	11	12	13	14	15
Potential for growth	6	3	1	2	4	5	11	10	7	8	12	9	14	13	15

10.10 Ⓒ The following table shows, for a random sample of college sophomores, grades made in a statistics course and the scores the students assigned the course on a course-evaluation form. Can we conclude from these data that the two variables are directly correlated? Let $\alpha = 0.05$. Find the p value.

Statistics grade	70	88	85	84	90	95
Course evaluation score	4	8	6	5	9	2

10.11 Ⓒ A random sample of 10 employees take part in a study to assess the relationship between the employees' scores on a job-aptitude test and their supervisors' evaluations of the employees' job performance. Compute r_s and test to determine whether the two variables are directly related. Let $\alpha = 0.05$. Find the p value. The data are as follows.

Aptitude score	13	41	72	24	57	100	84	36	92	63
Supervisors' evaluation	31	19	81	43	50	74	63	24	100	96

10.7 THE WILCOXON SIGNED-RANK TEST FOR LOCATION

Use the Wilcoxon test for hypotheses about μ when neither t nor z is appropriate.

Sometimes a business researcher wished to test a null hypothesis about a population mean, but for some reason cannot use either z or t as a test statistic. The z statistic may be ruled out, for example, because the researcher has a small (less than 30) sample from a population that is known to be grossly nonnormally distributed. Therefore the central limit theorem is not applicable. The t statistic may not work well because the sampled population does not sufficiently approximate a normal distribution. In such a situation, a possible alternative is to use a nonparametric procedure.

A nonparametric procedure that the researcher can often use for the one-sample case in which neither the z statistic nor the t statistic is appropriate is the *Wilcoxon signed-rank test for location*. This procedure is based on the following assumptions about the data.

The Assumptions

1. The sample is random.
2. The variable is continuous
3. The population is symmetrically distributed about its mean μ.
4. The measurement scale is at least interval.

The Hypotheses

Here are the null hypotheses about some unknown population mean μ_0 that may be tested, and their alternatives.

$$(a)\, H_0: \mu = \mu_0 \qquad (b)\, H_0: \mu \geq \mu_0 \qquad (c)\, H_0: \mu \leq \mu_0$$

$$H_1: \mu \neq \mu_0 \qquad\quad H_1: \mu < \mu_0 \qquad\quad H_1: \mu > \mu_0$$

The Calculations

The calculations involved in applying the Wilcoxon procedure are as follows.

1. Subtract the hypothesized mean μ_0 from each observation x_i, to obtain

$$d_i = x_i - \mu_0$$

If any x_i is equal to the mean, so that $d_i = 0$, eliminate it from the calculations and reduce n accordingly.

2. Rank the d_i from the smallest to the largest without regard to the sign of d_i. That is, consider only the absolute value of the d_i, designated by $|d_i|$, when ranking them. If two or more of the $|d_i|$ are equal, assign each tied value the mean of the rank positions the tied values occupy. If, for example, the three smallest $|d_i|$ are all equal, place them in rank positions 1, 2, and 3, but assign each a rank of $(1 + 2 + 3)/3 = 2$.

3. Assign each rank the sign of the d_i that yields that rank.

4. Find T_+, the sum of the ranks with positive signs, and T_-, the sum of the ranks with negative signs.

The Test Statistic

The test statistic is either T_+ or T_-, depending on the nature of the alternative hypothesis. To test for significance, enter Appendix Table I with the computed test statistic, the sample size n, and the chosen value of α. In Table I, the one-sided significance level is denoted by α' and the two-sided significance level by α''. If the test is two-sided, reject H_0 at the α level of significance if either T_+ or T_- (whichever has the smaller absolute value) is smaller than d for n and tabulated α (two-sided). If the alternative hypothesis is $H_1: \mu < \mu_0$, reject H_0 at the α level of significance if T_+ is less than d for n and tabulated α (one-sided). If the alternative hypothesis is $H_1: \mu > \mu_0$, reject H_0 at the α level of significance if T_- is less than d for n and tabulated α (one-sided).

The Rationale

Before we look at an example, let us consider the rationale underlying the Wilcoxon signed-rank test. Suppose that H_0 is true, that is, that the population mean μ is equal to the hypothesized mean μ_0. And suppose that the assumptions about the data are met. Then the probability of observing a positive difference d_i of a given magnitude is equal to the probability of observing a negative difference of the same magnitude. For a given sample, then, if H_0 is true, we would expect T_+ and T_- to be about equal. Therefore, a sufficiently small value of T_+ or a sufficiently small value of T_- (depending on the alternative hypothesis) will cause us to reject H_0.

The following example illustrates the use of the Wilcoxon signed-rank test.

EXAMPLE 10.6 A market analyst wants to know whether he can conclude, at the 0.05 level of significance, that the mean annual family income in a certain low-income area is less than \$15,000. Interviews with heads of household in a random sample of 20 families from the area yield the following incomes (in dollars per year): 8900, 9300, 10,100, 18,000, 10,300, 12,200, 7500, 9900, 11,200, 15,300, 17,200, 23,000, 12,500, 15,100, 14,900, 14,300, 16,200, 13,900, 15,000, and 18,000. The market analyst, who believes that the distribution of incomes in the area is symmetric, conducts the following hypothesis test.

SOLUTION

1. *Hypotheses*

$$H_0: \mu \geq \$15,000, \qquad H_1: \mu < \$15,000$$

2. *Test statistic.* Since the alternative is $\mu < \$15,000$, the test statistic is T_+.
3. *Significance level.* Let $\alpha = 0.05$.
4. *Decision rule.* Reject H_0 if the computed value of T_+ is smaller than the critical value.
5. *Calculations.* Table 10.5 gives the calculation of the test statistic.
6. *Statistical decision.* Reference to Table I, with $n = 19$ and $\alpha' = 0.052$, reveals that, since 57.5 is larger than 55, we cannot reject H_0 at the 0.05 level. In fact, for this test, $p > 0.052$.
7. *Conclusion.* We conclude, then, that the mean annual family income in the area may be \$15,000 or more.

TABLE 10.5
Calculation of the test statistic for Example 10.6

Annual family income (x_i)	$d_i = x_i - \mu_0$	Rank of $|d_i|$	Signed rank of $|d_i|$
8,900	−6,100	17	−17
9,300	−5,700	16	−16
10,100	−4,900	14	−14
18,000	+3,000	10.5	+10.5
10,300	−4,700	13	−13
12,200	−2,800	9	−9
7,500	−7,500	18	−18
9,900	−5,100	15	−15
11,200	−3,800	12	−12
15,300	+ 300	3	+3
17,200	+2,200	7	+7
23,000	+8,000	19	+19
12,500	−2,500	8	−8
15,100	+ 100	1.5	+1.5
14,900	− 100	1.5	−1.5
14,300	− 700	4	−4
16,200	+1,200	6	+6
13,900	−1,100	5	−5
15,000	0	Eliminate from analysis	
18,000	+3,000	10.5	+10.5
		$T_+ =$	57.5
		$T_- =$	132.5

The test statistic is $T_+ = 57.5$

Exercises

10.12 Ⓒ Sixteen laboratory animals are fed a special diet from birth through age twelve weeks. Their weight gains (in grams) are as follows: 64, 69, 80, 66, 65, 64, 66, 65, 77, 75, 67, 67, 68, 74, 70, 77. Can we conclude from these data that the diet results in a mean weight gain of less than 70 grams? Let $\alpha = 0.05$, and find the p value.

10.13 Ⓒ A psychologist selects a random sample of 25 handicapped assembly-line workers from among those employed at several factories of a large industry. Their manual dexterity scores are as follows: 32, 52, 21, 39, 23, 55, 36, 27, 37, 41, 34, 51, 51, 35, 46, 40, 31, 19, 41, 33, 52, 36, 34, 46, 41. Do these data provide sufficient evidence to indicate that the mean score for the population is not 45? Let $\alpha = 0.05$. Find the p value.

10.14 Ⓒ A population of adolescent laborers who dropped out of high school at age 16 has a mean reading comprehension score of 60. A random sample of 21 adolescents who ae still in school at age 16 make the following scores on the same test: 72, 62, 52, 57, 91, 78, 74, 67, 51, 62, 84, 59, 51, 57, 89, 64, 80, 72, 92, 64, 57. Do these data provide sufficient evidence to indicate that the mean score for adolescents still in school at age 16 is greater than that for dropouts employed as laborers? Let $\alpha = 0.05$. Find the p value.

10.8 THE MANN–WHITNEY TEST

Use the Mann–Whitney test with two independent samples when neither t nor z is appropriate.

Researchers sometimes have to test a null hypothesis about the difference between two location parameters under conditions that render both z and t inappropriate as test statistics. In such situations, researchers usually look for an appropriate nonparametric procedure. When the objective is to test for a significant difference between two location statistics computed from independent samples, the nonparametric procedure most often used is the *Mann–Whitney test*.

The test focuses on the median as the measure of location or central tendency. Recall that when a population is symmetric, the median and the mean are equal. Therefore, when the two sampled populations are symmetric, conclusions about their medians based on the Mann–Whitney test also apply to their means.

The Hypotheses

Let M_X = the median of population 1 and M_Y = the median of population 2. The following are the null hypotheses that may be tested, and their alternatives.

$$(a)\, H_0\!: M_X = M_Y, \qquad H_1\!: M_X \neq M_Y \qquad \text{Two-sided}$$

$$(b)\, H_0\!: M_X \geq M_Y, \qquad H_1\!: M_X < M_Y \qquad \text{One-sided}$$

$$(c)\, H_0\!: M_X \leq M_Y, \qquad H_1\!: M_X > M_Y \qquad \text{One-sided}$$

The Assumptions

The following are the assumptions underlying the Mann–Whitney test.

1. The samples have been randomly and independently drawn from their respective populations. Let $x_1, x_2, \ldots, x_{n_1}$ represent the sample values drawn from population 1, and let $y_1, y_2, \ldots, y_{n_2}$ represent the sample values drawn from population 2.

2. The variable of interest is continuous.

3. The measurement scale used is at least ordinal.

4. The distributions of the two sampled populations, if they differ at all, differ only with respect to location.

The Calculations

If the measurement scale for each sample is ordinal, you must be able to rank the observations of one sample with those of another when the two samples are combined as described below. In practice, you may need an interval scale in order for this to be possible.

   To compute the Mann–Whitney test statistic, combine the two samples and rank all sample observations from smallest to largest. Assign to tied observations the mean of the rank positions that they would have occupied had there been no ties. Then sum the ranks of the observations from population 1 (that is, the *X*'s). If the location parameter of population 1 is smaller than that of population 2, we expect (for equal sample sizes) the sum of the ranks for population 1 to be smaller than that for population 2. Similarly, if the location parameter of population 1 is larger than the location parameter of population 2, we expect the reverse to be true. The test statistic is based on this rationale. Depending on the null hypothesis, either a sufficiently small or a sufficiently large sum of ranks assigned to sample observations from population 1 causes us to reject the null hypothesis.

The Test Statistic

The test statistic is

$$T = S - \frac{n_1(n_1 + 1)}{2} \tag{10.5}$$

where S is the sum of the ranks assigned to the sample observations from population 1.

The Decision Rules

The appropriate decision rules for an α level of significance are as follows.

1. When we test $H_0: M_X = M_Y$, we reject H_0 for either a sufficiently small or a sufficiently large value of T. Therefore, we reject H_0 if the computed value of T is less than $W_{\alpha/2}$ or greater than $W_{1-\alpha/2}$, where $W_{\alpha/2}$ is the critical value of T given in Appendix Table J and $W_{1-\alpha/2}$ is given by

$$W_{1-\alpha/2} = n_1 n_2 - W_{\alpha/2} \tag{10.6}$$

2. When we test $H_0: M_X \geq M_Y$, we reject H_0 for sufficiently small values of T. We reject H_0 if the computed T is less than W_α, the critical value of T given in Table J for n_1, n_2, and α.

3. When we test $H_0: M_X \leq M_Y$, we reject H_0 for sufficiently large values of T. Therefore we reject H_0 if the computed T is greater than $W_{1-\alpha}$, where

$$W_{1-\alpha} = n_1 n_2 - W_\alpha \tag{10.7}$$

TABLE 10.6
Data for
Example 10.7

	Men's scores, X				Women's scores, Y	
18.50	17.00	12.40	25.00	19.10	15.00	18.00
14.00	16.00	15.20	23.00	18.75	21.00	18.25
20.00	12.50	12.50	16.20	21.10	18.50	24.00
19.00	12.00	19.25	19.75	17.50	17.25	18.30
19.50	10.00	11.00	20.00	17.75	16.30	19.20

In all cases, when we reject H_0, we conclude that H_1 is true. If we fail to reject H_0, we conclude that H_0 may be true. The following example illustrates the use of the Mann–Whitney test.

EXAMPLE 10.7 A researcher gives a random sample of 15 college men and an independent random sample of 20 college women a test to measure their knowledge of ecological issues. Table 10.6 shows the scores. We wish to know whether we can conclude on the basis of these data that the two populations of scores are different with respect to their medians. Let $\alpha = 0.05$.

SOLUTION

1. *Hypotheses*

$$H_0: M_X = M_Y, \qquad H_1: M_X \neq M_Y$$

2. *Test statistic.* Suppose that we are unwilling to assume that the populations are approximately normally distributed. In that case, t is not the appropriate test statistic. Since the sample sizes are small, we can't apply the central limit theorem. Therefore z is not a valid test statistic. We presume that the assumptions for the Mann–Whitney test statistic are met and use that procedure.

3. *Significance level.* Let $\alpha = 0.05$.

4. *Decision rule.* From Table J, $W_{\alpha/2} = 91$ for $n_1 = 15$, $n_2 = 20$, and $\alpha/2 = 0.025$. By Equation 10.6, we compute

$$W_{1-\alpha/2} = 15(20) - 91 = 209$$

We will reject H_0 if the computed value of T is either < 91 or > 209.

5. *Calculations.* Table 10.7 shows the scores of Table 10.6 in rank order, with the ranks attached. We see in Table 10.7 that $S = 186$. By Equation 10.5, then, the computed value of the test statistic is

$$T = 186 - \frac{15(15 + 1)}{2} = 66$$

6. *Statistical decision.* Since the computed value of the test statistic, $T = 66$, is less than 91, we reject H_0.

7. *Conclusion.* Since, for our present example, we reject H_0, we conclude that H_1 is true. That is, we conclude that the sampled populations of college men and women differ with respect to their medians when measuring knowledge of ecological issues.

TABLE 10.7
Data of Table 10.6 in rank order, with ranks attached

Men's scores, X	Ranks	Women's scores, Y	Ranks
10.00	1		
11.00	2		
12.00	3		
12.40	4		
12.50	5.5		
12.50	5.5		
14.00	7		
		15.00	8
15.20	9		
16.00	10		
		16.20	11
		16.30	12
17.00	13		
		17.25	14
		17.50	15
		17.75	16
		18.00	17
		18.25	18
		18.30	19
18.50	20.5	18.50	20.5
		18.75	22
19.00	23		
		19.10	24
		19.20	25
19.25	26		
19.50	27		
		19.75	28
20.00	29.5	20.00	29.5
		21.00	31
		21.10	32
		23.00	33
		24.00	34
		25.00	35
	Total = S = 186		

Finding p Values

Finding the p value in Table J can sometimes be tricky. The following example will help clarify the procedure.

Consider the two-sided test in which the computed value of the test statistic exceeds the largest value in Table J for $\alpha/2$, n_1, and n_2. Suppose that in our example the computed value of the test statistic had been 240. Since 240 exceeds $W_{1-\alpha/2} = (15)(20) - 91 = 209$, we would reject H_0. To find the one-sided p value, we would compute $T' = n_1 n_2 - T_0$, which for this example is $T' = (15)(20) - 240 = 60$. Since the probability, when the null hypothesis is true, of obtaining a value of the test statistic as small as 60 is 0.001, the one-sided p value is 0.001. The two-sided p value, then, would be 2(0.001) = 0.002. In the one-sided test in which the alternative hypothesis is $M_X > M_Y$, you may have to compute T' in order to determine the p value.

Since, for our present example, we reject H_0, we conclude that H_1 is true. That is, we conclude that the sampled populations of college men and women differ, on the average, with respect to knowledge of ecological issues.

Exercises   **10.15** Ⓒ A firm wishes to compare two methods of communicating information about a new product. Two groups of subjects are chosen to take part in an experiment. Subjects in the first group learn about the new product by Method A. Subjects in the second group learn about it by Method B. At the end of the experiment, each subject is given a test to measure knowledge of the new product. The results are shwn in the following table. Do these data provide sufficient evidence to indicate a difference in median scores among the two groups? Let $\alpha = 0.05$. Determine the p value.

Method A scores	50	59	60	71	80	81	80	78	72	77	73	75	75	77	76
Method B scores	52	54	58	78	65	69	61	60	72	60	59	65	69	68	65

  10.16 Ⓒ The following table gives the Brinell hardness numbers of specimens in random samples from two competing potential raw materials for a certain product. Can an investigator conclude that Material B has a higher Brinell hardness number, on the average, than Material A?

A	160	162	165	171	162	170	168	165	166	172	160	162	168	171	170
B	167	168	170	172	174	168	171	170	172	171	172	175	172	168	163	169

  10.17 Ⓒ The following table shows the monthly salaries of independent samples of 20 men and 20 women who do the same type of work. Do these data suggest that there is a difference in the median salaries for men and women who do this particular job? Let $\alpha = 0.05$. Determine the p value.

Men		Women	
$818	$954	$841	$886
942	946	795	955
963	881	887	983
893	788	836	970
819	863	892	894
941	891	875	877
935	749	960	763
865	847	934	767
840	902	771	961
973	965	715	800

  10.18 Ⓒ A team of industrial psychologists draws a sample of the records of those applicants for a certain job who have completed high school. They select an independent random sample of the records of applicants for the same job who were high school dropouts. The following table shows the emotional maturity test scores of the applicants in the two groups. Do these data provide sufficient evidence to indicate that the two sampled groups have different medians? Let $\alpha = 0.05$. Find the p value.

High school graduates				High school dropouts		
89	79	62	85	85	72	65
97	56	63	67	59	78	51
69	82	96	56	85	47	57
71	72	94	77	58	49	63
67	79	62		66	54	41
64	78	69		65	74	58
86	83	57		64	49	67

Summary

This chapter introduced a variety of statistical techniques that you may use under the following conditions:

1. When the assumptions underlying the parametric procedures, presented in previous chapters, are not met

2. When the data represent measurements on a weak measurement scale

3. When you need results in a hurry

4. When the hypothesis does not involve a parameter

You learned to test appropriate hypotheses using the following nonparametric procedures:

1. The one-sample runs test

2. The sign test

3. Spearman rank correlation

4. The Wilcoxon signed-rank test for location

5. The Mann–Whitney test

These procedures are characterized by either the fact that they do not depend on the form of the distribution from which the samples are drawn or the fact that the hypotheses tested are not statements about population parameters. Except for the runs test, the procedures presented in this chapter are nonparametric analogues of parametric procedures presented previously.

Review Questions

1. Define: **(a)** parametric statistics, **(b)** nonparametric statistics.

2. Under what conditions are nonparametric procedures used?

3. Define: **(a)** measurement, **(b)** nominal scale, **(c)** ordinal scale, **(d)** interval scale, **(e)** ratio scale.

4. List the advantages and disadvantages of nonparametric statistics.

5. Describe a situation from your area of interest in which each of the following nonparametric procedures could be used: **(a)** runs test, **(b)** sign test, **(c)** Spearman rank correlation, **(d)** Wilcoxon signed-rank test, **(e)** Mann–Whitney test. Use real or realistic data and carry out an appropriate hypothesis-testing procedure for each test.

6. A maker of sporting goods is testing a new material that can be used in the production of tennis balls. An attractive feature of the new material is the fact that it is less expensive than the material currently in use. To evaluate the new material, the company gives 15 expert tennis players a supply of balls made from both the new and the old materials. The players use each type of ball during 10 hours of practice. They then say which of the two they prefer. Twelve of the 15 players say that they prefer the balls made from the new material. Would you recommend that the company switch to the new material? Support your answer with an appropriate statistical analysis. Let $\alpha = 0.05$. Find the p value.

7. The desired mean length of a certain bolt produced in a factory is 80 mm. Slight random deviations from the desired mean are tolerable. Twenty consecutive bolts are measured, with the following results. Do these data provide sufficient evidence to indicate that deviations above and below the mean do not occur at random? Let $\alpha = 0.05$, and find the p value.

80.3	80.5	80.4	79.5	79.3	80.2	79.7	80.7	79.8	80.8
79.9	80.1	79.2	80.6	80.1	79.9	79.9	79.9	79.6	79.1

8. Each of 16 randomly selected homemakers in a small town is given a complimentary case of soft drinks for participating in a taste test. They have a choice of either "no-deposit, no-return" or returnable bottles. Thirteen choose the returnable bottles. Do these data provide sufficient evidence to indicate that homemakers in the town prefer soft drinks in returnable bottles? Let $\alpha = 0.05$, and find the p value.

9. © A market research team asks each member of a panel of consumers to guess the retail price of 16 small household items on the basis of a simple inspection of the items. The following table gives the actual retail price and the average prices guessed by members of the panel. Compute the rank-correlation coefficient between the average guessed price and the actual retail price. Test for significance. Let $\alpha = 0.01$, and determine the p value.

Item	Average guessed price	Actual retail price	Item	Average guessed price	Actual retail price
1	1.29	1.45	9	2.05	1.99
2	1.10	1.19	10	3.25	3.79
3	2.40	2.29	11	4.75	4.25
4	2.25	1.65	12	2.25	2.89
5	1.95	2.49	13	4.05	3.90
6	4.00	4.79	14	2.15	3.00
7	2.98	3.75	15	2.60	3.78
8	1.65	1.59	16	4.10	4.70

10. © Ten applicants for credit cards are ranked on their credit-risk potential by two officials (denoted X and Y) of the issuing bank. The results are given in the following table. Do these data suggest a lack of independence between the two officials' assessments of applicants' credit-risk potential? Let $\alpha = 0.05$, and find the p value.

Applicant	A	B	C	D	E	F	G	H	I	J
X	3	4	9	10	6	1	7	2	5	8
Y	5	3	7	9	6	2	8	4	1	10

11. © The following table shows data (in rank form) collected on 15 line managers with a large industrial firm. The X variable is the number of years of management experience. The Y variable is the quality of the managers' decision-making ability as assessed by their supervisors. Do these data provide sufficient evidence to indicate a lack of independence between the two variables? Let $\alpha = 0.01$, and determine the p value.

Rank of X	1	2	3	4.5	4.5	6	7	8	9.5	9.5	11	12	13	14	15
Rank of Y	3	2	1	7	8	5	4	6	14	15	12	9	10	11	13

12. © A random sample of 10 employees participates in a study to assess the relationship between scores on job aptitude tests and supervisors' evaluations of job performance. Compute r_S and perform a test to determine whether the two variables are directly related. Let $\alpha = 0.05$, and find the p value. The data are as follows.

Aptitude score	13	41	72	24	57	100	84	36	92	63
Supervisors' evaluation	31	19	81	43	50	74	63	24	100	96

13. © Select a simple random sample of size 20 from the population of employed heads of households in Appendix II. Use the rank correlation technique to see whether you can conclude that there is a direct relationship between age and annual salary. Let $\alpha = 0.05$, and find the p value. Compare your results with those of your classmates.

14. Ⓒ A team of research psychologists believes that male college students are more assertive than female college students. A random sample of $n_1 = 16$ college males made the following scores on a test designed to measure assertiveness (X): 22.3, 24.1, 28.9, 32.6, 29.3, 15.0, 39.9, 36.8, 21.3, 32.3, 27.0, 33.0, 25.5, 22.5, 33.3, 33.7. The scores (Y) made by a random sample of $n_2 = 19$ college females were: 18.1, 22.9, 10.0, 10.5, 19.1, 10.0, 10.0, 26.9, 12.5, 10.9, 19.1, 11.7, 14.6, 19.2, 11.4, 29.8, 33.4, 27.0, 25.3. Use the Mann–Whitney test to determine whether or not the psychologists are justified in their belief. Let $\alpha = 0.05$. Compute the p value. Higher scores indicate greater assertiveness.

15. Ⓒ At the end of a physical-fitness program, a random sample of 12 executives took a test to measure their endurance, with the following results: 936, 977, 891, 883, 844, 975, 978, 873, 945, 946, 826, 855. Can we conclude on the basis of these data that the population mean is not 900? Let $\alpha = 0.05$. Find the p value.

16. Select a simple random sample from the population of companies in Appendix III. (Ask your instructor how large the sample should be.) Formulate an appropriate hypothesis about the assets variable that can be tested by means of the Wilcoxon signed-rank test. Select a level of significance, carry out the seven-step hypothesis-testing procedure, and find the p value for the test.

17. Repeat Exercise 16 with the sales variable.

18. Repeat Exercise 16 with the market value variable.

19. Repeat Exercise 16 with the net profits variable.

20. Repeat Exercise 16 with the cash flow variable.

21. Repeat Exercise 16 with the number employed variable.

22. Select a simple random sample from the population of companies in Appendix III. (Ask your instructor how large the sample should be.) Formulate an appropriate hypothesis about assets and sales that can be tested by means of the Spearman rank correlation procedure. Choose a level of significance, carry out the seven-step hypothesis-testing procedure, and find the p value for the test.

23. Repeat Exercise 22 with assets and market value.

24. Repeat Exercise 22 with assets and net profits.

25. Repeat Exercise 22 with assets and cash flow.

26. Repeat Exercise 22 with assets and number employed.

27. Repeat Exercise 22 with sales and market value.

28. Repeat Exercise 22 with sales and net profits.

29. Repeat Exercise 22 with sales and cash flow.

30. Repeat Exercise 22 with sales and number employed.

31. Repeat Exercise 22 with market value and net profits.

32. Repeat Exercise 22 with market value and cash flow.

33. Repeat Exercise 22 with market value and number employed.

34. Repeat Exercise 22 with net profits and cash flow.

35. Repeat Exercise 22 with net profits and number employed.

36. Repeat Exercise 22 with cash flow and number employed.

PRACTICE WITH REAL DATA

1. Observe a sequence of 30 persons in some service line (a cafeteria line, for example). Test the null hypothesis that males and females occur in random order.

2. Select a random sample of American colleges and universities. For each, determine the size (number of students) and distance from a major metropolitan area (a city with a population of 100,000 or more, for example). Convert the data to ranks, compute the Spearman rank correlation coefficient, and make any inferences that you think are valid. Ask your reference librarian for help in locating the needed information and a list from which to select your sample.

- Experiment - process whereby we obtain info.
- Sample Space - all possible outcomes of an exper.
- Event - collection of 1 or more outcomes as a group
- Outcom - result of exper.
- Continuous Variable) - one that can assume any value w/in a specified interval
   EX. height
- Cluster Sample

Appendix I

85967	73152	14511	85285	36009	95892	36962	67835	63314	50162
07483	51453	11649	86348	76431	81594	95848	36738	25014	15460
96283	01898	61414	83525	04231	13604	75339	11730	85423	60698
49174	12074	98551	37895	93547	24769	09404	76548	05393	96770
97366	39941	21225	93629	19574	71565	33413	56087	40875	13351
90474	41469	16812	81542	81652	45554	27931	93994	22375	00953
28599	64109	09497	76235	41383	31555	12639	00619	22909	29563
25254	16210	89717	65997	82667	74624	36348	44018	64732	93589
28785	02760	24359	99410	77319	73408	58993	61098	04393	48245
84725	86576	86944	93296	10081	82454	76810	52975	10324	15457
41059	66456	47679	66810	15941	84602	14493	65515	19251	41642
67434	41045	82830	47617	36932	46728	71183	36345	41404	81110
72766	68816	37643	19959	57550	49620	98480	25640	67257	18671
92079	46784	66125	94932	64451	29275	57669	66658	30818	58353
29187	40350	62533	73603	34075	16451	42885	03448	37390	96328
74220	17612	65522	80607	19184	64164	66962	82310	18163	63495
03786	02407	06098	92917	40434	60602	82175	04470	78754	90775
75085	55558	15520	27038	25471	76107	90832	10819	56797	33751
09161	33015	19155	11715	00551	24909	31894	37774	37953	78837
75707	48992	64998	87080	39333	00767	45637	12538	67439	94914
21333	48660	31288	00086	79889	75532	28704	62844	92337	99695
65626	50061	42539	14812	48895	11196	34335	60492	70650	51108
84380	07389	87891	76255	89604	41372	10837	66992	93183	56920
46479	32072	80083	63868	70930	89654	05359	47196	12452	38234
59847	97197	55147	76639	76971	55928	36441	95141	42333	67483
31416	11231	27904	57383	31852	69137	96667	14315	01007	31929
82066	83436	67914	21465	99605	83114	97885	74440	99622	87912
01850	42782	39202	18582	46214	99228	79541	78298	75404	63648
32315	89276	89582	87138	16165	15984	21466	63830	30475	74729
59388	42703	55198	80380	67067	97155	34160	85019	03527	78140
58089	27632	50987	91373	07736	20436	96130	73483	85332	24384
61705	57285	30392	23660	75841	21931	04295	00875	09114	32101
18914	98982	60199	99275	41967	35208	30357	76772	92656	62318
11965	94089	34803	48941	69709	16784	44642	89761	66864	62803
85251	48111	80936	81781	93248	67877	16498	31924	51315	79921
66121	96986	84844	93873	46352	92183	51152	85878	30490	15974
53972	96642	24199	58080	35450	03482	66953	49521	63719	57615
14509	16594	78883	43222	23093	58645	60257	89250	63266	90858
37700	07688	65533	72126	23611	93993	01848	03910	38552	17472
85466	59392	72722	15473	73295	49759	56157	60477	83284	56367
52969	55863	42312	67842	05673	91878	82738	36563	79540	61935
42744	68315	17514	02878	97291	74851	42725	57894	81434	62041
26140	13336	67726	61876	29971	99294	96664	52817	90039	53211
95589	56319	14563	24071	06916	59555	18195	32280	79357	04224
39113	13217	59999	49952	83021	47709	53105	19295	88318	41626
41392	17622	18994	98283	07249	52289	24209	91139	30715	06604
54684	53645	79246	70183	87731	19185	08541	33519	07223	97413
89442	61001	36658	57444	95388	36682	38052	46719	09428	94012
36751	16778	54888	15357	68003	43564	90976	58904	40512	07725
98159	02564	21416	74944	53049	88749	02865	25772	89853	88714

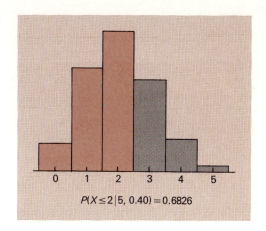

$$P(X \leq x | n, p) = \sum_{x=0}^{x} \binom{n}{x} p^x q^{n-x}$$

**TABLE B
Cumulative
binomial
probability
distribution**

# of successes x

	$n=5$									
x \\ p	0.01	0.02	0.03	0.04	0.05	0.06	0.07	0.08	0.09	0.10
0	0.9510	0.9039	0.8587	0.8154	0.7738	0.7339	0.6957	0.6591	0.6240	0.5905
1	0.9990	0.9962	0.9915	0.9852	0.9774	0.9681	0.9575	0.9456	0.9326	0.9185
2	1.0000	0.9999	0.9997	0.9994	0.9988	0.9980	0.9969	0.9955	0.9937	0.9914
3	1.0000	1.0000	1.0000	1.0000	1.0000	0.9999	0.9999	0.9998	0.9997	0.9995
4	1.0000	1.0000	1.0000	1.0000	1.0000	1.0000	1.0000	1.0000	1.0000	1.0000

x \\ p	0.11	0.12	0.13	0.14	0.15	0.16	0.17	0.18	0.19	0.20
0	0.5584	0.5277	0.4984	0.4704	0.4437	0.4182	0.3939	0.3707	0.3487	0.3277
1	0.9035	0.8875	0.8708	0.8533	0.8352	0.8165	0.7973	0.7776	0.7576	0.7373
2	0.9888	0.9857	0.9821	0.9780	0.9734	0.9682	0.9625	0.9563	0.9495	0.9421
3	0.9993	0.9991	0.9987	0.9983	0.9978	0.9971	0.9964	0.9955	0.9945	0.9933
4	1.0000	1.0000	1.0000	0.9999	0.9999	0.9999	0.9999	0.9998	0.9998	0.9997
5	1.0000	1.0000	1.0000	1.0000	1.0000	1.0000	1.0000	1.0000	1.0000	1.0000

x \\ p	0.21	0.22	0.23	0.24	0.25	0.26	0.27	0.28	0.29	0.30
0	0.3077	0.2887	0.2707	0.2536	0.2373	0.2219	0.2073	0.1935	0.1804	0.1681
1	0.7167	0.6959	0.6749	0.6539	0.6328	0.6117	0.5907	0.5697	0.5489	0.5282
2	0.9341	0.9256	0.9164	0.9067	0.8965	0.8857	0.8743	0.8624	0.8499	0.8369
3	0.9919	0.9903	0.9886	0.9866	0.9844	0.9819	0.9792	0.9762	0.9728	0.9692
4	0.9996	0.9995	0.9994	0.9992	0.9990	0.9988	0.9986	0.9983	0.9979	0.9976
5	1.0000	1.0000	1.0000	1.0000	1.0000	1.0000	1.0000	1.0000	1.0000	1.0000

x \\ p	0.31	0.32	0.33	0.34	0.35	0.36	0.37	0.38	0.39	0.40
0	0.1564	0.1454	0.1350	0.1252	0.1160	0.1074	0.0992	0.0916	0.0845	0.0778
1	0.5077	0.4875	0.4675	0.4478	0.4284	0.4094	0.3907	0.3724	0.3545	0.3370
2	0.8234	0.8095	0.7950	0.7801	0.7648	0.7491	0.7330	0.7165	0.6997	0.6826
3	0.9653	0.9610	0.9564	0.9514	0.9460	0.9402	0.9340	0.9274	0.9204	0.9130
4	0.9971	0.9966	0.9961	0.9955	0.9947	0.9940	0.9931	0.9921	0.9910	0.9898
5	1.0000	1.0000	1.0000	1.0000	1.0000	1.0000	1.0000	1.0000	1.0000	1.0000

TABLE B
(*continued*)

	$n=5$ (continued)									
x \ p	0.41	0.42	0.43	0.44	0.45	0.46	0.47	0.48	0.49	0.50
0	0.0715	0.0656	0.0602	0.0551	0.0503	0.0459	0.0418	0.0380	0.0345	0.0312
1	0.3199	0.3033	0.2871	0.2714	0.2562	0.2415	0.2272	0.2135	0.2002	0.1875
2	0.6651	0.6475	0.6295	0.6114	0.5931	0.5747	0.5561	0.5375	0.5187	0.5000
3	0.9051	0.8967	0.8879	0.8786	0.8688	0.8585	0.8478	0.8365	0.8247	0.8125
4	0.9884	0.9869	0.9853	0.9835	0.9815	0.9794	0.9771	0.9745	0.9718	0.9688
5	1.0000	1.0000	1.0000	1.0000	1.0000	1.0000	1.0000	1.0000	1.0000	1.0000

	$n=6$									
x \ p	0.01	0.02	0.03	0.04	0.05	0.06	0.07	0.08	0.09	0.10
0	0.9415	0.8858	0.8330	0.7828	0.7351	0.6899	0.6470	0.6064	0.5679	0.5314
1	0.9985	0.9943	0.9875	0.9784	0.9672	0.9541	0.9392	0.9227	0.9048	0.8857
2	1.0000	0.9998	0.9995	0.9988	0.9978	0.9962	0.9942	0.9915	0.9882	0.9841
3	1.0000	1.0000	1.0000	1.0000	0.9999	0.9998	0.9997	0.9995	0.9992	0.9987
4	1.0000	1.0000	1.0000	1.0000	1.0000	1.0000	1.0000	1.0000	1.0000	0.9999
5	1.0000	1.0000	1.0000	1.0000	1.0000	1.0000	1.0000	1.0000	1.0000	1.0000

x \ p	0.11	0.12	0.13	0.14	0.15	0.16	0.17	0.18	0.19	0.20
0	0.4970	0.4644	0.4336	0.4046	0.3771	0.3513	0.3269	0.3040	0.2824	0.2621
1	0.8655	0.8444	0.8224	0.7997	0.7765	0.7528	0.7287	0.7044	0.6799	0.6554
2	0.9794	0.9739	0.9676	0.9605	0.9527	0.9440	0.9345	0.9241	0.9130	0.9011
3	0.9982	0.9975	0.9966	0.9955	0.9941	0.9925	0.9906	0.9884	0.9859	0.9830
4	0.9999	0.9999	0.9998	0.9997	0.9996	0.9995	0.9993	0.9990	0.9987	0.9984
5	1.0000	1.0000	1.0000	1.0000	1.0000	1.0000	1.0000	1.0000	1.0000	0.9999
6	1.0000	1.0000	1.0000	1.0000	1.0000	1.0000	1.0000	1.0000	1.0000	1.0000

x \ p	0.21	0.22	0.23	0.24	0.25	0.26	0.27	0.28	0.29	0.30
0	0.2431	0.2252	0.2084	0.1927	0.1780	0.1642	0.1513	0.1393	0.1281	0.1176
1	0.6308	0.6063	0.5820	0.5578	0.5339	0.5104	0.4872	0.4644	0.4420	0.4202
2	0.8885	0.8750	0.8609	0.8461	0.8306	0.8144	0.7977	0.7804	0.7626	0.7443
3	0.9798	0.9761	0.9720	0.9674	0.9624	0.9569	0.9508	0.9443	0.9372	0.9295
4	0.9980	0.9975	0.9969	0.9962	0.9954	0.9944	0.9933	0.9921	0.9907	0.9891
5	0.9999	0.9999	0.9999	0.9998	0.9998	0.9997	0.9996	0.9995	0.9994	0.9993
6	1.0000	1.0000	1.0000	1.0000	1.0000	1.0000	1.0000	1.0000	1.0000	1.0000

x \ p	0.31	0.32	0.33	0.34	0.35	0.36	0.37	0.38	0.39	0.40
0	0.1079	0.0989	0.0905	0.0827	0.0754	0.0687	0.0625	0.0568	0.0515	0.0467
1	0.3988	0.3780	0.3578	0.3381	0.3191	0.3006	0.2828	0.2657	0.2492	0.2333
2	0.7256	0.7064	0.6870	0.6672	0.6471	0.6268	0.6063	0.5857	0.5650	0.5443
3	0.9213	0.9125	0.9031	0.8931	0.8826	0.8714	0.8596	0.8473	0.8343	0.8208
4	0.9873	0.9852	0.9830	0.9805	0.9777	0.9746	0.9712	0.9675	0.9635	0.9590
5	0.9991	0.9989	0.9987	0.9985	0.9982	0.9978	0.9974	0.9970	0.9965	0.9959
6	1.0000	1.0000	1.0000	1.0000	1.0000	1.0000	1.0000	1.0000	1.0000	1.0000

x \ p	0.41	0.42	0.43	0.44	0.45	0.46	0.47	0.48	0.49	0.50
0	0.0422	0.0381	0.0343	0.0308	0.0277	0.0248	0.0222	0.0198	0.0176	0.0156
1	0.2181	0.2035	0.1895	0.1762	0.1636	0.1515	0.1401	0.1293	0.1190	0.1094
2	0.5236	0.5029	0.4823	0.4618	0.4415	0.4214	0.4015	0.3820	0.3627	0.3437

TABLE B
(*continued*)

	$n=6$ (continued)									
x \ p	0.41	0.42	0.43	0.44	0.45	0.46	0.47	0.48	0.49	0.50
3	0.8067	0.7920	0.7768	0.7610	0.7447	0.7280	0.7107	0.6930	0.6748	0.6562
4	0.9542	0.9490	0.9434	0.9373	0.9308	0.9238	0.9163	0.9083	0.8997	0.8906
5	0.9952	0.9945	0.9937	0.9927	0.9917	0.9905	0.9892	0.9878	0.9862	0.9844
6	1.0000	1.0000	1.0000	1.0000	1.0000	1.0000	1.0000	1.0000	1.0000	1.0000

	$n=7$									
x \ p	0.01	0.02	0.03	0.04	0.05	0.06	0.07	0.08	0.09	0.10
0	0.9321	0.8681	0.8080	0.7514	0.6983	0.6485	0.6017	0.5578	0.5168	0.4783
1	0.9980	0.9921	0.9829	0.9706	0.9556	0.9382	0.9187	0.8974	0.8745	0.8503
2	1.0000	0.9997	0.9991	0.9980	0.9962	0.9937	0.9903	0.9860	0.9807	0.9743
3	1.0000	1.0000	1.0000	0.9999	0.9998	0.9996	0.9993	0.9988	0.9982	0.9973
4	1.0000	1.0000	1.0000	1.0000	1.0000	1.0000	1.0000	0.9999	0.9999	0.9998
5	1.0000	1.0000	1.0000	1.0000	1.0000	1.0000	1.0000	1.0000	1.0000	1.0000

x \ p	0.11	0.12	0.13	0.14	0.15	0.16	0.17	0.18	0.19	0.20
0	0.4423	0.4087	0.3773	0.3479	0.3206	0.2951	0.2714	0.2493	0.2288	0.2097
1	0.8250	0.7988	0.7719	0.7444	0.7166	0.6885	0.6604	0.6323	0.6044	0.5767
2	0.9669	0.9584	0.9487	0.9380	0.9262	0.9134	0.8995	0.8846	0.8687	0.8520
3	0.9961	0.9946	0.9928	0.9906	0.9879	0.9847	0.9811	0.9769	0.9721	0.9667
4	0.9997	0.9996	0.9994	0.9991	0.9988	0.9983	0.9978	0.9971	0.9963	0.9953
5	1.0000	1.0000	1.0000	1.0000	0.9999	0.9999	0.9999	0.9998	0.9997	0.9996
6	1.0000	1.0000	1.0000	1.0000	1.0000	1.0000	1.0000	1.0000	1.0000	1.0000

x \ p	0.21	0.22	0.23	0.24	0.25	0.26	0.27	0.28	0.29	0.30
0	0.1920	0.1757	0.1605	0.1465	0.1335	0.1215	0.1105	0.1003	0.0910	0.0824
1	0.5494	0.5225	0.4960	0.4702	0.4449	0.4204	0.3965	0.3734	0.3510	0.3294
2	0.8343	0.8159	0.7967	0.7769	0.7564	0.7354	0.7139	0.6919	0.6696	0.6471
3	0.9606	0.9539	0.9464	0.9383	0.9294	0.9198	0.9095	0.8984	0.8866	0.8740
4	0.9942	0.9928	0.9912	0.9893	0.9871	0.9847	0.9819	0.9787	0.9752	0.9712
5	0.9995	0.9994	0.9992	0.9989	0.9987	0.9983	0.9979	0.9974	0.9969	0.9962
6	1.0000	1.0000	1.0000	1.0000	0.9999	0.9999	0.9999	0.9999	0.9998	0.9998
7	1.0000	1.0000	1.0000	1.0000	1.0000	1.0000	1.0000	1.0000	1.0000	1.0000

x \ p	0.31	0.32	0.33	0.34	0.35	0.36	0.37	0.38	0.39	0.40
0	0.0745	0.0672	0.0606	0.0546	0.0490	0.0440	0.0394	0.0352	0.0314	0.0280
1	0.3086	0.2887	0.2696	0.2513	0.2338	0.2172	0.2013	0.1863	0.1721	0.1586
2	0.6243	0.6013	0.5783	0.5553	0.5323	0.5094	0.4866	0.4641	0.4419	0.4199
3	0.8606	0.8466	0.8318	0.8163	0.8002	0.7833	0.7659	0.7479	0.7293	0.7102
4	0.9668	0.9620	0.9566	0.9508	0.9444	0.9375	0.9299	0.9218	0.9131	0.9037
5	0.9954	0.9945	0.9935	0.9923	0.9910	0.9895	0.9877	0.9858	0.9836	0.9812
6	0.9997	0.9997	0.9996	0.9995	0.9994	0.9992	0.9991	0.9989	0.9986	0.9984
7	1.0000	1.0000	1.0000	1.0000	1.0000	1.0000	1.0000	1.0000	1.0000	1.0000

x \ p	0.41	0.42	0.43	0.44	0.45	0.46	0.47	0.48	0.49	0.50
0	0.0249	0.0221	0.0195	0.0173	0.0152	0.0134	0.0117	0.0103	0.0090	0.0078
1	0.1459	0.1340	0.1228	0.1123	0.1024	0.0932	0.0847	0.0767	0.0693	0.0625

TABLE B
(*continued*)

	$n=7$ (continued)									

x \ p	0.41	0.42	0.43	0.44	0.45	0.46	0.47	0.48	0.49	0.50
2	0.3983	0.3771	0.3564	0.3362	0.3164	0.2973	0.2787	0.2607	0.2433	0.2266
3	0.6906	0.6706	0.6502	0.6294	0.6083	0.5869	0.5654	0.5437	0.5219	0.5000
4	0.8937	0.8831	0.8718	0.8598	0.8471	0.8337	0.8197	0.8049	0.7895	0.7734
5	0.9784	0.9754	0.9721	0.9684	0.9643	0.9598	0.9549	0.9496	0.9438	0.9375
6	0.9981	0.9977	0.9973	0.9968	0.9963	0.9956	0.9949	0.9941	0.9932	0.9922
7	1.0000	1.0000	1.0000	1.0000	1.0000	1.0000	1.0000	1.0000	1.0000	1.0000

	$n=8$									

x \ p	0.01	0.02	0.03	0.04	0.05	0.06	0.07	0.08	0.09	0.10
0	0.9227	0.8508	0.7837	0.7214	0.6634	0.6096	0.5596	0.5132	0.4703	0.4305
1	0.9973	0.9897	0.9777	0.9619	0.9428	0.9208	0.8965	0.8702	0.8423	0.8131
2	0.9999	0.9996	0.9987	0.9969	0.9942	0.9904	0.9853	0.9789	0.9711	0.9619
3	1.0000	1.0000	0.9999	0.9998	0.9996	0.9993	0.9987	0.9978	0.9966	0.9950
4	1.0000	1.0000	1.0000	1.0000	1.0000	1.0000	0.9999	0.9999	0.9997	0.9996
5	1.0000	1.0000	1.0000	1.0000	1.0000	1.0000	1.0000	1.0000	1.0000	1.0000

x \ p	0.11	0.12	0.13	0.14	0.15	0.16	0.17	0.18	0.19	0.20
0	0.3937	0.3596	0.3282	0.2992	0.2725	0.2479	0.2252	0.2044	0.1853	0.1678
1	0.7829	0.7520	0.7206	0.6889	0.6572	0.6256	0.5943	0.5634	0.5330	0.5033
2	0.9513	0.9392	0.9257	0.9109	0.8948	0.8774	0.8588	0.8392	0.8185	0.7969
3	0.9929	0.9903	0.9871	0.9832	0.9786	0.9733	0.9672	0.9603	0.9524	0.9437
4	0.9993	0.9990	0.9985	0.9979	0.9971	0.9962	0.9950	0.9935	0.9917	0.9896
5	1.0000	0.9999	0.9999	0.9998	0.9998	0.9997	0.9995	0.9993	0.9991	0.9988
6	1.0000	1.0000	1.0000	1.0000	1.0000	1.0000	1.0000	1.0000	0.9999	0.9999
7	1.0000	1.0000	1.0000	1.0000	1.0000	1.0000	1.0000	1.0000	1.0000	1.0000

x \ p	0.21	0.22	0.23	0.24	0.25	0.26	0.27	0.28	0.29	0.30
0	0.1517	0.1370	0.1236	0.1113	0.1001	0.0899	0.0806	0.0722	0.0646	0.0576
1	0.4743	0.4462	0.4189	0.3925	0.3671	0.3427	0.3193	0.2969	0.2756	0.2553
2	0.7745	0.7514	0.7276	0.7033	0.6785	0.6535	0.6282	0.6027	0.5772	0.5518
3	0.9341	0.9235	0.9120	0.8996	0.8862	0.8719	0.8567	0.8406	0.8237	0.8059
4	0.9871	0.9842	0.9809	0.9770	0.9727	0.9678	0.9623	0.9562	0.9495	0.9420
5	0.9984	0.9979	0.9973	0.9966	0.9958	0.9948	0.9936	0.9922	0.9906	0.9887
6	0.9999	0.9998	0.9998	0.9997	0.9996	0.9995	0.9994	0.9992	0.9990	0.9987
7	1.0000	1.0000	1.0000	1.0000	1.0000	1.0000	1.0000	1.0000	0.9999	0.9999
8	1.0000	1.0000	1.0000	1.0000	1.0000	1.0000	1.0000	1.0000	1.0000	1.0000

x \ p	0.31	0.32	0.33	0.34	0.35	0.36	0.37	0.38	0.39	0.40
0	0.0514	0.0457	0.0406	0.0360	0.0319	0.0281	0.0248	0.0218	0.0192	0.0168
1	0.2360	0.2178	0.2006	0.1844	0.1691	0.1548	0.1414	0.1289	0.1172	0.1064
2	0.5264	0.5013	0.4764	0.4519	0.4278	0.4042	0.3811	0.3585	0.3366	0.3154
3	0.7874	0.7681	0.7481	0.7276	0.7064	0.6847	0.6626	0.6401	0.6172	0.5941
4	0.9339	0.9250	0.9154	0.9051	0.8939	0.8820	0.8693	0.8557	0.8414	0.8263
5	0.9866	0.9841	0.9813	0.9782	0.9747	0.9707	0.9664	0.9615	0.9561	0.9502
6	0.9984	0.9980	0.9976	0.9970	0.9964	0.9957	0.9949	0.9939	0.9928	0.9915
7	0.9999	0.9999	0.9999	0.9998	0.9998	0.9997	0.9996	0.9996	0.9995	0.9993
8	1.0000	1.0000	1.0000	1.0000	1.0000	1.0000	1.0000	1.0000	1.0000	1.0000

$n = 8$ (continued)

x \ p	0.41	0.42	0.43	0.44	0.45	0.46	0.47	0.48	0.49	0.50
0	0.0147	0.0128	0.0111	0.0097	0.0084	0.0072	0.0062	0.0053	0.0046	0.0039
1	0.0963	0.0870	0.0784	0.0705	0.0632	0.0565	0.0504	0.0448	0.0398	0.0352
2	0.2948	0.2750	0.2560	0.2376	0.2201	0.2034	0.1875	0.1724	0.1581	0.1445
3	0.5708	0.5473	0.5238	0.5004	0.4770	0.4537	0.4306	0.4078	0.3854	0.3633
4	0.8105	0.7938	0.7765	0.7584	0.7396	0.7202	0.7001	0.6795	0.6584	0.6367
5	0.9437	0.9366	0.9289	0.9206	0.9115	0.9018	0.8914	0.8802	0.8682	0.8555
6	0.9900	0.9883	0.9864	0.9843	0.9819	0.9792	0.9761	0.9728	0.9690	0.9648
7	0.9992	0.9990	0.9988	0.9986	0.9983	0.9980	0.9976	0.9972	0.9967	0.9961
8	1.0000	1.0000	1.0000	1.0000	1.0000	1.0000	1.0000	1.0000	1.0000	1.0000

$n = 9$

x \ p	0.01	0.02	0.03	0.04	0.05	0.06	0.07	0.08	0.09	0.10
0	0.9135	0.8337	0.7602	0.6925	0.6302	0.5730	0.5204	0.4722	0.4279	0.3874
1	0.9966	0.9869	0.9718	0.9522	0.9288	0.9022	0.8729	0.8417	0.8088	0.7748
2	0.9999	0.9994	0.9980	0.9955	0.9916	0.9862	0.9791	0.9702	0.9595	0.9470
3	1.0000	1.0000	0.9999	0.9997	0.9994	0.9987	0.9977	0.9963	0.9943	0.9917
4	1.0000	1.0000	1.0000	1.0000	1.0000	0.9999	0.9998	0.9997	0.9995	0.9991
5	1.0000	1.0000	1.0000	1.0000	1.0000	1.0000	1.0000	1.0000	1.0000	0.9999
6	1.0000	1.0000	1.0000	1.0000	1.0000	1.0000	1.0000	1.0000	1.0000	1.0000

x \ p	0.11	0.12	0.13	0.14	0.15	0.16	0.17	0.18	0.19	0.20
0	0.3504	0.3165	0.2855	0.2573	0.2316	0.2082	0.1869	0.1676	0.1501	0.1342
1	0.7401	0.7049	0.6696	0.6343	0.5995	0.5652	0.5315	0.4988	0.4670	0.4362
2	0.9327	0.9167	0.8991	0.8798	0.8591	0.8371	0.8139	0.7895	0.7643	0.7382
3	0.9883	0.9842	0.9791	0.9731	0.9661	0.9580	0.9488	0.9385	0.9270	0.9144
4	0.9986	0.9979	0.9970	0.9959	0.9944	0.9925	0.9902	0.9875	0.9842	0.9804
5	0.9999	0.9998	0.9997	0.9996	0.9994	0.9991	0.9987	0.9983	0.9977	0.9969
6	1.0000	1.0000	1.0000	1.0000	1.0000	0.9999	0.9999	0.9998	0.9998	0.9997
7	1.0000	1.0000	1.0000	1.0000	1.0000	1.0000	1.0000	1.0000	1.0000	1.0000

x \ p	0.21	0.22	0.23	0.24	0.25	0.26	0.27	0.28	0.29	0.30
0	0.1199	0.1069	0.0952	0.0846	0.0751	0.0665	0.0589	0.0520	0.0458	0.0404
1	0.4066	0.3782	0.3509	0.3250	0.3003	0.2770	0.2548	0.2340	0.2144	0.1960
2	0.7115	0.6842	0.6566	0.6287	0.6007	0.5727	0.5448	0.5171	0.4898	0.4628
3	0.9006	0.8856	0.8696	0.8525	0.8343	0.8151	0.7950	0.7740	0.7522	0.7297
4	0.9760	0.9709	0.9650	0.9584	0.9511	0.9429	0.9338	0.9238	0.9130	0.9012
5	0.9960	0.9949	0.9935	0.9919	0.9900	0.9878	0.9851	0.9821	0.9787	0.9747
6	0.9996	0.9994	0.9992	0.9990	0.9987	0.9983	0.9978	0.9972	0.9965	0.9957
7	1.0000	1.0000	0.9999	0.9999	0.9999	0.9999	0.9998	0.9997	0.9997	0.9996
8	1.0000	1.0000	1.0000	1.0000	1.0000	1.0000	1.0000	1.0000	1.0000	1.0000

x \ p	0.31	0.32	0.33	0.34	0.35	0.36	0.37	0.38	0.39	0.40
0	0.0355	0.0311	0.0272	0.0238	0.0207	0.0180	0.0156	0.0135	0.0117	0.0101
1	0.1788	0.1628	0.1478	0.1339	0.1211	0.1092	0.0983	0.0882	0.0790	0.0705
2	0.4364	0.4106	0.3854	0.3610	0.3373	0.3144	0.2924	0.2713	0.2511	0.2318
3	0.7065	0.6827	0.6585	0.6338	0.6089	0.5837	0.5584	0.5331	0.5078	0.4826
4	0.8885	0.8748	0.8602	0.8447	0.8283	0.8110	0.7928	0.7738	0.7540	0.7334
5	0.9702	0.9652	0.9596	0.9533	0.9464	0.9388	0.9304	0.9213	0.9114	0.9006
6	0.9947	0.9936	0.9922	0.9906	0.9888	0.9867	0.9843	0.9816	0.9785	0.9750

TABLE B
(continued)

					$n=9$ (continued)					

x \ p	0.31	0.32	0.33	0.34	0.35	0.36	0.37	0.38	0.39	0.40
7	0.9994	0.9993	0.9991	0.9989	0.9986	0.9983	0.9979	0.9974	0.9969	0.9962
8	1.0000	1.0000	1.0000	0.9999	0.9999	0.9999	0.9999	0.9998	0.9998	0.9997
9	1.0000	1.0000	1.0000	1.0000	1.0000	1.0000	1.0000	1.0000	1.0000	1.0000

x \ p	0.41	0.42	0.43	0.44	0.45	0.46	0.47	0.48	0.49	0.50
0	0.0087	0.0074	0.0064	0.0054	0.0046	0.0039	0.0033	0.0028	0.0023	0.0020
1	0.0628	0.0558	0.0495	0.0437	0.0385	0.0338	0.0296	0.0259	0.0225	0.0195
2	0.2134	0.1961	0.1796	0.1641	0.1495	0.1358	0.1231	0.1111	0.1001	0.0898
3	0.4576	0.4330	0.4087	0.3848	0.3614	0.3386	0.3164	0.2948	0.2740	0.2539
4	0.7122	0.6903	0.6678	0.6449	0.6214	0.5976	0.5735	0.5491	0.5246	0.5000
5	0.8891	0.8767	0.8634	0.8492	0.8342	0.8183	0.8015	0.7839	0.7654	0.7461
6	0.9710	0.9666	0.9617	0.9563	0.9502	0.9436	0.9363	0.9283	0.9196	0.9102
7	0.9954	0.9945	0.9935	0.9923	0.9909	0.9893	0.9875	0.9855	0.9831	0.9805
8	0.9997	0.9996	0.9995	0.9994	0.9992	0.9991	0.9989	0.9986	0.9984	0.9980
9	1.0000	1.0000	1.0000	1.0000	1.0000	1.0000	1.0000	1.0000	1.0000	1.0000

					$n=10$					

x \ p	0.01	0.02	0.03	0.04	0.05	0.06	0.07	0.08	0.09	0.10
0	0.9044	0.8171	0.7374	0.6648	0.5987	0.5386	0.4840	0.4344	0.3894	0.3487
1	0.9957	0.9838	0.9655	0.9418	0.9139	0.8824	0.8483	0.8121	0.7746	0.7361
2	0.9999	0.9991	0.9972	0.9938	0.9885	0.9812	0.9717	0.9599	0.9460	0.9298
3	1.0000	1.0000	0.9999	0.9996	0.9990	0.9980	0.9964	0.9942	0.9912	0.9872
4	1.0000	1.0000	1.0000	1.0000	0.9999	0.9998	0.9997	0.9994	0.9990	0.9984
5	1.0000	1.0000	1.0000	1.0000	1.0000	1.0000	1.0000	1.0000	0.9999	0.9999
6	1.0000	1.0000	1.0000	1.0000	1.0000	1.0000	1.0000	1.0000	1.0000	1.0000

x \ p	0.11	0.12	0.13	0.14	0.15	0.16	0.17	0.18	0.19	0.20
0	0.3118	0.2785	0.2484	0.2213	0.1969	0.1749	0.1552	0.1374	0.1216	0.1074
1	0.6972	0.6583	0.6196	0.5816	0.5443	0.5080	0.4730	0.4392	0.4068	0.3758
2	0.9116	0.8913	0.8692	0.8455	0.8202	0.7936	0.7659	0.7372	0.7078	0.6778
3	0.9822	0.9761	0.9687	0.9600	0.9500	0.9386	0.9259	0.9117	0.8961	0.8791
4	0.9975	0.9963	0.9947	0.9927	0.9901	0.9870	0.9832	0.9787	0.9734	0.9672
5	0.9997	0.9996	0.9994	0.9990	0.9986	0.9980	0.9973	0.9963	0.9951	0.9936
6	1.0000	1.0000	0.9999	0.9999	0.9999	0.9998	0.9997	0.9996	0.9994	0.9991
7	1.0000	1.0000	1.0000	1.0000	1.0000	1.0000	1.0000	1.0000	0.9999	0.9999
8	1.0000	1.0000	1.0000	1.0000	1.0000	1.0000	1.0000	1.0000	1.0000	1.0000

x \ p	0.21	0.22	0.23	0.24	0.25	0.26	0.27	0.28	0.29	0.30
0	0.0947	0.0834	0.0733	0.0643	0.0563	0.0492	0.0430	0.0374	0.0326	0.0282
1	0.3464	0.3185	0.2921	0.2673	0.2440	0.2222	0.2019	0.1830	0.1655	0.1493
2	0.6474	0.6169	0.5863	0.5558	0.5256	0.4958	0.4665	0.4378	0.4099	0.3828
3	0.8609	0.8413	0.8206	0.7988	0.7759	0.7521	0.7274	0.7021	0.6761	0.6496
4	0.9601	0.9521	0.9431	0.9330	0.9219	0.9096	0.8963	0.8819	0.8663	0.8497
5	0.9918	0.9896	0.9870	0.9839	0.9803	0.9761	0.9713	0.9658	0.9596	0.9527
6	0.9988	0.9984	0.9979	0.9973	0.9965	0.9955	0.9944	0.9930	0.9913	0.9894
7	0.9999	0.9998	0.9998	0.9997	0.9996	0.9994	0.9993	0.9990	0.9988	0.9984
8	1.0000	1.0000	1.0000	1.0000	1.0000	1.0000	0.9999	0.9999	0.9999	0.9999
9	1.0000	1.0000	1.0000	1.0000	1.0000	1.0000	1.0000	1.0000	1.0000	1.0000

TABLE B
(continued)

n = 10 (continued)

x \ p	0.31	0.32	0.33	0.34	0.35	0.36	0.37	0.38	0.39	0.40
0	0.0245	0.0211	0.0182	0.0157	0.0135	0.0115	0.0098	0.0084	0.0071	0.0060
1	0.1344	0.1206	0.1080	0.0965	0.0860	0.0764	0.0677	0.0598	0.0527	0.0464
2	0.3566	0.3313	0.3070	0.2838	0.2616	0.2405	0.2206	0.2017	0.1840	0.1673
3	0.6228	0.5956	0.5684	0.5411	0.5138	0.4868	0.4600	0.4336	0.4077	0.3823
4	0.8321	0.8133	0.7936	0.7730	0.7515	0.7292	0.7061	0.6823	0.6580	0.6331
5	0.9449	0.9363	0.9268	0.9164	0.9051	0.8928	0.8795	0.8652	0.8500	0.8338
6	0.9871	0.9845	0.9815	0.9780	0.9740	0.9695	0.9644	0.9587	0.9523	0.9452
7	0.9980	0.9975	0.9968	0.9961	0.9952	0.9941	0.9929	0.9914	0.9897	0.9877
8	0.9998	0.9997	0.9997	0.9996	0.9995	0.9993	0.9991	0.9989	0.9986	0.9983
9	1.0000	1.0000	1.0000	1.0000	1.0000	1.0000	1.0000	0.9999	0.9999	0.9999
10	1.0000	1.0000	1.0000	1.0000	1.0000	1.0000	1.0000	1.0000	1.0000	1.0000

x \ p	0.41	0.42	0.43	0.44	0.45	0.46	0.47	0.48	0.49	0.50
0	0.0051	0.0043	0.0036	0.0030	0.0025	0.0021	0.0017	0.0014	0.0012	0.0010
1	0.0406	0.0355	0.0309	0.0269	0.0233	0.0201	0.0173	0.0148	0.0126	0.0107
2	0.1517	0.1372	0.1236	0.1111	0.0996	0.0889	0.0791	0.0702	0.0621	0.0547
3	0.3575	0.3335	0.3102	0.2877	0.2660	0.2453	0.2255	0.2067	0.1888	0.1719
4	0.6078	0.5822	0.5564	0.5304	0.5044	0.4784	0.4526	0.4270	0.4018	0.3770
5	0.8166	0.7984	0.7793	0.7593	0.7384	0.7168	0.6943	0.6712	0.6474	0.6230
6	0.9374	0.9288	0.9194	0.9092	0.8980	0.8859	0.8729	0.8590	0.8440	0.8281
7	0.9854	0.9828	0.9798	0.9764	0.9726	0.9683	0.9634	0.9580	0.9520	0.9453
8	0.9979	0.9975	0.9969	0.9963	0.9955	0.9946	0.9935	0.9923	0.9909	0.9893
9	0.9999	0.9998	0.9998	0.9997	0.9997	0.9996	0.9995	0.9994	0.9992	0.9990
10	1.0000	1.0000	1.0000	1.0000	1.0000	1.0000	1.0000	1.0000	1.0000	1.0000

n = 11

x \ p	0.01	0.02	0.03	0.04	0.05	0.06	0.07	0.08	0.09	0.10
0	0.8953	0.8007	0.7153	0.6382	0.5688	0.5063	0.4501	0.3996	0.3544	0.3138
1	0.9948	0.9805	0.9587	0.9308	0.8981	0.8618	0.8228	0.7819	0.7399	0.6974
2	0.9998	0.9988	0.9963	0.9917	0.9848	0.9752	0.9630	0.9481	0.9305	0.9104
3	1.0000	1.0000	0.9998	0.9993	0.9984	0.9970	0.9947	0.9915	0.9871	0.9815
4	1.0000	1.0000	1.0000	1.0000	0.9999	0.9997	0.9995	0.9990	0.9983	0.9972
5	1.0000	1.0000	1.0000	1.0000	1.0000	1.0000	1.0000	0.9999	0.9998	0.9997
6	1.0000	1.0000	1.0000	1.0000	1.0000	1.0000	1.0000	1.0000	1.0000	1.0000

x \ p	0.11	0.12	0.13	0.14	0.15	0.16	0.17	0.18	0.19	0.20
0	0.2775	0.2451	0.2161	0.1903	0.1673	0.1469	0.1288	0.1127	0.0985	0.0859
1	0.6548	0.6127	0.5714	0.5311	0.4922	0.4547	0.4189	0.3849	0.3526	0.3221
2	0.8880	0.8634	0.8368	0.8085	0.7788	0.7479	0.7161	0.6836	0.6506	0.6174
3	0.9744	0.9659	0.9558	0.9440	0.9306	0.9154	0.8987	0.8803	0.8603	0.8389
4	0.9958	0.9939	0.9913	0.9881	0.9841	0.9793	0.9734	0.9666	0.9587	0.9496
5	0.9995	0.9992	0.9988	0.9982	0.9973	0.9963	0.9949	0.9932	0.9910	0.9883
6	1.0000	0.9999	0.9999	0.9998	0.9997	0.9995	0.9993	0.9990	0.9986	0.9980
7	1.0000	1.0000	1.0000	1.0000	1.0000	1.0000	0.9999	0.9999	0.9998	0.9998
8	1.0000	1.0000	1.0000	1.0000	1.0000	1.0000	1.0000	1.0000	1.0000	1.0000

x \ p	0.21	0.22	0.23	0.24	0.25	0.26	0.27	0.28	0.29	0.30
0	0.0748	0.0650	0.0564	0.0489	0.0422	0.0364	0.0314	0.0270	0.0231	0.0198
1	0.2935	0.2667	0.2418	0.2186	0.1971	0.1773	0.1590	0.1423	0.1270	0.1130

TABLE B
(*continued*)

| | | | | | *n* = 11 (continued) | | | | | |

x \ p	0.21	0.22	0.23	0.24	0.25	0.26	0.27	0.28	0.29	0.30
2	0.5842	0.5512	0.5186	0.4866	0.4552	0.4247	0.3951	0.3665	0.3390	0.3127
3	0.8160	0.7919	0.7667	0.7404	0.7133	0.6854	0.6570	0.6281	0.5989	0.5696
4	0.9393	0.9277	0.9149	0.9008	0.8854	0.8687	0.8507	0.8315	0.8112	0.7897
5	0.9852	0.9814	0.9769	0.9717	0.9657	0.9588	0.9510	0.9423	0.9326	0.9218
6	0.9973	0.9965	0.9954	0.9941	0.9924	0.9905	0.9881	0.9854	0.9821	0.9784
7	0.9997	0.9995	0.9993	0.9991	0.9988	0.9984	0.9979	0.9973	0.9966	0.9957
8	1.0000	1.0000	0.9999	0.9999	0.9999	0.9998	0.9998	0.9997	0.9996	0.9994
9	1.0000	1.0000	1.0000	1.0000	1.0000	1.0000	1.0000	1.0000	1.0000	1.0000

x \ p	0.31	0.32	0.33	0.34	0.35	0.36	0.37	0.38	0.39	0.40
0	0.0169	0.0144	0.0122	0.0104	0.0088	0.0074	0.0062	0.0052	0.0044	0.0036
1	0.1003	0.0888	0.0784	0.0690	0.0606	0.0530	0.0463	0.0403	0.0350	0.0302
2	0.2877	0.2639	0.2413	0.2201	0.2001	0.1814	0.1640	0.1478	0.1328	0.1189
3	0.5402	0.5110	0.4821	0.4536	0.4256	0.3981	0.3714	0.3455	0.3204	0.2963
4	0.7672	0.7437	0.7193	0.6941	0.6683	0.6419	0.6150	0.5878	0.5603	0.5328
5	0.9099	0.8969	0.8829	0.8676	0.8513	0.8339	0.8153	0.7957	0.7751	0.7535
6	0.9740	0.9691	0.9634	0.9570	0.9499	0.9419	0.9330	0.9232	0.9124	0.9006
7	0.9946	0.9933	0.9918	0.9899	0.9878	0.9852	0.9823	0.9790	0.9751	0.9707
8	0.9992	0.9990	0.9987	0.9984	0.9980	0.9974	0.9968	0.9961	0.9952	0.9941
9	0.9999	0.9999	0.9999	0.9998	0.9998	0.9997	0.9996	0.9995	0.9994	0.9993
10	1.0000	1.0000	1.0000	1.0000	1.0000	1.0000	1.0000	1.0000	1.0000	1.0000

x \ p	0.41	0.42	0.43	0.44	0.45	0.46	0.47	0.48	0.49	0.50
0	0.0030	0.0025	0.0021	0.0017	0.0014	0.0011	0.0009	0.0008	0.0006	0.0005
1	0.0261	0.0224	0.0192	0.0164	0.0139	0.0118	0.0100	0.0084	0.0070	0.0059
2	0.1062	0.0945	0.0838	0.0740	0.0652	0.0572	0.0501	0.0436	0.0378	0.0327
3	0.2731	0.2510	0.2300	0.2100	0.1911	0.1734	0.1567	0.1412	0.1267	0.1133
4	0.5052	0.4777	0.4505	0.4236	0.3971	0.3712	0.3459	0.3213	0.2974	0.2744
5	0.7310	0.7076	0.6834	0.6586	0.6331	0.6071	0.5807	0.5540	0.5271	0.5000
6	0.8879	0.8740	0.8592	0.8432	0.8262	0.8081	0.7890	0.7688	0.7477	0.7256
7	0.9657	0.9601	0.9539	0.9468	0.9390	0.9304	0.9209	0.9105	0.8991	0.8867
8	0.9928	0.9913	0.9896	0.9875	0.9852	0.9825	0.9794	0.9759	0.9718	0.9673
9	0.9991	0.9988	0.9986	0.9982	0.9978	0.9973	0.9967	0.9960	0.9951	0.9941
10	0.9999	0.9999	0.9999	0.9999	0.9998	0.9998	0.9998	0.9997	0.9996	0.9995
11	1.0000	1.0000	1.0000	1.0000	1.0000	1.0000	1.0000	1.0000	1.0000	1.0000

| | | | | | *n* = 12 | | | | | |

x \ p	0.01	0.02	0.03	0.04	0.05	0.06	0.07	0.08	0.09	0.10
0	0.8864	0.7847	0.6938	0.6127	0.5404	0.4759	0.4186	0.3677	0.3225	0.2824
1	0.9938	0.9769	0.9514	0.9191	0.8816	0.8405	0.7967	0.7513	0.7052	0.6590
2	0.9998	0.9985	0.9952	0.9893	0.9804	0.9684	0.9532	0.9348	0.9134	0.8891
3	1.0000	0.9999	0.9997	0.9990	0.9978	0.9957	0.9925	0.9880	0.9820	0.9744
4	1.0000	1.0000	1.0000	0.9999	0.9998	0.9996	0.9991	0.9984	0.9973	0.9957
5	1.0000	1.0000	1.0000	1.0000	1.0000	1.0000	0.9999	0.9998	0.9997	0.9995
6	1.0000	1.0000	1.0000	1.0000	1.0000	1.0000	1.0000	1.0000	1.0000	0.9999
7	1.0000	1.0000	1.0000	1.0000	1.0000	1.0000	1.0000	1.0000	1.0000	1.0000

x \ p	0.11	0.12	0.13	0.14	0.15	0.16	0.17	0.18	0.19	0.20
0	0.2470	0.2157	0.1880	0.1637	0.1422	0.1234	0.1069	0.0924	0.0798	0.0687

TABLE B
(continued)

n = 12 (continued)

x \ p	0.11	0.12	0.13	0.14	0.15	0.16	0.17	0.18	0.19	0.20
1	0.6133	0.5686	0.5252	0.4834	0.4435	0.4055	0.3696	0.3359	0.3043	0.2749
2	0.8623	0.8333	0.8023	0.7697	0.7358	0.7010	0.6656	0.6298	0.5940	0.5583
3	0.9649	0.9536	0.9403	0.9250	0.9078	0.8886	0.8676	0.8448	0.8205	0.7946
4	0.9935	0.9905	0.9867	0.9819	0.9761	0.9690	0.9607	0.9511	0.9400	0.9274
5	0.9991	0.9986	0.9978	0.9967	0.9954	0.9935	0.9912	0.9884	0.9849	0.9806
6	0.9999	0.9998	0.9997	0.9996	0.9993	0.9990	0.9985	0.9979	0.9971	0.9961
7	1.0000	1.0000	1.0000	1.0000	0.9999	0.9999	0.9998	0.9997	0.9996	0.9994
8	1.0000	1.0000	1.0000	1.0000	1.0000	1.0000	1.0000	1.0000	1.0000	0.9999
9	1.0000	1.0000	1.0000	1.0000	1.0000	1.0000	1.0000	1.0000	1.0000	1.0000

x \ p	0.21	0.22	0.23	0.24	0.25	0.26	0.27	0.28	0.29	0.30
0	0.0591	0.0507	0.0434	0.0371	0.0317	0.0270	0.0229	0.0194	0.0164	0.0138
1	0.2476	0.2224	0.1991	0.1778	0.1584	0.1406	0.1245	0.1100	0.0968	0.0850
2	0.5232	0.4886	0.4550	0.4222	0.3907	0.3603	0.3313	0.3037	0.2775	0.2528
3	0.7674	0.7390	0.7096	0.6795	0.6488	0.6176	0.5863	0.5548	0.5235	0.4925
4	0.9134	0.8979	0.8808	0.8623	0.8424	0.8210	0.7984	0.7746	0.7496	0.7237
5	0.9755	0.9696	0.9626	0.9547	0.9456	0.9354	0.9240	0.9113	0.8974	0.8822
6	0.9948	0.9932	0.9911	0.9887	0.9857	0.9822	0.9781	0.9733	0.9678	0.9614
7	0.9992	0.9989	0.9984	0.9979	0.9972	0.9964	0.9953	0.9940	0.9924	0.9905
8	0.9999	0.9999	0.9998	0.9997	0.9996	0.9995	0.9993	0.9990	0.9987	0.9983
9	1.0000	1.0000	1.0000	1.0000	1.0000	0.9999	0.9999	0.9999	0.9998	0.9998
10	1.0000	1.0000	1.0000	1.0000	1.0000	1.0000	1.0000	1.0000	1.0000	1.0000

x \ p	0.31	0.32	0.33	0.34	0.35	0.36	0.37	0.38	0.39	0.40
0	0.0116	0.0098	0.0082	0.0068	0.0057	0.0047	0.0039	0.0032	0.0027	0.0022
1	0.0744	0.0650	0.0565	0.0491	0.0424	0.0366	0.0315	0.0270	0.0230	0.0196
2	0.2296	0.2078	0.1876	0.1687	0.1513	0.1352	0.1205	0.1069	0.0946	0.0834
3	0.4619	0.4319	0.4027	0.3742	0.3467	0.3201	0.2947	0.2704	0.2472	0.2253
4	0.6968	0.6692	0.6410	0.6124	0.5833	0.5541	0.5249	0.4957	0.4668	0.4382
5	0.8657	0.8479	0.8289	0.8087	0.7873	0.7648	0.7412	0.7167	0.6913	0.6652
6	0.9542	0.9460	0.9368	0.9266	0.9154	0.9030	0.8894	0.8747	0.8589	0.8418
7	0.9882	0.9856	0.9824	0.9787	0.9745	0.9696	0.9641	0.9578	0.9507	0.9427
8	0.9978	0.9972	0.9964	0.9955	0.9944	0.9930	0.9915	0.9896	0.9873	0.9847
9	0.9997	0.9996	0.9995	0.9993	0.9992	0.9989	0.9986	0.9982	0.9978	0.9972
10	1.0000	1.0000	1.0000	0.9999	0.9999	0.9999	0.9999	0.9998	0.9998	0.9997
11	1.0000	1.0000	1.0000	1.0000	1.0000	1.0000	1.0000	1.0000	1.0000	1.0000

x \ p	0.41	0.42	0.43	0.44	0.45	0.46	0.47	0.48	0.49	0.50
0	0.0018	0.0014	0.0012	0.0010	0.0008	0.0006	0.0005	0.0004	0.0003	0.0002
1	0.0166	0.0140	0.0118	0.0099	0.0083	0.0069	0.0057	0.0047	0.0039	0.0032
2	0.0733	0.0642	0.0560	0.0487	0.0421	0.0363	0.0312	0.0267	0.0227	0.0193
3	0.2047	0.1853	0.1671	0.1502	0.1345	0.1199	0.1066	0.0943	0.0832	0.0730
4	0.4101	0.3825	0.3557	0.3296	0.3044	0.2802	0.2570	0.2348	0.2138	0.1938
5	0.6384	0.6111	0.5833	0.5552	0.5269	0.4986	0.4703	0.4423	0.4145	0.3872
6	0.8235	0.8041	0.7836	0.7620	0.7393	0.7157	0.6911	0.6657	0.6396	0.6128
7	0.9338	0.9240	0.9131	0.9012	0.8883	0.8742	0.8589	0.8425	0.8249	0.8062
8	0.9817	0.9782	0.9742	0.9696	0.9644	0.9585	0.9519	0.9445	0.9362	0.9270
9	0.9965	0.9957	0.9947	0.9935	0.9921	0.9905	0.9886	0.9863	0.9837	0.9807
10	0.9996	0.9995	0.9993	0.9991	0.9989	0.9986	0.9983	0.9979	0.9974	0.9968
11	1.0000	1.0000	1.0000	0.9999	0.9999	0.9999	0.9999	0.9999	0.9998	0.9998
12	1.0000	1.0000	1.0000	1.0000	1.0000	1.0000	1.0000	1.0000	1.0000	1.0000

TABLE B
(continued)

	$n = 13$									
x \ p	0.01	0.02	0.03	0.04	0.05	0.06	0.07	0.08	0.09	0.10
0	0.8775	0.7690	0.6730	0.5882	0.5133	0.4474	0.3893	0.3383	0.2935	0.2542
1	0.9928	0.9730	0.9436	0.9068	0.8646	0.8186	0.7702	0.7206	0.6707	0.6213
2	0.9997	0.9980	0.9938	0.9865	0.9755	0.9608	0.9422	0.9201	0.8946	0.8661
3	1.0000	0.9999	0.9995	0.9986	0.9969	0.9940	0.9897	0.9837	0.9758	0.9658
4	1.0000	1.0000	1.0000	0.9999	0.9997	0.9993	0.9987	0.9976	0.9959	0.9935
5	1.0000	1.0000	1.0000	1.0000	1.0000	0.9999	0.9999	0.9997	0.9995	0.9991
6	1.0000	1.0000	1.0000	1.0000	1.0000	1.0000	1.0000	1.0000	0.9999	0.9999
7	1.0000	1.0000	1.0000	1.0000	1.0000	1.0000	1.0000	1.0000	1.0000	1.0000

x \ p	0.11	0.12	0.13	0.14	0.15	0.16	0.17	0.18	0.19	0.20
0	0.2198	0.1898	0.1636	0.1408	0.1209	0.1037	0.0887	0.0758	0.0646	0.0550
1	0.5730	0.5262	0.4814	0.4386	0.3983	0.3604	0.3249	0.2920	0.2616	0.2336
2	0.8349	0.8015	0.7663	0.7296	0.6920	0.6537	0.6152	0.5769	0.5389	0.5017
3	0.9536	0.9391	0.9224	0.9033	0.8820	0.8586	0.8333	0.8061	0.7774	0.7473
4	0.9903	0.9861	0.9807	0.9740	0.9658	0.9562	0.9449	0.9319	0.9173	0.9009
5	0.9985	0.9976	0.9964	0.9947	0.9925	0.9896	0.9861	0.9817	0.9763	0.9700
6	0.9998	0.9997	0.9995	0.9992	0.9987	0.9981	0.9973	0.9962	0.9948	0.9930
7	1.0000	1.0000	0.9999	0.9999	0.9998	0.9997	0.9996	0.9994	0.9991	0.9988
8	1.0000	1.0000	1.0000	1.0000	1.0000	1.0000	1.0000	0.9999	0.9999	0.9998
9	1.0000	1.0000	1.0000	1.0000	1.0000	1.0000	1.0000	1.0000	1.0000	1.0000

x \ p	0.21	0.22	0.23	0.24	0.25	0.26	0.27	0.28	0.29	0.30
0	0.0467	0.0396	0.0334	0.0282	0.0238	0.0200	0.0167	0.0140	0.0117	0.0097
1	0.2080	0.1846	0.1633	0.1441	0.1267	0.1111	0.0971	0.0846	0.0735	0.0637
2	0.4653	0.4301	0.3961	0.3636	0.3326	0.3032	0.2755	0.2495	0.2251	0.2025
3	0.7161	0.6839	0.6511	0.6178	0.5843	0.5507	0.5174	0.4845	0.4522	0.4206
4	0.8827	0.8629	0.8415	0.8184	0.7940	0.7681	0.7411	0.7130	0.6840	0.6543
5	0.9625	0.9538	0.9438	0.9325	0.9198	0.9056	0.8901	0.8730	0.8545	0.8346
6	0.9907	0.9880	0.9846	0.9805	0.9757	0.9701	0.9635	0.9560	0.9473	0.9376
7	0.9983	0.9976	0.9968	0.9957	0.9944	0.9927	0.9907	0.9882	0.9853	0.9818
8	0.9998	0.9996	0.9995	0.9993	0.9990	0.9987	0.9982	0.9976	0.9969	0.9960
9	1.0000	1.0000	0.9999	0.9999	0.9999	0.9998	0.9997	0.9996	0.9995	0.9993
10	1.0000	1.0000	1.0000	1.0000	1.0000	1.0000	1.0000	1.0000	0.9999	0.9999
11	1.0000	1.0000	1.0000	1.0000	1.0000	1.0000	1.0000	1.0000	1.0000	1.0000

x \ p	0.31	0.32	0.33	0.34	0.35	0.36	0.37	0.38	0.39	0.40
0	0.0080	0.0066	0.0055	0.0045	0.0037	0.0030	0.0025	0.0020	0.0016	0.0013
1	0.0550	0.0473	0.0406	0.0347	0.0296	0.0251	0.0213	0.0179	0.0151	0.0126
2	0.1815	0.1621	0.1443	0.1280	0.1132	0.0997	0.0875	0.0765	0.0667	0.0579
3	0.3899	0.3602	0.3317	0.3043	0.2783	0.2536	0.2302	0.2083	0.1877	0.1686
4	0.6240	0.5933	0.5624	0.5314	0.5005	0.4699	0.4397	0.4101	0.3812	0.3530
5	0.8133	0.7907	0.7669	0.7419	0.7159	0.6889	0.6612	0.6327	0.6038	0.5744
6	0.9267	0.9146	0.9012	0.8865	0.8705	0.8532	0.8346	0.8147	0.7935	0.7712
7	0.9777	0.9729	0.9674	0.9610	0.9538	0.9456	0.9365	0.9262	0.9149	0.9023
8	0.9948	0.9935	0.9918	0.9898	0.9874	0.9846	0.9813	0.9775	0.9730	0.9679
9	0.9991	0.9988	0.9985	0.9980	0.9975	0.9968	0.9960	0.9949	0.9937	0.9922
10	0.9999	0.9999	0.9998	0.9997	0.9997	0.9995	0.9994	0.9992	0.9990	0.9987
11	1.0000	1.0000	1.0000	1.0000	1.0000	1.0000	0.9999	0.9999	0.9999	0.9999
12	1.0000	1.0000	1.0000	1.0000	1.0000	1.0000	1.0000	1.0000	1.0000	1.0000

n = 13 (continued)

x \ p	0.41	0.42	0.43	0.44	0.45	0.46	0.47	0.48	0.49	0.50
0	0.0010	0.0008	0.0007	0.0005	0.0004	0.0003	0.0003	0.0002	0.0002	0.0001
1	0.0105	0.0088	0.0072	0.0060	0.0049	0.0040	0.0033	0.0026	0.0021	0.0017
2	0.0501	0.0431	0.0370	0.0316	0.0269	0.0228	0.0192	0.0162	0.0135	0.0112
3	0.1508	0.1344	0.1193	0.1055	0.0929	0.0815	0.0712	0.0619	0.0536	0.0461
4	0.3258	0.2997	0.2746	0.2507	0.2279	0.2065	0.1863	0.1674	0.1498	0.1334
5	0.5448	0.5151	0.4854	0.4559	0.4268	0.3981	0.3701	0.3427	0.3162	0.2905
6	0.7476	0.7230	0.6975	0.6710	0.6437	0.6158	0.5873	0.5585	0.5293	0.5000
7	0.8886	0.8736	0.8574	0.8400	0.8212	0.8012	0.7800	0.7576	0.7341	0.7095
8	0.9621	0.9554	0.9480	0.9395	0.9302	0.9197	0.9082	0.8955	0.8817	0.8666
9	0.9904	0.9883	0.9859	0.9830	0.9797	0.9758	0.9713	0.9662	0.9604	0.9539
10	0.9983	0.9979	0.9973	0.9967	0.9959	0.9949	0.9937	0.9923	0.9907	0.9888
11	0.9998	0.9998	0.9997	0.9996	0.9995	0.9993	0.9991	0.9989	0.9986	0.9983
12	1.0000	1.0000	1.0000	1.0000	1.0000	1.0000	0.9999	0.9999	0.9999	0.9999
13	1.0000	1.0000	1.0000	1.0000	1.0000	1.0000	1.0000	1.0000	1.0000	1.0000

n = 14

x \ p	0.01	0.02	0.03	0.04	0.05	0.06	0.07	0.08	0.09	0.10
0	0.8687	0.7536	0.6528	0.5647	0.4877	0.4205	0.3620	0.3112	0.2670	0.2288
1	0.9916	0.9690	0.9355	0.8941	0.8470	0.7963	0.7436	0.6900	0.6368	0.5846
2	0.9997	0.9975	0.9923	0.9833	0.9699	0.9522	0.9302	0.9042	0.8745	0.8416
3	1.0000	0.9999	0.9994	0.9981	0.9958	0.9920	0.9864	0.9786	0.9685	0.9559
4	1.0000	1.0000	1.0000	0.9998	0.9996	0.9990	0.9980	0.9965	0.9941	0.9908
5	1.0000	1.0000	1.0000	1.0000	1.0000	0.9999	0.9998	0.9996	0.9992	0.9985
6	1.0000	1.0000	1.0000	1.0000	1.0000	1.0000	1.0000	1.0000	0.9999	0.9998
7	1.0000	1.0000	1.0000	1.0000	1.0000	1.0000	1.0000	1.0000	1.0000	1.0000

x \ p	0.11	0.12	0.13	0.14	0.15	0.16	0.17	0.18	0.19	0.20
0	0.1956	0.1670	0.1423	0.1211	0.1028	0.0871	0.0736	0.0621	0.0523	0.0440
1	0.5342	0.4859	0.4401	0.3969	0.3567	0.3193	0.2848	0.2531	0.2242	0.1979
2	0.8061	0.7685	0.7292	0.6889	0.6479	0.6068	0.5659	0.5256	0.4862	0.4481
3	0.9406	0.9226	0.9021	0.8790	0.8535	0.8258	0.7962	0.7649	0.7321	0.6982
4	0.9863	0.9804	0.9731	0.9641	0.9533	0.9406	0.9259	0.9093	0.8907	0.8702
5	0.9976	0.9962	0.9943	0.9918	0.9885	0.9843	0.9791	0.9727	0.9651	0.9561
6	0.9997	0.9994	0.9991	0.9985	0.9978	0.9968	0.9954	0.9936	0.9913	0.9884
7	1.0000	0.9999	0.9999	0.9998	0.9997	0.9995	0.9992	0.9988	0.9983	0.9976
8	1.0000	1.0000	1.0000	1.0000	1.0000	0.9999	0.9999	0.9998	0.9997	0.9996
9	1.0000	1.0000	1.0000	1.0000	1.0000	1.0000	1.0000	1.0000	1.0000	1.0000

x \ p	0.21	0.22	0.23	0.24	0.25	0.26	0.27	0.28	0.29	0.30
0	0.0369	0.0309	0.0258	0.0214	0.0178	0.0148	0.0122	0.0101	0.0083	0.0068
1	0.1741	0.1527	0.1335	0.1163	0.1010	0.0874	0.0754	0.0648	0.0556	0.0475
2	0.4113	0.3761	0.3426	0.3109	0.2811	0.2533	0.2273	0.2033	0.1812	0.1608
3	0.6634	0.6281	0.5924	0.5568	0.5213	0.4864	0.4521	0.4187	0.3863	0.3552
4	0.8477	0.8235	0.7977	0.7703	0.7415	0.7116	0.6807	0.6490	0.6168	0.5842
5	0.9457	0.9338	0.9203	0.9051	0.8883	0.8699	0.8498	0.8282	0.8051	0.7805
6	0.9848	0.9804	0.9752	0.9690	0.9617	0.9533	0.9437	0.9327	0.9204	0.9067
7	0.9967	0.9955	0.9940	0.9921	0.9897	0.9868	0.9833	0.9792	0.9743	0.9685
8	0.9994	0.9992	0.9989	0.9984	0.9978	0.9971	0.9962	0.9950	0.9935	0.9917
9	0.9999	0.9999	0.9998	0.9998	0.9997	0.9995	0.9993	0.9991	0.9988	0.9983
10	1.0000	1.0000	1.0000	1.0000	1.0000	0.9999	0.9999	0.9999	0.9998	0.9998
11	1.0000	1.0000	1.0000	1.0000	1.0000	1.0000	1.0000	1.0000	1.0000	1.0000

$n = 14$ (continued)

x \ p	0.31	0.32	0.33	0.34	0.35	0.36	0.37	0.38	0.39	0.40
0	0.0055	0.0045	0.0037	0.0030	0.0024	0.0019	0.0016	0.0012	0.0010	0.0008
1	0.0404	0.0343	0.0290	0.0244	0.0205	0.0172	0.0143	0.0119	0.0098	0.0081
2	0.1423	0.1254	0.1101	0.0963	0.0839	0.0729	0.0630	0.0543	0.0466	0.0398
3	0.3253	0.2968	0.2699	0.2444	0.2205	0.1982	0.1774	0.1582	0.1405	0.1243
4	0.5514	0.5187	0.4862	0.4542	0.4227	0.3920	0.3622	0.3334	0.3057	0.2793
5	0.7546	0.7276	0.6994	0.6703	0.6405	0.6101	0.5792	0.5481	0.5169	0.4859
6	0.8916	0.8750	0.8569	0.8374	0.8164	0.7941	0.7704	0.7455	0.7195	0.6925
7	0.9619	0.9542	0.9455	0.9357	0.9247	0.9124	0.8988	0.8838	0.8675	0.8499
8	0.9895	0.9869	0.9837	0.9800	0.9757	0.9706	0.9647	0.9580	0.9503	0.9417
9	0.9978	0.9971	0.9963	0.9952	0.9940	0.9924	0.9905	0.9883	0.9856	0.9825
10	0.9997	0.9995	0.9994	0.9992	0.9989	0.9986	0.9981	0.9976	0.9969	0.9961
11	1.0000	0.9999	0.9999	0.9999	0.9999	0.9998	0.9997	0.9997	0.9995	0.9994
12	1.0000	1.0000	1.0000	1.0000	1.0000	1.0000	1.0000	1.0000	1.0000	0.9999
13	1.0000	1.0000	1.0000	1.0000	1.0000	1.0000	1.0000	1.0000	1.0000	1.0000

x \ p	0.41	0.42	0.43	0.44	0.45	0.46	0.47	0.48	0.49	0.50
0	0.0006	0.0005	0.0004	0.0003	0.0002	0.0002	0.0001	0.0001	0.0001	0.0001
1	0.0066	0.0054	0.0044	0.0036	0.0029	0.0023	0.0019	0.0015	0.0012	0.0009
2	0.0339	0.0287	0.0242	0.0203	0.0170	0.0142	0.0117	0.0097	0.0079	0.0065
3	0.1095	0.0961	0.0839	0.0730	0.0632	0.0545	0.0468	0.0399	0.0339	0.0287
4	0.2541	0.2303	0.2078	0.1868	0.1672	0.1490	0.1322	0.1167	0.1026	0.0898
5	0.4550	0.4246	0.3948	0.3656	0.3373	0.3100	0.2837	0.2585	0.2346	0.2120
6	0.6645	0.6357	0.6063	0.5764	0.5461	0.5157	0.4852	0.4549	0.4249	0.3953
7	0.8308	0.8104	0.7887	0.7656	0.7414	0.7160	0.6895	0.6620	0.6337	0.6047
8	0.9320	0.9211	0.9090	0.8957	0.8811	0.8652	0.8480	0.8293	0.8094	0.7880
9	0.9788	0.9745	0.9696	0.9639	0.9574	0.9500	0.9417	0.9323	0.9218	0.9102
10	0.9951	0.9939	0.9924	0.9907	0.9886	0.9861	0.9832	0.9798	0.9759	0.9713
11	0.9992	0.9990	0.9987	0.9983	0.9978	0.9973	0.9966	0.9958	0.9947	0.9935
12	0.9999	0.9999	0.9999	0.9998	0.9997	0.9997	0.9996	0.9994	0.9993	0.9991
13	1.0000	1.0000	1.0000	1.0000	1.0000	1.0000	1.0000	1.0000	1.0000	0.9999
14	1.0000	1.0000	1.0000	1.0000	1.0000	1.0000	1.0000	1.0000	1.0000	1.0000

$n = 15$

x \ p	0.01	0.02	0.03	0.04	0.05	0.06	0.07	0.08	0.09	0.10
0	0.8601	0.7386	0.6333	0.5421	0.4633	0.3953	0.3367	0.2863	0.2430	0.2059
1	0.9904	0.9647	0.9270	0.8809	0.8290	0.7738	0.7168	0.6597	0.6035	0.5490
2	0.9996	0.9970	0.9906	0.9797	0.9638	0.9429	0.9171	0.8870	0.8531	0.8159
3	1.0000	0.9998	0.9992	0.9976	0.9945	0.9896	0.9825	0.9727	0.9601	0.9444
4	1.0000	1.0000	0.9999	0.9998	0.9994	0.9986	0.9972	0.9950	0.9918	0.9873
5	1.0000	1.0000	1.0000	1.0000	0.9999	0.9999	0.9997	0.9993	0.9987	0.9978
6	1.0000	1.0000	1.0000	1.0000	1.0000	1.0000	1.0000	0.9999	0.9998	0.9997
7	1.0000	1.0000	1.0000	1.0000	1.0000	1.0000	1.0000	1.0000	1.0000	1.0000

x \ p	0.11	0.12	0.13	0.14	0.15	0.16	0.17	0.18	0.19	0.20
0	0.1741	0.1470	0.1238	0.1041	0.0874	0.0731	0.0611	0.0510	0.0424	0.0352
1	0.4969	0.4476	0.4013	0.3583	0.3186	0.2821	0.2489	0.2187	0.1915	0.1671
2	0.7762	0.7346	0.6916	0.6480	0.6042	0.5608	0.5181	0.4766	0.4365	0.3980
3	0.9258	0.9041	0.8796	0.8524	0.8227	0.7908	0.7571	0.7218	0.6854	0.6482
4	0.9813	0.9735	0.9639	0.9522	0.9383	0.9222	0.9039	0.8833	0.8606	0.8358
5	0.9963	0.9943	0.9916	0.9879	0.9832	0.9773	0.9700	0.9613	0.9510	0.9389
6	0.9994	0.9990	0.9985	0.9976	0.9964	0.9948	0.9926	0.9898	0.9863	0.9819

TABLE B
(*continued*)

n = 15 (continued)

x \ p	0.11	0.12	0.13	0.14	0.15	0.16	0.17	0.18	0.19	0.20
7	0.9999	0.9999	0.9998	0.9996	0.9994	0.9990	0.9986	0.9979	0.9970	0.9958
8	1.0000	1.0000	1.0000	1.0000	0.9999	0.9999	0.9998	0.9997	0.9995	0.9992
9	1.0000	1.0000	1.0000	1.0000	1.0000	1.0000	1.0000	1.0000	0.9999	0.9999
10	1.0000	1.0000	1.0000	1.0000	1.0000	1.0000	1.0000	1.0000	1.0000	1.0000

x \ p	0.21	0.22	0.23	0.24	0.25	0.26	0.27	0.28	0.29	0.30
0	0.0291	0.0241	0.0198	0.0163	0.0134	0.0109	0.0089	0.0072	0.0059	0.0047
1	0.1453	0.1259	0.1087	0.0935	0.0802	0.0685	0.0583	0.0495	0.0419	0.0353
2	0.3615	0.3269	0.2945	0.2642	0.2361	0.2101	0.1863	0.1645	0.1447	0.1268
3	0.6105	0.5726	0.5350	0.4978	0.4613	0.4258	0.3914	0.3584	0.3268	0.2969
4	0.8090	0.7805	0.7505	0.7190	0.6865	0.6531	0.6190	0.5846	0.5500	0.5155
5	0.9252	0.9095	0.8921	0.8728	0.8516	0.8287	0.8042	0.7780	0.7505	0.7216
6	0.9766	0.9702	0.9626	0.9537	0.9434	0.9316	0.9183	0.9035	0.8870	0.8689
7	0.9942	0.9922	0.9896	0.9865	0.9827	0.9781	0.9726	0.9662	0.9587	0.9500
8	0.9989	0.9984	0.9977	0.9969	0.9958	0.9944	0.9927	0.9906	0.9879	0.9848
9	0.9998	0.9997	0.9996	0.9994	0.9992	0.9989	0.9985	0.9979	0.9972	0.9963
10	1.0000	1.0000	0.9999	0.9999	0.9999	0.9998	0.9998	0.9997	0.9995	0.9993
11	1.0000	1.0000	1.0000	1.0000	1.0000	1.0000	1.0000	1.0000	0.9999	0.9999
12	1.0000	1.0000	1.0000	1.0000	1.0000	1.0000	1.0000	1.0000	1.0000	1.0000

x \ p	0.31	0.32	0.33	0.34	0.35	0.36	0.37	0.38	0.39	0.40
0	0.0038	0.0031	0.0025	0.0020	0.0016	0.0012	0.0010	0.0008	0.0006	0.0005
1	0.0296	0.0248	0.0206	0.0171	0.0142	0.0117	0.0096	0.0078	0.0064	0.0052
2	0.1107	0.0962	0.0833	0.0719	0.0617	0.0528	0.0450	0.0382	0.0322	0.0271
3	0.2686	0.2420	0.2171	0.1940	0.1727	0.1531	0.1351	0.1187	0.1039	0.0905
4	0.4813	0.4477	0.4148	0.3829	0.3519	0.3222	0.2938	0.2668	0.2413	0.2173
5	0.6916	0.6607	0.6291	0.5968	0.5643	0.5316	0.4989	0.4665	0.4346	0.4032
6	0.8491	0.8278	0.8049	0.7806	0.7548	0.7278	0.6997	0.6705	0.6405	0.6098
7	0.9401	0.9289	0.9163	0.9023	0.8868	0.8698	0.8513	0.8313	0.8098	0.7869
8	0.9810	0.9764	0.9711	0.9649	0.9578	0.9496	0.9403	0.9298	0.9180	0.9050
9	0.9952	0.9938	0.9921	0.9901	0.9876	0.9846	0.9810	0.9768	0.9719	0.9662
10	0.9991	0.9988	0.9984	0.9978	0.9972	0.9963	0.9953	0.9941	0.9925	0.9907
11	0.9999	0.9998	0.9997	0.9996	0.9995	0.9994	0.9991	0.9989	0.9985	0.9981
12	1.0000	1.0000	1.0000	1.0000	0.9999	0.9999	0.9999	0.9998	0.9998	0.9997
13	1.0000	1.0000	1.0000	1.0000	1.0000	1.0000	1.0000	1.0000	1.0000	1.0000

x \ p	0.41	0.42	0.43	0.44	0.45	0.46	0.47	0.48	0.49	0.50
0	0.0004	0.0003	0.0002	0.0002	0.0001	0.0001	0.0001	0.0001	0.0000	0.0000
1	0.0042	0.0034	0.0027	0.0021	0.0017	0.0013	0.0010	0.0008	0.0006	0.0005
2	0.0227	0.0189	0.0157	0.0130	0.0107	0.0087	0.0071	0.0057	0.0046	0.0037
3	0.0785	0.0678	0.0583	0.0498	0.0424	0.0359	0.0303	0.0254	0.0212	0.0176
4	0.1948	0.1739	0.1546	0.1367	0.1204	0.1055	0.0920	0.0799	0.0690	0.0592
5	0.3726	0.3430	0.3144	0.2869	0.2608	0.2359	0.2125	0.1905	0.1699	0.1509
6	0.5786	0.5470	0.5153	0.4836	0.4522	0.4211	0.3905	0.3606	0.3316	0.3036
7	0.7626	0.7370	0.7102	0.6824	0.6535	0.6238	0.5935	0.5626	0.5314	0.5000
8	0.8905	0.8746	0.8573	0.8385	0.8182	0.7966	0.7735	0.7490	0.7233	0.6964
9	0.9596	0.9521	0.9435	0.9339	0.9231	0.9110	0.8976	0.8829	0.8667	0.8491
10	0.9884	0.9857	0.9826	0.9789	0.9745	0.9695	0.9637	0.9570	0.9494	0.9408
11	0.9975	0.9968	0.9960	0.9949	0.9937	0.9921	0.9903	0.9881	0.9855	0.9824
12	0.9996	0.9995	0.9993	0.9991	0.9989	0.9986	0.9982	0.9977	0.9971	0.9963
13	1.0000	1.0000	0.9999	0.9999	0.9999	0.9998	0.9998	0.9997	0.9996	0.9995
14	1.0000	1.0000	1.0000	1.0000	1.0000	1.0000	1.0000	1.0000	1.0000	1.0000

TABLE B
(continued)

						$n = 16$					

x \ p	0.01	0.02	0.03	0.04	0.05	0.06	0.07	0.08	0.09	0.10
0	0.8515	0.7238	0.6143	0.5204	0.4401	0.3716	0.3131	0.2634	0.2211	0.1853
1	0.9891	0.9601	0.9182	0.8673	0.8108	0.7511	0.6902	0.6299	0.5711	0.5147
2	0.9995	0.9963	0.9887	0.9758	0.9571	0.9327	0.9031	0.8688	0.8306	0.7892
3	1.0000	0.9998	0.9989	0.9968	0.9930	0.9868	0.9779	0.9658	0.9504	0.9316
4	1.0000	1.0000	0.9999	0.9997	0.9991	0.9981	0.9962	0.9932	0.9889	0.9830
5	1.0000	1.0000	1.0000	1.0000	0.9999	0.9998	0.9995	0.9990	0.9981	0.9967
6	1.0000	1.0000	1.0000	1.0000	1.0000	1.0000	0.9999	0.9999	0.9997	0.9995
7	1.0000	1.0000	1.0000	1.0000	1.0000	1.0000	1.0000	1.0000	1.0000	0.9999
8	1.0000	1.0000	1.0000	1.0000	1.0000	1.0000	1.0000	1.0000	1.0000	1.0000

x \ p	0.11	0.12	0.13	0.14	0.15	0.16	0.17	0.18	0.19	0.20
0	0.1550	0.1293	0.1077	0.0895	0.0743	0.0614	0.0507	0.0418	0.0343	0.0281
1	0.4614	0.4115	0.3653	0.3227	0.2839	0.2487	0.2170	0.1885	0.1632	0.1407
2	0.7455	0.7001	0.6539	0.6074	0.5614	0.5162	0.4723	0.4302	0.3899	0.3518
3	0.9093	0.8838	0.8552	0.8237	0.7899	0.7540	0.7164	0.6777	0.6381	0.5981
4	0.9752	0.9652	0.9529	0.9382	0.9209	0.9012	0.8789	0.8542	0.8273	0.7982
5	0.9947	0.9918	0.9880	0.9829	0.9765	0.9685	0.9588	0.9473	0.9338	0.9183
6	0.9991	0.9985	0.9976	0.9962	0.9944	0.9920	0.9888	0.9847	0.9796	0.9733
7	0.9999	0.9998	0.9996	0.9993	0.9989	0.9984	0.9976	0.9964	0.9949	0.9930
8	1.0000	1.0000	0.9999	0.9999	0.9998	0.9997	0.9996	0.9993	0.9990	0.9985
9	1.0000	1.0000	1.0000	1.0000	1.0000	1.0000	0.9999	0.9999	0.9998	0.9998
10	1.0000	1.0000	1.0000	1.0000	1.0000	1.0000	1.0000	1.0000	1.0000	1.0000

x \ p	0.21	0.22	0.23	0.24	0.25	0.26	0.27	0.28	0.29	0.30
0	0.0230	0.0188	0.0153	0.0124	0.0100	0.0081	0.0065	0.0052	0.0042	0.0033
1	0.1209	0.1035	0.0883	0.0750	0.0635	0.0535	0.0450	0.0377	0.0314	0.0261
2	0.3161	0.2827	0.2517	0.2232	0.1971	0.1733	0.1518	0.1323	0.1149	0.0994
3	0.5582	0.5186	0.4797	0.4417	0.4050	0.3697	0.3360	0.3041	0.2740	0.2459
4	0.7673	0.7348	0.7009	0.6659	0.6302	0.5940	0.5575	0.5212	0.4853	0.4499
5	0.9008	0.8812	0.8595	0.8359	0.8103	0.7831	0.7542	0.7239	0.6923	0.6598
6	0.9658	0.9568	0.9464	0.9342	0.9204	0.9049	0.8875	0.8683	0.8474	0.8247
7	0.9905	0.9873	0.9834	0.9786	0.9729	0.9660	0.9580	0.9486	0.9379	0.9256
8	0.9979	0.9970	0.9959	0.9944	0.9925	0.9902	0.9873	0.9837	0.9794	0.9743
9	0.9996	0.9994	0.9992	0.9988	0.9984	0.9977	0.9969	0.9959	0.9945	0.9929
10	0.9999	0.9999	0.9999	0.9998	0.9997	0.9996	0.9994	0.9992	0.9989	0.9984
11	1.0000	1.0000	1.0000	1.0000	1.0000	0.9999	0.9999	0.9999	0.9998	0.9997
12	1.0000	1.0000	1.0000	1.0000	1.0000	1.0000	1.0000	1.0000	1.0000	1.0000

x \ p	0.31	0.32	0.33	0.34	0.35	0.36	0.37	0.38	0.39	0.40
0	0.0026	0.0021	0.0016	0.0013	0.0010	0.0008	0.0006	0.0005	0.0004	0.0003
1	0.0216	0.0178	0.0146	0.0120	0.0098	0.0079	0.0064	0.0052	0.0041	0.0033
2	0.0856	0.0734	0.0626	0.0533	0.0451	0.0380	0.0319	0.0266	0.0222	0.0183
3	0.2196	0.1953	0.1730	0.1525	0.1339	0.1170	0.1018	0.0881	0.0759	0.0651
4	0.4154	0.3819	0.3496	0.3187	0.2892	0.2613	0.2351	0.2105	0.1877	0.1666
5	0.6264	0.5926	0.5584	0.5241	0.4900	0.4562	0.4230	0.3906	0.3592	0.3288
6	0.8003	0.7743	0.7469	0.7181	0.6881	0.6572	0.6254	0.5930	0.5602	0.5272
7	0.9119	0.8965	0.8795	0.8609	0.8406	0.8187	0.7952	0.7702	0.7438	0.7161
8	0.9683	0.9612	0.9530	0.9436	0.9329	0.9209	0.9074	0.8924	0.8758	0.8577
9	0.9908	0.9883	0.9852	0.9815	0.9771	0.9720	0.9659	0.9589	0.9509	0.9417
10	0.9979	0.9972	0.9963	0.9952	0.9938	0.9921	0.9900	0.9875	0.9845	0.9809
11	0.9996	0.9995	0.9993	0.9990	0.9987	0.9983	0.9977	0.9970	0.9962	0.9951
12	1.0000	0.9999	0.9999	0.9999	0.9998	0.9997	0.9996	0.9995	0.9993	0.9991

TABLE B
(continued)

n = 16 (continued)

x \ p	0.31	0.32	0.33	0.34	0.35	0.36	0.37	0.38	0.39	0.40
13	1.0000	1.0000	1.0000	1.0000	1.0000	1.0000	1.0000	0.9999	0.9999	0.9999
14	1.0000	1.0000	1.0000	1.0000	1.0000	1.0000	1.0000	1.0000	1.0000	1.0000

x \ p	0.41	0.42	0.43	0.44	0.45	0.46	0.47	0.48	0.49	0.50
0	0.0002	0.0002	0.0001	0.0001	0.0001	0.0001	0.0000	0.0000	0.0000	0.0000
1	0.0026	0.0021	0.0016	0.0013	0.0010	0.0008	0.0006	0.0005	0.0003	0.0003
2	0.0151	0.0124	0.0101	0.0082	0.0066	0.0053	0.0042	0.0034	0.0027	0.0021
3	0.0556	0.0473	0.0400	0.0336	0.0281	0.0234	0.0194	0.0160	0.0131	0.0106
4	0.1471	0.1293	0.1131	0.0985	0.0853	0.0735	0.0630	0.0537	0.0456	0.0384
5	0.2997	0.2720	0.2457	0.2208	0.1976	0.1759	0.1559	0.1374	0.1205	0.1051
6	0.4942	0.4613	0.4289	0.3971	0.3660	0.3359	0.3068	0.2790	0.2524	0.2272
7	0.6872	0.6572	0.6264	0.5949	0.5629	0.5306	0.4981	0.4657	0.4335	0.4018
8	0.8381	0.8168	0.7940	0.7698	0.7441	0.7171	0.6889	0.6596	0.6293	0.5982
9	0.9313	0.9195	0.9064	0.8919	0.8759	0.8584	0.8393	0.8186	0.7964	0.7728
10	0.9766	0.9716	0.9658	0.9591	0.9514	0.9426	0.9326	0.9214	0.9089	0.8949
11	0.9938	0.9922	0.9902	0.9879	0.9851	0.9817	0.9778	0.9732	0.9678	0.9616
12	0.9988	0.9984	0.9979	0.9973	0.9965	0.9956	0.9945	0.9931	0.9914	0.9894
13	0.9998	0.9998	0.9997	0.9996	0.9994	0.9993	0.9990	0.9987	0.9984	0.9979
14	1.0000	1.0000	1.0000	1.0000	0.9999	0.9999	0.9999	0.9999	0.9998	0.9997
15	1.0000	1.0000	1.0000	1.0000	1.0000	1.0000	1.0000	1.0000	1.0000	1.0000

n = 17

x \ p	0.01	0.02	0.03	0.04	0.05	0.06	0.07	0.08	0.09	0.10
0	0.8429	0.7093	0.5958	0.4996	0.4181	0.3493	0.2912	0.2423	0.2012	0.1668
1	0.9877	0.9554	0.9091	0.8535	0.7922	0.7283	0.6638	0.6005	0.5396	0.4818
2	0.9994	0.9956	0.9866	0.9714	0.9497	0.9218	0.8882	0.8497	0.8073	0.7618
3	1.0000	0.9997	0.9986	0.9960	0.9912	0.9836	0.9727	0.9581	0.9397	0.9174
4	1.0000	1.0000	0.9999	0.9996	0.9988	0.9974	0.9949	0.9911	0.9855	0.9779
5	1.0000	1.0000	1.0000	1.0000	0.9999	0.9997	0.9993	0.9985	0.9973	0.9953
6	1.0000	1.0000	1.0000	1.0000	1.0000	1.0000	0.9999	0.9998	0.9996	0.9992
7	1.0000	1.0000	1.0000	1.0000	1.0000	1.0000	1.0000	1.0000	1.0000	0.9999
8	1.0000	1.0000	1.0000	1.0000	1.0000	1.0000	1.0000	1.0000	1.0000	1.0000

x \ p	0.11	0.12	0.13	0.14	0.15	0.16	0.17	0.18	0.19	0.20
0	0.1379	0.1138	0.0937	0.0770	0.0631	0.0516	0.0421	0.0343	0.0278	0.0225
1	0.4277	0.3777	0.3318	0.2901	0.2525	0.2187	0.1887	0.1621	0.1387	0.1182
2	0.7142	0.6655	0.6164	0.5676	0.5198	0.4734	0.4289	0.3867	0.3468	0.3096
3	0.8913	0.8617	0.8290	0.7935	0.7556	0.7159	0.6749	0.6331	0.5909	0.5489
4	0.9679	0.9554	0.9402	0.9222	0.9013	0.8776	0.8513	0.8225	0.7913	0.7582
5	0.9925	0.9886	0.9834	0.9766	0.9681	0.9577	0.9452	0.9305	0.9136	0.8943
6	0.9986	0.9977	0.9963	0.9944	0.9917	0.9882	0.9837	0.9780	0.9709	0.9623
7	0.9998	0.9996	0.9993	0.9989	0.9983	0.9973	0.9961	0.9943	0.9920	0.9891
8	1.0000	0.9999	0.9999	0.9998	0.9997	0.9995	0.9992	0.9988	0.9982	0.9974
9	1.0000	1.0000	1.0000	1.0000	1.0000	0.9999	0.9999	0.9998	0.9997	0.9995
10	1.0000	1.0000	1.0000	1.0000	1.0000	1.0000	1.0000	1.0000	1.0000	0.9999
11	1.0000	1.0000	1.0000	1.0000	1.0000	1.0000	1.0000	1.0000	1.0000	1.0000

TABLE B
(*continued*)

						$n = 17$ (continued)					
x \ p	0.21	0.22	0.23	0.24	0.25	0.26	0.27	0.28	0.29	0.30
0	0.0182	0.0146	0.0118	0.0094	0.0075	0.0060	0.0047	0.0038	0.0030	0.0023
1	0.1004	0.0849	0.0715	0.0600	0.0501	0.0417	0.0346	0.0286	0.0235	0.0193
2	0.2751	0.2433	0.2141	0.1877	0.1637	0.1422	0.1229	0.1058	0.0907	0.0774
3	0.5073	0.4667	0.4272	0.3893	0.3530	0.3186	0.2863	0.2560	0.2279	0.2019
4	0.7234	0.6872	0.6500	0.6121	0.5739	0.5357	0.4977	0.4604	0.4240	0.3887
5	0.8727	0.8490	0.8230	0.7951	0.7653	0.7339	0.7011	0.6671	0.6323	0.5968
6	0.9521	0.9402	0.9264	0.9106	0.8929	0.8732	0.8515	0.8279	0.8024	0.7752
7	0.9853	0.9806	0.9749	0.9680	0.9598	0.9501	0.9389	0.9261	0.9116	0.8954
8	0.9963	0.9949	0.9930	0.9906	0.9876	0.9839	0.9794	0.9739	0.9674	0.9597
9	0.9993	0.9989	0.9984	0.9978	0.9969	0.9958	0.9943	0.9925	0.9902	0.9873
10	0.9999	0.9998	0.9997	0.9996	0.9994	0.9991	0.9987	0.9982	0.9976	0.9968
11	1.0000	1.0000	1.0000	0.9999	0.9999	0.9998	0.9998	0.9997	0.9995	0.9993
12	1.0000	1.0000	1.0000	1.0000	1.0000	1.0000	1.0000	1.0000	0.9999	0.9999
13	1.0000	1.0000	1.0000	1.0000	1.0000	1.0000	1.0000	1.0000	1.0000	1.0000

x \ p	0.31	0.32	0.33	0.34	0.35	0.36	0.37	0.38	0.39	0.40
0	0.0018	0.0014	0.0011	0.0009	0.0007	0.0005	0.0004	0.0003	0.0002	0.0002
1	0.0157	0.0128	0.0104	0.0083	0.0067	0.0054	0.0043	0.0034	0.0027	0.0021
2	0.0657	0.0556	0.0468	0.0392	0.0327	0.0272	0.0225	0.0185	0.0151	0.0123
3	0.1781	0.1563	0.1366	0.1188	0.1028	0.0885	0.0759	0.0648	0.0550	0.0464
4	0.3547	0.3222	0.2913	0.2622	0.2348	0.2094	0.1858	0.1640	0.1441	0.1260
5	0.5610	0.5251	0.4895	0.4542	0.4197	0.3861	0.3535	0.3222	0.2923	0.2639
6	0.7464	0.7162	0.6847	0.6521	0.6188	0.5848	0.5505	0.5161	0.4818	0.4478
7	0.8773	0.8574	0.8358	0.8123	0.7872	0.7605	0.7324	0.7029	0.6722	0.6405
8	0.9508	0.9405	0.9288	0.9155	0.9006	0.8841	0.8659	0.8459	0.8243	0.8011
9	0.9838	0.9796	0.9746	0.9686	0.9617	0.9536	0.9443	0.9336	0.9216	0.9081
10	0.9957	0.9943	0.9926	0.9905	0.9880	0.9849	0.9811	0.9766	0.9714	0.9652
11	0.9991	0.9987	0.9983	0.9977	0.9970	0.9960	0.9949	0.9934	0.9916	0.9894
12	0.9998	0.9998	0.9997	0.9996	0.9994	0.9992	0.9989	0.9985	0.9981	0.9975
13	1.0000	1.0000	1.0000	0.9999	0.9999	0.9999	0.9998	0.9998	0.9997	0.9995
14	1.0000	1.0000	1.0000	1.0000	1.0000	1.0000	1.0000	1.0000	1.0000	0.9999
15	1.0000	1.0000	1.0000	1.0000	1.0000	1.0000	1.0000	1.0000	1.0000	1.0000

x \ p	0.41	0.42	0.43	0.44	0.45	0.46	0.47	0.48	0.49	0.50
0	0.0001	0.0001	0.0001	0.0001	0.0000	0.0000	0.0000	0.0000	0.0000	0.0000
1	0.0016	0.0013	0.0010	0.0008	0.0006	0.0004	0.0003	0.0002	0.0002	0.0001
2	0.0100	0.0080	0.0065	0.0052	0.0041	0.0032	0.0025	0.0020	0.0015	0.0012
3	0.0390	0.0326	0.0271	0.0224	0.0184	0.0151	0.0123	0.0099	0.0080	0.0064
4	0.1096	0.0949	0.0817	0.0699	0.0596	0.0505	0.0425	0.0356	0.0296	0.0245
5	0.2372	0.2121	0.1887	0.1670	0.1471	0.1288	0.1122	0.0972	0.0838	0.0717
6	0.4144	0.3818	0.3501	0.3195	0.2902	0.2623	0.2359	0.2110	0.1878	0.1662
7	0.6080	0.5750	0.5415	0.5079	0.4743	0.4410	0.4082	0.3761	0.3448	0.3145
8	0.7762	0.7498	0.7220	0.6928	0.6626	0.6313	0.5992	0.5665	0.5333	0.5000
9	0.8930	0.8764	0.8581	0.8382	0.8166	0.7934	0.7686	0.7423	0.7145	0.6855
10	0.9580	0.9497	0.9403	0.9295	0.9174	0.9038	0.8888	0.8721	0.8538	0.8338
11	0.9867	0.9835	0.9797	0.9752	0.9699	0.9637	0.9566	0.9483	0.9389	0.9283
12	0.9967	0.9958	0.9946	0.9931	0.9914	0.9892	0.9866	0.9835	0.9798	0.9755
13	0.9994	0.9992	0.9989	0.9986	0.9981	0.9976	0.9969	0.9960	0.9950	0.9936
14	0.9999	0.9999	0.9998	0.9998	0.9997	0.9996	0.9995	0.9993	0.9991	0.9988
15	1.0000	1.0000	1.0000	1.0000	1.0000	1.0000	0.9999	0.9999	0.9999	0.9999
16	1.0000	1.0000	1.0000	1.0000	1.0000	1.0000	1.0000	1.0000	1.0000	1.0000

TABLE B
(continued)

					$n = 18$					

x \ p	0.01	0.02	0.03	0.04	0.05	0.06	0.07	0.08	0.09	0.10
0	0.8345	0.6951	0.5780	0.4796	0.3972	0.3283	0.2708	0.2229	0.1831	0.1501
1	0.9862	0.9505	0.8997	0.8393	0.7735	0.7055	0.6378	0.5719	0.5091	0.4503
2	0.9993	0.9948	0.9843	0.9667	0.9419	0.9102	0.8725	0.8298	0.7832	0.7338
3	1.0000	0.9996	0.9982	0.9950	0.9891	0.9799	0.9667	0.9494	0.9277	0.9018
4	1.0000	1.0000	0.9998	0.9994	0.9985	0.9966	0.9933	0.9884	0.9814	0.9718
5	1.0000	1.0000	1.0000	0.9999	0.9998	0.9995	0.9990	0.9979	0.9962	0.9936
6	1.0000	1.0000	1.0000	1.0000	1.0000	1.0000	0.9999	0.9997	0.9994	0.9988
7	1.0000	1.0000	1.0000	1.0000	1.0000	1.0000	1.0000	1.0000	0.9999	0.9998
8	1.0000	1.0000	1.0000	1.0000	1.0000	1.0000	1.0000	1.0000	1.0000	1.0000

x \ p	0.11	0.12	0.13	0.14	0.15	0.16	0.17	0.18	0.19	0.20
0	0.1227	0.1002	0.0815	0.0662	0.0536	0.0434	0.0349	0.0281	0.0225	0.0180
1	0.3958	0.3460	0.3008	0.2602	0.2241	0.1920	0.1638	0.1391	0.1176	0.0991
2	0.6827	0.6310	0.5794	0.5287	0.4797	0.4327	0.3881	0.3462	0.3073	0.2713
3	0.8718	0.8382	0.8014	0.7618	0.7202	0.6771	0.6331	0.5888	0.5446	0.5010
4	0.9595	0.9442	0.9257	0.9041	0.8794	0.8518	0.8213	0.7884	0.7533	0.7164
5	0.9898	0.9846	0.9778	0.9690	0.9581	0.9449	0.9292	0.9111	0.8903	0.8671
6	0.9979	0.9966	0.9946	0.9919	0.9882	0.9833	0.9771	0.9694	0.9600	0.9487
7	0.9997	0.9994	0.9989	0.9983	0.9973	0.9959	0.9940	0.9914	0.9880	0.9837
8	1.0000	0.9999	0.9998	0.9997	0.9995	0.9992	0.9987	0.9980	0.9971	0.9957
9	1.0000	1.0000	1.0000	1.0000	0.9999	0.9999	0.9998	0.9996	0.9994	0.9991
10	1.0000	1.0000	1.0000	1.0000	1.0000	1.0000	1.0000	0.9999	0.9999	0.9998
11	1.0000	1.0000	1.0000	1.0000	1.0000	1.0000	1.0000	1.0000	1.0000	1.0000

x \ p	0.21	0.22	0.23	0.24	0.25	0.26	0.27	0.28	0.29	0.30
0	0.0144	0.0114	0.0091	0.0072	0.0056	0.0044	0.0035	0.0027	0.0021	0.0016
1	0.0831	0.0694	0.0577	0.0478	0.0395	0.0324	0.0265	0.0216	0.0176	0.0142
2	0.2384	0.2084	0.1813	0.1570	0.1353	0.1161	0.0991	0.0842	0.0712	0.0600
3	0.4586	0.4175	0.3782	0.3409	0.3057	0.2728	0.2422	0.2140	0.1881	0.1646
4	0.6780	0.6387	0.5988	0.5586	0.5187	0.4792	0.4406	0.4032	0.3671	0.3327
5	0.8414	0.8134	0.7832	0.7512	0.7174	0.6824	0.6462	0.6093	0.5719	0.5344
6	0.9355	0.9201	0.9026	0.8829	0.8610	0.8370	0.8109	0.7829	0.7531	0.7217
7	0.9783	0.9717	0.9637	0.9542	0.9431	0.9301	0.9153	0.8986	0.8800	0.8593
8	0.9940	0.9917	0.9888	0.9852	0.9807	0.9751	0.9684	0.9605	0.9512	0.9404
9	0.9986	0.9980	0.9972	0.9961	0.9946	0.9927	0.9903	0.9873	0.9836	0.9790
10	0.9997	0.9996	0.9994	0.9991	0.9988	0.9982	0.9975	0.9966	0.9954	0.9939
11	1.0000	0.9999	0.9999	0.9998	0.9998	0.9997	0.9995	0.9993	0.9990	0.9986
12	1.0000	1.0000	1.0000	1.0000	1.0000	0.9999	0.9999	0.9999	0.9998	0.9997
13	1.0000	1.0000	1.0000	1.0000	1.0000	1.0000	1.0000	1.0000	1.0000	1.0000

x \ p	0.31	0.32	0.33	0.34	0.35	0.36	0.37	0.38	0.39	0.40
0	0.0013	0.0010	0.0007	0.0006	0.0004	0.0003	0.0002	0.0002	0.0001	0.0001
1	0.0114	0.0092	0.0073	0.0058	0.0046	0.0036	0.0028	0.0022	0.0017	0.0013
2	0.0502	0.0419	0.0348	0.0287	0.0236	0.0193	0.0157	0.0127	0.0103	0.0082
3	0.1432	0.1241	0.1069	0.0917	0.0783	0.0665	0.0561	0.0472	0.0394	0.0328
4	0.2999	0.2691	0.2402	0.2134	0.1886	0.1659	0.1451	0.1263	0.1093	0.0942
5	0.4971	0.4602	0.4241	0.3889	0.3550	0.3224	0.2914	0.2621	0.2345	0.2088
6	0.6889	0.6550	0.6202	0.5849	0.5491	0.5133	0.4776	0.4424	0.4079	0.3743
7	0.8367	0.8122	0.7859	0.7579	0.7283	0.6973	0.6651	0.6319	0.5979	0.5634
8	0.9280	0.9139	0.8981	0.8804	0.8609	0.8396	0.8165	0.7916	0.7650	0.7368
9	0.9736	0.9671	0.9595	0.9506	0.9403	0.9286	0.9153	0.9003	0.8837	0.8653

TABLE B
(continued)

n = 18 (continued)

x \ p	0.31	0.32	0.33	0.34	0.35	0.36	0.37	0.38	0.39	0.40
10	0.9920	0.9896	0.9867	0.9831	0.9788	0.9736	0.9675	0.9603	0.9520	0.9424
11	0.9980	0.9973	0.9964	0.9953	0.9938	0.9920	0.9898	0.9870	0.9837	0.9797
12	0.9996	0.9995	0.9992	0.9989	0.9986	0.9981	0.9974	0.9966	0.9956	0.9942
13	0.9999	0.9999	0.9999	0.9998	0.9997	0.9996	0.9995	0.9993	0.9990	0.9987
14	1.0000	1.0000	1.0000	1.0000	1.0000	0.9999	0.9999	0.9999	0.9998	0.9998
15	1.0000	1.0000	1.0000	1.0000	1.0000	1.0000	1.0000	1.0000	1.0000	1.0000

x \ p	0.41	0.42	0.43	0.44	0.45	0.46	0.47	0.48	0.49	0.50
0	0.0001	0.0001	0.0000	0.0000	0.0000	0.0000	0.0000	0.0000	0.0000	0.0000
1	0.0010	0.0008	0.0006	0.0004	0.0003	0.0002	0.0002	0.0001	0.0001	0.0001
2	0.0066	0.0052	0.0041	0.0032	0.0025	0.0019	0.0015	0.0011	0.0009	0.0007
3	0.0271	0.0223	0.0182	0.0148	0.0120	0.0096	0.0077	0.0061	0.0048	0.0038
4	0.0807	0.0687	0.0582	0.0490	0.0411	0.0342	0.0283	0.0233	0.0190	0.0154
5	0.1849	0.1628	0.1427	0.1243	0.1077	0.0928	0.0795	0.0676	0.0572	0.0481
6	0.3418	0.3105	0.2807	0.2524	0.2258	0.2009	0.1778	0.1564	0.1368	0.1189
7	0.5287	0.4938	0.4592	0.4250	0.3915	0.3588	0.3272	0.2968	0.2678	0.2403
8	0.7072	0.6764	0.6444	0.6115	0.5778	0.5438	0.5094	0.4751	0.4409	0.4073
9	0.8451	0.8232	0.7996	0.7742	0.7473	0.7188	0.6890	0.6579	0.6258	0.5927
10	0.9314	0.9189	0.9049	0.8893	0.8720	0.8530	0.8323	0.8098	0.7856	0.7597
11	0.9750	0.9693	0.9628	0.9551	0.9463	0.9362	0.9247	0.9117	0.8972	0.8811
12	0.9926	0.9906	0.9882	0.9853	0.9817	0.9775	0.9725	0.9666	0.9598	0.9519
13	0.9983	0.9978	0.9971	0.9962	0.9951	0.9937	0.9921	0.9900	0.9875	0.9846
14	0.9997	0.9996	0.9994	0.9993	0.9990	0.9987	0.9983	0.9977	0.9971	0.9962
15	1.0000	0.9999	0.9999	0.9999	0.9999	0.9998	0.9997	0.9996	0.9995	0.9993
16	1.0000	1.0000	1.0000	1.0000	1.0000	1.0000	1.0000	1.0000	0.9999	0.9999
17	1.0000	1.0000	1.0000	1.0000	1.0000	1.0000	1.0000	1.0000	1.0000	1.0000

n = 19

x \ p	0.01	0.02	0.03	0.04	0.05	0.06	0.07	0.08	0.09	0.10
0	0.8262	0.6812	0.5606	0.4604	0.3774	0.3086	0.2519	0.2051	0.1666	0.1351
1	0.9847	0.9454	0.8900	0.8249	0.7547	0.6829	0.6121	0.5440	0.4798	0.4203
2	0.9991	0.9939	0.9817	0.9616	0.9335	0.8979	0.8561	0.8092	0.7585	0.7054
3	1.0000	0.9995	0.9978	0.9939	0.9868	0.9757	0.9602	0.9398	0.9147	0.8850
4	1.0000	1.0000	0.9998	0.9993	0.9980	0.9956	0.9915	0.9853	0.9765	0.9648
5	1.0000	1.0000	1.0000	0.9999	0.9998	0.9994	0.9986	0.9971	0.9949	0.9914
6	1.0000	1.0000	1.0000	1.0000	1.0000	0.9999	0.9998	0.9996	0.9991	0.9983
7	1.0000	1.0000	1.0000	1.0000	1.0000	1.0000	1.0000	0.9999	0.9999	0.9997
8	1.0000	1.0000	1.0000	1.0000	1.0000	1.0000	1.0000	1.0000	1.0000	1.0000

x \ p	0.11	0.12	0.13	0.14	0.15	0.16	0.17	0.18	0.19	0.20
0	0.1092	0.0881	0.0709	0.0569	0.0456	0.0364	0.0290	0.0230	0.0182	0.0144
1	0.3658	0.3165	0.2723	0.2331	0.1985	0.1682	0.1419	0.1191	0.0996	0.0829
2	0.6512	0.5968	0.5432	0.4911	0.4413	0.3941	0.3500	0.3090	0.2713	0.2369
3	0.8510	0.8133	0.7725	0.7292	0.6841	0.6380	0.5915	0.5451	0.4995	0.4551
4	0.9498	0.9315	0.9096	0.8842	0.8556	0.8238	0.7893	0.7524	0.7136	0.6733
5	0.9865	0.9798	0.9710	0.9599	0.9463	0.9300	0.9109	0.8890	0.8643	0.8369
6	0.9970	0.9952	0.9924	0.9887	0.9837	0.9772	0.9690	0.9589	0.9468	0.9324
7	0.9995	0.9991	0.9984	0.9974	0.9959	0.9939	0.9911	0.9874	0.9827	0.9767
8	0.9999	0.9998	0.9997	0.9995	0.9992	0.9986	0.9979	0.9968	0.9953	0.9933
9	1.0000	1.0000	1.0000	0.9999	0.9999	0.9998	0.9996	0.9993	0.9990	0.9984

TABLE B
(continued)

n = 19 (continued)

x \ p	0.11	0.12	0.13	0.14	0.15	0.16	0.17	0.18	0.19	0.20
10	1.0000	1.0000	1.0000	1.0000	1.0000	1.0000	0.9999	0.9999	0.9998	0.9997
11	1.0000	1.0000	1.0000	1.0000	1.0000	1.0000	1.0000	1.0000	1.0000	1.0000

x \ p	0.21	0.22	0.23	0.24	0.25	0.26	0.27	0.28	0.29	0.30
0	0.0113	0.0089	0.0070	0.0054	0.0042	0.0033	0.0025	0.0019	0.0015	0.0011
1	0.0687	0.0566	0.0465	0.0381	0.0310	0.0251	0.0203	0.0163	0.0131	0.0104
2	0.2058	0.1778	0.1529	0.1308	0.1113	0.0943	0.0795	0.0667	0.0557	0.0462
3	0.4123	0.3715	0.3329	0.2968	0.2631	0.2320	0.2035	0.1776	0.1542	0.1332
4	0.6319	0.5900	0.5480	0.5064	0.4654	0.4256	0.3871	0.3502	0.3152	0.2822
5	0.8071	0.7749	0.7408	0.7050	0.6677	0.6295	0.5907	0.5516	0.5125	0.4739
6	0.9157	0.8966	0.8751	0.8513	0.8251	0.7968	0.7664	0.7343	0.7005	0.6655
7	0.9693	0.9604	0.9497	0.9371	0.9225	0.9059	0.8871	0.8662	0.8432	0.8180
8	0.9907	0.9873	0.9831	0.9778	0.9713	0.9634	0.9541	0.9432	0.9306	0.9161
9	0.9977	0.9966	0.9953	0.9934	0.9911	0.9881	0.9844	0.9798	0.9742	0.9674
10	0.9995	0.9993	0.9989	0.9984	0.9977	0.9968	0.9956	0.9940	0.9920	0.9895
11	0.9999	0.9999	0.9998	0.9997	0.9995	0.9993	0.9990	0.9985	0.9980	0.9972
12	1.0000	1.0000	1.0000	0.9999	0.9999	0.9999	0.9998	0.9997	0.9996	0.9994
13	1.0000	1.0000	1.0000	1.0000	1.0000	1.0000	1.0000	1.0000	0.9999	0.9999
14	1.0000	1.0000	1.0000	1.0000	1.0000	1.0000	1.0000	1.0000	1.0000	1.0000

x \ p	0.31	0.32	0.33	0.34	0.35	0.36	0.37	0.38	0.39	0.40
0	0.0009	0.0007	0.0005	0.0004	0.0003	0.0002	0.0002	0.0001	0.0001	0.0001
1	0.0083	0.0065	0.0051	0.0040	0.0031	0.0024	0.0019	0.0014	0.0011	0.0008
2	0.0382	0.0314	0.0257	0.0209	0.0170	0.0137	0.0110	0.0087	0.0069	0.0055
3	0.1144	0.0978	0.0831	0.0703	0.0591	0.0495	0.0412	0.0341	0.0281	0.0230
4	0.2514	0.2227	0.1963	0.1720	0.1500	0.1301	0.1122	0.0962	0.0821	0.0696
5	0.4359	0.3990	0.3634	0.3293	0.2968	0.2661	0.2373	0.2105	0.1857	0.1629
6	0.6294	0.5927	0.5555	0.5182	0.4812	0.4446	0.4087	0.3739	0.3403	0.3081
7	0.7909	0.7619	0.7312	0.6990	0.6656	0.6310	0.5957	0.5599	0.5238	0.4878
8	0.8997	0.8814	0.8611	0.8388	0.8145	0.7884	0.7605	0.7309	0.6998	0.6675
9	0.9595	0.9501	0.9392	0.9267	0.9125	0.8965	0.8787	0.8590	0.8374	0.8139
10	0.9863	0.9824	0.9777	0.9720	0.9653	0.9574	0.9482	0.9375	0.9253	0.9115
11	0.9962	0.9949	0.9932	0.9911	0.9886	0.9854	0.9815	0.9769	0.9713	0.9648
12	0.9991	0.9988	0.9983	0.9977	0.9969	0.9959	0.9946	0.9930	0.9909	0.9884
13	0.9998	0.9998	0.9997	0.9995	0.9993	0.9991	0.9987	0.9983	0.9977	0.9969
14	1.0000	1.0000	0.9999	0.9999	0.9999	0.9998	0.9998	0.9997	0.9995	0.9994
15	1.0000	1.0000	1.0000	1.0000	1.0000	1.0000	1.0000	1.0000	0.9999	0.9999
16	1.0000	1.0000	1.0000	1.0000	1.0000	1.0000	1.0000	1.0000	1.0000	1.0000

x \ p	0.41	0.42	0.43	0.44	0.45	0.46	0.47	0.48	0.49	0.50
0	0.0000	0.0000	0.0000	0.0000	0.0000	0.0000	0.0000	0.0000	0.0000	0.0000
1	0.0006	0.0005	0.0004	0.0003	0.0002	0.0001	0.0001	0.0001	0.0001	0.0000
2	0.0043	0.0033	0.0026	0.0020	0.0015	0.0012	0.0009	0.0007	0.0005	0.0004
3	0.0187	0.0151	0.0122	0.0097	0.0077	0.0061	0.0048	0.0037	0.0029	0.0022
4	0.0587	0.0492	0.0410	0.0340	0.0280	0.0229	0.0186	0.0150	0.0121	0.0096
5	0.1421	0.1233	0.1063	0.0912	0.0777	0.0658	0.0554	0.0463	0.0385	0.0318
6	0.2774	0.2485	0.2213	0.1961	0.1727	0.1512	0.1316	0.1138	0.0978	0.0835
7	0.4520	0.4168	0.3824	0.3491	0.3169	0.2862	0.2570	0.2294	0.2036	0.1796
8	0.6340	0.5997	0.5647	0.5294	0.4940	0.4587	0.4238	0.3895	0.3561	0.3238
9	0.7886	0.7615	0.7328	0.7026	0.6710	0.6383	0.6046	0.5701	0.5352	0.5000

TABLE B
(continued)

						$n = 19$ (continued)					
x \ p	0.41	0.42	0.43	0.44	0.45	0.46	0.47	0.48	0.49	0.50
10	0.8960	0.8787	0.8596	0.8387	0.8159	0.7913	0.7649	0.7369	0.7073	0.6762
11	0.9571	0.9482	0.9379	0.9262	0.9129	0.8979	0.8813	0.8628	0.8425	0.8204
12	0.9854	0.9817	0.9773	0.9720	0.9658	0.9585	0.9500	0.9403	0.9291	0.9165
13	0.9960	0.9948	0.9933	0.9914	0.9891	0.9863	0.9829	0.9788	0.9739	0.9682
14	0.9991	0.9988	0.9984	0.9979	0.9972	0.9964	0.9954	0.9940	0.9924	0.9904
15	0.9999	0.9998	0.9997	0.9996	0.9995	0.9993	0.9990	0.9987	0.9983	0.9978
16	1.0000	1.0000	1.0000	0.9999	0.9999	0.9999	0.9999	0.9998	0.9997	0.9996
17	1.0000	1.0000	1.0000	1.0000	1.0000	1.0000	1.0000	1.0000	1.0000	1.0000

						$n = 20$					
x \ p	0.01	0.02	0.03	0.04	0.05	0.06	0.07	0.08	0.09	0.10
0	0.8179	0.6676	0.5438	0.4420	0.3585	0.2901	0.2342	0.1887	0.1516	0.1216
1	0.9831	0.9401	0.8802	0.8103	0.7358	0.6605	0.5869	0.5169	0.4516	0.3917
2	0.9990	0.9929	0.9790	0.9561	0.9245	0.8850	0.8390	0.7879	0.7334	0.6769
3	1.0000	0.9994	0.9973	0.9926	0.9841	0.9710	0.9529	0.9294	0.9007	0.8670
4	1.0000	1.0000	0.9997	0.9990	0.9974	0.9944	0.9893	0.9817	0.9710	0.9568
5	1.0000	1.0000	1.0000	0.9999	0.9997	0.9991	0.9981	0.9962	0.9932	0.9887
6	1.0000	1.0000	1.0000	1.0000	1.0000	0.9999	0.9997	0.9994	0.9987	0.9976
7	1.0000	1.0000	1.0000	1.0000	1.0000	1.0000	1.0000	0.9999	0.9998	0.9996
8	1.0000	1.0000	1.0000	1.0000	1.0000	1.0000	1.0000	1.0000	1.0000	0.9999
9	1.0000	1.0000	1.0000	1.0000	1.0000	1.0000	1.0000	1.0000	1.0000	1.0000

x \ p	0.11	0.12	0.13	0.14	0.15	0.16	0.17	0.18	0.19	0.20
0	0.0972	0.0776	0.0617	0.0490	0.0388	0.0306	0.0241	0.0189	0.0148	0.0115
1	0.3376	0.2891	0.2461	0.2084	0.1756	0.1471	0.1227	0.1018	0.0841	0.0692
2	0.6198	0.5631	0.5080	0.4550	0.4049	0.3580	0.3146	0.2748	0.2386	0.2061
3	0.8290	0.7873	0.7427	0.6959	0.6477	0.5990	0.5504	0.5026	0.4561	0.4114
4	0.9390	0.9173	0.8917	0.8625	0.8298	0.7941	0.7557	0.7151	0.6729	0.6296
5	0.9825	0.9740	0.9630	0.9493	0.9327	0.9130	0.8902	0.8644	0.8357	0.8042
6	0.9959	0.9933	0.9897	0.9847	0.9781	0.9696	0.9591	0.9463	0.9311	0.9133
7	0.9992	0.9986	0.9976	0.9962	0.9941	0.9912	0.9873	0.9823	0.9759	0.9679
8	0.9999	0.9998	0.9995	0.9992	0.9987	0.9979	0.9967	0.9951	0.9929	0.9900
9	1.0000	1.0000	0.9999	0.9999	0.9998	0.9996	0.9993	0.9989	0.9983	0.9974
10	1.0000	1.0000	1.0000	1.0000	1.0000	0.9999	0.9999	0.9998	0.9996	0.9994
11	1.0000	1.0000	1.0000	1.0000	1.0000	1.0000	1.0000	1.0000	0.9999	0.9999
12	1.0000	1.0000	1.0000	1.0000	1.0000	1.0000	1.0000	1.0000	1.0000	1.0000

x \ p	0.21	0.22	0.23	0.24	0.25	0.26	0.27	0.28	0.29	0.30
0	0.0090	0.0069	0.0054	0.0041	0.0032	0.0024	0.0018	0.0014	0.0011	0.0008
1	0.0566	0.0461	0.0374	0.0302	0.0243	0.0195	0.0155	0.0123	0.0097	0.0076
2	0.1770	0.1512	0.1284	0.1085	0.0913	0.0763	0.0635	0.0526	0.0433	0.0355
3	0.3690	0.3289	0.2915	0.2569	0.2252	0.1962	0.1700	0.1466	0.1256	0.1071
4	0.5858	0.5420	0.4986	0.4561	0.4148	0.3752	0.3375	0.3019	0.2685	0.2375
5	0.7703	0.7343	0.6965	0.6573	0.6172	0.5765	0.5357	0.4952	0.4553	0.4164
6	0.8929	0.8699	0.8442	0.8162	0.7858	0.7533	0.7190	0.6831	0.6460	0.6080
7	0.9581	0.9464	0.9325	0.9165	0.8982	0.8775	0.8545	0.8293	0.8018	0.7723
8	0.9862	0.9814	0.9754	0.9680	0.9591	0.9485	0.9360	0.9216	0.9052	0.8867
9	0.9962	0.9946	0.9925	0.9897	0.9861	0.9817	0.9762	0.9695	0.9615	0.9520
10	0.9991	0.9987	0.9981	0.9972	0.9961	0.9945	0.9926	0.9900	0.9868	0.9829

TABLE B
(*continued*)

	$n = 20$ (continued)									
x \ p	0.21	0.22	0.23	0.24	0.25	0.26	0.27	0.28	0.29	0.30
11	0.9998	0.9997	0.9996	0.9994	0.9991	0.9986	0.9981	0.9973	0.9962	0.9949
12	1.0000	1.0000	0.9999	0.9999	0.9998	0.9997	0.9996	0.9994	0.9991	0.9987
13	1.0000	1.0000	1.0000	1.0000	1.0000	1.0000	0.9999	0.9999	0.9998	0.9997
14	1.0000	1.0000	1.0000	1.0000	1.0000	1.0000	1.0000	1.0000	1.0000	1.0000

x \ p	0.31	0.32	0.33	0.34	0.35	0.36	0.37	0.38	0.39	0.40
0	0.0006	0.0004	0.0003	0.0002	0.0002	0.0001	0.0001	0.0001	0.0001	0.0000
1	0.0060	0.0047	0.0036	0.0028	0.0021	0.0016	0.0012	0.0009	0.0007	0.0005
2	0.0289	0.0235	0.0189	0.0152	0.0121	0.0096	0.0076	0.0060	0.0047	0.0036
3	0.0908	0.0765	0.0642	0.0535	0.0444	0.0366	0.0300	0.0245	0.0198	0.0160
4	0.2089	0.1827	0.1589	0.1374	0.1182	0.1011	0.0859	0.0726	0.0610	0.0510
5	0.3787	0.3426	0.3082	0.2758	0.2454	0.2171	0.1910	0.1671	0.1453	0.1256
6	0.5695	0.5307	0.4921	0.4540	0.4166	0.3803	0.3453	0.3118	0.2800	0.2500
7	0.7409	0.7078	0.6732	0.6376	0.6010	0.5639	0.5265	0.4892	0.4522	0.4159
8	0.8660	0.8432	0.8182	0.7913	0.7624	0.7317	0.6995	0.6659	0.6312	0.5956
9	0.9409	0.9281	0.9134	0.8968	0.8782	0.8576	0.8350	0.8103	0.7837	0.7553
10	0.9780	0.9721	0.9650	0.9566	0.9468	0.9355	0.9225	0.9077	0.8910	0.8725
11	0.9931	0.9909	0.9881	0.9846	0.9804	0.9753	0.9692	0.9619	0.9534	0.9435
12	0.9982	0.9975	0.9966	0.9955	0.9940	0.9921	0.9898	0.9868	0.9833	0.9790
13	0.9996	0.9994	0.9992	0.9989	0.9985	0.9979	0.9972	0.9963	0.9951	0.9935
14	0.9999	0.9999	0.9999	0.9998	0.9997	0.9996	0.9994	0.9991	0.9988	0.9984
15	1.0000	1.0000	1.0000	1.0000	1.0000	0.9999	0.9999	0.9998	0.9998	0.9997
16	1.0000	1.0000	1.0000	1.0000	1.0000	1.0000	1.0000	1.0000	1.0000	1.0000

x \ p	0.41	0.42	0.43	0.44	0.45	0.46	0.47	0.48	0.49	0.50
0	0.0000	0.0000	0.0000	0.0000	0.0000	0.0000	0.0000	0.0000	0.0000	0.0000
1	0.0004	0.0003	0.0002	0.0002	0.0001	0.0001	0.0001	0.0000	0.0000	0.0000
2	0.0028	0.0021	0.0016	0.0012	0.0009	0.0007	0.0005	0.0004	0.0003	0.0002
3	0.0128	0.0102	0.0080	0.0063	0.0049	0.0038	0.0029	0.0023	0.0017	0.0013
4	0.0423	0.0349	0.0286	0.0233	0.0189	0.0152	0.0121	0.0096	0.0076	0.0059
5	0.1079	0.0922	0.0783	0.0660	0.0553	0.0461	0.0381	0.0313	0.0255	0.0207
6	0.2220	0.1959	0.1719	0.1499	0.1299	0.1119	0.0958	0.0814	0.0688	0.0577
7	0.3804	0.3461	0.3132	0.2817	0.2520	0.2241	0.1980	0.1739	0.1518	0.1316
8	0.5594	0.5229	0.4864	0.4501	0.4143	0.3793	0.3454	0.3127	0.2814	0.2517
9	0.7252	0.6936	0.6606	0.6264	0.5914	0.5557	0.5196	0.4834	0.4474	0.4119
10	0.8520	0.8295	0.8051	0.7788	0.7507	0.7209	0.6896	0.6568	0.6229	0.5881
11	0.9321	0.9190	0.9042	0.8877	0.8692	0.8489	0.8266	0.8024	0.7762	0.7483
12	0.9738	0.9676	0.9603	0.9518	0.9420	0.9306	0.9177	0.9031	0.8867	0.8684
13	0.9916	0.9893	0.9864	0.9828	0.9786	0.9735	0.9674	0.9603	0.9520	0.9423
14	0.9978	0.9971	0.9962	0.9950	0.9936	0.9917	0.9895	0.9867	0.9834	0.9793
15	0.9996	0.9994	0.9992	0.9989	0.9985	0.9980	0.9973	0.9965	0.9954	0.9941
16	0.9999	0.9999	0.9999	0.9998	0.9997	0.9996	0.9995	0.9993	0.9990	0.9987
17	1.0000	1.0000	1.0000	1.0000	1.0000	0.9999	0.9999	0.9999	0.9999	0.9998
18	1.0000	1.0000	1.0000	1.0000	1.0000	1.0000	1.0000	1.0000	1.0000	1.0000

TABLE B
(continued)

						$n = 25$					
x \ p	0.01	0.02	0.03	0.04	0.05	0.06	0.07	0.08	0.09	0.10
0	0.7778	0.6035	0.4670	0.3604	0.2774	0.2129	0.1630	0.1244	0.0946	0.0718
1	0.9742	0.9114	0.8280	0.7358	0.6424	0.5527	0.4696	0.3947	0.3286	0.2712
2	0.9980	0.9868	0.9620	0.9235	0.8729	0.8129	0.7466	0.6768	0.6063	0.5371
3	0.9999	0.9986	0.9938	0.9835	0.9659	0.9402	0.9064	0.8649	0.8169	0.7636
4	1.0000	0.9999	0.9992	0.9972	0.9928	0.9850	0.9726	0.9549	0.9314	0.9020
5	1.0000	1.0000	0.9999	0.9996	0.9988	0.9969	0.9935	0.9877	0.9790	0.9666
6	1.0000	1.0000	1.0000	1.0000	0.9998	0.9995	0.9987	0.9972	0.9946	0.9905
7	1.0000	1.0000	1.0000	1.0000	1.0000	0.9999	0.9998	0.9995	0.9989	0.9977
8	1.0000	1.0000	1.0000	1.0000	1.0000	1.0000	1.0000	0.9999	0.9998	0.9995
9	1.0000	1.0000	1.0000	1.0000	1.0000	1.0000	1.0000	1.0000	1.0000	0.9999
10	1.0000	1.0000	1.0000	1.0000	1.0000	1.0000	1.0000	1.0000	1.0000	1.0000

x \ p	0.11	0.12	0.13	0.14	0.15	0.16	0.17	0.18	0.19	0.20
0	0.0543	0.0409	0.0308	0.0230	0.0172	0.0128	0.0095	0.0070	0.0052	0.0038
1	0.2221	0.1805	0.1457	0.1168	0.0931	0.0737	0.0580	0.0454	0.0354	0.0274
2	0.4709	0.4088	0.3517	0.3000	0.2537	0.2130	0.1774	0.1467	0.1204	0.0982
3	0.7066	0.6475	0.5877	0.5286	0.4711	0.4163	0.3648	0.3171	0.2734	0.2340
4	0.8669	0.8266	0.7817	0.7332	0.6821	0.6293	0.5759	0.5228	0.4708	0.4207
5	0.9501	0.9291	0.9035	0.8732	0.8385	0.7998	0.7575	0.7125	0.6653	0.6167
6	0.9844	0.9757	0.9641	0.9491	0.9305	0.9080	0.8815	0.8512	0.8173	0.7800
7	0.9959	0.9930	0.9887	0.9827	0.9745	0.9639	0.9505	0.9339	0.9141	0.8909
8	0.9991	0.9983	0.9970	0.9950	0.9920	0.9879	0.9822	0.9748	0.9652	0.9532
9	0.9998	0.9996	0.9993	0.9987	0.9979	0.9965	0.9945	0.9917	0.9878	0.9827
10	1.0000	0.9999	0.9999	0.9997	0.9995	0.9991	0.9985	0.9976	0.9963	0.9944
11	1.0000	1.0000	1.0000	1.0000	0.9999	0.9998	0.9997	0.9994	0.9990	0.9985
12	1.0000	1.0000	1.0000	1.0000	1.0000	1.0000	0.9999	0.9999	0.9998	0.9996
13	1.0000	1.0000	1.0000	1.0000	1.0000	1.0000	1.0000	1.0000	1.0000	0.9999
14	1.0000	1.0000	1.0000	1.0000	1.0000	1.0000	1.0000	1.0000	1.0000	1.0000

x \ p	0.21	0.22	0.23	0.24	0.25	0.26	0.27	0.28	0.29	0.30
0	0.0028	0.0020	0.0015	0.0010	0.0008	0.0005	0.0004	0.0003	0.0002	0.0001
1	0.0211	0.0162	0.0123	0.0093	0.0070	0.0053	0.0039	0.0029	0.0021	0.0016
2	0.0796	0.0640	0.0512	0.0407	0.0321	0.0252	0.0196	0.0152	0.0117	0.0090
3	0.1987	0.1676	0.1403	0.1166	0.0962	0.0789	0.0642	0.0519	0.0417	0.0332
4	0.3730	0.3282	0.2866	0.2484	0.2137	0.1826	0.1548	0.1304	0.1090	0.0905
5	0.5675	0.5184	0.4701	0.4233	0.3783	0.3356	0.2956	0.2585	0.2245	0.1935
6	0.7399	0.6973	0.6529	0.6073	0.5611	0.5149	0.4692	0.4247	0.3817	0.3407
7	0.8642	0.8342	0.8011	0.7651	0.7265	0.6858	0.6435	0.6001	0.5560	0.5118
8	0.9386	0.9212	0.9007	0.8772	0.8506	0.8210	0.7885	0.7535	0.7162	0.6769
9	0.9760	0.9675	0.9569	0.9440	0.9287	0.9107	0.8899	0.8662	0.8398	0.8106
10	0.9918	0.9883	0.9837	0.9778	0.9703	0.9611	0.9498	0.9364	0.9205	0.9022
11	0.9976	0.9964	0.9947	0.9924	0.9893	0.9852	0.9801	0.9736	0.9655	0.9558
12	0.9994	0.9990	0.9985	0.9977	0.9966	0.9951	0.9931	0.9904	0.9870	0.9825
13	0.9999	0.9998	0.9996	0.9994	0.9991	0.9986	0.9979	0.9970	0.9957	0.9940
14	1.0000	1.0000	0.9999	0.9999	0.9998	0.9997	0.9995	0.9992	0.9988	0.9982
15	1.0000	1.0000	1.0000	1.0000	1.0000	0.9999	0.9999	0.9998	0.9997	0.9995
16	1.0000	1.0000	1.0000	1.0000	1.0000	1.0000	1.0000	1.0000	0.9999	0.9999
17	1.0000	1.0000	1.0000	1.0000	1.0000	1.0000	1.0000	1.0000	1.0000	1.0000

TABLE B
(*continued*)

x \ p	0.31	0.32	0.33	0.34	0.35	0.36	0.37	0.38	0.39	0.40
0	0.0001	0.0001	0.0000	0.0000	0.0000	0.0000	0.0000	0.0000	0.0000	0.0000
1	0.0011	0.0008	0.0006	0.0004	0.0003	0.0002	0.0002	0.0001	0.0001	0.0001
2	0.0068	0.0051	0.0039	0.0029	0.0021	0.0016	0.0011	0.0008	0.0006	0.0004
3	0.0263	0.0207	0.0162	0.0126	0.0097	0.0074	0.0056	0.0043	0.0032	0.0024
4	0.0746	0.0610	0.0496	0.0400	0.0320	0.0255	0.0201	0.0158	0.0123	0.0095
5	0.1656	0.1407	0.1187	0.0994	0.0826	0.0682	0.0559	0.0454	0.0367	0.0294
6	0.3019	0.2657	0.2321	0.2013	0.1734	0.1483	0.1258	0.1060	0.0886	0.0736
7	0.4681	0.4253	0.3837	0.3439	0.3061	0.2705	0.2374	0.2068	0.1789	0.1536
8	0.6361	0.5943	0.5518	0.5092	0.4668	0.4252	0.3848	0.3458	0.3086	0.2735
9	0.7787	0.7445	0.7081	0.6700	0.6303	0.5896	0.5483	0.5067	0.4653	0.4246
10	0.8812	0.8576	0.8314	0.8025	0.7712	0.7375	0.7019	0.6645	0.6257	0.5858
11	0.9440	0.9302	0.9141	0.8956	0.8746	0.8510	0.8249	0.7964	0.7654	0.7323
12	0.9770	0.9701	0.9617	0.9515	0.9396	0.9255	0.9093	0.8907	0.8697	0.8462
13	0.9917	0.9888	0.9851	0.9804	0.9745	0.9674	0.9588	0.9485	0.9363	0.9222
14	0.9974	0.9964	0.9950	0.9931	0.9907	0.9876	0.9837	0.9788	0.9729	0.9656
15	0.9993	0.9990	0.9985	0.9979	0.9971	0.9959	0.9944	0.9925	0.9900	0.9868
16	0.9998	0.9998	0.9996	0.9995	0.9992	0.9989	0.9984	0.9977	0.9968	0.9957
17	1.0000	1.0000	0.9999	0.9999	0.9998	0.9997	0.9996	0.9994	0.9992	0.9988
18	1.0000	1.0000	1.0000	1.0000	1.0000	0.9999	0.9999	0.9999	0.9998	0.9997
19	1.0000	1.0000	1.0000	1.0000	1.0000	1.0000	1.0000	1.0000	1.0000	0.9999
20	1.0000	1.0000	1.0000	1.0000	1.0000	1.0000	1.0000	1.0000	1.0000	1.0000

x \ p	0.41	0.42	0.43	0.44	0.45	0.46	0.47	0.48	0.49	0.50
0	0.0000	0.0000	0.0000	0.0000	0.0000	0.0000	0.0000	0.0000	0.0000	0.0000
1	0.0000	0.0000	0.0000	0.0000	0.0000	0.0000	0.0000	0.0000	0.0000	0.0000
2	0.0003	0.0002	0.0002	0.0001	0.0001	0.0000	0.0000	0.0000	0.0000	0.0000
3	0.0017	0.0013	0.0009	0.0007	0.0005	0.0003	0.0002	0.0002	0.0001	0.0001
4	0.0073	0.0055	0.0042	0.0031	0.0023	0.0017	0.0012	0.0009	0.0006	0.0005
5	0.0233	0.0184	0.0144	0.0112	0.0086	0.0066	0.0050	0.0037	0.0028	0.0020
6	0.0606	0.0495	0.0401	0.0323	0.0258	0.0204	0.0160	0.0124	0.0096	0.0073
7	0.1308	0.1106	0.0929	0.0773	0.0639	0.0523	0.0425	0.0342	0.0273	0.0216
8	0.2407	0.2103	0.1823	0.1569	0.1340	0.1135	0.0954	0.0795	0.0657	0.0539
9	0.3849	0.3465	0.3098	0.2750	0.2424	0.2120	0.1840	0.1585	0.1354	0.1148
10	0.5452	0.5044	0.4637	0.4235	0.3843	0.3462	0.3098	0.2751	0.2426	0.2122
11	0.6971	0.6603	0.6220	0.5826	0.5426	0.5022	0.4618	0.4220	0.3829	0.3450
12	0.8203	0.7920	0.7613	0.7285	0.6937	0.6571	0.6192	0.5801	0.5402	0.5000
13	0.9059	0.8873	0.8664	0.8431	0.8173	0.7891	0.7587	0.7260	0.6914	0.6550
14	0.9569	0.9465	0.9344	0.9203	0.9040	0.8855	0.8647	0.8415	0.8159	0.7878
15	0.9829	0.9780	0.9720	0.9647	0.9560	0.9457	0.9337	0.9197	0.9036	0.8852
16	0.9942	0.9922	0.9897	0.9866	0.9826	0.9778	0.9719	0.9648	0.9562	0.9461
17	0.9983	0.9977	0.9968	0.9956	0.9942	0.9923	0.9898	0.9868	0.9830	0.9784
18	0.9996	0.9994	0.9992	0.9988	0.9984	0.9977	0.9969	0.9959	0.9945	0.9927
19	0.9999	0.9999	0.9998	0.9997	0.9996	0.9995	0.9992	0.9989	0.9985	0.9980
20	1.0000	1.0000	1.0000	1.0000	0.9999	0.9999	0.9998	0.9998	0.9997	0.9995
21	1.0000	1.0000	1.0000	1.0000	1.0000	1.0000	1.0000	1.0000	0.9999	0.9999
22	1.0000	1.0000	1.0000	1.0000	1.0000	1.0000	1.0000	1.0000	1.0000	1.0000

between
−2.51 .0060
to
−0.10 .4602
.4542

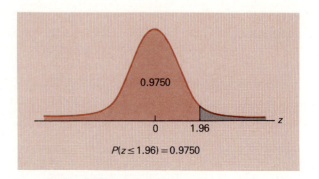

$P(z \le 1.96) = 0.9750$

Entries in the body of the table
are areas between $-\infty$ and z.

Ex
−3.61

−3.60
.00
−3.61

$P(z > 2.58) - 1.00$
.9951 − 1.00
.00049
OR
.49.03

TABLE C
Normal curve areas
$P(z \le z_0)$

z	−0.09	−0.08	−0.07	−0.06	−0.05	−0.04	−0.03	−0.02	−0.01	0.00	z
−3.80	.0001	.0001	.0001	.0001	.0001	.0001	.0001	.0001	.0001	.0001	−3.80
−3.70	.0001	.0001	.0001	.0001	.0001	.0001	.0001	.0001	.0001	.0001	−3.70
−3.60	.0001	.0001	.0001	.0001	.0001	.0001	.0001	.0001	.0002	.0002	−3.60
−3.50	.0002	.0002	.0002	.0002	.0002	.0002	.0002	.0002	.0002	.0002	−3.50
−3.40	.0002	.0003	.0003	.0003	.0003	.0003	.0003	.0003	.0003	.0003	−3.40
−3.30	.0003	.0004	.0004	.0004	.0004	.0004	.0004	.0005	.0005	.0005	−3.30
−3.20	.0005	.0005	.0005	.0006	.0006	.0006	.0006	.0006	.0007	.0007	−3.20
−3.10	.0007	.0007	.0008	.0008	.0008	.0008	.0009	.0009	.0009	.0010	−3.10
−3.00	.0010	.0010	.0011	.0011	.0011	.0012	.0012	.0013	.0013	.0013	−3.00
−2.90	.0014	.0014	.0015	.0015	.0016	.0016	.0017	.0018	.0018	.0019	−2.90
−2.80	.0019	.0020	.0021	.0021	.0022	.0023	.0023	.0024	.0025	.0026	−2.80
−2.70	.0026	.0027	.0028	.0029	.0030	.0031	.0032	.0033	.0034	.0035	−2.70
−2.60	.0036	.0037	.0038	.0039	.0040	.0041	.0043	.0044	.0045	.0047	−2.60
−2.50	.0048	.0049	.0051	.0052	.0054	.0055	.0057	.0059	.0060	.0062	−2.50
−2.40	.0064	.0066	.0068	.0069	.0071	.0073	.0075	.0078	.0080	.0082	−2.40
−2.30	.0084	.0087	.0089	.0091	.0094	.0096	.0099	.0102	.0104	.0107	−2.30
−2.20	.0110	.0113	.0116	.0119	.0122	.0125	.0129	.0132	.0136	.0139	−2.20
−2.10	.0143	.0146	.0150	.0154	.0158	.0162	.0166	.0170	.0174	.0179	−2.10
−2.00	.0183	.0188	.0192	.0197	.0202	.0207	.0212	.0217	.0222	.0228	−2.00
−1.90	.0233	.0239	.0244	.0250	.0256	.0262	.0268	.0274	.0281	.0287	−1.90
−1.80	.0294	.0301	.0307	.0314	.0322	.0329	.0336	.0344	.0351	.0359	−1.80
−1.70	.0367	.0375	.0384	.0392	.0401	.0409	.0418	.0427	.0436	.0446	−1.70
−1.60	.0455	.0465	.0475	.0485	.0495	.0505	.0516	.0526	.0537	.0548	−1.60
−1.50	.0559	.0571	.0582	.0594	.0606	.0618	.0630	.0643	.0655	.0668	−1.50
−1.40	.0681	.0694	.0708	.0721	.0735	.0749	.0764	.0778	.0793	.0808	−1.40
−1.30	.0823	.0838	.0853	.0869	.0885	.0901	.0918	.0934	.0951	.0968	−1.30
−1.20	.0985	.1003	.1020	.1038	.1056	.1075	.1093	.1112	.1131	.1151	−1.20
−1.10	.1170	.1190	.1210	.1230	.1251	.1271	.1292	.1314	.1335	.1357	−1.10
−1.00	.1379	.1401	.1423	.1446	.1469	.1492	.1515	.1539	.1562	.1587	−1.00
−0.90	.1611	.1635	.1660	.1685	.1711	.1736	.1762	.1788	.1814	.1841	−0.90
−0.80	.1867	.1894	.1922	.1949	.1977	.2005	.2033	.2061	.2090	.2119	−0.80
−0.70	.2148	.2177	.2206	.2236	.2266	.2296	.2327	.2358	.2389	.2420	−0.70
−0.60	.2451	.2483	.2514	.2546	.2578	.2611	.2643	.2676	.2709	.2743	−0.60
−0.50	.2776	.2810	.2843	.2877	.2912	.2946	.2981	.3015	.3050	.3085	−0.50
−0.40	.3121	.3156	.3192	.3228	.3264	.3300	.3336	.3372	.3409	.3446	−0.40
−0.30	.3483	.3520	.3557	.3594	.3632	.3669	.3707	.3745	.3783	.3821	−0.30
−0.20	.3859	.3897	.3936	.3974	.4013	.4052	.4090	.4129	.4168	.4207	−0.20
−0.10	.4247	.4286	.4325	.4364	.4404	.4443	.4483	.4522	.4562	.4602	−0.10
0.00	.4641	.4681	.4721	.4761	.4801	.4840	.4880	.4920	.4960	.5000	0.00

between

$\frac{.9997}{.9938}$ $\begin{array}{l} +2.50 \quad .9938 \\ \quad to \\ +3.40 \quad .9997 \end{array}$

$-\ \frac{.9997}{.9938}$

$\frac{5.9 \cdot 9^{-03}}{.00059}$ R

TABLE C
(continued)

z	0.00	0.01	0.02	0.03	0.04	0.05	0.06	0.07	0.08	0.09	z
0.00	.5000	.5040	.5080	.5120	.5160	.5199	.5239	.5279	.5319	.5359	0.00
0.10	.5398	.5438	.5478	.5517	.5557	.5596	.5636	.5675	.5714	.5753	0.10
0.20	.5793	.5832	.5871	.5910	.5948	.5987	.6026	.6064	.6103	.6141	0.20
0.30	.6179	.6217	.6255	.6293	.6331	.6368	.6406	.6443	.6480	.6517	0.30
0.40	.6554	.6591	.6628	.6664	.6700	.6736	.6772	.6808	.6844	.6879	0.40
0.50	.6915	.6950	.6985	.7019	.7054	.7088	.7123	.7157	.7190	.7224	0.50
0.60	.7257	.7291	.7324	.7357	.7389	.7422	.7454	.7486	.7517	.7549	0.60
0.70	.7580	.7611	.7642	.7673	.7704	.7734	.7764	.7794	.7823	.7852	0.70
0.80	.7881	.7910	.7939	.7967	.7995	.8023	.8051	.8078	.8106	.8133	0.80
0.90	.8159	.8186	.8212	.8238	.8264	.8289	.8315	.8340	.8365	.8389	0.90
1.00	.8413	.8438	.8461	.8485	.8508	.8531	.8554	.8577	.8599	.8621	1.00
1.10	.8643	.8665	.8686	.8708	.8729	.8749	.8770	.8790	.8810	.8830	1.10
1.20	.8849	.8869	.8888	.8907	.8925	.8944	.8962	.8980	.8997	.9015	1.20
1.30	.9032	.9049	.9066	.9082	.9099	.9115	.9131	.9147	.9162	.9177	1.30
1.40	.9192	.9207	.9222	.9236	.9251	.9265	.9279	.9292	.9306	.9319	1.40
1.50	.9332	.9345	.9357	.9370	.9382	.9394	.9406	.9418	.9429	.9441	1.50
1.60	.9452	.9463	.9474	.9484	.9495	.9505	.9515	.9525	.9535	.9545	1.60
1.70	.9554	.9564	.9573	.9582	.9591	.9599	.9608	.9616	.9625	.9633	1.70
1.80	.9641	.9649	.9656	.9664	.9671	.9678	.9686	.9693	.9699	.9706	1.80
1.90	.9713	.9719	.9726	.9732	.9738	.9744	.9750	.9756	.9761	.9767	1.90
2.00	.9772	.9778	.9783	.9788	.9793	.9798	.9803	.9808	.9812	.9817	2.00
2.10	.9821	.9826	.9830	.9834	.9838	.9842	.9846	.9850	.9854	.9857	2.10
2.20	.9861	.9864	.9868	.9871	.9875	.9878	.9881	.9884	.9887	.9890	2.20
2.30	.9893	.9896	.9898	.9901	.9904	.9906	.9909	.9911	.9913	.9916	2.30
2.40	.9918	.9920	.9922	.9925	.9927	.9929	.9931	.9932	.9934	.9936	2.40
2.50	.9938	.9940	.9941	.9943	.9945	.9946	.9948	.9949	.9951	.9952	2.50
2.60	.9953	.9955	.9956	.9957	.9959	.9960	.9961	.9962	.9963	.9964	2.60
2.70	.9965	.9966	.9967	.9968	.9969	.9970	.9971	.9972	.9973	.9974	2.70
2.80	.9974	.9975	.9976	.9977	.9977	.9978	.9979	.9979	.9980	.9981	2.80
2.90	.9981	.9982	.9982	.9983	.9984	.9984	.9985	.9985	.9986	.9986	2.90
3.00	.9987	.9987	.9987	.9988	.9988	.9989	.9989	.9989	.9990	.9990	3.00
3.10	.9990	.9991	.9991	.9991	.9992	.9992	.9992	.9992	.9993	.9993	3.10
3.20	.9993	.9993	.9994	.9994	.9994	.9994	.9994	.9995	.9995	.9995	3.20
3.30	.9995	.9995	.9995	.9996	.9996	.9996	.9996	.9996	.9996	.9997	3.30
3.40	.9997	.9997	.9997	.9997	.9997	.9997	.9997	.9997	.9997	.9998	3.40
3.50	.9998	.9998	.9998	.9998	.9998	.9998	.9998	.9998	.9998	.9998	3.50
3.60	.9998	.9998	.9999	.9999	.9999	.9999	.9999	.9999	.9999	.9999	3.60
3.70	.9999	.9999	.9999	.9999	.9999	.9999	.9999	.9999	.9999	.9999	3.70
3.80	.9999	.9999	.9999	.9999	.9999	.9999	.9999	.9999	.9999	.9999	3.80

.9938

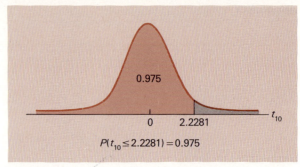

$P(t_{10} \leq 2.2281) = 0.975$

TABLE D
Percentiles of the
***t* distribution**
$P(t \leq t_0)$

df	$t_{0.90}$	$t_{0.95}$	$t_{0.975}$	$t_{0.99}$	$t_{0.995}$
1	3.078	6.3138	12.706	31.821	63.657
2	1.886	2.9200	4.3027	6.965	9.9248
3	1.638	2.3534	3.1825	4.541	5.8409
4	1.533	2.1318	2.7764	3.747	4.6041
5	1.476	2.0150	2.5706	3.365	4.0321
6	1.440	1.9432	2.4469	3.143	3.7074
7	1.415	1.8946	2.3646	2.998	3.4995
8	1.397	1.8595	2.3060	2.896	3.3554
9	1.383	1.8331	2.2622	2.821	3.2498
10	1.372	1.8125	2.2281	2.764	3.1693
11	1.363	1.7959	2.2010	2.718	3.1058
12	1.356	1.7823	2.1788	2.681	3.0545
13	1.350	1.7709	2.1604	2.650	3.0123
14	1.345	1.7613	2.1448	2.624	2.9768
15	1.341	1.7530	2.1315	2.602	2.9467
16	1.337	1.7459	2.1199	2.583	2.9208
17	1.333	1.7396	2.1098	2.567	2.8982
18	1.330	1.7341	2.1009	2.552	2.8784
19	1.328	1.7291	2.0930	2.539	2.8609
20	1.325	1.7247	2.0860	2.528	2.8453
21	1.323	1.7207	2.0796	2.518	2.8314
22	1.321	1.7171	2.0739	2.508	2.8188
23	1.319	1.7139	2.0687	2.500	2.8073
24	1.318	1.7109	2.0639	2.492	2.7969
25	1.316	1.7081	2.0595	2.485	2.7874
26	1.315	1.7056	2.0555	2.479	2.7787
27	1.314	1.7033	2.0518	2.473	2.7707
28	1.313	1.7011	2.0484	2.467	2.7633
29	1.311	1.6991	2.0452	2.462	2.7564
30	1.310	1.6973	2.0423	2.457	2.7500
35	1.3062	1.6896	2.0301	2.438	2.7239
40	1.3031	1.6839	2.0211	2.423	2.7045
45	1.3007	1.6794	2.0141	2.412	2.6896
50	1.2987	1.6759	2.0086	2.403	2.6778
60	1.2959	1.6707	2.0003	2.390	2.6603
70	1.2938	1.6669	1.9945	2.381	2.6480
80	1.2922	1.6641	1.9901	2.374	2.6388
90	1.2910	1.6620	1.9867	2.368	2.6316
100	1.2901	1.6602	1.9840	2.364	2.6260
120	1.2887	1.6577	1.9799	2.358	2.6175
140	1.2876	1.6558	1.9771	2.353	2.6114
160	1.2869	1.6545	1.9749	2.350	2.6070
180	1.2863	1.6534	1.9733	2.347	2.6035
200	1.2858	1.6525	1.9719	2.345	2.6006
∞	1.282	1.645	1.96	2.326	2.576

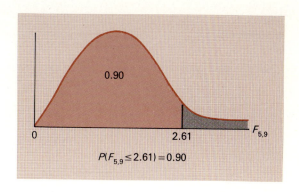

$$P(F_{5,9} \leq 2.61) = 0.90$$

**TABLE E
Percentiles of the
F distribution
$P(F \leq F_0)$**

					$F_{0.90}$				
Denominator degrees of freedom				Numerator degrees of freedom					
	1	2	3	4	5	6	7	8	9
1	39.86	49.50	53.59	55.83	57.24	58.20	58.91	59.44	59.86
2	8.53	9.00	9.16	9.24	9.29	9.33	9.35	9.37	9.38
3	5.54	5.46	5.39	5.34	5.31	5.28	5.27	5.25	5.24
4	4.54	4.32	4.19	4.11	4.05	4.01	3.98	3.95	3.94
5	4.06	3.78	3.62	3.52	3.45	3.40	3.37	3.34	3.32
6	3.78	3.46	3.29	3.18	3.11	3.05	3.01	2.98	2.96
7	3.59	3.26	3.07	2.96	2.88	2.83	2.78	2.75	2.72
8	3.46	3.11	2.92	2.81	2.73	2.67	2.62	2.59	2.56
9	3.36	3.01	2.81	2.69	2.61	2.55	2.51	2.47	2.44
10	3.29	2.92	2.73	2.61	2.52	2.46	2.41	2.38	2.35
11	3.23	2.86	2.66	2.54	2.45	2.39	2.34	2.30	2.27
12	3.18	2.81	2.61	2.48	2.39	2.33	2.28	2.24	2.21
13	3.14	2.76	2.56	2.43	2.35	2.28	2.23	2.20	2.16
14	3.10	2.73	2.52	2.39	2.31	2.24	2.19	2.15	2.12
15	3.07	2.70	2.49	2.36	2.27	2.21	2.16	2.12	2.09
16	3.05	2.67	2.46	2.33	2.24	2.18	2.13	2.09	2.06
17	3.03	2.64	2.44	2.31	2.22	2.15	2.10	2.06	2.03
18	3.01	2.62	2.42	2.29	2.20	2.13	2.08	2.04	2.00
19	2.99	2.61	2.40	2.27	2.18	2.11	2.06	2.02	1.98
20	2.97	2.59	2.38	2.25	2.16	2.09	2.04	2.00	1.96
21	2.96	2.57	2.36	2.23	2.14	2.08	2.02	1.98	1.95
22	2.95	2.56	2.35	2.22	2.13	2.06	2.01	1.97	1.93
23	2.94	2.55	2.34	2.21	2.11	2.05	1.99	1.95	1.92
24	2.93	2.54	2.33	2.19	2.10	2.04	1.98	1.94	1.91
25	2.92	2.53	2.32	2.18	2.09	2.02	1.97	1.93	1.89
26	2.91	2.52	2.31	2.17	2.08	2.01	1.96	1.92	1.88
27	2.90	2.51	2.30	2.17	2.07	2.00	1.95	1.91	1.87
28	2.89	2.50	2.29	2.16	2.06	2.00	1.94	1.90	1.87
29	2.89	2.50	2.28	2.15	2.06	1.99	1.93	1.89	1.86
30	2.88	2.49	2.28	2.14	2.05	1.98	1.93	1.88	1.85
40	2.84	2.44	2.23	2.09	2.00	1.93	1.87	1.83	1.79
60	2.79	2.39	2.18	2.04	1.95	1.87	1.82	1.77	1.74
120	2.75	2.35	2.13	1.99	1.90	1.82	1.77	1.72	1.68
∞	2.71	2.30	2.08	1.94	1.85	1.77	1.72	1.67	1.63

TABLE E
(continued)

Denominator degrees of freedom	$F_{0.90}$									
	Numerator degrees of freedom									
	10	12	15	20	24	30	40	60	120	∞
1	60.19	60.71	61.22	61.74	62.00	62.26	62.53	62.79	63.06	63.33
2	9.39	9.41	9.42	9.44	9.45	9.46	9.47	9.47	9.48	9.49
3	5.23	5.22	5.20	5.18	5.18	5.17	5.16	5.15	5.14	5.13
4	3.92	3.90	3.87	3.84	3.83	3.82	3.80	3.79	3.78	3.76
5	3.30	3.27	3.24	3.21	3.19	3.17	3.16	3.14	3.12	3.10
6	2.94	2.90	2.87	2.84	2.82	2.80	2.78	2.76	2.74	2.72
7	2.70	2.67	2.63	2.59	2.58	2.56	2.54	2.51	2.49	2.47
8	2.54	2.50	2.46	2.42	2.40	2.38	2.36	2.34	2.32	2.29
9	2.42	2.38	2.34	2.30	2.28	2.25	2.23	2.21	2.18	2.16
10	2.32	2.28	2.24	2.20	2.18	2.16	2.13	2.11	2.08	2.06
11	2.25	2.21	2.17	2.12	2.10	2.08	2.05	2.03	2.00	1.97
12	2.19	2.15	2.10	2.06	2.04	2.01	1.99	1.96	1.93	1.90
13	2.14	2.10	2.05	2.01	1.98	1.96	1.93	1.90	1.88	1.85
14	2.10	2.05	2.01	1.96	1.94	1.91	1.89	1.86	1.83	1.80
15	2.06	2.02	1.97	1.92	1.90	1.87	1.85	1.82	1.79	1.76
16	2.03	1.99	1.94	1.89	1.87	1.84	1.81	1.78	1.75	1.72
17	2.00	1.96	1.91	1.86	1.84	1.81	1.78	1.75	1.72	1.69
18	1.98	1.93	1.89	1.84	1.81	1.78	1.75	1.72	1.69	1.66
19	1.96	1.91	1.86	1.81	1.79	1.76	1.73	1.70	1.67	1.63
20	1.94	1.89	1.84	1.79	1.77	1.74	1.71	1.68	1.64	1.61
21	1.92	1.87	1.83	1.78	1.75	1.72	1.69	1.66	1.62	1.59
22	1.90	1.86	1.81	1.76	1.73	1.70	1.67	1.64	1.60	1.57
23	1.89	1.84	1.80	1.74	1.72	1.69	1.66	1.62	1.59	1.55
24	1.88	1.83	1.78	1.73	1.70	1.67	1.64	1.61	1.57	1.53
25	1.87	1.82	1.77	1.72	1.69	1.66	1.63	1.59	1.56	1.52
26	1.86	1.81	1.76	1.71	1.68	1.65	1.61	1.58	1.54	1.50
27	1.85	1.80	1.75	1.70	1.67	1.64	1.60	1.57	1.53	1.49
28	1.84	1.79	1.74	1.69	1.66	1.63	1.59	1.56	1.52	1.48
29	1.83	1.78	1.73	1.68	1.65	1.62	1.58	1.55	1.51	1.47
30	1.82	1.77	1.72	1.67	1.64	1.61	1.57	1.54	1.50	1.46
40	1.76	1.71	1.66	1.61	1.57	1.54	1.51	1.47	1.42	1.38
60	1.71	1.66	1.60	1.54	1.51	1.48	1.44	1.40	1.35	1.29
120	1.65	1.60	1.55	1.48	1.45	1.41	1.37	1.32	1.26	1.19
∞	1.60	1.55	1.49	1.42	1.38	1.34	1.30	1.24	1.17	1.00

TABLE E
(continued)

$F_{0.95}$

Denominator degrees of freedom	Numerator degrees of freedom								
	1	2	3	4	5	6	7	8	9
1	161.4	199.5	215.7	224.6	230.2	234.0	236.8	238.9	240.5
2	18.51	19.00	19.16	19.25	19.30	19.33	19.35	19.37	19.38
3	10.13	9.55	9.28	9.12	9.01	8.94	8.89	8.85	8.81
4	7.71	6.94	6.59	6.39	6.26	6.16	6.09	6.04	6.00
5	6.61	5.79	5.41	5.19	5.05	4.95	4.88	4.82	4.77
6	5.99	5.14	4.76	4.53	4.39	4.28	4.21	4.15	4.10
7	5.59	4.74	4.35	4.12	3.97	3.87	3.79	3.73	3.68
8	5.32	4.46	4.07	3.84	3.69	3.58	3.50	3.44	3.39
9	5.12	4.26	3.86	3.63	3.48	3.37	3.29	3.23	3.18
10	4.96	4.10	3.71	3.48	3.33	3.22	3.14	3.07	3.02
11	4.84	3.98	3.59	3.36	3.20	3.09	3.01	2.95	2.90
12	4.75	3.89	3.49	3.26	3.11	3.00	2.91	2.85	2.80
13	4.67	3.81	3.41	3.18	3.03	2.92	2.83	2.77	2.71
14	4.60	3.74	3.34	3.11	2.96	2.85	2.76	2.70	2.65
15	4.54	3.68	3.29	3.06	2.90	2.79	2.71	2.64	2.59
16	4.49	3.63	3.24	3.01	2.85	2.74	2.66	2.59	2.54
17	4.45	3.59	3.20	2.96	2.81	2.70	2.61	2.55	2.49
18	4.41	3.55	3.16	2.93	2.77	2.66	2.58	2.51	2.46
19	4.38	3.52	3.13	2.90	2.74	2.63	2.54	2.48	2.42
20	4.35	3.49	3.10	2.87	2.71	2.60	2.51	2.45	2.39
21	4.32	3.47	3.07	2.84	2.68	2.57	2.49	2.42	2.37
22	4.30	3.44	3.05	2.82	2.66	2.55	2.46	2.40	2.34
23	4.28	3.42	3.03	2.80	2.64	2.53	2.44	2.37	2.32
24	4.26	3.40	3.01	2.78	2.62	2.51	2.42	2.36	2.30
25	4.24	3.39	2.99	2.76	2.60	2.49	2.40	2.34	2.28
26	4.23	3.37	2.98	2.74	2.59	2.47	2.39	2.32	2.27
27	4.21	3.35	2.96	2.73	2.57	2.46	2.37	2.31	2.25
28	4.20	3.34	2.95	2.71	2.56	2.45	2.36	2.29	2.24
29	4.18	3.33	2.93	2.70	2.55	2.43	2.35	2.28	2.22
30	4.17	3.32	2.92	2.69	2.53	2.42	2.33	2.27	2.21
40	4.08	3.23	2.84	2.61	2.45	2.34	2.25	2.18	2.12
60	4.00	3.15	2.76	2.53	2.37	2.25	2.17	2.10	2.04
120	3.92	3.07	2.68	2.45	2.29	2.17	2.09	2.02	1.96
∞	3.84	3.00	2.60	2.37	2.21	2.10	2.01	1.94	1.88

$F_{0.95}$

Denominator degrees of freedom	Numerator degrees of freedom									
	10	12	15	20	24	30	40	60	120	∞
1	241.9	243.9	245.9	248.0	249.1	250.1	251.1	252.2	253.3	254.3
2	19.40	19.41	19.43	19.45	19.45	19.46	19.47	19.48	19.49	19.50
3	8.79	8.74	8.70	8.66	8.64	8.62	8.59	8.57	8.55	8.53
4	5.96	5.91	5.86	5.80	5.77	5.75	5.72	5.69	5.66	5.63
5	4.74	4.68	4.62	4.56	4.53	4.50	4.46	4.43	4.40	4.36
6	4.06	4.00	3.94	3.87	3.84	3.81	3.77	3.74	3.70	3.67
7	3.64	3.57	3.51	3.44	3.41	3.38	3.34	3.30	3.27	3.23
8	3.35	3.28	3.22	3.15	3.12	3.08	3.04	3.01	2.97	2.93
9	3.14	3.07	3.01	2.94	2.90	2.86	2.83	2.79	2.75	2.71
10	2.98	2.91	2.85	2.77	2.74	2.70	2.66	2.62	2.58	2.54
11	2.85	2.79	2.72	2.65	2.61	2.57	2.53	2.49	2.45	2.40
12	2.75	2.69	2.62	2.54	2.51	2.47	2.43	2.38	2.34	2.30
13	2.67	2.60	2.53	2.46	2.42	2.38	2.34	2.30	2.25	2.21
14	2.60	2.53	2.46	2.39	2.35	2.31	2.27	2.22	2.18	2.13
15	2.54	2.48	2.40	2.33	2.29	2.25	2.20	2.16	2.11	2.07
16	2.49	2.42	2.35	2.28	2.24	2.19	2.15	2.11	2.06	2.01
17	2.45	2.38	2.31	2.23	2.19	2.15	2.10	2.06	2.01	1.96
18	2.41	2.34	2.27	2.19	2.15	2.11	2.06	2.02	1.97	1.92
19	2.38	2.31	2.23	2.16	2.11	2.07	2.03	1.98	1.93	1.88
20	2.35	2.28	2.20	2.12	2.08	2.04	1.99	1.95	1.90	1.84
21	2.32	2.25	2.18	2.10	2.05	2.01	1.96	1.92	1.87	1.81
22	2.30	2.23	2.15	2.07	2.03	1.98	1.94	1.89	1.84	1.78
23	2.27	2.20	2.13	2.05	2.01	1.96	1.91	1.86	1.81	1.76
24	2.25	2.18	2.11	2.03	1.98	1.94	1.89	1.84	1.79	1.73
25	2.24	2.16	2.09	2.01	1.96	1.92	1.87	1.82	1.77	1.71
26	2.22	2.15	2.07	1.99	1.95	1.90	1.85	1.80	1.75	1.69
27	2.20	2.13	2.06	1.97	1.93	1.88	1.84	1.79	1.73	1.67
28	2.19	2.12	2.04	1.96	1.91	1.87	1.82	1.77	1.71	1.65
29	2.18	2.10	2.03	1.94	1.90	1.85	1.81	1.75	1.70	1.64
30	2.16	2.09	2.01	1.93	1.89	1.84	1.79	1.74	1.68	1.62
40	2.08	2.00	1.92	1.84	1.79	1.74	1.69	1.64	1.58	1.51
60	1.99	1.92	1.84	1.75	1.70	1.65	1.59	1.53	1.47	1.39
120	1.91	1.83	1.75	1.66	1.61	1.55	1.50	1.43	1.35	1.25
∞	1.83	1.75	1.67	1.57	1.52	1.46	1.39	1.32	1.22	1.00

TABLE E
(continued)

Denominator degrees of freedom	\multicolumn{9}{c}{$F_{0.975}$ Numerator degrees of freedom}

Denominator degrees of freedom	1	2	3	4	5	6	7	8	9
1	647.8	799.5	864.2	899.6	921.8	937.1	948.2	956.7	963.3
2	38.51	39.00	39.17	39.25	39.30	39.33	39.36	39.37	39.39
3	17.44	16.04	15.44	15.10	14.88	14.73	14.62	14.54	14.47
4	12.22	10.65	9.98	9.60	9.36	9.20	9.07	8.98	8.90
5	10.01	8.43	7.76	7.39	7.15	6.98	6.85	6.76	6.68
6	8.81	7.26	6.60	6.23	5.99	5.82	5.70	5.60	5.52
7	8.07	6.54	5.89	5.52	5.29	5.12	4.99	4.90	4.82
8	7.57	6.06	5.42	5.05	4.82	4.65	4.53	4.43	4.36
9	7.21	5.71	5.08	4.72	4.48	4.32	4.20	4.10	4.03
10	6.94	5.46	4.83	4.47	4.24	4.07	3.95	3.85	3.78
11	6.72	5.26	4.63	4.28	4.04	3.88	3.76	3.66	3.59
12	6.55	5.10	4.47	4.12	3.89	3.73	3.61	3.51	3.44
13	6.41	4.97	4.35	4.00	3.77	3.60	3.48	3.39	3.31
14	6.30	4.86	4.24	3.89	3.66	3.50	3.38	3.29	3.21
15	6.20	4.77	4.15	3.80	3.58	3.41	3.29	3.20	3.12
16	6.12	4.69	4.08	3.73	3.50	3.34	3.22	3.12	3.05
17	6.04	4.62	4.01	3.66	3.44	3.28	3.16	3.06	2.98
18	5.98	4.56	3.95	3.61	3.38	3.22	3.10	3.01	2.93
19	5.92	4.51	3.90	3.56	3.33	3.17	3.05	2.96	2.88
20	5.87	4.46	3.86	3.51	3.29	3.13	3.01	2.91	2.84
21	5.83	4.42	3.82	3.48	3.25	3.09	2.97	2.87	2.80
22	5.79	4.38	3.78	3.44	3.22	3.05	2.93	2.84	2.76
23	5.75	4.35	3.75	3.41	3.18	3.02	2.90	2.81	2.73
24	5.72	4.32	3.72	3.38	3.15	2.99	2.87	2.78	2.70
25	5.69	4.29	3.69	3.35	3.13	2.97	2.85	2.75	2.68
26	5.66	4.27	3.67	3.33	3.10	2.94	2.82	2.73	2.65
27	5.63	4.24	3.65	3.31	3.08	2.92	2.80	2.71	2.63
28	5.61	4.22	3.63	3.29	3.06	2.90	2.78	2.69	2.61
29	5.59	4 20	3.61	3.27	3.04	2.88	2.76	2.67	2.59
30	5.57	4.18	3.59	3.25	3.03	2.87	2.75	2.65	2.57
40	5.42	4.05	3.46	3.13	2.90	2.74	2.62	2.53	2.45
60	5.29	3.93	3.34	3.01	2.79	2.63	2.51	2.41	2.33
120	5.15	3.80	3.23	2.89	2.67	2.52	2.39	2.30	2.22
∞	5.02	3.69	3.12	2.79	2.57	2.41	2.29	2.19	2.11

TABLE E
(*continued*)

$$F_{0.975}$$

Denominator degrees of freedom	Numerator degrees of freedom									
	10	12	15	20	24	30	40	60	120	∞
1	968.6	976.7	984.9	993.1	997.2	1001	1006	1010	1014	1018
2	39.40	39.41	39.43	39.45	39.46	39.46	39.47	39.48	39.49	39.50
3	14.42	14.34	14.25	14.17	14.12	14.08	14.04	13.99	13.95	13.90
4	8.84	8.75	8.66	8.56	8.51	8.46	8.41	8.36	8.31	8.26
5	6.62	6.52	6.43	6.33	6.28	6.23	6.18	6.12	6.07	6.02
6	5.46	5.37	5.27	5.17	5.12	5.07	5.01	4.96	4.90	4.85
7	4.76	4.67	4.57	4.47	4.42	4.36	4.31	4.25	4.20	4.14
8	4.30	4.20	4.10	4.00	3.95	3.89	3.84	3.78	3.73	3.67
9	3.96	3.87	3.77	3.67	3.61	3.56	3.51	3.45	3.39	3.33
10	3.72	3.62	3.52	3.42	3.37	3.31	3.26	3.20	3.14	3.08
11	3.53	3.43	3.33	3.23	3.17	3.12	3.06	3.00	2.94	2.88
12	3.37	3.28	3.18	3.07	3.02	2.96	2.91	2.85	2.79	2.72
13	3.25	3.15	3.05	2.95	2.89	2.84	2.78	2.72	2.66	2.60
14	3.15	3.05	2.95	2.84	2.79	2.73	2.67	2.61	2.55	2.49
15	3.06	2.96	2.86	2.76	2.70	2.64	2.59	2.52	2.46	2.40
16	2.99	2.89	2.79	2.68	2.63	2.57	2.51	2.45	2.38	2.32
17	2.92	2.82	2.72	2.62	2.56	2.50	2.44	2.38	2.32	2.25
18	2.87	2.77	2.67	2.56	2.50	2.44	2.38	2.32	2.26	2.19
19	2.82	2.72	2.62	2.51	2.45	2.39	2.33	2.27	2.20	2.13
20	2.77	2.68	2.57	2.46	2.41	2.35	2.29	2.22	2.16	2.09
21	2.73	2.64	2.53	2.42	2.37	2.31	2.25	2.18	2.11	2.04
22	2.70	2.60	2.50	2.39	2.33	2.27	2.21	2.14	2.08	2.00
23	2.67	2.57	2.47	2.36	2.30	2.24	2.18	2.11	2.04	1.97
24	2.64	2.54	2.44	2.33	2.27	2.21	2.15	2.08	2.01	1.94
25	2.61	2.51	2.41	2.30	2.24	2.18	2.12	2.05	1.98	1.91
26	2.59	2.49	2.39	2.28	2.22	2.16	2.09	2.03	1.95	1.88
27	2.57	2.47	2.36	2.25	2.19	2.13	2.07	2.00	1.93	1.85
28	2.55	2.45	2.34	2.23	2.17	2.11	2.05	1.98	1.91	1.83
29	2.53	2.43	2.32	2.21	2.15	2.09	2.03	1.96	1.89	1.81
30	2.51	2.41	2.31	2.20	2.14	2.07	2.01	1.94	1.87	1.79
40	2.39	2.29	2.18	2.07	2.01	1.94	1.88	1.80	1.72	1.64
60	2.27	2.17	2.06	1.94	1.88	1.82	1.74	1.67	1.58	1.48
120	2.16	2.05	1.94	1.82	1.76	1.69	1.61	1.53	1.43	1.31
∞	2.05	1.94	1.83	1.71	1.64	1.57	1.48	1.39	1.27	1.00

TABLE E
(*continued*)

$F_{0.99}$

Denominator degrees of freedom	Numerator degrees of freedom								
	1	2	3	4	5	6	7	8	9
1	4052	4999.5	5403	5625	5764	5859	5928	5981	6022
2	98.50	99.00	99.17	99.25	99.30	99.33	99.36	99.37	99.39
3	34.12	30.82	29.46	28.71	28.24	27.91	27.67	27.49	27.35
4	21.20	18.00	16.69	15.98	15.52	15.21	14.98	14.80	14.66
5	16.26	13.27	12.06	11.39	10.97	10.67	10.46	10.29	10.16
6	13.75	10.92	9.78	9.15	8.75	8.47	8.26	8.10	7.98
7	12.25	9.55	8.45	7.85	7.46	7.19	6.99	6.84	6.72
8	11.26	8.65	7.59	7.01	6.63	6.37	6.18	6.03	5.91
9	10.56	8.02	6.99	6.42	6.06	5.80	5.61	5.47	5.35
10	10.04	7.56	6.55	5.99	5.64	5.39	5.20	5.06	4.94
11	9.65	7.21	6.22	5.67	5.32	5.07	4.89	4.74	4.63
12	9.33	6.93	5.95	5.41	5.06	4.82	4.64	4.50	4.39
13	9.07	6.70	5.74	5.21	4.86	4.62	4.44	4.30	4.19
14	8.86	6.51	5.56	5.04	4.69	4.46	4.28	4.14	4.03
15	8.68	6.36	5.42	4.89	4.56	4.32	4.14	4.00	3.89
16	8.53	6.23	5.29	4.77	4.44	4.20	4.03	3.89	3.78
17	8.40	6.11	5.18	4.67	4.34	4.10	3.93	3.79	3.68
18	8.29	6.01	5.09	4.58	4.25	4.01	3.84	3.71	3.60
19	8.18	5.93	5.01	4.50	4.17	3.94	3.77	3.63	3.52
20	8.10	5.85	4.94	4.43	4.10	3.87	3.70	3.56	3.46
21	8.02	5.78	4.87	4.37	4.04	3.81	3.64	3.51	3.40
22	7.95	5.72	4.82	4.31	3.99	3.76	3.59	3.45	3.35
23	7.88	5.66	4.76	4.26	3.94	3.71	3.54	3.41	3.30
24	7.82	5.61	4.72	4.22	3.90	3.67	3.50	3.36	3.26
25	7.77	5.57	4.68	4.18	3.85	3.63	3.46	3.32	3.22
26	7.72	5.53	4.64	4.14	3.82	3.59	3.42	3.29	3.18
27	7.68	5.49	4.60	4.11	3.78	3.56	3.39	3.26	3.15
28	7.64	5.45	4.57	4.07	3.75	3.53	3.36	3.23	3.12
29	7.60	5.42	4.54	4.04	3.73	3.50	3.33	3.20	3.09
30	7.56	5.39	4.51	4.02	3.70	3.47	3.30	3.17	3.07
40	7.31	5.18	4.31	3.83	3.51	3.29	3.12	2.99	2.89
60	7.08	4.98	4.13	3.65	3.34	3.12	2.95	2.82	2.72
120	6.85	4.79	3.95	3.48	3.17	2.96	2.79	2.66	2.56
∞	6.63	4.61	3.78	3.32	3.02	2.80	2.64	2.51	2.41

TABLE E
(*continued*)

$F_{0.99}$

Denominator degrees of freedom	Numerator degrees of freedom									
	10	12	15	20	24	30	40	60	120	∞
1	6056	6106	6157	6209	6235	6261	6287	6313	6339	6366
2	99.40	99.42	99.43	99.45	99.46	99.47	99.47	99.48	99.49	99.50
3	27.23	27.05	26.87	26.69	26.60	26.50	26.41	26.32	26.22	26.13
4	14.55	14.37	14.20	14.02	13.93	13.84	13.75	13.65	13.56	13.46
5	10.05	9.89	9.72	9.55	9.47	9.38	9.29	9.20	9.11	9.02
6	7.87	7.72	7.56	7.40	7.31	7.23	7.14	7.06	6.97	6.88
7	6.62	6.47	6.31	6.16	6.07	5.99	5.91	5.82	5.74	5.65
8	5.81	5.67	5.52	5.36	5.28	5.20	5.12	5.03	4.95	4.86
9	5.26	5.11	4.96	4.81	4.73	4.65	4.57	4.48	4.40	4.31
10	4.85	4.71	4.56	4.41	4.33	4.25	4.17	4.08	4.00	3.91
11	4.54	4.40	4.25	4.10	4.02	3.94	3.86	3.78	3.69	3.60
12	4.30	4.16	4.01	3.86	3.78	3.70	3.62	3.54	3.45	3.36
13	4.10	3.96	3.82	3.66	3.59	3.51	3.43	3.34	3.25	3.17
14	3.94	3.80	3.66	3.51	3.43	3.35	3.27	3.18	3.09	3.00
15	3.80	3.67	3.52	3.37	3.29	3.21	3.13	3.05	2.96	2.87
16	3.69	3.55	3.41	3.26	3.18	3.10	3.02	2.93	2.84	2.75
17	3.59	3.46	3.31	3.16	3.08	3.00	2.92	2.83	2.75	2.65
18	3.51	3.37	3.23	3.08	3.00	2.92	2.84	2.75	2.66	2.57
19	3.43	3.30	3.15	3.00	2.92	2.84	2.76	2.67	2.58	2.49
20	3.37	3.23	3.09	2.94	2.86	2.78	2.69	2.61	2.52	2.42
21	3.31	3.17	3.03	2.88	2.80	2.72	2.64	2.55	2.46	2.36
22	3.26	3.12	2.98	2.83	2.75	2.67	2.58	2.50	2.40	2.31
23	3.21	3.07	2.93	2.78	2.70	2.62	2.54	2.45	2.35	2.26
24	3.17	3.03	2.89	2.74	2.66	2.58	2.49	2.40	2.31	2.21
25	3.13	2.99	2.85	2.70	2.62	2.54	2.45	2.36	2.27	2.17
26	3.09	2.96	2.81	2.66	2.58	2.50	2.42	2.33	2.23	2.13
27	3.06	2.93	2.78	2.63	2.55	2.47	2.38	2.29	2.20	2.10
28	3.03	2.90	2.75	2.60	2.52	2.44	2.35	2.26	2.17	2.06
29	3.00	2.87	2.73	2.57	2.49	2.41	2.33	2.23	2.14	2.03
30	2.98	2.84	2.70	2.55	2.47	2.39	2.30	2.21	2.11	2.01
40	2.80	2.66	2.52	2.37	2.29	2.20	2.11	2.02	1.92	1.80
60	2.63	2.50	2.35	2.20	2.12	2.03	1.94	1.84	1.73	1.60
120	2.47	2.34	2.19	2.03	1.95	1.86	1.76	1.66	1.53	1.38
∞	2.32	2.18	2.04	1.88	1.79	1.70	1.59	1.47	1.32	1.00

TABLE E
(continued)

$F_{0.995}$

Denominator degrees of freedom	Numerator degrees of freedom								
	1	2	3	4	5	6	7	8	9
1	16211	20000	21615	22500	23056	23437	23715	23925	24091
2	198.5	199.0	199.2	199.2	199.3	199.3	199.4	199.4	199.4
3	55.55	49.80	47.47	46.19	45.39	44.84	44.43	44.13	43.88
4	31.33	26.28	24.26	23.15	22.46	21.97	21.62	21.35	21.14
5	22.78	18.31	16.53	15.56	14.94	14.51	14.20	13.96	13.77
6	18.63	14.54	12.92	12.03	11.46	11.07	10.79	10.57	10.39
7	16.24	12.40	10.88	10.05	9.52	9.16	8.89	8.68	8.51
8	14.69	11.04	9.60	8.81	8.30	7.95	7.69	7.50	7.34
9	13.61	10.11	8.72	7.96	7.47	7.13	6.88	6.69	6.54
10	12.83	9.43	8.08	7.34	6.87	6.54	6.30	6.12	5.97
11	12.23	8.91	7.60	6.88	6.42	6.10	5.86	5.68	5.54
12	11.75	8.51	7.23	6.52	6.07	5.76	5.52	5.35	5.20
13	11.37	8.19	6.93	6.23	5.79	5.48	5.25	5.08	4.94
14	11.06	7.92	6.68	6.00	5.56	5.26	5.03	4.86	4.72
15	10.80	7.70	6.48	5.80	5.37	5.07	4.85	4.67	4.54
16	10.58	7.51	6.30	5.64	5.21	4.91	4.69	4.52	4.38
17	10.38	7.35	6.16	5.50	5.07	4.78	4.56	4.39	4.25
18	10.22	7.21	6.03	5.37	4.96	4.66	4.44	4.28	4.14
19	10.07	7.09	5.92	5.27	4.85	4.56	4.34	4.18	4.04
20	9.94	6.99	5.82	5.17	4.76	4.47	4.26	4.09	3.96
21	9.83	6.89	5.73	5.09	4.68	4.39	4.18	4.01	3.88
22	9.73	6.81	5.65	5.02	4.61	4.32	4.11	3.94	3.81
23	9.63	6.73	5.58	4.95	4.54	4.26	4.05	3.88	3.75
24	9.55	6.66	5.52	4.89	4.49	4.20	3.99	3.83	3.69
25	9.48	6.60	5.46	4.84	4.43	4.15	3.94	3.78	3.64
26	9.41	6.54	5.41	4.79	4.38	4.10	3.89	3.73	3.60
27	9.34	6.49	5.36	4.74	4.34	4.06	3.85	3.69	3.56
28	9.28	6.44	5.32	4.70	4.30	4.02	3.81	3.65	3.52
29	9.23	6.40	5.28	4.66	4.26	3.98	3.77	3.61	3.48
30	9.18	6.35	5.24	4.62	4.23	3.95	3.74	3.58	3.45
40	8.83	6.07	4.98	4.37	3.99	3.71	3.51	3.35	3.22
60	8.49	5.79	4.73	4.14	3.76	3.49	3.29	3.13	3.01
120	8.18	5.54	4.50	3.92	3.55	3.28	3.09	2.93	2.81
∞	7.88	5.30	4.28	3.72	3.35	3.09	2.90	2.74	2.62

TABLE E
(*continued*)

					$F_{0.995}$					

Denominator degrees of freedom	Numerator degrees of freedom									
	10	12	15	20	24	30	40	60	120	∞
1	24224	24426	24630	24836	24940	25044	25148	25253	25359	25465
2	199.4	199.4	199.4	199.4	199.5	199.5	199.5	199.5	199.5	199.5
3	43.69	43.39	43.08	42.78	42.62	42.47	42.31	42.15	41.99	41.83
4	20.97	20.70	20.44	20.17	20.03	19.89	19.75	19.61	19.47	19.32
5	13.62	13.38	13.15	12.90	12.78	12.66	12.53	12.40	12.27	12.14
6	10.25	10.03	9.81	9.59	9.47	9.36	9.24	9.12	9.00	8.88
7	8.38	8.18	7.97	7.75	7.65	7.53	7.42	7.31	7.19	7.08
8	7.21	7.01	6.81	6.61	6.50	6.40	6.29	6.18	6.06	5.95
9	6.42	6.23	6.03	5.83	5.73	5.62	5.52	5.41	5.30	5.19
10	5.85	5.66	5.47	5.27	5.17	5.07	4.97	4.86	4.75	4.64
11	5.42	5.24	5.05	4.86	4.76	4.65	4.55	4.44	4.34	4.23
12	5.09	4.91	4.72	4.53	4.43	4.33	4.23	4.12	4.01	3.90
13	4.82	4.64	4.46	4.27	4.17	4.07	3.97	3.87	3.76	3.65
14	4.60	4.43	4.25	4.06	3.96	3.86	3.76	3.66	3.55	3.44
15	4.42	4.25	4.07	3.88	3.79	3.69	3.58	3.48	3.37	3.26
16	4.27	4.10	3.92	3.73	3.64	3.54	3.44	3.33	3.22	3.11
17	4.14	3.97	3.79	3.61	3.51	3.41	3.31	3.21	3.10	2.98
18	4.03	3.86	3.68	3.50	3.40	3.30	3.20	3.10	2.99	2.87
19	3.93	3.76	3.59	3.40	3.31	3.21	3.11	3.00	2.89	2.78
20	3.85	3.68	3.50	3.32	3.22	3.12	3.02	2.92	2.81	2.69
21	3.77	3.60	3.43	3.24	3.15	3.05	2.95	2.84	2.73	2.61
22	3.70	3.54	3.36	3.18	3.08	2.98	2.88	2.77	2.66	2.55
23	3.64	3.47	3.30	3.12	3.02	2.92	2.82	2.71	2.60	2.48
24	3.59	3.42	3.25	3.06	2.97	2.87	2.77	2.66	2.55	2.43
25	3.54	3.37	3.20	3.01	2.92	2.82	2.72	2.61	2.50	2.38
26	3.49	3.33	3.15	2.97	2.87	2.77	2.67	2.56	2.45	2.33
27	3.45	3.28	3.11	2.93	2.83	2.73	2.63	2.52	2.41	2.29
28	3.41	3.25	3.07	2.89	2.79	2.69	2.59	2.48	2.37	2.25
29	3.38	3.21	3.04	2.86	2.76	2.66	2.56	2.45	2.33	2.21
30	3.34	3.18	3.01	2.82	2.73	2.63	2.52	2.42	2.30	2.18
40	3.12	2.95	2.78	2.60	2.50	2.40	2.30	2.18	2.06	1.93
60	2.90	2.74	2.57	2.39	2.29	2.19	2.08	1.96	1.83	1.69
120	2.71	2.54	2.37	2.19	2.09	1.98	1.87	1.75	1.61	1.43
∞	2.52	2.36	2.19	2.00	1.90	1.79	1.67	1.53	1.36	1.00

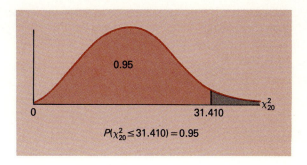

$$P(\chi_{20}^2 \leq 31.410) = 0.95$$

**TABLE F
Percentiles of
the chi-square
distribution
$P(X^2 \leq \chi^2)$**

df	$\chi_{0.005}^2$	$\chi_{0.025}^2$	$\chi_{0.05}^2$	$\chi_{0.90}^2$	$\chi_{0.95}^2$	$\chi_{0.975}^2$	$\chi_{0.99}^2$	$\chi_{0.995}^2$
1	0.0000393	0.000982	0.00393	2.706	3.841	5.024	6.635	7.879
2	0.0100	0.0506	0.103	4.605	5.991	7.378	9.210	10.597
3	0.0717	0.216	0.352	6.251	7.815	9.348	11.345	12.838
4	0.207	0.484	0.711	7.779	9.488	11.143	13.277	14.860
5	0.412	0.831	1.145	9.236	11.070	12.832	15.086	16.750
6	0.676	1.237	1.635	10.645	12.592	14.449	16.812	18.548
7	0.989	1.690	2.167	12.017	14.067	16.013	18.475	20.278
8	1.344	2.180	2.733	13.362	15.507	17.535	20.090	21.955
9	1.735	2.700	3.325	14.684	16.919	19.023	21.666	23.589
10	2.156	3.247	3.940	15.987	18.307	20.483	23.209	25.188
11	2.603	3.816	4.575	17.275	19.675	21.920	24.725	26.757
12	3.074	4.404	5.226	18.549	21.026	23.336	26.217	28.300
13	3.565	5.009	5.892	19.812	22.362	24.736	27.688	29.819
14	4.075	5.629	6.571	21.064	23.685	26.119	29.141	31.319
15	4.601	6.262	7.261	22.307	24.996	27.488	30.578	32.801
16	5.142	6.908	7.962	23.542	26.296	28.845	32.000	34.267
17	5.697	7.564	8.672	24.769	27.587	30.191	33.409	35.718
18	6.265	8.231	9.390	25.989	28.869	31.526	34.805	37.156
19	6.844	8.907	10.117	27.204	30.144	32.852	36.191	38.582
20	7.434	9.591	10.851	28.412	31.410	34.170	37.566	39.997
21	8.034	10.283	11.591	29.615	32.671	35.479	38.932	41.401
22	8.643	10.982	12.338	30.813	33.924	36.781	40.289	42.796
23	9.260	11.688	13.091	32.007	35.172	38.076	41.638	44.181
24	9.886	12.401	13.848	33.196	36.415	39.364	42.980	45.558
25	10.520	13.120	14.611	34.382	37.652	40.646	44.314	46.928
26	11.160	13.844	15.379	35.563	38.885	41.923	45.642	48.290
27	11.808	14.573	16.151	36.741	40.113	43.194	46.963	49.645
28	12.461	15.308	16.928	37.916	41.337	44.461	48.278	50.993
29	13.121	16.047	17.708	39.087	42.557	45.722	49.588	52.336
30	13.787	16.791	18.493	40.256	43.773	46.979	50.892	53.672
35	17.192	20.569	22.465	46.059	49.802	53.203	57.342	60.275
40	20.707	24.433	26.509	51.805	55.758	59.342	63.691	66.766
45	24.311	28.366	30.612	57.505	61.656	65.410	69.957	73.166
50	27.991	32.357	34.764	63.167	67.505	71.420	76.154	79.490
60	35.535	40.482	43.188	74.397	79.082	83.298	88.379	91.952
70	43.275	48.758	51.739	85.527	90.531	95.023	100.425	104.215
80	51.172	57.153	60.391	96.578	101.879	106.629	112.329	116.321
90	59.196	65.647	69.126	107.565	113.145	118.136	124.116	128.299
100	67.328	74.222	77.929	118.498	124.342	129.561	135.807	140.169

TABLE Ga
Table of critical values of r in the runs test

Table Ga and Table Gb contain various critical values of r for various values of n_1 and n_2. For the one-sample runs test, any value of r that is equal to or smaller than that shown in Table Ga or equal to or larger than that shown in Table Gb is significant at the 0.05 level.

$n_1 \backslash n_2$	2	3	4	5	6	7	8	9	10	11	12	13	14	15	16	17	18	19	20
2											2	2	2	2	2	2	2	2	2
3				2	2	2	2	2	2	2	2	2	3	3	3	3	3	3
4			2	2	2	3	3	3	3	3	3	3	3	4	4	4	4	4
5		2	2	3	3	3	3	3	4	4	4	4	4	4	4	4	5	5	5
6	2	2	3	3	3	3	4	4	4	4	5	5	5	5	5	5	6	6	6
7	2	2	3	3	3	4	4	5	5	5	5	5	6	6	6	6	6	6	6
8		2	3	3	3	4	4	5	5	5	6	6	6	6	6	7	7	7	7
9		2	3	3	4	4	5	5	5	6	6	6	7	7	7	7	8	8	8
10		2	3	3	4	5	5	5	6	6	7	7	7	7	8	8	8	8	9
11		2	3	4	4	5	5	6	6	7	7	7	8	8	8	9	9	9	9
12	2	2	3	4	4	5	6	6	7	7	7	8	8	8	9	9	9	10	10
13	2	2	3	4	5	5	6	6	7	7	8	8	9	9	9	10	10	10	10
14	2	2	3	4	5	5	6	7	7	8	8	9	9	9	10	10	10	11	11
15	2	3	3	4	5	6	6	7	7	8	8	9	9	10	10	11	11	11	12
16	2	3	4	4	5	6	6	7	8	8	9	9	10	10	11	11	11	12	12
17	2	3	4	4	5	6	7	7	8	9	9	10	10	11	11	11	12	12	13
18	2	3	4	5	5	6	7	8	8	9	9	10	10	11	11	12	12	13	13
19	2	3	4	5	6	6	7	8	8	9	10	10	11	11	12	12	13	13	13
20	2	3	4	5	6	6	7	8	9	9	10	10	11	12	12	13	13	13	14

TABLE Gb
Table of critical values of r in the runs test

$n_1 \backslash n_2$	2	3	4	5	6	7	8	9	10	11	12	13	14	15	16	17	18	19	20
2																			
3																			
4				9	9														
5			9	10	10	11	11												
6			9	10	11	12	12	13	13	13	13								
7				11	12	13	13	14	14	14	14	15	15	15					
8				11	12	13	14	14	15	15	16	16	16	16	17	17	17	17	17
9					13	14	14	15	16	16	16	17	17	18	18	18	18	18	18
10					13	14	15	16	16	17	17	18	18	18	19	19	19	20	20
11					13	14	15	16	17	17	18	19	19	19	20	20	20	21	21
12					13	14	16	16	17	18	19	19	19	20	20	21	21	22	22
13						15	16	17	18	19	19	20	20	21	21	22	22	23	23
14						15	16	17	18	19	20	20	21	22	22	23	23	23	24
15						15	16	18	18	19	20	21	22	22	23	23	24	24	25
16							17	18	19	20	21	21	22	23	23	24	25	25	25
17							17	18	19	20	21	22	23	23	24	25	25	26	26
18							17	18	19	20	21	22	23	24	25	25	26	26	27
19							17	18	20	21	22	23	23	24	25	26	26	27	27
20							17	18	20	21	22	23	24	25	25	26	27	27	28

**TABLE H
Critical values of
the Spearman test
statistic**

Approximate upper-tail critical values, r_s^*, where $P(r_s > r_s^*) \leq \alpha$, $n = 4(1)30$

Significance Level, α

n	0.001	0.005	0.010	0.025	0.050	0.100
4	——	——	——	——	.8000	.8000
5	——	——	.9000	.9000	.8000	.7000
6	——	.9429	.8857	.8286	.7714	.6000
7	.9643	.8929	.8571	.7450	.6786	.5357
8	.9286	.8571	.8095	.7143	.6190	.5000
9	.9000	.8167	.7667	.6833	.5833	.4667
10	.8667	.7818	.7333	.6364	.5515	.4424
11	.8364	.7545	.7000	.6091	.5273	.4182
12	.8182	.7273	.6713	.5804	.4965	.3986
13	.7912	.6978	.6429	.5549	.4780	.3791
14	.7670	.6747	.6220	.5341	.4593	.3626
15	.7464	.6536	.6000	.5179	.4429	.3500
16	.7265	.6324	.5824	.5000	.4265	.3382
17	.7083	.6152	.5637	.4853	.4118	.3260
18	.6904	.5975	.5480	.4716	.3994	.3148
19	.6737	.5825	.5333	.4579	.3895	.3070
20	.6586	.5684	.5203	.4451	.3789	.2977
21	.6455	.5545	.5078	.4351	.3688	.2909
22	.6318	.5426	.4963	.4241	.3597	.2829
23	.6186	.5306	.4852	.4150	.3518	.2767
24	.6070	.5200	.4748	.4061	.3435	.2704
25	.5962	.5100	.4654	.3977	.3362	.2646
26	.5856	.5002	.4564	.3894	.3299	.2588
27	.5757	.4915	.4481	.3822	.3236	.2540
28	.5660	.4828	.4401	.3749	.3175	.2490
29	.5567	.4744	.4320	.3685	.3113	.2443
30	.5479	.4665	.4251	.3620	.3059	.2400

Note: The corresponding lower-tail critical value for r_s is $-r_s^*$.

TABLE I
d-factors for
Wilcoxon signed-
rank test

(α' = one-sided significance level, α'' = two-sided significance level)

n	d	α''	α'	n	d	α''	α'	n	d	α''	α'
3	1	.250	.125	13	10	.008	.004	20	38	.009	.005
4	1	.125	.063		11	.010	.005		39	.011	.005
5	1	.062	.031		18	.048	.024		53	.048	.024
	2	.125	.063		19	.057	.029		54	.053	.027
6	1	.031	.016		22	.094	.047		61	.097	.049
	2	.063	.031		23	.110	.055		62	.105	.053
	3	.094	.047	14	13	.009	.004	21	43	.009	.005
	4	.156	.078		14	.011	.005		44	.010	.005
7	1	.016	.008		22	.049	.025		59	.046	.023
	2	.031	.016		23	.058	.029		60	.050	.025
	4	.078	.039		26	.091	.045		68	.096	.048
	5	.109	.055		27	.104	.052		69	.103	.052
8	1	.008	.004	15	16	.008	.004	22	49	.009	.005
	2	.016	.008		17	.010	.005		50	.010	.005
	4	.039	.020		26	.048	.024		66	.046	.023
	5	.055	.027		27	.055	.028		67	.050	.025
	6	.078	.039		31	.095	.047		76	.098	.049
	7	.109	.055		32	.107	.054		77	.105	.053
9	2	.008	.004	16	20	.009	.005	23	55	.009	.005
	3	.012	.006		21	.011	.006		56	.010	.005
	6	.039	.020		30	.044	.022		74	.048	.024
	7	.055	.027		31	.051	.025		75	.052	.026
	9	.098	.049		36	.093	.047		84	.098	.049
	10	.129	.065		37	.105	.052		85	.105	.052
10	4	.010	.005	17	24	.009	.005	24	62	.010	.005
	5	.014	.007		25	.011	.006		63	.011	.005
	9	.049	.024		35	.045	.022		82	.049	.025
	10	.064	.032		36	.051	.025		83	.053	.026
	11	.084	.042		42	.098	.049		92	.095	.048
	12	.105	.053		43	.109	.054		93	.101	.051
11	6	.010	.005	18	28	.009	.005	25	69	.010	.005
	7	.014	.007		29	.010	.005		70	.011	.005
	11	.042	.021		41	.048	.024		90	.048	.024
	12	.054	.027		42	.054	.027		91	.052	.026
	14	.083	.042		48	.099	.049		101	.096	.048
	15	.102	.051		49	.108	.054		102	.101	.051
12	8	.009	.005	19	33	.009	.005				
	9	.012	.006		34	.011	.005				
	14	.042	.021		47	.049	.025				
	15	.052	.026		48	.055	.027				
	18	.092	.046		54	.096	.048				
	19	.110	.055		55	.104	.052				

Note: For $n > 25$ use $d \approx \frac{1}{2}[\frac{1}{2}n(n+1) + 1 - z\sqrt{n(n+1)(2n+1)/6}]$, where z is read from Table C.

TABLE J
Quantiles of the Mann–Whitney test statistic

n_1	p	$n_2=2$	3	4	5	6	7	8	9	10	11	12	13	14	15	16	17	18	19	20
2	.001	0	0	0	0	0	0	0	0	0	0	0	0	0	0	0	0	0	0	0
	.005	0	0	0	0	0	0	0	0	0	0	0	0	0	0	0	0	0	1	1
	.01	0	0	0	0	0	0	0	0	0	0	0	1	1	1	1	1	1	2	2
	.025	0	0	0	0	0	0	1	1	1	1	2	2	2	2	2	3	3	3	3
	.05	0	0	0	1	1	1	2	2	2	2	3	3	4	4	4	4	5	5	5
	.10	0	1	1	2	2	2	3	3	4	4	5	5	5	6	6	7	7	8	8
3	.001	0	0	0	0	0	0	0	0	0	0	0	0	0	0	0	1	1	1	1
	.005	0	0	0	0	0	0	0	1	1	1	2	2	2	3	3	3	3	4	4
	.01	0	0	0	0	0	1	1	2	2	2	3	3	3	4	4	5	5	5	6
	.025	0	0	0	1	2	2	3	3	4	4	5	5	6	6	7	7	8	8	9
	.05	0	1	1	2	3	3	4	5	5	6	6	7	8	8	9	10	10	11	12
	.10	1	2	2	3	4	5	6	6	7	8	9	10	11	11	12	13	14	15	16
4	.001	0	0	0	0	0	0	0	0	1	1	1	2	2	2	3	3	4	4	4
	.005	0	0	0	0	1	1	2	2	3	3	4	4	5	6	6	7	7	8	9
	.01	0	0	0	1	2	2	3	4	4	5	6	6	7	9	8	9	10	10	11
	.025	0	0	1	2	3	4	5	5	6	7	8	9	10	11	12	12	13	14	15
	.05	0	1	2	3	4	5	6	7	8	9	10	11	12	13	15	16	17	18	19
	.10	1	2	4	5	6	7	8	10	11	12	13	14	16	17	18	19	21	22	23
5	.001	0	0	0	0	0	0	1	2	2	3	3	4	4	5	6	6	7	8	8
	.005	0	0	0	1	2	2	3	4	5	6	7	8	8	9	10	11	12	13	14
	.01	0	0	1	2	3	4	5	6	7	8	9	10	11	12	13	14	15	16	17
	.025	0	1	2	3	4	6	7	8	9	10	12	13	14	15	16	18	19	20	21
	.05	1	2	3	5	6	7	9	10	12	13	14	16	17	19	20	21	23	24	26
	.10	2	3	5	6	8	9	11	13	14	16	18	19	21	23	24	26	28	29	31
6	.001	0	0	0	0	0	0	2	3	4	5	5	6	7	8	9	10	11	12	13
	.005	0	0	1	2	3	4	5	6	7	8	10	11	12	13	14	16	17	18	19
	.01	0	0	2	3	4	5	7	8	9	10	12	13	14	16	17	19	20	21	23
	.025	0	2	3	4	6	7	9	11	12	14	15	17	18	20	22	23	25	26	28
	.05	1	3	4	6	8	9	11	13	15	17	18	20	22	24	26	27	29	31	33
	.10	2	4	6	8	10	12	14	16	18	20	22	24	26	28	30	32	35	37	39
7	.001	0	0	0	0	1	2	3	4	6	7	8	9	10	11	12	14	15	16	17
	.005	0	0	1	2	4	5	7	8	10	11	13	14	16	17	19	20	22	23	25
	.01	0	1	2	4	5	7	8	10	12	13	15	17	18	20	22	24	25	27	29
	.025	0	2	4	6	7	9	11	13	15	17	19	21	23	25	27	29	31	33	35
	.05	1	3	5	7	9	12	14	16	18	20	22	25	27	29	31	34	36	38	40
	.10	2	5	7	9	12	14	17	19	22	24	27	29	32	34	37	39	42	44	47
8	.001	0	0	0	1	2	3	5	6	7	9	10	12	13	15	16	18	19	21	22
	.005	0	0	2	3	5	7	8	10	12	14	16	18	19	21	23	25	27	29	31
	.01	0	1	3	5	7	8	10	12	14	16	18	21	23	25	27	29	31	33	35
	.025	1	3	5	7	9	11	14	16	18	20	23	25	27	30	32	35	37	39	42
	.05	2	4	6	9	11	14	16	19	21	24	27	29	32	34	37	40	42	45	48
	.10	3	6	8	11	14	17	20	23	25	28	31	34	37	40	43	46	49	52	55
9	.001	0	0	0	2	3	4	6	8	9	11	13	15	16	18	20	22	24	26	27
	.005	0	1	2	4	6	8	10	12	14	17	19	21	23	25	28	30	32	34	37
	.01	0	2	4	6	8	10	12	15	17	19	22	24	27	29	32	34	37	39	41
	.025	1	3	5	8	11	13	16	18	21	24	27	29	32	35	38	40	43	46	49
	.05	2	5	7	10	13	16	19	22	25	28	31	34	37	40	43	46	49	52	55
	.10	3	6	10	13	16	19	23	26	29	32	36	39	42	46	49	53	56	59	63
10	.001	0	0	1	2	4	6	7	9	11	13	15	18	20	22	24	26	28	30	33
	.005	0	1	3	5	7	10	12	14	17	19	22	25	27	30	32	35	38	40	43
	.01	0	2	4	7	9	12	14	17	20	23	25	28	31	34	37	39	42	45	48
	.025	1	4	6	9	12	15	18	21	24	27	30	34	37	40	43	46	49	53	56
	.05	2	5	8	12	15	18	21	25	28	32	35	38	42	45	49	52	56	59	63
	.10	4	7	11	14	18	22	25	29	33	37	40	44	48	52	55	59	63	67	71

n_1	p	$n_2=2$	3	4	5	6	7	8	9	10	11	12	13	14	15	16	17	18	19	20
11	.001	0	0	1	3	5	7	9	11	13	16	18	21	23	25	28	30	33	35	38
	.005	0	1	3	6	8	11	14	17	19	22	25	28	31	34	37	40	43	46	49
	.01	0	2	5	8	10	13	16	19	23	26	29	32	35	38	42	45	48	51	54
	.025	1	4	7	10	14	17	20	24	27	31	34	38	41	45	48	52	56	59	63
	.05	2	6	9	13	17	20	24	28	32	35	39	43	47	51	55	58	62	66	70
	.10	4	8	12	16	20	24	28	32	37	41	45	49	53	58	62	66	70	74	79
12	.001	0	0	1	3	5	8	10	13	15	18	21	24	26	29	32	35	38	41	43
	.005	0	2	4	7	10	13	16	19	22	25	28	32	35	38	42	45	48	52	55
	.01	0	3	6	9	12	15	18	22	25	29	32	36	39	43	47	50	54	57	61
	.025	2	5	8	12	15	19	23	27	30	34	38	42	46	50	54	58	62	66	70
	.05	3	6	10	14	18	22	27	31	35	39	43	48	52	56	61	65	69	73	78
	.10	5	9	13	18	22	27	31	36	40	45	50	54	59	64	68	73	78	82	87
13	.001	0	0	2	4	6	9	12	15	18	21	24	27	30	33	36	39	43	46	49
	.005	0	2	4	8	11	14	18	21	25	28	32	35	39	43	46	50	54	58	61
	.01	1	3	6	10	13	17	21	24	28	32	36	40	44	48	52	56	60	64	68
	.025	2	5	9	13	17	21	25	29	34	38	42	46	51	55	60	64	68	73	77
	.05	3	7	11	16	20	25	29	34	38	43	48	52	57	62	66	71	76	81	85
	.10	5	10	14	19	24	29	34	39	44	49	54	59	64	69	75	80	85	90	95
14	.001	0	0	2	4	7	10	13	16	20	23	26	30	33	37	40	44	47	51	55
	.005	0	2	5	8	12	16	19	23	27	31	35	39	43	47	51	55	59	64	68
	.01	1	3	7	11	14	18	23	27	31	35	39	44	48	52	57	61	66	70	74
	.025	2	6	10	14	18	23	27	32	37	41	46	51	56	60	65	70	75	79	84
	.05	4	8	12	17	22	27	32	37	42	47	52	57	62	67	72	78	83	88	93
	.10	5	11	16	21	26	32	37	42	48	53	59	64	70	75	81	86	92	98	103
15	.001	0	0	2	5	8	11	15	18	22	25	29	33	37	41	44	48	52	56	60
	.005	0	3	6	9	13	17	21	25	30	34	38	43	47	52	56	61	65	70	74
	.01	1	4	8	12	16	20	25	29	34	38	43	48	52	57	62	67	71	76	81
	.025	2	6	11	15	20	25	30	35	40	45	50	55	60	65	71	76	81	86	91
	.05	4	8	13	19	24	29	34	40	45	51	56	62	67	73	78	84	89	95	101
	.10	6	11	17	23	28	34	40	46	52	58	64	69	75	81	87	93	99	105	111
16	.001	0	0	3	6	9	12	16	20	24	28	32	36	40	44	49	53	57	61	66
	.005	0	3	6	10	14	19	23	28	32	37	42	46	51	56	61	66	71	75	80
	.01	1	4	8	13	17	22	27	32	37	42	47	52	57	62	67	72	77	83	88
	.025	2	7	12	16	22	27	32	38	43	48	54	60	65	71	76	82	87	93	99
	.05	4	9	15	20	26	31	37	43	49	55	61	66	72	78	84	90	96	102	108
	.10	6	12	18	24	30	37	43	49	55	62	68	75	81	87	94	100	107	113	120
17	.001	0	1	3	6	10	14	18	22	26	30	35	39	44	48	53	58	62	67	71
	.005	0	3	7	11	16	20	25	30	35	40	45	50	55	61	66	71	76	82	87
	.01	1	5	9	14	19	24	29	34	39	45	50	56	61	67	72	78	83	89	94
	.025	3	7	12	18	23	29	35	40	46	52	58	64	70	76	82	88	94	100	106
	.05	4	10	16	21	27	34	40	46	52	58	65	71	78	84	90	97	103	110	116
	.10	7	13	19	26	32	39	46	53	59	66	73	80	86	93	100	107	114	121	128
18	.001	0	1	4	7	11	15	19	24	28	33	38	43	47	52	57	62	67	72	77
	.005	0	3	7	12	17	22	27	32	38	43	48	54	59	65	71	76	82	88	93
	.01	1	5	10	15	20	25	31	37	42	48	54	60	66	71	77	83	89	95	101
	.025	3	8	13	19	25	31	37	43	49	56	62	68	75	81	87	94	100	107	113
	.05	5	10	17	23	29	36	42	49	56	62	69	76	83	89	96	103	110	117	124
	.10	7	14	21	28	35	42	49	56	63	70	78	85	92	99	107	114	121	129	136
19	.001	0	1	4	8	12	16	21	26	30	35	41	46	51	56	61	67	72	78	83
	.005	1	4	8	13	18	23	29	34	40	46	52	58	64	70	75	82	88	94	100
	.01	2	5	10	16	21	27	33	39	45	51	57	64	70	76	83	89	95	102	108
	.025	3	8	14	20	26	33	39	46	53	59	66	73	79	86	93	100	107	114	120
	.05	5	11	18	24	31	38	45	52	59	66	73	81	88	95	102	110	117	124	131
	.10	8	15	22	29	37	44	52	59	67	74	82	90	98	105	113	121	129	136	144
20	.001	0	1	4	8	13	17	22	27	33	38	43	49	55	60	66	71	77	83	89
	.005	1	4	9	14	19	25	31	37	43	49	55	61	68	74	80	87	93	100	106
	.01	2	6	11	17	23	29	35	41	48	54	61	68	74	81	88	94	101	108	115
	.025	3	9	15	21	28	35	42	49	56	63	70	77	84	91	99	106	113	120	128
	.05	5	12	19	26	33	40	48	55	63	70	78	85	93	101	108	116	124	131	139
	.10	8	16	23	31	39	47	55	63	71	79	87	95	103	111	120	128	136	144	152

ACKNOWLEDGMENTS FOR TABLES

A. From the Rand Corporation, *A Million Random Digits with 100,000 Normal Deviates*. The Free Press, Glencoe, Illinois, 1955. Used by permission of The Rand Corporation.

D. Reproduced from *Documenta Geigy Scientific Tables*, 7th ed., Basel, 1970. Courtesy CIBA-GEIGY Limited, Basel, Switzerland.

E. From *Biometrika Tables for Statisticians*, 3d ed., vol. I, Bentley House, London, 1966. Reprinted by permission of the Biometrika Trustees.

F. From A. Hald and S. A. Sinkbaek, ''A Table of Percentage Points of the χ^2 Distribution,'' *Skandinavisk Aktuarietidskrift* 33(1950):168–175. Used by permission.

G. Table Ga and Gb adapted from Frieda S. Swed and C. Eisenhart, ''Tables for Testing Randomness of Grouping in a Sequence of Alternatives,'' *Annals of Mathematical Statistics* 14(1943):66–87. Used by permission.

H. From Gerald J. Glasser and Robert Winter, ''Critical Values of the Coefficient of Rank Correlation for Testing the Hypothesis of Independence,'' *Biometrika* 48(1961):444–448. Used by permission of the Biometrika Trustees. The table as reprinted here contains corrections given in W. J. Conover, *Practical Nonparametric Statistics,* © 1971 by John Wiley & Sons, Inc., New York.

I. F. Wilcoxon, S. Katti, and R. A. Wilcox, *Critical Values and Probability Levels for the Wilcoxon Rank Sum Test and the Wilcoxon Signed Rank Test*, Pearl River, N.Y.: American Cyanamid Co., 1949; reproduced with the permission of American Cyanamid Company.

J. Adapted from L. R. Verdooren, ''Extended Tables of Critical Values for Wilcoxon's Test Statistic,'' *Biometrika* 50(1963), 177–186. Used by permission of the Biometrika Trustees.

Appendix II
Hypothetical Population of Employed Heads of Households

VARIABLE

1. Sex
   1 = male
   2 = female
2. Marital status
   1 − single
   2 = married
   3 = widowed or divorced
3. Age
4. Occupation
   1 = professional
   2 = managerial
   3 = sales
   4 = clerical and technical
   5 = other
5. Education (years of school completed)
6. Commuting distance to work (miles)
7. Number of years with current employer
8. Annual income (thousands of dollars)
9. Family size (number of persons)
10. Size of residence (hundreds of square feet of floor space)

					Variable					
Subject	1	2	3	4	5	6	7	8	9	10
1	1	2	29	4	14	12	5	24	4	26
2	1	2	48	1	16	34	10	27	4	22
3	1	2	41	5	12	12	11	16	4	20
4	1	2	54	4	14	18	20	23	3	20
5	1	2	44	4	12	5	20	21	3	19
6	1	2	57	3	16	30	21	44	2	36
7	1	1	45	2	16	22	22	48	1	8
8	1	2	59	2	12	20	29	32	2	25
9	1	1	18	3	12	17	1	12	1	6
10	1	2	49	3	14	24	24	37	3	32
11	1	2	43	2	16	7	18	38	3	33
12	1	2	44	4	16	14	20	31	4	30
13	1	2	43	2	12	29	15	28	4	29
14	1	2	45	5	12	28	14	17	3	18
15	1	2	50	1	16	17	23	24	3	20
16	1	1	44	4	14	28	20	22	1	19
17	1	2	52	3	12	17	21	30	3	30
18	1	2	60	2	16	22	25	60	2	39
19	1	2	43	2	16	9	12	39	4	31
20	1	2	53	4	12	26	16	18	3	17
21	1	3	45	5	16	21	20	29	1	28
22	1	2	55	3	12	5	30	27	2	20
23	1	3	20	5	14	33	2	10	1	6
24	1	2	58	4	14	32	16	24	2	19
25	1	2	43	4	12	31	21	17	4	17
26	1	3	43	3	12	34	24	24	1	26
27	2	1	21	3	12	13	2	10	1	5
28	1	2	41	2	16	31	14	38	4	32
29	1	2	44	2	16	17	12	42	3	4
30	1	2	40	4	16	17	10	29	4	28
31	1	2	56	2	12	13	16	23	2	20
32	1	2	47	3	16	29	18	41	4	34
33	1	2	51	2	12	24	16	30	3	32
34	2	3	26	2	16	17	3	16	2	24
35	2	1	18	4	12	6	1	11	1	6
36	1	2	30	2	16	5	1	31	3	27
37	1	2	49	2	12	32	9	28	3	31
38	1	2	42	4	16	33	12	24	4	20
39	1	2	50	4	14	25	14	20	3	18
40	1	2	54	3	16	5	13	37	3	34
41	1	2	45	4	14	31	23	24	4	20
42	1	2	57	2	16	11	20	60	2	38
43	2	3	25	1	17	20	3	18	2	12
44	2	1	24	1	18	10	1	19	1	5
45	1	2	59	2	16	10	19	51	2	36
46	2	1	34	1	16	13	7	14	1	7
47	1	2	43	2	12	25	16	21	4	20
48	2	3	30	2	16	14	5	12	3	12
49	1	2	45	4	16	17	15	22	3	19
50	1	2	58	3	15	33	20	31	2	33

	Variable									
Subject	1	2	3	4	5	6	7	8	9	10
51	2	1	25	1	16	4	3	15	1	5
52	1	2	29	3	16	32	2	34	5	30
53	1	2	52	2	14	32	7	28	3	25
54	1	2	18	4	12	23	1	10	2	4
55	1	2	53	4	14	12	11	21	2	20
56	1	2	55	3	16	27	15	41	2	34
57	2	3	35	3	13	19	10	12	2	9
58	1	2	40	2	12	16	10	26	4	27
59	2	1	42	4	16	30	6	13	1	5
60	1	2	44	2	16	32	15	32	3	34
61	1	2	48	4	16	27	21	30	3	32
62	1	1	20	5	12	28	2	12	1	6
63	1	2	42	2	16	9	12	38	4	34
64	1	2	60	3	14	8	20	27	2	28
65	1	3	21	3	12	16	1	12	1	5
66	1	2	56	2	15	32	26	29	2	27
67	1	2	41	2	16	20	15	34	4	33
68	1	2	51	4	14	30	20	21	3	19
69	1	2	44	4	12	20	12	20	4	18
70	1	2	47	5	12	29	17	16	3	17
71	1	2	31	2	13	14	6	35	4	38
72	1	2	20	4	13	35	3	11	3	6
73	1	2	50	3	12	34	22	27	4	23
74	1	2	47	4	16	16	16	25	3	22
75	1	2	54	4	14	32	28	23	3	21
76	2	1	31	5	12	7	11	11	1	6
77	1	2	57	4	14	27	22	24	2	21
78	2	3	29	1	18	21	5	20	2	24
79	1	2	59	5	12	9	31	17	2	27
80	1	2	42	3	16	28	19	41	3	38
81	1	2	42	3	16	9	14	38	4	37
82	2	2	48	5	12	9	8	12	4	10
83	2	2	49	4	12	7	14	13	5	16
84	1	2	55	2	16	8	15	44	3	36
85	1	2	49	4	12	16	10	17	4	18
86	1	1	21	5	12	32	2	12	1	7
87	1	2	30	4	14	20	3	29	4	27
88	2	1	26	1	16	29	4	17	1	70
89	2	1	35	3	14	28	12	10	1	5
90	1	2	52	4	14	30	12	19	2	18
91	1	1	18	3	12	20	1	10	1	6
92	1	2	53	5	12	29	24	15	3	16
93	1	2	43	2	16	14	21	38	4	37
94	1	2	58	3	16	35	16	37	2	39
95	2	1	44	2	18	11	20	19	1	11
96	1	2	40	2	12	34	12	27	4	34
97	1	2	41	2	16	11	11	36	3	37
98	1	2	48	4	16	34	10	28	3	27
99	1	2	40	2	14	25	12	30	4	28
100	1	1	60	4	14	10	24	25	1	21

					Variable					
Subject	1	2	3	4	5	6	7	8	9	10
101	2	3	31	1	18	24	7	19	3	15
102	1	2	56	3	16	20	20	42	2	38
103	1	2	51	3	12	9	21	31	3	23
104	2	1	33	1	16	28	10	20	1	23
105	1	2	29	1	18	15	5	29	3	27
106	1	2	22	1	16	29	1	22	2	12
107	1	1	29	5	12	17	4	28	1	6
108	2	1	36	2	16	25	11	17	1	12
109	1	2	32	1	16	26	2	30	4	27
110	1	2	21	4	13	10	2	11	3	7
111	1	2	48	1	16	23	14	20	4	29
112	1	2	43	2	12	29	12	24	3	30
113	1	2	50	2	12	22	30	27	3	21
114	2	1	37	3	14	26	10	14	1	8
115	1	2	54	1	16	19	26	22	2	29
116	2	2	48	4	14	23	8	13	6	11
117	1	2	57	3	16	9	20	38	2	34
118	2	1	38	5	16	28	3	12	1	7
119	1	1	59	4	14	9	32	21	1	19
120	1	2	47	2	16	31	24	32	3	33
121	1	3	58	4	16	32	20	24	2	20
122	1	2	55	1	16	34	25	29	3	22
123	1	2	52	3	14	30	22	27	4	24
124	1	2	31	1	16	33	4	32	4	27
125	2	1	43	1	16	16	3	17	1	10
126	2	1	27	4	12	15	8	10	1	5
127	1	2	53	2	12	15	18	30	2	24
128	2	3	28	5	13	5	8	12	3	18
129	1	2	40	2	12	6	15	21	4	19
130	1	2	41	4	14	17	17	19	3	16
131	1	2	42	2	16	29	14	35	4	34
132	1	1	20	5	12	19	2	14	1	8
133	1	2	43	4	12	16	18	21	3	19
134	1	2	42	3	16	12	14	40	3	34
135	1	2	60	3	12	32	27	30	2	30
136	1	2	56	2	16	15	28	38	2	33
137	1	2	18	3	12	26	1	12	3	6
138	1	2	51	2	16	30	19	44	3	37
139	1	2	49	2	12	34	10	32	5	30
140	1	2	30	3	12	14	8	34	3	27
141	1	2	30	4	14	26	5	25	5	17
142	1	2	38	3	12	5	10	38	3	35
143	1	2	49	2	14	35	11	24	3	30
144	1	3	50	2	16	22	15	38	4	33
145	2	2	47	3	14	15	20	16	2	23
146	1	2	54	3	16	9	21	41	3	35
147	1	2	43	4	16	8	20	26	4	30
148	1	1	57	3	12	34	24	27	1	31
149	1	1	18	3	12	21	1	14	1	5
150	1	2	59	2	14	17	32	28	2	30

			Variable							
Subject	1	2	3	4	5	6	7	8	9	10
151	1	2	40	2	12	13	20	24	5	31
152	1	2	20	5	14	14	2	16	2	5
153	1	1	49	4	16	9	22	22	1	19
154	1	3	55	5	12	20	26	18	1	5
155	1	1	22	2	16	31	2	20	1	6
156	1	1	21	4	15	9	2	15	1	6
157	1	2	29	3	15	28	1	37	6	18
158	1	1	23	2	16	11	1	20	1	7
159	1	2	32	2	16	33	1	41	5	18
160	1	1	20	5	12	30	1	11	1	5
161	1	1	52	5	12	28	27	17	1	8
162	1	3	41	4	16	13	14	20	1	6
163	1	2	53	3	16	13	21	35	3	34
164	1	2	44	5	14	33	20	18	4	20
165	1	2	58	4	14	14	30	21	2	19
166	1	1	47	2	16	32	22	33	3	32
167	1	2	60	5	12	23	28	15	2	15
168	1	2	42	4	16	9	20	22	4	20
169	2	2	47	5	12	25	22	18	4	12
170	1	2	43	3	16	11	14	42	3	33
171	1	2	48	2	16	23	17	45	2	34
172	1	1	56	2	12	6	21	30	1	30
173	1	2	42	5	12	12	22	18	4	20
174	1	2	51	4	14	27	20	21	3	20
175	1	2	31	2	16	16	5	45	5	38
176	1	2	31	4	14	10	7	30	3	26
177	1	2	21	4	12	27	3	16	3	8
178	1	2	48	3	14	35	20	20	3	20
179	1	1	42	2	16	10	20	31	1	33
180	1	2	50	4	16	20	16	24	3	21
181	1	2	44	1	16	26	20	22	4	19
182	1	1	54	4	12	34	26	17	1	12
183	2	1	28	2	16	5	3	20	1	5
184	1	2	34	2	16	28	7	40	3	36
185	1	2	56	3	14	29	26	30	2	20
186	2	1	32	3	12	12	6	14	1	6
187	1	2	55	2	16	22	22	24	2	24
188	1	2	41	2	14	24	13	20	3	19
189	1	2	53	4	16	23	20	21	3	20
190	2	3	27	2	18	29	5	22	2	19
191	2	1	18	5	12	15	1	11	1	5
192	1	3	30	5	12	20	3	30	1	5
193	2	1	22	1	16	24	1	17	1	7
194	1	2	33	2	12	34	7	29	2	36
195	1	1	24	1	16	21	2	21	1	4
196	1	2	18	5	12	11	1	12	2	4
197	1	2	49	4	14	20	28	19	4	18
198	1	2	52	5	12	35	26	16	3	17
199	1	2	23	2	15	30	2	15	3	12
200	1	2	51	2	16	10	28	42	3	23

					Variable					
Subject	1	2	3	4	5	6	7	8	9	10
201	1	1	20	3	12	31	2	10	1	5
202	1	2	47	3	16	27	20	31	4	20
203	1	2	45	2	12	23	25	22	3	18
204	1	2	22	3	12	10	3	12	2	6
205	1	2	43	2	12	35	19	20	4	19
206	2	3	36	4	14	10	9	13	3	18
207	2	3	32	1	16	25	8	16	4	12
208	1	2	32	2	18	7	5	42	2	39
209	1	1	20	4	12	25	1	10	1	7
210	1	2	29	2	16	30	4	38	2	29
211	1	2	20	3	12	10	2	11	2	4
212	1	1	25	1	16	14	2	18	1	7
213	1	2	29	3	12	31	6	27	3	28
214	1	1	18	4	12	15	1	10	1	5
215	1	1	32	1	16	14	10	30	1	9
216	1	1	22	4	14	32	2	12	1	4
217	1	2	35	4	14	12	5	26	4	15
218	1	2	34	3	16	30	4	42	4	29
219	1	2	20	5	12	27	2	14	3	6
220	1	2	36	2	15	14	4	27	3	16
221	1	3	23	1	16	15	1	21	1	15
222	1	2	47	2	12	13	17	22	3	19
223	1	2	41	2	16	7	16	34	3	31
224	1	2	49	3	16	9	19	37	2	33
225	1	2	42	4	12	8	14	18	4	27
226	1	2	50	3	12	17	29	24	3	30
227	2	1	42	2	16	21	15	22	1	8
228	1	2	31	1	17	8	1	39	2	9
229	1	3	53	4	12	16	27	21	1	19
230	1	1	21	3	12	8	3	14	1	4
231	1	2	54	3	16	10	16	36	3	35
232	1	2	48	2	16	19	20	41	3	37
233	2	1	32	3	16	25	8	21	1	14
234	2	3	25	2	16	11	2	23	2	14
235	1	2	52	2	12	14	30	24	2	21
236	1	2	44	3	12	20	21	30	3	33
237	2	1	29	2	16	27	3	24	1	14
238	1	2	51	2	16	16	26	55	3	39
239	1	2	43	2	12	31	19	22	4	20
240	1	2	24	3	12	7	1	17	3	20
241	1	2	46	3	16	10	16	37	3	23
242	1	2	45	2	16	31	19	35	4	29
243	1	2	33	3	16	24	6	45	4	39
244	1	2	30	1	17	16	3	32	4	28
245	2	3	33	4	12	9	12	14	4	12
246	2	3	27	4	12	15	4	12	1	8
247	1	2	26	1	16	12	2	25	3	28
248	1	2	21	3	12	22	3	10	2	4
249	1	2	30	2	12	13	7	28	4	16
250	1	2	24	2	16	35	3	24	3	24

	Variable									
Subject	1	2	3	4	5	6$'$	7	8	9	10
251	1	2	33	2	16	5	4	42	3	30
252	2	1	33	5	12	15	9	11	1	6
253	1	2	35	3	12	34	14	22	3	15
254	2	3	45	5	12	5	15	12	3	17
255	1	2	34	4	14	35	9	22	4	15
256	1	2	46	5	16	22	17	24	4	20
257	2	3	26	1	18	25	2	18	1	18
258	1	2	48	4	12	23	24	17	2	21
259	1	2	42	4	14	8	20	22	3	20
260	1	1	20	5	13	11	2	12	1	6
261	1	2	36	3	16	6	5	40	4	38
262	1	3	29	4	15	17	6	30	1	8
263	1	1	25	2	12	7	1	14	1	7
264	1	2	18	4	12	18	1	10	2	5
265	1	2	32	4	14	12	8	31	4	17
266	1	2	47	2	16	13	25	42	2	32
267	2	1	25	3	14	10	3	19	1	8
268	2	3	34	3	12	16	7	19	2	12
269	2	3	35	2	16	10	7	26	3	19
270	2	3	37	5	12	15	14	13	4	20
271	1	2	45	3	16	32	24	41	4	33
272	1	2	22	2	16	8	1	14	3	10
273	1	2	44	3	12	19	21	31	3	31
274	2	3	40	4	12	22	10	13	5	14
275	1	3	43	2	16	17	19	49	1	26
276	1	2	37	2	12	7	12	29	4	15
277	1	1	20	4	13	20	2	12	1	6
278	1	2	41	3	16	16	20	30	4	24
279	1	1	23	4	16	26	1	19	1	7
280	1	3	31	5	12	32	1	25	1	7
281	1	1	18	5	12	27	1	12	1	6
282	1	1	18	4	12	22	2	10	1	4
283	1	1	18	3	12	17	1	10	1	7
284	2	3	46	3	12	9	21	15	3	16
285	1	2	23	2	16	13	2	22	3	20
286	1	2	27	1	17	16	3	20	4	19
287	2	1	26	4	14	21	2	14	1	6
288	1	2	31	2	16	12	3	28	3	15
289	1	1	20	3	14	8	3	10	1	6
290	1	2	34	1	18	24	2	21	3	16
291	1	3	22	5	15	10	3	15	1	7
292	1	2	35	2	16	23	10	46	5	39
293	2	1	31	2	16	7	3	16	1	5
294	1	2	42	2	16	15	11	47	2	34
295	1	2	45	3	16	20	16	52	3	35
296	2	3	27	5	12	15	5	12	1	13
297	1	2	26	4	12	12	6	15	3	18
298	1	2	30	3	16	11	5	45	5	39
299	1	1	33	1	17	28	3	35	1	19
300	1	1	21	5	15	18	1	12	1	6

					Variable					
Subject	1	2	3	4	5	6	7	8	9	10
301	1	2	36	4	14	33	9	24	4	16
302	2	1	41	1	18	8	12	19	1	5
303	2	1	39	2	16	19	9	21	1	6
304	1	1	44	1	18	26	20	20	1	6
305	1	1	41	2	16	12	13	36	1	8
306	1	3	43	4	12	28	17	19	1	7
307	1	1	18	5	12	25	1	12	1	5
308	1	2	38	3	16	25	14	45	5	20
309	1	2	20	3	12	26	3	13	3	12
310	1	2	36	3	16	12	10	45	5	38
311	1	2	32	3	12	10	7	30	5	25
312	2	3	34	4	15	11	10	13	3	12
313	1	1	24	2	16	5	1	20	1	15
314	1	2	25	3	14	10	3	15	3	16
315	1	2	29	2	13	28	8	32	3	27
316	1	1	18	4	12	11	1	14	1	6
317	2	3	18	3	12	9	1	16	1	6
318	1	2	25	5	12	8	3	18	4	18
319	1	1	20	4	12	31	1	15	1	6
320	1	2	28	5	12	20	2	20	5	19
321	1	2	29	2	16	15	7	30	4	27
322	2	3	47	3	16	14	20	14	4	17
323	2	1	34	5	13	10	13	15	1	6
324	2	3	25	4	12	16	9	13	2	6
325	2	1	40	1	16	9	16	19	1	7
326	1	2	32	3	16	13	6	45	5	34
327	2	1	27	1	16	13	1	17	1	5
328	1	1	34	2	16	25	7	36	1	15
329	2	3	33	1	18	24	11	20	3	19
330	1	2	35	1	16	35	7	21	4	16
331	1	2	21	3	12	16	2	14	2	10
332	1	2	23	1	16	29	1	20	2	21
333	1	2	36	4	12	9	8	29	5	27
334	1	1	19	5	12	12	1	12	1	6
335	1	2	27	2	13	15	5	19	3	18
336	1	2	24	3	14	16	2	16	2	20
337	1	2	31	4	15	19	5	30	5	36
338	2	3	38	3	12	6	9	14	2	17
339	2	3	48	5	12	13	16	11	4	18
340	1	2	20	4	14	8	3	14	3	11
341	1	2	38	2	12	25	16	31	5	29
342	1	2	37	2	16	8	11	52	4	38
343	1	1	22	2	16	22	1	18	1	7
344	1	2	33	4	14	15	2	32	5	28
345	1	2	30	1	16	9	4	34	3	39
346	1	2	26	3	15	25	2	14	3	15
347	2	1	49	4	13	11	26	11	1	6
348	1	1	20	5	12	32	2	10	1	4
349	1	1	19	5	12	27	1	12	1	7
350	2	3	28	2	16	18	3	24	3	18

					Variable					
Subject	1	2	3	4	5	6	7	8	9	10
351	1	1	21	4	12	21	1	12	1	6
352	1	1	24	1	16	20	3	19	1	20
353	1	2	26	2	16	28	3	27	4	19
354	1	1	20	3	12	25	1	14	1	4
355	1	2	30	3	16	7	4	42	5	38
356	1	2	33	2	16	7	5	41	4	37
357	1	3	34	3	16	26	7	50	5	31
358	1	2	19	5	12	10	2	15	2	12
359	1	2	45	2	16	30	15	45	2	34
360	1	2	39	2	12	6	12	30	3	30
361	1	2	43	3	16	32	10	41	4	38
362	1	1	22	4	14	28	2	14	1	6
363	1	2	34	3	12	29	10	37	5	38
364	1	2	44	4	14	33	22	21	3	21
365	1	2	40	2	13	7	12	18	5	20
366	1	3	32	3	12	26	5	32	1	17
367	2	3	29	2	16	20	5	14	1	5
368	1	2	25	4	16	28	2	22	3	18
369	1	2	28	4	14	12	3	24	6	19
370	1	2	29	3	16	6	7	40	4	30
371	1	1	36	1	16	14	6	21	1	8
372	1	2	20	4	14	23	2	15	3	12
373	1	3	42	4	12	20	16	17	1	4
374	2	3	32	2	18	15	3	22	2	14
375	1	1	41	3	16	19	14	31	1	4
376	2	1	23	1	16	21	1	19	1	6
377	2	1	28	2	16	8	4	20	1	7
378	1	2	38	1	18	32	12	22	3	18
379	1	2	37	4	12	5	16	20	5	14
380	1	1	18	3	12	27	1	10	1	4
381	1	2	31	4	16	30	2	35	4	38
382	1	2	27	3	16	13	4	24	5	28
383	1	1	23	3	12	9	3	19	1	7
384	2	3	41	1	16	19	17	16	4	12
385	2	1	30	2	18	25	4	23	1	8
386	1	1	20	4	12	22	2	12	1	4
387	1	2	27	4	12	9	3	18	4	16
388	1	1	23	5	13	10	4	17	1	8
389	2	1	39	3	14	25	12	14	1	6
390	1	2	31	3	16	12	7	45	4	39
391	1	2	35	5	12	7	1	15	2	15
392	2	3	21	5	12	12	2	11	2	9
393	1	2	38	4	14	34	14	20	4	18
394	1	2	45	2	12	24	10	22	3	20
395	1	2	43	4	14	12	23	19	2	19
396	1	1	18	4	12	27	1	13	1	5
397	1	2	46	3	16	18	22	55	2	36
398	1	2	34	2	16	14	11	45	4	38
399	1	3	22	1	16	23	1	16	1	6
400	1	2	30	5	12	21	4	32	5	27

	Variable									
Subject	1	2	3	4	5	6	7	8	9	10
401	1	2	33	3	14	31	6	34	3	38
402	2	1	19	3	12	7	1	13	1	5
403	1	1	26	5	13	33	4	17	1	7
404	1	2	36	3	16	16	5	42	5	30
405	1	2	40	2	16	9	20	39	3	31
406	1	2	39	2	12	7	18	28	2	29
407	1	2	44	3	16	30	14	40	4	32
408	1	1	19	3	12	31	2	12	1	4
409	1	2	42	4	15	30	12	18	3	19
410	1	2	21	5	12	25	2	11	2	10
411	1	2	41	5	14	8	13	17	3	18
412	1	3	37	5	12	11	8	22	1	8
413	1	1	20	3	12	21	1	11	1	4
414	1	2	32	5	12	31	4	28	4	16
415	1	2	29	2	18	13	5	43	5	39
416	1	2	28	1	16	6	6	21	3	18
417	1	3	24	2	15	33	2	18	1	6
418	1	3	25	5	15	6	1	20	1	6
419	2	1	35	5	12	14	9	14	1	6
420	2	1	29	3	12	7	7	12	1	7
421	1	1	25	2	16	33	3	24	1	18
422	1	2	28	2	18	24	1	32	2	26
423	1	2	29	1	16	23	3	30	4	36
424	1	1	18	4	12	12	1	10	1	5
425	1	2	32	5	12	9	2	21	4	22
426	1	2	35	4	14	34	3	29	3	25
427	1	2	19	4	12	26	2	11	2	9
428	1	3	38	5	12	5	7	18	1	7
429	1	3	23	4	15	23	5	15	1	6
430	1	3	41	2	16	35	20	52	1	20
431	1	2	46	2	12	22	16	29	3	21
432	2	3	25	4	16	15	2	14	2	14
433	1	2	34	3	16	28	4	35	5	38
434	1	1	43	3	16	27	14	37	1	22
435	1	2	24	4	16	33	3	21	3	22
436	1	1	20	4	12	29	2	12	1	4
437	1	2	27	5	12	27	5	21	2	19
438	1	2	31	3	12	30	6	42	3	28
439	1	1	21	4	12	29	3	14	1	6
440	1	2	36	2	12	8	7	28	4	28
441	1	2	42	1	18	18	13	26	4	28
442	1	2	39	4	16	30	12	28	5	22
443	1	3	47	4	14	13	21	24	3	21
444	2	1	25	5	12	13	3	16	1	5
445	1	2	48	2	12	16	19	22	4	20
446	1	3	44	5	12	25	20	15	1	6
447	1	2	40	3	16	30	17	35	3	34
448	1	2	45	3	12	34	20	23	3	20
449	1	2	37	2	16	33	9	28	4	28
450	1	2	33	3	12	14	2	31	2	26

					Variable					
Subject	1	2	3	4	5	6	7	8	9	10
451	1	2	20	5	12	17	1	13	2	10
452	2	3	24	4	14	13	4	14	2	12
453	1	1	30	3	16	18	3	41	1	14
454	1	1	22	5	13	11	3	15	1	6
455	1	2	26	4	13	17	8	18	3	15
456	1	1	20	5	13	15	2	12	1	4
457	1	2	26	2	16	28	1	26	4	21
458	1	2	22	2	16	35	1	18	2	5
459	1	2	30	4	13	30	2	30	4	18
460	1	2	33	3	16	28	10	48	3	30
461	2	1	36	4	12	15	11	11	1	6
462	1	2	35	5	12	6	3	18	2	7
463	1	2	37	3	16	7	14	45	5	35
464	2	3	31	1	17	6	8	18	2	13
465	1	1	39	2	12	21	9	21	1	7
466	1	2	44	2	16	28	14	34	3	23
467	1	2	21	3	12	8	2	11	2	5
468	1	1	34	5	12	22	3	20	1	7
469	1	1	23	1	16	9	1	22	1	9
470	1	2	28	3	14	16	3	32	4	30
471	2	3	26	4	13	15	4	12	2	9
472	1	2	25	3	12	5	3	20	3	17
473	2	1	26	3	14	19	2	11	1	4
474	1	2	29	2	16	8	4	42	4	21
475	1	2	32	3	16	30	4	45	5	39
476	2	1	38	2	18	8	13	20	1	5
477	1	2	36	2	18	13	12	36	4	16
478	1	2	24	4	14	6	1	17	3	18
479	1	1	18	4	12	13	1	12	1	4
480	1	2	40	4	14	12	15	21	2	20
481	2	3	39	3	16	13	13	13	2	10
482	1	2	43	3	16	6	18	38	3	31
483	1	1	42	2	12	10	17	18	1	6
484	1	2	19	4	12	34	1	13	2	6
485	1	2	41	4	16	9	11	31	4	25
486	1	2	20	3	12	20	2	14	1	5
487	1	2	37	1	18	24	6	19	3	15
488	1	2	31	5	12	11	7	38	4	27
489	2	1	48	4	12	11	18	12	1	5
490	1	2	27	4	14	22	7	22	4	16
491	2	3	30	3	12	8	6	14	2	14
492	2	1	27	3	14	22	3	11	1	4
493	1	1	22	2	16	25	1	20	1	7
494	1	2	24	5	12	9	2	16	3	17
495	1	1	19	5	¹2	26	1	10	1	4
496	1	1	27	2	18	12	3	25	1	8
497	2	1	34	4	14	9	3	10	1	4
498	1	1	31	1	18	26	2	26	1	9
499	2	3	27	4	12	8	5	11	2	9
500	1	1	35	3	16	19	6	48	5	37

					Variable					
Subject	1	2	3	4	5	6	7	8	9	10
501	1	2	38	2	16	34	15	32	5	30
502	2	1	47	1	18	25	12	21	1	11
503	1	2	33	2	16	17	11	50	4	37
504	1	2	23	2	16	34	1	23	2	19
505	1	2	34	5	12	33	1	21	3	15
506	1	2	26	1	16	23	2	23	3	21
507	1	2	30	2	16	9	4	44	2	30
508	1	1	20	5	12	14	2	10	1	4
509	1	3	36	5	12	14	5	18	1	7
510	1	2	39	1	18	13	12	20	5	20
511	1	1	40	2	16	15	17	30	1	8
512	2	1	46	2	18	15	10	24	1	11
513	2	1	37	2	16	5	7	22	1	5
514	1	2	43	3	16	32	13	46	2	26
515	1	1	21	4	15	10	1	15	1	6
516	1	2	42	4	12	16	16	17	3	21
517	1	1	20	4	14	7	1	12	1	4
518	1	2	44	2	12	18	20	22	3	20
519	1	2	41	2	14	35	20	23	4	19
520	1	2	37	2	12	8	12	27	4	26
521	1	1	18	3	12	28	1	13	1	4
522	1	3	32	2	16	21	6	44	1	9
523	1	2	29	3	14	25	2	39	3	29
524	1	1	28	1	18	25	5	24	1	4
525	1	2	25	4	13	11	1	19	3	18
526	1	1	25	2	16	15	2	26	1	20
527	2	1	37	3	14	8	6	13	1	4
528	1	2	28	2	16	34	2	34	4	31
529	1	2	32	2	12	18	8	30	3	16
530	2	3	28	3	14	25	2	12	3	14
531	2	3	39	1	18	14	4	15	1	5
532	1	2	21	5	12	23	2	15	3	6
533	1	2	35	2	12	34	14	27	4	16
534	2	3	31	4	13	23	6	11	2	6
535	1	2	38	4	12	10	17	21	5	19
536	1	2	23	2	14	5	2	16	3	18
537	1	2	42	2	16	24	16	49	4	32
538	1	1	18	3	12	23	2	10	1	4
539	1	2	34	2	16	31	6	48	5	38
540	1	2	43	1	12	31	15	25	3	18
541	1	3	20	5	12	32	1	12	1	6
542	1	1	22	3	12	35	3	17	1	7
543	1	2	27	3	14	10	4	27	5	20
544	1	2	31	4	14	16	5	22	4	24
545	2	3	42	1	16	24	4	24	3	12
546	1	2	36	3	12	21	9	28	3	25
547	1	1	19	4	12	23	2	13	1	6
548	1	1	24	2	13	23	2	15	1	7
549	1	2	44	3	12	5	24	24	2	19
550	1	2	41	5	16	25	15	34	3	29

	Variable									
Subject	1	2	3	4	5	6	7	8	9	10
551	1	2	20	4	12	25	3	14	3	4
552	1	2	40	4	12	24	16	15	4	16
553	1	2	39	2	12	12	13	12	5	18
554	1	1	37	3	16	32	11	47	1	10
555	1	3	33	2	13	8	1	25	1	15
556	2	1	24	1	16	25	2	20	1	6
557	1	3	30	4	14	32	8	35	1	10
558	1	2	29	4	13	20	4	27	4	17
559	2	1	28	2	16	18	5	21	1	5
560	1	2	26	3	14	16	5	28	4	22
561	2	3	48	2	18	22	15	24	4	20
562	1	3	26	4	12	23	8	20	1	7
563	1	1	20	4	12	15	1	12	1	4
564	1	2	29	2	16	26	6	45	5	38
565	1	2	30	1	16	11	4	28	4	26
566	2	3	38	3	14	16	8	14	4	18
567	1	2	33	1	16	35	3	29	5	27
568	1	2	35	1	18	23	5	23	3	25
569	1	1	19	5	12	29	1	15	1	6
570	1	2	38	3	16	5	14	52	5	38
571	1	2	42	2	16	18	14	25	3	20
572	1	1	20	5	14	5	2	13	1	6
573	1	2	34	2	12	5	10	28	5	29
574	1	2	24	2	16	33	3	20	3	16
575	1	3	25	1	16	11	1	20	1	7
576	2	3	31	4	13	20	8	12	2	6
577	2	3	49	4	12	13	13	10	3	10
578	2	3	49	3	14	18	20	14	5	16
579	2	3	32	2	16	6	5	21	1	5
580	1	2	28	3	16	9	4	25	2	16
581	1	2	32	1	16	26	10	29	2	25
582	2	1	29	4	14	7	4	13	1	6
583	1	2	36	2	16	27	9	35	5	38
584	1	2	40	4	12	22	15	19	2	18
585	2	1	36	1	18	8	3	19	1	11
586	1	1	41	3	16	21	12	32	1	9
587	2	3	29	3	12	14	9	15	2	6
588	1	2	39	4	14	13	10	21	3	18
589	1	2	37	4	14	13	15	22	5	17
590	1	2	23	2	12	30	4	16	3	17
591	1	1	18	3	12	33	2	14	1	6
592	1	1	21	5	12	29	3	10	1	4
593	1	2	31	3	16	35	4	47	4	39
594	1	1	22	2	16	35	1	19	1	7
595	1	2	27	1	18	10	2	20	3	18
596	1	2	22	2	12	8	3	18	2	12
597	1	2	27	3	15	12	5	22	4	17
598	2	3	32	1	18	18	6	18	2	13
599	2	3	37	4	12	20	7	13	3	13
600	1	2	31	2	16	31	6	41	4	39

					Variable					
Subject	1	2	3	4	5	6	7	8	9	10
601	1	2	21	3	14	11	2	12	2	6
602	1	2	35	4	12	9	10	25	4	17
603	2	3	33	3	14	21	11	15	1	7
604	1	2	38	2	16	12	13	40	5	34
605	2	3	43	2	16	17	16	19	3	14
606	1	3	34	3	16	15	8	39	1	8
607	1	1	39	2	16	23	14	37	1	9
608	2	1	25	3	16	10	2	14	1	9
609	1	2	29	3	16	35	4	46	5	38
610	1	2	30	3	15	32	7	40	4	38
611	1	2	33	4	12	19	5	32	2	16
612	2	1	33	4	12	24	9	15	1	6
613	1	2	26	4	14	33	3	19	3	18
614	1	2	41	3	12	18	19	21	4	21
615	2	1	19	4	12	14	1	12	1	4
616	1	2	36	2	16	11	5	38	5	27
617	1	2	24	1	16	9	1	18	4	18
618	1	1	19	4	13	6	2	10	1	4
619	1	2	20	4	12	6	3	13	2	6
620	1	3	42	3	16	26	14	23	1	7
621	1	3	18	4	12	12	1	14	1	7
622	1	2	40	2	14	35	12	38	3	22
623	1	2	20	4	14	33	2	15	3	5
624	1	2	37	2	16	10	10	45	5	38
625	2	1	38	3	12	18	9	11	1	5
626	1	2	32	2	12	19	9	27	3	17
627	2	3	29	4	12	18	3	10	2	5
628	1	1	23	1	16	5	2	21	1	9
629	1	2	28	4	12	17	6	20	3	15
630	1	2	25	4	14	23	3	22	2	16
631	1	1	20	4	12	15	2	12	1	4
632	1	2	25	5	12	8	3	19	4	15
633	1	1	23	3	12	18	1	17	1	5
634	1	2	28	2	12	17	5	21	4	17
635	1	2	32	3	14	32	7	24	4	16
636	1	3	18	3	12	7	1	13	1	6
637	1	2	35	2	16	20	9	40	2	10
638	1	2	38	3	16	26	12	52	4	36
639	1	1	21	5	12	33	1	15	1	4
640	1	2	44	2	16	29	21	32	4	24
641	1	2	45	3	16	11	20	40	3	35
642	1	2	19	4	13	9	2	14	2	6
643	1	2	34	4	14	32	3	19	3	16
644	1	3	40	3	12	7	19	26	1	9
645	1	3	20	4	14	11	2	12	1	4
646	1	1	24	5	16	35	2	22	1	7
647	1	2	27	2	16	31	1	25	5	20
648	2	1	32	1	18	7	5	17	1	8
649	1	1	31	3	14	10	7	24	1	7
650	1	1	22	3	12	24	4	17	1	6

					Variable					
Subject	1	2	3	4	5	6	7	8	9	10
651	1	1	36	3	12	33	7	27	1	9
652	2	1	45	2	17	11	12	22	1	8
653	1	2	46	4	14	25	22	20	3	19
654	1	2	42	3	12	25	17	24	4	20
655	2	3	28	4	14	6	4	12	1	4
656	1	2	43	2	16	8	19	31	3	32
657	1	2	39	2	16	21	12	33	4	33
658	1	2	41	5	12	5	11	16	3	19
659	1	2	33	5	16	19	7	41	3	39
660	2	1	26	4	14	12	1	13	1	6
661	2	3	34	1	18	17	3	21	2	19
662	1	2	37	3	15	24	17	20	4	16
663	1	2	30	3	16	5	4	45	4	38
664	1	1	29	1	17	14	4	29	1	14
665	1	2	26	5	16	14	1	25	4	20
666	2	3	47	3	14	24	19	14	5	14
667	2	1	39	2	18	16	8	25	1	12
668	1	3	24	2	15	19	2	19	1	7
669	1	2	26	5	13	25	6	20	3	18
670	1	1	30	4	14	33	5	37	1	9
671	2	3	27	4	14	5	3	12	1	4
672	1	2	33	1	18	5	9	30	4	17
673	2	3	36	4	13	22	11	11	2	12
674	1	3	35	2	12	29	2	20	1	9
675	1	2	38	4	14	17	14	26	5	20
676	1	1	20	5	12	5	3	12	1	4
677	1	2	42	4	12	35	22	19	4	17
678	1	2	41	2	14	31	16	21	3	16
679	1	2	34	1	18	34	4	19	3	16
680	2	1	27	3	12	12	4	12	1	4
681	2	3	44	4	12	19	16	10	3	13
682	1	1	25	3	14	35	5	18	1	6
683	1	1	19	3	12	17	2	10	1	4
684	1	2	28	3	16	5	4	35	5	30
685	1	2	32	4	15	23	5	22	4	16
686	1	3	18	3	12	29	1	10	1	4
687	1	2	36	1	16	13	9	19	4	15
688	2	1	31	2	16	7	5	18	1	5
689	1	2	40	2	16	17	17	38	2	18
690	2	1	35	1	18	5	8	19	1	8
691	1	2	21	5	15	7	1	15	3	8
692	1	2	20	5	12	6	2	12	2	6
693	1	2	39	3	12	30	15	20	4	19
694	1	3	22	1	16	26	1	21	1	8
695	2	3	33	3	16	5	6	17	2	16
696	1	1	37	1	18	32	2	16	1	7
697	1	2	23	5	12	6	3	15	3	20
698	2	3	34	1	18	18	7	20	3	14
699	1	2	31	2	16	11	3	38	4	37
700	1	2	27	1	16	28	3	21	3	17

					Variable					
Subject	1	2	3	4	5	6	7	8	9	10
701	1	2	27	4	16	19	4	28	4	20
702	1	1	22	2	13	9	2	20	1	5
703	1	3	31	3	16	34	1	44	1	10
704	1	1	20	4	12	5	2	14	1	6
705	1	2	35	3	14	14	5	34	3	36
706	1	1	21	4	12	6	1	15	1	6
707	1	1	38	5	12	17	1	17	1	7
708	1	2	46	2	16	17	17	28	3	20
709	1	2	39	2	16	14	18	30	4	20
710	1	2	45	4	14	26	14	21	3	20
711	2	1	28	3	12	28	3	12	1	4
712	1	1	50	2	12	11	23	23	2	19
713	1	2	42	3	16	16	20	40	3	35
714	1	2	34	2	16	26	1	47	4	39
715	1	1	19	4	12	26	1	10	1	4
716	1	2	24	3	16	20	2	18	2	17
717	1	2	26	1	16	19	2	23	4	19
718	1	2	33	2	15	31	2	40	3	38
719	1	2	36	5	12	15	4	19	4	14
720	1	2	48	4	16	7	22	26	3	21
721	2	3	22	4	12	10	2	11	1	4
722	1	3	51	3	16	5	16	42	2	34
723	1	2	43	3	14	32	15	29	3	20
724	2	1	23	4	12	17	1	12	1	4
725	1	3	49	2	12	25	19	27	1	21
726	1	2	47	3	16	22	21	42	4	33
727	1	2	40	2	16	15	14	31	4	24
728	1	3	44	2	12	10	24	25	1	20
729	1	2	37	5	12	27	15	19	4	15
730	1	2	32	4	14	34	3	30	4	27
731	2	3	26	4	14	6	2	12	2	10
732	1	2	28	5	12	20	3	21	3	25
733	1	2	25	2	16	24	2	26	3	29
734	2	3	32	3	14	9	7	10	2	5
735	1	3	23	4	12	5	2	17	1	4
736	1	3	25	4	12	11	6	17	1	5
737	1	3	27	1	18	16	2	19	1	6
738	1	2	28	3	16	24	1	33	3	27
739	2	1	30	2	16	27	3	21	1	5
740	1	2	23	2	16	14	2	23	3	22
741	1	1	32	3	16	7	1	40	1	15
742	1	2	35	3	16	24	4	48	5	39
743	2	3	31	4	12	29	4	14	3	19
744	1	2	46	2	12	27	14	28	3	21
745	1	2	38	1	18	18	7	38	4	27
746	1	2	48	2	16	16	19	32	3	20
747	1	1	45	2	16	27	16	26	1	5
748	1	2	22	5	16	22	1	22	3	13
749	1	2	34	5	12	7	2	19	4	14
750	1	2	36	2	16	18	7	32	5	18

					Variable					
Subject	1	2	3	4	5	6	7	8	9	10
751	1	2	49	3	16	9	22	41	3	33
752	1	3	39	4	14	15	14	22	5	23
753	1	2	47	3	12	27	19	29	3	22
754	2	1	29	2	16	8	6	20	1	5
755	1	2	50	4	16	12	28	23	2	20
756	1	1	43	3	16	33	13	34	1	15
757	1	2	51	3	12	35	28	27	2	20
758	1	2	20	4	12	7	1	12	2	6
759	1	2	52	2	16	24	22	52	3	36
760	1	1	19	4	12	9	2	13	1	6
761	1	2	53	3	16	20	27	36	3	31
762	1	2	40	3	12	22	21	24	4	22
763	1	2	52	5	16	8	22	27	2	20
764	1	2	33	3	12	9	4	35	2	16
765	2	3	25	4	14	12	1	13	2	5
766	1	2	44	1	16	7	22	22	3	18
767	2	3	31	1	18	21	7	19	1	12
768	1	1	24	1	16	22	1	20	1	5
769	1	2	37	3	16	19	16	51	5	20
770	1	2	26	3	14	15	4	21	4	17
771	1	2	24	2	12	6	2	17	2	16
772	1	1	26	2	15	7	3	21	1	7
773	1	1	33	2	16	32	6	38	1	9
774	1	2	35	5	12	15	6	27	4	6
775	1	2	52	2	12	14	22	24	3	20
776	1	2	38	3	16	14	11	52	5	36
777	1	2	53	4	16	21	26	20	3	19
778	1	2	48	3	16	24	22	27	4	24
779	2	1	30	2	16	19	6	26	1	10
780	1	2	50	4	14	27	25	21	3	19
781	1	2	54	3	16	10	27	39	4	36
782	2	3	30	4	12	21	5	13	2	14
783	1	2	55	2	16	34	30	34	3	31
784	1	3	51	3	12	24	29	30	3	30
785	1	2	34	4	12	23	9	22	5	15
786	2	3	44	3	12	10	16	11	3	8
787	2	1	31	4	13	25	4	12	1	6
788	1	2	25	5	12	35	4	19	4	15
789	1	2	23	3	14	35	3	18	3	21
790	1	2	27	2	12	22	7	22	5	19
791	1	1	22	4	13	13	2	15	1	6
792	1	2	36	4	14	32	8	29	3	27
793	1	2	49	3	12	12	24	22	2	19
794	1	2	39	3	12	16	19	24	4	31
795	1	2	47	2	16	33	18	21	3	20
796	1	1	40	3	16	15	16	32	1	32
797	1	2	46	4	16	34	24	30	4	30
798	1	1	20	5	12	20	1	12	1	5
799	1	2	45	4	14	31	24	22	4	29
800	1	1	19	5	12	5	1	10	1	4

					Variable					
Subject	1	2	3	4	5	6	7	8	9	10
801	1	2	44	4	16	35	22	26	4	30
802	2	1	35	3	14	25	11	12	1	6
803	2	1	44	2	18	23	10	25	1	5
804	1	2	37	4	13	20	16	18	3	16
805	1	3	28	4	12	31	2	22	1	5
806	1	1	19	4	12	30	1	10	1	4
807	1	2	28	2	16	10	3	31	4	29
808	1	2	35	4	14	31	12	29	4	26
809	2	1	32	1	18	7	4	20	1	5
810	1	1	20	4	12	23	1	11	1	6
811	1	2	49	2	12	16	14	24	4	21
812	1	2	45	3	16	29	15	32	3	24
813	2	3	31	3	14	17	6	12	3	10
814	1	1	50	4	14	21	22	20	1	20
815	1	2	38	2	16	11	14	30	4	30
816	1	2	51	2	16	35	20	35	3	33
817	1	2	39	2	16	28	16	41	4	36
818	1	1	48	3	16	15	21	30	1	20
819	1	1	47	2	12	33	20	20	1	19
820	1	1	34	3	12	29	13	32	1	10
821	2	3	35	2	16	5	4	19	2	12
822	1	2	26	3	12	35	8	22	4	16
823	1	2	36	3	16	13	9	36	3	37
824	2	1	20	3	12	16	2	10	1	4
825	1	2	52	4	12	23	18	19	2	17
826	1	2	53	3	16	34	17	41	2	30
827	2	3	46	4	14	22	11	12	2	4
828	2	1	34	1	18	20	9	22	1	4
829	1	2	54	2	12	35	24	29	3	20
830	1	2	40	2	16	28	16	31	4	21
831	1	2	55	1	16	7	27	21	2	20
832	1	2	23	1	16	24	2	20	2	19
833	1	2	56	4	16	25	26	25	2	20
834	1	1	24	3	15	13	2	16	1	7
835	1	2	46	3	14	14	20	31	3	23
836	1	3	37	2	16	12	13	39	1	14
837	2	3	30	2	16	20	6	23	2	15
838	1	2	27	3	16	10	4	29	5	20
839	1	2	25	3	16	17	2	26	3	20
840	2	1	39	3	12	24	13	15	1	5
841	1	2	27	4	14	25	5	26	4	18
842	2	3	45	4	14	19	14	12	2	5
843	1	1	35	1	18	11	5	23	1	9
844	1	1	49	2	16	26	16	43	2	26
845	1	2	50	2	12	5	14	27	3	19
846	2	3	43	4	14	10	9	13	2	5
847	1	3	54	3	16	23	12	32	1	22
848	1	1	38	3	16	35	14	54	1	38
849	1	2	57	2	14	25	30	23	3	20
850	1	2	39	4	16	14	14	27	5	23

					Variable					
Subject	1	2	3	4	5	6	7	8	9	10
851	1	2	59	2	16	10	21	28	2	22
852	1	3	60	2	12	15	30	21	2	20
853	1	2	40	4	16	15	19	20	3	19
854	1	2	55	4	14	33	14	18	3	17
855	2	3	31	3	14	7	3	17	3	25
856	1	3	36	2	12	25	11	22	1	10
857	1	2	24	2	16	29	2	22	4	19
858	1	2	28	3	15	15	5	32	4	38
859	1	2	48	5	12	14	13	16	3	20
860	1	2	52	4	14	18	20	18	3	19
861	2	1	33	2	17	7	8	21	1	12
862	1	2	46	4	14	28	18	19	4	20
863	1	2	58	3	16	10	16	38	3	36
864	2	3	39	1	18	13	13	18	3	24
865	1	3	56	2	12	35	14	24	2	23
866	1	2	53	2	16	29	14	29	4	23
867	2	3	35	1	17	20	8	19	2	20
868	1	2	51	3	16	31	23	37	5	36
869	1	1	19	4	12	16	2	10	1	4
870	1	2	47	2	16	25	20	43	3	38
871	1	2	37	2	12	7	17	28	5	27
872	2	3	34	2	16	6	5	27	2	26
873	1	2	26	2	12	19	5	24	5	17
874	2	3	32	4	12	7	4	12	1	6
875	1	1	25	2	15	20	3	19	1	5
876	1	3	25	5	12	15	2	16	1	7
877	2	3	32	4	12	8	7	13	4	18
878	1	2	26	3	12	29	2	20	4	15
879	1	2	49	2	12	18	14	31	3	24
880	1	1	19	3	12	21	2	11	1	6
881	1	2	50	2	16	26	22	38	4	36
882	1	2	38	2	16	13	12	32	4	30
883	1	2	54	3	16	18	20	40	3	37
884	1	2	47	2	16	25	19	33	3	32
885	1	2	56	4	14	5	16	18	2	17
886	2	1	24	1	16	15	1	19	1	11
887	1	2	57	2	12	9	21	21	2	20
888	2	1	34	3	12	8	6	14	1	7
889	1	2	27	5	16	32	3	27	4	20
890	1	1	55	2	16	10	22	34	1	23
891	1	2	40	4	14	5	14	18	4	20
892	1	1	58	2	12	11	31	21	1	20
893	2	1	33	3	12	17	5	10	1	5
894	1	3	59	2	16	29	20	42	2	24
895	1	2	52	2	16	14	16	37	3	32
896	2	3	36	2	16	12	3	21	4	27
897	1	2	60	3	12	19	32	23	2	20
898	2	3	23	1	16	17	1	18	2	18
899	2	3	38	2	16	13	8	24	4	30
900	2	3	20	4	12	9	1	11	1	6

					Variable					
Subject	1	2	3	4	5	6	7	8	9	10
901	1	2	40	2	12	7	16	24	4	24
902	1	2	48	2	16	25	14	41	4	37
903	2	1	43	1	18	11	7	19	1	5
904	2	1	38	4	12	20	14	13	1	7
905	1	1	51	3	14	9	20	24	1	22
906	1	3	39	2	15	12	12	25	5	23
907	1	1	53	3	14	30	14	20	1	20
908	1	2	37	2	16	33	14	40	4	39
909	2	3	33	1	18	7	4	20	2	6
910	1	2	28	4	14	11	3	21	2	15
911	2	3	34	2	18	10	8	28	3	28
912	1	3	28	2	16	33	6	34	1	15
913	1	2	49	3	16	9	11	42	3	24
914	1	2	38	5	12	16	9	17	3	16
915	1	2	54	2	12	11	21	29	3	19
916	2	1	37	4	12	12	13	13	1	6
917	2	3	34	3	12	8	7	16	2	12
918	1	3	48	2	12	8	22	27	1	23
919	1	2	56	2	16	17	14	35	2	25
920	2	3	37	3	12	20	8	17	1	6
921	1	2	57	4	14	11	24	24	2	21
922	1	2	47	3	16	22	21	32	3	22
923	1	3	50	3	12	27	28	26	1	5
924	1	2	58	2	16	28	33	30	2	21
925	1	3	40	2	16	12	10	35	1	20
926	1	2	55	1	16	8	14	27	2	19
927	1	1	19	3	12	31	1	10	1	4
928	1	2	59	4	14	22	21	21	2	20
929	1	2	60	4	15	33	29	22	2	19
930	2	1	30	1	18	6	3	18	1	8
931	1	2	40	2	16	34	11	41	4	34
932	1	2	42	4	16	6	12	28	3	19
933	2	3	37	4	12	16	5	13	4	10
934	1	2	43	2	16	13	14	34	4	25
935	1	2	44	3	12	33	21	29	4	19
936	1	2	37	2	12	8	15	26	5	18
937	2	3	42	2	16	15	14	25	2	24
938	1	2	36	4	12	25	16	19	5	15
939	1	2	53	3	16	20	25	33	4	20
940	1	2	39	2	16	23	16	35	4	37
941	1	3	52	2	14	24	12	26	3	19
942	2	1	36	3	14	15	7	16	1	5
943	1	2	51	4	12	34	15	24	3	20
944	1	3	27	2	16	19	3	31	1	10
945	1	3	26	5	16	5	2	27	1	5
946	1	1	19	4	12	14	1	11	1	6
947	1	1	27	3	14	34	5	30	1	9
948	1	3	49	2	16	16	17	40	1	19
949	1	2	54	2	16	17	12	45	3	24
950	2	3	33	2	18	19	4	27	3	21

					Variable					
Subject	1	2	3	4	5	6	7	8	9	10
951	1	1	57	3	12	9	17	30	1	8
952	1	2	47	4	14	33	17	26	4	20
953	1	2	59	5	12	10	29	18	2	19
954	1	2	48	2	16	22	22	37	4	21
955	1	2	60	4	12	23	24	20	2	19
956	1	2	52	3	16	18	21	32	3	30
957	1	2	40	2	16	35	14	35	4	33
958	2	1	32	1	18	15	8	23	1	6
959	1	2	58	2	12	24	30	26	2	20
960	1	2	55	4	14	23	15	21	2	18
961	2	3	33	4	12	13	11	14	2	14
962	1	2	28	1	18	6	4	27	4	17
963	1	2	43	2	12	33	13	25	4	20
964	1	2	45	2	16	7	17	35	3	32
965	1	2	49	3	16	27	12	40	4	34
966	1	2	39	1	16	21	10	28	5	18
967	1	2	50	4	16	15	21	30	3	21
968	1	2	48	3	12	35	22	24	3	19
969	2	3	39	3	12	8	14	13	4	19
970	2	3	41	4	12	8	13	14	3	15
971	2	1	31	1	18	9	4	21	1	6
972	1	2	44	2	14	12	14	26	4	20
973	2	3	36	2	16	11	5	24	2	30
974	1	2	42	2	12	11	14	25	3	19
975	1	2	40	4	12	23	15	20	4	18
976	1	2	56	2	14	16	16	27	2	20
977	1	2	39	3	12	35	19	26	4	21
978	1	2	53	3	16	29	23	45	3	37
979	2	3	38	1	16	13	6	20	2	8
980	1	2	51	4	16	23	25	33	3	24
981	1	3	47	3	16	14	17	33	1	24
982	1	1	48	2	16	22	19	37	1	25
983	1	2	49	2	12	28	20	28	3	20
984	2	3	40	2	16	20	14	22	2	18
985	1	2	54	4	16	7	24	21	3	19
986	1	2	57	3	14	33	28	30	2	22
987	2	3	35	3	14	10	7	18	1	7
988	1	2	56	3	12	25	32	26	2	19
989	1	2	55	4	16	5	24	24	2	18
990	1	2	40	3	16	23	16	32	4	23
991	1	2	53	2	16	7	20	29	3	21
992	2	3	39	4	12	8	9	13	1	6
993	2	1	22	1	16	9	1	20	1	6
994	1	2	52	2	12	20	24	21	3	20
995	2	3	24	5	12	19	1	12	2	6
996	1	2	51	2	14	5	20	20	3	19
997	1	2	50	3	12	35	19	27	3	22
998	1	3	19	5	12	15	1	10	1	4
999	1	1	28	3	16	11	1	36	1	10
1000	2	3	32	4	12	9	3	13	2	6

Appendix III
Ranking the Forbes 500s (Data on 808 Different Companies)

Company	Assets ($mil)	Sales ($mil)	Market value ($mil)	Net profits ($mil)	Cash flow ($mil)	Number employed (thou)
1. Abbott Laboratories	2,824	2,928	5,480	347.6	448.2	33.2
2. Advanced Micro Devices	414	488	1,813	47.2	85.6	11.5
3. Aetna Life & Casualty	47,626	14,411	3,583	325.2	356.5	52.8
4. Affiliated Bkshs Colo	2,248	248	147	21.5	28.3	2.3
5. H F Ahmanson	20,226	2,213	859	107.9	128.7	6.5
6. Air Prods & Chems	2,256	1,662	1,387	115.0	300.4	17.8
7. Albertson's	936	4,279	863	70.3	115.2	33.0
8. Alco Standard	1,085	2,939	676	59.9	91.1	15.7
9. Alexander & Baldwin	745	430	468	53.1	83.8	3.7
10. Allegheny Intl	1,940	2,348	366	-3.9	57.6	38.8
11. Allegheny Power	3,561	1,724	1,297	169.7	283.1	5.8
12. Allied Bancshares	7,895	785	853	98.8	109.5	3.7
13. Allied Corp	7,647	10,022	2,980	410.0	878.0	117.8
14. Allied Stores	2,427	3,676	1,001	128.5	209.1	63.0
15. Allis-Chalmers	1,054	1,300	223	-133.2	-91.2	17.3
16. ALLTEL	1,370	606	459	55.2	143.5	6.2
17. Alcoa	6,267	5,263	3,632	164.5	510.6	39.1
18. AMAX	4,448	2,290	1,578	-489.0	-304.1	13.3

Source: From *Forbes Annual Directory,* © 1984, pp. 218–242. Used by permission.

General notes: (1) This list includes U.S.-based companies that are publicly owned. (2) Fiscal year-end results are used for companies with fiscal years that end in December and January. For all other companies, trailing 12-month results are used for sales and profits, and assets are as of the most recent quarter. (3) For nonfinancial companies, sales includes net sales and other operating revenue, excluding excise taxes for oil, liquor and tobacco companies. For financial companies, sales includes total operating income and other income. (4) Market value is calculated by multiplying the Dec. 30, 1983 closing price of common stock by the number of shares outstanding at that time. (5) Net profits and cash flow are from continuing operations before unusual and extraordinary items. In prior years profits included discontinued operations, so some 1982 profit ranks may not be comparable. Profits for insurance operations exclude realized gains or losses. (6) Cash flow is net profits plus depreciation, depletion and amortization. (7) The number of employees is an average figure for the year.

Company	Assets ($mil)	Sales ($mil)	Market value ($mil)	Net profits ($mil)	Cash flow ($mil)	Number employed (thou)
19. Amdahl	724	778	711	43.3	100.4	5.8
20. Amerada Hess	6,217	8,369	2,396	205.3	611.1	8.1
21. American Brands	4,304	4,436	3,256	390.3	489.4	70.9
22. Amer Broadcasting	2,090	2,940	1,631	159.8	213.0	13.8
23. American Can	2,830	3,346	1,001	97.5	180.8	29.8
24. American Cyanamid	3,056	3,535	2,450	166.4	349.4	39.5
25. American Elec Power	12,832	4,368	3,079	428.0	796.0	24.7
26. American Express	43,981	9,770	6,961	514.7	514.7	67.2
27. American Fletcher	3,377	320	136	22.1	27.3	2.4
28. American General	15,061	3,953	1,513	289.8	311.8	13.8
29. American Greetings	683	804	828	54.8	70.1	17.8
30. American Home Prod	3,086	4,856	7,735	627.2	722.8	54.6
31. Amer Hospital Supply	2,280	3,310	2,932	211.9	287.9	33.2
32. American Intl Group	10,556	3,996	4,665	427.3	457.5	24.0
33. Amer Medical Intl	1,706	1,386	1,144	108.2	185.2	31.0
34. American Motors	1,724	3,272	514	−258.3	−171.3	25.1
35. American Natl Ins	3,429	752	623	93.5	98.8	8.1
36. Am Natural Resources	3,944	3,354	1,130	171.3	389.1	11.3
37. American Petrofina	1,399	2,069	597	55.3	139.8	2.6
38. Amer Savings & Loan	3,278	331	111	17.5	20.6	0.9
39. American Security	3,724	334	215	31.4	36.0	1.5
40. American Standard	1,622	2,181	865	62.6	128.8	38.6
41. American Stores	1,627	7,984	1,171	117.9	205.2	61.0
42. American Tel & Tel*	149,530	69,403	59,392	5,746.6	15,600.8	977.3
43. Amerifin	7,112	3	362	−22.4	−21.6	1.9
44. Ameritech	18,512	9,041	6,229	1,064.8	2,435.3	99.5
45. AmeriTrust	5,797	573	452	51.1	60.6	4.0
46. Amfac	1,439	2,253	490	−21.3	25.4	26.6
47. AMP	1,238	1,515	4,101	163.1	226.4	20.5
48. AMR	4,728	4,763	1,747	227.9	525.1	42.0
49. AmSouth Bancorp	3,637	375	242	33.6	40.1	3.4
50. Analog Devices	235	238	726	23.6	37.2	3.4
51. Anderson, Clayton	472	1,402	352	27.5	53.5	16.4
52. Anheuser-Busch Cos	4,330	6,034	3,025	348.0	535.3	38.7
53. Apple Computer	607	1,085	1,443	57.6	81.3	4.0
54. ARA Services	1,407	3,156	609	54.2	154.9	116.0
55. Archer Daniels Midland	2,550	4,733	1,786	110.4	230.4	8.5
56. Arizona Bancwest	2,760	270	162	19.1	26.0	2.2
57. Arizona Public Service	4,386	1,074	1,292	264.8	354.9	7.3
58. Arkla	1,732	1,297	1,112	59.1	112.2	5.3
59. Armco	3,609	4,165	1,383	−273.0	−66.4	50.0
60. Armstrong World Inds	955	1,439	684	63.1	118.5	19.8
61. ASARCO	2,227	1,512	848	58.3	113.3	9.9
62. Ashland Oil	4,063	7,838	787	94.7	279.0	29.8
63. Associated Dry Goods	2,004	3,718	897	115.5	188.1	60.0
64. Atlantic Bancorp	3,330	311	243	28.8	36.5	3.1
65. Atlantic City Electric	1,140	517	401	66.2	104.6	2.0
66. Atlantic Richfield	23,282	25,147	10,802	1,547.9	3,519.8	50.6
67. Auto Data Processing	705	816	1,247	68.8	133.5	16.3

*Predivestiture results; operating companies also included in tables.

Company	Assets ($mil)	Sales ($mil)	Market value ($mil)	Net profits ($mil)	Cash flow ($mil)	Number employed (thou)
68. Avco	6,388	2,806	727	102.9	145.7	26.0
69. Avnet	847	1,375	1,614	66.3	78.6	8.1
70. Avon Products	2,286	3,000	1,872	164.4	231.7	38.6
71. Bacardi	282	175	638	58.8	63.0	0.7
72. Baker International	2,165	1,788	1,342	55.4	55.4	23.0
73. Baltimore Gas & Elec	3,810	1,639	1,221	216.5	375.2	9.1
74. Banc One	7,270	743	802	83.3	99.2	5.9
75. BanCal Tri-State	3,867	402	228	10.7	15.5	2.6
76. Banco Popular PR	2,974	295	119	26.8	31.1	4.3
77. BancOhio	6,062	608	185	18.5	30.1	5.5
78. BancOklahoma	2,103	162	138	15.1	17.6	1.1
79. Bancorp Hawaii	3,377	345	210	31.0	37.3	2.8
80. BancTEXAS Group	2,123	205	124	3.6	7.5	1.1
81. Bank of Boston	19,538	2,599	766	135.7	168.0	14.0
82. Bank of New England	5,801	622	204	36.6	41.8	4.2
83. Bank of New York	12,797	1,340	485	90.6	106.9	8.4
84. Bank of Virginia	3,850	412	197	30.2	36.0	2.8
85. BankAmerica	121,176	13,299	3,140	390.5	642.6	88.2
86. Bankers Trust N Y	40,003	3,852	1,338	254.0	286.9	11.8
87. Barnett Banks Fla	9,397	988	612	81.9	106.8	9.4
88. Baxter Travenol Labs	2,127	1,842	3,275	218.1	304.2	32.3
89. BayBanks	4,639	466	243	32.0	46.2	4.8
90. Beatrice Foods	4,788	9,441	3,163	200.1	390.7	78.0
91. Becton, Dickinson	1,076	1,120	762	73.5	130.0	20.2
92. Bell Atlantic	18,930	8,883	6,301	1,026.1	2,403.6	102.7
93. BellSouth	24,083	10,681	8,136	1,371.5	3,041.5	125.9
94. Beneficial Corp	6,716	1,582	753	105.6	138.0	13.1
95. Bergen Brunswig	353	1,585	299	21.7	25.0	2.5
96. Berkshire Hathaway	1,856	624	1,502	48.6	56.6	4.5
97. Best Products	1,423	2,081	466	37.1	72.2	18.0
98. Bethlehem Steel	4,457	4,898	1,318	−314.2	−62.5	52.8
99. Big Three Industries	1,098	669	906	45.3	119.4	5.2
100. Black & Decker	1,049	1,227	1,239	40.5	93.2	15.1
101. Blue Bell	654	1,216	425	51.0	72.5	28.0
102. Boatmen's Bancshares	3,505	265	182	25.4	30.2	2.2
103. Boeing	7,471	11,129	4,242	355.0	720.0	84.6
104. Boise Cascade	2,838	3,451	1,170	60.4	222.2	28.0
105. Borden	2,720	4,265	1,582	160.4	255.9	32.6
106. Borg-Warner	2,617	3,542	2,115	182.6	297.3	77.1
107. Boston Edison	1,995	1,069	430	67.9	154.9	4.0
108. Bristol-Myers	3,007	3,917	5,760	408.0	474.6	35.7
109. Broadview Financial	2,019	199	22	8.4	11.5	0.7
110. Brown-Forman Dist	1,012	786	818	80.6	98.1	4.8
111. Brown Group	646	1,529	660	70.1	93.3	28.0
112. Browning-Ferris Inds	787	875	1,402	83.2	176.0	15.5
113. Brunswick	817	1,216	610	66.1	110.5	18.6
114. Burlington Industries	2,195	3,121	1,004	111.5	245.0	53.0
115. Burlington Northern	10,901	4,508	3,678	413.2	670.6	45.1
116. Burroughs	4,098	4,296	2,289	192.5	597.9	62.9
117. Cabot	1,328	1,579	805	62.0	137.1	7.4
118. CalFed	14,329	1,548	434	80.5	91.5	4.4

Company	Assets ($mil)	Sales ($mil)	Market value ($mil)	Net profits ($mil)	Cash flow ($mil)	Number employed (thou)
119. California First Bank	4,347	461	172	18.2	26.5	3.9
120. Campbell Soup	2,173	3,483	1,967	178.0	275.0	40.5
121. Capital Cities Comm	1,053	762	1,887	114.7	155.0	7.6
122. Capital Holding	4,784	1,581	960	123.5	134.1	8.3
123. Carnation	1,748	3,365	1,944	194.8	249.3	21.1
124. Carolina Power & Light	5,294	1,647	1,375	239.3	419.9	8.7
125. Carter Hawley Hale	2,029	3,633	830	67.5	142.4	58.0
126. Carteret Savings	4,396	523	68	12.2	22.8	8.1
127. Castle & Cooke	1,079	1,642	499	34.5	64.5	35.5
128. Caterpillar Tractor	6,968	5,424	4,496	−288.0	218.0	58.4
129. CBS	2,990	4,458	1,966	187.2	284.2	31.6
130. CBT	6,072	585	241	38.5	48.4	5.4
131. Celanese	2,869	3,261	1,082	112.0	325.0	37.0
132. Centel	2,352	1,272	970	113.3	279.8	13.6
133. Centerre Bancorp	5,354	495	200	20.8	30.3	3.6
134. Central & South West	5,716	2,613	1,783	267.4	460.2	9.0
135. Central Bancorp	2,822	285	158	22.3	28.9	1.5
136. Central Bancshares	2,769	286	155	24.8	29.4	2.2
137. Central Fidelity Banks	2,702	302	196	24.5	31.0	2.6
138. Central Ill Pub Svc	1,536	733	530	85.5	144.3	2.9
139. Central Maine Power	1,055	456	267	52.2	78.0	2.1
140. Central Soya	636	1,575	216	23.3	43.4	8.2
141. Centran	2,884	304	74	15.1	20.4	2.4
142. CFS Continental	327	1,233	203	17.0	31.5	4.3
143. Champion International	3,576	4,264	1,588	82.2	268.9	39.3
144. Charter	1,813	5,566	187	50.4	88.3	4.2
145. CharterCorp	2,701	272	178	19.2	19.2	2.1
146. Chase Manhattan	81,921	8,523	1,581	429.6	510.9	37.0
147. Chemical New York	51,165	4,903	1,325	305.6	347.8	19.5
148. Chesebrough-Pond's	1,172	1,685	1,321	127.9	154.3	21.6
149. Chrysler	6,772	13,240	3,365	525.8	983.0	81.5
150. Chubb	3,539	1,761	852	84.4	90.4	7.7
151. CIGNA	35,117	12,564	3,206	400.5	400.5	41.6
152. Cincinnati G & E	2,928	1,369	541	145.9	221.8	5.1
153. Cincinnati Milacron	629	559	744	−10.3	12.8	9.3
154. Citadel Holding	2,207	206	40	6.8	10.0	0.8
155. Citicorp	134,655	17,037	4,625	860.0	1,059.0	62.2
156. Citizens & Southern Ga	6,933	684	442	57.9	79.2	5.7
157. Citizens & Southern SC	2,052	201	185	20.2	27.7	2.5
158. Citizens Fidelity	2,668	275	255	28.8	33.0	1.8
159. City Federal S & L	6,795	698	147	43.9	50.0	3.2
160. City Investing	8,361	5,948	1,374	175.0	313.0	63.2
161. City National	2,071	215	202	17.3	22.1	1.8
162. Cleveland Elec Illum	4,267	1,210	1,214	246.0	340.3	5.4
163. Clorox	631	935	694	70.7	90.9	5.6
164. Coastal Corp	3,338	5,963	695	91.6	240.4	6.0
165. Coca-Cola	5,228	6,829	7,295	558.3	785.6	40.3
166. Colgate-Palmolive	2,664	4,865	1,763	186.2	248.1	43.0
167. Colonial Penn Group	1,105	1,241	387	46.7	46.7	3.1
168. Colorado Natl Bnkshs	2,463	283	181	22.2	37.3	2.8

Company	Assets ($mil)	Sales ($mil)	Market value ($mil)	Net profits ($mil)	Cash flow ($mil)	Number employed (thou)
169. Colt Industries	1,177	1,576	1,271	99.3	137.0	21.4
170. Columbia Gas System	5,238	5,078	1,369	191.0	395.4	12.0
171. Columbia S & L	4,990	287	51	39.9	42.3	0.4
172. Combined International	2,514	1,235	1,105	131.3	183.6	7.4
173. Combustion Engineering	2,585	3,092	1,052	76.2	163.4	37.9
174. Comerica	8,556	780	315	48.7	58.1	5.3
175. Commerce Bancshares	3,477	336	238	34.9	39.5	3.0
176. Commerce Union	2,369	249	97	14.4	19.0	1.9
177. Commonwealth Edison	15,048	4,634	4,348	802.3	1,212.7	17.5
178. Computervision	349	400	1,228	35.3	64.3	4.6
179. ConAgra	1,290	2,485	631	53.2	81.9	18.2
180. Consolidated Edison	8,247	5,516	3,227	575.8	865.6	22.4
181. Consolidated Foods	2,720	6,789	1,478	179.6	303.1	91.2
182. Consol Freightways	990	1,355	817	65.5	129.1	17.4
183. Consol Natural Gas	3,358	3,445	1,382	162.8	365.2	7.5
184. Consumers Power	8,469	2,974	1,228	347.8	534.4	13.0
185. Continental Bancorp	3,239	322	243	30.1	33.4	2.2
186. Continental Corp	9,278	3,947	1,354	14.5	34.4	18.0
187. Continental Group	3,653	4,819	1,529	199.2	429.2	43.3
188. Continental Illinois	42,097	4,381	878	101.2	158.7	12.6
189. Continental Telecom	4,228	2,101	1,493	172.4	459.2	21.8
190. Control Data	8,778	4,583	1,725	161.7	361.0	55.9
191. Convergent Technologies	255	163	861	14.9	18.9	0.7
192. Cooper Industries	1,949	1,850	1,492	71.2	139.1	30.4
193. Adolph Coors	1,156	1,110	709	89.3	156.3	9.0
194. CoreStates Financial	8,587	896	477	83.0	98.2	5.6
195. Corning Glass Works	1,775	1,589	1,470	59.5	165.6	28.3
196. Cox Communications	940	615	1,277	78.0	173.9	7.0
197. CPC International	2,483	4,011	1,868	191.6	305.8	38.1
198. Cray Research	279	170	811	26.1	45.5	1.5
199. Crocker National	23,393	2,560	508	−10.4	37.0	14.9
200. Crown Central Petrol	653	1,668	112	4.0	48.3	3.7
201. Crown Cork & Seal	822	1,298	492	51.5	89.9	12.9
202. Crown Zellerbach	2,411	2,709	993	87.8	186.9	22.2
203. CSX	10,835	5,787	3,614	271.6	586.6	61.4
204. Cullen/Frost Bankers	3,064	322	213	−22.3	−14.0	2.5
205. Cummins Engine	1,259	1,605	756	24.7	94.8	18.8
206. Dana	2,095	2,865	1,581	109.1	196.6	31.8
207. Dart & Kraft	5,418	9,714	3,653	435.1	613.7	77.1
208. Data General	885	867	843	29.0	94.8	15.0
209. Dauphin Deposit	2,260	183	135	16.7	16.7	1.7
210. Dayton-Hudson	3,586	6,963	3,013	243.2	376.9	85.5
211. Dayton Power & Light	2,287	957	509	123.2	177.7	3.1
212. Deere	5,947	3,995	2,608	29.5	233.8	47.1
213. Delmarva Power & Light	1,533	650	571	85.1	137.1	2.5
214. Delta Air Lines	3,230	3,883	1,580	−13.9	321.3	37.5
215. Deluxe Check Printers	403	620	893	76.6	97.5	10.0
216. Deposit Guaranty	2,294	233	126	17.7	23.8	1.7
217. Detroit Edison	8,195	2,310	1,792	364.6	547.0	11.1
218. Diamond Shamrock	6,024	4,026	2,515	113.7	596.4	12.1

Company	Assets ($mil)	Sales ($mil)	Market value ($mil)	Net profits ($mil)	Cash flow ($mil)	Number employed (thou)
219. Digital Equipment	4,950	4,827	4,070	262.2	262.2	75.8
220. Walt Disney	2,466	1,339	1,819	84.9	247.0	29.0
221. Dominion Bankshares	3,826	376	206	24.5	30.3	3.1
222. Dominion Resources	7,691	2,612	1,834	266.0	561.3	12.7
223. Donaldson, Lufkin	5,445	723	200	24.0	31.3	3.7
224. R R Donnelley & Sons	1,204	1,546	1,467	114.4	186.3	16.5
225. Dorchester Gas	521	1,182	360	14.2	39.7	1.2
226. Dover	704	1,010	1,072	77.5	116.1	12.9
227. Dow Chemical	11,981	10,951	6,536	293.0	1,134.0	55.6
228. Dow Jones	700	866	3,116	114.2	151.6	6.1
229. Dresser Industries	3,181	3,435	1,646	22.1	220.1	40.3
230. E I du Pont	24,432	35,173	12,421	1,127.0	2,846.0	162.1
231. Duke Power	7,379	2,420	2,503	431.3	755.9	20.6
232. Dun & Bradstreet	1,186	1,510	3,496	142.0	189.4	26.0
233. Duquesne Light	3,146	800	789	145.2	225.0	5.0
234. E-Systems	371	827	923	49.9	62.0	12.0
235. Eastern Air Lines	3,758	3,942	233	−305.1	−21.4	38.2
236. Eastern Gas & Fuel	1,266	1,200	548	42.7	100.2	7.9
237. Eastman Kodak	10,928	10,170	12,606	565.0	1,217.0	125.5
238. Eaton	2,279	2,674	1,769	109.6	200.8	41.0
239. Jack Eckerd	1,034	2,486	1,040	80.6	113.8	31.3
240. EG&G	339	904	981	46.6	56.5	19.0
241. El Paso Electric	1,393	302	435	87.3	99.0	1.1
242. Electronic Data Systems	451	695	1,849	65.2	90.7	13.3
243. Emerson Electric	2,519	3,599	4,558	311.0	417.4	51.4
244. Emhart	1,018	1,686	783	84.3	126.5	29.4
245. Engelhard	889	2,099	1,033	73.5	107.4	7.1
246. ENSERCH	3,259	3,502	1,222	69.6	259.5	20.3
247. Entex	997	1,293	452	63.2	108.4	5.0
248. Equimark	3,254	339	24	−11.1	−8.2	2.3
249. Equitable Bancorp	2,874	307	363	14.5	23.4	2.6
250. Esmark	3,338	4,587	1,719	128.7	217.3	60.0
251. Ethyl	1,510	1,745	1,014	115.4	211.2	13.5
252. Evans Products	872	1,352	132	−63.9	−40.5	13.0
253. Exxon	62,963	88,561	31,623	4,978.0	8,505.8	156.0
254. Farm & Home Savings	2,695	283	93	−2.4	0.9	0.7
255. Farm House foods	285	1,515	51	0.8	0.8	4.7
256. Farmers Group	2,041	790	1,417	137.7	136.2	12.2
257. Federal Co	348	1,168	253	25.2	53.8	13.0
258. Federal Express	1,127	1,194	2,038	106.4	199.2	19.1
259. Fedl National Mortgage	78,917	8,472	1,514	75.5	75.5	1.2
260. Federated Dept Strs	4,901	8,690	2,605	338.3	544.5	124.0
261. Fidelcor	5,662	525	202	46.8	52.1	3.3
262. Fidelity Union Bancorp	3,766	340	181	16.7	22.1	3.3
263. Fin Corp of America	22,700	1,827	887	172.5	198.9	4.0
264. Fin Corp Santa Barbara	2,463	217	35	−22.1	−22.1	0.7
265. Firestone	2,579	3,998	1,077	98.0	224.0	62.9
266. First Alabama Bshs	3,214	346	284	39.7	46.8	3.5
267. First American	3,497	350	181	26.1	32.3	2.7
268. First Atlanta	5,762	546	341	52.3	62.5	4.2

Company	Assets ($mil)	Sales ($mil)	Market value ($mil)	Net profits ($mil)	Cash flow ($mil)	Number employed (thou)
269. First Bank System	20,871	1,928	809	129.7	155.3	9.8
270. First Boston	22,003	1,482	470	80.2	85.1	2.1
271. First Chicago	35,323	3,675	1,057	183.5	217.8	11.2
272. First City Bancorp	17,263	1,624	608	49.8	77.7	8.7
273. First Commerce	2,024	213	203	12.8	17.4	1.6
274. First Empire State	2,071	227	108	5.3	8.8	2.1
275. First Executive	4,810	1,342	598	44.1	44.1	0.4
276. First Federal Michigan	7,971	800	85	31.6	34.8	1.4
277. First Florida Banks	2,798	278	288	34.0	44.0	2.6
278. First Hawaiian	2,605	267	135	21.1	25.4	2.1
279. First Interstate Bancorp	44,423	4,341	1,726	247.4	315.8	31.7
280. First Kentucky Natl	3,318	309	236	29.9	34.6	3.0
281. First Maryland Bancorp	3,655	387	141	19.2	27.3	3.5
282. First National Cinc	2,633	254	202	25.6	31.4	1.7
283. First Natl State Bcp	6,417	526	242	47.4	54.6	4.6
284. First Natl Supermkts	271	1,246	41	1.9	14.8	12.8
285. First of America Bank	4,109	433	119	26.1	42.5	3.9
286. First Oklahoma Bancorp	2,862	307	140	−43.5	−36.1	1.5
287. First Pennsylvania	5,152	541	108	−15.7	−9.4	3.7
288. First Security	4,943	521	255	21.2	30.5	4.7
289. First Tennessee Natl	4,617	425	223	30.2	45.6	3.3
290. First Union	6,803	657	504	58.5	69.0	5.1
291. First Virginia Banks	2,360	270	207	29.0	35.1	3.4
292. First Wisconsin	5,062	529	172	33.6	44.2	4.3
293. Fischbach	477	1,293	183	23.8	37.9	12.0
294. Fleet Financial	5,736	569	356	52.0	65.7	4.3
295. Fleetwood Enterprises	327	1,313	628	58.1	63.3	10.3
296. Fleming Cos	679	4,898	514	41.7	64.9	11.6
297. Flickinger	186	1,489	113	12.3	20.6	7.1
298. Florida Federal S&L	3,896	377	142	0.9	3.8	1.3
299. Florida National Banks	3,550	403	273	29.5	38.3	4.2
300. Florida Power & Light	7,721	3,352	2,268	314.0	579.0	12.8
301. Florida Progress	3,140	1,338	845	103.9	229.0	4.9
302. Fluor	4,085	5,042	1,357	79.3	299.3	38.6
303. FMC	2,783	3,498	1,537	168.8	331.1	32.2
304. Food Lion	274	1,172	537	27.7	41.8	9.4
305. Ford Motor	23,869	44,455	7,755	1,926.9	4,219.0	380.1
306. Fort Howard Paper	1,200	786	1,725	107.0	151.0	9.6
307. Foster Wheeler	908	1,541	529	44.2	58.8	14.4
308. Freeport-McMoRan	1,418	786	1,478	90.1	263.5	4.9
309. Fruehauf	1,596	2,129	586	8.4	99.1	24.5
310. Gannett	1,690	1,704	3,149	191.7	258.7	26.5
311. GATX	2,531	849	431	15.3	103.3	8.4
312. GEICO	1,776	873	1,185	94.8	99.1	4.9
313. Gelco	2,470	904	293	−5.8	239.9	8.4
314. General Cinema	673	920	506	59.0	96.6	12.5
315. General Dynamics	2,836	7,146	3,064	286.6	458.4	88.9
316. General Electric	23,288	26,797	26,653	2,024.0	3,108.0	340.0
317. General Foods	4,349	8,573	2,672	309.6	460.9	62.0
318. General Instrument	827	892	1,024	52.0	122.0	25.6

Company	Assets ($mil)	Sales ($mil)	Market value ($mil)	Net profits ($mil)	Cash flow ($mil)	Number employed (thou)
319. General Mills	3,164	5,520	2,501	245.7	380.5	80.5
320. General Motors	45,694	74,582	23,419	3,730.2	8,849.8	691.0
321. General Public Utils	5,334	2,480	487	66.9	317.8	12.6
322. General Re	5,440	1,659	3,088	192.0	195.8	2.7
323. General Signal	1,314	1,575	1,447	89.7	131.6	23.3
324. General Tire & Rubber	1,853	2,184	828	70.8	148.2	33.0
325. Genuine Parts	868	2,068	1,628	103.6	118.9	12.4
326. Georgia-Pacific	4,979	6,469	2,512	105.0	476.0	41.5
327. Giant Food	500	1,957	331	40.5	68.8	15.4
328. Gibraltar Financial	6,047	640	171	32.6	36.6	1.5
329. Gibraltar Savings	3,902	490	199	46.8	48.7	0.7
330. Gillette	1,696	2,183	1,494	145.9	222.0	29.8
331. Glendale Federal S&L	9,741	1,013	205	35.2	35.2	3.6
332. Golden West Financial	8,186	922	457	77.4	97.7	2.1
333. B F Goodrich	2,576	3,192	715	14.7	136.6	29.7
334. Goodyear	5,985	9,736	3,202	331.5	628.2	128.8
335. Gould	1,488	1,325	1,352	79.2	141.0	20.3
336. W R Grace	5,035	6,219	2,194	159.7	464.3	76.6
337. W W Grainger	617	880	886	51.7	72.0	5.8
338. Great American Federal	4,897	550	126	28.4	35.1	2.1
339. Great Atl & Pac Tea	1,139	5,222	459	31.4	80.1	40.0
340. Great Northern Nekoosa	1,818	1,565	1,002	84.0	162.7	12.4
341. Gt Western Financial	18,639	1,991	779	73.7	90.6	5.5
342. Greyhound	1,965	2,131	1,221	70.3	118.5	33.6
343. Grumman	1,088	2,220	682	110.7	144.8	28.1
344. GTE	24,223	12,944	8,341	964.0	2,731.0	187.2
345. Guarantee Finl Calif	2,394	254	39	3.6	8.8	1.2
346. Gulf	20,964	26,581	7,130	864.0	2,324.0	47.1
347. Gulf & Western Inds	4,425	4,198	2,330	297.3	367.3	60.0
348. Gulf States Utilities	4,353	1,436	1,067	229.8	333.1	4.9
349. Gulfstream Aerospace	516	576	554	53.1	67.1	3.5
350. Halliburton	5,834	5,511	4,778	314.8	690.7	78.5
351. Hammermill Paper	1,031	1,623	414	32.5	82.2	12.2
352. Harris Bankcorp	7,425	780	465	31.3	46.4	3.9
353. Harris Corp	1,588	1,474	1,584	56.1	140.8	25.2
354. Hartford National	4,676	421	249	38.4	46.3	3.7
355. G Heileman Brewing	530	1,151	790	57.0	80.5	6.0
356. H J Heinz	2,421	3,843	2,682	232.9	306.6	42.5
357. Hercules	2,175	2,629	1,893	151.0	279.2	24.3
358. Hershey Foods	984	1,706	991	100.2	139.3	14.0
359. Hewlett-Packard	4,444	4,933	10,620	442.0	682.0	70.0
360. Hilton Hotels	1,099	683	1,523	85.9	126.0	32.0
361. Holiday Inns	1,936	1,585	1,777	124.4	228.4	43.6
362. Home Federal S&L-Cal	6,803	773	286	37.0	55.5	3.3
363. Homestake Mining	505	223	1,107	43.5	64.3	2.3
364. Honeywell	4,675	5,753	3,046	231.2	562.1	93.8
365. Horizon Bancorp	2,428	204	164	18.8	23.0	2.2
366. George A Hormel	514	1,440	298	33.5	60.5	6.9
367. Hospital Corp of Am	4,083	3,203	3,402	243.2	399.2	73.5
368. Household Intl	8,446	7,912	1,511	206.4	438.1	80.5

Company	Assets ($mil)	Sales ($mil)	Market value ($mil)	Net profits ($mil)	Cash flow ($mil)	Number employed (thou)
369. Houston Industries	6,575	3,993	1,809	303.7	502.8	11.0
370. Houston Natural Gas	3,129	2,972	1,757	186.2	534.3	10.8
371. Hughes Tool	2,098	1,157	1,158	−37.3	94.5	14.1
372. Humana	2,272	1,847	2,096	171.4	272.0	40.6
373. Huntington Bancshares	5,426	558	221	24.5	33.8	4.4
374. E F Hutton Group	13,164	2,172	878	110.6	132.7	14.6
375. IC Industries	3,985	3,724	799	76.1	212.1	41.9
376. Idaho Power	1,520	376	545	88.1	127.1	1.7
377. Illinois Power	3,437	1,278	998	207.7	277.7	4.0
378. Imperial Corp of Am	6,110	586	129	−34.6	−29.2	1.4
379. Indiana National	3,068	280	117	14.3	20.4	2.1
380. Ingersoll-Rand	2,311	2,274	1,039	−25.4	56.4	33.6
381. Inland Steel	2,626	3,046	772	−52.3	70.9	28.7
382. Integrated Resources	928	322	205	57.8	60.8	2.1
383. Intel	1,680	1,122	4,691	116.1	219.1	20.5
384. Interco	1,650	2,658	986	105.0	146.5	51.5
385. InterFirst	21,736	2,150	1,110	−172.0	−147.0	9.7
386. Intergraph	251	252	983	29.3	35.1	2.2
387. IBM	37,243	40,180	74,508	5,485.0	9,423.0	367.2
388. Intl Flavors & Frag	458	461	999	68.4	80.1	3.6
389. Intl Harvester	3,214	3,863	412	−324.4	−199.3	37.9
390. Intl Minerals & Chem	1,980	1,493	1,158	84.5	201.1	8.4
391. International Paper	5,617	4,357	2,935	211.6	436.4	33.7
392. InterNorth	5,010	4,997	1,751	231.0	477.9	10.2
393. Iowa-Illinois G & E	1,112	514	297	59.5	100.0	1.6
394. IPALCO Enterprises	1,337	427	484	67.4	110.4	2.2
395. Irving Bank	18,586	1,836	462	92.5	118.0	9.6
396. ITT	13,967	14,155	6,160	623.9	1,144.6	280.5
397. IU International	1,156	2,039	623	34.4	111.4	35.0
398. James River Corp Va	1,369	2,104	920	85.5	138.9	19.8
399. Jefferson-Pilot	3,277	921	803	98.7	101.0	6.0
400. Jewel Cos	1,562	5,723	553	83.1	172.8	37.1
401. Jim Walter	2,638	2,093	603	79.7	154.7	19.4
402. Johnson & Johnson	4,461	5,973	7,820	547.0	756.8	78.6
403. Johnson Controls	966	1,325	681	61.3	102.1	20.6
404. K Mart	8,183	18,598	4,186	492.3	756.8	245.0
405. Kaiser Alum & Chem	3,506	2,858	857	−98.0	18.8	17.2
406. Kansas City Pwr & Lt	2,071	562	531	126.5	172.8	2.7
407. Kansas Gas & Electric	1,778	393	546	107.5	137.4	1.9
408. Kansas Power & Light	1,711	860	491	83.6	128.7	3.4
409. Kellogg	1,467	2,381	2,476	242.7	305.5	18.8
410. Kemper	6,838	2,222	572	68.4	68.4	14.9
411. Kentucky Utilities	1,176	512	418	65.1	109.5	1.9
412. Kerr-McGee	3,807	3,508	1,616	144.9	427.5	9.6
413. Key Banks	3,492	342	214	33.1	38.8	3.4
414. Kidde	1,686	2,052	641	72.6	116.8	38.0
415. Kimberly-Clark	2,904	3,274	2,071	188.8	299.6	33.3
416. Knight-Ridder News	1,180	1,473	1,700	119.4	170.9	21.5
417. Koppers	1,175	1,566	622	23.4	101.2	14.5
418. Kroger	3,502	15,236	1,655	127.1	306.7	159.3

Company	Assets ($mil)	Sales ($mil)	Market value ($mil)	Net profits ($mil)	Cash flow ($mil)	Number employed (thou)
419. Lear Siegler	868	1,527	758	73.4	107.1	20.4
420. Leaseway Transportation	901	1,267	467	37.3	238.9	16.1
421. Levi Strauss	1,736	2,689	1,744	170.3	215.3	44.5
422. Libbey-Owens-Ford	838	1,168	431	40.4	80.3	15.2
423. Liberty National	2,261	238	110	14.4	17.7	1.1
424. Eli Lilly	3,414	3,034	4,253	457.4	555.7	29.3
425. Limited	377	1,086	1,445	70.9	99.3	14.4
426. Lincoln First Banks	4,179	423	213	26.0	33.4	3.3
427. Lincoln National	11,086	3,899	1,379	168.1	196.4	12.7
428. Litton Industries	4,273	5,021	2,956	242.7	438.2	72.1
429. Lockheed	2,830	6,490	2,527	262.8	375.0	71.0
430. Loews	11,510	4,693	2,027	252.7	307.6	30.0
431. Long Island Lighting	6,390	1,788	1,080	365.0	428.4	6.0
432. Longs Drug Stores	318	1,214	516	36.4	44.3	8.2
433. Louisiana Land	1,682	1,245	838	94.0	315.5	1.6
434. Louisiana-Pacific	1,265	1,102	840	23.1	111.8	13.0
435. Louisville Gas & Elec	1,394	637	423	59.7	101.1	3.6
436. Lowe's Companies	521	1,431	811	50.6	62.6	7.9
437. LTV	4,406	4,578	1,004	−238.3	−128.3	34.0
438. Lubrizol	683	800	857	57.2	94.2	4.2
439. Lucky Stores	1,713	8,388	958	105.4	183.3	64.5
440. M/A-Com	660	654	857	31.6	63.0	9.1
441. Mack Trucks	973	1,217	644	−26.2	0.0	11.6
442. R H Macy	2,104	3,827	2,634	212.7	296.9	49.0
443. Malone & Hyde	486	2,681	452	37.3	58.3	8.0
444. Manufacturers Hanover	64,332	6,596	1,343	337.0	385.6	28.1
445. Manufacturers Natl	5,807	552	191	34.6	43.7	3.7
446. Manville	2,253	1,729	264	60.1	136.5	20.6
447. MAPCO	1,641	2,065	702	50.5	131.9	6.4
448. Marine	2,455	259	80	16.8	21.1	2.0
449. Marine Midland Banks	22,872	2,156	473	101.1	124.2	11.1
450. Marion Laboratories	156	199	712	20.0	26.1	1.7
451. Marriott	2,501	3,037	1,915	115.2	211.5	109.3
452. Marsh & McLennan	779	968	1,765	123.5	148.3	17.4
453. Marshall & Ilsley	3,362	345	238	31.5	38.3	2.9
454. Martin Marietta	2,738	3,899	1,229	141.3	303.2	41.8
455. Maryland National	5,740	548	268	38.6	48.4	5.0
456. Masco	1,271	1,059	1,899	106.6	155.5	11.5
457. May Dept Stores	2,845	4,229	1,550	177.5	276.6	69.8
458. Maytag	322	597	712	60.7	73.9	4.7
459. MCA	1,768	1,584	2,054	147.2	625.7	16.3
460. McDonald's	3,727	3,001	4,183	342.6	528.1	125.0
461. McDonnell Douglas	4,792	8,111	2,338	274.9	486.2	73.5
462. McGraw-Edison	1,520	2,094	685	31.7	104.5	28.5
463. McGraw-Hill	1,053	1,295	2,119	126.5	154.2	14.0
464. MCI Communications	3,500	1,521	3,371	202.9	373.9	7.2
465. McKesson	1,447	4,365	683	69.4	108.4	12.2
466. Mead	2,087	2,367	1,165	30.0	143.3	17.5
467. Medtronic	448	422	676	58.6	81.7	5.2
468. Mellon National	26,433	2,519	1,315	183.8	212.2	11.9

Company	Assets ($mil)	Sales ($mil)	Market value ($mil)	Net profits ($mil)	Cash flow ($mil)	Number employed (thou)
469. Melville	1,493	3,923	1,829	176.3	231.9	65.0
470. Mercantile Bancorp	5,508	525	262	41.5	49.0	3.7
471. Mercantile Bankshares	2,124	236	229	29.5	34.6	2.3
472. Mercantile Stores	931	1,626	810	83.2	116.6	20.0
473. Mercantile Texas	11,884	1,113	669	100.4	115.0	6.6
474. Merchants National	2,082	230	61	9.0	12.5	1.5
475. Merck	4,215	3,246	6,683	450.9	600.3	32.3
476. Meridian Bancorp	3,728	398	216	32.3	37.4	2.9
477. Merrill Lynch	26,139	5,687	2,865	313.2	387.1	40.9
478. Mesa Petroleum	2,306	388	895	70.2	207.3	0.8
479. Metromedia	1,311	533	979	32.8	71.9	6.5
480. MGM/UA Entertainment	1,353	711	728	29.4	64.6	3.0
481. MGM/UA Home Entertainment	146	171	704	41.6	41.8	0.1
482. Michigan National	6,891	779	186	15.9	36.0	7.2
483. MidCon	3,293	3,597	1,039	123.9	363.9	5.1
484. Middle South Utilities	11,101	2,910	2,221	378.1	561.3	13.4
485. Midlantic Banks	6,413	516	370	48.9	58.3	4.2
486. Minn Mining & Mfg	5,760	7,039	9,672	667.0	1,033.0	86.5
487. Minnesota Power	1,073	374	335	54.1	85.4	1.6
488. Mitchell Energy & Dev	1,981	931	1,127	72.8	175.5	3.7
489. Mobil	35,072	54,607	11,696	1,503.0	3,395.0	183.1
490. Molex	196	213	786	29.8	42.6	3.3
491. Monfort Of Colorado	208	1,373	67	14.4	25.3	3.4
492. Monsanto	6,427	6,299	4,307	369.0	886.0	51.5
493. Montana Power	1,692	489	601	88.6	121.4	2.9
494. Moore Financial	2,766	287	153	22.7	26.7	2.4
495. J P Morgan	58,023	5,764	2,742	460.0	491.0	12.8
496. Morrison-Knudsen	859	2,166	280	41.5	69.7	22.1
497. Morton Thiokol	1,184	1,830	1,289	98.0	157.8	17.3
498. Motorola	3,236	4,328	5,366	244.0	533.0	83.8
499. Mountain Fuel Supply	927	567	470	55.7	99.9	2.8
500. Murphy Oil	2,808	2,388	1,079	131.9	411.5	5.9
501. Nabisco Brands	3,625	5,985	2,603	322.6	460.8	62.4
502. Nalco Chemical	489	659	1,235	71.0	100.5	4.6
503. Natl Bancshares Texas	2,346	230	200	17.6	21.5	1.8
504. National Can	809	1,648	259	37.1	75.4	10.5
505. National City	6,586	631	351	41.4	53.3	4.2
506. National Distillers	1,973	2,267	879	66.7	134.5	12.0
507. National Intergroup	2,649	2,993	711	−120.8	−1.0	19.7
508. Natl Medical Entrprs	1,978	1,918	1,501	108.1	164.2	49.3
509. Natl Semiconductor	1,087	1,505	1,333	44.4	157.7	37.8
510. National Svc Inds	498	996	637	58.1	82.1	16.9
511. NBD Bancorp	13,245	1,151	538	81.7	96.9	6.8
512. NCNB	12,808	1,252	707	92.2	109.1	7.7
513. NCR	3,560	3,731	3,383	287.7	533.5	62.5
514. New England Electric	3,131	1,374	957	132.6	266.5	5.1
515. N Y State Elec & Gas	3,143	994	976	156.7	226.8	4.4
516. New York Times	774	1,091	1,111	70.3	117.6	8.6
517. Newmont Mining	2,091	721	1,537	52.9	109.3	7.0
518. Niagara Mohawk Power	5,358	2,632	1,638	312.4	451.6	10.5

Company	Assets ($mil)	Sales ($mil)	Market value ($mil)	Net profits ($mil)	Cash flow ($mil)	Number employed (thou)
519. NICOR	2,684	2,237	692	49.8	211.3	5.7
520. A C Neilsen	524	690	825	51.2	81.7	21.5
521. Nike	464	861	540	52.6	62.8	4.4
522. NL Industries	1,927	1,390	973	−18.8	110.0	14.8
523. Noble Affiliates	720	270	749	23.3	103.6	1.8
524. Norfolk Southern	8,172	3,148	3,972	315.4	549.4	37.7
525. Norstar Bancorp	5,351	472	432	58.3	67.2	5.2
526. North American Philips	2,252	3,800	1,114	93.6	169.2	51.2
527. Northeast Savings	3,373	337	44	−3.9	−1.9	8.6
528. Northeast Utilities	4,629	1,889	1,205	221.5	345.1	8.8
529. No Indiana Pub Svc	3,696	1,956	976	137.8	252.6	6.3
530. Northern States Power	3,395	1,696	1,164	183.9	374.6	7.5
531. Northern Trust	6,438	683	294	18.3	29.0	4.2
532. Northrop	1,596	3,261	1,312	100.7	210.5	36.3
533. Northwest Airlines	1,602	2,196	972	50.1	197.0	14.0
534. Northwest Industries	1,811	1,608	987	7.3	84.7	29.6
535. Northwestern Financial	2,489	271	156	17.5	25.1	3.0
536. Norton	1,043	1,128	727	28.7	77.4	20.2
537. Norwest	19,854	2,319	940	125.2	156.2	16.5
538. NYNEX	20,100	10,143	5,939	982.7	2,273.2	118.8
539. Occidental Petroleum	11,775	19,116	2,399	480.2	1,487.9	47.3
540. Ogden	1,053	1,728	571	52.5	95.3	45.0
541. Ohio Casualty	1,678	946	522	55.7	59.8	5.3
542. Ohio Edison	5,905	1,516	1,329	272.4	399.5	7.8
543. Oklahoma Gas & Elec	2,128	972	848	117.7	178.4	3.9
544. Old Kent Financial	3,706	349	174	32.4	40.3	2.6
545. Old Stone	2,316	266	89	15.4	18.2	1.3
546. Olin	1,829	1,935	737	71.7	205.0	17.9
547. Owens-Corning Fbrgls	1,640	2,753	1,071	79.7	196.0	22.8
548. Owens-Illinois	2,936	3,422	1,037	82.1	244.6	45.3
549. PACCAR	896	1,412	1,047	37.5	56.6	8.1
550. Pacific Gas & Electric	14,721	6,647	4,470	788.0	1,184.6	26.6
551. Pacific Lighting	3,719	4,586	1,202	157.2	280.2	10.7
552. Pacific Power & Light	4,451	1,598	1,396	277.1	486.5	9.2
553. Pacific Resources	637	1,550	141	11.1	20.4	0.8
554. Pacific Telesis Group	18,973	8,015	5,360	675.7	1,772.4	101.9
555. Paine Webber	8,314	1,527	496	69.5	82.6	9.9
556. Pan Am World Airways	2,910	3,789	837	−59.9	155.9	28.5
557. Panhandle Eastern	5,194	3,405	1,531	177.6	403.9	7.2
558. Parker-Hannifin	791	1,111	908	44.2	84.1	19.0
559. Payless Cashways	442	914	704	33.8	46.4	7.7
560. Pay'N Save	491	1,220	394	30.1	45.4	11.0
561. Penn Central	2,874	2,539	1,194	133.5	250.9	36.0
562. J C Penney	7,438	12,078	4,190	467.0	620.0	174.0
563. Penn Power & Light	6,049	1,248	1,451	296.0	403.9	8.2
564. Pennzoil	3,584	2,317	1,749	164.2	446.5	8.8
565. Peoples Energy	1,359	1,547	302	48.6	91.9	3.8
566. PepsiCo	4,638	7,896	3,579	284.1	544.8	143.5
567. Perkin-Elmer	899	1,067	1,269	51.8	84.3	14.2
568. Petrolane	835	960	757	−40.4	29.3	12.2

Company	Assets ($mil)	Sales ($mil)	Market value ($mil)	Net profits ($mil)	Cash flow ($mil)	Number employed (thou)
569. Pfizer	3,936	3,750	5,705	447.1	561.6	40.7
570. Phibro-Salomon	42,017	29,757	4,539	470.0	501.0	6.7
571. Philadelphia Electric	8,144	2,596	2,053	389.1	554.4	10.4
572. Philip Morris	9,667	9,466	8,967	903.5	1,230.5	70.0
573. Phillips Petroleum	13,094	15,249	5,286	721.0	1,706.0	29.0
574. Pillsbury	2,931	3,948	1,574	173.6	287.9	56.0
575. Pioneer	973	1,025	1,008	72.9	135.5	2.3
576. Pioneer Hi-Bred Intl	721	512	958	41.2	63.6	2.6
577. Pitney Bowes	1,473	1,606	1,120	117.7	193.2	26.5
578. Pittston	1,060	1,230	530	−71.8	−7.6	12.8
579. PNC Financial	12,245	1,218	889	117.0	129.7	6.4
580. Pneumo	486	1,235	422	39.0	55.6	9.3
581. Polaroid	1,319	1,254	1,037	49.7	101.5	14.2
582. Portland Genl Elec	2,348	586	575	162.7	237.2	3.2
583. Potomac Elec Power	2,807	1,170	1,028	140.1	237.9	5.4
584. PPG Industries	3,615	3,682	2,437	244.3	432.4	37.0
585. Premier Industrial	234	358	708	36.6	40.9	3.0
586. Price Co	191	789	725	17.8	20.5	1.7
587. Primark	1,471	1,967	242	31.2	86.0	4.2
588. Prime Computer	445	516	839	32.5	61.8	5.6
589. Procter & Gamble	8,361	12,633	9,469	886.0	1,219.0	63.1
590. Provident Life & Acc	3,194	1,149	612	89.2	100.5	4.1
591. PSFS	11,922	1,118	394	26.2	65.5	2.5
592. Public Service Colo	2,665	1,629	910	106.4	207.0	6.8
593. Public Service Ind	4,345	874	625	255.8	338.1	5.3
594. Public Service N H	2,086	463	425	151.7	172.7	2.4
595. Public Service N M	2,487	397	861	116.4	167.5	2.9
596. Pub Svc Elec & Gas	8,565	3,963	2,340	389.8	682.3	13.2
597. Puget Sound Pwr & Lt	2,127	518	628	102.0	146.4	2.4
598. Quaker Oats	1,629	2,919	1,179	134.7	199.0	26.2
599. Rainier Bancorp	6,413	696	380	47.2	60.2	5.3
600. Ralston Purina	2,098	4,964	2,651	261.3	371.2	57.7
601. Raychem	507	605	745	28.2	59.2	8.6
602. Raytheon	3,729	5,937	3,649	300.1	517.2	74.1
603. RCA	7,656	8,977	2,842	240.8	781.7	109.5
604. Republic Airlines	1,109	1,511	115	−111.0	−40.4	14.3
605. Republic New York	10,119	990	489	84.7	94.2	2.3
606. Republic Steel	2,876	2,701	506	−195.3	−52.0	25.3
607. RepublicBank	19,082	1,721	844	119.5	136.0	8.1
608. Revco D S	676	2,001	1,112	78.4	99.1	22.3
609. Revlon	2,215	2,379	1,179	109.0	185.3	31.2
610. R J Reynolds Inds	9,874	10,371	6,881	835.0	1,309.0	93.8
611. Reynolds Metals	3,293	3,341	836	−29.1	117.2	28.2
612. Richardson-Vicks	983	1,213	646	48.3	69.5	10.9
613. Riggs National	4,766	380	203	23.4	27.6	2.0
614. RIHT Financial	2,041	223	111	5.2	8.5	2.1
615. Rite Aid	510	1,432	938	56.1	78.2	15.0
616. Roadway Services	812	1,253	1,385	99.2	135.2	18.5
617. A H Robins	510	563	536	58.2	68.5	5.7
618. Rochester Gas & Elec	1,498	756	427	86.2	142.8	2.7

Company	Assets ($mil)	Sales ($mil)	Market value ($mil)	Net profits ($mil)	Cash flow ($mil)	Number employed (thou)
619. Rockwell International	5,339	8,309	5,098	410.7	657.7	101.5
620. Rohm & Haas	1,511	1,876	1,568	137.6	232.1	11.5
621. ROLM	812	549	1,307	34.1	52.8	7.3
622. Ryder Systems	2,257	2,384	1,309	101.1	365.9	21.4
623. Safeco	3,415	1,643	1,032	133.3	133.3	10.1
624. Safeway Stores	4,174	18,585	1,513	183.3	447.9	159.3
625. St Paul Cos	5,595	2,321	1,212	126.8	139.0	10.0
626. St Regis Paper	2,880	2,775	1,216	55.2	169.1	26.0
627. San Diego Gas & Elec	2,840	1,530	1,014	187.4	266.7	5.0
628. Sanders Associates	477	646	952	42.6	63.9	8.6
629. Santa Fe Southern	11,388	5,976	4,989	333.4	860.0	75.3
630. Schering-Plough	2,397	1,808	1,881	178.5	228.8	25.2
631. SCM	1,110	1,767	346	29.7	78.3	22.7
632. SCOA Industries	501	1,305	490	41.8	55.9	19.0
633. Scott Paper	2,723	2,465	1,522	123.7	270.1	17.8
634. G D Searle	1,343	946	2,165	110.0	153.4	12.6
635. Sears, Roebuck	46,176	35,883	13,163	1,300.8	1,658.4	426.8
636. Security Pacific	40,382	4,323	1,878	264.3	329.0	22.5
637. SEDCO	936	544	823	132.2	199.6	4.8
638. Service Merchandise	756	1,458	486	44.9	63.3	15.0
639. ServiceMaster Inds	95	701	710	25.6	29.8	6.1
640. Shared Medical Systems	158	211	807	27.3	42.4	2.2
641. Shawmut	5,755	586	261	32.9	43.6	5.4
642. Shell Oil	22,169	19,678	12,364	1,633.0	3,041.0	35.8
643. Sherwin-Williams	940	1,973	598	51.2	77.7	20.2
644. Signal Cos	5,203	6,151	3,592	114.0	222.0	48.8
645. Singer	1,420	2,478	468	16.2	68.5	56.5
646. SmithKline Beckman	3,170	2,835	4,706	486.0	578.7	30.9
647. Society	4,283	426	191	29.3	36.7	3.2
648. SONAT	3,222	2,687	1,330	210.2	406.6	6.6
649. So Carolina E & G	2,358	975	687	103.9	148.9	3.7
650. South Carolina Natl	2,308	250	170	25.4	33.5	2.8
651. Southeast Banking	8,883	867	429	54.5	88.3	6.8
652. Southern Calif Edison	11,292	4,464	4,004	690.8	980.2	16.0
653. Southern Company	15,034	5,418	3,759	583.5	1,093.7	30.4
654. So New England Tel	2,128	1,183	1,009	120.6	269.1	13.4
655. Southland	3,309	8,512	1,505	131.8	276.9	55.4
656. Southland Royalty	676	321	728	25.7	89.7	0.6
657. Southmark	919	379	296	59.4	66.4	3.0
658. SouthTrust	3,001	297	190	27.9	31.8	2.5
659. Southwest Airlines	587	448	800	40.9	70.8	3.2
660. Southwest Bancshares	7,989	727	425	3.0	13.5	4.3
661. Southwestern Bell	18,360	7,904	5,686	892.7	1,991.1	94.8
662. Southwestern Pub Svc	1,398	754	753	100.4	145.6	2.4
663. Sovran Financial	7,187	811	517	62.9	82.1	8.2
664. Sperry	5,376	5,158	2,483	170.7	392.3	74.8
665. Square D	945	1,144	1,143	60.1	99.0	21.2
666. Squibb	1,946	1,769	2,417	173.3	207.7	23.9
667. A E Staley Mfg	1,155	1,815	669	10.8	77.7	4.5
668. Standard Oil Calif	24,010	27,342	11,813	1,590.0	3,757.0	40.9

Company	Assets ($mil)	Sales ($mil)	Market value ($mil)	Net profits ($mil)	Cash flow ($mil)	Number employed (thou)
669. Standard Oil Indiana	25,805	27,635	14,829	1,868.0	3,626.0	57.3
670. Standard Oil Ohio	16,362	11,599	11,082	1,731.0	2,929.0	46.9
671. Stanley Works	704	984	764	49.5	84.9	13.9
672. State Street Boston	4,044	443	251	38.5	43.1	3.7
673. Stauffer Chemical	2,119	1,326	1,104	−3.4	134.0	10.5
674. Sterling Drug	1,470	1,901	1,654	136.8	172.6	23.8
675. J P Stevens	1,164	2,043	365	23.5	78.2	34.6
676. Stop & Shop Cos	811	2,791	556	50.8	91.7	31.5
677. Student Loan Marketing	9,118	904	1,028	66.1	67.2	0.6
678. Suburban Bancorp	2,580	233	162	22.7	27.6	1.8
679. Sumitomo Bank Cal	2,454	251	64	8.8	13.2	1.6
680. Sun Banks	8,901	594	571	46.3	61.6	7.5
681. Sun Company	12,466	14,730	5,081	613.0	1,533.0	39.6
682. Sundstrand	917	909	892	51.4	106.6	13.3
683. Super Food Services	158	1,254	85	6.5	10.5	1.9
684. Super Valu Stores	1,062	5,750	1,079	75.0	126.2	24.1
685. Superior Oil	5,267	1,793	4,676	171.4	557.8	6.6
686. Supermarkets General	751	3,517	419	40.7	86.5	33.0
687. Swift Independent	307	2,624	151	22.0	34.6	6.2
688. Sysco	556	2,119	767	42.0	60.9	7.7
689. Tandem Computers	446	451	1,376	33.8	53.4	4.1
690. Tandon	356	344	1,015	27.3	36.4	4.3
691. Tandy	1,077	2,662	4,524	292.7	335.6	31.5
692. TECO Energy	1,649	677	654	74.3	125.3	3.8
693. Tecumseh Products	516	829	495	55.2	76.4	9.8
694. Tektronix	1,118	1,209	1,424	48.3	119.4	20.9
695. Tele-Communications	1,222	347	876	16.0	80.2	3.5
696. Teledyne	3,852	2,979	3,407	303.8	357.6	44.6
697. Telerate	127	75	1,007	22.8	29.7	0.2
698. Temple-Inland	1,209	1,175	788	48.2	112.6	10.0
699. Tenneco	17,994	14,449	5,714	716.0	1,696.0	96.5
700. Teradyne	253	251	782	21.4	36.0	3.6
701. Tesoro Petroleum	1,067	3,046	192	45.0	96.9	3.3
702. Texaco	27,199	40,068	9,292	1,233.0	2,950.0	57.5
703. Texas Air	1,178	1,246	86	−177.9	76.6	12.3
704. Texas American Bshs	5,409	528	389	34.9	53.0	3.3
705. Texas Commerce Bshs	19,499	1,668	1,333	177.0	201.0	8.1
706. Texas Eastern	4,644	5,393	1,522	154.6	374.0	6.4
707. Texas Instruments	2,713	4,580	3,331	−145.4	206.0	80.4
708. Texas Oil & Gas	2,970	1,894	5,010	306.6	491.7	3.4
709. Texas Utilities	8,781	3,488	2,876	461.5	689.4	16.3
710. Textron	2,105	2,980	1,125	88.7	153.3	41.0
711. Third National	3,726	390	210	32.3	39.0	3.2
712. Thrifty Corp	478	1,217	349	23.0	38.1	14.0
713. TIE/Communications	359	324	881	35.1	42.4	1.2
714. Tiger International	1,114	1,250	117	−95.6	−13.5	12.0
715. Time Inc	2,273	2,717	3,095	143.2	233.7	17.1
716. Times Mirror	2,384	2,478	2,575	179.5	298.9	27.7
717. Timken	1,108	937	759	0.5	71.7	16.6
718. Toledo Edison	2,402	505	534	128.3	179.4	2.4

Company	Assets ($mil)	Sales ($mil)	Market value ($mil)	Net profits ($mil)	Cash flow ($mil)	Number employed (thou)
719. Toledo Trustcorp	2,151	196	144	20.7	24.2	1.5
720. Torchmark	3,217	1,133	812	98.0	115.6	6.4
721. Tosco	953	2,494	90	−81.0	−48.4	2.5
722. Toys 'R' Us	820	1,320	1,905	92.3	105.7	13.7
723. Trans World	1,473	1,889	855	60.2	124.2	70.0
724. Trans World Airlines	2,738	3,354	372	−35.9	185.0	27.5
725. Transamerica	10,952	4,681	2,001	175.9	318.7	28.8
726. Transco Energy	3,625	3,845	895	133.0	491.4	3.5
727. TRANSOHIO Financial	2,447	250	36	4.2	6.2	0.8
728. Travelers	32,876	12,002	2,658	342.6	382.5	29.1
729. Tribune	1,635	1,586	1,237	71.6	144.5	18.7
730. Trust Co of Georgia	4,850	545	743	73.0	86.9	4.6
731. TRW	3,321	5,493	2,895	199.6	392.8	86.7
732. Tucson Electric Power	1,868	367	880	103.4	148.1	1.1
733. Turner Construction	435	1,709	76	11.4	14.9	2.6
734. UAL	5,134	6,022	1,267	142.0	553.3	58.0
735. Union Camp	2,381	1,688	2,011	132.7	250.6	16.8
736. Union Carbide	10,295	9,001	4,422	220.0	697.0	101.4
737. Union Electric	5,206	1,401	1,219	276.2	368.5	7.3
738. Union National	2,185	197	112	13.7	23.4	2.0
739. Union Pacific	10,218	8,353	5,824	414.0	938.0	46.9
740. Uniroyal	1,486	2,040	572	52.3	110.8	20.7
741. United Banks of Colo	3,868	399	162	26.4	34.2	3.2
742. United Brands	1,005	2,232	193	−102.3	−69.4	43.0
743. Utd Energy Resources	2,710	4,035	692	28.9	299.4	3.9
744. United Financial Group	3,504	355	59	−1.7	0.0	0.7
745. United Illuminating	1,179	450	267	80.5	97.9	1.5
746. United Jersey Banks	3,635	343	195	23.8	28.5	2.9
747. United Missouri Bshs	2,639	219	185	25.7	32.7	2.0
748. U S Bancorp	6,511	653	410	52.4	61.7	5.5
749. United States Gypsum	1,194	1,611	990	80.3	127.7	16.1
750. United States Shoe	678	1,428	811	71.1	90.4	25.0
751. United States Steel	19,314	16,869	3,178	−1,161.0	8.0	98.7
752. U S Tobacco	373	383	1,122	70.6	81.2	3.7
753. U S Trust	2,333	235	153	18.4	23.3	1.6
754. U S WEST	17,370	7,705	5,372	894.0	2,098.5	93.5
755. United Technologies	8,720	14,669	4,334	509.2	909.7	188.8
756. United Telecom	4,945	2,511	1,793	232.6	659.4	28.3
757. United Virginia Bshs	5,415	563	371	51.5	63.5	5.0
758. Unocal	9,228	10,066	5,493	625.9	1,674.8	20.2
759. Upjohn	2,195	1,986	1,803	160.2	217.9	21.3
760. USAir Group	1,318	1,432	725	80.6	144.1	11.5
761. USF&G	5,279	2,387	1,498	171.5	178.5	9.2
762. USLIFE	3,158	931	534	76.5	85.8	3.0
763. Utah Power & Light	2,838	855	1,248	144.5	224.5	4.5
764. Valero Energy	1,477	1,495	466	44.7	77.5	1.8
765. Valley Fed Sav & Loan	2,272	241	43	1.6	4.9	1.0
766. Valley National	8,146	814	419	45.8	66.2	6.8
767. Varian Associates	600	791	1,177	47.1	59.9	13.1
768. VF	567	1,101	989	119.4	139.5	22.7

Company	Assets ($mil)	Sales ($mil)	Market value ($mil)	Net profits ($mil)	Cash flow ($mil)	Number employed (thou)
769. Vulcan Materials	735	820	783	54.2	120.9	5.9
770. Wachovia	7,850	781	697	84.6	96.0	6.4
771. Wal-Mart Stores	1,652	4,667	5,457	196.2	246.0	54.0
772. Waldbaum	314	1,587	79	13.9	33.8	7.0
773. Walgreen	796	2,447	1,172	71.9	97.8	31.7
774. Wang Laboratories	1,918	1,793	4,895	179.0	313.1	26.5
775. Warner Communications	3,122	3,425	1,763	−417.8	−316.4	21.9
776. Warner-Lambert	2,919	3,108	2,370	200.5	299.8	42.0
777. Washington Mutual Sav	3,400	324	81	7.3	10.7	1.0
778. Washington National	3,360	824	267	22.4	27.3	5.8
779. Washington Post	571	878	1,035	68.4	99.9	5.3
780. Washington Water Power	1,227	339	395	67.7	86.6	1.4
781. Waste Management	1,338	1,040	2,224	120.4	209.4	16.9
782. Weis Markets	339	892	745	50.1	64.0	10.0
783. Wells Fargo	27,018	2,980	946	154.9	205.3	16.7
784. Wendy's International	507	715	851	55.2	81.5	32.5
785. West Point-Pepperell	740	1,300	532	59.5	98.5	21.5
786. Western Savings & Loan	2,964	333	80	19.0	23.5	1.2
787. Western Union	2,123	1,045	878	−59.1	84.1	14.7
788. Westinghouse Elec	8,569	9,533	4,792	449.0	832.0	132.9
789. Westvaco	1,611	1,564	1,094	74.7	172.3	14.8
790. Wetterau	436	2,565	204	21.4	38.5	7.6
791. Weyerhaeuser	5,946	4,883	4,445	204.8	545.5	40.4
792. Whirlpool	1,466	2,668	1,772	163.0	224.3	20.8
793. White Consolidated	1,315	2,058	751	51.8	90.7	23.0
794. Whitney Holding	2,122	212	279	32.3	32.3	0.9
795. Whittaker	974	1,603	268	37.6	61.4	17.0
796. Wickes Cos	958	2,875	70	9.5	46.9	31.4
797. Williams Cos	4,686	2,167	944	54.0	244.6	7.2
798. Wilson Foods	264	2,085	51	−44.4	−34.3	8.7
799. Winn-Dixie Stores	1,129	7,133	1,204	114.3	235.1	66.5
800. Wisconsin Elec Pwr	2,491	1,418	948	150.0	263.6	6.2
801. Wisconsin Pwr & Lt	881	555	363	54.6	115.3	2.5
802. Witco Chemical	733	1,386	511	52.0	95.6	8.0
803. Wometco Enterprises	534	520	767	30.9	72.0	6.2
804. F W Woolworth	2,364	5,456	1,106	117.7	217.5	105.9
805. Xerox	9,297	8,463	4,707	459.2	1,307.4	107.0
806. Zayre	908	2,614	776	61.4	95.2	36.0
807. Zenith Radio	739	1,361	780	46.3	76.1	27.0
808. Zions Utah Bancorp	2,311	245	195	24.5	27.9	1.7

Appendix IV
Summation Notation

The symbol Σ, which we use extensively in this text, is mathematical shorthand notation. We use it to indicate that the items following it are to be added. When necessary for clarity, we include an index of summation, usually i, as part of the notation. For example,

$$\sum_{i=1}^{4} x_i$$

instructs us to add the values of x from x_1 through x_4. That is,

$$\sum_{i=1}^{4} x_i = x_1 + x_2 + x_3 + x_4$$

Similarly, Σx or Σx_i instructs us to add all values of x, where the meaning of "all" is apparent from the context.

The following are some algebraic properties of summation that you will find useful.

1. The summation of a constant c is n times the constant, when n is the number of values of the index of summation. That is,

$$\sum_{i=1}^{n} c = nc$$

For example,

$$\sum_{i=1}^{4} 5 = 4(5) = 20$$

2. The summation of a constant times a variable is equal to the constant times the summation of the variable. That is, given that c is a constant, then

$$\sum_{i=1}^{n} c x_i = c \sum_{i=1}^{n} x_i$$

For example,

$$\sum_{i=1}^{4} 5(x_i) = 5 \sum_{i=1}^{4} x_i$$

If $x_1 = 2$, $x_2 = 3$, $x_3 = 6$, and $x_4 = 10$, we have

$$5(2 + 3 + 6 + 10) = 5(21) = 105$$

3. The summation of a sum (or difference) is the sum (or difference) of the individual sums. In symbols,

$$\sum_{i=1}^{n} (x_i \pm y_i) = \sum_{i=1}^{n} x_i \pm \sum_{i=1}^{n} y_i$$

This last property extends to more than two components. For example,

$$\sum_{i=1}^{n} (x_i + y_i - z_i) = \sum_{i=1}^{n} x_i + \sum_{i=1}^{n} y_i - \sum_{i=1}^{n} z_i$$

Double Subscript Notation   In some cases a population may be composed of two or more identifiable groups or subpopulations. It is frequently convenient in such cases both to distinguish one observation from another and to identify the subpopulation to which each observation belongs. We can accomplish this by using a double subscript on each observation. For example, consider a population consisting of four groups or subpopulations, each containing three observations, as shown in the following table.

	Group		
1	2	3	4
10	8	2	8
15	9	6	11
25	14	1	4
50	31	9	23

We refer to the first observation in group 2 as x_{12}, and we may write $x_{12} = 8$. The second observation in group 4 is designated x_{24}, and we may write $x_{24} = 11$, and so on.

The total of a given group is obtained by adding the observations in that group as shown in the table. The total for the entire population of 12 observations is obtained by adding the group totals. For the population shown in the table, the population total is $50 + 31 + 9 + 23 = 113$. This system of notation and summation may be generalized for the case of k groups as follows.

x_{ij} = the ith observation in the jth group, where j identifies the group and i distinguishes one observation from another within the group

$$\sum_{i=1}^{n_j} x_{ij} = \text{the total for the } j\text{th group}$$

$$\sum_{j=1}^{k} \sum_{i=1}^{n_j} x_{ij} = \text{the grand total of all observations}$$

GREEK ALPHABET

α	Alpha	ι	Iota	ρ	Rho
β	Beta	κ	Kappa	$\sigma\ (\Sigma)$	Sigma
γ	Gamma	λ	Lambda	τ	Tau
δ	Delta	μ	Mu	υ	Upsilon
ϵ	Epsilon	ν	Nu	ϕ	Phi
ζ	Zeta	ξ	Xi	χ	Chi
η	Eta	o	Omicron	ψ	Psi
θ	Theta	π	Pi	ω	Omega

Answers to Odd-Numbered Exercises

Note: Many of the following answers were obtained by computer and, consequently, may differ from answers obtained by hand calculations because of rounding.

CHAPTER 2

2.3

Class interval	f_i	Cumulative frequency
0–4.9	20	20
5.0–9.9	29	49
10.0–14.9	18	67
15.0–19.9	11	78
20.0–24.9	9	87
25.0–29.9	8	95
30.0–34.9	5	100
	100	

2.5

Class interval	f_i	Cumulative frequency	Relative frequency	Cumulative relative frequency	x_i
0–4	43	43	0.3583	0.3583	2
5–9	30	73	0.2500	0.6083	7
10–14	17	90	0.1417	0.7500	12
15–19	16	106	0.1333	0.8833	17
20–24	10	116	0.0833	0.9666	22
25–29	4	120	0.0333	0.9999	27
	120				

2.7

Stem	Leaf
0	7
1	2 8 7 6
2	5 1 7 0 6 7 1
3	0 4 5 6 0 0 5 0 0
4	2 0 6
5	1

2.9

Adult male:	
Stem	Leaf
17	1
18	4
19	1 5
20	1 2 5 1 9
21	2 3 4 4 3 7
22	2 5 2 9
23	9 8 3
24	9 5 8

Adult female:	
Stem	Leaf
12	5
13	5
14	3 5
15	2 4 4 0 5
16	5 6 8 7
17	8 3
18	6 6 4
19	0 0 5 9
20	3
21	2 4

2.11 (a) Females   Percent satisfied: $100\left(\dfrac{650}{2500}\right) = 26$

Percent dissatisfied: $100\left(\dfrac{975}{2500}\right) = 39$

Percent no opinion: $100 - 26 - 39 = 35$

Males   Percent satisfied: $100\left(\dfrac{2279}{4300}\right) = 53$

Percent dissatisfied: $100\left(\dfrac{1720}{4300}\right) = 40$

Percent no opinion: $100 - 53 - 40 = 7$

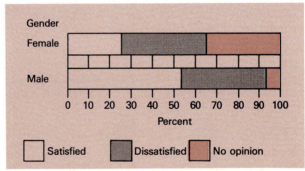

(b)

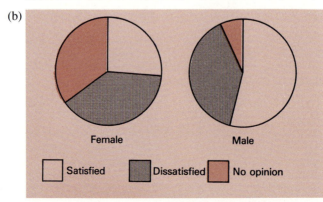

2.13

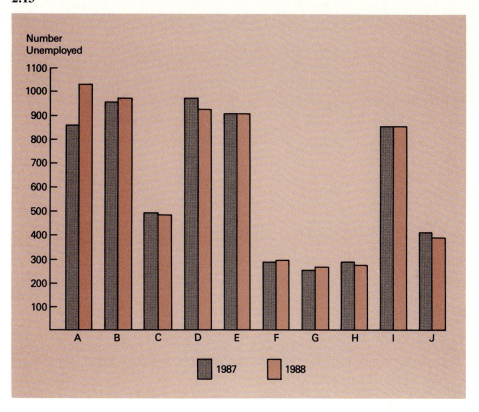

2.15 (a) 27.5 (b) 28.5 (c) 30 (d) 20 (e) 38.28 (f) 6.2
2.17 (a) 57.1 (b) 56 (c) 56 and 59 (d) 10 (e) 9.0 (f) 3.0
2.19 (a) 75 (b) 50–150

2.21

Class interval	f_i	x_i	x_if_i	$x_i^2f_i$
0–4.9	20	2.45	49.00	120.05
5.0–9.9	29	7.45	21.05	1,609.57
10.0–14.9	18	12.45	216.10	2,790.04
15.0–19.9	11	17.45	191.95	3,349.53
20.0–24.9	9	22.45	202.05	4,536.02
25.0–29.9	8	27.45	219.60	6,028.02
30.0–34.9	5	32.45	162.25	5,265.01
	100		1265.00	23,698.24

$$\bar{x} = \frac{1265.00}{100} = 12.65, \qquad \text{Median} = 9.95 + \left(\frac{1}{18}\right)(5) = 10.23,$$

$$s^2 = \frac{100(23,698.24) - (1265.00)}{100(99)} = \frac{769,599}{9900} = 77.74, \qquad s = 8.82$$

2.23 $\bar{x} = 152.9$,   Median $= 149.5 + \left(\dfrac{1}{23}\right)(10) = 149.5 + 0.43 = 149.93$

$s^2 = 332.7677$, $s = 18.24$

2.25 $\bar{x} = 274.1875$, $s^2 = 10{,}613.11$, $s = 103.02$,   Median $= 261.50$,
$P_{25} = 191.5$, $P_{75} = 352.44$, $P_{95} = 459.5$

Review Questions

15.

(b) Age (years)	Hundreds of contestants (f_i)	x_i	$x_i f_i$	Relative frequency
10–14	4	12	48	0.04
15–19	8	17	136	0.08
20–24	15	22	330	0.15
25–29	19	27	513	0.19
30–34	21	32	672	0.21
35–39	12	37	444	0.12
40–44	8	42	336	0.08
45–49	6	47	282	0.06
50–54	4	52	208	0.04
55–59	3	57	171	0.03
	100		3140	1.00

$$\bar{x} = \frac{3140}{100} = 31.4$$

(c) $0.15 + 0.19 + 0.21 + 0.12 = 0.67$
(d) $0.04 + 0.08 + 0.15 + 0.19 = 0.46$
(e) $0.08 + 0.06 + 0.04 + 0.03 = 0.21$

17. $\bar{x} = \dfrac{3.7 + 3.1 + \cdots + 4.6}{20} = 3.395$,   Median $= 3.25$

$s^2 = \dfrac{20[(3.7)^2 + (3.1)^2 + \cdots + (4.6)^2] - (67.9)^2}{(20)(19)} = 0.66997$,

$s = 0.8185$

19. $\bar{x} = \dfrac{9.1 + 2.5 + \cdots + 5.9}{15} = 5.7133$,   Median $= 6.4$

$s^2 = \dfrac{15[(9.1)^2 + (2.5)^2 + \cdots + (5.9)^2] - (85.7)^2}{(15)(14)} = 7.0141$, $s = 2.65$

21. $\bar{x} = \dfrac{59 + 97 + \cdots + 51}{20} = 73.5$,   Median $= 65$

$s^2 = \dfrac{20[(59)^2 + (97)^2 + \cdots + (51)^2] - (1470)^2}{(20)(19)} = 584.37$, $s = 24.174$

23. $\bar{x} = \dfrac{4 + 2 + \cdots + 1}{15} = 3$,   Median $= 3$

$s^2 = \dfrac{15[(4)^2 + (2)^2 + \cdots + (1)^2] - (45)^2}{(15)(14)} = 3.1429$, $s = 1.7728$

25. $\bar{x} = \dfrac{1 + 5 + 3 + \cdots + 2}{20} = 5.4,$ Median $= 5$

$s^2 = \dfrac{20[(1)^2 + (5)^2 + (3)^2 + \cdots + (2)^2] - (108)^2}{(20)(19)} = 7.9368,$

$s = 2.8172$

27. $\bar{x} = \dfrac{7 + 9 + 6 + \cdots + 0}{20} = 4.75,$ Median $= 4.5$

$s^2 = \dfrac{20[(7)^2 + (9)^2 + (6)^2 + \cdots + (0)^2] - (95)^2}{(20)(19)} = 7.3553,$

$s = 2.7121$

29. (a) $\bar{x} = \dfrac{1 + 1 + \cdots + 10}{20} = 3.9$ (b) Median $= 3$

(c) $s^2 = \dfrac{20[(1)^2 + (1)^2 + \cdots + (10)^2] - (78)^2}{(20)(19)} = 5.5684,$ $s = 2.3598$

31.

Number of days	Number of items
0–4	8
5–9	22
10–14	38
15–19	16
20–24	15
25–29	8
30–34	3
	$\overline{110}$

$\bar{x} = \dfrac{8(2) + 22(7) + 38(12) + 16(17) + 15(22) + 8(27) + 3(32)}{110}$

$= \dfrac{1540}{110} = 14$

37. 220.17

39. Frequency distribution:

Class interval	Frequency
120–139	2
140–159	12
160–179	36
180–199	89
200–219	151
220–239	165
240–259	91
260–279	42
280–299	8
300–319	4

41. 220.71

CHAPTER 3

3.1   (a) 56   (b) 60   (c) 362,880   (d) 5040   (e) 30   (f) 120   (g) 120   (h) 35
(i) 5   (j) 70

3.3   35   **3.5**   (a) 120   (b) 60   **3.7**   (a) 720   (b) 360

3.9   (a) (i) 0.10   (ii) 0.142   (iii) 0.015   (iv) 0.106   (v) 0.3500   (vi) 0.227
(b) (i) 0.075   (ii) 0.165   (iii) 0.010   (iv) 0.010   (v) 0.230   (vi) 0.438
(vii) 0.600
(c) No. $P(A_1 \cap B_1) \neq P(A_1)P(B_1)$, for example.

3.11   (a) 0.33   (b) 0.17   (c) 0.50

3.13   (a) 0.427   (b) 0.257   (c) 0.197   (d) 0.120

3.15   (a) 0.2490   (b) 0.1120   (c) 0.4149   (d) 0.2241

Review Questions

11.   4

13.   (a) $P(\text{1st}) = \dfrac{400}{1000} = 0.40$ (b) $P(\text{2nd}) = \dfrac{350}{1000} = 0.35$

(c) $P(\text{3rd}) = \dfrac{250}{1000} = 0.25$ (d) $P(\text{1st or 2nd}) = 0.40 + 0.35 = 0.75$

15.   (a) $\dfrac{30}{100}$ (b) $\dfrac{(25 + 44 - 15)}{100} = \dfrac{54}{100}$ (c) $\dfrac{33}{100}$

(d) $\dfrac{(100 - 15)}{100} = \dfrac{85}{100}$ (e) $\dfrac{100}{100}$ (f) $\dfrac{(100 - 23)}{100} = \dfrac{77}{100}$

(g) $\dfrac{7}{100}$ (h) $\dfrac{(100 - 20)}{100} = \dfrac{80}{100}$

17. $_7P_7 = 7! = 5040$

19.   (a) (1) $\dfrac{300}{500} = 0.60$ (2) $\dfrac{135}{500} = 0.27, \dfrac{65}{500} = 0.13$

(3) $\dfrac{125}{500} = 0.25$ for each area

(4) $\dfrac{115}{125} = 0.92$ (5) $\dfrac{65}{500} + \dfrac{125}{500} - \dfrac{15}{500} = 0.35$

(b) (1) $\dfrac{5}{500} = 0.01$ (2) $\dfrac{125}{500} + \dfrac{300}{500} - \dfrac{115}{500} = 0.62$ (3) $\dfrac{375}{500} = 0.75$

(4) $\dfrac{60}{125} = 0.48$ (5) $\dfrac{5}{65} = 0.08$ (6) $\dfrac{300}{500} = 0.60$

21. $P(\text{not a college graduate}) = 1 - 0.55 = 0.45$

23.   (a) $_6C_2 = \dfrac{6!}{2!4!} = 15$

$M_1M_2 \quad M_2F_1 \quad F_1F_3$

$$M_1F_1 \quad M_2F_2 \quad F_1F_4$$

$$M_1F_2 \quad M_2F_3 \quad F_2F_3$$

$$M_1F_3 \quad M_2F_4 \quad F_2F_4$$

$$M_1F_4 \quad F_1F_2 \quad F_3F_4$$

(b) $\dfrac{14}{15} = 0.9333$ (c) $\dfrac{8}{15} = 0.5333$ (d) $\dfrac{9}{15} = 0.6000$ (e) $\dfrac{1}{15} = 0.0667$

25. (a) $P(E_1 \cap E_2) = P(E_1)P(E_2) = (0.20)(0.30) = 0.06$ (b) 0

(c) $P(E_1 \cup E_2) = P(E_1) + P(E_2) = 0.20 + 0.30 = 0.50$

27. (a) $\dfrac{1}{_9P_3} = \dfrac{1}{504}$ (b) $\dfrac{(_3C_1)(_6C_2)}{_9C_3} + \dfrac{(_3C_2)(_6C_1)}{_9C_3} + \dfrac{(_3C_3)(_6C_0)}{_9C_3} = \dfrac{64}{84} = \dfrac{16}{21}$

29. (a) $0.05 + 0.10 + 0.10 + 0.15 + 0.20 = 0.60$ (b) $0.15 + 0.20 + 0.40$
$= 0.75$ (c) $0.10 + 0.15 = 0.25$ (d) $0.20 + 0.40 = 0.60$

31. (a) $\dfrac{800}{1400} = 0.5714$ (b) $\dfrac{500}{1400} = 0.3571$

(c) $P(E|MC) = \dfrac{P(E \cap MC)}{P(MC)} = \dfrac{500/1400}{900/1400} = 0.5556$

33. The total number of ways to fill the four positions $= _{10}C_4 = 210$. If no minority is selected, the selections must come from the others. The number of these combinations $= _6C_4 = 15$. The probability of one of these combinations, then, is $15/210 = 0.0714$.

35. (a) $P(D \cup C) = P(D) + P(C) - P(D \cap C) = 0.75 + 0.60 - 0.40 = 0.95$

(b) $P(C|D) = \dfrac{0.4}{0.75} = 0.53$ (c) $P(D|C) = \dfrac{0.4}{0.6} = 0.67$

37. Let A = recruited from outside current firm
B = would like to change firms

(a) $P(A \cap B) = P(B)P(A|B) = (0.2)(0.6) = 0.12$

(b) $P(A \cup B) = P(A) + P(B) - P(A \cap B) = 0.3 + 0.2 - 0.12 = 0.38$

(c) $P(B|A) = \dfrac{P(B \cap A)}{P(A)} = \dfrac{0.12}{0.30} = 0.4$

CHAPTER 4

4.1 (a) $P(X = x_i)$: 0.05, 0.08, 0.10, 0.12, 0.18, 0.14, 0.10, 0.09, 0.08, 0.04, 0.02
(b) $P(X \le x_i)$: 0.05, 0.13, 0.23, 0.35, 0.53, 0.67, 0.77, 0.86, 0.94, 0.98, 1.00

4.3 (a) 0.05 (b) 0.02 (c) 0.33 (d) 0.67 (e) 0.63

4.5. (c) (1) $1 - \dfrac{42}{80} = \dfrac{38}{80}$ (2) $\dfrac{15}{80}$ (3) $1 - \dfrac{74}{80} = \dfrac{6}{80}$ (4) $\dfrac{56}{80}$

(d) $\mu = 1.85,$ $\sigma^2 = 2.4775$

4.7   (a) 0.3125   (b) 0.5   (c) 0.5   (d) 0.0312   (e) 0.0312
4.9   (a) 0.0170   (b) 0.9984   (c) 0.3430
4.11 Yes   **4.13** (a) 0.5846   (b) 0.0338   (c) 0.5846   (d) 0.9906
4.15 (a) 0.4670   (b) $1 - 0.4670 = 0.5330$ (c) $0.9999 - 0.4670 = 0.5329$
          (d) $1 - 0.9999 = 0.0001$ (e) 0
4.17 (a) $P(X = 6|15, 0.75) = P(X = 9|15, 0.25) = 0.9992 - 0.9958 = 0.0034$
          (b) $P(X \geq 7|15, 0.75) = P(X \leq 8|15, 0.25) = 0.9958$
          (c) $P(X \leq 5|15, 0.75) = P(X \geq 10|15, 0.25) = 1 - 0.9992 = 0.0008$
          (d) $P(6 \leq X \leq 9|15, 0.75) = P(9 \geq X \geq 6|15, 0.25) = 0.9992 - 0.8516$
$$= 0.1476$$
4.19 0.9709   **4.21** 0.7422   **4.23** 0.9901   **4.25** 0.9902
4.27 $0.9997 - 0.9292 = 0.0705$
4.29 $P(z \leq -2.67) = 0.0038$ $P(z \leq z_1) = 0.0038 + 0.9718 = 0.9756$ $z_1 = 1.97$
4.31 $P(z \leq 2.98) = 0.9986$ **4.33** $\mu = 76$, $\sigma = 10$
          $P(z \leq z_1) = 0.9986 - 0.1117$ (a) 0.4172
          $= 0.8869$ (b) 0.5398
          $z_1 = 1.21$ (c) 0.5793
4.35 $\mu = 120$, $\sigma^2 = 16$, $\sigma = 4$,   0.4013
4.37 (a) 0.5328   (b) 0.0228   (c) 0.0228
4.39 $(0.30)(50) = 15$, $\sqrt{15(0.7)} = \sqrt{10.5} = 3.24$
          $P(19.5 \leq X \leq 24.5) = P(1.39 \leq z \leq 2.93) = 0.9983 - 0.9177 = 0.0806$

Review Questions **17.** (a) $P(X = x_i)$: 0.10, 0.15, 0.20, 0.25, 0.15, 0.05, 0.03, 0.02, 0.02, 0.02, 0.01
                               (c) $P(X \leq x_i)$: 0.10, 0.25, 0.45, 0.70, 0.85, 0.90, 0.93, 0.95, 0.97, 0.99, 1.00
          19. (a) 0.0480   (b) 0.0171   (c) 0.7454   (d) 0.0003
          21. 0.9010   **33.** 0.2131
          23. 3.33   **35.** 0.8414
          25. 265.30   **37.** (a) 0.0228   (b) 309
          27. (a) 0.0013   (b) 0.0062   **39.** (a) 64.75   (b) $k = 118.45$
                   (c) 0.7745   (d) 728   (c) 130.15
                   (e) 2.28%   (d) $k = 131.80$, $k' = 68.20$
          29. 0.1320
          31. (a) 0.1935   (b) 0.0018   **41.** 14.90
                   (c) 0.0018   **43.** 10.6
          45. (a) 2, 1.8   (b) 4, 3.2   (c) 6, 4.2   (d) 8, 4.8   (e) 10, 5   (f) 12, 4.8
                   (g) 14, 4.2   (h) 16, 3.2
                   (i) 18, 1.8; σ^2 largest for $p = 0.5$; σ^2 smallest for $p = 0.1$ and $p = 0.9$
          47. $\mu = 70(0.10) = 7$, $\sigma = \sqrt{70(0.10)(0.90)} = 2.51$,
                   $P(x \geq 12|70, 0.10) = 0.0367$

CHAPTER 5

5.1 (a) 99.8, 0.548   (b) 0.5554   **5.3**   0.9237

5.5 Sample:

	2,4	2,6	2,8	2,10	4,6	4,8	4,10	6,8	6,10	8,10
$\bar{x}$	3	4	5	6	5	6	7	7	8	9

$\bar{x}$	3	4	5	6	7	8	9
$f(\bar{x})$	1	1	2	2	2	1	1

$$\mu = \frac{2 + 4 + 6 + 8 + 10}{5} = 6,$$

$$\sigma^2 = \frac{5(4 + 16 + 36 + 64 + 100) - (30)^2}{(5)(5)} = 8,$$

$$\mu_{\bar{x}} = \frac{3 + 4 + 2(5) + 2(6) + 2(7) + 8 + 9}{10} = 6,$$

$$\sigma_{\bar{x}}^2 = \frac{(3-6)^2 + (4-6)^2 + 2(5-6)^2 + 2(6-6)^2 + 2(7-6)^2 + (8-6)^2 + (9-6)^2}{10} = 3$$

5.7	0.0071	**5.15**	0.2358
5.9	0.4778	**5.17**	0.0038
5.11	0.8413	**5.19**	0.1190
5.13	0.4658		

Review Questions

13. (a) 32, 1.5 (b) 0.8854 (c) 0.0228 (d) 0.0918 (f) random
15. 0.0475 **21.** 0.0212 **27.** 0.2005
17. 0.0351 **23.** 0.8764, 0.0618 **29.** 0.0475
19. 0.0089 **25.** 0.0668 **33.** 0.0034

CHAPTER 6

6.1 8.6, 9.0 **6.3** 63, 67 **6.5** 18.67, 28.67
6.7 $\bar{x} = 15.50$, $s = 8$, $t = 2.1315$; \$11.24, \$19.76
6.9 $\bar{d} = 2$, $s_d^2 = 96.5333$, $s_d = 9.825$, $t = 2.1315$; $-3.24, 7.24$
6.11 (a) 109.32, 140.68 (b) 104.36, 145.64
6.13 $\bar{x}_1 = 112.88$, $\bar{x}_2 = 104.0625$; 1.7506, 15.8844
6.15 $s_p^2 = 229.4$; 5.6, 24.6 **6.17** $s_p^2 = 0.019$; $-0.17, 0.05$
6.19 0.45, 0.55 **6.21** 0.64, 0.76 **6.23** 0.14, 0.26 **6.25** $-0.02, 0.16$
6.27 82 **6.29** 157 **6.31** 385 **6.33** 218

Review Questions

15. 2.482, 2.498
19. 0.02, 0.08
21. 0.02, 0.08 **33.** 0.82, 0.92 **37.** 171
23. 12, 18 **35.** \$34, \$50 **39.** 7.8, 20.2
25. 0.07, 0.23 **41.** 1476
27. 0.53, 0.67 **43.** 0.004, 0.216
29. 5.1, 7.6 **45.** 12.706, 23.161
31. 0.36, 0.44 **47.** 167.559, 182.041
49. (a) 15.6 (b) 16 (c) $s^2 = 9.6667$, $s = 3.1091$ (d) 14.3, 16.9
(e) Is the sampled population at least approximately normally distributed?
(f) Yes, since 16 is contained in the confidence interval.
51. $\bar{x} = 48.3$, $s = 22.9991$; 38, 59 Since 50 is contained in the interval, we
conclude that the salesperson may be spending an average of 50 minutes on each
call.
59. 0.50, 0.70
61. 0.58, 0.74

63. $-0.26, 0.06$

65. $\bar{x}_F = \dfrac{43 + 48 + \cdots + 62}{40} = 55.25, \qquad s_F^2 = 151.1667,$

$\bar{x}_M = 73.67, \qquad s_M^2 = 428.9040$

67. 66.77, 80.57
69. 0.56, 0.84
71. 0.11, 0.49
73. 0.53, 0.61

CHAPTER 7

7.1 Reject null hypothesis, $z = -3.00$; $p = 0.0026$
7.3 Since $3.00 \not< 1.96$, reject H_0; $p = 0.0026$
7.5 Yes, $t = 2.50$; $\quad$ **7.11** $z = -2.00$; $p = 0.0456$
$0.01 < p < 0.025$
7.7 $t = 3.115$; $p < 0.005$ $\quad$ **7.13** $z = 2$; $p = 0.0228$
7.9 Yes, $t = 2.264$; $\quad$ **7.15** Yes, $z = -2.346$; $p \approx 0.0094$
$0.025 > p > 0.01$

7.17 $s_p^2 = \dfrac{9(144) + 7(110)}{16} = 129.125 \qquad t = \dfrac{26.1 - 17.6}{\sqrt{129.125[(1/10) + (1/8)]}} = \dfrac{8.5}{5.39}$
$= 1.58$

Cannot reject H_0. Conclude that the average time required on second shift may not be less than that required on first shift. $0.10 > p > 0.05$
7.19 $s_p^2 = 119.48$, $t = -3.9418$ Reject H_0, since $-3.9418 < -2.485$; $p < 0.005$
7.21 Yes, $z = 6.35$; $p < 0.001$ $\quad$ **7.29** Yes, $z = 2.50$; $p = 0.0062$
7.23 Yes, $z = -4.00$; $p < 0.001$ $\quad$ **7.31** No, $z = -1.11$; $p = 0.2670$
7.25 Yes, $z = -8.5888$; $p < 0.0002$ $\quad$ **7.33** $z = 0.88$; $p = 0.1894$
7.27 No, $z = -1.31$; $p = 0.0951$

Review Questions

17. Yes, $z = -1.67$; $p = 0.0475$
19. Yes, $t = -2.50$; $0.025 > p > 0.01$
21. Yes, $z = -3.00$; $p = 0.0013$
23. Yes, $t = -4.84$. The samples were randomly and independently drawn from normally distributed populations. $p < 0.005$
27. No, $z \approx 1.00$; $p = 0.1587$
29. $H_0: p_A \leq p_B$, $H_1: p_A > p_B$; No, $\bar{p} = 0.504$, $z = 0.62$; $p = 0.2676$
31. $z = -2.5$; $p = 0.0062$ $\quad$ **41.** $t = -2.763$; $0.01 > p > 0.005$
35. $z = 2.67$; $p = 0.0038$ $\quad$ **43.** $z = 1.72$; $p = 0.0427$
37. $t = 1.421$; $0.10 > p > 0.05$
45. Since $z = 3 > 1.645$, we reject H_0. $p = 0.0013$
47. No, $t = -1.3474$; $0.20 > p > 0.10$ $\quad$ **53.** Yes, $\bar{d} = -5.5$, $s_d = 4.58$, $t = -4.160$; $p < 0.005$
49. Yes, $t = -3.5841$; $p < 0.01$ $\quad$ **55.** Yes, $t = 4.704$
51. No, $z = 1.02$; $p = 0.1539$ $\quad$ **57.** No, $t = 1.337$; $p = 0.0901$

63. $\bar{x} = 3.928.$ Since $3.928 < 3.98$, conclude that the process is out of control.
65. (b) The process was out of control for samples 4, 7, and 10.
67. $\bar{x}_A = 7.54,$ $s_A^2 = 24.3657,$ $\bar{x}_B = 10.03,$ $s_B^2 = 21.2491$
69. $H_0: \mu_A \geq \mu_B$ $H_1: \mu_A < \mu_B,$ $z = -4.88,$
Reject H_0, since $-4.88 < -1.645.$ Since $-4.88 < -3.89, p < 0.0001.$
71. $H_0: p_B \geq p_A$ $H_1: p_B < p_A,$ $\bar{p} = \dfrac{30 + 20}{100} = 0.5,$
$z = -2.00,$ Reject H_0, since $-2.00 < -1.645.$ $p = 0.0228$
73. $\hat{p} = \dfrac{486}{700} = 0.69$
75. $H_0: p \geq 0.75$ $H_1: p < 0.75,$ $z = -3.67,$
Reject H_0, since $-3.67 < -1.645.$ $p = 0.0001$

CHAPTER 8

8.1 $F = 94.04;$ $p < 0.005$ 8.3 Yes, $F = 10.24;$ $p < 0.005$
8.5 $F = 9.83;$ $p < 0.005$
8.7 $X^2 = 46.626,$ $p < 0.005$
8.9 $X^2 = 53.8575,$ $p < 0.005$
8.11 $X^2 = 206.45;$ $p < 0.005$ Reject H_0.
8.13 $X^2 = 1.37883;$ $p > 0.10$ Do not reject H_0.
8.15 $X^2 = 17.8854;$ $0.01 > p > 0.005$ Reject H_0.
8.17 $X^2 = 22.0;$ $p < 0.005$
8.19 $X^2 = 10.367,$ $0.025 > p > 0.01$

Review Questions

15. $F = 39.63,$ $p < 0.005$
17. $F = 50.04,$ $p < 0.005$
19. $F = 16.73,$ $p < 0.005$
21. $F = 1.94,$ $p > 0.10$
23. $F = 7.55,$ $p < 0.005$
25. (a) 3 (b) 30 (c) No, because $1.0438 < 3.35.$
27. Yes. Since $6.49 > 2.98$, reject the null hypothesis of equal population means. Since $6.48 > 5.41, p < 0.005.$
29. $X^2 = 2.647,$ $p > 0.10$
31. $X^2 = 9.148,$ $0.10 > p > 0.05$
33. $X^2 = 18.5,$ $p < 0.005$
35. $X^2 = 6.774,$ $0.10 > p > 0.05$
37. $X^2 = 18.1343,$ $p < 0.005$
39. $X^2 = 137.952,$ $p < 0.005$
41. $X^2 = 83.0307,$ $p < 0.005$
45. $X^2 = 7,$ $0.05 > p > 0.025$
47. $X^2 = 26.6667,$ $p < 0.005$
49. $X^2 = 99.1259,$ $p < 0.005$

CHAPTER 9

9.1 $\hat{y} = -0.1329 + 0.0618x$ **9.3** $\hat{y} = 78.2210 + 1.5161x$

9.5   (a) $r^2 = 0.92$ (b) $F = 145.8; p < 0.005$ (c) $t = 12.12; p < 0.01$
(e) 0.05, 0.07

9.7   (a) $r^2 = 0.90$ (b) $F = 122.89; p < 0.005$ (c) $t = 11.08; p < 0.01$
(e) 1.22, 1.81

9.9   (a) $2.96 \pm (2.1604)(1.16447)(0.3182)$ (b) $2.96 \pm (2.1604)(1.16447)(1.0494)$

9.11   (a) $169.19 \pm (2.1604)(7.1924)(0.2947)$
(b) $169.19 \pm (2.1604)(7.1924)(1.0425)$

9.13

Confidence Limits for $\mu_{y\vert x}$		
x	Lower	Upper
20	9.06	12.52
30	15.25	18.12
40	21.38	23.77
50	27.42	29.52
60	33.34	35.39
70	39.11	41.40
80	44.79	47.51
25	12.16	15.31
90	50.41	53.68
100	55.99	59.88

$\hat{y} = -0.9954 + 0.5893x$

9.15   (b) $b = 0.7694$, $r^2 = 0.85496$, $r = 0.9246$, $t = 6.87$
Since computed $t >$ critical t (2.306), reject H_0. $p < 0.01$
(c) $z = -1.87$; $p = 2(0.0307) = 0.0614$

9.17   (a) $\hat{y} = -30.5761 + 1.0406x_{1j} + 0.8390x_{2j}$ (b) 0.98   (c) $F = 173.77$;
$p < 0.005$ (d) $t(b_1) = 5.46; p < 0.01; t(b_2) = 6.36; p < 0.01$

9.19   (a) $\hat{y} = -3.8162 + 68.9486x_{1j} + 0.2457x_{2j}$ (b) 0.98   (c) $F = 146.48$;
$p < 0.005$ (d) $t(b_1) = 4.02; p < 0.01; t(b_2) = 1.31; p > 0.20$

Review Questions

15.   (a) $\hat{y} = 54.61229 + 0.394782x$ (b) $r = 0.2151$ (c) $t = 0.934$
(d) $p > 0.20$

17.   (a) $\hat{y} = 22.6046 + 12.6714x$

(b)

Source	SS	df	MS	
Regression	18,535.15	1	18,535.15	7
Error	3,313.85	14	236.70	
Total	21,849.00	15		

(c) $p < 0.005$ (d) $\hat{y} = \$111.30$

19.   (b) $\hat{y} = 0.78336 + 0.56821x$ (c) $t = 18.148, p < 0.005$ (d) 0.962
(e) 22.69, 35.70

23.   (a) $\hat{y} = 4.78014 + 0.0897922x$

(b) Source	SS	df	MS	F
Regression	40.4723	1	40.4723	10.264
Error	51.2613	13	3.9432	
Total	91.7336	14		

(c) Since $10.264 > 4.67$, reject H_0.

25. $\hat{y}_j = 13.45 + 4.02x_1 + 2.81x_2$; $R^2_{y.12} = 0.6682$; $F = 7.05$, $0.01 < p < 0.025$; $t_1 = 3.75$, $p < 0.01$; $t_2 = 2.04$, $0.05 < p < 0.10$; $\hat{y} = 50.41$

27. $b_1 = -4.06$, $b_2 = 3.20$; $R^2_{y.12} = 0.7437$, $F = 11.61$, $p < 0.005$

29. $\hat{y}_j = 0.395081 + 0.257827x_1 + 2.96621x_2$; $R^2_{y.12} = 0.7526$; $t_1 = 0.520753$, $p > 0.10$; $t_2 = 2.95103$, $0.01 < p < 0.05$

31. (a) $\hat{y}_j = 4.6004 + 0.6701x_1 + 4.8692x_2 - 0.033619x_3$
(b) $R^2_{y.123} = 0.48793$, $\qquad F = 3.49$, $0.05 < p < 0.10$
(c) $t_1 = 1.11$, $p > 0.20$; $t_2 = 0.84$, $p > 0.20$; $\qquad t_3 = -0.06$, $p > 0.20$

35. $r^2 = \dfrac{6757.2015}{10191.999} = 0.66299079$

37. $s_b = 0.1139165$, $\qquad t = 8.6462$, $\qquad$ Reject H_0: $\beta = 0$. $\qquad p < 0.01$
39. $r = 0.8142425$
41. $\hat{y} = 12.229786 + 0.9849433(80) = 91.02525$

CHAPTER 10

10.1 $r = 6$, not significant $\qquad$ **10.3** $\qquad$ Since $2 < 7 < 9$, H_0 cannot be rejected.
10.5 H_0: No difference in preference
H_1: Candy bar packaged by Method A is preferred
20 pluses, 5 minuses, 2 zeros, $n = 25$, $k = 5$

$$z = \frac{5.5 - 12.5}{0.5(5)} = \frac{-7}{2.5} = -2.8$$

Critical $z = -1.645$. Reject H_0. Conclude that candy bar packaged by Method A is preferred.
10.7 $r_S = 0.703$, $\qquad p < 0.001$
10.9 $r_S = 0.864$, $\qquad p < 0.001$
10.11 $r_S = 0.7455$, $\qquad 0.005 < p < 0.010$
10.13 Since $T_+ = 55.5 > 69$, reject H_0. $\qquad p < 0.01$
10.15 Since $178.5 > 160$, reject H_0. $\qquad 0.01 > p > 0.002$
10.17 Since $272 > 227 > 128$, do not reject H_0. $\qquad p > 0.20$

Review Questions

7. Since $6 < 12 < 16$, do not reject H_0. $\qquad p > 0.05$
9. $r_s = 0.918$; $\qquad p < 0.001$ (one-sided test). $\qquad$ Reject H_0.
11. $r_s = 0.7804$; $\qquad$ Since $0.7804 > 0.7464$, $p < 2(0.001) = 0.002$. $\qquad$ Reject H_0.
15. $T_+ = 49.5$; $T_- = 28.5$; $\qquad p > 0.110$

Index

NOTES

SOME FREQUENTLY USED SYMBOLS

General

X	Random variable of interest Independent variable in linear regression
x	Observed value of random variable X
N	Population size (finite)
n	Sample size
Σ	Summation sign (Greek capital letter sigma)
$E(X)$	Expected value of X

Probability

$P(A)$	Probability that event A occurs
$P(\bar{A})$	Probability that event A does not occur
$P(A\|B)$	Probability of A given B (conditional probability)
$P(A \cap B)$	Probability that both A and B occur (joint probability)
$P(A \cup B)$	Probability that A or B or both occur

Parameters and Their Estimators

μ	Population mean (Greek letter mu)
$\bar{x}$	Sample mean (estimator of μ)
$\mu_{\bar{x}}$	Mean of the sampling distribution of $\bar{x}$
$\mu_1 - \mu_2$	Difference between two population means
$\bar{x}_1 - \bar{x}_2$	Difference between two sample means (estimator of $\mu_1 - \mu_2$)
$\mu_{\bar{x}_1 - \bar{x}_2}$	Mean of the sampling distribution of the difference between two sample means
d_i	Difference between paired observations or ranks
μ_d	Population mean difference (paired observations)
$\bar{d}$	Sample mean difference (paired observations)
σ^2	Population variance
σ	Population standard deviation ($\sqrt{\sigma^2}$) (Greek lower-case sigma)
s^2	Sample variance (estimator of σ^2)
s	Sample standard deviation ($\sqrt{s^2}$)
$\sigma_{\bar{x}}^2$	Variance of the sampling distribution of $\bar{x}$
$s_{\bar{x}}^2$	Estimator of $\sigma_{\bar{x}}^2$
$\sigma_{\bar{x}_1 - \bar{x}_2}^2$	Variance of the sampling distribution of the difference between two sample means
$s_{\bar{x}_1 - \bar{x}_2}^2$	Estimator of $\sigma_{\bar{x}_1 - \bar{x}_2}^2$
p	Population proportion
$\hat{p}$	Sample proportion (estimator of p)
$\mu_{\hat{p}}$	Mean of the sampling distribution of $\hat{p}$
$\sigma_{\hat{p}}^2$	Variance of the sampling distribution of $\hat{p}$
$p_1 - p_2$	Difference between two population proportions
$\hat{p}_1 - \hat{p}_2$	Difference between two sample proportions (estimator of $p_1 - p_2$)
$\mu_{\hat{p}_1 - \hat{p}_2}$	Mean of the sampling distribution of the difference between two sample proportions
$\sigma_{\hat{p}_1 - \hat{p}_2}^2$	Variance of the sampling distribution of the difference between two sample proportions
σ_d^2	Variance of population d_i's
σ_d	Standard deviation of d_i's
s_d^2	Variance of sample d_i's (Estimator of σ_d^2)
s_d	Standard deviation of sample d_i's (Estimator of σ_d)